THE CAMBRIDGE HISTORY OF
THE GOTHIC

This second volume of *The Cambridge History of the Gothic* provides a rigorous account of the Gothic in British, American and Continental European culture, from the Romantic period through to the Victorian *fin de siècle*. Here, leading scholars in the fields of literature, theatre, architecture and the history of science and popular entertainment explore the Gothic in its numerous interdisciplinary forms and guises, as well as across a range of different international contexts. As much a cultural history of the Gothic in this period as an account of the ways in which the Gothic mode has participated in the formative historical events of modernity, the volume offers fresh perspectives on familiar themes while also drawing new critical attention to a range of hitherto overlooked concerns. From Romanticism, to Penny Bloods, Dickens and even the railway system, the volume provides a compelling and comprehensive study of nineteenth-century Gothic culture.

DALE TOWNSHEND is Professor of Gothic Literature in the Manchester Centre for Gothic Studies, Manchester Metropolitan University. He has published widely on Gothic writing of the eighteenth and nineteenth centuries. His most recent monograph is *Gothic Antiquity: History, Romance, and the Architectural Imagination, 1760–1840* (Oxford University Press, 2019).

ANGELA WRIGHT is Professor of Romantic Literature at the University of Sheffield, and a former co-president of the International Gothic Association (IGA). Her books include *Britain, France and the Gothic: The Import of Terror, 1764–1820* (Cambridge University Press, 2013), *Mary Shelley* (University of Wales Press, 2018), and the co-edited volumes *Ann Radcliffe, Romanticism and the Gothic* (with Dale Townshend, Cambridge University Press, 2014) and *Romantic Gothic: An Edinburgh Companion* (with Dale Townshend, Edinburgh University Press, 2016).

THE CAMBRIDGE HISTORY OF
THE GOTHIC

How to write the history of a cultural mode that, for all its abiding fascination with the past, has challenged and complicated received notions of history from the very start? *The Cambridge History of the Gothic* rises to this challenge, charting the history of the Gothic even as it reflects continuously upon the mode's tendency to question, subvert and render incomplete all linear historical narratives. Taken together, the three chronologically sequenced volumes in the series provide a rigorous account of the origins, efflorescence and proliferation of the Gothic imagination, from its earliest manifestations in European history through to the present day. The chapters in Volume I span antiquity and the long eighteenth century (c. 1680–1800), covering such topics as the Gothic Sack of Rome in AD 410, the construction and reception of the Gothic past in eighteenth-century Britain, the revival of Gothic architecture, art and literature in British and European culture and their imbrication during the revolutionary decades, 1770–1800. Elaborating upon several of the themes introduced in the first volume, the chapters in Volume II address the Gothic cultures of Britain, America and Europe during the nineteenth century (1800–1900), thus covering while moving well beyond those areas that have traditionally been demarcated as the 'Romantic' and the 'Victorian'. Engaging with the themes of the earlier volumes, the chapters in Volume III also explore some of the myriad forms that the Gothic has assumed in the twentieth and twenty-first centuries (c. 1896–present), beginning with an account of the appropriation of the mode in early cinema and concluding with the apocalyptic Gothic turns of much recent cultural production. Resolutely interdisciplinary in focus, *The Cambridge History of the Gothic* extends the critical focus well beyond literature and film to include discussions of Gothic historiography, politics, art, architecture and counterculture. All three volumes in the series are attentive to the ways in which history has been refracted through a Gothic lens, and are as keen to chart the inscription of Gothic in some of the formative events of Western history as they are to provide a history of the Gothic mode itself. Written by an international cast of contributors, the chapters bring fresh scholarly attention to bear upon established Gothic themes while also highlighting a number of new critical concerns. As such, they are of relevance to the general reader, the student and the established scholar alike.

THE CAMBRIDGE HISTORY OF THE GOTHIC

*

VOLUME 2
Gothic in the Nineteenth Century

*

Edited by
DALE TOWNSHEND
Manchester Metropolitan University

ANGELA WRIGHT
University of Sheffield

CAMBRIDGE
UNIVERSITY PRESS

Shaftesbury Road, Cambridge CB2 8EA, United Kingdom

One Liberty Plaza, 20th Floor, New York, NY 10006, USA

477 Williamstown Road, Port Melbourne, VIC 3207, Australia

314–321, 3rd Floor, Plot 3, Splendor Forum, Jasola District Centre, New Delhi – 110025, India

103 Penang Road, #05–06/07, Visioncrest Commercial, Singapore 238467

Cambridge University Press is part of Cambridge University Press & Assessment, a department of the University of Cambridge.

We share the University's mission to contribute to society through the pursuit of education, learning and research at the highest international levels of excellence.

www.cambridge.org
Information on this title: www.cambridge.org/9781108460187

DOI: 10.1017/9781108561082

© Cambridge University Press & Assessment 2020

This publication is in copyright. Subject to statutory exception and to the provisions of relevant collective licensing agreements, no reproduction of any part may take place without the written permission of Cambridge University Press & Assessment.

First published 2020
First paperback edition 2025

A catalogue record for this publication is available from the British Library

Library of Congress Cataloging-in-Publication data
NAMES: Wright, Angela, 1969 May 14– editor. | Townshend, Dale, editor.
TITLE: The Cambridge history of the Gothic / edited by Angela Wright, University of Sheffield ; Dale Townshend, Manchester Metropolitan University.
DESCRIPTION: Cambridge, UK ; New York : Cambridge University Press, 2020–. | Includes bibliographical references and indexes. | Contents: v. 1. Gothic in the long eighteenth century – v. 2. Gothic in the nineteenth century –
IDENTIFIERS: LCCN 2019058624 (print) | LCCN 2019058625 (ebook) | ISBN 9781108662017 (three-volume set) | ISBN 9781108472708 (v. 1 ; hardback) | ISBN 9781108472715 v. 2 ; hardback) | ISBN 9781108561044 (v. 1 ; ebook) | ISBN 9781108561082 (v. 2 ; ebook))
SUBJECTS: LCSH: Gothic fiction (Literary genre) – History and criticism. | Gothic revival (Literature) – History and criticism. | Fantastic fiction – History and criticism. | Architecture, Gothic. | Art, Gothic.
CLASSIFICATION: LCC PN3435 .C285 2020 (print) | LCC PN3435 (ebook) | DDC 809.3/8729–dc23
LC record available at https://lccn.loc.gov/2019058624
LC ebook record available at https://lccn.loc.gov/2019058625

ISBN	- 3 Volume Set	978 1 108 66201 7
ISBN	- Volume I	978 1 108 47270 8
ISBN	- Volume II	978 1 108 47271 5
ISBN	- Volume III	978 1 108 47272 2
ISBN	978-1-108-47271-5	Hardback
ISBN	978-1-108-46018-7	Paperback

Cambridge University Press & Assessment has no responsibility for the persistence or accuracy of URLs for external or third-party internet websites referred to in this publication and does not guarantee that any content on such websites is, or will remain, accurate or appropriate.

Contents

List of Figures page x
List of Tables xi
Notes on Contributors xii
Acknowledgements xvi

Introduction: Gothic in the Nineteenth Century, 1800–1900   1
DALE TOWNSHEND

2.1. Gothic Romanticism and the Summer of 1816   19
MADELEINE CALLAGHAN AND ANGELA WRIGHT

2.2. *Fantasmagoriana*: The Cosmopolitan Gothic and *Frankenstein*   41
MAXIMILIAAN VAN WOUDENBERG

2.3. The Mutation of the Vampire in Nineteenth-Century Gothic   65
JERROLD E. HOGLE

2.4. From Romantic Gothic to Victorian Medievalism: 1817 and 1877   85
TOM DUGGETT

2.5. Nineteenth-Century Gothic Architectural Aesthetics: A. W. N. Pugin, John Ruskin and William Morris   118
ALEXANDRA WARWICK

2.6. Gothic Fiction, from Shilling Shockers to Penny Bloods   139
ANTHONY MANDAL

2.7. The Theatrical Gothic in the Nineteenth Century   162
KELLY JONES

2.8. 'Spectrology': Gothic Showmanship in Nineteenth-Century Popular Shows and Media 182
JOE KEMBER

2.9. The Gothic in Victorian Poetry 204
SERENA TROWBRIDGE

2.10. The Genesis of the Victorian Ghost Story 224
SCOTT BREWSTER

2.11. Charles Dickens and the Gothic 246
JOHN BOWEN

2.12. Victorian Domestic Gothic Fiction 265
TAMAR HELLER

2.13. The Gothic in Nineteenth-Century Spain 285
XAVIER ALDANA REYES AND ROCÍO RØDTJER

2.14. The Gothic in Nineteenth-Century Italy 303
FRANCESCA SAGGINI

2.15. The Gothic in Nineteenth-Century Scotland 328
SUZANNE GILBERT

2.16. The Gothic in Nineteenth-Century Ireland 359
CHRISTINA MORIN

2.17. The Gothic in Nineteenth-Century America 376
CHARLES L. CROW

2.18. Nineteenth-Century British and American Gothic and the History of Slavery 394
MAISHA WESTER

2.19. Genealogies of Monstrosity: Darwin, the Biology of Crime and Nineteenth-Century British Gothic Literature 416
CORINNA WAGNER

2.20. Gothic and the Coming of the Railways 445
WILLIAM HUGHES

2.21. Gothic Imperialism at the *Fin de siècle* 463
ANDREW SMITH

Select Bibliography 482
Index 520

Illustrations and Captions for Volume II

Fig.4.1:	Malory in the black-letter manner. Anon., Frontispiece to Robert Southey's *The Byrth, Lyf, and Actes of Kyng Arthur* (1817). The British Library Board, 634.1.6, p. 7.	*page 101*
Fig.4.2:	The old house in the hereafter. William Morris (and W. H. Hooper and C. M. Gere), Frontispiece to *News from Nowhere*, the Kelmscott Press edition of 1890. The Trustees of the British Museum.	*109*
Fig.4.3:	From symbolic historicism to historical feel. Charles Francis Annesley Voysey, Designs for Perrycroft, Jubilee Drive, Colwall, Herefordshire: north and east elevations (1st preliminary design). RIBA Collections.	*111*
Fig.4.4:	As if alive in the thirteenth century. Martin Charles, Exterior view of William Morris and Philip Speakman Webb's Red House, Bexleyheath, London. RIBA Collections.	*112*
Fig.8.1:	Pepper's Ghost illusion. Image courtesy of the Bill Douglas Cinema Museum.	*190*
Fig.8.2:	'The Whiskey Demon; or, The Dream of the Reveller' (Newton and Co., 1888), slide 12 of 12. Philip and Rosemary Banham Collection, reproduced by permission.	*198*
Fig.19.1:	Moreau, *L'homme fossile*, from Pierre Boitard, *Paris Before Man* (1861). Author's photograph.	*419*
Fig.19.2:	Charles Darwin, 'Tree of Life', from *On the Origin of Species* (1859). Author's photograph.	*421*
Fig.19.3:	Richard Louis Dugdale, showing the fifth to the six generations of the Juke Family, *The Jukes* (1877; 1910). Author's photograph.	*422*
Fig.19.4:	Illustration from 'Pallinghurst Barrow', *Illustrated London News* (1892). Author's photograph.	*424*
Fig.19.5:	'The skull of Villella', Gina Lombroso-Ferrero, *Criminal Man* (c. 1864–71). Author's photograph.	*433*
Fig.19.6:	George Darwin, for Charles Darwin, 'Drosera rotundifolia', *Insectivorous Plants* (1875). Author's photograph.	*439*
Fig.19.7:	Daniel Hack Tuke, 'W. B.' 'Case of Moral Insanity' (1885). Author's photograph.	*442*

Tables

Table 2.1: Table showing the provenance of the stories read by the Byron-Shelley circle in Geneva in 1816   *page 44*

Notes on Contributors

XAVIER ALDANA REYES is Reader in English Literature and Film at Manchester Metropolitan University. He is the author of *Gothic Cinema* (2020), *Spanish Gothic* (2017), *Horror Film and Affect* (2016) and *Body Gothic* (2014), and the editor of *Twenty-First-Century Gothic: An Edinburgh Companion* (with Maisha Wester, 2019) and *Horror: A Literary History* (2016).

JOHN BOWEN is Professor of Nineteenth-Century Literature at the University of York. His books include *Other Dickens: Pickwick to Chuzzlewit* (2000), *Palgrave Advances in Charles Dickens Studies* (with Robert L. Patten, 2006) and editions of novels by Dickens and Anthony Trollope. He has served as president of the Dickens Fellowship and is currently writing a monograph entitled *Reading Charles Dickens*.

SCOTT BREWSTER is Reader in Modern English Literature at the University of Lincoln. He is co-editor, with Luke Thurston, of *The Routledge Handbook to the Ghost Story* (2017) and, with Lucie Armitt, is currently completing *Climates of Fear: Gothic Travel through Haunted Landscapes* (2020).

MADELEINE CALLAGHAN is Senior Lecturer in Romantic Literature at the University of Sheffield. Her research speciality is the poetry of Wordsworth, Byron, Shelley and Yeats. Her first monograph, *Shelley's Living Artistry*, was published in 2017, and her second, *The Poet-Hero in the Work of Byron and Shelley*, in 2019. She has published various articles and chapters on Romantic and post-Romantic poetry, and, with Michael O'Neill, co-authored *The Romantic Poetry Handbook* (2018).

CHARLES L. CROW is Professor Emeritus of English at Bowling Green State University, USA. His publications include *A Companion to the Regional Literatures of America* (2003), *American Gothic* (2009), *American Gothic: An Anthology from Salem Witchcraft to H. P. Lovecraft* (2012), *A Companion to American Gothic* (2013), and, with Susan Castillo Street, *The Palgrave Handbook of the Southern Gothic* (2016).

TOM DUGGETT is Associate Professor in Romantic and Victorian Literature at Xi'an Jiaotong – Liverpool University (XJTLU, the University of Liverpool in China). He is the author of a study of Wordsworth's poetry and politics, *Gothic Romanticism: Architecture,*

Politics, and Literary Form (2010), and the editor of Robert Southey's 1829 prose work, *Sir Thomas More: or, Colloquies on the Progress and Prospects of Society* (2018).

SUZANNE GILBERT has recently retired from the University of Stirling, Scotland. She shares with Ian Duncan the general editorship of the Stirling/South Carolina Research Edition of *The Collected Works of James Hogg*. She has served as volume editor of Hogg's *The Mountain Bard* (2007) and *Queen Hynde* (1998) with Douglas S. Mack, and is currently working on *Scottish Pastorals, Other Early Poems and Letters on Poetry*. With Sarah Dunnigan, she edited a collection of essays, *Scottish Traditional Literatures* (2013). She has published articles and chapters on eighteenth- and nineteenth-century Scottish literature, women's writing and oral traditions, particularly ballads.

TAMAR HELLER is Associate Professor of English and Comparative Literature at the University of Cincinnati. She is the author of *Dead Secrets: Wilkie Collins and the Female Gothic* (1992), and a number of articles on Victorian Gothic and sensation fiction. The editor of two novels by Rhoda Broughton, *Cometh Up as a Flower* (2004) and *Not Wisely, but Too Well* (2013), she is currently completing a book on Broughton entitled *A Plot of Her Own: Rhoda Broughton and English Fiction*.

JERROLD E. HOGLE is Professor Emeritus of English and University Distinguished Professor at the University of Arizona. A former president of the International Gothic Association and still on its Executive Committee, he has been a Guggenheim and Mellon Fellow for research as well as a recent winner of the Distinguished Scholar Award from the Keats-Shelley Association of America. He has published widely on English Romantic Literature, literary and cultural theory, and the many forms of the Gothic. His books include *Shelley's Process: Radical Transference and the Development of His Major Works* (1988); *The Undergrounds of The Phantom of the Opera: Sublimation and the Gothic in Leroux's Novel and Its Progeny* (2002); *The Cambridge Companion to Gothic Fiction* (2002); its more recent successor, *The Cambridge Companion to the Modern Gothic* (2014); and, with Robert Miles, *The Gothic and Theory: An Edinburgh Companion* (2019).

WILLIAM HUGHES is Professor of Literature in English at the University of Macau, China. He is a founder member of the International Gothic Association, and served as its first secretary, as well as being the editor of the IGA's journal, *Gothic Studies*, for 20 years. He is the author, editor or co-editor of over twenty books, including *Beyond Dracula: Bram Stoker's Fiction and Its Cultural Contexts* (2000); *The Historical Dictionary of Gothic Literature* (2013); *That Devil's Trick: Hypnotism and the Victorian Popular Imagination* (2015); and *Key Concepts in the Gothic* (2018). He is currently writing a monograph on phrenology in Victorian popular culture.

KELLY JONES is Senior Lecturer in Drama at the University of Lincoln. Her research focuses upon staging the Gothic as well as theatrical realisations of the supernatural. She has published on staging the ghost story, recent stage adaptations of Mary Shelley's *Frankenstein* and the monstrous child in contemporary Gothic theatre. She has most recently co-edited the book, *Contemporary Gothic Drama: Attraction, Consummation and*

Consumption on the Modern British Stage (with Benjamin Poore and Robert Dean, 2018) and is currently working on a monograph, *The Ghost Story on the English Stage*.

JOE KEMBER is Professor of Film and Visual Culture at the University of Exeter. He has written and researched extensively on nineteenth-century popular shows and early cinema and is currently completing research projects concerning the magic lantern and other Victorian media.

ANTHONY MANDAL is Professor of Print and Digital Cultures at Cardiff University, where he directs the Centre for Editorial and Intertextual Research. He is the author of books and articles on the Gothic, nineteenth-century fiction, Jane Austen, the history of the book and digital humanities. He is the founding editor of the online journal, *Romantic Textualities: Literature and Print Culture, 1780–1840*, and one of the General Editors of *The New Edinburgh Edition of the Works of Robert Louis Stevenson*, to be completed in thirty-nine volumes. In summer 2019, he was elected as president of the British Association for Romantic Studies.

CHRISTINA MORIN lectures in English literature at the University of Limerick. She is the author of *The Gothic Novel in Ireland, c. 1760–1829* (2018) and *Charles Robert Maturin and the Haunting of Irish Romantic Fiction* (2011). She has also edited, with Marguérite Corporaal, *Traveling Irishness in the Long Nineteenth Century* (2017) and, with Niall Gillespie, *Irish Gothics: Genres, Forms, Modes and Traditions* (2014). Current projects include a monograph on Irish writers and the Minerva press and a special issue of *Romantic Textualities*, edited with Elizabeth Neiman, on 'The Minerva Press and the Romantic-era Literary Marketplace'.

ROCÍO RØDTJER is a research associate at King's College London and recipient of an AHGBI-Spanish Embassy Doctoral Publication Prize. Her thesis *Women and Nationhood in Restoration Spain 1874–1931: The State as Family* is forthcoming as a monograph. Additionally, she has written on both the Spanish Gothic and the nineteenth-century scientific imaginary.

FRANCESCA SAGGINI is Professor in English Literature at the Universita' della Tuscia, Italy. Recent works in the area of Gothic Studies include essays on Bram Stoker, the Italian legacy of John Polidori's *The Vampyre* and Frances Burney's Gothic. She is the author of *The Gothic Novel and the Stage: Romantic Appropriations* (2015; Honourable Mention at the 2016 ESSE Book Awards); recently, she co-edited, with Anna Enrichetta Soccio, *Transmedia Creatures: Frankenstein's Afterlives* (2018).

ANDREW SMITH is Professor of Nineteenth-Century English Literature at the University of Sheffield. His published books include *Gothic Death 1740–1914: A Literary History* (2016); *The Ghost Story 1840–1920: A Cultural History* (2010); *Gothic Literature* (2007; revised 2013); *Victorian Demons* (2004); and *Gothic Radicalism* (2000). He is a past president of the International Gothic Association.

DALE TOWNSHEND FSA is Professor of Gothic Literature in the Manchester Centre for Gothic Studies, Manchester Metropolitan University. His most recent publications include

Writing Britain's Ruins (with Peter N. Lindfield and Michael Carter, 2017) and *Gothic Antiquity: History, Romance, and the Architectural Imagination, 1760–1840* (2019).

SERENA TROWBRIDGE is Reader in Victorian Literature at Birmingham City University. Her research focuses on the Pre-Raphaelites and Gothic in literature and art, and her most recent publication is *My Ladys Soul: The Poetry of Elizabeth Siddall* (2018). Recent publications include '"Truth to Nature": the pleasures and dangers of the environment in Christina Rossetti's poetry', in *Victorian Writers and the Environment*, ed. Laurence W. Mazzeno and Ronald D. Morrison (2017) and a chapter on Graveyard poetry for *Gothic and Death*, ed. Carol Margaret Davison (2017). Her monograph, *Christina Rossetti's Gothic*, was published in 2013.

MAXIMILIAAN VAN WOUDENBERG is a Visiting Fellow at Clare Hall, Cambridge. He is the author of *Coleridge and Cosmopolitan Intellectualism 1794–1804: The Legacy of Göttingen University* (2018). He has also written on the *Fantasmagoriana* stories that Mary Shelley read before she created *Frankenstein*. Along with Anthony Mandal, he co-edits the online journal, *Romantic Textualities: Literature and Print Culture, 1780–1840*.

CORINNA WAGNER is Associate Professor in Literature and the History of Art at the University of Exeter. Her research interests include medical history and the arts, Victorian Gothic literature and architecture, the body in art, and the history of photography. She has co-edited *The Oxford Handbook to Victorian Medievalism* (2020) and *A Body of Work: An Anthology of Poetry and Medicine* (2016) and edited *Gothic Evolutions: Poetry, Tales, Context, Theory* (2014). Her books include *Pathological Bodies: Medicine and Political Culture* (2013) and *Art, Anatomy and the Real* (2021). She has also co-curated an exhibition on Victorian Gothic and is working with partners on a series of exhibitions on water and cities.

ALEXANDRA WARWICK is Professor of English Studies and Head of the School of Humanities at the University of Westminster. She has published on a variety of aspects of nineteenth-century literature and culture, including Gothic architecture, Andrew Lang, archaeology and the Whitechapel murders. Her current work is on Victorian archaeology.

MAISHA WESTER is Associate Professor at Indiana University, Bloomington and Fulbright Scholar (2017–18). Her research is on racial representation and politics of otherness in Gothic literature and American horror film, Gothic literature in the Black Diaspora, and mobilisations of Gothic discourses in sociopolitical discussions of race and ethnicity. In addition to a number of essays and book chapters, she is the author of *African American Gothic: Screams From Shadowed Places* (2012) and co-editor of *Twenty-First-Century Gothic: An Edinburgh Companion* (2019), with Xavier Aldana Reyes.

ANGELA WRIGHT is Professor of Romantic Literature in the School of English at the University of Sheffield. A former co-president of the International Gothic Association (IGA), she is completing a Leverhulme-funded project entitled *Fostering Romanticism* and working upon the author Ann Radcliffe. Her books include *Britain, France and the Gothic: The Import of Terror* (2013) and *Mary Shelley* (2018). With Dale Townshend, she has also edited *Ann Radcliffe, Romanticism and the Gothic* (2014) and *Romantic Gothic: An Edinburgh Companion* (2016).

Acknowledgements

The *Cambridge History of the Gothic* was conceived in 2015, when Linda Bree, then Editorial Director at Cambridge University Press, first suggested the idea to us. After much discussion and writing, what began life as a modest single-volume project became a larger and far more ambitious three-volume work. Our thanks are due to Linda Bree for her early encouragement, and for taking this project at proposal stage through peer review, syndicate and contracting. Shalini Bisa and Tim Mason efficiently oversaw much of the initial paperwork. Since then, Bethany Thomas has become our patient, encouraging and responsive editor who has supported the project indefatigably. We are enormously grateful to both Linda and Bethany, and to the extraordinary team who has worked alongside them at Cambridge University Press, including Natasha Burton, content manager Sarah Starkey, copy-editor Denise Bannerman and indexer Eric Anderson of Arc Indexing Inc. Jayavel Radhakrishnan at Integra Software Services has been the most helpful and efficient of project managers.

Of course, there would be no *Cambridge History of the Gothic* were it not for the exciting scholarship on the Gothic that has been produced by researchers across the globe. Our heartfelt thanks are also thus due to the scholars who, with such enthusiasm and diligence, signed up to write chapters for these volumes, and who patiently endured the sometimes arduous processes of review, editing and revision. They have been extremely generous with their time and scholarship, and we remain forever in their debt. Our respective institutions have been encouraging of, and patient with, us as we have wrestled with the enormity of this project. Angela Wright wishes to thank the School of English at the University of Sheffield, and especially those colleagues who have listened and, in several cases, contributed work to these volumes. Particular thanks are due to Andy Smith, Maddy Callaghan, Joe Bray, Hamish Mathison, Anna Barton, Amber Regis and Frances Babbage. Dale Townshend wishes to thank his friends and colleagues in the Manchester Centre for Gothic Studies at

Acknowledgements

Manchester Metropolitan University, as well as Jess Edwards and Antony Rowland. In a more personal capacity, the editors also wish to thank their families. For Angela, Hamish, Jess and Antonia have provided fun, amusement and understanding, and for Dale, Howard, Shannon and Stephen have, as ever, been long-suffering sources of laughter, comfort and support.

Introduction: Gothic in the Nineteenth Century, 1800–1900

DALE TOWNSHEND

> Does any one now read Mrs. Radcliffe, or am I the only wanderer in her windy corridors, listening timidly to groans and hollow voices, and shielding the flame of a lamp, which, I fear, will presently flicker out, and leave me in darkness? People know the name of 'The Mysteries of Udolpho'; They know that boys would say to Thackeray, at school, 'Old fellow, draw us Vivaldi in the Inquisition.' But have they penetrated into the chill galleries of the Castle of Udolpho? Have they shuddered for Vivaldi in face [sic] of the sable-clad and masked Inquisition?
> (Andrew Lang, 'Mrs. Radcliffe's Novels', 1900)[1]

Literary History and the Invention of 'Gothic Fiction', 1800–1900.

The history of the Gothic in the nineteenth century is subtly yet legibly sketched out in some of the semantic changes that were effected in the period to the word 'Gothic' itself. A notoriously overdetermined noun and adjective in English since at least the early seventeenth century – the OED lists the King James Bible of 1611 as its earliest recorded use in print – 'Gothic' for much of the long eighteenth century signified that which concerned or pertained to the ancient Gothic tribes or their language; by extension, that which we now refer to as Teutonic or Germanic; that which belonged to, or was characteristic of, the Middle Ages; that which, in all its apparent opposition to the Classicism of ancient Greece and Rome, was perceived as barbarous, rude, unpolished or in generally bad taste; and the style of architecture that was prevalent in Europe from the twelfth to the sixteenth century, the chief

---

[1] Andrew Lang, 'Mrs. Radcliffe's novels', *The Cornhill Magazine* 9:49 (July 1900): 23–34 (p. 23).

characteristic of which was the pointed arch.² Though these significations often clustered together simultaneously, attempts to localise one or two more particular meanings of the word were not uncommon. Chapters 1–8 in the first volume of *The Cambridge History of the Gothic* provide near-exhaustive coverage of the circulation of the term 'Gothic' in these and other related contexts in antiquity and throughout the period 1680–1800.

Within this range of discrete yet closely interrelated historical, political and architectural meanings, notions of the literary were somewhat eclipsed, although, as Nick Groom's and Dale Townshend's chapters in Volume I show, it is clear that, even if it was not always named as such, a very particular understanding of what we would now term a Gothic literary aesthetic was already beginning to take shape in the work of William Temple; John Dennis; Anthony Ashley Cooper, 3rd Earl of Shaftesbury; John Dryden; Joseph Addison; and other writers of the late seventeenth and early eighteenth centuries. What distinguished such early invocations of the 'Gothic' in these more narrowly literary senses, however, was that this was a descriptive category that was almost exclusively reserved for works of purportedly 'ancient' provenance, be they by writers such as Petrarch, Pierre de Ronsard, Ludovico Ariosto and Torquato Tasso in the Continental tradition, or Geoffrey Chaucer, William Shakespeare, Edmund Spenser, John Milton and other early modern dramatists and the poets in the English. The term 'Gothic', in this respect, was for the long eighteenth century as much a marker of a writer's historical positioning – his perceived relations to the sometimes noble, sometimes barbaric Gothic past – as a means of describing any text's particular formal and thematic properties. When, in February 1765, John Langhorne, with more than a modicum of scepticism, remarked in his review of the first edition of *The Castle of Otranto* (published 24 December 1764) that the text teemed with 'the absurdities of Gothic fiction', he was seemingly unaware of the fact that this was really a modern hoax that had issued from the pen of a contemporary writer; the term 'Gothic' that he employed here referred instead to the fiction's purported origins in what Horace Walpole's translator William Marshal in the first Preface described as 'the darkest ages of christianity', that is, the period somewhere between '1095, the æra of the first crusade, and 1243, the date of the last'.³ Langhorne was

---

2 See the entry for 'Gothic' in the *Oxford English Dictionary* (Oxford: Oxford University Press, 2018) <www.oed.com> (last accessed 12 September 2019).
3 Horace Walpole, *The Castle of Otranto*, edited by Nick Groom (Oxford: Oxford University Press, 2014), p. 5. John Langhorne's review of first edition of *The Castle of Otranto* in the *Monthly Review* in February 1765, vol. 32, pp. 97–9 is reprinted in Peter

altogether less complimentary, however, when, with Walpole's disclosure of authorship in the second edition in 1765, *The Castle of Otranto* was revealed to be no antique relic of 'Gothic fiction' at all, but a fabrication of disconcertingly modern origins:

> When this book was published as a translation from an old Italian romance, we had the pleasure of distinguishing in it the marks of genius, and many beautiful characteristic paintings; we were dubious, however, concerning the antiquity of the work upon several considerations, but being willing to find some excuse for the absurd and monstrous fictions it contained, we wished to acquiesce in the declaration of the title-page, that it was really a translation from an ancient writer. While we considered it as such, we could readily excuse its preposterous phenomena, and consider them as sacrifices to a gross and unenlightened age.—But when, as in this edition, *The Castle of Otranto* is declared to be a modern performance, that indulgence we afforded to the foibles of a supposed antiquity, we can by no means extend to the singularity of a false taste in a cultivated period of learning.[4]

For Langhorne, the absurdity that was deemed appropriate to the dark 'Gothic' past was unconscionable in the England of the enlightened, modern present. Not even after Walpole added the subtitle of 'A Gothic Story' to the second edition of *Otranto* did 'Gothic' come to assume quite the same set of meanings that the word mobilises in literary studies today, and this despite the fact that several late eighteenth-century writers in Walpole's wake, including Clara Reeve, Richard Warner, Isabella Kelly, Mary Tuck and Eliza Ratcliffe, had all employed variations on his 'Gothic Story' in the subtitles to their own fictions. Variously known instead as 'modern romances', the 'German school or horror' or the 'terrorist system of novel writing', and loosely grouped together in the fashion of those 'horrid' novels that Isabella Thorpe excitedly lists in Jane Austen's *Northanger Abbey* (written 1798–9; published late 1817; dated 1818), such fictions, though certainly perceived as belonging to a singular and recognisable literary type, were by no means marketed and read as 'Gothic'.[5] Indeed, as Austen's novel so clearly illustrates, the devotees of the circulating libraries, those influential cultural

---

Sabor (ed.), *Horace Walpole: The Critical Heritage* (London: Routledge & Kegan Paul, 1987), pp. 70–1.
4 John Langhorne's review of the second edition of *The Castle of Otranto* in the *Monthly Review* in May 1765, vol. 32, p. 394 is reprinted in Sabor (ed.), *Horace Walpole*, pp. 71–2.
5 On the naming of what we now call 'Gothic fiction' in the eighteenth century, see E. J. Clery, 'The Genesis of "Gothic" Fiction', in Jerrold E. Hogle (ed.), *The Cambridge Companion to Gothic Fiction* (Cambridge: Cambridge University Press, 2002), pp. 21–40 (p. 22).

establishments through which these 'horrid romances' were habitually disseminated and consumed, could never possibly have identified themselves as having particularly 'Gothic' literary tastes, since the word in the period, far from designating a literary genre, was primarily reserved for notions of the 'ancestral' or associated with what we would now term the 'medieval'.[6] As critics have frequently pointed out, it would not be until the early nineteenth century that 'Gothic' would lose many of its older historical and political meanings and come to serve as the name for the modern literature of horror and terror, wonder and supernatural enchantment, meanings that the *OED* added in a draft addition to its entry on the word as recently as December 2007: 'Of or designating a genre of fiction characterized by suspenseful, sensational plots involving supernatural or macabre elements and often (esp. in early use) having a medieval theme or setting.'

Such changes to the meaning of 'Gothic', from a primarily historical category to a term of literary-critical description, are clearly evidenced in the work of the English essayist and surgeon, Nathan Drake. In the first edition of his *Literary Hours; or, Sketches Critical and Narrative* of 1798, Drake paid sustained attention to what he termed 'Gothic superstition', that imaginative literary strain that, for all the 'polished' tastes of the late eighteenth-century present, remains 'yet alive to all the horrors of witchcraft, to all the solemn and terrible graces of the appalling spectre'.[7] Characterised by wayward flights of fancy and tales of elves and fairies, this 'vulgar Gothic' tradition was internally divided for Drake between what he referred to as 'sportive' and 'terrible' varieties, yet both strains trading in the signature generation of horror and terror, and eliciting in those who consumed them the responses of 'grateful astonishment' and the 'welcome sensation of fear'.[8] Though it was said to be epitomised by the enchanted forest in Tasso's *Jerusalem Delivered* (1581), the ghostliness of *The Lusiads* (1572) by the sixteenth-century Portuguese poet Luís de Camões and the spectres and sprites of some of Shakespeare's plays, Drake in *Literary Hours* also pioneeringly extended this Gothic literary tradition into the work of a number of more recent and contemporary writers who, he argued, had all sought to emulate it, including, most notably, the poetry of William Collins, Thomas Gray and William Cooper; Walpole's *The Castle of Otranto*; John Aikin's 'Sir Bertrand: A Fragment' (1773); Clara Reeve's *The Old English Baron* (1778); Gottfried August

---

6 See Alfred E. Longueil, 'The word "gothic" in eighteenth century criticism', *Modern Language Notes* 38:8 (December 1923): 453–60.
7 Nathan Drake, *Literary Hours; or, Sketches Critical and Narrative* (London, 1798), p. 87.
8 Drake, *Literary Hours*, p. 90.

Introduction: Gothic in the Nineteenth Century, 1800–1900

Bürger's 'Lenore' (1773); Christoph Martin Wieland's *Oberon* (1780–96); and the romances of Ann Radcliffe and Matthew Gregory Lewis.[9] Here, at the very end of the eighteenth century, texts and writers that were hitherto otherwise not specifically referred to as such are drawn together into a distinctive literary category of the 'Gothic', the term thus serving as a generic marker of sorts for some of the popular literary productions of Drake's own day. Albeit in a far more cautious and localised fashion, the otherwise largely anti-Gothic T. J. Mathias would achieve much the same when, in the one-volume reissue of the four-part *The Pursuits of Literature* of 1798, he paid tribute to 'the mighty magician of THE MYSTERIES OF UDOLPHO, bred and nourished by the Florentine Muses amid the paler shrines of Gothic superstition and in all the dreariness of Inchantment [sic]', a rhetorical move that similarly forged an important connection between the word 'Gothic' and the fictions of Ann Radcliffe.[10]

After Drake and Mathias, and throughout the course of the nineteenth century, such generic uses of the term became increasingly common-place. In his discussion of the work of Horace Walpole in his *Lives of the Novelists* of 1825, for example, a compilation of the Prefaces that he had written earlier for the reprints of several eighteenth-century novels and romances in Ballantyne's Novelists' Library series, Walter Scott repeated his by-now familiar tendency to distinguish between the unabashed supernaturalism of writers such as Walpole and the explained supernatural of Radcliffe through the use of the term 'Gothic' in a notably modern, literary sense:

> Romantic narrative is of two kinds—that which, being in itself possible, may be matter [sic] of belief at any period; and that which, though held impossible by more enlightened ages, was yet consonant with the faith of earlier times. The subject of *The Castle of Otranto* is of the latter class. Mrs. Radcliffe, a name not to be mentioned without the high respect due to genius, has endeavoured to effect a compromise between those different styles of narrative, by referring her prodigies to an explanation founded on natural causes, in the latter chapters of her romances. To this improvement upon the gothic romance there are so many objections that we own ourselves inclined to prefer, as more simple and impressive, the narrative of Walpole, which details supernatural

---

9 Like many writers of his day, including Horace Walpole, Drake misattributes 'Sir Bertrand' in *Literary Hours* to John Aikin's sister, Anna Laetitia Aikin (later Barbauld).
10 T. J. Mathias, *The Pursuits of Literature: A Satirical Poem in Four Dialogues. With Notes*, 8th edition (London: Printed for T. Becket, 1798), p. 58.

incidents as they would have been readily believed and received in the eleventh or twelfth century.[11]

Though, as of old, 'Gothic' in this extract continues to signify that which is 'of the eleventh and twelfth centuries', it also serves for Scott as a means of identifying and naming a specific and recognisable strand in modern literature, one that is said to be distinguished by its supernatural contents and exemplified by the romances of Walpole and Radcliffe. There is evidence of such usages in circulation across the Atlantic, too. In his *Six Months in Italy* of 1853, the Massachusetts-based lawyer and author George Stillman Hillard invoked a distinct category of 'Gothic fiction' in order to comment on the altogether more sanguine literary tastes of the Italian people:

> They have no liking for dark and supernatural terrors which make the flesh creep. Their facile and impressible nature demands gay, airy, and smiling fancies. The shapes and conceptions of Gothic fiction—the sheeted ghost gliding from the churchyard—the midnight bell struck by airy hands—the groan mingling with the wind that sweeps through the aisles of a ruined chapel—the damp vault, and the bloody shroud—have no charm for these children of the sun. The gloomy and spectral shadows which flit through Mrs. Radcliffe's Italian romances, are of Northern, not Italian origin.[12]

Though the word as Hillard employs it continues to suggest Britain's mythical northern European ancestors, the Goths, 'Gothic', perhaps with greater insistence, also signifies the fictional tradition comprising many of the characteristics that are most often associated with the mode today: darkness and death, gloom and mystery, and the host of supernatural terrors, from sheeted ghosts to spectral shadows, that 'make the flesh creep'. The 'Gothic' literary tradition that eighteenth-century writers such as Richard Hurd and Thomas Percy had identified and located in the 'antique' poems and dramas of the fifteenth, sixteenth and seventeenth centuries had, by the mid nineteenth century, been transposed and applied generically to modern or more recent horrid fictions. Thus, by 1889, Edmund Gosse in *A History of Eighteenth Century Literature (1660–1780)*, could describe Horace Walpole as the 'father' of the modern British Gothic strain, noting of *The Castle of Otranto* that 'This Gothic novel positively frightened grown-up people to the extent of making them

---

11 Walter Scott, *Lives of the Novelists*, 2 vols (Philadelphia and New York, 1825), vol. 2, pp. 131–2.
12 George Stillman Hillard, *Six Months in Italy*, 2 vols (Boston: Ticknor, Reed, and Fields, 1853), vol. 2, p. 233.

unwilling to seek their beds.'[13] Though it was not without its literary implications in earlier periods, 'Gothic' over the course of the nineteenth century forfeited many of its older political and historical meanings in order to serve with greater clarity and precision as the name for a modern literary genre or type, one accompanied, as such, by canonical or iconically 'Gothic' writers the likes of Horace Walpole, Ann Radcliffe and Matthew Gregory Lewis.

The Gothic and the Romantic in Nineteenth-Century Literary Historiography

This critical construction of 'Gothic literature' in the nineteenth century largely occurred against and in relation to the formation of canonical British 'Romanticism', that other retrospectively applied category of literary periodisation with which it has remained in constant tension ever since. The distaste of the poets whom we now refer to as 'Romantic' for the 'Gothic' writers and texts with whom they were contemporary are well known, and include Samuel Taylor Coleridge's censorious review of Matthew Gregory Lewis's *The Monk* (1796) in *The Critical Review* in February 1797; William Wordsworth's claims to have 'counteracted' the taste for 'frantic novels, sickly and stupid German Tragedies, and deluges of idle and extravagant stories in verse' in the Preface to the second, two-volume edition of *Lyrical Ballads* in 1800;[14] Coleridge's dismissal of the lurid popular fictions of the circulating library in a footnote to chapter three of *Biographia Literaria* (1817); and the various indictments and anti-Gothic pronouncements of figures such as Robert Southey, Walter Scott, Lord Byron and Percy Bysshe Shelley.[15] William Hazlitt's Lecture VIII 'On the Living Poets' (1818) gives some indication of how the Romantic literati perceived the popular taste for the Gothic that prevailed among many readers of their own day. Here, Hazlitt

---

13 Edmund Gosse, *A History of Eighteenth Century Literature (1660–1780)* (London and New York: Macmillan and Co., 1889), p. 301.
14 See Samuel Taylor Coleridge and William Wordsworth, *Lyrical Ballads, 1798 and 1800*, edited by Michael Gamer and Dahlia Porter (Peterborough, Ont.: Broadview, 2008), p. 177.
15 For an overview of Romantic reactions to the Gothic, see Dale Townshend and Angela Wright, 'Gothic and Romantic: An Historical Overview', in Angela Wright and Dale Townshend (eds), *Romantic Gothic: An Edinburgh Companion* (Edinburgh: Edinburgh University Press, 2016), pp. 1–34. For other important accounts of the relationship between the Gothic and the Romantic, see Michael Gamer, *Romanticism and the Gothic: Genre, Reception, and Canon Formation* (Cambridge: Cambridge University Press, 2000) and Tom Duggett, *Gothic Romanticism: Architecture, Politics, and Literary Form* (Basingstoke and New York: Palgrave Macmillan, 2010).

argued that if the *Lyrical Ballads* (1798) of Wordsworth and Coleridge could be said to have had one major advantage for contemporary letters, it was that it rejuvenated a simple, native tradition in English verse by retrieving the nation's literature from the clutches of the extravagant and marvellous 'German' Gothic strain:

> It was a time of promise, a renewal of the world of letters; and the Deucalions, who were to perform this feat of regeneration, were the present poet-laureat [sic] [Robert Southey] and the authors of the Lyrical Ballads. The Germans, who made heroes of robbers, and honest women of cast-off mistresses, had already exhausted the extravagant and marvellous in sentiment and situation: our native writers adopted a wonderful simplicity of style and matter.[16]

While the Romantic imagination was native, original, organic and visionary, the Gothic was a foreign and debased association-driven formula that barely aspired even to the lowly realms of fancy. Using the extraordinary fictions, poetic and otherwise, that were conceived during the Summer of 1816 in Switzerland as a particular, localised example, Madeleine Callaghan and Angela Wright's chapter in this volume explores the relationship between the Gothic and the Romantic further, showing that the relationship between the two was far more complex, and by no means as absolute and clear-cut as the comments of Hazlitt and other Romantic writers suggest. Maximiliaan van Woudenberg's chapter, in turn, reveals the extent to which Mary Shelley's *Frankenstein* (1818; 1831), today lauded as a central text of both Gothic literature and canonical British Romanticism, drew upon the 'cosmopolitan' Gothic conventions of early nineteenth-century Germany and France, particularly as these were realised in actual and literary manifestations of the phantasmagoria or magic-lantern show.

And yet, taking Romantic writers at their word, and overlooking the extent to which they too often made recourse to some of the characteristics of the Gothic aesthetic, literary historians of the nineteenth century routinely installed a sense of 'Romanticism' on the basis of its perceived differences from what was simultaneously being constructed as the genre of 'Gothic fiction'. In *A History of English Literature* (1864), for example, Thomas B. Shaw, a graduate of St John's College, Cambridge, and eventually tutor and Professor of English to the Grand Dukes of Russia, ambitiously sought to write for his students a history of English letters that stretched from the

---

16 William Hazlitt, *Lectures on the English Poets. Delivered at the Surrey Institution* (London: Printed for Taylor and Hessey, 1818), p. 320.

Anglo-Saxon period through to the reigns of Kings George I and II. His account of the 'Dawn of Romantic Poetry' – a section of his history that surveys such earlier poets as William Collins, Mark Akenside, Thomas Gray and William Cowper, before going on to consider the more familiarly 'Romantic' figures of Walter Scott, Wordsworth, Coleridge, Southey, Thomas Moore, P. B. Shelley, Keats, Byron and Thomas Campbell – sets in place many of the assumptions about so-called 'Big-Six' Romanticism that are still prevalent today:

> The great revolution in popular taste and sentiment which substituted what is called the romantic type in literature for the cold and clear-cut artificial spirit of that classicism which is exhibited in its highest form in the writings of [Alexander] Pope was, like all powerful and desirable movements, whether in politics or in letters, gradual.[17]

Though slow to take effect, Romanticism by this reckoning was a revolutionary and resolutely anti-Classical literary 'movement' that demonstrated a perceptible tendency 'to seek for subjects and forms of expressions in a wider, more passionate, and more natural sphere of nature and emotion'.[18] But what is particularly notable about Shaw's construction of the category of the 'Romantic' in *A History of English Literature* is the way in which he cautiously negotiates the Gothic qualities of the literature that he includes within it, be that the 'necromantic agency' and the 'midnight expedition of Deloraine to the wizard's tomb in Melrose Abbey' in Scott's *The Lay of the Last Minstrel* (1805); the 'tragic and gloomy' tone of Scott's *The Bride of Lammermoor* (1819); the 'atmosphere of mystical and supernatural influences' and the 'superhuman purity and unearthliness of the characters' in Wordsworth's *The White Doe of Rylstone* (1815); or the 'wild, mystical phantasmagoric narrative' that is Coleridge's 'The Rime of the Ancyent Marinere' (1798).[19] Although, as these phrases suggest, Shaw at least countenances the poignantly Gothic moments in some of the best-known novels and poems of the Romantic canon, he tends either to condemn them as examples of aesthetic failure, or to apologise for their existence as merely the necessary paraphernalia of the writer's quest for antiquarian authenticity. The supernaturalism of Coleridge's 'Christabel' (1816), for example, he deems too unrealistic, dream-like and ultimately 'fatal to the poem as a work of art', while the fantastic elements in Wordsworth are said to lend to the poetry a 'somewhat affected air'; the Gothicism of Scott,

---

17 Thomas B. Shaw, *A History of English Literature* (London: John Murray, 1864), p. 374.
18 Shaw, *A History of English Literature*, p. 374.
19 Shaw, *A History of English Literature*, pp. 407, 415, 449, 453.

for its part, is modestly commended as an example of the 'completeness with which the poet throws himself back into past ages' in order to 'speak and think' like 'a minstrel of the fourteenth century'.[20] As in Langhorne's review of Walpole a century earlier, Gothic could only be excused if it were explained as a deliberate echo or trace of the ancient Gothic past.

The depth of Shaw's anti-Gothic biases becomes especially apparent when, in a section of *A History of English Literature* entitled 'Modern Novelists', he turns to discuss the romances of Horace Walpole, Clara Reeve, Ann Radcliffe, Matthew Gregory Lewis, Mary Shelley and Charles Robert Maturin. Though aspects of his appraisal of these writers are surprisingly positive – the 'wonderful fictions' of Radcliffe, he maintains, 'exhibit a surprising power (perhaps never equalled) over the emotions of fear and undefined mysterious suspense' – Shaw for the most part rehearses the opprobrium that earlier nineteenth-century critics had levied against the tradition of eighteenth- and nineteenth-century Gothic romance.[21] Of *Otranto*, for instance, he claims that 'The manners are totally absurd and unnatural, the heroine being one of those inconsistent portraits in which the sentimental languor of the eighteenth century is superadded to the female character of the Middle Ages—in short, one of those incongruous contradictions which we meet in all the romantic fictions before Scott.'[22] Clara Reeve's *The Old English Baron* (1778), by the same token, is said to contain 'the same defects' as Walpole's haunted castle, while, for all her powers of narrative suspense, Radcliffe is said to be a poor portrayer of literary character whose fictional repertoire remains, in the end, decidedly limited.[23] Writing about Lewis, Shaw cuttingly claims that *The Monk* 'owes its continued popularity (though, we are happy to say, only among half-educated men and ecstatic milliners) chiefly to the licentious warmth of its scenes', and while Maturin's imagination was often vivid, his works in general 'are full of the most outrageous absurdities', *Melmoth the Wanderer* (1820) in particular a 'farrago of impossible and inconceivable adventures, without plan or coherence'.[24] Even Shaw's comments on *Frankenstein* are, at best, ambivalent: some of the scenes in this otherwise 'powerful tale' are 'managed with a striking and breathless effect' that 'makes us for a moment forget the childish improbability and melodramatic extravagance of the

---

20 Shaw, *A History of English Literature*, pp. 449, 454, 407.
21 Shaw, *A History of English Literature*, p. 463.
22 Shaw, *A History of English Literature*, p. 462.
23 Shaw, *A History of English Literature*, p. 463.
24 Shaw, *A History of English Literature*, p. 464.

tale'.²⁵ Perhaps the key to Shaw's disapproval lies in his revealing observation concerning the use of the explained supernatural in the work of Ann Radcliffe: 'after all, pure fear—*sensual*, not moral, fear—is by no means a legitimate object of high art'.²⁶ For the nineteenth century, the Gothic was tasteless, formulaic, tawdry, immature and resolutely popular, the Romantic imagination, by contrast, the inspired and inspirational preserve of higher aesthetic realms.

Similar assumptions were written into literary historiography throughout the Victorian period. In William John Courthope's *The Liberal Movement in English Literature* (1885), for example, the Gothic was described as little more than a strain of proto-Romanticism, a markedly undeveloped mode that would only later develop into the 'mature' aesthetic visions of a Wordsworth, Coleridge, Scott, Byron, Keats or P. B. Shelley:

> Towards the close of the eighteenth century the taste for the supernatural and the marvellous was quickened by German influences, which inspired the fictions of Monk Lewis and Mrs. Radcliffe; and the stream of romance added to its volume the French Revolutionary ethics advocated in the imaginative and philosophical works of William Godwin. In all these writers two leading characteristics are manifest; a Conservative adherence to classical form, and a Liberal tendency to encourage romantic feeling; a tendency which, it is evident, may be either so chastened by judgment and reflection as simply to intensify the pleasures of the imagination, or, if unchecked by reason, may ripen into revolt against the whole order of existing society.²⁷

In Edward Dowden's later study *The French Revolution and English Literature* (1897) too, 'the Romantic movement' is figured as an exclusively masculine category that includes William Blake, Robert Burns, Southey, Coleridge, Wordsworth, Keats, Byron and P. B. Shelley, and which strenuously excludes as such all intimations of the feminised Gothic tradition. Even as it formulated a modern sense of 'Gothic fiction', the nineteenth century habitually subordinated it to the tradition of high poetic Romanticism.

Even so, there is evidence to suggest that, dismissed and undervalued though it was, the Gothic remained a secret and somewhat illicit source of readerly pleasure and enjoyment throughout much of the Victorian period. One such Gothic reader was none other than Wilkie Collins, a writer who, as Tamar Heller's chapter in this volume elaborates, himself made innovative

---

25 Shaw, *A History of English Literature*, p. 465.
26 Shaw, *A History of English Literature*, p. 464.
27 William John Courthope, *The Liberal Movement in English Literature* (London: John Murray, 1885), pp. 121–2.

use of the Gothic aesthetic in his short stories and sensation novels of the 1850s and 1860s. As Collins, recounting his regaling of members of his family with a selection of Gothic stories, wrote to his father in August 1842,

> It turned (it generally somehow does whenever I am in her company) upon literature, and I sat with my back to the window, and my hand in my pocket, freezing my horrified auditors by a varied recital of the most terrible portions of the Monk and Frankenstein. Every sentence that fell from my lips was followed in rapid succession by – 'Lor!' – 'oh!' 'ah!' 'He! He!' 'Good gracious!' etc etc. None of our country relations I am sure ever encountered in their whole lives before such a hash of diablerie, demonology, massacre, with their [?] and bread and butter. I intend to give them another course, comprising, The Ancient Mariner, Jack the Giant Killer, the Mysteries of Udolpho and an inquiry into the life and actions (when they were little girls) of the witches of Macbeth.[28]

Returning a number of eighteenth-century Gothic fictions and Romantic poems to their roots in the oral tradition of storytelling, Collins entertains his enraptured audience with tales of the ghastly and the supernatural. Others remained powerfully drawn to the Gothic romances published towards the end of the previous century. In Charlotte Brontë's *Shirley* (1849), for instance, a novel set in Yorkshire during the industrial depression of 1811–12, the narrator at one point describes the young Rose Yorke as being deeply engrossed in a reading of Radcliffe's *The Italian* (1796–7). As the dialogue between Rose and Caroline Helstone develops, so we gain some insight into the ways in which Radcliffe and her works were largely associated with the reading habits of children and inexperienced young women in the period:

> Caroline stole a quiet gaze towards [Rose], dwelling on her young, absorbed countenance, and observing a certain unconscious movement of the mouth as she read, – a movement full of character. Caroline had tact, and she had fine instinct: she felt that Rose Yorke was a peculiar child, – one of the unique: she knew how to treat her. Approaching quietly, she knelt on the carpet at her side, and looked over her little shoulder at her book. It was a romance of Mrs. Radcliffe's – 'The Italian'.
>
> Caroline read on with her, making no remark: presently Rose showed her the attention of asking, ere she turned a leaf,–
>
> 'Are you ready?'

---

28 This extract from Collins's letter of 25 August 1842 is reprinted in Victor Sage (ed.), *The Gothick Novel: A Casebook* (Basingstoke: Macmillan, 1990), p. 72. Other editions of Collins's letters render the illegible word in parenthesis as the tea 'Souchong'.

Caroline only nodded.
'Do you like it?' inquired Rose, ere long.
'Long since, when I read it as a child, I was wonderfully taken with it.'
'Why?'
'It seemed to open with such promise, – such foreboding of a most strange tale to be unfolded.'
'And in reading it, you feel as if you were far away from England, – really in Italy, – under another sort of sky, – that blue sky of the south which travellers describe.'
'You are sensible of that, Rose?'
'It makes me long to travel, Miss Helstone.'[29]

This coupling of Gothic with the tastes of younger female readers, however, was not without exception. We know, for example, that the Victorian novelist William Makepeace Thackeray read *The Mysteries of Udolpho* (1794) and *The Italian* as a schoolboy, and remained particularly delighted by Maturin's *Melmoth the Wanderer* (1820).[30] Moreover, Montague Summers, the early twentieth century's greatest Gothic champion, looked back fondly on his late-Victorian childhood of the 1880s to conjure up in the opening paragraph of *The Gothic Quest* (1938) a powerful scene of literary enchantment, evocatively describing how he, a young but precocious reader, came to access, and fall under the spell of, the works of Ann Radcliffe:

> My love for the romances of Mrs. Radcliffe dates from my very first years. Among my earliest recollections is an edition of her Works in one rather formidable fat volume, double-coloured—which offered no difficulties then—and embellished with woodcuts that were a perpetual delight, not least because of their close affinity to the plays of Webb and Pollock of which one was giving nightly performances. Bound in dull black morocco, gilt-tooled, Mrs. Radcliffe lived on the summit of the highest shelves in a sombre and shadowy but by no means large old library, where the books stood ranged [sic] in very neat rows in tall mahogany cases behind heavy glass doors. Most sections were locked and keyless, but the particular bookcase whence Mrs. Radcliffe could be reached by mounting upon a chair and stretching rather far was always left unfastened, as I suppose containing standard literature and works approved for general and uncensored perusal, Scott, Dickens, Thackeray, Trollope, Marryat, Fenimore

---

29 Charlotte Brontë, *Shirley*, edited by Herbert Rosengarten, intro. by Margaret Smith (Oxford: Oxford University Press, 1981), pp. 398–9.
30 See [William Makepeace Thackeray], 'Roundabout papers, No. VIII: De Juventute', *The Cornhill Magazine* 2:10 (October 1860): 501–12; and Benjamin Franklin Fisher IV (ed.), *The Gothic's Gothic: Study Aids to the Tradition of the Tale of Terror* (New York: Routledge, 2018), entry no. 1295.

> Cooper, Lingard, Miss Strickland, Prescott, and the more sober historians. *Tom Jones*, I remember, was banished to the remotest altitudes, and jailed beyond all hope of release. What a day it was—diem numera meliore lapillo, as old Persius bids—that day when I discovered how an alien key would fit the bookcase locks![31]

What is notable, here, is that Summers recalls Radcliffe's works being kept in an almost inaccessible yet unlocked bookcase alongside such other legitimate, canonical or 'uncensored' nineteenth-century British and American writers as Scott, Charles Dickens, Thackeray, Anthony Trollope, James Fenimore Cooper and Florence Marryat. Nonetheless, she remained somewhat of an antiquarian curiosity, albeit one that was no less desirable for being so. Although, in the extract from his essay on Ann Radcliffe that I cited as the epigraph to this Introduction, the Scottish poet, critic, anthropologist and 'psychical researcher' Andrew Lang in 1900 had rhetorically enquired whether 'any one now read[s] Mrs Radcliffe', it is quite clear that she and those writers of the Gothic school remained popular if somewhat unorthodox literary fare throughout the nineteenth century: the volume of her novels that Lang reads in the public library is the 'dirtiest, greasiest, most dog's-eared, and most bescribbled tome in the collection', all sufficient proof for him that the Great Enchantress has, indeed, 'been read diligently, and copiously annotated'.[32]

The Gothic in Nineteenth-Century British, American and European Culture

The great irony of Gothic in the nineteenth century, of course, is that, generically localised in, and restricted to, the Gothic romances of Walpole, Radcliffe, Lewis and other writers of the previous century, it was not a term that was generally applied to any of the later fictions of the period 1800–1900 that we now readily describe as 'Gothic' or 'Gothic-inflected'. The point is made clear when we survey contemporary responses to Mary Shelley's *Frankenstein* (1818; 1831) and Bram Stoker's *Dracula* (1897), the two influential and subsequently mythologised texts of Gothic monstrosity that loom large over the century so as almost to book-end it. Of the several early reviews of Shelley's novel that were published in 1818 and 1831, not one of them made use of the term

---

31 Montague Summers, *The Gothic Quest: A History of the Gothic Novel*, 2nd edition (London: Fortune Press, 1968), p. 7.
32 Lang, 'Mrs. Radcliffe's Novels', p. 23.

'Gothic' in order to describe or generically classify it.³³ That 'Gothic' as a specifically literary concept remained for much of the Victorian period restricted primarily to works of the previous century is similarly attested to by responses to Stoker's iconic vampire fiction in the late 1890s: of the reviews that were published in *The Athenaeum* (June 1897), *The Spectator* (July 1897) and *Punch* (June 1897), not one made reference to the text as 'Gothic', and nor, as the interview with the author that was published in *British Weekly* in July of the same year indicates, did Stoker think of himself as writing within a Gothic literary tradition.³⁴ Across the Atlantic, the works of Edgar Allan Poe in the middle of the century largely escaped this label too, one notable exception being John Moncure Daniel's altogether dismissive reference to Poe's *oeuvre* as 'unequal and uneven, gothic and grotesque' in a review that was published in *The Southern Literary Messenger* in March 1850.³⁵ Even in the American context, though, the term continued to function in its older sense as a marker of the unruly, the uncivilised and the barbaric. Consequently, though Lang's 1900 essay on Radcliffe persuasively traced her influence in the works of a number of nineteenth-century British and American writers – Jane Austen's *Northanger Abbey*; Charlotte Brontë's *Jane Eyre* (1847); the novels of Walter Scott; Byron's poetry; Robert Louis Stevenson's *Kidnapped* (1886); Nathaniel Hawthorne's *The Marble Faun* (1860); the historical romances of Stanley John Weyman – not once did he feel it necessary or appropriate to designate this post-Radcliffean literary tradition as 'Gothic'. The significance of such linguistic suspensions is twofold. First, and as Jarlath Killeen has claimed, the Gothic nineteenth century is largely the construct of the twentieth and twenty-first centuries, the monstrous 'Mr Hyde' that all too conveniently serves as the dark double to the 'Dr Jekyll' of modern progress and sexual liberation.³⁶ 'Nineteenth-century Gothic' is as much a retrospective

---

33 This includes those reviews published in *The Quarterly Review* (by John Wilson Croker, January 1818); *La Belle Assemblée* (March 1818); *Blackwood's Edinburgh Magazine* (by Walter Scott, March 1818); *The British Critic* (April 1818); *The Edinburgh Magazine, and Literary Miscellany* (1818); *The Gentleman's Magazine* (April 1818); and *The Anthenaeum* (written by P. B. Shelley in 1817, published in November 1831). For a useful compilation of this material, see the early reviews published online at <http://knarf.english.up enn.edu/Reviews/reviews.html> (last accessed 21 August 2019).

34 For some contemporary reviews of Stoker's novel, see Bram Stoker, *Dracula*, edited by Glennis Byron (Peterborough, Ont.: Broadview, 1998), pp. 481–8.

35 This review is reprinted in Ian Malcolm Walker (ed.), *Edgar Allan Poe: The Critical Heritage* (London and New York: Routledge & Kegan Paul, 1986), pp. 356–76 (p. 365).

36 See Jarlath Killeen's argument in *Gothic Literature 1825–1914* (Cardiff: University of Wales Press, 2009).

construct as 'Victorianism' or the 'Victorian period' itself. Second, it is during the nineteenth century that the literary Gothic, as Julian Wolfreys has pointed out, loses much of its formal and generic stability, fragmenting and dissolving instead into a mercurial mode that stealthily works its way into the most unsuspecting and unlikely of cultural forms: 'The gothic' in this period, Wolfreys writes, 'becomes truly haunting in that it can never be pinned down as a single identity, while it returns through various apparitions and manifestations, seemingly everywhere', from comic discourse and photographic images and into the social construction of childhood, sexuality and the modern technologies of the uncanny.[37] Though, even in the earlier period, the Gothic had always been more a fluid 'mode' of cultural expression than a fixed and static literary 'genre', it is during the nineteenth century that, as Peter J. Kitson has argued, this shift from genre to mode became especially pronounced.[38]

The essays assembled here all variously attest to the acuity of such critical claims. Joe Kember's chapter, for example, pays welcome attention to the ways in which the Gothic mode influenced the popular entertainment industry in nineteenth-century Britain, while Anthony Mandal shows how it was absorbed into the chapbooks, shilling shockers and penny bloods of the so-called 'trade Gothic'. As Scott Brewster's chapter shows, it was in the ghost stories of the Victorian period that the Gothic tradition in fiction most securely anchored itself. But the Gothic worked its way into more self-consciously realist modes of representation, too: John Bowen, for instance, discusses how Charles Dickens put Gothic to the service of writing what Sigmund Freud would later describe as 'the Uncanny', while Serena Trowbridge shows how Gothic enriched and nourished the work of several nineteenth-century poets, both canonical and lesser known. Corinna Wagner provides a fresh and searching account of the ways in which several Victorian Gothic fictions responded to the writings of Charles Darwin and other evolutionary scientists of the nineteenth century, while Jerrold E. Hogle's

---

37 Julian Wolfreys, 'Preface: "I could a tale unfold" or, the Promise of Gothic', in Ruth Robbins and Julian Wolfreys (eds), *Victorian Gothic: Literary and Cultural Manifestations in the Nineteenth Century* (Basingstoke: Palgrave Macmillan, 2000), pp. xi–xx (p. xv). For a continuation of this argument, see Julian Wolfreys, 'Victorian Gothic', in Anna Powell and Andrew Smith (eds), *Teaching the Gothic* (Basingstoke: Palgrave Macmillan, 2006), pp. 62–77.

38 Peter J. Kitson, 'The Victorian Gothic', in William Baker and Kenneth Womack (eds), *A Companion to the Victorian Novel* (Westport, CT: Greenwood Press, 2002), pp. 163–76 (p. 165).

Introduction: Gothic in the Nineteenth Century, 1800–1900

chapter advances a rigorous history of the vampire, perhaps the period's most characteristic monster, from Romanticism to the century's end. Andrew Smith closes the volume with an account of the complex and often ambivalent role that the Gothic fictions of writers such as Henry Rider Haggard, Rudyard Kipling and Arthur Conan Doyle played in the project of British imperialism at the very end of the period. Together, these scholars, in the critical tradition inaugurated by Robert Mighall in *A Geography of Victorian Gothic Fiction* (2003), all continue the work of revising the once-prominent assumption that, after its belated expression in fictions such as Maturin's *Melmoth the Wanderer* (1820), Thomas De Quincey's *Confessions of an English Opium-Eater* (1821) and James Hogg's *The Private Memoirs and Confessions of a Justified Sinner* (1824), the Gothic went 'underground' for much of the Victorian era in Britain, only later to be 'resurrected' in the popular fictions of Stevenson, Oscar Wilde and Stoker at the *fin de siècle*.

This volume moves well beyond received critical notions of the 'Victorian Gothic' in other respects, too, particularly in its inclusion of a suite of chapters devoted to exploring different national manifestations of the mode beyond nineteenth-century England.[39] Xavier Aldana Reyes and Rocío Rødtjer, for instance, consider the Gothic in nineteenth-century Spanish literature, providing a fascinating counterpoint to the Gothic depictions of Spain found in many late eighteenth-century British fictions. Revising the opinions of those who, like George Stillman Hillard in 1853, held that Italian culture showed no natural penchant for Gothic imaginings, Francesca Saggini shows the extent to which nineteenth-century Italian literature engaged with the Gothic mode, both in translation and in the vernacular Italian. The chapters by Suzanne Gilbert and Christina Morin respectively deal with the Gothic literature of nineteenth-century Scotland and Ireland, while Charles L. Crow provides a comprehensive and wide-ranging account of nineteenth-century American Gothic. As in Volume I of *The Cambridge History of the Gothic*, though, we remain attuned in this volume to the ways in which the Gothic registered, and participated within, some of the important historical events of the period 1800–1900. Maisha Wester's chapter, in this regard, reads a selection of British and American nineteenth-century Gothic texts in relation to the history of slavery on both continents, while William Hughes

---

39 In addition to the other critical studies of the Victorian Gothic cited in this Introduction, see Julian Wolfreys, *Victorian Hauntings: Spectrality, Gothic, the Uncanny and Literature* (Basingstoke: Palgrave Macmillan, 2002) and Andrew Smith and William Hughes (eds), *The Victorian Gothic: An Edinburgh Companion* (Edinburgh: Edinburgh University Press, 2012).

provides a pioneering account of the ways in which Gothic was used to express the perceived ramifications of, and anxieties pertaining to, the rise of the British railway system from the mid-1820s onwards.

Literature, of course, was the only realm to have witnessed a new sense of 'Gothic' in the nineteenth century, and as the chapters brought together here demonstrate, the word underwent equally significant changes in the field of historiography. Following the coinage of the terms 'medieval' and 'renaissance' in 1817 and 1836 respectively, the 'Gothic' past, that once capacious period of British antiquity that stretched from the fifth century right up to the sixteenth and beyond, fractured into two discrete historical epochs. Though not without exception, the 'Gothic' became the 'medieval', and with this suspension of what had long been an injurious term connoting savagery and violence, darkness and superstition, so perceptions of the past changed radically too. Tom Duggett's chapter explores some of the literary and historical ramifications of the shift from the 'Romantic Gothic' to 'Victorian medievalism', its argument pivoting on the years 1817 and 1877. One area in which 'Gothic' retained its currency, though, was in architectural theory and practice, an important aspect of the interdisciplinary nature of Gothic culture in nineteenth-century Britain that is explored by Alexandra Warwick. But even here, the Revivalist Gothic architecture of A. C. and A. W. N Pugin, Charles Barry, John Ruskin, William Morris and others was wilfully and self-consciously different from the whimsical and irresponsible 'Gothick' confections of Walpole, Beckford and other amateur architects and patrons of the previous century. Indeed, the architectural style that, in earlier periods, was often denounced as 'Gothic' in the barbarous sense of that word became from Charles Locke Eastlake's *A History of the Gothic Revival* (1872) onwards designated by the term 'Gothick', the intentional linguistic archaism signifying the frivolousness, sentimental antiquarianism and misplaced archaeological rigour that the Gothic Revivalists of the late nineteenth century identified in the work of earlier practitioners.[40]

---

40 For more on this, see Michael Hall, 'Introduction', in Michael Hall (ed.), *Gothic Architecture and Its Meanings, 1550–1830* (Reading: Spire Books, 2002), pp. 7–24.

2.1

Gothic Romanticism and the Summer of 1816

MADELEINE CALLAGHAN AND ANGELA WRIGHT

> A thousand fantasies
> Begin to throng into my memory
> Of calling shapes, and beck'ning shadows dire,
> And airy tongues, that syllable men's names
> (John Milton, *Comus: A Mask* [1634], ll. 205–9)[1]

It is no exaggeration to say that the Summer of 1816 has attained near-mythological status in accounts of Romantic poetry, Gothic fiction and poetry, and literary biography. One of the most well-documented seasons of literary creativity in the history of English literature, its extraordinary intensity derived in part from exceptional meteorological conditions across the globe. Known otherwise as 'the year without a summer', 1816 was marked as particularly cold, wet and inclement following the eruption of Mount Tambora in Indonesia the year before. As Gillen D'Arcy Wood has observed, the time in 1816 that the individuals whom we explore in this chapter spent on the banks of lac Léman still 'remains the coldest, wettest Geneva summer since records began in 1753', with a record 130 days of rain recorded between April and September.[2] In his apocalyptic poem 'Darkness', composed in July 1816, Lord Byron would observe that 'men forgot their passions in the dread / Of this their desolation; and all hearts / Were chill'd into a selfish prayer for light' as they confronted a world without sun.[3]

Inhospitable climate events, including heavy cloud cover, flooding and uncharacteristically low temperatures can, of course, prove conducive to

---

[1] John Milton, 'A Masque of the Same Author Presented at Ludlow Castle, 1634, before the Earl of Bridgewater then President of Wales (Comus)', in *John Milton: The Complete Poems*, edited by John Leonard (London: Penguin, 1998), p. 52.
[2] Gillen D'Arcy Wood, *Tambora: The Eruption that Changed the World* (Princeton, NJ and Oxford: Princeton University Press, 2014), p. 46.
[3] Lord Byron, 'Darkness' (1816), in *The Prisoner of Chillon and Other Poems* (London: Printed for John Murray, 1816), pp. 27–31, ll. 7–9.

remarkable feats of creativity. Prolonged and intensified due to the poor weather, the formative meeting in Switzerland between Mary Wollstonecraft Godwin, Percy Bysshe Shelley, Lord Byron, Jane [Claire] Clairmont and John William Polidori set in place an explosive chain of imaginative and personal events, the consequences of which are still culturally significant today. For out of this summer came some of the most significant achievements of Gothic and Romantic literature, from Mary Shelley's *Frankenstein* (1818; 1831) and John Polidori's *The Vampyre* (1819) to Byron's *Manfred* (1817) and Canto III of *Childe Harold's Pilgrimage* (1816); the establishment of vital artistic connections between both Mary and Percy Shelley with Byron; and the abrupt departure of the youthful Polidori, the spurned physician and companion of Lord Byron.

But the Summer of 1816 was not simply the beginning of the 'Satanic School', as Robert Southey would hyperbolise.[4] Instead, it marked the culmination of the intense programme of reading and fervent intellectual and creative exchange between the individuals concerned, a crucial time in which the conversations and connections that they enjoyed would immeasurably enrich the artistic output of each writer. From Percy Shelley and Mary Godwin's fascination with the poetry and personae of William Wordsworth and Samuel Taylor Coleridge, and the works of Ann Radcliffe and Matthew Gregory Lewis, to the group's burgeoning interest in, and poetic recasting of, the first-generation Romantic poets, the Summer of 1816 saw the personal and intellectual connections between Byron, Mary and Percy magnify their engagement with the British literary world that they had left behind. For certain members of the party, this period witnessed the beginning of important personal relationships, but it was a beginning built upon the solid foundations of their previous intellectual and artistic experiences. The months of June, July, August and September of 1816 saw those gathered at and around the Villa Diodati innovatively extending what has subsequently been termed 'Romantic' and 'Gothic' literature in hitherto unprecedented directions, even if, in effect, much of the work that these writers produced during this time bears testament to the artificial nature of that very distinction itself.

Literary precursors from both the immediate and remote pasts were read and discussed at Diodati in 1816. We know that later, during the month of

---

[4] Robert Southey, *The Poetical Works of Robert Southey, Collected by Himself*, 10 vols (London: Longman, Orme, Brown, Green & Longmans, 1838), vol. 10, p. 206.

August, Matthew Gregory Lewis, author of, most notably, the Gothic romance *The Monk* (1796), visited the Byron's rented villa, and translated *viva voce* Johann Wolfgang von Goethe's *Faust* (1790) for Byron and Shelley.[5] The reading aloud of some texts and the spontaneous translations of others have become significant in subsequent accounts of the gathering. Richard Holmes summarises the power that, even from afar, Coleridge's poetry had on this group of expatriates and self-imposed exiles in Europe, observing that 'when Byron read "Christabel" aloud at the Villa Diodati, one stormy night in June 1816, Shelley ran out in a fit and Mary Shelley began her novel *Frankenstein*'.[6] Coleridge's 'Christabel' was only published in 1816, but its origin in the 1790s, as well as its long period of percolation before that, is a perfect illustration of how literary remnants from the eighteenth century came to be debated, contested and transmitted at the Villa Diodati. Like most accounts, Holmes places the reading of 'Christabel' prior to Byron's suggestion of the ghost storytelling competition. Polidori's *The Diary of Dr. John William Polidori, 1816, Relating to Byron, Shelley, Etc.* (published 1911) differed, however, in its account of the sequence of events. There, on Monday June 17, Polidori noted that 'The ghost-stories are begun by all but me' – that is to say that Byron, Shelley, Mary Godwin and Jane Claire Clairmont had all begun to compose supernatural tales, the results of which were *Frankenstein* by Mary Wollstonecraft Shelley and Byron's fragment of 'The Vampyre', first published with *Mazeppa* in 1819. The following day, Tuesday 18 June, Polidori notes that he commenced his contribution, subsequently to be published under the title *Ernestus Berchtold; or, The Modern Oedipus* (1819), and then that 'Lord B. repeated some verses of Coleridge's "Christabel" of the witch's breast' and that Shelley 'then had a seizure'.[7] Punctilious though it may seem to draw attention to Polidori's slight chronological alteration of the events, it is nonetheless important to note the differing accounts by those present and active during the famed literary competition: although we aim to produce here a history of those extraordinary few months, disagreements in the order of certain crucial occurrences leave some questions of literary precedent and influence more intangible and unanswerable than others.

---

[5] For further information on the meeting, see David Ellis, *Byron in Geneva: The Summer of 1816* (Oxford: Oxford University Press, 2011), p. 100.
[6] Richard Holmes (ed.), *Coleridge: Selected Poems* (London: HarperCollins, 1996), p. 68.
[7] John William Polidori, *The Diary of Dr John William Polidori, 1816, Relating to Byron, Shelley, Etc.*, edited by William Michael Rossetti (London: Elkin Matthews, 1911), pp. 125–6.

Monstrous Progenies

The short Preface that Percy Bysshe Shelley wrote for the first edition of *Frankenstein* (1818) in 1817 made no mention of 'Christabel' at all, but instead foregrounded the fiction's Classical and canonical English or 'Gothic' precedents, noting that 'The *Iliad*, the tragic poetry of Greece, – Shakespeare, in *The Tempest* and *Midsummer Night's Dream*, – and most especially Milton, in *Paradise Lost*, conform to the rule' of preserving 'the truth of the elementary principles of human nature'.[8] This Preface followed an impulse similar to that of Horace Walpole in the Preface to the second edition of *The Castle of Otranto* in 1765, where, with more than a hint of false modesty, Walpole claimed to 'shelter' his 'own daring under the cannon of the brightest genius this country, at least, has produced'.[9] Walpole was sheltering the attempts of his 'humble' novelistic synthesis of ancient and modern romance beneath the protective shield of Shakespearean emulation, unwittingly setting an example for the first Preface to *Frankenstein* so many years later. Having cited such Classical and canonical precedent, Percy's Preface went on to state that:

> the most humble novelist, who seeks to confer or receive amusement from his labours, may, without presumption, apply to prose fiction a licence, or rather a rule, from the adoption of which so many exquisite combinations of human feeling have resulted in the highest specimens of poetry.[10]

'Humble' was indeed the appropriate adjectival descriptor to be applied to any novelist's attempts to imitate a Milton or Shakespeare's 'combinations of human feeling'. Whereas poetry was a vocational duty, the novelist's work was to 'confer or receive amusement'. In this first Preface to *Frankenstein*, the adverse weather of the Summer of 1816 was cited as being key to the indoor reading of ghost stories, and the challenge of the ghost story-writing competition that ensued. 'The season was cold and rainy', it observes, 'and in the evenings we crowded around a blazing wood fire, and occasionally amused ourselves with some German stories of ghosts, which happened to fall into our hands.'[11] Mary Shelley would later confirm her late husband's sense of the significance of the poor weather conditions to the act of authorship in her

---

[8] [P. B. Shelley], 'Preface' to the first edition, in Mary Shelley, *Frankenstein; or, The Modern Prometheus*, edited by Marilyn Butler (Oxford: Oxford University Press, 2008), pp. 3–4 (p. 3). All references to Shelley's novel are taken from Marilyn Butler's edition of the 1818 text.

[9] Horace Walpole, *The Castle of Otranto*, edited by Nick Groom (Oxford: Oxford University Press, 2014), p. 13.

[10] [P. B. Shelley], 'Preface' to the first edition of *Frankenstein* (1818), p. 3.

[11] [P. B. Shelley], 'Preface' to the first edition of *Frankenstein* (1818), p. 4.

'Introduction' to the Standard Novels edition of *Frankenstein* in 1831, observing that 'incessant rain often confined us for days to the house'.[12]

Both paratexts foregrounded the reading of Jean-Baptiste Benoît Eyriès's French translation of a selection of German ghost stories, *Fantasmagoriana, ou Recueil d'Histoires d'Apparitions de Spectres, Revenants, Fantômes, etc.* (1812), an aspect of the compositional history of *Frankenstein* that is explored to fuller effect by Maximiliaan van Woudenberg in Chapter 2 of this volume. Mary Shelley's memory of the collection in the 1831 'Author's Introduction', however, went way beyond Percy's brief allusion to it in the 1818 Preface. Long after the deaths of Byron, Shelley and Polidori, Mary's recollections returned quite particularly to the ghost in Shakespeare's *Hamlet*:

> There was the *History of the Inconstant Lover,* who, when he thought to clasp the bride to whom he had pledged his vows, found himself in the arms of the pale ghost of her whom he had deserted. There was the tale of the sinful founder of his race whose miserable doom it was to bestow the kiss of death on all the younger sons of his fated house, just when they reached the age of promise. His gigantic, shadowy form, clothed like the ghost in *Hamlet,* in complete armour, but with the beaver up, was seen at midnight, by the moon's fitful beams, to advance slowly along the gloomy avenue. The shape was lost beneath the shadow of the castle walls; but soon a gate swung back, a step was heard, the door of the chamber opened, and he advanced to the couch of the blooming youths, cradled in healthy sleep.[13]

It is difficult to pinpoint precisely which scene in Eyriès's collection that Shelley has in mind here. Instead, her memories of Shakespeare seem to have been sharpened by Ann Radcliffe's posthumously published 'On the Supernatural in Poetry', which appeared in the *New Monthly Magazine* in 1826. Here, Radcliffe's fictional mouthpiece had argued that:

> The dark watch upon the remote platform, the dreary aspect of the night, the very expression of the office on guard, 'the air bites shrewdly; it is very cold;', the recollection of a star, an unknown world, are all circumstances which excite forlorn, melancholy, and solemn feelings, and dispose us to welcome, with trembling curiosity, the awful being that draws near; and to indulge in that strange mixture of horror, pity and indignation, produced by the tale it reveals.[14]

---

[12] Mary Wollstonecraft Shelley, 'Author's Introduction to the Standard Novels Edition (1831)', in Mary Shelley, *Frankenstein; or, The Modern Prometheus*, edited by Marilyn Butler (Oxford: Oxford University Press, 2008), pp. 192–7 (p. 192).
[13] Shelley, 'Author's Introduction', p. 194.
[14] Ann Radcliffe, 'On the supernatural in poetry', *New Monthly Magazine* 16:1 (1826): 145–52 (pp. 147–8).

Mary Shelley's recollection of *Hamlet* is conditioned by Radcliffe's earlier evocation of the play, becoming a half-fabricated recollection of another writer's interpretation of a 'Gothic' literary text. Radcliffe's descriptions in 'On the Supernatural in Poetry' also continually stressed the emotions that preceded the appearance of the ghost of Hamlet's father, including the 'forlorn melancholy' 'solemn feelings' and 'trembling curiosity' excited by the 'dreary aspect of the night', something that Shelley here transmuted into the 'gloomy avenue' and the attention to visual and acoustic aspects.[15]

Of course, well beyond this short essay from 1826, Mary Shelley's craft was deeply indebted to the works of the Great Enchantress. She and Percy Shelley together had read Radcliffe's *The Mysteries of Udolpho* (1794) in 1815 and *The Italian* (1796–7) in 1814, and this, together with their close study of both Wordsworth and Coleridge, guaranteed a constant quest in *Frankenstein* to unite, in the fashion of these earlier Gothic and Romantic writers, 'the exquisite combinations of human feeling' with accordant circumstances.[16] This is evident, for instance, in the way in which chapter IV, the account of creation with which Mary Shelley commenced the story in 1816, foregrounds the 'dreary night of November', when the 'rain pattered dismally against the panes' as crucial components of the Creature's coming to life. These are Radcliffean 'accordant circumstances' in all but name, scenes that echo the unseasonably cold weather during the Summer of 1816 as well as the moment of Shelley's first conceptualisation of *Frankenstein*, a text that, like Victor in relation to the Creature, she would refer to as her own 'hideous progeny' in the 1831 Introduction.

As critics have frequently pointed out, *Frankenstein* was to a large extent generated by the synergies of scientific endeavour during the Romantic period and the literary and scientific readings that the company at the Villa Diodati undertook in consequence of being confined to close quarters.[17] Nonetheless, the immediate climatic conditions of 1816 continued to play a

---

[15] For further readings of this, see Angela Wright, *Mary Shelley* (Cardiff: University of Wales Press, 2018), pp. 110–12.

[16] In the journal maintained by Mary Godwin and Percy Bysshe Shelley, Mary records on Sunday 27 November 1814, 'Read The Italian and talk all day – a very happy day indeed', and the year 1815 records the joint rereading of *The Mysteries of Udolpho*. See Mary Shelley, journal entry for Sunday 27 November, in Paula R. Feldman and Diana Scott-Kilvert (eds), *The Journals of Mary Shelley, 1814–1844*, 2 vols (Oxford: Clarendon Press, 1987), vol. 1, p. 48. See also the reading list for 1815, vol. 1, pp. 88–91.

[17] For accounts of the scientific contexts of Romanticism, especially in relation to electricity and Humphry Davy, see Marilyn Butler, 'The first *Frankenstein* and radical science', *Times Literary Supplement* 9 (April 1993), pp. 12–14 and Sharon Ruston, *Creating Romanticism: Case Studies in the Literature, Science and Medicine of the 1790s* (Basingstoke: Palgrave Macmillan, 2013), pp. 124–5.

determining role in the fiction, not least in the framing narrative of Arctic explorer Robert Walton, which was subsequently added to the tale in 1817. Walton draws equal amounts of pain and pleasure from the 'cold northern breeze' in his very first letter to his sister, the silent addressee Margaret Walton Saville, whose initials uncannily echo those of the married Mary Wollstonecraft Shelley.[18] As he at this point confesses to his sister, the icy climate of St Petersburg acts as both brace for Walton's nerves and the source of considerable 'delight'. The precision and optimism that Walton applies in equal measure to his description of the climate combine in the group's literary readings and experience of the weather in 1816. Coleridge's 'Christabel', for example, read either immediately before or after the announcing of the ghost storytelling competition, foregrounds atmospheric conditions as early as Part I, stanza 3:

> Is the Night chilly and dark?
> The night is chilly but not dark.
> The thin grey Cloud is spread on high,
> It covers but not hides the Sky.
> The Moon is behind, and at the Full;
> And yet she looks both small and dull.
> The Night is chill, the Cloud is grey:
> Tis a Month before the Month of May,
> And the Spring comes slowly up this way.[19]

The speaker in the poem inhabits a dual perspective, simultaneously anticipating *and* responding to questions on the night's atmosphere in a manner that seems teasingly reminiscent of Wordsworth's pedantic speaker in 'The Thorn' from *Lyrical Ballads* (1798). Coleridge dissolves and dissipates doubts about the night's clear skies, but through the clarity and precision of the descriptions, reintroduces elements of that self-same doubt. The night may not be 'dark', but the 'thin grey Cloud' 'covers but not hides' the sky. The indeterminacy here would serve to temper the later optimism of Robert Walton in *Frankenstein*. In his second letter to his sister, dated four months later, Walton notes that he is 'encompassed' by 'frost and snow', that the 'winter has been dreadfully severe' but that 'the spring promises well'. The

---

[18] For further readings of this, see Anne K. Mellor, *Mary Shelley: Her Life, Her Fiction, Her Monsters* (London and New York: Routledge, 1988), pp. 52–69 and Wright, *Mary Shelley*, pp. 44–9.

[19] Samuel Taylor Coleridge, 'Christabel', Part I, ll. 14–22, in *The Collected Works of Samuel Taylor Coleridge: Poetical Works; Poems (Variorum Text), Part I*, Vol. XVI, edited by J. C. C. Mays (Princeton, NJ: Princeton University Press, 2001), pp. 483–4.

explorer's optimism is, however, qualified through literary allusion: the allusions in 'Christabel' to the reluctant advance of spring lurk behind Walton's hopeful observations. As if to underline the inspiration from Coleridge, Walton then ventriloquises Coleridge's ancient mariner, quoting from him directly when he states that he is going to 'the land of mist and snow; but I shall kill no albatross, therefore do not be alarmed for my safety.'[20] Walton's optimism is first assuaged by the implicit connection to 'Christabel', and then by the more explicit allusions to 'The Rime of the Ancient Mariner' (1798). In the 1831 Standard Novels edition, Mary Shelley would make the connection with Coleridge's 'Ancient Mariner' even more pronounced, having Walton observe that 'I have often attributed my attachment to, my passionate enthusiasm for, the dangerous mysteries of the ocean, to that production of the most imaginative of modern poets.'[21] Walton in no way acts as a mouthpiece for Shelley, and the fact that it is he, and later Victor Frankenstein, who ventriloquises Coleridge's ancient mariner places ideological distance between the authorial position and these literary characters. Nonetheless, Mary Shelley's familiarity with Samuel Taylor Coleridge, both through her father's friendship with him and through her own close reading of his poetry, is well known.[22] Walton's assessment of Coleridge as 'the most imaginative of modern poets' no doubt echoes the views of the author.[23]

As the borrowings from the work of Coleridge ('Christabel'; 'Ancient Mariner'), Wordsworth ('Tintern Abbey') and Percy Shelley ('Mutability') in the text suggest, the literary past weighs heavily upon the present in *Frankenstein*. Mary Shelley is acutely aware of this, and presents it to us in her Creature's indiscriminate reading of Milton's *Paradise Lost*, showing her own readers the dangers of the subjectivism that infects his acts of literary sense-making and interpretation: 'As I read, however, I applied much personally to my own feelings and condition.'[24] The text thus grapples with a paradox that inflected all of the works generated during the Summer of 1816: the need to accept, embrace and account for the past while acknowledging its

---

[20] Shelley, *Frankenstein*, p. 10.
[21] Shelley, *Frankenstein*, Appendix B (Collation of the texts of 1818 and 1831), p. 201.
[22] For further biographical readings of the friendship between Samuel Taylor Coleridge and the Godwins, see, for example, William St Clair's chapter 'The Discovery of Poetry', in *The Godwins and the Shelleys* (London: Faber and Faber, 1989), pp. 221–7 and Miranda Seymour, *Mary Shelley* (London: Faber and Faber, 2011), pp. 39–40.
[23] Shelley, *Frankenstein*, Appendix B (Collation of the texts of 1818 and 1831), p. 201.
[24] Shelley, *Frankenstein*, p. 103.

failure – the failure of influence fully to explain or guarantee the experience of the present.

This is why *Frankenstein*, while formally and thematically innovative, participates so strongly in a Gothic literary tradition: it brings the past back as a revenant, as an echo, a memory of a memory. The narrative's success lies in bringing to the foreground shards, fragments and ghosts of the creature's possible influences, of the shards, fragments and ghosts of Victor's motives, but never an organic, coherent account or explanation. Mary Shelley's instinct is to prevent the aggregation of influence into a whole – we are permitted incomplete glimpses of influence, but never a composite entity. The Creature's body itself is representative of this: despite anatomically appearing as a unity of sorts, we remain unconvinced that it is ever really such; instead, it is, like the body of the text itself, always a failed totality, an entity that is never simply the sum of its parts, an indescribable or inconsolable simulacra of the real. In *Frankenstein*, Mary Shelley bequeaths to the Gothic the unruly figure of textual and corporeal monstrosity, an innovation that would become central to the mode from 1818 onwards.

Albeit on a more literal level, the irreducibility of influence haunted another of the fictions to come out of the Summer of 1816, too: John Polidori's *The Vampyre* (1819). In his chapter in this volume, Jerrold E. Hogle addresses this influential text, charting its significance to the evolving tradition of vampire tales in the nineteenth century and its connections with the reading of Coleridge's 'Christabel' in 1816. The fact that, during the ghost story competition at Diodati, it was Byron who first produced a fragment called 'The Vampyre', and that, when Polidori's tale was first published by Henry Colburn in the *New Monthly Magazine* in 1819 it was described as 'A Tale By Lord Byron', has been the subject of much critical speculation. How did Colburn come by Polidori's manuscript, and was Polidori actively engaged in an act of plagiarism, piracy or identity-theft? William Michael Rossetti, who edited Polidori's diary of the Summer of 1816 in 1911 after John Hobhouse prohibited Polidori from publishing in 1820, at last vindicated his uncle from the charge of imposture, while many, including Dr Richard Garnett in an entry on Polidori for the *Dictionary of National Biography* as late as 1896, continued to attribute the tale to Byron.[25] Polidori, for his part, devoted much time and considerable effort to dispelling these charges. The tale of aristocratic degeneracy, embodied in the vampiric and strongly

---

[25] Richard Garnett, 'Polidori, John William (1795–1821)', *Oxford Dictionary of National Biography* <www.oxforddnb.com/view/10.1093/odnb/9780192683120.001.0001/odnb-9 780192683120-e-22466> (last accessed 18 September 2018).

Byronic form of Lord Ruthven, was, Polidori admitted in an open letter to the same journal in May 1819, first conceived by Byron, but 'in its present form', he insisted, the tale belonged entirely to himself.[26] He returned to this in the Introduction to *Ernestus Berchtold*, claiming that, while *The Vampyre* was founded upon the 'groundwork' of Byron's fragment, the tale itself was his own creation; the manuscript, having been entrusted to the Countess of Breuss, he continued, 'appears to have fallen into the hands of some person, who sent it to the Editor [Colburn] in such a way, as to leave it so doubtful from his words, whether it was his lordship's or not, that I found some difficulty in vindicating it to myself'.[27] As Patricia L. Skarda has pointed out, *The Vampyre* is, indeed, highly Byronic in places, perhaps even self-consciously so.[28] But in Polidori's defence, we witness here the tussle between the origins of a tale and that same story in 'its present form', suggesting not simply a struggle between a definitive past version and its published form, but a broader, near-impossible struggle of detecting and attributing relations of influence. The tangled origins and challenged authorship of *The Vampyre* reveal much about how the reciprocity of the debating, editing, transcribing, translating, reading and composing of ghost stories during the Summer of 1816 at the Villa Diodati complicates and problematises any singular account of origin and influence at this particularly rich moment in literary history.

The Poetry of 1816: Gothic and Romantic Impulses

For Percy Shelley, Wordsworth and Coleridge were a pressing influence and abiding spur to creativity, and 1816 was the year that he would meet Byron and attempt to convert him to such intense interest in their poetic forebears. Polidori was a first-hand observer of the effects caused by Lord Byron's reading of the verses of 'Christabel', and, with a physician's eye, combined the effects with the remedy in his record of the event: 'LB repeated some verses of Coleridge's Christabel, of the witch's breast; when silence ensued, & Shelley, shrieking and putting his hands to his head, ran out of the room with a candle. Threw water in his face and after gave him ether.'[29] Despite the high pitch of the initial reception to 'Christabel', the artistic ramifications of

---

[26] John W. Polidori, 'Letter to the editor', *New Monthly Magazine* 11:64 (May 1819): p. 332.
[27] John Polidori, *Ernestus Berchtold; or, The Modern Oedipus. A Tale* (London: Printed for Longman, Hurst, Rees, Orme, and Brown, 1819), p. vi.
[28] Patricia L. Skarda, 'Vampirism and plagiarism: Byron's influence and Polidori's practice', *Studies in Romanticism* 28:2 (Summer 1989): 249–69.
[29] *The Diary of Dr John William Polidori*, 18 June, 1816, p. 126.

contact with Coleridge's poetry ran deep and generated subtle and complex responses from the group. Percy Shelley had recently published *Alastor; or, The Spirit of Solitude; And Other Poems* (1815), a volume that, including the titular poem, formulated a multifaceted and challenging response to Wordsworth's poetry and which revealed a careful and not entirely positive reading of the older poet's work. For despite Percy Shelley having enjoyed relatively small success in comparison to Byron, he was, in 1816, no poetic neophyte. As well as the *Alastor* volume, Shelley had published his ambitious epic, *Queen Mab* (1813) and had also written the poems later published in *The Esdaile Notebook* (1964), a volume which Donald H. Reiman and Neil Fraistat compare with Wordsworth's *The Prelude* (1799; 1805; 1850) and *The Excursion* (1814).[30] Shelley also had a further four publications to his name – *Zastrozzi* (1810); *Original Poetry by Victor and Cazire* (1810); *St Irvyne; or, The Rosicrucian* (published 1810; dated 1811); and *Posthumous Fragments of Margaret Nicholson* (1810) – as well as his anonymously published pamphlet, *Poetical Essay on the Existing State of Things* (1811). Shelley had already sought to engage directly with Wordsworth and Coleridge in his work, with *The Esdaile Notebook*'s 'Falshood and Vice: a Dialogue' bearing a strong resemblance to Coleridge's 'Fire, Famine, and Slaughter',[31] and 'The Retrospect. Cwm Elan 1812' displaying both its influence by and departure from Wordsworth's 'Lines Composed a Few Miles above Tintern Abbey, On Revisiting the Banks of the Wye during a Tour. July 13, 1798' (1798). But Shelley's meeting with Byron in Geneva galvanised his imaginative power, as he sought and found within himself a voice still more capable of challenging, responding to and thinking with his peers. Charles E. Robinson succinctly draws attention to the vital nature of the Byron–Shelley relationship from this point onwards: 'Byron and Shelley's letters to and about each other demonstrate the thoroughness of their literary association: in a very real sense, each was a student of the other, whose works he read, criticized, and remembered.'[32] Shelley, perhaps inspired by his deepening relationship with Byron, discovers individuality through influence as he creates a dialogue between himself and others that lasted throughout his lifetime.

---

[30] See *The Complete Poetry of Percy Bysshe Shelley*, edited by Donald Reiman, Neil Fraistat and Nora Crook, 3 vols to date (Baltimore, MD: Johns Hopkins University Press, 2004), vol. 2, p. xvii. Hereafter cited as *Complete Poetry* with volume number and page number provided.
[31] See Sally West, *Coleridge and Shelley: Textual Engagement* (Aldershot: Ashgate, 2007), p. 32.
[32] Charles E. Robinson, *Shelley and Byron: The Snake and Eagle Wreathed in Fight* (Baltimore, MD: The Johns Hopkins University Press, 1976), p. 4.

Shelley's work of 1816, including 'Mont Blanc', 'Hymn to Intellectual Beauty', 'To Laughter' and 'Upon the wandering winds', shows the poet making his verse the site of confrontation with his peers, with poetic inspiration as well as with his surroundings.[33] For, as he wrote to Thomas Love Peacock in 1816, when Shelley considered 'England's literature', Coleridge was 'in my thoughts'.[34] 'Mont Blanc' was published in two versions: the first is the version found in the Shelleys' collaborative *History of a Six Weeks' Tour* (1817), and the second is a version that came to light in the Scrope Davies Notebook that was discovered in December 1976. Both versions of the poem reveal Shelley's subtle technical accomplishments and the ways in which he showcases imaginative power while critiquing its instincts. As Nancy Moore Goslee writes with reference to Shelley's larger poetic achievement, 'Mont Blanc' shows how far Shelley's poems 'both overthrow idols and posit new idols – emergent truths that are no longer voiceless or imageless yet are still subject to a Demogorgon-like skepticism',[35] and both versions of 'Mont Blanc' see Shelley situate the self as the primary conduit of experience capable of weighing up the previous imaginative achievements and beliefs of his peers only to affirm his own hard-won poetic doubt.

Entering the wider conversation about Romantic ideas of nature, 'Mont Blanc' stands as reply to the poetry of Wordsworth and Coleridge, particularly the latter's 'Hymn Before Sun-rise, in the Vale of Chamouni' (1802). In the Preface to his poem, Coleridge asks, 'Who *would* be, who *could* be, an Atheist, in this valley of wonders!',[36] and though Shelley might not have read this provocation, 'Mont Blanc' seems to offer a rather different response from that which Coleridge might have expected. Coleridge had ended his poem with confirmation of God's power, enjoining the mountain to 'tell thou the silent Sky / And tell the Stars, and tell yon rising Sun, / Earth, with her thousand voice, praises GOD' (ll. 83–5).[37] For Coleridge by the close of the poem, there is one God, and one way of reading the mountain. In 'Mont

---

[33] The latter two poems are sonnets that are more obscure for only being discovered in 1976 in a Barclay vault as part of the *Scrope Davies Notebook*. See *Complete* Poetry, vol. 3, pp. 69–70.

[34] *The Letters of Percy Bysshe Shelley*, edited by Frederick L. Jones, 2 vols (Oxford: Clarendon Press, 1964), vol. 1, p. 490.

[35] Nancy Moore Goslee, *Shelley's Visual Imagination* (Cambridge: Cambridge University Press, 2011), p. 27.

[36] Samuel Taylor Coleridge, 'Prefatory Note to "Hymn before Sun-rise, in the Vale of Chamouny"', in *The Collected Works of Samuel Taylor Coleridge: Poetical Works; Poems (Variorum Text), Part II, Vol. VXI*, p. 925.

[37] Samuel Taylor Coleridge, 'Hymn before Sun-rise, in the Vale of Chamouny', in *The Collected Works of Samuel Taylor Coleridge*, p. 723.

Blanc', by contrast, Shelley, instead of focusing on faith, turns the spotlight onto awful doubt, moving the reader through perspective after perspective on the mountain and its surroundings. Frances Ferguson's emphasis on the 'human mind's imaginings' suggests the speaker-centred nature of the poem,[38] where the reader seems less to see a mimetic representation of nature than to watch the poet experiencing nature. Rather than leaving his reader with an affirming statement or a mode of experience that might teach the reader how to respond to the mountain in the way that Coleridge had done, Shelley's final verse paragraph casts the burden of understanding onto the reader's imagination, challenging us to look inwards towards our own methods of interpretation:

> The secret strength of things
> Which governs thought, and to the infinite dome
> Of heaven is as a law, inhabits thee!
> And what were thou, and earth, and stars, and sea,
> If to the human mind's imaginings
> Silence and solitude were vacancy? (5. ll. 139–44)

Shelley's distinctiveness lies in the openness of the lines. Rather than being led towards a conclusion that might unify the poem, or an ending that casts the poet speaker as a teacher or leader of his readers, Shelley has his reader confront the mystery of nature itself. The beginning of the quoted lines almost gives way to a softening of Shelley's stance, where he seems to discover a single way of reading this 'secret strength of things' that 'governs thought', but, before the reader can settle into any certainty, Shelley moves to a dizzying open question that refuses to become mere rhetorical flourish. Asking us to strip away the manifold preconceptions that could ossify into a single way of seeing, Shelley's question demands that we consider the possibility that 'the human mind's imaginings' project readings of nature that rest on nothing more than their own thoughts. Certainties evaporate; Shelley's poetic voice in 1816, bolstered by his creative exchange with the Villa Diodati circle, takes on a challenging and individual hue.

Shelley's sonnet, 'To Laughter'[39] has been linked to Byron, with Judith Chernaik and Thomas Burnett, for example, reading the poem as Shelley viewing Byron as one of those who is in danger of falling prey to laughter's

---

[38] See Frances Ferguson, 'Shelley's "Mont Blanc": What the Mountain Said', in Michael O'Neill (ed.), *Shelley* (London: Longman, 1993), pp. 43–55. Shelley's poetry is quoted from *Complete Poetry*, vol. 3.

[39] The recent nature of the discovery of 'To Laughter' and 'Upon the wandering winds' has meant that they have received slighter critical attention than *Scene – Pont Pellisier in*

more dangerous effects, even as they see the sonnet as primarily a precursor to Shelley's 'When the lamp is shattered'.[40] In this sonnet, Shelley returns to one of his primary concerns: the role of the poet. His relationship with Byron becomes a fascinating lens through which to read 'To Laughter', as Shelley's speaker, as John Bleasdale perceptively writes, adopts 'the pose of the exile [more] than the spirit of the tourist'.[41] Uniting himself with Byron by having his speaker adopt the 'pose of exile' – a pose which Byron would designate for Harold and himself in 1816's Canto III of *Childe Harold's Pilgrimage* and for *Manfred* (1817) in the eponymous dramatic poem – Shelley situates the poet as outside of the collective, able to reveal and then survive laughter's deforming possibilities:

> Thy friends were never mine though heartless fiend:
> Silence and solitude and calm and storm,
> Hope, before whose veiled shrine all spirits bend
> In worship, and the rainbow-vested form
> Of conscience, that within thy hollow heart
> Can find no throne—the love of such great powers
> Which has requited mine in many hours
> Of loneliness, thou ne'er hast felt; depart!
> Thou canst not bear the moon's great eye, thou fearest
> A fair child clothed in smiles—aught that is high
> Or good or beautiful. —Thy voice is dearest
> To those who mock at truth and Innocency.
> I, now alone, weep without shame to see
> How many broken hearts lie bare to thee.   (ll. 1–14)

Immediately combative, Shelley draws an unassailable line between himself and laughter, his powerful antagonist. Laughter is exposed as a 'heartless fiend' that is bent upon destruction as the poet reveals the precise nature of its authoritarian power and his own determination to resist. Even at the level of form, Shelley inscribes the same message: the sonnet's authoritarian formal rules come to be subverted by the poet's mastery. Taking his cue from Byron's experimental attitude to form in *Childe Harold's Pilgrimage* Canto III, in which the opening stanza seems broken in two by the force of emotion caged in the Spenserian stanza, Shelley seeks to make the sonnet bend to his

---

the *Vale of Servox*, the Scrope Davies Notebook version of *Mont Blanc*, and 'Hymn to Intellectual Beauty'. See *Complete Poetry*, vol. 3, pp. 69–70 for details of the discovery.

[40] Judith Chernaik and Timothy Burnett, 'The Byron and Shelley notebooks in the Scrope Davies find', *The Review of English Studies* 29:113 (1978): 36–49 (p. 41).

[41] John Bleasdale, '"To Laughter": Shelley's sonnet and solitude', *Romanticism on the Net* 22 (2001) <http://id.erudit.org/iderudit/005972ar> (last accessed 19 September 2019).

will. Choosing to refuse the conventional patterns of the Petrarchan sonnet or the Shakespearean sonnet, Shelley breaks formal boundaries with daring half rhyme in lines 1 and 3, the swelling of the closing couplet into a triplet and opting for feminine rhymes that resist possible comic effect. Going beyond Byron's experimentation, Shelley makes himself both the superior ethical poet and the more formally adventurous artist. Hope, which in Shelley's later work is far more dangerous than in this sonnet,[42] is enshrined as the most powerful virtue, a point that Shelley, quoting Coleridge, made to Byron in a letter of 1816,[43] suggesting how carefully Shelley would consider the kind of advice he offered his peer and that he would often choose to embed his thought into his poetry and his letters. The octave's description of hope's dominion offers an alternative to laugher, lending the speaker the courage to demand that laughter depart. Yet such a victory is not sustained: the sestet, after showing that laughter fears 'aught that is high / Or good or beautiful', swiftly performs a tonal switch to admit that laughter's voice is still 'dearest' to mockers before the speaker bares his emotional pain 'without shame' at the thought of those prey to laughter. These closing lines, in their vulnerability, reveal that laughter might well have a power beyond hope's worshipped form. Admitting '[h]ow many broken hearts lie bare to thee', the lines stop just short of allowing that, for all the defiance of the sonnet, the speaker has not converted anyone from laughter to the hope that he adores. Likewise, his avowal that he weeps 'without shame' suggests that others, including Byron, may consider such emotional overflow deeply shameful. Matthew Ward points out that '[n]o doubt Shelley could be rather po-faced',[44] and that Shelley builds into the poem a defiance of how his sonnet may easily be understood as the work of an over-earnest poet, open to precisely the kind of mockery his poem enjoins against. 'To Laughter' takes formal and personal risks to create a sonnet in which ethical and aesthetic principles work in tandem even as it admits its own susceptibility to being misunderstood.

Byron's *Manfred*, like Mary Shelley's *Frankenstein* and Shelley's lyrics, is similarly preoccupied with how the ethical and aesthetic collide in literature. *Manfred* sees Byron shape a protagonist that is both the apotheosis and a near

---

[42] Hope is often coupled with despair in Shelley's poetry. See, for example, *Alastor*, 639 or *Hellas*, 39. For the complete range of Shelley's use of 'hope', see F. S. Ellis, *A Lexical Concordance to the Poetical Works of Percy Bysshe Shelley* (London: Bernard Quadrich, 1892; rpt. Johnson Reprint Company 1967), pp. 335–6.

[43] *The Letters of Percy Bysshe Shelley*, vol. 2, p. 125.

[44] Matthew Ward, 'Laughter as sympathy in Percy Shelley's poetics', *Cambridge Quarterly* 44:2 (2015): 146–65 (p. 151).

condemnation of a hero type that he had explored throughout his earlier *Tales*, but with a clear Promethean twist and more than a gestural nod to the villain in Walpole's *The Castle of Otranto*. The influence of Shelley, whose *Queen Mab* and *Alastor* form vital connections to Byron's dramatic poem, is significant for the specifically satanic quality of *Manfred*. Peter A. Schock claims that 'Shelley was in advance of Byron, establishing modes of blaspheming Satanism which the other poet went on to adapt (despite the remarks of both men that deprecate the influence of Shelley's irreligion on Byron).'[45] More than satanic, Byron, in line with his peers of the Summer of 1816, aimed to create a version of the Promethean hero who dabbles in forbidden sciences in a manner that recalls the Poet of Percy Shelley's *Alastor* and Mary Shelley's *Frankenstein*. In his first soliloquy in Act I, scene I, Manfred makes the following Promethean observations:

> in my heart
> There is a vigil, and these eyes but close
> To look within; and yet I live, and bear
> The aspect and the form of breathing men.
> But grief should be the instructor of the wise;
> Sorrow is knowledge: they who know the most
> Must mourn o'er the fatal truth,
> The Tree of Knowledge is not that of Life.[46]   (I.i.5–12)

With the phrase 'these eyes but close / To look within', Byron insinuates an echo of Aeschylus's Prometheus's constant vigil, which Percy Shelley would recall in *Prometheus Unbound* when Prometheus addresses Jupiter to affirm that 'Thou and I alone of living things / Behold with sleepless eyes!' (*Prometheus Unbound* I. 3–4). There is no rest for these Promethean characters. Introspection becomes the prison in which Promethean characters must exist. Manfred's maxim that 'sorrow is knowledge' is freighted with the literary Promethean tradition that runs from Aeschylus, through Milton, and up to the Romantic period. Science, as for the original Prometheus, is a dangerous pursuit that aligns him with the Promethean and satanic (anti)heroes:

> And then I dived,
> In my lone wanderings, to the caves of death,
> Searching its cause in its effect; and drew

---

[45] Peter A. Schock, *Romantic Satanism: Myth and the Historical Moment in Blake, Shelley, and Byron* (Basingstoke: Palgrave Macmillan, 2003), p. 79.

[46] Byron's poetry is quoted from Lord George Gordon Byron, *Lord Byron: The Major Works*, edited by Jerome McGann (Oxford: Oxford University Press, 2000).

> From wither'd bones, and skulls, and heap'd up dust,
> Conclusions most forbidden. Then I pass'd
> The nights of years in sciences untaught,
> Save in the old-time ... (*Manfred*, II. ii. 79–85)

Such scientific exploration, as for Percy Shelley's *Alastor* Poet and Mary Shelley's Victor Frankenstein, becomes a haunting site of sin. The obsession with death, isolation and finding out what was hidden sees Byron insist on the transgressive nature of Manfred's research. Overreaching into 'forbidden' knowledge separates Manfred from society, but, paradoxically, despite the Promethean solitude of Byron's hero, his hero's Promethean quality draws Byron into the community of writers and thinkers at the Villa Diodati, underscoring their group as a new generation of thinkers that would succeed the Lake Poets, and forging new directions in Romantic and Gothic literature in the process.

Perhaps as a result of Shelley dosing him with 'Wordsworth physic even to nausea',[47] Byron saw the poet 'c[o]me into competition with Wordsworth upon his own ground, and with his own weapons; and in the first encounter he vanquished and overthrew him'.[48] But Byron does not simply compete with Wordsworth. Taking his bearings from elements of the elder poet's work that had so impressed Shelley, Byron in Canto III of *Childe Harold's Pilgrimage* fashions a version of the self in nature that both builds on and radically departs from the Wordsworthian model. Stanzas 72 to 76 engage directly with the nature that Wordsworth had hailed as 'The anchor of my purest thoughts, the nurse, / The guide, the guardian of my heart, and soul / Of all my moral being' ('Tintern Abbey', ll. 110–12).[49] Byron's stanzas stand as test of this Wordsworthian formula to decide on whether such an understanding of nature's role in relation to the self was possible in his own poetry.

> I live not in myself, but I become
> Portion of that around me; and to me,
> High mountains are a feeling, but the hum
> Of human cities torture: I can see
> Nothing to loathe in nature, save to be
> A link reluctant in a fleshly chain,
> Class'd among creatures, when the soul can flee,

---

[47] Thomas Medwin, *Conversations of Lord Byron* (London: Colburn, 1824), p. 237.
[48] John Wilson, review of *Manfred*, *Blackwood's Magazine* I (June 1817): 289–95, quoted in Andrew Rutherford (ed.), *Byron: The Critical Heritage* (London and New York: Routledge & Kegan Paul; New York: Barnes & Noble, 1970), pp. 111–14 (p. 113).
[49] Wordsworth's poetry is quoted from *William Wordsworth: The Major Works, including The Prelude*, edited by Stephen Gill (Oxford: Oxford University Press, 2011).

> And with the sky, the peak, the heaving plain
> Of ocean, or the stars, mingle, and not in vain.
> (*Childe Harold's Pilgrimage*, III. 72: ll. 680–8)

Opening with assertion, Byron insists on himself as mingled with nature in a way that is clearly indebted to Wordsworth. But whereas, for Wordsworth, this was a hard-won revelation, for Byron this is a starting point from which he will depart. The mountains are an unspecified form of feeling, but cities 'torture', as the anti-urban sentiment seems a more powerful force than any emotional attachment to the rural landscape. The stanza continues to decline from the height and pitch at which it began. Deliberately underwhelming his reader, Byron claims 'I can see / Nothing to loathe in nature', failing to offer more than a lack of hatred rather than positive love of nature as Byron returns to the theme he had developed previously: the isolation of the self. The self as a 'link reluctant in a fleshly chain' offers both a horror of the self as a corporeal creature and a tiny part of something larger, as if this were also a troubled acceptance of Alexander Pope's approving claim in *An Essay on Man* (1733–4) that all creatures form part of the 'Vast chain of being'.[50] By stanza 73, Byron's acceptance seems like stoicism, where he claims 'thus I am absorb'd, and this is life' (*Childe Harold's Pilgrimage*, III. 73: l. 689). The speaker, characterised as one who must 'act and suffer' by what is implied to be divine decree, can but aspire to spurn 'the clay-cold bonds which round our being cling' (*Childe Harold's Pilgrimage*, III. 73: l. 697). Aiming to break free from the limits and restrictions, an impulse that Bernard Beatty and Vincent Newey rightly see as a cornerstone of Byron's art,[51] the speaker tries to slough off the body's 'degraded form' (*Childe Harold's Pilgrimage*, III. 74: l. 699) in favour of the mind's ethereal life. But the self cannot remain satisfied with aspiration alone. The return to nature breeds questions that go unanswered – questions that seem to demand an affirmative response, but which hauntingly remain unsatisfied:

> Are not the mountains, waves, and skies, a part
> Of me and of my soul, as I of them?
> Is not the love of these deep in my heart
> With a pure passion? should I not contemn
> All objects, if compared with these? and stem
> A tide of suffering, rather than forgo

---

[50] Alexander Pope's poetry is quoted from Alexander Pope, *Alexander Pope: The Major Works*, edited by Pat Rogers (Oxford: Oxford University Press, 2006), I. VIII. 237.
[51] See Bernard Beatty and Vincent Newey (eds), *Byron and the Limits of Fiction* (Liverpool: Liverpool University Press, 1988), especially 'Preface'.

Such feelings for the hard and worldly phlegm
Of those whose eyes are only turn'd below,
Gazing upon the ground, with thoughts which dare not glow?
(*Childe Harold's Pilgrimage*, III, 75: ll. 707–15).

Rather than the stanzas enacting an ascent from doubt to affirmation, as Wordsworth had done in 'Tintern Abbey', these lines magnify uncertainty to the point that the entire stanza is taken over by questions that seem less rhetorical than begging the reader for a positive response. We are asked to evaluate if the speaker can lay claim to any such 'pure passion' for nature on the basis of the lines we have read, and the speaker's position seems increasingly weak. Where Wordsworth finds solace when he claims 'Therefore am I still / A lover of the meadows and the woods' ('Tintern Abbey', ll. 103–4), Byron can only ask if he can 'contemn / All objects, if compared with these' where, again, a fatigued contempt for all that is not nature triumphs over any active love of nature's pleasures. As in Shelley's *Alastor*, published in 1816, Byron turns his contempt on those who meet Shelley's description of people, 'who, deluded by no generous error, instigated by no sacred thirst of doubtful knowledge, duped by no illustrious superstition, loving nothing on this earth, and cherishing no hopes beyond'.[52] But Byron does not, finally, think about nature itself. Instead, Byron's condemnation is of those who have 'thoughts which dare not glow'. Imagination rather than nature has leapt to the fore as Byron supplants Wordsworth's version of the self in nature with a darker and more fraught, even 'Gothic', portrait of a mind that cannot find in nature the consolation it seems to seek. Stanza 76 opens with 'But this is not my theme' (*Childe Harold's Pilgrimage*, III. 76: 716): Byron's encounter with Wordsworthian poetics leaves him certain that the formula beloved of the first-generation Romantic poet cannot be his own.

The 'Epistle to Augusta' openly performs its deliberate failure to succeed in the Wordsworthian mode. More directly than in Canto III of *Childe Harold's Pilgrimage*, Byron responds to 'Tintern Abbey' and the difference between Wordsworth's address to his sister and Byron's poem to his half-sister.[53] Byron parades the dissimilarity as much as the likeness between the poems, reminding the reader, even in the title, that Byron writes rather than speaks to his sibling, and that another level of intimacy beyond familial bonds might exist between Byron and Augusta. Nature,

---

[52] Shelley, 'Preface to *Alastor*', *Complete Poems*, vol. 3, p. 5.
[53] For more on this connection, see Robert R. Harson, 'Byron's "Tintern Abbey"', *Keats-Shelley Journal* 20 (1971): 113–21.

in the context of the separation endured by Byron, cannot soothe and salve the shattered self:

> Here are the Alpine landscapes—which create
> A fund for contemplation—to admire
> Is a brief feeling of a trivial date—
> But something worthier do such scenes inspire:
> Here to be lonely is not desolate—
> For much I view which I could most desire—
> And above all a lake I can behold—
> Lovelier—not dearer—than our own of old.
>
> ('Epistle to Augusta', 8. ll. 57–64)

Almost as if to distract himself from the pain of separation, Byron draws attention to his environment as a means of transcending suffering, the *ottava rima*'s rhymes working to undermine any stable sense of landscape as healer. The rhymes of 'admire', 'inspire' and 'desire' offer a formula of sorts for poetic creation, but after admiring nature, the inspired poet is still left with desire, unable to convert loss into fulfilment even after he writes poetry out of his awe-inspired state. The Alpine scenes he enjoys offer a 'fund for contemplation', but the line offers more a functional view of how the poet might make use of nature than any true interchange between the two. After admitting nature cannot just be admired, Byron claims that its beauty inspires 'something worthier'. But Byron does not or cannot reveal what that something is. What nature offers, that which he 'can behold', is far less emotionally affecting than the lake that Augusta and the speaker viewed 'of old'. Nature itself is not enough to transform the poet. It is what a particular part of nature meant to him that clinches the couplet's nostalgic pang. The sense that a complete union between the self and nature will not take place sponsors the following stanza, as Byron admits to his own complicity in his suffering:

> Oh that thou wert but with me!—but I grow
> The fool of my own wishes—and forget
> The solitude which I have vaunted so
> Has lost its praise in this but one regret—
> There may be others which I less may show—
> I am not of the plaintive mood—and yet
> I feel an ebb in my philosophy
> And the tide rising in my altered eye.
>
> ('Epistle to Augusta', 9. ll. 65–72)

Wishing for Augusta's presence, before the first line of the stanza even finishes, Byron immediately wryly undercuts his feeling, where the foolishness of wishes jostles with his longing. 'The solitude which I have vaunted so' speaks directly to *Childe Harold's Pilgrimage* Canto III's frequent and impassioned hopes to avoid humankind, and *Manfred's* tormented but self-willed alienation. Having referred to solitude in *Childe Harold's Pilgrimage* as 'where we are least alone' (III. 90: l. 843), Byron turns a self-ironising eye upon the poem that he had composed immediately before the 'Epistle to August', witnessing how quickly Byronic emotion can turn on a dime. The mobility that Byron would make the centre of *Beppo* and *Don Juan*, also written in *ottava rima*, is vital to this poem as Byron's 'altered eye' invites speculation on how Byron is altered, and how such alteration may play out in his literary productions in and after 1816. Byron's experimentation with Wordsworthian poetics, where Byron seemed to summon and then send packing his older peer, show 1816 to be the year where, even from the distance of the Swiss Alps, Byron, Percy Shelley, Mary Shelley and Polidori became a self-fashioned counterforce to Wordsworth in English poetry. Just as Mary Shelley and Polidori set the Gothic aesthetic in new directions, so Byron and Percy radically reformulated the Romantic mode.

A brief but extraordinarily vivid period in the lives of those involved, the Summer of 1816 produced a remarkable and enduring legacy: a rethinking and reworking of the legacies of poetic predecessors, a continuity and departure from the Gothic romances of the 1790s, and a new strain of vampire fiction. But the debates, readings and translations that took place during these legendary few months dissolve the contours of the generic boundaries within which each author worked, showing us more than any other moment in the history of this period the symbiotic nature of Romantic and Gothic works. The fates of the participants involved are well known: John Polidori committed suicide by poison in 1821; Percy Shelley drowned alongside his friend Edward Williams in the Gulf of Spezia in 1822; and Byron died in Greece in 1824. Claire Clairmont survived the longest of all of them, living until 1879, but she lived separately from Mary Shelley. Four months during the Summer of 1816 were sufficient to seal literary friendships and to change our conceptions of the dynamic interplay that persisted not just between Romantic and the Gothic forms, but between the pasts and presents of those literary forms. Mary Shelley was to edit the work of both Byron and Percy Shelley, as well as to continue writing her own fiction, drama, essays, biographies and poetry well into the Victorian period. But writing in her journal on 14 May 1824, as she commenced a new novel of apocalyptic and personal catastrophe, she alluded to the theme of her new work as follows: 'The last man! Yes I may well describe that solitary being's feelings, feeling myself as the last relic of a beloved race, my companions extinct before me.'[54] 'Extinction' offers us a vivid snapshot into how she experienced her solitary state in 1824: it suggests, as she then wrote large in *The Last Man* (1826), that Mary Shelley perceived herself to be the very last of a species, surviving beyond her allocated time, a 'relic' of a vivid summer that was now definitively consigned to literary history and myth-making.

---

[54] Mary Shelley, journal entry for 24 May 1824, in *The Journals of Mary Shelley*, vol. 2, pp. 476–7.

2.2

Fantasmagoriana: The Cosmopolitan Gothic and Frankenstein

MAXIMILIAAN VAN WOUDENBERG

Maurice Hindle has remarked that the critical preoccupation with the antecedents of Mary Shelley's *Frankenstein; or, The Modern Prometheus* (1818; 1831) 'can easily become a "hunt the source for *Frankenstein*" game'.[1] If this is so, it was a game that was perhaps initiated by Mary Wollstonecraft Shelley herself. In her 'Author's Introduction' to Henry Colburn and Richard Bentley's Standard Novels edition of 1831, Shelley famously made mention of a collection of German ghost stories in French translation that the group gathered together at the Villa Diodati, Geneva, had read:

> In the summer of 1816, we visited Switzerland, and became the neighbours of Lord Byron. . . . But it proved a wet, ungenial summer, and incessant rain often confined us for days to the house. Some volumes of ghost stories, translated from the German into French, fell into our hands. . . . I have not seen these stories since then; but their incidents are as fresh in my mind as if I had read them yesterday.
> 'We will each write a ghost story', said Lord Byron; and his proposition was acceded to.[2]

The 'volumes of ghost stories' referred to here was, of course, *Fantasmagoriana* (1812), Jean-Baptiste Benoît Eyriès's translation and compilation of a selection of German supernatural tales.[3] While, to literary historians and scholars of Gothic fiction, the ghost storytelling contest at the Villa Diodati and its literary offspring – Shelley's *Frankenstein* (1818) and John

---

1 Maurice Hindle, 'Introduction', in Mary Shelley, *Frankenstein*, edited by Maurice Hindle (Harmondsworth: Penguin, 1985), pp. 7–42 (p. 34).
2 Mary Shelley, 'Introduction [1831]', in Mary Shelley, *Frankenstein*, edited by David Lorne Macdonald and Kathleen Scherf (Peterborough, Ont.: Broadview, 2000), pp. 353–59 (pp. 354–5). All citations from the novel are from this edition, followed by volume and chapter numbers for readers of other editions.
3 Jean-Baptiste Benoît Eyriès, *Fantasmagoriana, ou Recueil d'Histoires d'Apparitions de Spectres, Revenans, Fantômes, etc.; Traduit de l'allemand, par un Amateur*, 2 vols (Paris: Schoell, 1812).

Polidori's *The Vampyre* (1819) – are well known, the original tales read by the Byron-Shelley circle have somewhat fallen into obscurity.[4] As Terry Hale noted in 1992, 'so scarce has the work become that it is rarely discussed even by biographers of the Byron-Shelley circle'.[5]

Recently, however, and after an hiatus of over 200 years, modern editions and translations of *Fantasmagoriana* have begun to appear,[6] occasioning not only the reappraisal of the significance of this collection as a source of influence and inspiration at the Villa Diodati, but also prompting critical enquiries into the significance of *Fantasmagoriana* as a text itself.[7] This chapter subjects these concerns to further scrutiny, examining in the first section the provenance of *Fantasmagoriana* as it travelled between European cultures of the Romantic period; exploring in the second section the text in the historical context of popular magic-lantern shows and musing on further possible residual influences on the ghost storytelling contest at the Villa Diodati; and, finally, considering the impact of particular stories in Eyriès's compilation on the genesis of the English Gothic masterpiece that is Mary Shelley's *Frankenstein*.

Fantasmagoriana: The German Provenance of a French Collection

Fantasmagoriana was Eyriès's anonymous French translation of the first two volumes of the German *Gespensterbuch* (1810–11).[8] Literally meaning 'ghost

---

4 Schulze's story 'Die Verwandtschaft mit der Geisterwelt', translated as 'L'Heure Fatale' in *Fantasmagoriana*, also had an influence on Byron's composition of *Manfred* (1817), in particular the Astarte scene. See Manfred Eimer, 'Einflüsse deutscher Räuber- und Schauerromantik auf Shelley, Mrs. Shelley und Byron', *Englische Studien* 48 (1914–15): 231–45 (pp. 241–4), and n.66 and p. 56 below.

5 Terry Hale, 'Introduction', in Terry Hale (ed.), *Tales of the Dead: The Ghost Stories of the Villa Diodati* (Chislehurst: The Gothic Society, 1992), pp. 8–19 (p. 9). Hale's edition is based on the English translation of *Fantasmagoriana* in 1813: Sarah Elizabeth Brown Utterson, *Tales of the Dead* (London: White, Cochrane, and Co., 1813).

6 A French edition and Italian translation appeared in 2015, followed by a German translation in 2017. See *Fantasmagoriana ou Recueil d'histoires d'apparitions, de spectres, revenants, fantômes, etc.* (La Fresnaie-Fayel: Otrante, 2015); Fabio Camilletti, trans. *Fantasmagoriana* (Rome: Nova Delphi, 2015); Markus Bernauer (ed.), *Fantasmagoriana: Geisterbarbiere, Totenbräute, und mordende Porträts* (Berlin: Ripperger & Kremers, 2017); and A. J. Day (ed.), *Fantasmagoriana (Tales of the Dead)* (St Ives: Fantasmagoriana Press, 2005).

7 Anglo-centric interpretations 'tend to overemphasize' the role of *Fantasmagoriana* 'in Geneva, thereby marginalizing the actual book'. Fabio Camilletti, 'Beyond the uncanny: *Fantasmagoriana*, intertextuality, and the pleasure principle', *Compar(a)ison* 1–2 (2009): 61–81 (p. 66).

8 Johann August Apel and Friedrich Laun, *Gespensterbuch*, 5 vols (Leipzig: Göschen, 1810–15). Laun was the pseudonym of Friedrich August Schulze.

book' or 'book of spectres', *Gespensterbuch* was a popular collection of ghost stories written by Johann Apel and Friedrich Schulze, itself purporting to have been inspired by the telling of 'Grausigere Sagen' [grisly sagas] at a social gathering in Leipzig. In his memoirs of 1837, Schulze recounts how he and Apel conceived of *Gespensterbuch* during a so-called *Gespensterthee* or 'ghost tea':

> ... und so kam endlich das allgemeine Verlangen nach Constituirung eines von Zeit zu Zeit zu haltenden Gespensterthee's, das hieß, eines geselligen Abends, zu Stande, dem das ungewisse Mondlicht der Geistergeschichten nicht fehlen durfte.
> Und diese sogenannte Gespenstertheee wurden bald darauf Veranlassung zu dem gemeinschaftlich von Apel und mir herausgegebenen Gespensterbuche.[9]
>
> [... and so finally came forth general demands to hold, from time to time, a ghost tea, that is to say, a sociable evening which should not fail the uncertain moonlight of ghost stories.
> And these so-called ghost teas soon became the occasion for the jointly-published *Gespensterbuch* by Apel and myself.][10]

Given this point of genesis, it is perhaps not so surprising to note that several of the stories in *Gespensterbuch* employ layered narrative structures that feature anecdotes about ghosts told in a social gathering.

The first two volumes of *Gespensterbuch* contained twelve stories. The two volumes of *Fantasmagoriana* comprised a total of eight stories, translating five stories from *Gespensterbuch*, and adding three from other German sources. With the publication of the English translation of *Fantasmagoriana* by Sarah Utterson as *Tales of the Dead* in 1813, only three of the original *Gespensterbuch* stories remained.[11] With three editions in three different languages published in three countries over three years, it is clear that these short supernatural fictions enjoyed considerable popularity in north-western Europe during the early 1810s. With each new edition or iteration of the collection, stories were both added and excluded, resulting in multi-authored variants. As I have suggested elsewhere, *Fantasmagoriana* and its variants are thus best conceptualised as travelling texts, as cosmopolitan collections that traverse geographical, linguistic and cultural boundaries, adapting and transforming

---

9   Friedrich August Schulze, *Memoiren von Friedrich Laun*, 3 vols (Bunzlau: Appun's Buchhandlung, 1837), vol. 2, p. 20.
10 Unless noted, all translations from German into English are my own.
11 See stories 3, 4, and 5 in table 2.1. All three stories are by Schulze. See also Maximiliaan van Woudenberg, 'The variants and transformations of *Fantasmagoriana*: tracing a travelling text to the Byron-Shelley circle', *Romanticism* 20:3 (2014): 306–320.

Table 2.1: Table showing the provenance of the stories read by the Byron-Shelley circle in Geneva in 1816

	Fantasmagoriana	German Original	Provenance
1.	'L'Amour Muet, anecdote du seizième siècle', vol. 1, pp. 1–113.	'Stumme Liebe'	Musäus, Volksmährchen der Deutschen, vol. 4 (1786).[12]
2.	'Les Portraits de Famille', vol. 1, pp. 117–225.	'Die Bilder der Ahnen. Erzählung'	Apel, anonymous in Kind, Malven, vol. 1 (1805), pp. 97–196.[13]
3.	'La Tête de Mort', vol. 1, pp. 229–76.	'Der Todtenkopf'	Schulze, Gespensterbuch, vol. 2 (1811), pp. 143–80.
4.	'La Morte Fiancée', vol. 2, pp. 1–101.	'Die Todtenbraut'	Schulze, Gespensterbuch, vol. 2 (1811), pp. 1–72.
5.	'L'Heure Fatale', vol. 2, pp. 105–60.	'Die Verwandtschaft mit der Geisterwelt'	Schulze, Gespensterbuch, vol. 1 (1810), pp. 239–80.
6.	'Le Revenant', vol. 2, pp. 163–224.	'Der Geist des Verstorbenen'	Schulze, Gespensterbuch, vol. 1 (1810), pp. 125–74.
7.	'La Chambre Grise, histoire véritable', vol. 2, pp. 227–44.	'Die graue Stube. (Eine buchstäblich wahre Geschichte.)'	Clauren, Der Freimüthige, nr. 71 (9 April 1810), pp. 281–2 and nr. 72 (10 April 1810), pp. 286–8.[14]
8.	'La Chambre Noire', vol. 2, pp. 247–303.	'Die schwarze Kammer. Anekdote' and 'Die graue Stube'	Apel, Gespensterbuch, vol. 2 (1811), pp. 181–206. Clauren, Der Freimüthige, nr. 88 (3 May 1810), pp. 349–50; nr. 89 (4 May 1810), pp. 355–6; and nr. 90 (5 May 1810), pp. 357–8.

themselves culturally, typographically, materially and even generically as they do so.[15]

12 Johann August Musäus, Volksmährchen der Deutschen, 5 vols (Gotha: Ettinger, 1782–6), vol. 4. Several pre-1812 editions are also possible sources for Eyriès's text. See Musäus, 'Stumme Liebe', in Volksmährchen der Deutschen, 5 vols (Vienna: s.n., 1788), vol. 4, pp. 5–149; Musäus, 'Stumme Liebe', in Christoph Martin Wieland (ed.), Die deutschen Volksmährchen von Johann August Musäus, 5 vols (Gotha: Ettinger, 1804), vol. 4, pp. 5–174.

13 There are several pre-1812 printings of this story: Friedrich Kind, 'Die Bilder der Ahnen', in Malven, 2 vols (Züllichau und Freystadt: Darnmann, 1805), vol. 1, pp. 97–196; Friedrich Kind (ed.), 'Die Bilder der Ahnen', in Romantische Erzählungen (Leipzig: s. n., 1807), pp. 67–132; [Johann] August Apel, 'Die Bilder der Ahnen', in Cicaden, 3 vols (Berlin: Kunst und Industrie-Comptoir, 1810–11), vol. 1, pp. 11–106. Eyriès may have used any of these editions for his translation.

14 Heinrich Clauren, 'Die graue Stube. (Ein buchstäblich wahre Geschichte.)', Der Freimüthige oder Berlinisches Unterhaltungsblatt für gebildete, unbefangene Leser 71 (9 April 1810): 281–2; 72 (10 April 1810): 286–8.

15 Van Woudenberg, 'The variants', pp. 308–9.

The provenance of the stories read by the Byron-Shelley circle in Geneva in 1816 is shown in Table 2.1.

As the table shows, these ghost stories were carefully selected and placed in a specific order by their French translator. For instance, the last two stories – 'La Chambre Grise' and 'La Chambre Noire' – are companion pieces that appear together only in the French collection. The original publication of 'La Chambre Grise' as 'Die graue Stube' in the Berlin entertainment journal *Der Freimüthige* in April 1810 included a description of a ghostly visitation at the midnight hour to the bedside of the protagonist Blendau. This caused some measure of public outcry, with both author and publication reprimanded in the *Allgemeiner Anzeiger der Deutschen* on 4 May 1810 as follows:

> Was dem Verfasser dieses Aufsatzes die Feder dazu in die Hand gab, war, daß ihm ein rechtlicher Mann sagte, er habe die erwähnte Spukgeschichte am Abend seiner Gattin vorgelesen, weil er geglaubt habe, der Ausgang werde einen Beytrag zur Zerstörung des Aberglaubens liefern; allein da ganz das Gegentheil dabey Statt finde, so habe sie einen so tiefen Eindruck auf seine Frau gemacht, daß sie die ganze Nacht in der größten Unruhe zugebracht, und in ihrer Furcht vor Gespenstern sehr gestärkt worden sey.[16]
>
> [What it was for the author of this essay [in the *Allgemeiner Anzeiger*] to take the quill into his hand, was, that he was told by a law-abiding man, that he read the mentioned ghost story in the evening to his wife, because he believed that it would provide a contribution to the destruction of superstition; only the complete opposite occurred thereby, and so you have made such a deep impression [with *Die graue Stube*] on his wife, that she spent the whole night in the greatest turmoil, and her fear for ghosts is very much strengthened.]

The *Allgemeiner Anzeiger* objected to the portrayal of superstition, in particular because Blendau is characterised in the narrative as a man of logic and reason, a well-educated person who, as the subtitle of 'a literally true story' indicates, vouches for the existence of ghosts.

It is this sense of authenticity that was challenged by the *Allgemeiner Anzeiger*, with the reviewer calling upon both author and journal to prove that Blendau was real and that the narrative was true by publishing details of the time, place and names of witnesses concerned:

---

16 'Etwas über die Spukgeschichte betitelt: die graue Stube; im Freymüthigen Nr. 71', *Allgemeiner Anzeiger der Deutschen* 119 (4 May 1810): 1297–9 (p. 1298).

Gedachter Secretär Blandau [sic], „ein gewissenhafter, zuverlässiger junger Mann," verbürgt nach dem Zeugnisse des Berichterstatters, H. C., die Wahrheit jedes Wortes in dieser, wie es dem Unterzeichneten vorkommen will, höchst absurden Geschichte, „mit seiner Ehre, mit seinem Leben." . . . so hofft Unterzeichneter, daß derselbe wenigstens den Erzähler dieser buchstäblich wahren Geschichte vermögen werde, aus seinem Incognito hervorzutreten, und zugleich sämmtliche Namen, Zeiten und Orte genau anzugeben, oder aber zu erklären, er habe die „gebildeten und unbefangenen" Leser des Freymüthigen bloß zum Beßten haben wollen.[17]

[The imaginary Secretary Blandau, 'a conscientious, reliable young man' witnessed by the correspondent, H[einrich].C[lauren]., vouches the truth of each word in this, as it seems to this writer, highly absurd story, 'with his honour, with his life'. . . . thus hopes the undersigned, that the author at the very least will be able to produce the narrator of this literally true story, to emerge out of his incognito, and simultaneously specify the names, times, and places, or explain that he tried to [deceive] the 'educated and unbiased' readers of the *Freimüthige*.]

Here, the requested evidence of names, times and places to prove the existence of ghosts follows an almost legal format. It is exactly this process that becomes a significant component of Apel's 'La Chambre Noire', which opens directly with, and so continues, the public controversy:

Ich ergriff den Anzeiger, der in mein Lieser- und Lese-Departement gehörte, und las.
Das erste Blatt enthielt gerade die Vorhaltung an den Freimüthigen, wegen der grauen Stube. Ich las mit heimlicher Freude, denn ich hatte schon früher mit dem Stadtphysikus über die graue Stube disputirt, und hoffte mit diesem Alliirten in der Hand, ihn und seinen Gespensterglauben auf das Haupt zu schlagen.[18]

[I seized the *Allgemeiner Anzeiger*, which belonged to my reading department, and read.
The first page contained a reproach of the *Freimüthige* concerning the story of *Die graue Stube* [the grey room]. I read with secret joy because I had

17 'Aufforderung', *Allgemeiner Anzeiger der Deutschen* 127 (12 May 1810): 1385–6. A footnote further laments the increasing belief in ghosts: 'Mit dem Gespenster- und Geisterwesen wird es von Tage zu Tage ärger; auch übrigens wackere und brave Menschen sind diesen Albernheiten zugethan.' [It is becoming worse from day to day with ghosts and spiritual beings; even upright and good people are subjected to this silliness.] 'Aufforderung', *Allgemeiner Anzeiger* (p. 1386). Public discussion continues with the *Allgemeiner Anzeiger* questioning the enlightened scholarship of the editor of the *Freymüthigen* and with a response by Clauren in August 1810.
18 Apel and Laun, *Gespensterbuch*, vol. 2, p. 184.

already disputed *Die graue Stube* before with the town doctor and hoped that with this ally in my hand, I could deliver a blow to him and his belief in ghosts.]

This demand for evidence in the *Allgemeiner Anzeiger* furnishes a key narrative device in 'La Chambre Noire', a story in which the bedside visitation by a ghost is investigated by a magistrate. Undoubtedly, the north-German readers of *Gespensterbuch* in the 1810s were familiar with both the narrative and the stir about the veracity surrounding it. In citing the actual newspaper reports concerned, Apel thus frames 'La Chambre Noire' with the redoubtable forces of realism, authenticity and authority.

For his part, Eyriès most likely became aware of this public controversy while reading Apel's story in *Gespensterbuch* and included Heinrich Clauren's original as the prequel in ordering the companion pieces. In citing the exact source and date in his French title – 'La Chambre Grise, histoire véritable. Extrait du Journal intitulé: Le Sincère. Lundi 9 avril 1810' – Eyriès cultivates a literary continuity between the two stories and its public debacle for a French readership. However, Eyriès's role as editor and mediator of the German Gothic did not end there. At the same time that the *Allgemeiner Anzeiger* published their reproach of 'Die graue Stube' on 4 May 1810, Clauren was publishing a sequel to his story in three issues of *Der Freimüthige* on 3, 4, and 5 May 1810.[19] It is likely that Clauren was responding to the public controversy, since his continuation explains the ghostly bedside visitation in the original story as a hoax. It is worth noting that Eyriès did not translate the sequel as a continuation of Clauren's original story. Instead, Eyriès inserted the three issues of *Der Freimüthige* directly into Apel's story as an extract from the *Freimüthige* – 'Le Sincère, Journal destiné à l'amusement des lecteurs instruits et sans prévention. Berlin, jeudi 3 mai 1810' – transforming 'La Chambre Noire' into a pastiche jointly authored by Apel and Clauren. It is important to emphasise that the combination of these two stories circulated in tandem only in *Fantasmagoriana*; both are excluded from Utterson's *Tales of the Dead*. In reading *Fantasmagoriana* in 1816, the Byron-Shelley circle was thus exposed to a unique example of the German Gothic that had been deliberately curated and assembled by their French translator.

The stories anthologised in *Fantasmagoriana* are most representative of *Schauerliteratur* (literally 'shudder-literature'), the late eighteenth-century

---

19 Heinrich Clauren, 'Die graue Stube', *Der Freimüthige oder Berlinisches Unterhaltungsblatt für gebildete, unbefangene Leser* 88 (3 May 1810): 349–50; 89 (4 May 1810): 355–6; 90 (5 May 1810): 357–8.

German literary tradition that, as Wolfgang Trautwein explains, aimed specifically to create a 'shudder' effect in the reader: 'Schauerliteratur als eine literarische Form, die im Rezeptionsvorgang Schauer hervorruft, d. h. auf eine bestimmte Weise Angst aktiviert.' [*Schauerliteratur* as a literary form, that in the reception process causes shudder [and horror], that is, in a certain manner activates fear and anxiety.][20] It is clearly this tradition upon which the participants in the ghost storytelling competition at the Villa Diodati in 1816 drew. In the Preface that he wrote for the 1818 edition of *Frankenstein*, Percy Bysshe Shelley had made cautious reference to the 'playful desire of imitation' that *Fantasmagoriana* had inspired.[21] But by 1831, Mary Shelley herself was content to rephrase this relation of 'imitation' as one of outright literary 'rivalry':

> I busied myself *to think of a story*, – a story to rival those which had excited us to this task. One which would speak to the mysterious fears of our nature, and awaken thrilling horror – one to make the reader dread to look around, to curdle the blood, and quicken the beatings of the heart. If I did not accomplish these things, my ghost story would be unworthy of its name.[22]

As Shelley herself saw it, the challenge of the ghost storytelling contest was to arouse 'thrilling horror', to write a ghost story that would make its readers physically shudder with fear. It was Eyriès's selection of *Schauerliteratur* in *Fantasmagoriana* that mediated this aspect of the German Gothic to the Byron-Shelley circle in 1816.

Phantasmagoria: Magic-Lantern Shows and Story Telling

What Eyriès had in mind for his collection was not simply a solitary consumption of ghost stories, but a performance of sorts, too, an act of communal reading that was intended to create and foster a more intense and thrilling aesthetic experience. This is to say that, in titling his volume *Fantasmagoriana*, Eyriès deliberately evoked the cultural phenomenon of the phantasmagoria, those popular magic-lantern shows of late eighteenth- and early nineteenth-century Europe that called up and projected onto a screen vivid visual images

---

20 Wolfgang Trautwein, *Erlesene Angst. Schauerliteratur im 18. und 19. Jahrhundert* (Munich and Vienna: Carl Hanser Verlag, 1980), p. 11.
21 Shelley, 'Preface [1818]', p. 48.
22 Shelley, 'Introduction [1831]', pp. 355–6; emphasis in original.

as if they were the ghosts of the dead.[23] These ghost-shows were, indeed, a dalliance with the supernatural, the apparitions and spectres that characteristically flitted across their screens all designed to provoke in the audience the emotional and psychological responses of fear, horror and terror. Terry Castle summarises the reaction of the audiences attending a typical phantasmagoric magic-lantern show as follows:

> Plunged in darkness and assailed by unearthly sounds, spectators were subjected to an eerie, estranging, and ultimately baffling spectral parade. The illusion was apparently so convincing that surprised audience members sometimes tried to fend off the moving 'phantoms' with their hands or fled the room in terror. Even as it supposedly explained apparitions away, the spectral technology of the phantasmagoria mysteriously re-created the emotional aura of the supernatural. One knew ghosts did not exist, yet one saw them anyway, without knowing precisely how.[24]

Not insignificantly, these shows travelled throughout Europe via the same Leipzig–Paris–London route of cultural transmission, as the travelling texts of the German ghost stories would do only a few years later.

Phantasmagoric shows began around the 1770s with the necromancer Johann Georg Schröpfer.[25] Nicknamed the *Gespenstermacher*[26] [ghost-maker], Schröpfer and his coffee house in Leipzig became 'the focus of necromantic interest in Saxony in the early 1770s', when he started to perform his spectacles.[27] According to Greffarth, these 'necromantic performances ... captivated his spectators throughout all-night sessions ... He raised the spirits of deceased celebrities of old and recent times ... The apparitions were said to be clearly visible ... hanging in the air, and screaming awfully ... the faces of the spirits ... looked more like smoke or vapor than flesh and skin'.[28] While contemporaries debated various explanations for these *séances*,[29] it is generally thought that Schröpfer's 'ability in summoning ghosts' was achieved 'via a

---

23 Terry Castle, 'Phantasmagoria: spectral technology and the metaphorics of modern reverie', *Critical Inquiry* 15:1 (1988): 26–61.
24 Castle, 'Phantasmagoria', p. 30.
25 Gustav Wustmann, 'Schrepfer [a.k.a. Schröpfer], Johann Georg', in *Allgemeine Deutsche Biographie* 32 (1891). <www.deutsche-biographie.de/pnd120914042.html> (last accessed 14 May 2019). See also: David J. Jones, *Gothic Machine: Textualities, Pre-cinematic Media and Film in Popular Visual Culture, 1670–1910* (Cardiff: University of Wales Press, 2011), pp. 26–7, 29–33.
26 Camilletti, 'Beyond the Uncanny', pp. 67–8.
27 Renko Geffarth, 'The Masonic Necromancer: Shifting Identities in the Lives of Johann Georg Schrepfer', in Olav Hammer and Kocku von Stuckrad (eds), *Polemical Encounters: Esoteric Discourse and Its Others* (Leiden and Boston: Brill, 2007), pp. 181–97 (p. 182).
28 Geffarth, 'The Masonic Necromancer', p. 185.
29 See Geffarth, 'The Masonic Necromancer', pp. 187–92.

hidden magic lantern'.³⁰ Given this background, it is perhaps no coincidence that *Gespensterbuch*, itself a collection of spectral narratives, was published in Leipzig a few decades later.

Almost two decades after Schröpfer's death in December 1792, Paul Philidor staged the phantasmagoria at Rue de Richelieu in Paris.³¹ Credited by Mannoni with the 'invention of mobile back-projection', Philidor was able to position 'his lantern, mounted on wheels or rails' at a closer or further distance from the screen, resulting in the size of the image becoming gradually larger or smaller.³² Significantly, Philidor intended his phantasmagoria not as a ghost-show, but rather as part of the larger Enlightenment project of debunking popular superstition. As Mannoni explains, however, he was also 'somewhat ambiguously exploiting the public taste for the occult' at the same time.³³

Philidor 'vanished from France around April 1793',³⁴ and consequently it would be Robertson, the stage name of Étienne-Gaspard Robert, who gained great popularity with his magic-lantern shows during the late 1790s and early 1800s.³⁵ Robertson presented his first phantasmagoria show at the Pavillon de l'Echiquier in Paris in 1798,³⁶ a moment that, as Mannoni notes, temporally coincided with the popularity of the Gothic novel in Europe.³⁷ Castle further observes that Robertson 'staged his first "fantasmagorie" as a Gothic extravaganza, complete with fashionably Radcliffean décor'.³⁸ In selecting the

---

30 Camilletti, 'Beyond the Uncanny', p. 67. Mannoni notes: 'Schröpfer [a.k.a. Schrepfer] organized shows of necromancy . . . in which the ghosts of the departed were called up using the "nebulous lantern" which Edme-Gilles Guyot had been first to describe in 1769–70. This was used to project illuminated images, not onto the traditional textile screen, but onto a curtain of smoke . . . it is not known whether . . . Schröpfer used moving back projection', Laurent Mannoni, 'The Phantasmagoria', in Laurent Mannoni, *The Great Art of Light and Shadow: Archaeology of the Cinema*, edited and trans. by Richard Crangle (Exeter: University of Exeter Press, 2000), pp. 136–75 (pp. 138–9). See also Geffarth, 'The Masonic Necromancer', pp. 188 and 188 n.37, for contemporary views 'attributing the effects to mere optical illusions caused by using pseudomagic apparatuses like the *laterna magica*, concave mirrors, or opaque smoke'.
31 Mannoni, 'The Phantasmagoria', p. 142.
32 Mannoni, 'The Phantasmagoria', pp. 141, 145.
33 Mannoni, 'The Phantasmagoria', pp. 143–4.   34 Mannoni, 'The Phantasmagoria', p. 146.
35 'Robertson was the most celebrated and skilled projectionist of his time . . . He stole everything from Philidor, but he did so with such a scientific approach, such an impassioned mastery, and in such a lasting manner . . . that he played a far more prominent role in pre-cinema history than his unfortunate predecessor', Mannoni, 'The Phantasmagoria', p. 147.
36 See Castle, 'Phantasmagoria', p. 31, and Mannoni, 'The Phantasmagoria', p. 147. Mannoni informs further: 'This "Pavillon" still stands today, as 48 Rue de l'Échiquier. It is a small château . . . ', Mannoni, 'The Phantasmagoria', p. 150.
37 Mannoni, 'The Phantasmagoria', p. 137.   38 Castle, 'Phantasmagoria', p. 34.

content for his shows, 'Robertson drew frequently on the "graveyard" and Gothic iconography' that was so popular in the 1790s.[39]

What distinguished Robertson's phantasmagoria from other magic-lantern shows was Philidor's innovation of projecting images of ghosts and apparitions in such a manner as to approach towards, or recede away from, the audience.[40] Robertson accomplished this with moving slides, and by placing his 'whole apparatus on rollers', the latter a technological innovation that allowed his ghosts to 'grow or shrink in front of the viewer's eyes'.[41] Mannoni identifies this as 'the crucial technical component of the phantasmagoria show: the image which advanced and grew, or retreated and diminished, and always remained sharp ... now animated figures crossed the screen in all directions ... came towards the viewer at an astonishing speed, and then disappeared suddenly'.[42]

Like Philidor, Robertson too framed his phantasmagoria show as a scientific technique intended for the purpose of 'the destruction of "absurd beliefs, the childish terrors which dishonor the intelligence of man"'.[43] But what is especially relevant to the Byron-Shelley circle in 1816 is that this rational approach to the dispelling of superstition included experiments in Galvanism. The published announcement for Robertson's first show reads as follows:

> Fantasmagoria at the Pavillon in the rue de l'Échiquier, by citizen E-G. Robertson: apparitions of Spectres, Phantoms and Ghosts, such as they must have appeared or could appear in any time, in any place and among any people. *Experiments with the new fluid known by the name of Galvanism, whose application gives temporary movement to bodies whose life has departed.* An artist noted for his talents will play the Harmonica. One may subscribe for the first showing, which will take place on Tuesday 4 Pluviose [23 January 1798].[44]

---

39 Castle, 'Phantasmagoria', p. 36. Castle further explains that Robertson adapted Henry Fuseli's 'The Nightmare', as well as scenes from 'Macbeth and the Ghost of Banquo', 'The Bleeding Nun', 'A Witches' Sabbath' and 'Young Interring his Daughter', among others, Castle, 'Phantasmagoria', pp. 36–7.
40 '... images appearing to approach and recede from the spectator, [was] the essential component which separated the phantasmagoria from the simple lantern show of diabolical scenes', Mannoni, 'The Phantasmagoria', p. 138.
41 Castle, 'Phantasmagoria', p. 33.
42 'The combination of the movable lantern and the moving slide were an essential step forward in the history of "moving" projection', Mannoni, 'The Phantasmagoria', p. 141.
43 Mannoni, 'The Phantasmagoria', p. 161.
44 *Affiches, Annonces et Avis Divers* 121 (20 January 1798): 2224. English translation here quoted from Mannoni, 'The Phantasmagoria', p. 150; emphasis mine.

As Mannoni observes, Robertson 'was one of the very earliest practitioners in France of Galvanism . . . had long been fascinated by electricity; [and] he later became the friend and faithful supporter of . . . Alessandro Volta'.[45] Jones explains that 'Spectators also saw electrical charges passed through dead frogs' legs which twitched as if revivified', noting that 'Robertson was again planting subliminal messages in the minds of his audience . . . If dead frogs could move again, could Robespierre rise?'[46] Looking back on the genesis of *Frankenstein* in 1831, Mary Shelley recounted how, shortly before her famous 'waking nightmare' at the Villa Diodati, topics of discussion among the members of the group included whether 'a corpse would be reanimated', noting that 'galvanism had given token of such things', and continuing that 'perhaps the component parts of a creature might be manufactured, brought together, and endued with vital warmth'.[47] It is not inconceivable that such topics of conversation were prompted by the group's prior knowledge of Robertson's phantasmagoric shows and the interest in Galvanism that accompanied them.

At the end of 1798, Robertson announced the moving of his show to larger quarters at the Couvent des Capucines, and the phantasmagoria opened here in early January 1799. Intriguingly, this old convent was just a short distance from the bookshop that would publish *Fantasmagoriana* in 1812.[48] Against this backdrop, and as Camilletti has pointed out, it is clear that Eyriès carefully assembled the ghost stories under the title *Fantasmagoriana* in order to evoke in literature the spirit of Robertson's magic-lantern shows.[49] Even Eyriès's subtitle – *ou Recueil d'Histoires d'Apparitions de Spectres, Revenans, Fantômes, etc.;* – echoes Philidor's advertisement of 1792: 'La Phantasmagorie, ou apparitions des Spectres & évocations des Ombres des Personnages célebres & autres.'[50]

---

45 Mannoni, 'The Phantasmagoria', p. 150.
46 Jones, *Gothic Machine*, p. 65. For a discussion of Robertson, see p. 67.
47 Shelley, 'Introduction [1831]', p. 357.   48 Camilletti, 'Beyond the Uncanny', pp. 67–8.
49 Fabio Camilletti, 'On this day in 1816: John Polidori finds a book', *BARS Blog*, 12 June 2016 <www.bars.ac.uk/blog/?p=1214> (last accessed 14 May 2019). On the title, see also Camilletti: 'The title *Fantasmagoriana* . . . was not . . . a reference to ghosts (*fantôme*), but rather to the visual creations of imagination (*fantasme*). At the same time, of course, it was an allusion to Robertson's phantasmagoria shows . . . ', Fabio Camilletti, 'From Villa Diodati to Villa Gabrielli: a manuscript appendix to *Fantasmagoriana*', *Gothic Studies* 20:1–2 (November 2018), pp. 214–26 (pp. 220–2).
50 *Affiches, Annonces et Avis Divers, ou Journal Général de France* 73 (14 March 1793): 1083. On adding the suffix 'ana' to 'Fantasmagoria', as emphasising 'the collective and plural nature of books' and '*Fantasmagoriana*, the first "-ana book" explicitly related to supernatural matters', see Camilletti, 'From Villa Diodati', p. 217.

In the early 1800s, phantasmagoria came to England. This time it was the 'Parisian showman, Paul de Philipst[h]al,[51] [who] offered extremely successful specter-shows on the Robertsonian model at the Lyceum Theatre in London in late 1801 and 1802, and later [in] ... Edinburgh and Dublin'.[52] William Nicholson provides a contemporary account of Philipsthal's show at the Lyceum:

> In this gloomy and wavering light the curtain was drawn up, and presented to the spectator a cave or place exhibiting skeletons, and other figures of terror, in relief, and painted on the sides or walls ... These appearances were followed by figures of departed men, ghosts, skeletons, transmutations, &c. produced on the screen by the magic lanthorn [sic] on the other side, and moving their eyes, mouths, &c. by the well known contrivance of two or more sliders ... Several figures of celebrated men were thus exhibited with some transformations; such as the head of Dr. Franklin being converted into a skull, and these were succeeded by phantoms, skeletons, and various terrific figures, which instead of seeming to recede and then vanish, were (by enlargement) made suddenly to advance; to the surprize and astonishment of the audience, and then disappear by seeming to sink into the ground.[53]

The success of Philipsthal's shows spawned numerous imitators.[54] Under the phantasmagoria rubric, magic-lantern ghost shows were still being performed in London in 1812. Henry Crabb Robinson records that in September of that year he 'went to the Mechanical and Optical theatre ... The Phantasmagoria also gratified me. I had never before seen the effect of magic lanthornes [sic] throwing their figures on a thin transparent surface which enables the operator to establish elaborate machinery and produce a powerful effect.'[55]

---

51 Mannoni and others have questioned if Philidor and Philipsthal were the same individual. 'Philipstahl [sic], whose surname shared a first syllable with Philidor and Philadelphia, also had the same first name (Paul) as the lanternist of Rue de Richelieu, whose work in 1792–3 was of such importance.' See Mannoni, 'The Phantasmagoria', p. 173. For a detailed account of Philipsthal in Great Britain, see Mervyn Heard, 'Paul de Philipsthal & the phantasmagoria in England, Scotland and Ireland', *New Magic Lantern Journal* 8:1 (October 1996): 2–7; 8.2 (October 1997): 11–16, and 8:4 (December 1999): 6–13.
52 Castle, 'Phantasmagoria', p. 37. See also p. 37 n. 9.
53 William Nicholson, 'Narrative and Explanation of the Appearance of Phantoms and other Figures in the Exhibition of Phantasmagoria. With Remarks on the Philosophical use of common Occurrences', *A Journal of Natural Philosophy, Chemistry, and The Arts* (London: G. and J. Robinson, 1802), vol. 1, pp. 147–50 (p. 148).
54 For a sample between 1802 and 1812, see Castle, 'Phantasmagoria', pp. 38–9.
55 Henry Crabb Robinson, 'September 23 [1812]', in *The London Theatre 1811–1866. Selections from the Diary of Henry Crabb Robinson*, edited by Eluned Brown (London: The Society for Theatre Research, 1966), p. 47.

The question that remains, of course, is the extent to which the members of the Byron-Shelley circle were familiar with the phantasmagoria before reading Eyriès's *Fantasmagoriana* in 1816. In her journal entry for Wednesday 28 December 1814, the young Mary Wollstonecraft records: 'in the evening S[helley]. & I go to Gray's Inn to get Hogg ... cant find him – go to Garnerin's lecture – on Electricity – the gasses – & the Phantasmagoria'.[56] David Jones explains that 'Garnerin, Robertson's future rival, had copied his show *in toto* from Robertson's.'[57] It is not known whether the electrical components of Garnerin's show featured the animation of dead frogs.[58] In any event, the Shelleys were personally acquainted with Garnerin's version of Robertson's phantasmagoria show a year-and-a-half before the contest at Villa Diodati.

From the early 1800s onwards, phantasmagoria circulated as a term and concept in British print culture and the public sphere. Henry Lemoine's poem 'Phantasmagoria', for example, appeared in *The Gentleman's Magazine* on 30 June 1802. Lemoine locates the genesis of his poem in the 'popularity of the above subject [Phantasmagoria], the taste for terror, and the long train of terrific romances or novels of the late years published, I hope may plead for an excuse for ... the following lines'.[59] In the same month, Lawrence Sulivan published a poem in *The Gentleman's Magazine* that contained the lines: 'What's the Greek word for all this *Goblinstoria?* / I have it pat – It is *Phantasmagoria.*'[60] Phantasmagoria also circulated prominently in political cartoons of the day, including in the satirical *A New Phantasmagoria for John Bull!!* (after George Moutard Woodward, 1805); in Williams's etching of William Heath's *The Flushing Phantasmagoria–or–Kings Conjurors Amuseing [sic] John Bull* (1809); and in Thomas Rowlandson's *Phantasmagoria, A View of Elephanta* (1816). All three of these images feature a magic lantern projecting

---

56 Mary Shelley, 'Wednesday [December] 28th', in *The Journals of Mary Shelley, 1814–1844*, Vol. I: *1814–1822*, edited by Paula R. Feldman and Diana Scott-Kilvert (Oxford: Oxford University Press, 2015), p. 56. For André-Jacques Garnerin, see also Mannoni, 'The Phantasmagoria', p. 158, and Simon During, *Modern Enchantments: The Cultural Power of Secular Magic* (Cambridge, MA and London: Harvard University Press, 2002), pp. 252–8.
57 Jones, *Gothic Machine*, p. 70.
58 *The Morning Post* advertised 'Professor Garnerin's Grand Philosophical Recreations' at Spring Gardens where 'Electricity, Gas, Aerostation, Phantasmagoria, and Hydraulic Sports, will be varied every night, for the entertainment of the Public'. *The Morning Post*, Tuesday 8 November 1814, p. 2.
59 Henry Lemoine, 'Phantasmagoria', *The Gentleman's Magazine* 72 (June 1802): no pag.
60 Lawrence Sulivan, 'Prologue. To Julius Caesar, performed at Mr. Newcome's School, Hackney, in May 1802', *The Gentleman's Magazine* 72 (June 1802): 543–4 (p. 544); emphasis Sulivan.

the caricatured subject matter.[61] As Richard D. Altick explains, 'the phantasmagoria served the caricaturists well ... The persistence of imitations and variations of the show, as well as the memories people had of their experience in the darkened room, kept the phantasmagoria topical down to the time of Waterloo at least'.[62] In light of this circulation, and given the prominence of phantasmagoria shows in London during the early 1810s, it is likely that, in addition to the Shelleys, Byron, Claire Clairmont and Polidori were also familiar with these forms of popular visual entertainment before they left for the Continent. Perhaps, in reading the *Fantasmagoriana* collection at the Villa Diodati, the Byron-Shelley circle were in quest of similar phantasmagoric experiences, the communal reading of *Fantasmagoriana* in part recreating the ghostly horror and terror of the magic-lantern shows in their own parlour.

Just as the *Gespensterbuch* found its genesis in a *Gespensterthee*, so Apel and Schulze, in turn, encouraged the telling of ghost stories to their readers. Indeed, the Afterword to *Gespensterbuch* claimed that both volumes were intended to incite further acts of supernatural reading and listening:

> Ob es Gespenster gebe, soll eine sehr unentschiedene und streitige Sache seyn, aber entschieden und unstreitig ist es, daß es Gespenstergeschichten giebt, und die Erfahrung, welche über Gespenster selbst sehr zweideutig belehrt, zeigt unwidersprechlich, daß sehr viel Leute die Gespenstergeschichten außerordentlich gern hören und lesen. Der geneigte Leser bezeugt mir dieses willig, denn wär es nicht so, warum hätte er sich denn durch dieses Bändchen bis zur Nachrede durchgelesen?[63]

> [Whether there are ghosts is a very undecided and disputed matter, but what is decided and not up for debate is that there are ghost stories, and while the experience with ghosts is very ambiguous, it shows, incontrovertibly, that many people extraordinarily enjoy hearing and reading ghost-stories. The inclined reader willingly testifies to this, because if it was not so, why did the reader then read through this little book all the way to the afterword?]

It is a small step from here to Byron's suggestion that each write their own ghost story. While these particular events were undoubtedly significant in inspiring a number of well-known Gothic fictions, it appears that the practice of telling one's own ghost stories was more widespread than the mythologising of the Summer of 1816 might have us believe. In any case, the ghost-storytelling contest is a particularly cosmopolitan event: an English literary coterie reading a French-

---

61 See Richard D. Altick, *The Shows of London* (Cambridge, MA and London: Harvard University Press, 1978), p. 218.
62 Altick, *The Shows of London*, p. 218.
63 Apel and Laun, *Gespensterbuch*, vol. 1, pp. 282–3.

edited translation of popular German ghost stories acquired from a Swiss library or bookstore that inspired English Gothic classics of enduring fame.

Fantasmagoriana and *Frankenstein*

For almost a century, the influence of *Fantasmagoriana* on the Gothic productions of the Byron-Shelley circle was almost forgotten. Polidori's diary entry for 17 June 1816 notes that 'The ghost-stories are begun by all but me',[64] but the editor of the diary in 1911 dismissed *Fantasmagoriana* outright as 'a poor sort of book'.[65] It was not until 1914 that one of the first scholarly treatises on the influences of *Schauerliteratur* on Byron and the Shelleys appeared. Manfred Eimer identified the stories in *Fantasmagoriana* and compared particular passages from 'L'Heure Fatale' to scenes in Byron's dramatic poem *Manfred*.[66] Polidori's *The Vampyre* might also be added to this list of texts inspired by *Fantasmagoriana*,[67] but in the discussion that follows, I wish to focus specifically on the influence that the conventions of German *Schauerliteratur*, particularly as they feature in the tales anthologised in *Fantasmagoriana*, had upon the composition of *Frankenstein*.

One of the most poignant scenes in Shelley's novel is the midnight visitation by the monster to Victor Frankenstein's bedside. Shortly after having created – and subsequently abandoned – his creation, Victor narrates:

> I started from my sleep with horror; a cold dew covered my forehead, my teeth chattered, and every limb became convulsed; when, by the dim and yellow light of the moon, as it forced its way through the window-shutters, I beheld the wretch – the miserable monster whom I had created. He held up the curtain of the bed; and his eyes, if eyes they may be called, were fixed on me.[68]

This scene is transposed from Shelley's own 'waking nightmare' described in her 1831 Introduction. After reading the ghost stories and listening to discussions on Galvanism, Shelley recounts that:

---

64 William Michael Rossetti (ed.), *The Diary of Dr. John William Polidori, 1816, Relating to Byron, Shelley, Etc.* (Cambridge: Cambridge University Press, 2014), p. 125.
65 Rossetti, *The Diary of Dr. John William Polidori*, p. 126.
66 See Eimer, 'Einflüsse deutscher Räuber- und Schauerromantik', pp. 241–4, .
67 For a brief discussion of 'L'Heure Fatale', and Byron's *Manfred* and 'La Morte Fiancée', and Polidori's *The Vampyre*, see Maximiliaan van Woudenberg, 'The Gothic Galaxy of the Byron-Shelley Circle: The Metamorphosis of Friedrich Schulze and *Fantasmagoriana*', in Maurizio Ascari, Serena Baiesi and David Levente Palatinus (eds), *Gothic Metamorphoses Across the Centuries: Contexts, Legacies, Media* (Bern: Peter Lang, 2020), pp. 53–68.
68 Shelley, *Frankenstein*, pp. 85–6; vol. 1, chapter 4.

Fantasmagoriana: The Cosmopolitan Gothic and *Frankenstein*

> Night waned upon this talk, and even the witching hour had gone by, before we retired to rest. When I placed my head on the pillow, I did not sleep, nor could I be said to think... I saw the hideous phantasm of a man stretched out ... He sleeps; but he is awakened; he opens his eyes; behold the horrid thing stands at his bedside, opening his curtains, and looking on him with yellow, watery, but speculative eyes.
> I opened mine in terror.[69]

What Shelley does not recall here is that the waking terror of bedside visitation was a common motif in *Schauerliteratur*, and one that featured in six of the eight stories brought together in Eyriès's *Fantasmagoriana*.

Specifically, Shelley in 1831 remembers two stories from the collection 'as if I had read them yesterday'.[70] The first of these is 'the History of the Inconstant Lover, who, when he thought to clasp the bride to whom he had pledged his vows, found himself in the arms of the pale ghost of her whom he had deserted'.[71] While it echoes the episode of the Bleeding Nun in Matthew Gregory Lewis's *The Monk* (1796) and, through this, Gottfried August Bürger's 'Lenore' (1774), this, of course, is Schulze's 'La Morte Fiancée', a story in which the groom is found dead in the bridal chamber by his bride. Mary Shelley masterfully transforms the curse in the story into an exquisite misdirection in *Frankenstein*. Here, it is not Victor the groom but his innocent bride Elizabeth that is the target of the monster's threatening vow to Victor that 'remember, I shall be with you on your wedding-night'.[72] The curse in 'La Morte Fiancée' is reversed in *Frankenstein* in terms of both plot and gender, as the innocent and faithful bride is punished instead of the inconstant groom. 'La Morte Fiancée', however, does not show the wedding-bed death of the groom, and this unrealised bedside visitation also does not describe a 'waking terror'.

The second story that Mary Shelley remembers reading at the Villa Diodati is Apel's 'Les Portraits de Famille', a narrative that, as Terry Hale notes, features a curse that 'offers one close parallel with Mary Shelley's novel in that both works deal with the annihilation of an entire family'.[73] Shelley particularly recalls this 'tale of the sinful founder of his race, whose miserable doom it was to bestow the kiss of death on all the younger sons of his fated house ... Eternal sorrow sat upon his face as he bent down and kissed the forehead of the boys, who from that hour withered like flowers snapt upon

---

69 Shelley, 'Introduction [1831]', p. 357.   70 Shelley, 'Introduction [1831]', p. 355.
71 Shelley, 'Introduction [1831]', pp. 354–5.
72 Shelley, *Frankenstein*, p. 193; vol. 3, chapter 3.   73 Hale, *Tales of the Dead*, p. 16.

the stalk'.⁷⁴ In 'Les Portraits de Famille', it is Ditmar – misremembered by Shelley as being 'clothed like the ghost in Hamlet, in complete armour, but with the beaver up'⁷⁵ – who curses with a kiss his young ancestors while they are asleep. As Ferdinand narrates:

> L'agitation m'ôta le sommeil; je me tournai pour éveiller un des enfans et causer avec lui ... Qui pourra dépeindre mon épouvante, quand je vis devant le lit de l'enfant l'effroyable figure?
> Le saisissement, l'horreur me glacèrent; je n'osai ni remuer, ni même fermer les yeux. Je vis le spectre se pencher vers l'enfant, et lui baiser doucement le front. Il se pencha ensuite par dessus mon lit, et baisa le front de l'autre enfant.
> Je perdis connoissance en ce moment; ... .⁷⁶

> [The agitation I had endured took from me the power of sleep, and I turned to awake one of the children to talk with me: but no powers can depict the horrors I endured when I saw the frightful figure [of Ditmar] at the side of the child's bed.
> I was petrified with horror, and dared neither move nor shut my eyes. I beheld the spectre stoop towards the child and softly kiss his forehead: he then went round the bed, and kissed the forehead of the other boy.
> I lost all recollection at that moment; ... .]⁷⁷

The cursing of descendants is replayed in *Frankenstein* in the monster's murdering of his first victim, William: like the young boys in 'Les Portraits de Famille', William, 'my darling infant' in Elizabeth's phrase, is young and innocent.⁷⁸ This bedside description in Apel's story, however, is far from the terror of Victor's and Shelley's own 'waking nightmare'. Ferdinand awakens due to his own agitation, and while 'petrified with horror', he is not the target of the ghostly visitation. In Schulze's 'Le Revenant', the widow Julien sees her dead husband in her bedroom and becomes a firm believer in ghosts and the paranormal. The terror of a 'waking nightmare', however, is absent. In all three stories, in fact, the bedroom visitation scene is largely a plot device, and does not focus on the horror of the awakened sleeper.

---

74 Shelley, 'Introduction [1831]', p. 355.
75 Shelley, 'Introduction [1831]', p. 355. Rieger notes that Shelley recalls the story 'in an altered form. Eyriès's ghost wears "un manteau gris," but no armor; his journey from the garden to the children's bedside is silent and invisible', James Rieger, 'Dr Polidori and the genesis of *Frankenstein*', *Studies in English Literature, 1500–1900* 3:4 (1963): 461–72 (p. 466).
76 Eyriès, *Fantasmagoriana*, vol. 1, pp. 152–3.
77 English translation: Utterson, *Tales of the Dead*, pp. 22–3.
78 Shelley, *Frankenstein*, p. 99. vol. 1, chapter 6.

Instead, it is Musäus's 'L'Amour Muet' and the companion stories – Clauren's 'La Chambre Grise' and Apel's 'La Chambre Noire' – that feature lengthy passages describing the terror of a bedside encounter with the supernatural. The protagonist in 'L'Amour Muet' – Franz Melchior – however, is awakened not by a ghost, but by the sudden shock of a palpitation. Thus, Franz is already fully awake when the ghost first approaches, and then enters, his bedchamber.[79] While this ghostly bedside encounter evokes terror, it does not feature the terror of a 'waking nightmare'.

In particular, then, it is the descriptions of a bedside visitation in Clauren's and Apel's tales that most closely resemble the 'waking nightmare' in *Frankenstein*. When the protagonist Blendau in 'La Chambre Grise' finally falls asleep, he is quickly awakened by *Burgfräulein* Gertrude, the ghost that haunts the castle. The horror and terror of a bedside visitation – whether by supernatural ghost or scientifically created monster – is captured in some detail. It is revealing in this regard to compare the French translation read by Mary Shelley to the German original. The scene from Clauren reads as follows:

> Aber dieser Schlaf dauerte nicht lange. Nach zwei Stunden erwachte er; noch mit zugemachten Augen hörte er die nahe Thurmglocke zwölfe brummen. Er schlug die Augen auf. Licht im Zimmer. Er richtete sich im Bette auf. Der Schreck machte ihn völlig munter. Sein Blick fiel durch die Spalte der Bettvorhänge auf den Spiegel.
>
> Da stand das Burgfräulein Gertrude im Leichenhemde mit dem Kruzifixe in der linken, und einem großen blinkenden Stahl-Dolch in der rechten Hand.
>
> Blendau war ganz wach. Er sah mit hellen Augen.
>
> Das Blut erkaltete ihm in allen Adern. Das war kein Gesicht, kein Traum, das war eine schreckliche Wahrheit.[80]

[But this sleep did not last long. After two hours he [Blendau] awoke; with his eyes still closed he heard the nearby tower-bell drone twelve. He opened his eyes. Light in the room. He straightened up in bed. Fear made him entirely awake. His gaze fell through the gap in the bed curtains upon the mirror.

There stood *Burgfräulein* Gertrude in a shroud with a crucifix in her left hand and a large shiny steel-dagger in her right hand.

Blendau was entirely awake. He saw with bright eyes.

---

79 Johann August Musäus, 'Stumme Liebe', in *Volksmährchen der Deutschen*, 5 vols (Vienna: s.n., 1788), vol. 4, pp. 5–149 (pp. 96–9). Eyriès, *Fantasmagoriana*, vol. 1, pp. 68–70.
80 Clauren, 'Die graue Stube', p. 287.

The blood cooled in all his veins. This was not a vision – not a dream. This was the terrible truth.]

Eyriès renders the French translation of the scene as follows:

> Mais environ deux heures après il s'éveille, et il entend l'horloge de la tour voisine sonner minuit; il ouvre les yeux, il voit la chambre éclairée; il se lève sur son séant; la frayeur le tient éveillé; les rideaux du pied du lit sont entr'ouverts; ses regards tombent sur le miroir qui est en face de lui.
> Il aperçoit le spectre de Gertrude vêtu d'un linceul, un crucifix dans la main gauche, un poignard dans la main droite.
> Blendau étoit complétement éveillé, il voyoit tout très-distinctement.
> Son sang se glace dans ses veines; ce qu'il a devant les yeux n'est point un songe, une apparence vaine, c'est une réalité effrayante; ... [81]

> [But after around two hours he wakes up, and he hears the clock of the neighbouring tower ring midnight; he opens his eyes, he sees the room lit; he sits up; fear keeps him awake; the curtains at the foot of the bed are ajar; his eyes fall on the mirror in front of him.
> He sees the spectre of Gertude wearing a shroud, a crucifix in her left hand, a dagger in her right hand.
> Blendau was completely awake, he saw everything distinctly.
> His blood is ice-cold in his veins; what he has before his eyes is not a dream, not a vain appearance, it is a frightening reality;]

The sudden opening of eyes is described in detail – and, like Victor and Mary Shelley, narrated in the first person – in Apel's 'La Chambre Noire'. While asleep in bed, the town doctor, Bärmann, hears his name called:

> Ich war noch im ersten Schlafe, da dünkte es mich, als hört' ich meinen Namen ganz leise nennen. Ich fuhr zusammen und horchte auf, da hört' ich nochmals ganze deutlich rufen: August! Der Schall kam, wie es schien, aus den Vorhängen meines Bettes. *Ich riß die Augen weit auf*, sah aber nichts als dichte Dunkelheit um mich. Indessen hatte mich doch der leise Ruf mit einem Fieberfrost übergossen, ich drückte die Augen fest zu und fing an wieder einzuschlummern. Auf einmal weckt mich ein Rauschen in den Bettvorhängen und der Ruf meines Namens tönt mir noch deutlicher zu.[82]

> [I was still in the first sleep, when it seemed to me I heard my name called very softly. I collected myself and listened; there I heard again, clearly calling: 'August!' The sound came, so it seemed, from the curtains of my bed. *I tore*

---

81 Eyriès, *Fantasmagoriana*, vol. 2, pp. 237–8.
82 Apel, 'Die schwarze Kammer', in Apel and Laun, *Gespensterbuch*, vol. 2, pp. 191–2; emphasis mine.

my eyes wide open, but saw nothing around me but dense darkness. Meantime, however, this soft call had poured a feverish cold over me, I squeezed my eyes firmly closed and started to doze asleep again. All at once I am awakened by a rustling in the bed-curtains and the call of my name sounds even more clearly.]

The equivalent passage in *Fantasmagoriana* reads as follows:

J'étois dans mon premier sommeil, lorsqu'il me sembla que j'entendois prononcer mon nom tout bas; je fus saisi et j'écoutai: j'entendis encore appeler très-distinctement Auguste. La voix paroissoit venir du grand rideau du lit. *J'ouvris les yeux*; mais autour de moi régnoit une obscurité profonde; cependant le bruit léger qui s'étoit fait entendre, m'avoit occasionné un frisson. Je fermai les yeux et je recommençai à sommeiller. Soudain je suis réveillé par un bruit que fait le grand rideau, et mon nom est articulé encore plus distinctement.[83]

[I was in my first sleep, when it seemed to me that I heard my name whispered; I was seized and listened: I heard again very distinctly called August. The voice seemed to come from the big curtain of the bed. *I opened my eyes*; but around me reined a profound darkness; however, the soft noise which was heard made me shudder. I closed my eyes and began to slumber again. Suddenly I'm awakened by a noise made by the big curtain, and my name is articulated again even more distinctly.]

In Apel's original, Bärmann describes his awakening as: 'Ich riß die Augen weit auf' [I tore my eyes wide open]. The meaning here is of a sudden and unanticipated opening of one's eyes, an awakening with a start that is captured later in Shelley's and Victor's 'waking terror'. In the French edition, however, Eyriès translates the German simply as 'J'ouvris les yeux' [I opened my eyes]. The French translation clearly ignores the impact of the German verb *riß*, derived from *reißen*, meaning to rip or to tear, thus omitting the connotation of a sudden opening of the eyes as if in a state of absolute horror. Though she apparently did not read the story in German, Mary Shelley instinctively restores the impact of the German Gothic captured in the word *riß* with Victor's 'started from sleep with horror' and her own description: 'I opened mine in terror'. Thus, in *Frankenstein*, the horror and terror of a sudden awakening captured in the German are imaginatively restored in the monster's bedside visitation, as well as in Mary Shelley's own 'waking nightmare'. If Mary Shelley did not read the German originals of these tales – and there is no evidence that she did – she seems instinctively to have

---

83 Eyriès, *Fantasmagoriana*, vol. 2, p. 259; emphasis mine.

appropriated the shudders of the *Schauerliteratur* for her own Gothic narrative.

Eyes are not the only Gothic trope of 'waking terror' that Shelley seems to draw from these *Schauerliteratur* stories. Other tropes employed in scenes of bedside visitations include a cold fever,[84] and the opening of bed curtains.[85] Certainly, such Gothic conventions were widespread in early nineteenth-century literature, and do not feature solely in the stories collected in *Fantasmagoriana*. Nevertheless, it is of interest to note how closely the sequence of these two bedside scenes, and the details in the passages above, resembles Victor's sudden awakening. Clearly, the bedside visitations in these German ghost stories were an inspirational prompt for *Frankenstein*. It is Mary Shelley's genius that masterfully transforms these *Schauerliteratur* tropes into the 'waking nightmare' of her own story for an English audience.

This transformation is perhaps best illustrated through a brief return to the controversy of the two companion stories that I outlined above. The legal analysis of the bedside ghost in 'La Chambre Noire' is a rational, indeed, enlightened response to the supernatural bedside visit in 'La Chambre Grise'. Where Clauren's original story firmly establishes the existence of the supernatural and the unexplainable with an oath by the educated Blendau, Apel's narrative provides a rational explanation: it is a mechanical devise that is the source for the illusion of the supernatural in the tale. Echoing the scientific framework of the phantasmagoria shows, Apel concludes his narrative not by establishing the existence of the spirit world, but by confirming the power of ghost stories:

> Geht mir – rief er – wir leben in einer schlechten Zeit! Alles Alte geht zu Grunde, nicht einmal ein rechtschaffenes Gespenst kann sich mehr halten. Komme mir keiner wieder mit einer Gespensterhistorie!
> Bewahre! – erwiderten wir andern beiden – Gerade wenn es mit den Gespenstern aus ist, geht das rechte Zeitalter für ihre Geschichte an. Kommt doch jede Geschichte erst hinter der Wirklichkeit, und den Leser dadurch, wenn das Glück gut ist, hinter die Wahrheit![86]

---

84 See Clauren, 'Die graue Stube', p. 287. Apel and Laun, *Gespensterbuch*, vol. 2, p. 191. Shelley, *Frankenstein*, pp. 85–6; vol. 1, chapter 4.

85 Compare 'Die Schaudervolle bog die Vorhänge des Himmelbettes zurück, ihr stieres kaltes Auge schoß einen entsetzlichen Blick . . . ' [The horrible [ghost] bent back the curtains of the four-poster bed, her vacant cold eyes shot a terrible look . . .] in Clauren, 'Die graue Stube', p. 287, to: 'He [monster] held up the curtain of the bed; and his eyes, if eyes they may be called, were fixed on me', Shelley, *Frankenstein*, p. 86, vol. 1, chapter 4.

86 Apel and Laun, *Gespensterbuch*, vol. 2, p. 206. See also Eyriès, *Fantasmagoriana*, vol. 2, pp. 302–3. As the last story in the French translation, the ending of this story also

['Away' – the town doctor shouted – 'we are living in a bad time. Everything old goes to ruin, not even a righteous ghost can exist anymore. No one approach me again with a ghost story!'

'Heaven forbid!' – we both responded – 'Just when one is done with ghosts, the right era for their stories begins. Every story first comes after reality, and through it the reader, when their luck is good, after the truth.']

Like Apel, Shelley in *Frankenstein* consolidates the rationale of the Enlightenment with the unexplainable supernatural: after all, the novel never fully and satisfactorily explains exactly how the monster comes to life. This is not Shelley's purpose. Instead, her primary aim, as we have seen above, is *'to think of a story, –* a story to rival those which had excited us to this task. One which would . . . awaken thrilling horror'. This commences with the 'waking nightmare' of a bedside visitation inspired by German ghost stories mediated in a French collection. Shelley achieves this by focusing on the powerful shudder effects of her 'ghost' story that are evoked neither by the ghostly supernatural of 'La Chambre Grise', nor by the rational and mechanical explanation of 'La Chambre Noire', but rather through the rationalisation of faith in the promise of science and technology. In place of requiring of the reader a suspension of disbelief in the face of Gothic supernaturalism, Shelley embraces the enlightened promises of science and technology, discourses that serve as the source for the rational yet still, in some senses, profoundly supernatural creation of the monster by a Promethean overreacher.

Conclusion

Jean-Baptiste Benoît Eyriès's *Fantasmagoriana* is a singular collection of European ghost stories that invoked the spirit of the phantasmagoria magic-lantern shows of the late eighteenth and early nineteenth centuries. The reading of *Fantasmagoriana* to arouse 'shudder' and 'horror' was an event that followed in the footsteps of the *Gespensterthee* of Apel and Schulze, inspiring those gathered at the Villa Diodati in 1816 to host their own ghost-telling session and compose their own ghost stories. Shelley's 'waking nightmare' was a direct result of discussions of Galvanism and the reading of German ghost stories in French translation. Her creative process in *Frankenstein* consists of blending the waking residue of the shuddering effect

marked the conclusion to the Byron-Shelley circle's reading of German ghost stories. It is easy to see how this passage provided a prompt for Byron's suggestion to write their own ghost stories.

produced by the reading of ghost stories into an imaginative creation of a new creative narrative. The global fascination with *Frankenstein* today is thus at least partly attributable to the fact that Shelley's text is a palimpsest of European Gothic in the early years of the nineteenth century, of bedroom visitations derived from German *Schauerliteratur* and mediated via the French translations collected in *Fantasmagoriana*. In *Frankenstein*, the tropes and conventions of the German Gothic undergo a transformation into a staple of the English Gothic literary tradition, effectively obscuring the German origins of generic frameworks and authorial sources of the ghost stories in the process. In reading *Frankenstein*, English readers were – and, indeed, still are – engaging with a cosmopolitan Gothic fiction, the constituent elements of which are as diverse as the body-parts that comprise its resident creature.

2.3
The Mutation of the Vampire in Nineteenth-Century Gothic

JERROLD E. HOGLE

The figure of the vampire and 'Gothic' fiction by that name came into English writing quite separately in the eighteenth century. One of the first published references in English to 'vampire' in its most common sense appeared in a travel narrative of 1745. There, 'Vampyres are supposed to be the Bodies of deceased Persons, animated by evil Spirits, which come out of the Graves, in the Night-time, suck the Blood of many of the Living, and thereby destroy them.'[1] Even so, despite its haunted medieval castle just 20 years later that forecasts the initial setting of Bram Stoker's *Dracula* (1897), Horace Walpole's *The Castle of Otranto* (1764), the first narrative to be labelled 'A Gothic Story' in its second edition (1765), includes no such ravenous elements in its ghosts or monstrosities. It limits them to enlarged spectral fragments from the statue on the tomb of the castle's original owner that obscurely manifest his murder by the current Prince's grandfather; the image of that very grandsire walking out of his portrait 'with a grave and melancholy air'; and the reanimated bones of the Hermit of Joppa, like a skeleton in a fifteenth-century *danse macabre* painting, who confronts the Marquis Frederic, Prince Manfred's rival for the ownership of Otranto, with death as the wage for his conspiracy to marry Manfred's daughter in exchange for Manfred marrying his.[2] While Walpole's scheme was inspiring variations over the next three decades, the vampire legend in the West followed a separate path, most often in German poetry, albeit in verses soon translated for English readers: Heinrich August Ossenfelder's dramatic monologue of 1748, 'The Vampire', has its speaker promise a 'little girl' that 'I will become a vampire' and 'suck up / The fresh crimson of your cheeks' if she accepts 'the old teachings / Of her devout mother' about the 'deadly vampires' in which 'people of the Theyse

---

1 'Vampire, *n.*, 1a.' in the *Oxford English Dictionary* (hereafter cited in my text as *OED*).
2 See Horace Walpole, *The Castle of Otranto*, edited by W. S. Lewis with intro. and notes by E. J. Clery (Oxford: Oxford University Press, 1996), pp. 18–21, 25–6, 106–7 and 113–14.

[river in Hungary] / Have [long] believed'; Gottfried August Bürger's much-translated 'Lenore' (1773) lets its heroine call out at night for her long-lost soldier-lover only to be swept up by his skeleton on horseback and carried off to his grave because he is already dead; Johann Wolfgang von Goethe's verse-play *The Bride of Corinth* (1797) centres on a young man in ancient Greece awakened at midnight by the deceased object of his love who moans that she is 'From the silent graveyard ... driven / ... Still to love him' by draining 'his life-blood from his heart with gust'; and Robert Southey's *Thalaba the Destroyer* (1800) embraces this German turn to the female vampire, while also incorporating the vampiric drives in the vengeful ancestors of supposedly Oriental myths, so much so that the attempts of sorcerers to draw the Muslim hero towards Hell lead to him facing the 'livid' illusion of his dead wife, whose 'terrible ... Brightness' in her 'eye' in Canto 8, verses 9–10, leaves Thalaba 'palsied of all power' until his older guide 'through the vampire corpse / Thrust his lance'.[3]

How the Vampire Entered the Gothic, 1800–1816

It is by combining all these influences while adding some others, right at the start of the nineteenth century, that Samuel Taylor Coleridge offered Western readers the first truly *Gothic* transmutation of the vampire-figure in his poem 'Christabel', which he left unfinished in 1800 and circulated privately before its publication in 1816. It is then this version that George Gordon, the already (in)famous Lord Byron, recited aloud to his guests – including Percy Bysshe Shelley, Mary Godwin (soon to be Mary Shelley) and Byron's physician-in-residence, Dr John Polidori – at the Villa Diodati near Geneva during the summer of that year and made one impetus of a challenge for all of them to write their own 'ghost stories'.[4] From that challenge, we now know, emerged Mary Shelley's *Frankenstein* (1818), in which the title character comes to see his creature 'in the light of my own vampire, my own spirit let loose from the grave',[5] and Polidori's novella *The Vampyre* (1819), the

---

3 For all these texts and my quotations from them (sometimes translations of them), see Roxana Stuart, *Stage Blood: Vampires of the Nineteenth-Century Stage* (Bowling Green, OH: Bowling Green State University Popular Press, 1994), pp. 31–3.

4 See John Polidori, *The Diary of Dr. John William Polidori 1816, Relating to Byron, Shelley, Etc.*, edited by William Michael Rossetti (London: Elkin Matthews, 1911), p. 128, and Jerrold E. Hogle, 'The gothic image at the Villa Diodati', *The Wordsworth Circle* 47 (2017): 16–26.

5 Mary Wollstonecraft Shelley, *Frankenstein; or, The Modern Prometheus: The 1818 Text*, edited by James Rieger, Phoenix edition (Chicago: University of Chicago Press, 1982), p. 72.

site of the first male aristocratic vampire, based partly on Byron, that helped spawn a succession of others over the next eight decades, culminating most famously in Stoker's Count Dracula. 'Christabel' had and still has that kind of power, despite its never using the word 'vampire', partly because it follows Walpole's stated prescription for a 'Gothic Story' in the Preface to the second edition of *Otranto*: a 'blend' of 'the two kinds of romance, the ancient and the modern', a looking backwards and forwards like the two faces of the Roman god Janus, in which the 'ancient' is nearly all 'imagination' as it recalls the supernatural chivalric romances of the twelfth through the sixteenth centuries, and the 'modern' is a discourse that insists on 'probability' within the standards of 'common life' based on the empirical epistemology of the Enlightenment, as in the emerging novel of the 1740s and after.[6] On the one hand, ancient romance is clearly invoked when Coleridge's young title character, who wanders, like Bürger's Lenore, outside her father's castle longing for her absent lover, is 'suddenly' faced with the statuesque and 'lovely' figure of Geraldine (ll. 39–40),[7] reminiscent of the very tall spectre of the statue in *Otranto*. This 'strange' figure's initial luminosity (l. 69), once Christabel is seduced into sneaking that 'lady' into her bed within the castle, turns out, when Geraldine undresses, to be but a cover for the horror of 'her bosom and half her side – / A sight to dream of, not to tell!' (ll. 199–201), later remembered by Christabel as a 'vision of fear' with a reptilian 'bosom old' and 'bosom cold' (ll. 436–41). With those features, Geraldine recalls the disguised, evil succubus 'Duessa' in Edmund Spenser's epic-romance *The Faerie Queene* (1590–6), who is ultimately 'dispoild' to expose 'her misshaped parts', 'wrinckled' and 'old', including 'neather' regions of which 'My chaster Muse for shame doeth blush to write'.[8] Such is one old-romance pre-text for a figure to whom Coleridge adds the powers of a Goethean-Southeyan vampire so that she rises after sleeping with Christabel with engorged, 'heaving breasts', having 'drunken deep' during the night and now looking 'yet more fair', leaving her young bedmate enervated 'With such perplexity of mind / As dreams too lively leave behind' (ll. 357–67).

On the other hand, during this very awakening, Christabel thinks back to the previous night when 'the lady leaps up suddenly' near a 'huge oak tree'

---

6 Walpole, *The Castle of Otranto*, p. 9.
7 All my citations from this poem come from the first printed text in Samuel Taylor Coleridge, *Christabel 1816*, intro. by Jonathan Wordsworth (Oxford: Woodstock Books, 1991).
8 *Faerie Queene* I. viii. 46 in *Edmund Spenser's Poetry: A Norton Critical Edition*, edited by Hugh Maclean and Anne Lake Prescott (New York: Norton, 1968), pp. 96–7.

(ll. 37–9). Now, though, 'The same who lay down by her side', her mind tells her, is 'the same *whom she / Raised up* beneath the old oak tree' (ll. 353–5; my emphasis). At this and other moments, 'Christabel' adopts the assumptions of what Walpole has called 'modern' romance. In his 1764 first Preface to *Otranto*, he urges his readers not to believe in the 'preternatural' parts of his tale 'exploded now even from romances', and in his 1765 Preface he adds that his characters behave 'according to the rules of probability' in more enlightened fiction, because he is rendering them as believing what was 'established' in their minds by the belief-system of their day and thus as acting like 'mere men and women would do' when faced with anything 'extraordinary'.[9] Hence, for example, when Walpole's Frederic, quite alone and feeling 'portents' of guilt in his thoughts, beholds the skeletal shade of the Hermit that no one else sees, he breaks into 'a flood' of repentant 'tears' because he has empirically learned the assumptions behind a *danse macabre* figure that exposes the sins within the postures of the prideful nobility.[10] The first Gothic Story thus starts developing an aporia basic to the Gothic mode from that point onwards: a hesitation between seeing spectres or monsters as supernatural entities outside their observers and seeing them as projections by the observing subjects, as symbolic figures who reflect back both the ideas their projectors have consciously come to believe in (as per the assumptions of Enlightenment empiricism) and feelings of which they have hitherto been only dimly conscious or even unconscious (as is clearly the case with Frederic in *Otranto*). Given what Christabel admits about 'raising up' Geraldine herself, then, she is also a modern-romance character by Walpole's standards. Recalling the Ossenfelder poem and longing for the mother who 'died the hour I was born' (l. 191) – as well as seeking a female, perhaps even lesbian, self-empowerment denied to her by her father – this daughter of the castle calls up a powerful, older and maternal projection of these very desires. Soon, however, she feels guilty about her dream-projection. She comes to fear its consequences (a death like her mother's in that 'bosom old' and 'cold') and its overweening, forbidden tendencies that now operate outside her, vampirically draining her of her own energy while siphoning off her personal responsibility, as when she breathes out the 'hissing sound' (l. 442) of the 'serpent' version of herself that she finally sees Geraldine to be (l. 587) while her easily-seduced father remains deceived and ensnared.[11] This

---

9 Walpole, *The Castle of Otranto*, pp. 9–10.   10 Walpole, *The Castle of Otranto*, pp. 106–7.
11 This kind of reading of 'Christabel' was first offered thoroughly in James Twitchell, '"Desire with loathing strangely mixed": the dream-work of *Christabel*', *Psychoanalytic Review* 61:1 (1974): 33–44.

ancient-modern romance combination, which therefore leaves vampirism caught between both tendencies, even replays Walpole's emptying-out of 'exploded' old Catholic romance-figures, as Geraldine jettisons many aspects of Duessa, that then become re-filled with more modern and Protestant assumptions about the processes, fears and guilt in the individual mind and its projected imaginings.

The Expansion of the Vampire, 1816–1819

Consequently, when the strong influence of 'Christabel' during the summer at Diodati reappears in the *Frankenstein* and *Vampyre* novels that famously emerged from it, this Janus-faced Gothicism is reenacted, now using the word 'vampire', to suggest an even wider range of meanings connected to it. Frankenstein's creature is deeply conflicted, of course, because his very creation is pulled between the ancient and the modern by being half-recollective of old medieval alchemy and half-imitative of the post-Enlightenment life-sciences as Mary Shelley knew them. But it/he becomes Victor Frankenstein's 'own vampire' and 'spirit let loose from the grave' less because he is reminiscent of the *homunculi* supposedly created by alchemists and more because his composition is deeply rooted in a pre-conscious internal longing for the dead mother that is even greater than Christabel's. Right after he first beholds his finished artificial man, Victor falls into a swoon, where he dreams of embracing his fiancée, Elizabeth, only to see her 'features ... change' into 'the corpse of my dead mother' who died after catching a fever from Elizabeth, whereupon this whole vision dissolves into the multi-coloured and anamorphic face of 'the miserable monster who I created',[12] now at least as much a *doppelgänger* for Frankenstein as Geraldine is for Christabel. Here, though, a creature created ostensibly without a mother is an inverted sublimation, far more than Geraldine, of the unconscious desire to rejoin the mother, possibly even in death, and to destroy any substitute that stands in the way. It is this combination of drives (towards a site of birth and death together) that comes to motivate, again pre-consciously, the creature's later killing of Elizabeth, who bears some blame for the death of Victor's mother. Frankenstein's nightmare even suggests that, if the creature is really created as an enactor of his creator's unconscious drives, the murders of Victor's little brother William and his best friend, Henry Clerval, are equally driven by

---

12 Shelley, *Frankenstein*, p. 53, which both recalls pp. 37–8 (the death of Victor's mother from nursing Elizabeth) and foretells p. 193 (the strangled Elizabeth left 'lifeless and inanimate').

Victor's repressed wishes displaced into his fabrication,[13] which can act out what he dare not. It is all this that Frankenstein is really saying, if not consciously, when he speaks of his creature as his 'own vampire', his 'own spirit let loose', as though his reanimation of combined corpses does indeed rise up, with Victor's hidden 'evil spirit' driving it (as in that 1745 definition of 'vampire'), to choke off the lives of all those dearest to him, as blood-sucking familial vampires, like the one in Southey's *Thalaba*, had been known to do by 1816–18.

The creature thus joins the skeletal Hermit-ghost in *Otranto* and Geraldine as an example of what Sigmund Freud has called the 'uncanny', now a staple of 'modern romance', in an essay of 1919 almost exactly one hundred years after *Frankenstein* first appeared. Freud's *unheimlich* (or un-home-like) feeling that creeps up on a subject on beholding what seems an alien monstrosity is actually a carrying-out, and thus a calling-forth, of what is primordially desired but repressed in the subject him/herself (the deeply home-like, *heimlich*, which does include a primal drive towards death as much as erotic love).[14] The same creature, like his most Gothic pre-texts, is thus also an instance of what Julia Kristeva has seen as a process underlying uncanny projection: '*abjection*' as defined in her book *Powers of Horror* (1980). There the human subject, seeking the illusion of a clear identity without anomalies that could make it other-than-itself within itself, *throws off* (ject + ab) into a seemingly absolute and grotesque 'other' the most anomalous aspects at the very foundation of its being. These include the 'archaism' of the most 'pre-objectal relationship', the primal state of being half-inside/half-outside the mother and half-alive/half-not at the moment of birth.[15] This state is what Frankenstein, a lot like Christabel, is recalling in the dream of rejoining the dead mother that intimates the hidden motivation behind the making of his 'other', a site of the uncanny for him but also of his now-'abject' otherness-from-himself as though it were outside him. 'Vampire' in the Gothic, it turns out, between 'Christabel' and *Frankenstein*, comes to mean, in the first two decades of the nineteenth century, a former bogey for older Christianity (or 'ancient' romance) that has now become a site (in 'modern' romance) for

---

13 This long-standing interpretation of the original *Frankenstein* was fully articulated first in Morton Kaplan and Robert Kloss, *The Unspoken Motive: A Guide to Psychoanalytic Literary Criticism* (New York: Free Press, 1973), especially pp. 131–45.
14 See Sigmund Freud, 'The "Uncanny"', in *Collected Papers of Sigmund Freud*, edited and trans. by Joan Riviere, 5 vols (London: Hogarth Press, 1949), vol. 4, pp. 368–407.
15 Julia Kristeva, *Powers of Horror: An Essay on Abjection*, trans. by Leon S. Roudiez (New York: Columbia University Press, 1982), p. 10.

projections of a post-Enlightenment subjectivity that has conflicting layers, refusing to acknowledge consciously what it most unconsciously pursues.

Those contradictions appear, not obviously in 'mere men and women', but in a vampiric figure that is both dead and alive, as well as ancient and modern. It gives back to 'normal' characters and us as readers an illusion of self-consistency by sucking the *in*consistencies in their and our natures supposedly out of us, including our in-human longings for physical immortality and overweening power, so that we can condemn what we deeply desire. Indeed, the resulting 'abject' also reflects, while it still obscures and distorts, the anomalies – the collective fears about deep-seated contradictions of many kinds – that inhabit the *cultural* unconscious, as well the personal one, and intimate a human society seething with conflicts within, alongside schemes for unifying, itself. Scholars have therefore analysed the Geraldine-vampire in 'Christabel' as an uncanny throwing-off of widespread fears about and desires for the rise of strong, independent, sexually frank women in the face of staunch resistance to just that transformation, all in 1790s England.[16] Others have persuasively seen Frankenstein's uncanny creature-vampire as symbolically coalescing, and thus abjecting as fearful, numerous social contradictions for readers of 1818, including quandaries about the status of women (here removed from the birth process) but also about the middle-class creation of a threatening working class (epitomised by the creature); the attempt to perfect the human race that confronts Anglo prejudices against the racial differences in humanity (the many colours in the creature's face); and uncertainties and disagreements within the rising life-sciences both as they strive to overcome older systems based on religion that still assert themselves and as they help further the emerging – and frightening – Industrial Revolution that could replace human with mechanical reproduction.[17]

The Gothic vampire by 1820 is thus not just an externalised repository for primal drives, and guilts about them in the individual psyche, but also a modern-romance locus for unresolved, and therefore repressed, cultural conflicts and anomalies, now abjected into what appears to be partly, but not fully, human, the ultimate anomaly – and consequently a terrifying threat to the dominant culture of the moment. Polidori's *The Vampyre*, even as first published in 1819, employs all these dimensions in the process of making more literal what is only a metaphoric employment of 'vampire' in

---

16 See Jerrold E. Hogle, '"Christabel" as gothic: the abjection of instability', *Gothic Studies* 7:1 (2005): 18–28.

17 For a more comprehensive list of these cultural conflicts and the scholars who have best revealed them, see Hogle, 'The Gothic Image', pp. 16–17.

Frankenstein. Influenced by, yet pointedly turning away from, the figure of the centuries-old 'Augustus Darvell', who has the 'power of giving to one passion the appearance of another' (and is not explicitly termed a vampire) in the 1816 'Fragment' Byron wrote as *his* 'ghost story',[18] Polidori instead offers his readers the cadaverous 'nobleman' Lord Ruthven, using the family name of the caricature of Byron in Lady Caroline Lamb's novel *Glenarvon* (from earlier in 1816).[19] His Ruthven is passionless and vacant within, like an empty tomb, with a 'dead grey eye' that cannot 'pierce through to' *or* reveal 'the inward workings of the heart' and a 'deadly hue [in] his face' which conveys no 'emotion' and seems 'beautiful' only in 'outline'.[20] While joining the already-dead nature of the standard vampire to his sense of Byron as an unfeeling 'taker' who had likened one of his autobiographical heroes *to* a vampire in his poem *The Giaour* (1813),[21] Polidori also renders the aristocracy associated with both his title character and his former employer as the merest sepulchre of itself, as void of all enduring or practical social value and instead a mere, though superficially attractive, feeder off of other lives, be it of their feelings, their money, or (eventually, in this case) their blood. *The Vampyre*, by thus reenacting Walpole's emptying of believable grounds from marvels in 'ancient romance' which nevertheless still attract people, thereby vampirises and abjects the psychological and cultural sense of the aristocrat that has become Janus-faced in the nineteenth century. Now it is alluring to all other classes as they harken back to what their world has long assumed about ordained hierarchies, yet it is also superannuated, a husk of itself, to the point of sucking life from others rather than providing real labour or substance of its own. So begins the abjection of a persistent and unresolved conflict of feelings about the upper class that is henceforth absorbed symbolically by several aristocratic vampires, all the way from adaptations of Polidori's novella to Bram Stoker's *Dracula* (1897) nearly 80 years later.

Moreover, the most 'passion' that is projected towards the 'dead grey' Ruthven comes from the younger 'Aubrey' in *The Vampyre*, a sort of Polidori gazing on a version of Lord Byron. It is Aubrey who projects his own 'high romantic feeling of honour and candour', itself based on a Quixotic indulgence in 'romances', onto a fancied idol, so much so that he turns the hollow

---

18 See Lord Byron, '"A Fragment", June 17, 1816', in Mary Shelley, *Frankenstein; or, The Modern Prometheus: The 1818 Text*, pp. 260–5 (especially p. 261).
19 D. L. Macdonald, *Poor Polidori: A Critical Biography of the Author of The Vampyre* (Toronto: University of Toronto Press, 1991), pp. 96–8.
20 [John Polidori], *The Vampyre; A Tale* (London: Sherwood, Neeley, and Jones, 1819), pp. 27–8.
21 See Hogle, 'The Gothic Image', pp. 22–3.

Lord 'into the hero of a romance' by whom he wants to be guided on an old-style Grand Tour of Europe so as to attain 'an equality with the aged' as he imagines them.[22] He tries, in other words, to fill up an emptiness in both Ruthven and himself with a romantic tradition that is already as antiquated and empty within itself as it is still compelling. Consequently, the attraction of Aubrey to an exemplar who turns out to be truly a vampire is the further abjection, alongside its harbouring of the conflicts over aristocrats, of an anomalous state of being greatly feared by increasingly educated, class-climbing people in the early 1800s. In this state, the old certainties, now 'exploded', linked to romances and estate-centred agriculture are giving way to other methods for defining the self in a more cosmopolitan, less strictly class-based world. Yet this prospect holds out a present and future that offer no scheme as certain as the old ones by which to configure that self, making all questors for new groundings cling to old shapes (such as ancient vampires) that suck hope and desire back into them. Nina Auerbach has perceptively seen that the vampire-symbol sought by many class-climbers for self-definition in the early 1800s was a 'friend' offering 'a bond between companions' that turned 'vassals into peers', that provided a self-fulfilment unavailable to the self by itself; but she also recognises that such friendship in Polidori's *Vampyre*, because it is being drawn as much towards old fictions as new possibilities, 'overwhelms conventional hierarchies' to the point of intimating 'homoerotic journeys' that must finally be condemned and suppressed by the realisation that it is the old and evil vampire who is offering this 'wider world' that 'makes familiar bonds fluid'.[23] In the vampire at this point, the possibilities of boundary-breaking and even sexual liberation that it seems to hold out have to be retracted by it as 'evil', as much as it encourages those very desires, because the vampire, now fully a Gothic site of contradiction, abjects that unresolved conflict in addition to others.

This achieved compounding of the vampire and the Gothic, though, should not be all that surprising, since the very nature of the vampire as a quite variable myth makes it like the Janus-faced spectres that Walpole offers in his first 'Gothic Story'. Like those figures, which are of statues, pictures or *dance macabre* icons rather than solid bodies, the vampire comes into the early nineteenth century as the re-figuration of earlier figurations with no solid grounding behind them, much as Polidori's Ruthven looks back to Byron's Darvell, whose face always hides a different one behind it, or to the Byron

---

22 Polidori, *The Vampyre*, pp. 30–2.
23 Nina Auerbach, *Our Vampires, Ourselves* (Chicago: University of Chicago Press, 1995), pp. 13–21.

behind *Glenarvon* who has already projected a version of himself as a vampire. In the Introduction prefixed to the first book-version of *The Vampyre* in 1819, the 'superstition' behind the 'tale' is admitted to be an amorphously 'general' one, vaguely traceable back to 'the East', that was then extended by 'the Greeks' only to 'spread' as a belief, 'with some ... variation, all over Hungary', where Ossenfelder located it, as well as other parts of Eastern Europe; even a supposedly '*credible* account of a particular case of vampirism', where a self-resurrected body seemed to prey on anyone available, according to 'magistrates' of 'Hungary' in 1732, should be seen as coloured by one set of beliefs about this figure as opposed to another, such as the Greek version in which the vampire-state is 'a sort of punishment after death' whereby the 'deceased' is 'compelled to confine his infernal visitations to those beings he loved most' when alive, a version that this Introduction exemplifies directly from Byron's *Giaour*[24] – and that Mary Shelley clearly adopts in *Frankenstein*, while Polidori does not in *The Vampyre*.

Hence the vampire-figure mutates because it is always already a mutation. It is like the Walpolean Gothic image in being a persistently antiquated and partly emptied symbol from which older beliefs can be withdrawn and into which newer ones, such as middle-class attitudes about the aristocracy, can be newly projected, provided that parts of the old beliefs, such as vampires being both dead and reanimated, remain at least haunting the transmuted figure, as they do in Walpole's ghosts. That way, there is some continuity in the use of the vampire that makes its ancient versions analogous enough to the modern variations on it and that therefore makes those variations sites for abjecting conflicted attitudes that, like Walpole's 'Gothic Story', are retrogressive and progressive at the same time. After all, even when definitions of the vampire as a physical revenant were being promulgated in England around the mid-eighteenth century, the same figure was already being used as a metaphor, which we can see in a 1741 British description of government officials as 'the vampires of the publick, and riflers of the kingdom' ('Vampire, n., 2a'; *OED*). The mating of the vampire and the Gothic between Coleridge in 1800–16 and Polidori in 1819 was thus truly a marriage of equal symbolic schemes – with the vampire, on its side, hovering constantly between monster and metaphor – and I would argue that it is such Janus-faced and shared figurative mechanisms that make possible the many abjected contradictions the vampire-figure is able to suggest-in-disguise as it is transmuted across nineteenth-century Gothic, including Gothic-inflected realistic,

---

24 See the 'Introduction' in Polidori, *The Vampyre*, pp. xix–xxiii.

fictions in the wake of 'Christabel', *Frankenstein*, and especially Polidori's *Vampyre*. Indeed, though there are far too many instances across the 1800s that enact this vampire-process for me to examine all of them here, I propose in what follows to highlight some indicative touchstones in some prominent examples. These all show how the Gothic vampire keeps widening and deepening its symbolic suggestiveness from the 1820s to the 1890s because of its special figurative capacity, coalesced between 1816 and 1819, for abjecting the psychological and cultural conflicts in the unconscious of the West as they themselves mutate from decade to decade.

The Nineteenth-Century Proliferation, 1820–1870

Many such vampires, as Roxana Stuart has shown, appeared on stage in plays and operas performed in French, English and German theatres from the 1820s onwards. The most-produced English ones, in fact, were actually adaptations, admittedly with some changes, of the Paris sensation of 1820, *Le Vampire*, billed as a *mélodrame* adaptation of Polidori's tale (thought to have been written by Byron) and co-authored by Pierre Carmouche, Achille Jouffrey and Charles Nodier. This highly influential play-with-music does retain the name 'Rutwen' as well that vampire's capacity to be brought back to life, when wounded, by moonlight as well as blood.[25] But it does entirely away with Polidori's 'dead grey' predator in favour of a new combination: a revenant endowed with Byron's Scottish ancestry (given French perceptions of Scotland as sadly oppressed by English conquerors) mixed with a dashing, insatiable lover of women, with genuine erotic appeal, fashioned after the title character in Mozart's opera *Don Giovanni* (1787), an allusion that plays on associations of Byron with the old Spanish Don Juan that Byron himself started to embrace with the first two cantos of his own *Don Juan* (published in 1819).[26] The result is a romantic figure almost as pitiable as he is traditionally Satanic – the first half-sympathetic Western vampire, then – who is self-conscious enough to articulate what drives his appetite for one female virgin after another. In Stuart's translation, he sees himself as 'blighted with unhappiness, alone on earth', the way the Byronic hero often sees his ill-fated condition, but as also inclined to kill-by-draining each of his brides, whom has to marry to kill, *quickly*

---

25 See Polidori, *The Vampyre*, p. 56, and Stuart, *Stage Blood*, p. 271.
26 Stuart, *Stage Blood*, pp. 45–8.

because he is 'always ready to leave without regret the emptiness which envelops me to search for another emptiness still unknown'.[27] With the sureties of an undoubted religious past and class-structure fading away and the figure of the Gothic vampire robbed at least partly of its older grounds, the achievement of traditional vampiric desire is almost instantly empty of value and fulfilment, and desire must pursue yet another object every time to fill up that ever-gaping void in a pursuit with no clear end, unless it is a pyrotechnic repetition (with which this version does conclude) of the traditional fiery dragging-into-Hell that ends *Don Giovanni*. This vampire thus abjects a half-hearted longing for hyperbolic exaggerations of established tradition (including wedding after wedding) struggling in conflict, as most traditions were in 1820, with the feared possibility that the basis of existence may be what the original French text calls *'le néant'*, a pre-existentialist nothingness from which all human effort keeps beginning again and which desire keeps pursuing attractive chimeras with conventional features to cover over and escape.

So great was the influence of this much-restaged rendering, often eclipsing Polidori's original, that further recastings of it did indeed penetrate more realistic fiction in the nineteenth century. A case in point, long noted as Byronic, is the character Heathcliff in Emily Brontë's *Wuthering Heights* (1847), whom the housekeeper Nelly Dean calls 'a ghoul, or a vampire' on observing his self-starved condition shortly before his death: 'those deep black eyes' and 'That smile, and ghastly paleness!', based on what Nelly has 'read of such hideous, such incarnate demons'.[28] On one level, Heathcliff fits this label by this point in the novel because he has harkened back to that 1741 metaphor, 'vampires' as 'riflers' of the 'publick'. As fitting retribution for having been treated as a low-class 'thing' because of his 'gypsy' blackness when he was taken into the Heights as a child from Liverpool, despite being given the name of the Earnshaws's dead male heir,[29] he has returned to Yorkshire now dressed up as a gentleman, having fleeced funds from others much as Ruthven did via gambling.[30] He has then proceeded to employ stratagems from inheritance law to marriage-for-convenience to appropriate all of the property in the novel's setting from the yeoman farm at the Heights to the upper-class Thrushcross Grange, ultimately owning even more than

---

27 Stuart, *Stage Blood*, p. 49.
28 Emily Brontë, *Wuthering Heights*, edited by Linda H. Peterson, 2nd edition (Boston: Bedford/St. Martin's, 2003), p. 281.
29 Brontë, *Wuthering Heights*, p. 52.   30 See Polidori, *The Vampyre*, pp. 25–34.

the *dead* 'Heathcliff' would have inherited. He thereby brings 'vampire' as a bleeder-off of property by post-Enlightenment means back to the forefront as a metaphor for the increasingly laissez-faire economic machinations that accompanied class mobility by the mid-nineteenth century. On another level, though, Heathcliff 'smiles' in his final 'pale' state because he is now very like he was when the novel's frame-narrator, Lockwood, first saw him: crying 'Oh! My heart's darling!' to an open window at the Heights, at which the sleepy Lockwood thinks he has seen the ghostly 'little fiend' of Catherine Earnshaw, Heathcliff's closest childhood companion and forever-unattainable love-object.[31] In a sense, *she* is the vampire-figure, like the Bride of Corinth, that has kept consuming his life because every dressing-up and property-acquisition of his has been a substitute for being-at-one with her; hence his starving himself to death as she does herself many years earlier.[32] He is therefore a variation on the French 'Rutwen' whose all-consuming desire moves from object to object, finding every one of them a location of his lack, empty of the fulfiling union that he seeks in them all. As metaphorically a vampire in the wake of the Byronic French *mélodrame*, Heathcliff, it turns out, is a site of abjection for a mid-nineteenth-century consumerist desire for rising in class towards a never-attainable object, as well as the fear that social standing will still interdict love as the basis for marriage. This complex is also mixed up in this 'abject' with an impulse – in Lockwood, Nelly, the reader and other characters – to cast these downsides of a conflicted modernity off into a racialised other, to see the fear of an ungrounded modern self without a clear origin or destiny as thrown over into an outcast 'feeder' off the rest of us, an upstart so uncannily like us that we must come (like Nelly) to see him as radically different, 'a ghoul, or a vampire'.

The acquisitive side of this figuration, as it happens, is made even more intense, at about the same time, in the most popular reincarnation of the un-dead in Victorian prose fiction: the title figure in *Varney the Vampire*, published (without any by-line) by either Thomas Peckett Prest or James Malcom Rymer from 1845 to 1847 as a multi-part serial in a series of 'penny dreadful' pamphlets for newly literate working-class, as well as lower-middle-class, audiences.[33] Yes, Varney does first appear in Flora Bannerworth's bedroom to

---

31 Brontë, *Wuthering Heights*, pp. 43–5.
32 See Brontë, *Wuthering Heights*, pp. 114–19, and Carol Senf, *The Vampire in Nineteenth-Century English Literature* (Madison: University of Wisconsin Press, 1988), pp. 79–83.
33 See Curt Herr, 'Introduction', in James Malcolm Rymer, *Varney the Vampire*, edited by Curt Herr (Crestline, CA: Zittaw Press, 2008), pp. 8–27 (especially pp. 9–16).

prey on her with the now-expected 'lofty stature ... sallow face ... projecting teeth ... [and] dark, lustrous, although somewhat sombre eyes'.[34] But he soon morphs, as in the face of Byron's Darvell, into subtly different, quasi-aristocratic and often charming, even sympathetic, disguises, with only those contradictory eyes as a constant. This 'perplexing amorphousness', possibly one product of rapid serial writing, includes a crucial change in the old tradition: that Varney is 'the first vampire who can transform his victims into his kind',[35] although some earlier non-fiction accounts of vampire legends had mentioned this possibility. Consequently, the many men who chase after him, thinking him another species, are also inclined to kill any suspicious person they meet, since 'who knows, if he ain't a vampire, how soon he may become one'.[36] By trying to make Varney a target, the 'normal' ones actually blur the boundaries between him and people like them – and why not? Virtually all the characters around him agree with his own prime motivation, to attain, as he puts it, 'that magician-like power over my kind, which the possession of ample means alone can give'.[37] With his attack on Flora for her blood being just a point of departure for a larger pursuit of the whole Bannerworth estate and many of its financial connections, Varney reaches beyond Heathcliff's acquisition of Catherine-substitutes to become an epitome of what came to be called the 'hungry '40s' in England; he is the hallmark (not really the 'other') of a 'feasting society' amassing capital voraciously by bleeding funds from its own members and breeding other capitalists, what Auerbach rightly terms 'the vampirism in all strata in British society' that is the true cause of Varney being a shape-shifter *and* reproducing himself[38] – and of course one reason why this serial's episodes kept being sold for two years so as to incite the next payment from a reader's resources, making the very form of this long novel unusually vampiric.

It is hardly surprising, then, that Karl Marx, in England while *Varney* was still popular, writes in *Das Kapital* (1867) that 'Capital is dead labor which, vampire-like, lives only by sucking on living labor, and lives the more, the more labor it sucks.'[39] Throughout Varney's and his neighbours' activities, every product of work is a bleeding of life from the worker that then goes into a capitalist pool to help bleed others and so provides ongoing fuel for the

---

34 James Malcolm Rymer, *Varney the Vampire; or, The Feast of Blood* (New York: Arno Press, 1970), p. 61.
35 Auerbach, *Our Vampires*, p. 29.   36 Rymer, *Varney the Vampire*, p. 339.
37 Rymer, *Varney the Vampire*, p. 151.   38 Auerbach, *Our Vampires*, pp. 31–32.
39 Karl Marx, *Capital: A Critique of Political Economy, Volume I*, trans. by Ben Fowkes (Harmondsworth: Penguin, 1990), p. 342.

endless vampiric reproduction of this whole process. The supreme 'penny dreadful' vampire is a site for the abjection, ostensibly of an aristocratic past (Varney's first life in the 1640s) coming back 'magician-like' to haunt Victorian England, but actually of what began to stir in the 1840s: the seeds of a bourgeoning capitalism that has so invaded human psychology by 1845–7 that the object of internal desire has become, much as people have tried to abject it, 'the possession of ample means' to pursue yet more desires by the exploitation of others. No wonder Charles Dickens can expect his readers readily to understand his quite Gothic association of vampirism with the greedy minor capitalists Krook and Vholes in *Bleak House* (serialised for middle- and higher-class audiences between 1852 and 1853), yet in which the overriding vampire, it turns out, and as Carol Senf has shown, is the amorphous Court of Chancery, which 'draws [nearly all the] good qualities' out of its plaintiffs as it bleeds them gradually of their financial and psychological resources year after year after year.[40]

The Late-Victorian Culmination, 1871–1897

By 1871–2, first in *The Dark Blue* magazine and then in a story-collection, Joseph Sheridan Le Fanu jolts the vampire tradition with another major mutation in his novella *Carmilla*, even though it centres on a relationship very like the one between the two women in 'Christabel'. An allusion back to the latter is unmistakable when 'a lady, with a commanding air', here the title character who turns out to be a vampire, appears suddenly, albeit in a 'carriage' accident, before Laura, the narrator, then a virgin girl of 19; she (on her own initiative, like Christabel's) begs her father, although they are English expatriates living in an East European 'schloss', 'to let her stay with us', since Laura is subtly drawn to 'a fine looking woman for her time of life' with already-lesbian overtones reminiscent of the ones briefly present in 'Christabel'.[41] Laura here, though, is far less externally seduced than Christabel, since the vision now before her recalls a dream (or was it a visitation?) from her childhood in which, despite being 'kept in ignorance of ghost stories', she sees a 'pretty face looking at me from the side of the bed', followed by 'a sensation as if two needles ran into my breast'.[42] Carmilla uncannily draws of out of the teenage Laura a return of long-repressed

---

40 Senf, *The Vampire*, pp. 110–13.
41 Joseph Sheridan Le Fanu, *Carmilla: A Critical Edition*, edited by Kathleen Costello-Sullivan (Syracuse, NY: Syracuse University Press, 2013), pp. 4, 14 and 16.
42 Le Fanu, *Carmilla*, p. 7.

feelings and memories already there, and, as these expand to 'the breaking out of suppressed instinct and emotion', they 'become a strange tumultuous excitement ... mingled with a vague sense of fear and disgust'.[43] The Carmilla–Laura interplay thus opens up a level of visceral, contradictory sensations that mingle the desire of same-sex attraction, or indeed sexual feeling in general, with the guilt that comes from all of it being childhood-based and increasingly forbidden by social convention. As Laura's narrative proceeds, the 'disgust' gets more and more worldly reinforcement as several senior men in her life, prompted by her father – fearing any increased power of the feminine, already an undercurrent in 'Christabel' – establish that Carmilla is really the animated corpse of the bloodthirsty 'Mircalla, Countess of Karnstein'. Centuries old and buried in a nearby chapel, she, like all vampires as these men see them, 'is prone to be fascinated with an engrossing vehemence, resembling the passion of love, by particular persons' and is therefore reanimated by that process as much as by her ongoing lust for blood.[44] Patriarchal discourse striving to contain a feminine boundlessness of feeling raises up the spectre of a vampire-figure into which all that amorphous 'vehemence' is finally abjected as though it were other-than-human. Such male-controlled narrative, in other words, employs ancient-romance absolutes of external good and evil, mediated by a Walpolean walking-image of the dead made into a vampire, to stand against and restrain a modern-romance possibility of pre-conscious internal feelings and drives being released from repression and projected between bodies, much as Walpole's Frederic projects his felt contradictions towards the Hermit-ghost that then dis-embodies them.

In this abjection, moreover, the undercurrent of a borderless and uncontainable sexuality is so attractive and threatening at the same time that this conundrum must be attached to an even more extreme otherness to become so finally horrific as to be beyond the norms of the Western world. Carmilla is seen by Laura's governesses as accompanied in her wrecked carriage by 'a hideous black woman, with a coloured turban on her head ... with gleaming eyes and large white eye-balls, and her teeth set in fury',[45] a sort of darker vampire lurking behind the primary one in the story. This double image echoes the blackness of Byron's Darvell when he returns to his primal state, the multi-coloured face that Mary Shelley gives Frankenstein's creature, the gypsy darkness of Emily Brontë's Heathcliff, and the rooting of Edward

43 Le Fanu, *Carmilla*, pp. 29–30.   44 Le Fanu, *Carmilla*, p. 94.
45 Le Fanu, *Carmilla*, p. 21.

Rochester's hidden and 'mad' wife, 'Bertha', in her 'dark' mixed-race origins as a Creole from Jamaica in Charlotte Brontë's *Jane Eyre* (1847), where she is explicitly likened to that 'foul German spectre – the vampire'.[46] The attraction and disgust aroused by Carmilla and her free-flowing sexuality is thereby thrown over into a cultural and racial otherness, and that effort to make her extreme humanity less than 'properly' human is even compounded by having her morph into a 'palpitating mass' and then a beastly 'dark creature' when the 'General' consulted by Laura's father observes Carmilla's final nocturnal attack on her sleeping victim.[47] A quite similar process of abjection is repeated 26 years later, as it happens, in Florence Marryat's novel *The Blood of the Vampire* (1897). There, a young woman who manifests an effusive personality, pronounced intellectual and artistic talent, and an unashamed desire to be loved (as though she were a Jane Eyre inspired by a Carmilla) turns out unwittingly be a *psychic* vampire, unintentionally – and never physically – draining the energy and life out of people around her by her mere presence. She unconsciously does so, we discover, because she is actually the Jamaican daughter of a 'half caste', echoing Bertha Rochester, of a massive, 'sensual' black woman with an insatiable 'lust for blood', whose 'slave mother' was 'bitten by a Vampire bat, which are formidable creatures in the West Indies',[48] first discovered and named in that part of the world in the late eighteenth century.

Nonetheless, it is Stoker's *Dracula*, published during the same year as *The Blood of the Vampire*, that displays, as we might expect, the culmination of all these mutations across its century that took the inherently mutative figure of the gothicized vampire and made it uncannily abject the most unsettling and unresolved pre-conscious conflicts in literate Western readers – more and more of them, we now see, over time. Indeed, with its title character conflating virtually all of the most standard vampire features that developed on the stage and the page since 'Christabel', enriched by its author's poring over such East European vampire lore as Emily Gerard's 'Transylvanian Superstitions' (1885),[49] *Dracula* (the novel and character) abjects and thus disguises, while also enhancing – as I hope all readers of it can now see – almost every

---

46 Charlotte Brontë, *Jane Eyre*, edited by Beth Newman (Boston: Bedford/St. Martins, 1996), pp. 281 and 302–7.
47 Le Fanu, *Carmilla*, p. 87.
48 Florence Marryat, *The Blood of the Vampire*, intro. by Brenda Hammack (Kansas City: Valancourt Books, 2009), p. 83.
49 See Emily Gerard, 'Transylvanian superstitions', *The Nineteenth Century* 20 (July 1885): 128–44.

complex of psychological and ideological conflict that we have seen uncannily vampirised in the examples we have discussed above. These include the continuous linkage of erotic desire and death, with even birth and death being fundamentally inextricable, made frighteningly visible when the Count 'inseminates' new vampires both dead and un-dead; the simultaneous attractiveness and repulsiveness of the European aristocracy, now more connected to its warlord foundations and its hoarding, instead of the free circulation, of money;[50] the possibility of unencumbered sexual fulfilment, seen also as a descent into rampant bestiality, as in the 'angry snarl' of the promiscuous Lucy Westenra once Dracula makes her a vampire; and the desire for the post-Enlightenment 'New Woman' to emerge, which the Count seems to enable, mixed with the fear that such a revolution will blur the boundaries of the sexes so as to make them hybrid or indistinguishable, as when Dracula feeds Mina Harker blood from his breast under 'moonlight' after sucking the same kind of fluid from her. Dracula even abjects the draw of capital investment and future profit, à la Varney, that makes the young lawyer-capitalist, here Jonathan Harker, seek 'old money' even from the East only to discover that he has both enabled foreign intrusion – including contagious diseases of the blood from abroad – and given his own being over to a rampant process of consumption that sucks up the products of his labour and leaves him behind, all too visible when he sees the Count assume Jonathan's own features on leaving Castle Dracula to suck up property, as well as blood, in England. Stoker's vampire also incarnates the appeal of the West, itself vampiric, drawing in the proceeds of its empires, particularly from the East, that finds itself simultaneously revolted by the fear of the racial and cultural other it imports, such as the Count Dracula of 'arched nostrils' and 'lofty domed forehead' that faces the Western explorer with the stereotypical face of the East European Jew at a time of resurgent anti-Semitism in the face of widespread Jewish immigration.[51]

Stoker's *Dracula*, of course, goes on to surpass its predecessors by adding to their range of abjected contradictions and to their projections,

---

50 Bram Stoker, *Dracula: A Norton Critical Edition*, edited by Nina Auerbach and David J. Skal (New York: Norton, 1997), pp. 27–30. See also, on this point, Franco Moretti, *Signs Taken for Wonders: Essays on the Sociology of Literary Forms*, trans. by Susan Fischer, David Forgacs and David Miller (New York: Verso, 1988), pp. 90–104.

51 Stoker, *Dracula*, pp. 187–90, 86–7, 246–7, 47, 23. See Howard L. Malchow, *Gothic Images of Race in Nineteenth-Century Britain* (Stanford: Stanford University Press, 1996), pp. 148–66.

and then subjugations, of 'abjects' in order to maintain hegemonic beliefs and standard constructions of the human self; hence its capacity to carry nineteenth-century mutations of the vampire into the future of the more recent adaptations of it and towards more transmogrifications of the vampire-figure beyond it so that the vampire can abject newer, pre-conscious quandaries as it keeps itself and its shape-shifting alive. One complex of conflicted feelings that it abjects, after all, is the comingled acceptance of and apprehensions about the theory of evolution, especially in the wake of Charles Darwin's *On the Origin of Species* (1859), that suggest the ongoing possibility of 'reversion' towards the pre-humanity of early primates amid the progressive evolution of the human race overall that modern advancements seem to validate.[52] Abraham Van Helsing, Stoker's leading vampire hunter, admits to Dracula's shape-shifting across stages of civilisation, but he also sees this process has driven by a 'child-brain' that counters that apparent evolution with a regressive pull back towards a more infant stage of the human race.[53] Moreover, evolution as metaphorised by the Count is less an ever-improving ascent than a frightening diffusion. With Dracula, more than any previous vampire, able to change shapes from man to bat to wolf to 'mist' to 'elemental dust', the vampire now abjects the instability of human identity, its regressive drift backwards into myriad other forms, that evolution brings with it as a believable future potential, as well as humanity's inheritance.[54] To counter this ultimate threat, part of the abjective drive in this Janus-faced Gothic novel takes its cue from the last third of *Carmilla* and endorses a severe, authoritarian clamping-down on all manifestations of this potential, employing even old Catholic icons (the cross and the wafer) alongside vampiric telepathy, that phallically stakes all manifestations of the vampire, from Lucy to Dracula, to restore at least the illusion of hegemonic progress and stable (and largely male-dominated) human identity. The original *Dracula*, the culminating mutation of all the vampire mutations in nineteenth-century Gothic, thus joins *The Blood of the Vampire* in the late 1890s to pose several questions for succeeding centuries to answer in their vampire tales: What do we need to continue to abject in the vampire-figure? What should we release from or add to symbolic repression as abjection enacts it? In what way will our newer vampires be 'uncanny' in both revealing and disguising

---

52 Charles Darwin, *The Origin of Species by Means of Natural Selection*, edited by John W. Burrow (Baltimore: Penguin, 1968), pp. 195–204.
53 Stoker, *Dracula*, p. 279.   54 Stoker, *Dracula*, p. 211.

our deepest ideological and psychological tugs of war between older and newer systems of belief? Vampire stories, films, television and video games are still arising to answer these questions, but only because of what was made possible by the mutation of the malleable vampire through the forms it took in the Gothic across the nineteenth century.

2.4

From Romantic Gothic to Victorian Medievalism: 1817 and 1877

TOM DUGGETT

No doubt within the last fifty years a new interest, almost like another sense, has arisen in these ancient monuments of art; and they have become the subject of one of the most interesting of studies, and of an enthusiasm, religious, historical, artistic, which is one of the undoubted gains of our time; yet we think that . . . those last fifty years of knowledge and attention have done more for their destruction than all the foregoing centuries of revolution, violence, and contempt. For Architecture, long decaying, died out, as a popular art at least, just as the knowledge of mediaeval art was born. So that the civilised world of the nineteenth century has no style of its own amidst its wide knowledge . . . of other centuries.

So runs the preamble to the 'Manifesto' of the Society for the Protection of Ancient Buildings (SPAB), founded by William* Morris in 1877.[1] Setting his face against the 'strange and most fatal idea' – John Ruskin's 'Lie' – of architectural 'Restoration', and the 'professional office-made versions' of antiquity represented by its 'Revivalist' twin, Morris developed a countervailing 'active view of history', involving hopes for a genuine revival of the 'master-art' of architecture, in a society remade by and for art.[2] In a lecture of

---

* For my mother, Gail Ann Eadie Duggett, gone to Scarborough Fair. This essay shares some materials with my chapter entitled 'Gothic and Architecture: Morris, Ruskin, Carlyle and the Gothic Legacies of the Lake Poets', in David Punter (ed.), *The Edinburgh Companion to Gothic and the Arts* (Edinburgh: Edinburgh University Press, 2019), pp. 15–35, and my edition of Robert Southey's *Sir Thomas More; or, Colloquies on the Progress and Prospects of Society*, 2 vols (London and New York: Routledge, 2018). I am grateful to the publishers for permission to use them here.

1 William Morris, 'The SPAB Manifesto' (1877), available from: <www.spab.org.uk/about-us/spab-manifesto> (last accessed 23 January 2019).
2 See John Ruskin, 'The Lamp of Memory', from *The Seven Lamps of Architecture*, in Dinah Birch (ed.), *John Ruskin: Selected Writings* (Oxford: Oxford University Press, 2004), pp. 24–7; W. R. Lethaby, quoted in E. P. Thompson, *William Morris: Romantic to Revolutionary*, 3rd edition (Pontypool: Spectre Classics, 2011), p. 227; Thompson, *William Morris*, p. 239; William Morris, 'The Lesser Arts', in *News from Nowhere and Other Writings*, edited by Clive Wilmer (London: Penguin, 1993), pp. 231–54 (p. 234); Richard Frith, '"The Worship of Courage": William Morris's *Sigurd the Volsung* and

85

the same year on the 'Decorative' or 'Lesser Arts', Morris spelt out the paradox that the discovery of the 'new sense' of 'history', within a national legacy of ancient architecture, had led to a mode of strangely unhistorical being. Before 'ecclesiastical zeal' and 'study' had led restorers into 'sweeping away' all changes 'at least since the Reformation', old churches had been 'altered and added to century after century, often beautifully, always historically', persisting through a combination – in itself historically valuable – of 'neglect' and 'violence', and 'ordinary obvious mending'.³ Morris saw that the 'symbolic' 'historicism' of the ecclesiological movement – epitomised in the work of architects such as A. W. N. Pugin and G. E. Street – had perhaps been an adequate vehicle for the 50-years' growth of the 'new sense' of art and history, or a whole conception of 'culture'.⁴ We were now determined, Morris said, 'to know the reality of all that has happened, and to be put off no longer with the dull records of the battles and intrigues of kings and scoundrels'.⁵ But another transformation was needed, he suggested in 1884, if the Gothic dream was not to lapse into nightmare:

> Surely it is a curious thing that while we are ready to laugh at the idea of . . . the Greek workman turning out a Gothic building, or a Gothic workman turning out a Greek one, we see nothing preposterous in the Victorian workman producing a Gothic one . . . I may be told, perhaps, that . . . historical knowledge . . . has enabled us to perform the miracle of raising the dead centuries to life. But to my mind it is a strange view to take of historical knowledge and insight, that it should set us on the adventure of trying to retrace our steps towards the past . . . Surely such a state of things is a token of change . . . of the visible end of one cycle and the beginning of another.⁶

Morris's perception of a pattern in history is in part an effect of his 'conversion' – the year before – to Marxism. But the same sense of Gothic architectural form as alternatively 'historic*ist*' death or 'historic*al*' rebirth, is equally present in his early short story for the *Oxford and Cambridge Magazine*, 'A Night in a Cathedral' (1856). In 'A Night', written after Morris's Anglo-French cathedral tour of summer 1855, the Gothic architecture of Amiens cathedral appears alternately in nightmares of monstrous finished forms and dream-visions of what Morris would later call 'inchoate' and 'half-conscious' 'moulding':

Victorian Medievalism', in L. M. Holloway and J. A. Palmgren (eds), *Beyond Arthurian Romances* (New York: Palgrave Macmillan, 2005), pp. 117–32 (p. 118).
3 Morris, 'The Lesser Arts', p. 247.
4 Morris, *News from Nowhere*, p. 247. On the conception of culture, see Raymond Williams, *Culture and Society, 1780–1950*, 2nd edition (New York: Columbia University Press, 1983), pp. 20–31.
5 Morris, *News from Nowhere*, p. 237.   6 Quoted in Thompson, *William Morris*, p. 239.

I looked out boldly into the darkness, and tried to fill up the details of the architecture, as I had seen them in the daylight ... I had been particularly struck by the calm pure beauty of some of [the stone-carvings in the aisles of the choir]; and now, standing before [them] in the darkness, I tried to recal those countenances, to still the tumult of my dread by their heavenly repose. They came out from the blankness, but with partial distinctness; after a little while passing off into foul and ugly faces, of demons and wicked men, which increased my fright.[7]

In his own 'inchoate' way, and with the half-suggestion of the 'historical sense' arising *in* achieved architectural forms, Morris adumbrates what Stephen Bann, following Michel Foucault, calls the early nineteenth-century 'dialectic' of the loss and rediscovery of history: the dawning of 'a deep historical perspective in which "man" was to lose his central position as the measure of all things, in which provinces of thought like natural history and the study of language would turn out to have their own separate genealogies and laws of development', and the past turned out not to be a single narrative of development but rather the congeries or ever-varying constellation of diverse temporalities.[8] As Nick Groom puts it in a recent essay on Thomas Chatterton and the 'catacthonic' or 'intra-historical', the arrival of Romanticism is bound up with the arrival of the new view of history: shifting out of eighteenth-century antiquarianism and Whig narratives of historical progress towards a sense of the past as an 'echo-chamber' or un-place with 'vertiginous depths'. The 'ultimately simple configuration [of defined] events' gives way to a perception of the 'histories-beneath-history' and the 'assemblages' of 'decentric thought'.[9]

The way had been prepared for Morris to grasp this 'deep historical perspective' by writers and artists going back beyond John Ruskin to Samuel Taylor Coleridge and Johann Wolfgang von Goethe, who had

---

7 William Morris, 'A night in a cathedral', *The Oxford and Cambridge Magazine*, vol. 5 (May 1856): 312–14. See also Morris's 1884 lecture, quoted in Thompson, pp. 236–7, which envisages the 'mists of pedantry' lifting, and superficial notions of civilisation and improvement relaced by a dynamic historical 'sense' of 'deep sympathy' with the 'half-conscious aims' of the past: '[I]nchoate order in the remotest times, varying indeed among different races and countries, but swayed always by the same laws, moving forward ever towards something that seems the very opposite of that which it started from, and yet the earlier order never dead but living in the new, and slowly moulding it to a recreation of its former self.'
8 Stephen Bann, *Romanticism and the Rise of History* (New York: Twayne Publishers, 1995), pp. 9–10.
9 Nick Groom, 'Catachthonic romanticism: buried history, deep ruins', *Romanticism* 24:2 (2018): 118–33. Groom's language draws on Gilles Deleuze and Félix Guattari, as well as Michel Foucault. See Gilles Deleuze and Félix A. Guattari, *A Thousand Plateaus*, trans. by Brian Massumi (London and New York: Continuum, 2004).

treated Gothic buildings as prime examples of such 'temporalised' 'things'; capable, as Foucault would put it, of 'reflecting' back a history newly understood not to exist except as 'interwoven in ["man's"] own being', his habits and acts.[10] Romantic antiquarianism 'makes manifest on the surface the naked fact that man found himself to be devoid of history, but that he was already working on the rediscovery deep inside him ... of a historicity which was bound essentially to himself'.[11] Architecture being, in Ruskin's phrase, 'a creation of his own, born of his necessities, and expressive of his nature', it was capable of being seen as 'in some sort, the work of the whole race ["of man"], while the picture or statue is the work of one only'.[12] As Coleridge had suggested in his 1818 lectures on 'The Gothic Mind' – 30 years before Ruskin on Gothic and the 'historical' admission 'of a richness of record altogether unlimited', and 40 years *after* Goethe (in the words of Friedrich Nietzsche) apprehending the 'soul' of the past in the 'intricate ... palimpsest' of Strasbourg cathedral looming up through the dark 'historical clouds' – Gothic architecture was 'sublime art' precisely because it was bound up with historical change, with the middle-ness of the 'Middle Ages' as such.[13] 'Imagine', said Coleridge,

> a Cathedral, of York, of Milan or of Strasburg, with all its many Chapels, its pillared stem and leaf-work Roof, as if some sacred [pagan] grove ... had been awed into stone at the approach of the true divinity ... [while] the chaunt of penitence and holy pity from consecrated Virgins sobbed and died away in its dark recesses ... [A]nd behold ... the warrior Monarch kneeling [before] the aged Bishop or mitred Abbot ... [A]nd in this assemblage thus collected before your imagination you will see and recognize the completion of the Æra –.[14]

What I propose in this chapter is, therefore, a serious (if not quite a literal) treatment of Morris's 1877 suggestion of a sort of 'fifty-year effect' for the architectural revival – as well as of his conception of progressive 'cycles' or

---

10 Michel Foucault, *The Order of Things: An Archaeology of the Human Sciences* (London and New York: Routledge, 2002), p. 402.
11 Foucault, quoted in Bann, *Romanticism and the Rise of History*, p. 10.
12 John Ruskin, 'The Nature of Gothic', in Birch (ed.), *John Ruskin: Selected Writings*, pp. 32–63 (p. 56).
13 See Ruskin, *Selected Writings*, pp. 21–2; Friedrich Nietzsche, 'On the Uses and Disadvantages of History for Life', in *Untimely Meditations*, edited by Daniel Breazeale, trans. by R. J. Hollingdale (Cambridge: Cambridge University Press, 1997), pp. 57–124 (p. 73); and Samuel Taylor Coleridge, *Lectures 1808–1819: On Literature*, edited by R. A. Foakes, 2 vols (London and Princeton, NJ: Routledge & Kegan Paul, Princeton University Press, 1987), vol. 2, pp. 74–5.
14 Coleridge, *Lectures 1808–1819: On Literature*, vol. 2, pp. 74–5.

cultural trends, moving through and then beyond 'visibility'.[15] Adopting a mode of historical reading that, as I will show, is itself a product of the earlier decades of the nineteenth century, I aim to link and to draw a dynamic contrast between these two 'moments' in the modern history of 'the Gothic'. If 'Romantic Gothic' and 'Victorian medievalism' constitute sequential 'chapters' within a single cultural narrative, they are also conceivable as adjacent but distinct formations, excavated here by way of two parallel 'sections' through the larger and more unevenly developed conceptual field (and 'feel') of 'Gothic'.[16] Each 'moment' has at least a 15-year penumbra, but for convenience, I encode them here as two years with a 60-year interval: 1817 and 1877.

A recent survey by David Matthews locates true cultural 'medievalism' in the 1840s: a decade not of 'inauguration' but of 'unique and never to be repeated ... cultural dominance'.[17] But there is a strong case to be made for both 1817 and 1877 – respectively, midwinter spring and St Martin's summer – as parallel moments of 'dominance' for (what Ruskin would call) this 'Gothic' 'form' of culture and society.[18] The year 1817 was marked by such works of Gothic imagination and of 'cultural Gothicism' (Nick Groom's term) as – to give only the most obvious examples – Coleridge's *Biographia Literaria*, Lord Byron's *Manfred*, Jane Austen's *Northanger Abbey* and the launch of *Blackwood's Magazine*. In this year, the 'Jacobin poet' turned poet laureate Robert Southey also published one of three new editions – following a gap in the publication record of almost two hundred years – of Thomas Malory's *Le Morte d'Arthur*.[19] And within the year, Southey alone had published or

---

15 The 'fifty-year effect' is Stephen Greenblatt's phrase for 'the time in the wake of the great, charismatic ideological struggle in which the revolutionary generation that made the decisive break with the past is all dying out and the survivors hear only hypocrisy in the sermons and look back with longing at the world they have lost'. See Stephen Greenblatt, *Hamlet in Purgatory: Expanded Edition* (Princeton, NJ and Oxford: Princeton University Press, 2013), pp. 248–9. Greenblatt is discussing the imaginative recuperation – occurring with Shakespeare in the 1590s – of the 'dismantle[d]' 'edifice' of Purgatory (see also p. 50). The resonances with Morris's 'Manifesto' for the SPAB are evident; though 'fifty years' will commonly tend to slip – as it does in Walter Scott's artful reflections on historical representation in *Waverley* (1814) and *Ivanhoe* (1819) – to 'sixty' and even 'sixty or seventy years' (see *Ivanhoe*, edited by Ian Duncan [Oxford: Oxford University Press, 1996], p. 14).
16 See Horace Walpole, *Anecdotes of Painting in England*, vol. 1 (Twickenham: Strawberry Hill, 1762), pp. 107–8.
17 David Matthews, *Medievalism: A Critical History* (Cambridge: D.S. Brewer, 2015), p. xi.
18 See John Ruskin, 'Traffic', in *The Crown of Wild Olive: Three Lectures on Work, Traffic, and War* (London: Smith, Elder, and Co., 1866), pp. 79–138 (pp. 82, 94–96, 102–12).
19 See Robert Southey to John May, 9 March 1803: '[F]ar more than ... Coleridge & Wordsworth ... it is I who in the language of Mr Canning & Mr Cobbet am [*par excellence*] the Jacobine [*sic*] poet.' See *The Collected Letters of Robert Southey*, 6 parts, edited by Lynda Pratt, Ian Packer, Tim Fulford and Carol Bolton, 2009–16. <www.rc

initiated no fewer than four further major works of medievalism, which also included a (pirated) play about the Peasants' Revolt, a history of the Jesuits and South America, and a two-part, four-volume history of the English 'Church and State'– an output that may amply justify Veronica Ortenberg's account of Southey as the Romantic poet, whether 'radical' or 'reactionary', 'most committed of all to medievalism'.[20] E. P. Thompson notes of the middle and late century that an 'attraction [to] medievalism and Catholicism' ran across the whole cultural scene: 'Revolutionary and reactionary alike were caught in the same current.'[21] But rarely was this cultural stream bridged quite so effectively or so interestingly as by Southey in 1817. With both the seditious *Wat Tyler* (1817) and the ultra-loyalist *Quarterly Review* to his name, Southey was not only – as his 'second generation' enemies would have it – an 'apostate' or 'epic renegade', but indeed, as Byron admitted, an 'entire man of letters'.[22] Southey in 1817 is thus my main case study in 'Romantic Gothic'. The year 1877, meanwhile, marked by the founding of the SPAB under the combined colours of Morris, Ruskin and Thomas Carlyle, represented a cultural moment so suffused with Gothicism that Morris came close to suggesting that the word itself ought to be retired – to lie fallow until it might again nourish meaningful thought.

1817 and 1877: Robert Southey and William Morris

Already in 1814, Robert Southey was being heralded as the foremost exponent of a new wave of 'Gothic' literary experimentation. Lord Byron woke the publisher John Murray in the middle of the night to compare notes on Southey's *Roderick, the Last of the Goths* (1814). *Roderick*, said Byron, was 'as near perfection as poetry can be – which considering how I dislike the school I

.umd.edu/editions/southeys_letters/> (last accessed 29 May 2019), letter no. 765. See also Robert Southey (ed.), *The byrth, lyf, and actes of Kyng Arthur: of his noble knyghtes of the Rounde Table, theyr merveyllous enquestes and aduentures, thachyeuyng of the Sanc Greal; and in the end le Morte D'Arthur, with the dolourous deth and departyng out of thys worlde of them al; With an Introduction and Notes by Robert Southey, Esq. . . . Printed from Caxton's Edition*, 1485, 2 vols (London: Longman, 1817).

20 The works described here are *Wat Tyler, A Dramatic Poem* (unpublished by Samuel Ridgeway in 1794, and published in three unauthorised editions in 1817 by W. T. Sherwin, J. Fairbarn and W. Hone); the second volume of Southey's three-part *History of Brazil* (1810–19); and *The Book of the Church* (2 vols, 1824) and *Sir Thomas More: or, Colloquies* (2 vols, 1829). See also Veronica Ortenberg, *In Search of the Holy Grail: The Quest for the Middle Ages* (London and New York: Continuum, 2006), p. 45.
21 Thompson, *William Morris*, p. 24.
22 See Byron's journal entry of 22 November 1813, in Lionel Madden (ed.), *Robert Southey: The Critical Heritage* (London: Routledge, 1972), p. 157.

wonder at', and adding that Southey 'might safely stake his fame upon the last of the Goths'.[23] For the reviewers in the *British Critic* and the *Quarterly Review*, meanwhile, the poem showed Southey to be at the leading edge of the 'Gothic' historical revival and the 'chivalrous spirit [now] revived amongst us'.[24] But in the 1820s, with the end of the Napoleonic Wars and what Jerome McGann describes as the second-generation turn away from an insular 'redemptive (cultural) scheme', and towards a more cosmopolitan imagination of 'loss' and open-ended 'failure', Southey had come to expect his 1817 works of occluded Gothic to have a long voyage into posterity.[25] His *Colloquies on Society* – a series of interlinked conversations with the ghost of Sir Thomas More, 'last of the old' world, as Morris would later call him, conceived in 1817 but not published until after Catholic Emancipation in 1829 – would, Southey predicted, 'be read hereafter, whatever be their fortune now'.[26] 'One edition will sell; some of the rising generation will be leavened by it, and in the third and fourth generations its foresight will be proved, and perhaps some of its effects may be seen.'[27]

Southey's pretensions to the historian's power of partial prophecy have often been mocked. As Thomas Babington Macaulay put it in his devastating piece on the *Colloquies* in the *Edinburgh Review*, Southey had 'foretold, we remember, on the very eve of the abolition of the Test and Corporation Acts, that these hateful laws were immortal'.[28] Southey had, indeed, 'the very alphabet to learn' of the historical and political-economic 'sciences' that he claimed to be explaining to the nation: his method, '[t]o stand on a hill, to look at a cottage and a factory, and to see which is the prettier'; making 'the

---

23 See Peter Cochran, *Byron and Bob: Lord Byron's Relationship with Robert Southey* (Newcastle upon Tyne: Cambridge Scholars, 2010), p. 46.
24 See *The British Critic* 3 (April 1815): 353–89 (p. 354); and *Eclectic Review* 7 (August 1811): 672–88 (p. 673).
25 See Jerome J. McGann, 'Poetry', in Iain McCalman (ed.), *An Oxford Companion to the Romantic Age* (Oxford: Oxford University Press, 1999), pp. 270–9 (pp. 277–8).
26 See Morris, 'Foreword to *Utopia*', in *News from Nowhere*, p. 373; and see Southey to Neville White, 20 January 1829, in Charles Cuthbert Southey (ed.), *Life and Correspondence of Robert Southey*, 6 vols (London: Longman, 1849–50), vol. 6, p. 22.
27 Southey to Walter Savage Landor, 14 August 1824, in John Wood Warter (ed.), *Selections from the Letters of Robert Southey*, 4 vols (London: Longman, 1856), vol. 3, pp. 437–38.
28 See Robert Southey, *Sir Thomas More: or, Colloquies on the Progress and Prospects of Society*, edited by Tom Duggett, 2 vols (London and New York: Routledge, 2018), pp. 808–9. Southey's defenders at *Fraser's Magazine* turned Macaulay's acknowledgement of Southey's 'considerable influence' back against him, pointing out that by his own progressive lights, such 'influence' as Southey's could not have come from a reputation as 'a prophet or an evangelist', but rather his 'accomplished scholars[hip]' in that 'General history' which is 'Philosophy teaching by example'. See Southey, *Sir Thomas More*, pp. 808, 831–2.

picturesque the test of political good'.[29] As Macaulay's review morphed into a 'classic' of liberalism, Southey's book dwindled to the status of a footnote.[30] But as R. J. Smith observes in *The Gothic Bequest*, the *Colloquies* were more quietly influential than mainstream literary history would suppose, containing 'in embryo ... much of the social criticism of Pugin, Carlyle, Ruskin, and Morris'.[31] Southey's set-piece contrasts between monasteries and cotton mills, and the cottages of manufacturing and agricultural labourers are, in effect, 'verbal sketch[es]' for 'the illustrations comparing medieval with nineteenth-century towns' in Pugin's *Contrasts* (1841). 'It was a fancydress version of Coleridge's clerisy and the literary equivalent of the Acts to build Anglican churches in the industrial towns ... a Tory version of the Alfredian myth.'[32]

This chapter seeks to amplify Smith's claim for the *Colloquies*, but to shift away from condescension to the poet's 'fancydress', and towards attending seriously to the sense of historical reenactment and what Stephen Bann and other historians of 'distance' call the post-Romantic desire to 'live the past'.[33] As Bill Shiels has argued, Southey, along with William Cobbett, was instrumental in reviving Thomas More as a complex figure of early modern Englishness, and was thus also a key figure in the framing of what Raymond Williams called the whole 'humanist challenge', with its English roots in More and his *Utopia* (1516).[34] The major mid-century statements of the 'culture' position were also lineal descendants of Southey's work. Thomas Carlyle at one point envisioned his *Past and Present* (1843) as a sort of sequel to Southey's *Colloquies* with More: a ghost-dialogue with the shade of Oliver Cromwell.[35] John Ruskin's 'The Nature of Gothic' (1853),

29 See Southey, *Sir Thomas More*, pp. 789, 799.
30 See Esther Wohlgemut, 'Southey, Macaulay and the Idea of a Picturesque History', *Romanticism on the Net*, 32–3 (2003/4), <http://id.erudit.org/iderudit/009261ar; §19–20> (last accessed 22 January 2019); and *Sir Thomas More*, pp. xxvi, xxxiii.
31 R. J. Smith, *The Gothic Bequest: Medieval Institutions in British Thought, 1688–1863* (Cambridge: Cambridge University Press, 1987), p. 157.
32 Smith, *The Gothic Bequest*, p. 157.
33 See Bann, *Romanticism and the Rise of History*, p. 130–62; Mark Salber Phillips, *On Historical Distance* (New Haven and London: Yale University Press, 2013), 'Introduction' and chapter 6; and Peter Burke, 'A Short History of Distance', in Mark Salber Phillips, Barbara Caine and Julia Adeney Thomas (eds), *Rethinking Historical Distance* (Basingstoke and New York: Palgrave Macmillan, 2013), pp. 21–33.
34 See William Shiels, 'Thomas More', in Gareth Atkins (ed.), *Making and Remaking Saints in Nineteenth-Century Britain* (Manchester University Press, 2016), pp. 112–26; and see also Williams, *Culture and Society*, p. 24: 'The very form of the *Colloquies* – the bringing of More to question the new society – indicates a conscious continuity with the first phase of the humanist challenge, in which many of the ideas now concentrated in the meaning of "culture" were in fact laid down.'
35 See Thomas Carlyle, *Past and Present*, edited by Chris R. Vanden Bossche (Berkeley, Los Angeles and London: University of California Press, 2005), p. xxvii.

meanwhile, is closely modelled upon the account of the 'fragmentation, mechanization, and enslavement of the modern factory worker' in Colloquy VII.[36] The impact of Southey's book in 1829-30 was indeed such as almost to short-circuit the supposed 'dichotomy' (as Stefan Collini and Philip Connell call it) within 'Victorian thought and sensibility' between 'political economy' and 'cultural critique' in its 'Carlylean ... Ruskinian or Morrisian' forms.[37] Going on transatlantic hearsay and positive reviews like the one in the *Quarterly* for July 1829, the US-based *Western Monthly Review* imagined Southey's book as a sustained historical contrast, liable to 'stagger' even the best-trained 'young republican', between the age of 'faith' and its 'huge gothic buildings' on the one hand, and the 'present times' of 'canals' and '*evidence* for every thing' on the other.[38]

Despite the admittedly few direct links between Southey and Morris, they make a particularly illuminating contrast for the history of the Gothic. Both 'entire men of letters', in Byron's phrase, Morris was by comparison – and in the terms that Southey used to describe his own 1816 meeting with Morris's forbear in industrial philanthropy, Robert Owen – the 'practical man' to Southey's dry scholar.[39] Both men built monasteries in their heads in early adulthood, looking back also to Nicholas Ferrar's early seventeenth-century Anglican religious community at Little Gidding.[40] But where Morris's 'FICTIONARY' at Merton Abbey at least bordered on 'social experiment', Southey restricted himself to visiting cooperatives and diagnosing the difficulty of their co-existence with commercial society.[41] And where Morris in later life became a sort of itinerant preacher of Socialism, overcoming his ingrained shyness and alienating old friends such as Sir Edward Burne-Jones in the process, Southey increasingly cleaved to his 'compleat

---

36 See Joseph Bizup, *Manufacturing Culture: Vindications of Early Victorian Industry* (Charlottesville and London: University of Virginia Press, 2003), pp. 19, 84, 180–1.
37 See Philip Connell, *Romanticism, Economics and the Question of 'Culture'* (Oxford: Oxford University Press, 2001), p. 5.
38 See Southey, *Sir Thomas More*, pp. 819–20.
39 Southey wrote to John Rickman of Owen as just 'such a Pantisocrat as I was', and imagined an influence that never was: 'Had we met twenty years ago the meeting might have influenced both his life & mine in no slight degree: during those years he has been a practical man, & I have been a student, – we do not differ in the main point, – but my mind has ripened more than his.' See Southey to John Rickman, 25 August 1816, *Collected Letters of Robert Southey*, letter no. 2832.
40 See Fiona MacCarthy, *William Morris: A Life for Our Time*, 2nd edition (London: Faber and Faber, 2010), pp. 63–8; and Southey, *Sir Thomas More*, pp. xliv–xlvi.
41 See MacCarthy, *A Life for Our Time*, pp. 452–60; and Southey, *Sir Thomas More*, pp. xxxvi–xliii.

seclusion [like] the monks of St Bernard' in his library at Greta Hall, even as he gained public notoriety and (among conservatives) political respect.[42] The two men travelled opposite political roads after leaving Oxford. The former 'Jacobin poet' picked up the laureateship from Walter Scott in 1813 as the best available establishment 'place'; Morris, the late Socialist convert, 'shuddered' at the prospect of taking over the mantle of Tennyson.[43] Southey is present in the text, but absent from the index, of Fiona MacCarthy's definitive biography of the Victorian 'life for our time' (as her subtitle calls Morris). And whatever Southey's evident role in staking out the 'culture' position in the 1820s and 1830s, as Raymond Williams and Philip Connell have shown, that terrain was fully occupied in Morris's day by subsequent, more immediate influences. In his lecture on 'How I became a Socialist' and his developing 'ideal' of social reformation by 'art', Morris states these important influences quite clearly. Among all those who were quite content with the 'mechanical' 'civilization of this century ... there were a few who were in open rebellion ... a few, say two, Carlyle and Ruskin'.[44] In a list of the 'basically conservative' ingredients from which Morris brewed his radical form of medievalism, Richard Frith thus places the laureate alongside Carlyle, Ruskin, Scott and Cobbett, and observes that 'all of these writers were important influences' – with 'the exception of Southey'.[45]

This formulation of the relationship, however – a key ingredient if not a direct 'influence' – seems about right. Southey was, as Tim Fulford has shown, a prime mover in the aesthetic and technological shift back towards illustrated books that would (arguably) culminate with the Kelmscott Chaucer and Morris's reinvention of the illuminated manuscript.[46] Southey devoted significant attention to the visual qualities of his books and experimented – like Wordsworth – with the historical encryption effect of the 'Gothic character' or 'black letter', which Morris in turn would seek to

---

42 See Thompson, *William Morris*, pp. 267–8, 274, 322, 701; W. A. Speck, *Robert Southey: Entire Man of Letters* (New Haven and London: Yale University Press, 2006), p. 174; and Southey, *Sir Thomas More*, p. 632 n. Southey rejected the various public roles that came his way in the 1820s and 1830s, including a seat in Parliament, a librarianship in Edinburgh, an editorship with the *Quarterly Review* and a Chair in History at the University of Durham.
43 See Speck, *Robert Southey*, pp. 154–5; and MacCarthy, *A Life for Our Time*, p. 632.
44 Morris, 'How I Became a Socialist', in *News from Nowhere*, p. 381
45 Richard Frith, 'The Worship of Courage', p. 118.
46 See Tim Fulford, 'Virtual Topography: Poets, Painters, Publishers and the Reproduction of the Landscape in the Early Nineteenth Century', *Romanticism and Victorianism on the Net*, 57–8 (February–May 2010) <http://id.erudit.org/iderudit/1006512ar> (last accessed 22 January 2019).

'redeem from the charge of unreadableness' with his 'Troy' and 'Chaucer' fonts for the Kelmscott Press.[47] In terms of 'historical feel', meanwhile, Southey was a precursor lastingly transumed by Carlyle, who moved in the late 1820s from youthful contempt towards a sort of emulous second-selfhood.[48] In his *Reminiscences* (1881), Carlyle represented Southey the *Quarterly* reviewer as a precursor in point of feeling, but also as a figure too mired in eighteenth-century orthodoxies – such as 'the Protestant Constitution of these kingdoms' – to grasp real truth:

> In spite of my Radicalism, I always found very much in these Toryisms which was greatly according to my heart; things rare and worthy, at once pious and true, which were always welcome to me, though I strove to base them on a better ground than his, – his being no eternal or time-defying one, as I could see.[49]

In 'Signs of the Times' (1829), an essay that ultimately replaced the review of *Colloquies* that Carlyle had been keen to write for the *Edinburgh Review*, Southey and his kind were relegated firmly to what Carlyle would later figure as the 'Dry Rubbish' heap of the 'Eighteenth Century'.[50] 'Signs' nevertheless reveals its debt to Southey in echoes of the passages in Southey's book attacking the heart-searing 'political system' founded on 'manufactures', decrying the 'mechanical character' of 'our whole manner of existence'.[51] Looking forward to the 'contrast' format of *Past and Present*, 'Signs' also looks back to Southey's use of parallel images of prehistoric and medieval monuments, and his sustained 'picturesque' description of the 'hamlet of Millbeck'

---

47 See Kenneth Curry, *Southey*, 2nd edition (London and New York: Routledge, 2016), p. 121; Steven H. Gale (ed.), *Encyclopedia of British Humorists: Geoffrey Chaucer to John Cleese*, 3 vols (New York and London: Garland, 1996), vol. 2, p. 1044; and Tom Duggett, *Gothic Romanticism: Architecture, Politics, and Literary Form* (Basingstoke and New York: Palgrave Macmillan, 2010), p. 172–6; MacCarthy, *A Life for Our Time*, pp. 613–4. Southey 'claimed' to have 'set the fashion' for using 'black letter on . . . title pages' (Speck, *Robert Southey*, p. 10), and the *Monthly Review* pointed out that the '*black letter* title-page (History of Brazil)' was itself '[a] warning . . . that this book is not composed in the fashionable manner of the present day' but rather that of 'the chronicles of other times' (*Monthly Review*, 69 [December 1812]: 337–52).
48 See Thomas Carlyle, *Past and Present*, pp. xxvi–xxvii. Transumption, as theorised by Harold Bloom, is a 'total, final act of taking up a poetic stance in relation to anteriority of poetic language', a dialectical development of belatedness to achieve a partial position of priority, or the 'illusion of having fathered one's own father'. See Harold Bloom, *A Map of Misreading* (Oxford: Oxford University Press, 1975), p. 136.
49 See Southey, *Sir Thomas More*, p. lxxxiii; and Thomas Carlyle, *Reminiscences*, edited by K. J. Fielding and Ian Campbell (Oxford: Oxford University Press, 1997), pp. 387–8.
50 See Connell, *Romanticism, Economics and the Question of 'Culture'*, p. 9; Carlyle, *Past and Present*, pp. 50–53; and Carlyle, *Chartism* in Alan Shelston (ed.), *Thomas Carlyle: Selected Writings* (London: Penguin, 1971), pp. 119–202 (p. 198).
51 See Southey, *Sir Thomas More*, p. 92; and Carlyle, *Selected Writings*, p. 67.

and its cottages belonging to the farming and the manufacturing poor. The farmers' cottages, 'built of the native stone without mortar', Southey had suggested, appeared 'beautifully' 'old', 'adjusted' to 'their place' by the 'scene' and 'time'. But for the 'new cottages of the manufacturers', built 'upon the manufacturing pattern ... naked, and in a row', Southey foresaw no such reversion: 'Time cannot mellow them; Nature will neither clothe nor conceal them; and they remain always as offensive to the eye as to the mind!'[52] The same part of Southey's book also provides the template for the cases made by both Carlyle and Ruskin against 'mechanism', with its contrast between the many-windowed 'manufactory' of modern times and the 'convent' of old.[53]

The sort of historical 'dialectic' that Morris would develop from Ruskin before finding it in Marx was also latent in Southey's *Colloquies*. In Colloquy XIII, the idea of a change of 'spirit', measurable in the building of cotton mills rather than monasteries, becomes a progressive speculation that the former may in some sense re-constitute the virtues of the latter: 'May not the manufacturing system be ... tending to work out, by means of the very excess to which it is carried, a remedy for the evils which it has brought with it ... a palingenesia, a restoration of national sanity and strength, a second birth [?]'.[54] This speculation is informed by Southey's long-running conversation with the census-taker and parliamentary official John Rickman, about the need for a whole range of new cooperative institutions, 'communities ... convents ... colleges', including 'Beguinages' or 'protestant nunneries' aimed at ameliorating the condition of destitute women.[55] Rickman promised to march in step with Southey on this 'chivalrous enterprize', but doubted that the time was yet 'ripe for this optimum grade of civilization', projecting 'a treatise on the due limits and administration of liberality, the excesses & aberrations of which in the shapes of Foundling Hospitals, Poor Rates, Gaols, &c. – &c. – &c. – will otherwise overturn the Society of which under due Regulation it would be [the] highest ornament'.[56] Southey was much more committed to what Raymond Williams terms 'the positive functions of government', believing 'the mass of mankind ... are what our institutions make us', as well as taking a more localist view that would restore 'economic independence' by 'multiply[ing] farms' and giving each 'labourer ... his grass plot and

---

52 Southey, *Sir Thomas More*, p. 96.
53 See Southey, *Sir Thomas More*, pp. xxxiv–xxxv, 296.
54 See Southey, *Sir Thomas More*, pp. 88, 297–8.
55 See Southey, *Sir Thomas More*, pp. xxxix, xliv–xlv.
56 See Southey, *Sir Thomas More*, pp. xliv–xxxix.

garden'.[57] But Southey shared Rickman's dialectical view of cooperative societies, as initially popularised by Robert Owen, as 'overturner' and 'highest ornament'. In August 1829 he wrote to Walter Savage Landor of cooperative societies such as one in Birmingham taking the dangerous step of declaring their aim as 'nothing short of a community in land and in goods'.[58] This was for 'plain, practicable, strong-headed men' to open the way for 'such fellows as Cobbett' to turn the good 'principle' to 'an engine of mischief'. A forthcoming article in the *Quarterly* by the physician and king's librarian Dr Robert Gooch was, Southey added, the first significant engagement with Owenism by a 'public writer'. Gooch's view of 'the bright side of the question' needed balancing with Southey's 'darker apprehensions'. 'Yet', Southey concluded,

> if we can keep this principle within its proper bounds, so as to secure the well-being of the whole lower order, without pulling down the higher orders ... I should then indeed gladly sing my *Nunc dimittis*! At present the ship is driving fast toward the breakers, and it behoves those who know their duty, to cast about in what manner they may best construct rafts from the wreck (they who may survive), when they shall have stood by it to the last.[59]

To 'cast about' to 'construct rafts' from the materials of existing society is both to insure against and to help precipitate the breakup of the old vessel. Standing by the old order, Southey both fears and relishes the utopian potential in its wreckage. He somehow hopes there can be communism for the 'lower order' and commercial society for the 'higher'; that is, a real-world achievement of the simultaneous subsistence within shared textual space of two incompatible 'worlds' as depicted in More's *Utopia*.[60] The vision is the Romantic-conservative, Carlylean one – of delving a yard beneath present-day radicals and liberals to effect more historically 'momentous' change. As Southey put it in a letter to his brother, Henry Herbert Southey, on 28 July 1829,

> Gooch is much interested about the Cooperative Societies: and so is Rickman and so am I. Lockhart, which I hardly expected, will print

---

57 See Williams, *Culture and Society*, p. 24; Southey to Robert Harry Inglis, 22 February 1829, *Life and Correspondence*, vol. 6, pp. 28–9.
58 Southey to Walter Savage Landor, 22 August 1829, *Selections*, vol. 4, pp. 144–7.
59 Southey to Landor, 22 August 1829, *Selections*, vol. 4, pp. 144–7.
60 For an account of this doubleness in More's *Utopia*, see Stephen Greenblatt, *Renaissance Self-Fashioning: From More to Shakespeare*, revised edition (Chicago: University of Chicago Press, 2005), pp. 22–3.

> Goochs paper upon them. It will be somewhat remarkable if H. M.'s Librarian and his P. L. should lend their hearty aid to an incipient change in society, likely to be more extensive and momentous in its consequences than any that has preceded it.[61]

But it was precisely the possession of such an 'incipient' or 'momentous' view of history that Carlyle denied to his Romantic precursor. A superficial presentism, Carlyle suggested in 'Signs', was evident in the predicament of such Church-and-State theorists as Southey and Coleridge, left bewildered by the submergence of the rough historical beast:

> The repeal of the Test Acts, and then of the Catholic disabilities, has struck many of their admirers with an incredible astonishment. Those things seemed fixed and immovable; deep as the foundations of the world; and lo, in a moment they have vanished, and their place knows them no more! Our worthy friends mistook the slumbering Leviathan for an island ... But now their Leviathan has suddenly dived under; and they can no longer be fastened in the stream of time; but must drift forward on it, even like the rest of the world ...[62]

This was far from fair to the time-sense actually developed in Southey's *Colloquies*, which rather approximates to Lorenz von Stein on a sense of modern history as a 'labyrinth of movement', and a way of reading that Stein's twentieth-century interpreter, Reinhart Koselleck, specifically figures as poetic or picturesque: 'If history is experienced as the movement of diverse streams whose mutual relations constantly undergo different degrees of intensification, petrifaction, or acceleration, then its general motion can be apprehended only from a consciously adopted point of view.'[63] According to the opening prospectus issued by the ghostly figure of Thomas More, the book uses landscape viewing as a heuristic for the re-education of the reader in the dynamic art of historical judgement:

> By comparing the great operating causes in the age of the Reformation, and in this age of revolutions, going back to the former age, looking at things as I then beheld them, perceiving wherein I judged rightly, and wherein I erred, and tracing the progress of those causes which are now developing their whole tremendous power, you will derive instruction ...[64]

---

61 Southey to Henry Herbert Southey, 28 July 1829, in Kenneth Curry (ed.), *New Letters of Robert Southey*, 2 vols (New York and London: Columbia University Press, 1965), vol. 2, pp. 341–2.
62 Carlyle, *Selected Writings*, pp. 62–3.
63 Reinhart Koselleck, *Futures Past: On the Semantics of Historical Time*, trans. and edited by Keith Tribe (New York and Chichester: Columbia University Press, 2004), pp. 60, 62.
64 See Southey, *Sir Thomas More*, p. 11.

Carlyle's 'Signs' does nevertheless represent the arrival of a still-more-mobile time-sense, both comparing and tracing the links between periods, and producing from this diorama-like moving contrast a 'Dynamical' sense of each 'Day' as the 'conflux of two Eternities', in among which we may wisely seek to 'adjust our own position'.[65] And it is arguably in 'Signs', written for the generally more optimistic or 'radical' *Edinburgh Review*, that the Morrisian 'active view of history' and 'moulding ... recreation' of the past first finds articulation. 'Nay, after all', Carlyle writes in 'Signs':

> our spiritual maladies are but of Opinion; we are but fettered by chains of our own forging, and which ourselves can also rend asunder ... Are the solemn temples, in which the Divinity was once visibly revealed among us, crumbling away? We can repair them, we can rebuild them. The wisdom, the heroic worth of our forefathers, which we have lost, we can recover. That admiration of old nobleness, which now so often shows itself as faint dilettantism, will one day become a generous emulation, *and man may again be all that he has been, and more than he has been.*[66]

Southey the antiquarian was thus a prophecy (in Carlyle) of Ruskin the historical visionary. To the extent that Southey was subsumed under the already archaic vision of Carlyle, he would have represented to Morris's generation of the 1850s an attitude to the past that was itself still moving but already unusable. As Fiona MacCarthy suggests, when Morris read Carlyle's *Past and Present* at Oxford in the early 1850s, he was 'affected deeply and lastingly', but found it ultimately 'too grotesque' in comparison with the 'high-flown clarities' emerging in the works of Ruskin – Carlyle falling between the two waves, as Jonathan Bate suggests, of the more radiant 'Wordsworthian ecology' that peaked again in Morris after Ruskin.[67] But this double disconnection between Morris and Southey remains odd inasmuch as Southey is almost unavoidable as a presence and key mediating figure in Morris's account of the books that influenced him. Items 51–3 in Morris's list of books, grouped together in the 'bible' category of works that 'I don't know how to class', are those where Southey was alternately a mediator and an influence: Thomas More (*Utopia*), and the *Works* of Ruskin and Carlyle.[68] On this view, Morris's claim for Ruskin's originality as the first to lay hold of the 'key' to social issues in the 'essence of art' reads

---

65 Carlyle, *Selected Writings*, p. 63.   66 Carlyle, *Selected Writings*, p. 83; my emphasis.
67 See MacCarthy, *A Life for Our Time*, p. 71; and Jonathan Bate, *Romantic Ecology: Wordsworth and the Environmental Tradition* (London: Routledge, 1991), pp. 58–9.
68 William Morris, *The Collected Letters of William Morris*, 4 vols, edited by Norman Kelvin (Princeton: Princeton University Press, 1984–96), vol. 2, p. 517.

rather like a belated reversal – ironically underwritten by the overwriting of Southey on both sides of the 'culture' debate – of Thomas Macaulay denouncing Southey's *Colloquies* as a merely 'picturesque' approach to economics and history.[69]

To reclaim Southey as a precursor of a future-oriented Morrisian Gothic is not to deny the element of retrograde eighteenth-century 'antiquarian humour' in his works.[70] Southey was, as he well knew himself, always liable to lapse into what Friedrich Nietzsche and Carlyle alike would decry as the 'repulsive spectacle' of the antiquary 'raking together' 'bibliographical' 'dust', 'encased in the stench of must and mould', degrading the impulse to serve the 'fresh life of the present' into to a mere 'insatiable thirst for … antiquity'.[71] But the rest of this chapter seeks to suggest that it was the distinctive work of first Ruskin and then Morris to extract and enhance the progressive potential and genuine social commitment lurking, 'inchoate' and 'imminent', in the antiquarian 'Gothic' of that Romantic first generation. And while such an argument inevitably proceeds by obliquities and observations of affinities, there is one evident 'hyperlink' between the generations in the shape of Southey's 1817 edition (taken over, like the laureateship, from Walter Scott) of Thomas Malory's *Le Morte d'Arthur* – a book that Dante Gabriel Rossetti linked with the Bible in 1857 as 'the two greatest books in the world'.[72] As noted earlier, Southey's edition is a landmark in the recovery of medieval romance. It is distinctive for its use of Gothic font and woodcut illustration on

---

69 'I know indeed', Morris conceded in his Preface, 'that Ruskin is not the first man who has put forward the possibility and the urgent necessity that men should take pleasure in Labour; for Robert Owen showed how by companionship and goodwill labour might be made at least endurable' (Morris, *News from Nowhere*, p. 368). The reference is to Robert Owen 'of Lanark' (1771–1858), 'that … most practical of all enthusiasts', as Southey called him (*Sir Thomas More*, p. 33) whose industrial 'villages of union' united in opposition both the establishment and the forces of plebian radicalism. For William Cobbett, writing in the crisis year of 1817, Owen's progressive-regressive utopian 'villages' looked more like a paternalist plot against the rights of the people: less communities of goods than 'parallelograms of paupers' (see *Political Register*, 2 August 1817). In Morris's account, Owen was too much a man of his time – at once too idealistic and too mechanistic – to have provided his system with an inherent 'motive power'. The difference in Ruskin's work, Morris claimed, was specifically the laying hold of the 'key' of 'art', which Owen in his 'tim[e] … could [not] possibly have found'. See Morris, *News from Nowhere*, pp. 368–9.
70 The phrase is Wordsworth's, from *The Excursion*. See William Wordsworth, *The Excursion*, edited by Sally Bushell, James A. Butler and Michael C. Jay, with the assistance of David Garcia, The Cornell Wordsworth (Ithaca, NY: Cornell University Press, 2007), III, l. 139.
71 Friedrich Nietzsche, 'On the Uses and Disadvantages of History for Life', p. 73.
72 J. W. Mackail, *The Life of William Morris*, 2 vols (London: Longman, Green, 1899), vol. 1, p. 91.

From Romantic Gothic to Victorian Medievalism: 1817 and 1877

Fig.4.1: Malory in the black-letter manner. Anon., Frontispiece to Robert Southey's *The Byrth, Lyf, and Actes of Kyng Arthur* (1817). The British Library Board, 634.1.6, p. 7.

the title page, as well as the liberal use throughout the text of illuminated initial letters (Fig.4.1). The book is also notable for its twenty-one-part Preface, designed in apparent imitation of the old text itself – which is said by Southey to resemble not a 'tree' but a sort of 'prickly pear', a set of joints growing upon each other, 'all equal in size and alike in shape, and the whole making a formless and misshapen mass'.[73]

Morris and Burne-Jones discovered Southey's edition of Malory in a Birmingham booksellers in the weeks immediately after their Anglo-French cathedral tour of summer 1855.[74] They were instantly galvanised. 'This', as MacCarthy significantly puts it, 'was the Malory summer'. Morris purchased the book immediately and worked from it in the composition of his first published volume of poems, *The Defence of Guenevere* (1858). Southey's *Malory* thus became for the Pre-Raphaelites a sort of portable Rouen cathedral – described later by Morris as the historic achievement of 'the work of the associated labour and thought of *the people*, the result of a chain of tradition unbroken from the earliest stages of art' (1895); this specific work of the older antiquarian an early material ground for Morris's later analogy, in a fragmentary essay of the 1890s, between the 'long[ing] for' beautiful buildings and beautiful books.[75] Both Southey and Morris distanced themselves from Thomas Dibdin's 'bibliomania'. Southey suggested that he was qualified to edit and comment upon Malory and other old texts precisely because his 'knowledge' was not over-encumbered with black-letter obsessions.[76] Morris would become famous for his instinctive ability to date and classify books and manuscripts.[77] And Southey's role in the bibliographical retransmission of Malory was, consciously or otherwise, one that Morris would later take on for himself. The *Morte d'Arthur* was one of the books that Morris projected to re-edit for the Kelmscott Press, 'with at least a hundred illustrations by Burne-Jones'.[78]

---

73 See Marylyn Parins (ed.), *Sir Thomas Malory: The Critical Heritage* (London and New York: Routledge, 2002), pp. 95, 101.
74 MacCarthy, *A Life for Our Time*, pp. 96–7.
75 'If I were asked to say what is at once the most important production of art and the thing to be most longed for, I should answer, a beautiful house; and if I were further asked to name the production next in importance and the thing next to be longed for, I should answer, a beautiful Book. To enjoy good houses and good books in self-respect and decent comfort, seems to me to be the pleasurable end towards which all societies of human beings ought now to struggle', William Morris, *The Ideal Book: Essays and Lectures on the Arts of the Book*, edited by William S. Peterson (Berkeley and Los Angeles: University of California Press, 1982), p. 1.
76 See *Collected Letters of Robert Southey*, letter no. 1360; and *Sir Thomas Malory: The Critical Heritage*, pp. 6–7.
77 See MacCarthy, *A Life for Our Time*, pp. 35, 42.
78 See 'An Annotated List of all the Books printed at the Kelmscott Press', p. 65, available at: <http://morrisedition.lib.uiowa.edu/BookArts/cockerell-kelmscott-annotated-list.pdf> (last accessed 22 January 2019); and MacCarthy, *A Life for Our Time*, p. 97.

But of more fundamental importance than this baton-pass between Southey and Morris as individual scholar-poets is the accomplishment of just the sort of generation-skipping transference that Southey had foreseen for his 1817 works of 'cultural Gothicism'. For Morris to work from Southey's 1817 edition of Malory was precisely to choose 'Romantic Gothic' over the intervening forms of 'Victorian medievalism'. Ruskin had defined 'mediaevalism' as a 'Gothic form' of society, fusing 'architecture', 'religion' and 'national life', and Morris would not distinguish the meaning or respective historical 'feel' of the two words until his autobiographical letter (to the Socialist Andreas Scheu) of 1883. The poems in *The Defence of Guenevere* were to be seen, he then told Scheu, with overtones of his contemporary assault on mere historicism and the 'Lie' of restoration, in the context of that early 'revival of Gothic architecture': 'exceedingly young ... very mediaeval'.[79] Before he had found a 'corrective' in the 'old Norse literature' of 'courage', Morris had thus erred upon what the letter to Scheu calls the 'maundering side of mediaevalism'.[80] But something like this later distinction of the 'Gothic' and the 'medieval' is already evident in *The Defence*, and in the choice of Southey as source text. For there were two other editions of Malory available, both published in 1816, and both based, unlike the Southey edition that had gone back to the Caxton text of 1485, on the 'more accessible' Stansby edition of 1634.[81] Tennyson knew Southey's edition but worked from a copy of one of the 1816 editions, by Walker and Edwards, a gift from Leigh Hunt, Southey's long-term enemy and poet of the technicolour medievalism of *The Story of Rimini* (1816).[82] In his survey of *Medievalism: The Middle Ages in Modern England* (2007), Michael Alexander devotes a chapter to the Victorian obsession with Malory, and draws a telling contrast between the 1816 editions, 'inexpensive and in modernised spelling', and the 'elaborate and scholarly' Southey edition.[83] In Southey's own words, his edition required of the reader a 'certain aptitude' for enjoying works for which 'the fashion ... has passed away'.[84] For Morris to work from Southey's old-form 'scholarly' 1817 edition, rather than the popular 'modern' 1816 editions, in

---

79 William Morris to Andreas Scheu, 15 September 1883, in *Letters*, vol. 2 (A), pp. 228–9; and see MacCarthy *A Life for Our Time*, pp. 142, 161.
80 Morris to Scheu, 15 September 1883, *Letters*, vol. 2 (A), pp. 228–9.
81 See *Sir Thomas Malory: The Critical Heritage*, p. 7.
82 See David Staines, *Tennyson's Camelot: The Idylls of the King and Its Medieval Sources* (Waterloo, Ont.: Wilfrid Laurier University Press, 1982), p. 27.
83 Michael Alexander, *Medievalism: The Middle Ages in Modern England* (New Haven and London: Yale University Press, 2007), pp. 105–26 (p. 113).
84 Alexander, *Medievalism*, p. 113.

effect reversing Tennyson's choice of sources, was thus to contest what MacCarthy calls the prevailing 'rotund' forms of mid-century medievalism, and to adumbrate what Morris would later define as a 'style historic in the true sense'.[85] What was a complaint against Southey in the 1810s – his anti-modern '*black letter* ... manner' – became the standard compliment paid to Morris in the 1870s: 'he occupies himself exclusively with old stories, and goes back to the old sources of language for words to put them in'.[86] And while contemporary reviews of Morris's *Defence* generally found the poetry deficient in comparison with Tennyson, there was also a dawning realisation of a loss of real history in the peak medievalism of the 1840s. The review in the *Literary Gazette* by Richard Garnett draws a telling contrast:

> The difference between the two poets obviously is that Tennyson writes of mediaeval things like a modern, and Mr. Morris like a contemporary. Tennyson's 'Sir Galahad' is Tennyson himself in an enthusiastic and devotional mood; Mr. Morris's is the actual champion, just as he lived and moved and had his being some twelve hundred years ago ... Tennyson is the modern *par excellence*, the man of his age; Rossetti and Morris are the men of the middle age; and while this at once places them in a position of inferiority as regards Tennyson [and the Romantic 'golden age of British poetry'], it increases their interest towards ourselves ...[87]

Southey's more granular, aphasic and rhizomatic approach to the art and culture of the Middle Ages thus underpins the 'difficult ... unsettling and demanding' poetry of Morris's *The Defence of Guenevere* (1858); and sets the terms for the oblique Gothic of *News from Nowhere* – framed in 1890 as a set of fugitive 'chapters' from a Utopian Romance.

The value of recovering a line of influence from Southey to Morris in a volume on the 'History of the Gothic' is now, I hope, becoming clear. In suggesting that much if not all of what was present in late-blooming Victorian medievalism was already present in first-generation Romanticism, I have been recovering a tradition that is about Gothic and History, and that has relatively little to do with the Gothic novel or other forms of Gothic in commercial pop culture. As Nick Groom has recently suggested, 'if [Walpole's] *Otranto* drafted the template that effectively redefined Gothic as a magical medievalist style, the [prevailing] political and social

---

85 Morris, *News from Nowhere*, pp. 347–8.
86 See Peter Faulkner (ed.), *William Morris, The Critical Heritage* (London: Routledge, 1973), pp. 208–9.
87 See Faulkner (ed.), *William Morris, The Critical Heritage*, pp. 33–6.

forms of Gothic' nevertheless 'continued'.[88] In recent work on Ruskin's articulation of the 'psychological' novelty of a 'wolfish life' that is *therefore* 'ennobling', Richard Adelman draws a telling contrast between Ruskin's 'Gothic' of the 'grey, shadowy, many-pinnacled image ... within us' and the 'Gothics' of Ann Radcliffe and 'Monk' Lewis, which rather deploy 'extreme moral depravity' within a rusticated discourse of enlightenment.[89] But if Adelman envisages Ruskin as in effect re-inventing Gothic as had Walpole before him, with other 'Gothic' works from Emily Brontë's *Wuthering Heights* (1847) onwards giving the term a markedly different inflection, a genealogical perspective linking Southey and Morris tends to suggest that this is more an effect of Ruskin working from quite different materials and in a quite different tradition. Ruskin is, in effect, going back past Horace Walpole, under the transumptive influence of the more authentically 'Gothic' first-generation Romantics, to the prevailing 'political and social forms' of the seventeenth and early eighteenth centuries. It is by this way that, as I have already been suggesting, Ruskin arrives at his account of 'mediaevalism' as a 'Gothic form' of society, fusing 'architecture', 'religion' and 'national life and character'. But the category of the 'Gothic' is not thus simply subsumed by the 'medieval'. By linking back to Southey and his self-consciously 'Gothic' writings on the one hand, and forward to Morris and his ultimate choice of a harder-edged (Nordic) 'Gothic' over the 'maundering ... mediaevalism' of Tennyson and Rossetti on the other, it seems possible both to reclaim 'Gothic' from critical misuse, and to reposition it as a *zeitgeist* term – a word in the process of becoming, through contestation and self-contradiction, a 'concept', or what the historical-semanticist Reinhart Kosselleck might call a category of historiographical reflection.[90]

The 'Style Historic': William Morris and Late-Victorian Gothic

It was not for the Lake Poets – not for Wordsworth or Coleridge, and still less for Southey – that Morris kept the key role in his narrative of Gothic

---

88 Nick Groom, 'Catachthonic romanticism', p. 120.
89 Richard Adelman, 'Ruskin & gothic literature', *The Wordsworth Circle* 48:3 (Summer 2017): 152–63 (p. 153).
90 See Reinhart Koselleck, *Futures Past*, pp. 75–92. On the expansion of 'Gothic' into a 'critical term' that has 'lost all substance', see also Maurice Lévy, '"Gothic" and the Critical Idiom', in Allan Lloyd Smith and Victor Sage (eds), *Gothick Origins and Innovations* (Amsterdam and Atlanta, GA: Rodopi, 1994), pp. 1–15; and Alexandra Warwick, 'Feeling gothicky?', *Gothic Studies* 9:1 (2007): 5–15.

resumption. Morris's taste in books was for those – as he put it – 'far more important than any literature': 'bibles' that seemed to have 'grown up from the very hearts of the *people*'.[91] Ruskin's *Stones* – 'one of the very few necessary and inevitable utterances of the century' – was evidently such a book.[92] Ruskin had grasped that in 'the element of sensuous pleasure, which is the essence of all true art', lay the intrinsic solution to the problem of 'pain' in 'labour' and the 'general unhappiness and universal degradation' accompanying the economic subjugation of 'material nature'. For to 'feel', as Ruskin put it, 'their souls withering within them ... to be counted off into a heap of mechanism ... – this, humanity for no long time is able to endure'.[93] And from the 'lesson' thus taught 'that art is the expression of man's pleasure in labour', for Morris it followed 'that the hallowing of labour by art is the one aim for us at the present day'.[94] As Ruskin had argued most influentially in his chapter, 'The Nature of Gothic' (1853), this mission for the arts was most entirely expressed in architecture. Not 'merely a science of the rule and compass', it was one of the highest and most distinctively *human* and 'poetic' of the arts: 'more than any other subject of art, the work of man, and the expression of [his] average power ... born of his necessities, and expressive of his nature'.[95] '[T]he common expression of our life', adds Morris the 'practical Socialist'. The 'true architectural work' is a 'harmonious' and all-inclusive 'co-operative ... art': 'a genuine thing'.[96]

Ruskin's 'The Nature of Gothic' may be, as Dinah Birch puts it, 'largely distinct from the historical context of Gothic buildings'.[97] But as Lars Spuybroek urges in 'The Digital Nature of Gothic' (2011), Ruskin forecasts a contemporary programme of 'digital' architecture in the broadest sense. '[I]mplanting craft into machinery' will not mean slowing 'modern' modes of replication to human speeds, but resuming the 'complex motor schema' of Ruskin's 'clumsy ... old Venetian', who works with pre-modern tools in a way productive of both 'imperfection' and 'transfiguration' at once.[98] Extending his reading all the way to the 'cut-and-paste' paradigm of the modern word-processor – essentially contested as it is by

---

91 See Morris, *News from Nowhere*, p. xxix. 92 See Morris, *News from Nowhere*, p. 367.
93 See Ruskin, *Selected Writings*, p. 43. 94 See Morris, *News from Nowhere*, p. 367.
95 See John Ruskin [Kata Phusin], 'The poetry of architecture: no. 1, introduction', *The Architectural Magazine and Journal* 4 (November 1837): 505–8 (p. 505); and Ruskin, *Selected Writings*, p. 56.
96 See Morris, *News from Nowhere*, pp. 331, 345.
97 See Dinah Birch, 'Clarity is Poetry', *Times Literary Supplement*, No. 5985, 15 December 2017 <www.the-tls.co.uk/articles/public/clarity-is-poetry-ruskin/> (last accessed 22 January 2019).
98 Ruskin, *Selected Writings*, pp. 46, 39–41.

Morris's manifesto for a re-creative 'art which we have made our own' – Spuybroek's 'vital' rereading of Ruskin leads towards a reconception of the computer 'not as a machine [but as] a way of positioning ... inside matter itself digital processes of 'stepwise' 'iterative' change.[99] With its failing 'majesty', its 'exhortation' to advance *beyond* mere 'engine-turned' efficiency, Ruskin's account of 'Gothic' is not only 'human' and poetic, but – as Morris put it in his 1892 preface – most characteristically 'ethical and political', indeed inherently social.[100] 'And it is, perhaps', says Ruskin of this 'dignifying' aspect of this 'subject of art',

> the principal admirableness of the Gothic schools of architecture, that they thus receive the results of the labour of inferior minds; and out of fragments full of imperfection, and betraying that imperfection in every touch, indulgently raise up a stately and unaccusable whole.[101]

In his 1889 lecture to the Arts and Crafts Exhibition Society, 'Gothic Architecture', Morris developed Ruskin's relatively static account of 'Gothic' edification into a dynamic vision of the Gothic future. To contrast the sort of 'eclectic' neo-classical architecture 'which is a mere imitation of what was once alive', and that 'organic' style 'which after a development of long centuries has still in it ... capacities for fresh developments', was to discover a way out of the unhistorical, style-less paralysis of the present:

> [W]hen the modern world [comes to] a change as wide and deep as that which destroyed Feudalism ... the style of architecture will have to be historic in the true sense; it will not be able to dispense with tradition; it cannot begin at least with doing something quite different from anything that has been done before; yet ... the form of it ... as well as the spirit, must be Gothic; an organic style cannot spring out of an eclectic one, but only from an organic one. In the future, therefore, our style of architecture must be Gothic Architecture.[102]

Delivered the year before the publication at the Kelmscott Press of his 'Utopian Romance' *News from Nowhere* (1890), it is one measure of the importance that Morris gave to this lecture that he later published it in a Kelmscott edition (1893). And its prime significance is its suggestion of a transformation of 'Gothic' into a prospective idea rather than a merely retrospective or nostalgic form: in Percy Bysshe Shelley's terms, a 'vitally metaphorical' recreation of the closed collocation and given associations of

---

99 Lars Spuybroek, *The Sympathy of Things: Ruskin and the Ecology of Design* (London and New York: Bloomsbury, 2011), pp. 15, 26–9.
100 See Ruskin, *Selected Writings*, pp. 39, 41, 48; and Morris, *News from Nowhere*, p. 369.
101 Ruskin, *Selected Writings*, p. 39.   102 Morris, *News from Nowhere*, pp. 347–8.

'Gothic Architecture'.[103] Those two plain words form Morris's lecture title, and his prediction of the future indeed ends on this common-sense (and, until the 1970s, long-dominant) collocation.[104] But what Morris does in both lecture and romance is to open up a space within the phrase similar to that in the 'dynamical' texts of Carlyle and Southey. As I shall suggest in more detail in a moment, his lecture ends up not really talking about 'Gothic Architecture' at all. The centre of interest lies rather in the space between those two words – in the notion of a 'style ... historic' and 'the future'.

There is an intriguing – and, I would suggest, specifically *Gothic* – temporality on display in Morris's lecture, one which has to do with historical distance and proximity and the contradictions involved in the 'organic' resumption of an artistic practice, cut off from its material and social conditions and contexts. In *News from Nowhere,* set in the London and Oxfordshire of the year 2102, Morris indulges himself in a revenge upon 'complacent' Victorian modernity. It is, the narrator William Guest learns, 'the nineteenth century, of which such big words have been said', that 'count[s] for nothing' among people 'who read Shakespeare and ha[ve] not forgotten the Middle Ages'.[105] The frontispiece of the Kelmscott edition draws similar mental brackets around the 'modern' world, presenting the 'old house' in the 'hereafter' (Fig.4.2) – and the end of the story in the beginning. 'Gothic' seems to lurk – a word on the precipice of becoming an historical concept – in the words of the beautiful but unattainable, gamine grey-eyed Ellen, touching the old grey stone walls of Kelmscott Manor itself: '[L]ovely still amidst all the beauty which these latter days have created', seeming to have 'waited for these happy days, and held in it the gathered crumbs of happiness of the confused and turbulent past.'[106]

---

103 See Percy Bysshe Shelley, 'A Defence of Poetry', in Richard Herne Shepherd (ed.), *The Prose Works of Percy Bysshe Shelley, Vol. II* (London: Chatto & Windus, 1906), pp. 1–38 (p. 4).

104 This is according to a Google Ngram search using the corpus 'English', and with the 'wildcard' function (which finds the 'top ten substitutions' for an asterisk placeholder) and the default 'smoothing' setting (which gives a 'moving average' to make 'trends more apparent') both enabled. Such a search shows the collocation 'Gothic style' overtaking 'Gothic Architecture' around 1969; the trajectory in 2008, the end-date of the corpus, shows the 'style' collocation dipping back beneath 'Architecture'. The research behind the Ngram Viewer is described in Jean-Baptiste Michel, Yuan Kui Shen, Aviva Presser Aiden, Adrian Veres, Matthew K. Gray, William Brockman, The Google Books Team, Joseph P. Pickett, Dale Hoiberg, Dan Clancy, Peter Norvig, Jon Orwant, Steven Pinker, Martin A. Nowak and Erez Lieberman Aiden, 'Quantitative analysis of culture using millions of digitized books', *Science* (14 January 2011), pp. 176–82 [published online 16 December 2010]. See also <http://books.google.com/ngrams> (last accessed 5 March 2020).

105 Morris, *News from Nowhere,* p. 84.   106 Morris, *News from Nowhere,* p. 220.

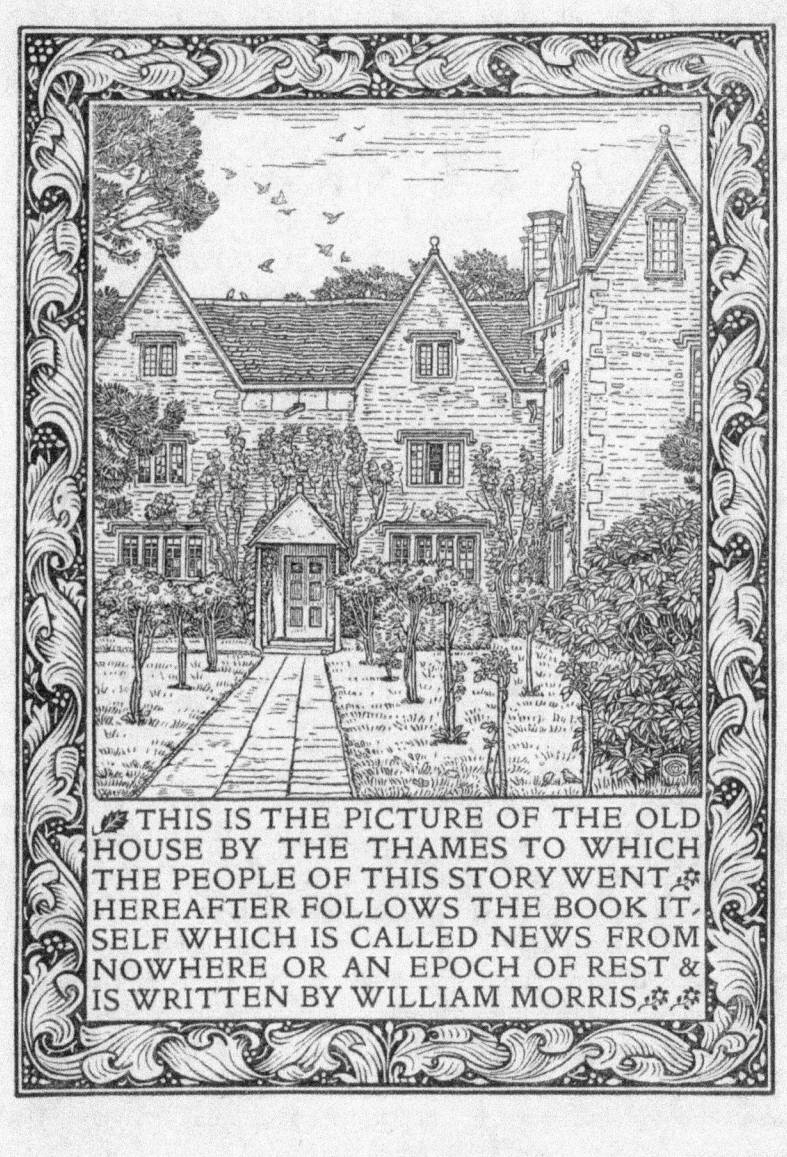

Fig.4.2: The old house in the hereafter. William Morris (and W. H. Hooper and C. M. Gere), Frontispiece to *News from Nowhere*, the Kelmscott Press edition of 1890. The Trustees of the British Museum.

This casting of the modern world as the true 'dark age' generates pathos and a pleasing historical 'shape', picking up on Ruskin's own classification of the historical sense into 'Classicalism, Mediaevalism, and Modernism', with 'medievalism' as the middling 'Gothic form'. But the access of historiographical pathos comes at the cost of opening Morris's desired Gothic resumption to the same charge of 'simulation' that he levels at neo-classicism. The 'brick box' nineteenth century being, by Morris's own account, almost as profoundly cut off from the 'graceful ... fourteenth-century type' of architecture as was the 'New Birth' from classical Rome and Greece, how could his Gothic Architecture be anything other than a rehearsal of dead 'forms' without their animating 'spirit'?[107] How was it, indeed, anything other than a re-tread of the same overly historicist 'tendency' that, as Nietzsche would put it, ultimately 'directed the Italians of the Renaissance' away from 'the fresh life of the present' and towards dust-heap-raking antiquarian irrelevance?[108]

The idea of a 'style ... historic in the true sense' seems to be Morris's solution to the problem. In *News from Nowhere*, the buildings of the new society 'embrace the best qualities of the Gothic of northern Europe' and of 'the Saracenic and Byzantine'.[109] But they do so without any 'copying'. The architecture of 2102 is thus not Gothic in particular 'historical' 'form', but in underlying historical identity – so as, ironically, much better to deserve the apparently forgotten name. There are only four uses of the word 'Gothic' in the text, and all of them are Guest's. 'Gothic' is thus simultaneously a governing trope and a term almost entirely unheard in Morris's 'new society'. The architecture of the early twenty-second century seems more in keeping with Charles Voysey's Colwall (1893) (Fig.4.3) and the 'general period flavour' somehow distilled from the 'period detail little ... kept', than even with Morris's own rebuttal of Puginesque 'gimcrack' 'Historicism' at his and Philip Webb's Red House (1859–60; see Fig.4.4).[110] Coming unexpectedly upon a 'whole mass of architecture', organically 'amidst' and 'bor[n]e upon' 'the pleasant fields' – as if Morris's ideally insular house-and-garden had been turned inside-out to make a whole garden-society – Guest finds himself transported far beyond the degraded 'modern' present, feeling the future in the weirdly nostalgic instant: he 'chuckle[s] for pleasure' at the sight, and feels

---

107 Morris, *News from Nowhere*, pp. 344, 226.
108 Nietzsche, 'On the Uses and Disadvantages of History for Life', pp. 73, 75.
109 Morris, *News from Nowhere*, p. 62.
110 See Nikolaus Pevsner, *An Outline of European Architecture*, revised edition (Layton, Utah: Gibbs Smith, 2009), p. 209; and MacCarthy, *A Life for Our Time*, pp. 45, 155, 353.

Fig.4.3: From symbolic historicism to historical feel. Charles Francis Annesley Voysey, Designs for Perrycroft, Jubilee Drive, Colwall, Herefordshire: north and east elevations (1st preliminary design). RIBA Collections.

'fairly ... as if I were alive in the fourteenth century'.[111] The historiographical equivalent of the 'dolly zoom', Morris's continual paralleling of 'the Mediaevals' and the people of Nowhere on the basis of an equally sharpened 'sense of architectural power' generates a prospect of open-ended futurity that is not one of alterity and anxiety, but strange familiarity and *rest*. In the words of the summative statement given by his historical interpreter and guide, old Hammond, this is a future-past not of vanished horizons of expectation, but rather of what Southey, writing at his most Wordsworthian, had called the 'palingenesis', the far-flung archaising renewal, or circuitous voyage forward into the past:

> This is how we stand. England was once a country of clearings amongst the woods and wastes, with a few towns interspersed, which were fortresses for the feudal army, markets for the folk, gathering places for craftsmen. It then became a country of huge and foul workshops and fouler gambling-dens,

[111] See Morris, *News from Nowhere*, pp. 105, 62.

Fig.4.4: As if alive in the thirteenth century. Martin Charles, Exterior view of William Morris and Philip Speakman Webb's Red House, Bexleyheath, London. RIBA Collections.

surrounded by an ill-kept, poverty-stricken farm, pillaged by the masters of the workshops. It is now a garden, where nothing is wasted and nothing is spoilt, with the necessary dwellings, sheds, and workshops scattered up and down the country, all trim and neat and pretty.[112]

112 Morris, *News from Nowhere*, p. 105.

'Gothic' thus features in *Nowhere*, like the 'art' that old Hammond says is now so 'necessarily' bound up with all production as to have 'no name amongst us', or the 'book-learned' 'history' that young Hammond can barely comprehend ('when a person can read, of course he reads what he likes to'), as a word in progressive litotic mood: self-cancelling and self-realising; withdrawing, like Voysey's Colway, from historic*ist* detail into historic*al* self-actualisation.[113]

Morris's contemporary lecture on 'Gothic Architecture' thus needs to be understood in the context of a sort of creative forgetting, a phasing-out *and* reconsecration, of the profaned word and collocation – which had peaked in English usage in the mid-to-late 1840s and again from the late 1860s up to around 1876.[114] The printing of the lecture in the Kelmscott Press series in 1893 – in black and red, on paper and on vellum, the press's first 16mo pocket-size edition – was part and parcel of an implicit programme of cultural revalidation. The 'master-art' of 'Architecture' had also been handled in precisely this way in Morris's early lecture, 'The Lesser Arts' (1877), as a name almost too sacred to be spoken. Refusing to 'meddle', Morris could 'scarcely ... more than ... echo' the Gothic chapter in Ruskin's *Stones*, and repeat that the seeds of social and industrial malaise lay in the contemporary 'divorce' of all the '*popular*', 'decorative' arts from architecture, painting and sculpture. But the way forward was the way back. 'Let us', Morris had urged, study to become unstudied, approaching the art of the ancients 'wisely': so as to be 'taught by it, kindled by it; all the while determining not to imitate or repeat it; to have either no art at all, or an art which we have made our own'.[115]

Speaking before his Socialist 'conversion', and expecting only 'to see in time' and perhaps not with 'our own eyes' the face of such a change, Morris in 1877 had prophesied first the 'death of all' arts, followed – as he conceded it was his 'comfort' to believe – by a re-birth from 'some tradition, some memory of the past', saved in the face of hopeless odds, from brutalising mechanical industry on the one hand, and the 'Lie' of 'restoration' on the other, by the defenders of the arts.[116] This was a catastrophic rather than an incremental or a dialectical vision. But it was – as Morris himself later implicitly conceded – more an 'echo' of Ruskin, and the binds and crutches of his tragically declining 'old buildings', used earlier the same year in the

---

113 Morris, *News from Nowhere*, p. 160.
114 According to the Google Ngram search detailed in note 104 above.
115 Morris, *News from Nowhere*, p. 244.   116 Morris, *News from Nowhere*, p. 244.

founding circular of the SPAB, than Morris's own vision.[117] And if the time-signature of Ruskin was thus the stop-gap *and* the *longue durée* – 'stay it ... where it declines; do not care about the unsightliness of the aid ... and many a generation will still be born and pass away beneath its shadow' – Morris after his 'conversion', and specifically in the 1889 lecture on 'Gothic Architecture', was obliged to give practical consideration of transformation, of means to ends. 'In the future ... ' he (almost) concludes, suggesting with the phrase both 'going forwards' and 'in the end', and hinting at the possible legitimacy of an initial phase of Gothic 'copying', distinct from the mere 'imitation' of neo-classicism. The way has already been prepared for this suggestion by oblique phrasing that seems to pull in a direction opposite to its content, so as to mime the induction of a fresh creative energy: the art of the future 'cannot begin at least *with* doing something quite different from anything that has been done before'.

The 'historic' character of Morris's resumed Gothic, it might be said, then, consists in its double time-signature, the backward-looking futurity of *departing from* the 'form' and 'style' of what has gone before. Morris thus produces an imaginable future out of the transumptive sense of the Gothic Revival – not quite present in Ruskin or Pugin, and more nearly there in Carlyle, writing after Southey – that a yet *better* spirit lies in waiting in the external forms of a reinvented tradition.

Coda

This chapter has been a story of the Gothic twice told and told backwards both ways. So I would like to conclude by briefly telling it forwards, moving towards William Morris from Robert Southey. In his thirteenth 'Colloquy', Southey's odd blend of antiquarianism and ghost story produces what I have called a sort of midwinter spring of Victorian medievalism. The ghost of Thomas More joins Montesinos overlooking a cotton mill beside the river Greta, which, 'with the dwelling-houses and other buildings appertaining to such an establishment', forms a settlement for which English has no word, but which inevitably 'reminds one of a convent'.[118] Invited to contemplate and compare the cotton mill and the convent, the 'hopeful' figure of Montesinos applies his 'great scale' of historical 'improvement'.[119] At different 'times and places', each

---

117 See Peter Faulkner, 'Ruskin and Morris', *Journal of the William Morris Society* 14:1 (2000): 6–17 (p. 11).
118 Southey, *Sir Thomas More*, p. 296.   119 Southey, *Sir Thomas More*, pp. 16, 390.

institution may promote or 'retard' 'progress'.[120] The 'manufacturing system' embodied in the mill is part of a continuous historical process from the sixteenth century, remaking the 'means' and 'men' previously 'devoured', as More had put it in *Utopia*, by enclosure and sheep farming.[121] Southey's Sir Thomas replies with a more timeless view of good and evil: 'Bad as the feudal times were, they were less injurious than these commercial ones to the kindly and generous feelings of human nature, and far, far more favourable to the principles of honour and integrity.'[122]

Between these statements, the 'prospect' nevertheless emerges of 'feudal times' being reconstituted in commercial society. This was a form of time for which, like the 'establishment' beside the Greta, English had as yet no word. 'Mediaeval' had only entered general usage in the 1820s, after being first attested in the peak-Gothic year of 1817, and 'mediaevalism' would not appear until a year after Southey's death, in 1844.[123] Southey actually wrote a review of the work in which 'mediaeval' first appeared.[124] But he seems never to have used the adjective himself, continuing in *Colloquies* and in his other works of the 1820s and 1830s to speak in more nominal terms of 'the middle ages', 'old times', the 'old English heart' and 'antiquity' in general.[125] This near-miss between Southey and the category of 'the medieval' may have been merely accidental. But in context, and bearing in mind the rapid senescence of the term, as in Morris's reference to 'maundering ...

---

120 Southey, *Sir Thomas More*, p. 296.   121 Southey, *Sir Thomas More*, pp. 41–4.
122 Southey, *Sir Thomas More*, p. 298.
123 See David Matthews, 'From mediaeval to medievalism: a new semantic history', *The Review of English Studies* 62:257 (November 2011): 695–715 (pp. 701, 705).
124 The word 'mediaeval' is first attested in Thomas Dudley Fosbrooke's *British Monachism: or, Manners and Customs of the Monks and Nuns of England*, 2nd edition, 2 vols (London: John Nichols, 1817), vol. 1, p. vi. See also Matthews, 'From mediaeval to medievalism', p. 701. Southey reviewed Fosbrooke's 1817 edition, having long owned and admired the 1802 first edition, in an essay published in the *Quarterly Review* in 1819. See 'British monachism' in *Quarterly Review* 22:43 (July 1819), pp. 59–102; and *Collected Letters of Robert Southey*, letters nos. 2494, 3149, 3197, 3335. 'Mediaeval' is already a capacious term in Fosbrooke's usage, used to describe variously 'customs', 'principles', 'fashions' and 'Architecture' (Fosbrooke, pp. vi, 18, 273). Southey's review describes Fosbrooke's book as 'a great store of curious and recondite information', which displays 'in the liveliness of [its] expression ... a vigorous and original mind' (p. 94n). But the new coinage of 'mediaeval' – a fairly simple matter of code-switching from the Latin *'medium aevum'*, as Matthews points out (p. 702) – goes unnoticed.
125 Southey's Anglican history in *The Book of the Church* (1824) describes the hope of 'every sound old English heart' in the early reign of Charles II 'that the constitution of their fathers, in Church, as well as in State, was now to be restored'. See Robert Southey, *The Book of the Church*, 2 vols (London: John Murray, 1824), vol. 2, p. 475. See also *Sir Thomas More*, pp. 112, 54, 242.

mediaevalism', the disconnection seems symptomatic of the sort of distinction in feeling for the past that this chapter has sought to recover. What David Matthews in his 'new semantic history' refers to as the greater neutrality and nicely delimiting periodicity of 'medieval' is, at its root, the 'modern' antithesis of the 'Gothic' historical perspective of Southey and the Lake Poets.[126] This is the 'catacthonic' or 'intra-historical' perspective of the inborn 'immensity' yet-remembered, the 'history' with 'no beginning' adumbrated by Wordsworth in the 'Intimations Ode' and in book two of the 1805 *Prelude* (ll. 109, 134; ll. 369, 237–8). It is the view that Coleridge, referring back beyond Edmund Burke's 'prescription' to Edward Coke's 'common-law' or 'immemorial' doctrine of usage 'time out of mind', phrased in terms of the gathering 'history of the Idea' and the 'potential' and 'latency' of an 'insular', 'self-evolving Constitution'.[127] And it is the historical orientation underpinning Southey's language, rejecting John Milner's charge of having misrepresented 'every vulgar superstition' as a Catholic doctrine, that he regarded not as present-day Catholic 'theory' but rather 'historical facts', being concerned to trace what the Roman Church's 'practice' '*has always been*' (my italics).[128] The very form of the *Colloquies*, staking out a space for a dialogue between ages, pre-emptively rejects any conception of the 'medieval' as the bad old – or even Carlyle's 'deep-buried' – past.[129] Indeed, nostalgia for 'feudal times' is clearly already beginning to turn into something much closer to John Ruskin's dynamic and recuperative force of 'mediaeva*lism*', as Southey's Sir Thomas asks his Montesinos: 'May not the manufacturing system be ... tending to work out, by means of the very excess to which it is carried, a remedy for the evils which it has brought with it?'[130] And Montesinos replies by envisioning just such a 'remedial process ... going on':

> [P]erhaps ... were time allowed ... we might then hope for a palingenesia, a restoration of national sanity and strength, a second birth ... perhaps, I say

---

[126] See Matthews, 'From Mediaeval to Medievalism', pp. 700, 704; and Matthews, *Medievalism: A Critical History*, p. 53; and see also my account of Wordsworth and the 'Gothic' political tradition in Tom Duggett, *Gothic Romanticism*, passim but especially pp. 19–20, 32–5, 102–6.

[127] See Samuel Taylor Coleridge, *On the Constitution of the Church and State*, edited by John Colmer (London and Princeton, NJ: Routledge & Kegan Paul, Princeton University Press, 1976), pp. 21–31, 85–103; Smith, *The Gothic Bequest*, pp. 3–12, 39–40, 92; Sean Silver, 'The Politics of Gothic Historiography, 1660-1800', in Glennis Byron and Dale Townshend (eds), *The Gothic World* (Abingdon and New York: Routledge, 2014), pp. 3–14 (p. 9).

[128] See Stuart Andrews, *Robert Southey: History, Politics, Religion* (New York: Palgrave Macmillan, 2011), pp. 122–33.

[129] Carlyle, *Past and Present*, p. 52.   [130] Southey, *Sir Thomas More*, pp. 297–8.

... and were time allowed ... for I say this doubtfully, and that ghostly shake of the head with which it is received does not lessen the melancholy distrust wherewith it is expressed.[131]

The hesitations and ellipses mime the effect of ghostly apparition. Montesinos falters in his speech at Sir Thomas's 'ghostly shake of the head'. Thus registering what Wordsworth's 1821 sonnet 'Mutability' calls 'the unimaginable touch of time', the simultaneous 'drop' and 'sustain' of 'outward forms', of ancient 'towers' in 'silent air', Southey at the heart of the *Colloquies* opens the way towards the transfiguring vision of Morris's *Nowhere*: the recrudescence within – or *after* – 'modernity' of the Gothic past, a genuine 'second birth' rather than a merely formal after-echo of old England.[132] Albeit that this will be a cultural rebirth of 'doubt' and 'melancholy', rather than of naïve religion or simple faith; the revivalism of the less deceived.

---

131 Southey, *Sir Thomas More*, p. 298.
132 See William Wordsworth, *Sonnet Series and Itinerary Poems, 1819–1850*, edited by Geoffrey Jackson (Ithaca, NY: Cornell University Press, 2004), p. 197.

2.5

Nineteenth-Century Gothic Architectural Aesthetics: A. W. N. Pugin, John Ruskin and William Morris

ALEXANDRA WARWICK

On the evening of 16 October 1834 fire broke out in the Palace of Westminster, London, the complex of buildings that housed the chambers and offices of Parliament. Watched by huge crowds, the fire burned until early the next morning, destroying most of the site, including the House of Lords, the House of Commons and its Library, and considerable portions of St Stephen's Chapel. Only Westminster Hall and some other medieval parts of the Palace were saved. On the following day *The Times* described the fire as 'a spectacle of terrible beauty' and continued:

> For the Houses of Parliament, their ruin through such agency will, of course, be felt as an afflicting accident by all Englishmen who appreciate them according to the high political and national ends to which they have through many ages, with more or less useful ministration, been made tributary: but they rank not among the finer specimens of art, nor are identified, as are the Hall and the Abbey of Westminster, almost as much with the material frame of England, as with her historical and moral grandeur.

The author concluded with a wish that rebuilding might be 'made in a style harmonizing with the original building, instead of exhibiting a heterogeneous mass of architectural erections, in which taste, chronology and convenience, were equally set at naught'.[1] A Select Committee was appointed to consider reconstruction, and in June 1835 it recommended that a design competition should be held, specifying that designs submitted should be either 'Gothic or Elizabethan' in style.[2]

Among the observers of the fire was one who also recognised the spectacle as sublime, calling it in a letter to the architect and antiquary Edward James

---

1 Anon., 'London, Friday, October 17, 1834', *The Times*, p. 2.
2 Chris Brooks, *The Gothic Revival* (London: Phaidon, 1999), p. 206.

Willson 'truly curious & awfully grand', but finding, in his poorly written and punctuated style, that there was 'nothing much to regret & a great deal to rejoice in. a vast quantity of Soanes mixtures & Wyatts heresies have been effectually consigned to oblivion ... the old walls stood triumphantly amidst this scene of ruin'.[3] The rejoicing observer was none other than Augustus Welby Northmore Pugin, seeing the triumph of the medieval 'old walls' and the destruction of the recent 'mixtures' and 'heresies' of the Georgian architects John Soane and James Wyatt. Pugin the Younger would come to play an important part in the development of Gothic, in the rebuilding of Parliament and in the intense debates about what should properly constitute 'the material frame of England'.

The destruction of the Houses of Parliament could hardly have been a more obvious emblem of the moment. The aftershocks of the European and American Revolutions of the late eighteenth century continued to disrupt British politics and culture, and many of the effects of the Industrial Revolution were already starkly apparent across the countryside and in the new towns and cities. There was a palpable sense of historical rupture: as Thomas Carlyle put it in 1829, the signs of the times pointed to 'a mighty change in our whole manner of existence'.[4] Parliament had reacted; the 1820s and 1830s saw a series of legislative changes, including the Roman Catholic Relief Act (1829); the Great Reform Act (1832); the Abolition of Slavery (1833) and the much-hated Poor Law Amendment Act (1834). The fire was seen by some as a higher judgement on Parliament, even as a repeal of its more unpopular Acts, or as a chance for further reform for those who thought the 1832 Act insufficient. Carlyle, another observer of the fire, noted the crowd's response: '"A judgement for the Poor Law Bill!" – "There go their acts!" Such exclamations seemed to be the prevailing ones. A man sorry I did not anywhere see.'[5]

The parliamentary design competition, then, was pitched into the heart of the debate about Britain's present and future, and its relationship to its past, what Carlyle would articulate as the 'Condition of England' question. In the early decades of the nineteenth century, Pugin was convinced that Gothic was the answer to that question and, after Pugin, John Ruskin was equally convinced of the same. By the 1880s

---

3 Margaret Belcher (ed.), *The Letters of A. W. N. Pugin, 1830–1842*, 5 vols (Oxford: Oxford University Press, 2001) vol. 1, p. 42. Pugin's spelling and punctuation retained.
4 [Thomas Carlyle], 'Signs of the times', *Edinburgh Review*, 49 (1829): 439–59 (p. 444).
5 Caroline Shenton, *The Day Parliament Burned Down* (Oxford: Oxford University Press, 2012), p. 131.

William Morris, although for rather different reasons, asserted Socialism as the 'fourth stage' of the Gothic Revival, again passionately believing that the Gothic style was the past, the present and the future of England. It is a measure of the imbrication of architecture in particular with questions of the contemporary that the term 'Victorian' is used for the first time in relation to it. Before Victoria had even been crowned, an article discussing London architecture concluded with the 'hope that the Victorian æra will give a new name to a new, a national, and a noble style of architecture'.[6]

The struggle for a 'Victorian Architecture' was thus already well under way when the competition for the rebuilding of the Houses of Parliament was announced in 1835, but the confident designation of 'Gothic or Elizabethan' belied the clarity with which either of those terms was understood. Despite the subtitle of the second edition of Horace Walpole's *The Castle of Otranto*, 'A Gothic Story', it is worth noting that, in the late eighteenth and nineteenth centuries, 'Gothic' was not primarily a literary genre at all. Antiquarian collections such as Thomas Percy's *Reliques of Ancient English Poetry* (1765), or literary criticism such as Richard Hurd's *Letters on Chivalry and Romance* (1762) had begun to designate 'Gothic' as particularly English, the name for a deep-seated imaginative tendency characterised by a natural inventiveness that was different from the orderly Classical forms, and evident in its native writers such as Edmund Spenser or William Shakespeare. However, the term was very rarely used to refer to contemporary literary productions, and never applied to those works, like Bram Stoker's *Dracula* (1897), that twentieth-century criticism has identified so closely with it. It is William Morris's writing that is most often described as 'Gothic' in the nineteenth century, while more recent criticism never places him in this tradition. Partly because of the work of Pugin and Ruskin, 'Gothic' in the nineteenth century referred instead principally to architecture and its associated crafts.

The history of architecture at the time was patchy, as the valorisation of Classical models since the Renaissance had meant that only in the later eighteenth century had anyone begun systematically collecting examples of medieval work. Gothic had long been thought of just as the orderless 'other' to the Classical style: as Roger North defined 'Gothick' in 1695, it was often

6 Kelly J. Mays, 'How the Victorians un-invented themselves: architecture, the battle of the styles, and the history of the term "Victorian"', *Journal of Victorian Culture* 19:1 (2014): 1–23 (p. 14).

thought to comprise 'all that is not Regular'.⁷ New 'Gothic' buildings, such as William Kent's designs for Esher Place (1733), Surrey, or the 'gothicising' of Alnwick Castle, Northumberland, by James Paine, Daniel Garett and Robert Adam (from 1756), were improvised on an eclectic range of sources. Walpole's Strawberry Hill (1749–76) was the first to be based on copies of actual medieval structures, but it too came to be seen as embarrassingly inauthentic in design and materials – a stagy 'heap of inconsistencies', as A. W. N. Pugin's father, Auguste Charles Pugin or Pugin the Elder, put it.⁸ Medieval architecture was rather like the 'Middle Ages' themselves, conceived of as having no characteristics of their own, and being instead simply the period of time between the fall of the Roman Empire and the recovery of Classical culture in the Renaissance. In the mid-eighteenth century, attempts at systematising Gothic began with Batty Langley's widely derided *Ancient Architecture Restored, and Improved* (1741–2) and continued through the second edition of Thomas Warton's *Observations on the Fairy Queen of Spenser* (1754; 1762) and collections of engravings of medieval architecture. In 1807 John Britton published the first volume of *The Architectural Antiquities of Great Britain*. The series ran until 1827 and, like Walter's Scott's historical novels, showed a more detailed panorama of the life of the past than had been the case with earlier antiquarian collections of isolated examples or objects. In 1811 John Milner proposed three identifiable phases of the Gothic 'Pointed' style, and in 1817 Thomas Rickman published his *An Attempt to Discriminate the Styles of English Architecture, from the Conquest to the Reformation*, renaming the phases the Norman, Early English, Decorated English and Perpendicular English.

There are several things emerging in these texts, most obviously a distinction between the Gothic fantasy of someone like Walpole, on the one hand, and an historical or 'archaeological' medievalism on the other. The first use of the word 'medieval' is in 1817,⁹ a term that was self-consciously proposed as an alternative to the 'Gothic' Middle Ages, and a coinage that suggested that the period was now coming to be thought of as having its own distinct features. This is partly the product and partly the fuel of a new sense of history and a more acute consciousness of the present. The Gothic is crucial

---

7 Howard M. Colvin and John Newman (eds), *Of Building: Roger North's Writings on Architecture* (Oxford: Clarendon, 1981), p. 111.
8 Auguste Charles Pugin and Edward J. Willson, *Specimens of Gothic Architecture Selected From Various Ancient Edifices in England*, 2 vols (London: J. Taylor, 1821–3), vol. 1, p. xiv.
9 Michael Alexander, *Medievalism: The Middle Ages in Modern England* (New Haven and London: Yale University Press, 2007), p. 73.

to this because of its relation to time. No one, enthusiast, critic or neutral, ever contests that Gothic is historical, or indeed modern; that is, of the time in which it is made. This is in contrast to the Greek and Roman Classical or 'ancient', which is conceived of as *timeless*, its eternal values transcending history. Much of the contest between Gothic and Classical thus revolves around the question of whether Classical values were indeed appropriate for the newness of the age, or whether the dynamic relation of the medieval to its own historical moments represented a continuity of progressive spirit capable of reinvention in modernity. The Goths' arguments emphasised the living, fluid and progressive character of Gothic against the rigid, static values of the ancient. Gothic has meaning precisely because it expresses its time, whenever that time is.

Equally, they argue, Gothic expresses its place. In the early nineteenth-century publications there is increasing identification of Gothic with Britain (or more usually England) and an insistence that a new national style should be one reclaimed from England's past. 'Gothic or Elizabethan', then, signifies history and politics as well as architectural style. It points to the question of the character and constitution of the 'English' people and their relation to foreign conquerors and kings. As Rosemary Jann notes, the Civil Wars of the seventeenth century had depended upon the issue of whether history sanctioned the supremacy of the king or Parliament.[10] Gothic, in this argument, is the democratic political organisation of the original Teutonic tribes of Britain, threatened successively by Roman and other invaders, William the Conqueror and lines of kings asserting a divine right of rule. As a parliamentarian stated in 1645, 'Nor can any nation on earth shew so much of the ancient Gothique Law as this island hath'. The pre-Roman Britons were 'a free people, governed by laws, and those made not ... by great men, but by the people'.[11] Various political positions interpreted this Gothic liberty differently. Jann outlines the development of Whig history in the nineteenth century, which relied upon the assertion of a heritage of Gothic democracy in which monarchy is constrained by parliamentary law and the will of the people. For Whigs, the success of Victorian Britain was the proof of the wisdom of its evolution of a government balanced between freedom and constraint, whereas the example of France showed the terrible effects of the

---

[10] Rosemary Jann, 'Democratic myths in Victorian medievalism', *Browning Institute Studies* 8 (1980): 129–49 (p. 130).

[11] Samuel Kliger, 'The "Goths" in England: an introduction to the gothic vogue in eighteenth-century aesthetic discussion', *Modern Philology* 43:2 (1945): 107–17 (pp. 107, 112).

revolutionary seizure of liberty from unchecked monarchy. For conservatives like the Young England movement of the 1840s, feudal hierarchical order guaranteed the freedom of the people, but for socialists like Morris, such freedom could only be attained by equality. Nineteenth-century medievalism continues to play out the tensions of political Gothic, not least in the rebuilt Houses of Parliament, whose floor-plan holds in permanent parallel the traditions of feudal authority and Gothic liberty, an architectural structure in which the people are simultaneously subjects whose rights are concessions and fellow-citizens whose rights are inherent.[12]

The Gothic aesthetics of Pugin, Ruskin and Morris, then, are a critical part of the Condition of England question and the pervading consciousness that this was an unprecedented moment in history. The question of their influence on one another is complex: Pugin appears to have had little interest in Ruskin[13] and Ruskin was dismissive of Pugin, calling him 'one of the smallest possible or conceivable architects'.[14] Morris venerated Ruskin's work, especially his essay on 'The Nature of Gothic' from *The Stones of Venice* (1851–3), which he called 'one of the very few necessary and inevitable utterances of the century',[15] but only later in his life did Ruskin appear to value Morris.[16] Morris rarely mentions Pugin, even in his lectures on the Gothic Revival. Despite this, and despite their differing conceptions of the definition and meaning of Gothic, they all share an absolute conviction that architecture *does* have meaning and that architecture is the most important sign of the spiritual, moral and political health and progress of the societies that produce it. Each believed that architecture did not simply indicate, but that it was *part* of that which it indicated, that the material is a part of an otherwise invisible order to which it refers. In this it resembles Samuel Taylor Coleridge's idea of the living symbol that, he says, 'always partakes of the Reality which it renders intelligible, and while it enunciates the whole, abides itself a living part in that Unity, of which it is the representative'.[17] For Pugin, Ruskin and Morris, architecture and design are symbolic in the same sense, not merely

---

12 Brooks, *Revival*, p. 219.
13 Rosemary Hill, *God's Architect: Pugin and the Building of Romantic Britain* (London: Allen Lane, 2007), p. 459.
14 E. T. Cook and Alexander Wedderburn (eds), *The Works of John Ruskin*, 39 vols (London: George Allen, 1903–12), vol. 9, p. 438.
15 William Morris, Preface to Kelmscott edition, *The Nature of Gothic* (London: George Allen, 1892), p. i.
16 Derrick Leon, *Ruskin, the Great Victorian* (London: Routledge and Kegan Paul, 1949), p. 577.
17 Samuel Taylor Coleridge, *The Statesman's Manual* (London: Gale and Jenner, 1816), p. 30.

representative or metaphorical, but a living part of a greater unity. For all three, the terms 'living' and 'life' are central, and while for its critics Gothic is moribund because the past is dead, for revivalists it is a vital and living force, albeit one in need of urgent attention.

A. W. N. Pugin

In January 1836 Charles Barry was announced as the winner of the Houses of Parliament competition. Pugin had produced the Gothic drawings for Barry's submission and had already taken a vigorous part in the flurry of pamphlets and open letters on style that intensified after the competition's announcement. In a pamphlet of 1835, for example, he finds Christopher Wren's Classical remodelling of St Paul's, London, inferior to medieval cathedrals, denouncing all other 'half-English, half-Pagan erections' and ending with the hope that 'Anglo-Greek will shortly cease to exist'.[18] In 1836 he published *Contrasts*, a book whose subtitle, '*a parallel between the noble edifices of the fourteenth and fifteenth centuries, and similar buildings of the present day; shewing the present decay of taste*', left no doubt as to his position. *Contrasts* is a work enabled by literary antiquarianism, Walter Scott's historical fiction and the architectural topographies of the late eighteenth and early nineteenth centuries. It relies upon a full sense of life in the past, especially on the daily life of people, and not, as had the eighteenth-century literary Gothic, on extreme experience or its architecture as an assemblage of antique curiosities. *Contrasts* is a fierce polemic, and a recognisable contribution to the genre that Carlyle called 'Götzism', after Goethe's *Götz von Berlichingen* (1773) in which a last relic of medieval heroism is shown in contrast to degraded modern society. As its title suggests, *Contrasts* systematically juxtaposes pairs of medieval and contemporary images. In an image of the present, a small boy is driven away from a flimsy, locked water pump inscribed with the names of its donors – watched by an officer lounging in the doorway of a police station. The contrast of 1479, however, is a large, beautiful drinking fountain, not the self-aggrandising gift of wealthy men but part of the communal space where a man stands upright, refreshing himself, unmolested by petty officialdom. These medieval contrasts emphasise the integrated social life of the people, and Gothic as a form for living.

When *Contrasts* was published the arguments between Goths and Classicists were already entrenched, each side often accusing the other of

18 Belcher (ed.), *Letters*, vol. 1, p. 52.

the same failings: dark, ugly, liable to attract dirt, expensive, not properly 'English' and not appropriate for a modern state.[19] But what is implicit or explicit in many of the arguments, however, is one of the fundamental difficulties of medievalism itself. Behind the rhetoric of nationality and taste lay the awkward realisation that Britain's medieval past was Catholic. Catholicism was still seen by some as a persistently threatening foreign force, further complicated by the fact that the vast majority of Catholics in England were poor immigrants from Ireland.[20] The Roman Catholic Relief Act of 1829 had removed most of the disenfranschising legislation, but anti-Catholic feeling still ran high and often burst into verbal and physical violence as the revival of elements of pre-Reformation Christianity gathered theological strength in Tractarianism and the Oxford Movement, and architectural expression in the Camden Society. The reinstatement of some pre-Reformation tenets and liturgical practices, along with 'restoration' of church interiors, produced a 'High Church' Anglo-Catholicism within the Church of England. More scandalously, it also produced some converts to the Church of Rome, most notably in 1845 John Henry Newman, who had published the first of the *Tracts for the Times* in 1833.

Pugin recorded his own conversion to Catholicism on 6 June 1835: 'Finished alterations at Chapel received into Holy Catholic Church.'[21] The laconic note understates the strength of his conviction, but also indicates how absolutely inseparable faith and architecture are for him. Earlier he had written to a friend, 'I feel perfectly convinced the roman Catholick church is the only true one—and the only one in which the grand & sublime style of church architecture can ever be restored.'[22] His letter shows his conviction, but it also reveals Pugin's naïvety about the politics of Catholicism. He was to become embroiled in the painful and sometimes bitter complexities of Roman versus Anglo-Catholicism, disputes with Newman (who disliked both Pugin and Gothic) and others, and actually endangered during the papal aggression crisis of 1850.[23] The course of his historical/religious education parallels the course of his development in Gothic architecture: he revises his position on both. In the first edition of *Contrasts* he pinpoints the Reformation as an attack on true religion that led ultimately to the material

---

19 See, for example, Anon., 'Article VIII', *Edinburgh Review* 65:131 (1837): 174–9 (p. 131) and Anon., 'Article III', *Quarterly Review* 58:115 (1837): 61–82 (p. 115).
20 See Edward R. Norman, *The English Catholic Church in the Nineteenth Century* (Oxford: Clarendon, 1984).
21 Hill, *God's Architect*, p. 144.   22 Hill, *God's Architect*, p. 121.
23 Hill, *God's Architect*, p. 449.

expression of spiritual degradation in architecture. In the second edition of 1841, he recognises in a new Preface that his original argument was 'indistinctly developed'. He restates his claim that Gothic 'was produced in England by the Catholic faith' and that it was 'destroyed in England by the ascendancy of Protestantism', but now believes that he was wrong in treating Protestantism 'as the primary cause instead of [it] being the effect of some other powerful agency' which was the decayed state of faith throughout Europe that allowed the two 'monsters of revived Paganism and Protestantism' to gain a footing.[24] He sees Christian faith as an energetic force, its weakening causing the distorted outgrowth of Protestantism. Protestantism is thus not an evil opposition, but an energy that has become diverted from its natural course. The cure is not to kill the monster but to reclaim its vigour for the true faith; Gothic is both the means and the manifestation of such restoration.

Pugin added two more plates to the 1841 edition, both showing an even more developed notion of the fully 'living' society. Where the 1836 Contrasts had views of single buildings and monuments seen from ground level, the two new plates, 'Contrasted Residences of the Poor' and 'Catholic Town of 1440 versus the same town in 1840', are bird's- (or God's-)eye views of whole settlements. The first is a clear criticism of the Poor Law Amendment Act of 1834. As had others, such as Charles Dickens in *Oliver Twist* (1837–9), Pugin picks out the notorious elements: the lack of food, disrespectful treatment of the dead, corruption of officials and separation of families. In the contrasted towns, the town of 1840 is very obviously an English one, containing gas and iron works, an asylum, a 'Socialist Hall of Science' a town hall and a number of nondescript chapels. It is shown as an atomised society, with the various functions of society divided and housed in box-like buildings, whereas in 1440, music, worship, care of the poor and sick, governance, intellectual and artistic pursuits are all carried out together in the integrated religious institutions. Stiff, blunt vertical and horizontal lines describe the divided society; in 1440 the lines are in movement: branching, arching and tapering into the infinite sky. By 1840 the sky has become just a space into which the industrial chimneys void their waste.

In 1841 Pugin published *The True Principles of Pointed or Christian Architecture*, followed in 1843 by *An Apology for the Revival of Christian Architecture in England*, firmly aligning Catholicism, Christianity, Gothic and, significantly, England with one another, and declaring in a letter of

---

24 A. W. N. Pugin, *Contrasts*, 2nd revised edition (London: Charles Dolman, 1841), p. iv.

1841, 'I will never perpetrate anything foreign in England again... the revival of our national antiquities must be our cry.'[25] Pugin lays claim to Christianity by making it synonymous with Gothic and then firmly places the Gothic in England. For Pugin, 'true principles' are simultaneously those of Catholic faith and of construction. He insists that ornament and materials should be honest, with ornament arising from structure rather than being mere decoration and eschewing the fakery of plaster and cement of earlier revivalist experiments at Walpole's Strawberry Hill and William Beckford's Fonthill Abbey. Such truth to materials and form was not only emphasised by Ruskin, who makes Truth one of his architectural principles in *The Seven Lamps of Architecture* (1849), but became one of the central tenets of Modernist architecture.

Through his career, Pugin is increasingly explicit about the place of the past in the present, not as an alien, disruptive force but a natural survival, a true principle that could be revived to set the present along the lines that it should have followed. In the 1840s such views were appearing in many places as responses to the 'Condition of England' question and the turbulent decade that produced the 'year of revolutions' in Europe in 1848. Carlyle's *Past and Present* (1843) makes its 'Götzism' evident in its title, and contrasts the life and works of a twelfth-century abbot with the sorry state of the modern worker. Carlyle emphatically did not draw the same religious conclusions as Pugin, focusing instead on the importance of work and the dignity of labour, while also criticising the idle aristocracy and the commercialisation of social relations. The 'Young England' movement, whose most notable member was Benjamin Disraeli, later Prime Minister, also saw an idle aristocracy, a middle class driven by economic individualism and a church that was neglecting its social function, especially in relation to the poor. Their medieval ideal also appealed to Gothic precedent, but proposed a conservative version of a feudal hierarchy of mutual dependence, headed by a monarch and stabilised by the Church of England. Young England overlapped with the Oxford Movement and Tractarianism, but Pugin's description of Birmingham's 'Greek buildings & Smoking chimneys—radicals & disenters blended together'[26] could have served as the summary of all that Young England and the Tractarians were reacting to.

Catholicism cast a shadow over Pugin's reputation. For Charles Locke Eastlake, in his triumphalist *A History of the Gothic Revival* (1872), Pugin is clearly an awkward presence. The first mention of Pugin points out that he is

25 Belcher (ed.), *Letters*, vol. 1, p. 133.   26 Belcher (ed.), *Letters*, vol. 1, p. 23.

a Roman Catholic.[27] After faint praise of some of his work, Eastlake concludes that Pugin is a minor architect who had little real effect on the Revival because of his 'absolute assumption ... that the moral and social condition of England was infinitely superior in the Middle Ages to that of the present, and secondly that a good architect ought to inaugurate his professional career by adopting the faith of the Roman Catholic Church'. Eastlake carefully quarantines Pugin in the early period, saying that if he had lived longer he might have been more important, as he would have 'gone with the stream' of the Revival,[28] but implies that he had a retarding influence in producing 'a sort of chronological propriety [that] hampered the inventive faculties of men ... no one was safe from critics who knew to a nicety the coiffure of a thirteenth-century angel, and who damned a moulding that was half an hour too late'.[29] Eastlake thus consigns Pugin to the quaintly enthusiastic but regrettably misguided league of the antiquarians.

Pugin's last work was the Medieval Court at the Great Exhibition, London, of 1851; Gothic was at the heart of a revolutionary building of glass and iron in an exhibition that presented Britain as a stable, powerful nation at the cutting edge of the modern world. His death in 1852 is sometimes seen as end of a phase of the Revival, and in some sense it was. The second 'Battle of the Styles' that broke out in 1855 over the design and building of a new Foreign Office was more than a re-staging of the argument over the House of Parliament of the later 1830s. Bernard Porter calls it 'one of the worst-run public competitions in British building history' and the confusion of the competition continued throughout its construction.[30] George Gilbert Scott's Gothic design had eventually been commissioned, but he and his designs were implacably opposed by the Prime Minister, Lord Palmerston. Palmerston deployed the familiar arguments of expense, dirt, lack of light, undesirable religious associations, and refuted Gothic's claim to Englishness since, as he claimed, he had 'never heard of the Goths, the Vandals or the Saracens doing much in this country'.[31] Palmerston's stance may just have been political contrariness, but Scott was nevertheless forced to compromise and the new Foreign Office was built in an Italianate style. Despite this defeat, however, the new generation of architects looked to be realising

---

27 Charles Locke Eastlake, *A History of the Gothic Revival* (London: Longmans, Green and Co., 1872), p. 118.
28 Eastlake, *History*, pp. 151–2.   29 Eastlake, *History*, p. 137.
30 Bernard Porter, *The Battle of the Styles: Society, Culture and the Design of the New Foreign Office, 1855–1861* (London: Continuum, 2011), p. 7.
31 Porter, *Battle*, p. 10.

Palmerston's fear that they would Gothicize the whole country.[32] By the 1870s the revived Gothic style was everywhere, from the ecclesiastical, academic and domestic to the secular and commercial, in London, in new industrial cities, older towns and villages, and exported to the reaches of the Empire.

Porter suggests that the Battle of the Styles was ostensibly a struggle between those who thought that architecture should be taken seriously and those who, equally seriously, thought that it should not.[33] Although the new generation of Gothic architects may have succeeded in having architecture taken seriously, this was achieved by professionalisation rather than through religious or political conviction. The Institute of British Architects in London had been formed in 1834 and granted a royal charter in 1837. Eastlake was secretary to RIBA from 1866 to 1877 and his *History* accordingly sidelines Pugin and Ruskin as amateurs who endangered the Revival's professional progress. Eastlake's conclusion declares that 'the grammar of an ancient art has been mastered' but asks

> Will a time ever arrive when, freed from the idle prejudices, the pedantry, the false sentiment and the vulgarisms that have hampered its utterance and confounded its phraseology, this noble and expressive language shall be used throughout the land ... employed for majestic emphasis in our public buildings, telling of rural beauty in the village homestead, exciting devotion in every church, proclaiming comfort in every home, and stability in every warehouse?[34]

Stripped of faith, politics and history, this is professional 'Victorian Architecture', a non-signifying Gothic, or at least a Gothic that signifies only 'Gothic' itself.

John Ruskin

Eastlake consigns Ruskin to a past phase in the history of the Revival even though, in 1872, Ruskin was still a significant public figure. He is fulsome in his praise of Ruskin's critical acuity, but remarks that if he 'had been content to limit his researches, his criticism, and the dissemination of his principles to the field of pictorial art alone, he would have won for himself a name not easily forgotten'.[35] Ruskin is obliquely acknowledged as having rescued the

---

32 George Gilbert Scott, *Personal and Professional Recollections* (London: Sampson Low, 1879), p. 185.
33 Porter, *Battle*, p. 129.   34 Eastlake, *History*, p. 372.   35 Eastlake, *History*, p. 264.

Revival from Catholicism by extending, in *The Stones of Venice*, the possibilities of a post-Reformation Gothic,[36] but then is dismissed for his amateurism, his 'imperfect acquaintance with the science of construction'.[37] The accusation of impracticality is the basis of Eastlake's more serious criticism: 'His views on the subject of art may in the main be sound; his philanthropical intentions are, we doubt not, sincere; but considered in combination as they are usually associated, they present a scheme which is utterly impracticable.'[38] It was, Eastlake says, 'wild and impetuous reasoning ... which broke the spell of Mr Ruskin's authority', thus 'People began to ask themselves whether ... even such as guide as this was to be trusted when he allowed his theories to waft him into dreamland, or to culminate in plans which would have been considered unfeasible in Utopia.'[39] Ruskin's fault, therefore, is to assert that there is any social or moral meaning in architecture. Eastlake also accuses Pugin and Ruskin of having imperilled the Revival by introducing a dangerous liberty: 'Under the influence first of Pugin and then of Ruskin, architects found themselves suddenly emancipated from the conditions and restrictions which had hampered their efforts ... freedom from national traditions, freedom from structural and decorative conventionality ... they had their liberty, and like all liberty thus suddenly and lawlessly attained it was woefully misused.'[40] It is an odd contradiction of the more frequent accusation that the early Revival was stiffly historicist; what Eastlake sees in Pugin and Ruskin is the assertion of a freedom of spirit in design against what, by this time, had become a professionally controlled style. It also registers (though Pugin and Ruskin did not) the revolutionary potential of the old Gothic liberty, where a democratic commonwealth stands against the reimposition of conservative traditions.

Ruskin was acutely conscious of a need to distance himself from Pugin; he claimed to 'owe nothing' to him and to have read none of his work apart from a glance at *Contrasts*, 'not feeling, from the style of his architecture, the smallest interest in his opinions'.[41] The claim is certainly untrue,[42] and Ruskin's aversion perhaps lay in his own conflicted attitude to Catholicism. In *The Seven Lamps of Architecture* he wrote, 'No man was ever more inclined than I to a sympathy with the principles and forms of the Romanist Church' but he then immediately says of Catholicism that 'its lying and Idolatrous

36 Eastlake, *History*, p. 266.   37 Eastlake, *History*, p. 277.   38 Eastlake, *History*, p. 272.
39 Eastlake, *History*, pp. 273–4.   40 Eastlake, *History*, p. 357.
41 Cook and Wedderburn (eds), *The Works*, vol. 3, pp. 428–9.
42 See Patrick R. M. Conner, 'Pugin and Ruskin', *Journal of the Warburg and Courtauld Institutes* 41 (1978): 344–50.

power is the darkest plague ever to have held commission to hurt the earth'.[43] *Seven Lamps* also contained Appendix 12, 'Romanist Modern Art', which is a violent and personal attack on Pugin. Ruskin renounced Evangelicalism in 1858 and withdrew Appendix 12 from subsequent editions, along with other notes that he described as 'rabid and utterly false Protestantism'.[44] He was nevertheless obliged to continue reassuring his readers, in 1877 writing 'don't be afraid that I am going to become a Roman Catholic, or that I am one in disguise. I can no more become a *Roman*-Catholic than again an Evangelical Protestant'.[45] Ruskin identifies the Renaissance (rather than the Reformation, as Pugin had) as the moment when Gothic falls away from its true principles, after which 'instant degradation followed in every direction,—a flood of folly and hypocrisy', but his point is often strikingly similar to Pugin's in arguing that Catholicism only produced great art and architecture when it had, as it were, Protestantism still inside it and that the schism had exacerbated the loss of energy in the Church.[46] Kenneth Clark, in *The Gothic Revival* (1928), suggests that 'the dissociation of Gothic and Rome was, perhaps, Ruskin's most complete success'[47] and that 'for the majority of readers Ruskin succeeded in disinfecting Gothic architecture', but then continues to treat him as a 'dangerous' conduit of foreignness, where those 'deceived by Ruskin's superficial resemblance to themselves' introduced 'exotic weeds' into the garden of England.[48]

The dangerous gift that both Eastlake and Clark identify in Ruskin is his persuasive power to make his readers see differently. His first major work, *Modern Painters* (1843–60), contains an exercise: 'Place an object as close to the eye as you like, there is always something which you *cannot* see . . . and place an object as far from the eye as you like . . . there is always something in it which you *can* see.'[49] Whatever other inconsistencies emerged over his long career, this injunction to look and to think about what is seen or not seen remains constant because, as he put it in an address to the Cambridge School of Art (1858), 'we want, in this world of ours, very often to be able to see in the dark'.[50]

---

43 Cook and Wedderburn (eds), *The Works*, vol. 8, pp. 267–8.
44 Cook and Wedderburn (eds), *The Works*, vol. 7, p. 15.
45 Cook and Wedderburn (eds), *The Works*, vol. 29, p. 92.
46 Cook and Wedderburn (eds), *The Works*, vol. 9, p. 58.
47 Kenneth Clark, *The Gothic Revival: An Essay on the History of Taste*, revised and enlarged edition (London: Constable, 1950), p. 180.
48 Clark, *Revival*, p. 196.   49 Cook and Wedderburn (eds), *The Works*, vol. 3, p. 329.
50 Cook and Wedderburn (eds), *The Works*, vol. 16, p. 180.

For Ruskin, seeing in the dark begins with seeing the dark itself. Stephen Kite calls this darkness 'energetic shadow', and its visualisation 'a practice of active—often precarious—engagement'.[51] In *The Seven Lamps of Architecture* Ruskin writes:

> the use of that shadow is entirely to show the confines of the figures; and it is to *their lines*, and not to the shapes of the shadows behind them, that the art and the eye are addressed ... the sculptors have dispensed with, or even struggled to avoid, all shadows which were not absolutely necessary to the explaining of the form. On the contrary, in Gothic sculpture, the shadow becomes itself a subject of thought.[52]

Across the three volumes of *The Stones of Venice* (1851–3), the energetic shadows are the subject of thought. 'The Nature of Gothic' appears in the very centre of the work, in the middle of volume II, and is pivotal to the argument. Having made the shift to Venice, Ruskin carefully anatomises the 'external forms and internal elements' of Gothic, insisting that:

> It is not enough that it has the Form, if it have not also the power and life. It is not enough that it has the Power, if it have not the form. We must therefore inquire into each of these characters successively; and determine first, what is the Mental Expression, and secondly, what the Material Form of Gothic architecture, properly so called.[53]

This again is the Coleridgean living symbol; the architecture is part of that which it indicates, both having the same 'power and life'. Six qualities are given by Ruskin in order of importance: savageness; love of change; naturalism; grotesqueness; obstinacy and redundance (generosity), and through them Ruskin instates a cultural and aesthetic geography that distinguishes 'northern Gothic' from southern or eastern in 'a perpetual reflection of the contrast between Goth and Roman in their first encounter'.[54] With some sleight of hand in his selection of examples of geology, weather and animals he establishes the northern 'Gothic heart', formed by its landscape, as having 'strength of will, independence of character, resoluteness of purposes, impatience of undue control, and that general tendency to set the individual reason against authority, and the individual deed against destiny', this

---

51 Stephen Kite, 'Shaping the Darks; Ruskin's "Energetic Shadow"', in Timothy Brittain-Catlin, Jan de Meyer and Martin Bressani (eds), *Gothic Revival Worldwide: A. W. N. Pugin's Global Influence* (Leuven: Leuven University Press, 2016), pp. 228–39 (p. 233).
52 Cook and Wedderburn (eds), *The Works*, vol. 8, p. 238.
53 Cook and Wedderburn (eds), *The Works*, vol. 9, p. 183.
54 Cook and Wedderburn (eds), *The Works*, vol. 10, pp. 184–5.

being, he argues, opposed to the southern 'languid submission of thought to tradition and purpose to fatality'.[55] The implicit gendering of the north and south also becomes explicit. Gothic is masculine, and it is the dignity of *male* labour that is being assaulted by modern industrial capitalism.

Having set out the nature of Gothic, Ruskin produces his own set of contrasts: 'reader, look around this English room of yours ... Examine again all those accurate mouldings, and perfect polishings, and unerring adjustments of seasoned wood and tempered steel'. The reader is then instructed to 'go forth again to gaze on the old cathedral front', to 'examine once more those ugly goblins and formless monsters'. He says that 'If read rightly' the sharp, bright surfaces of the mass-produced ornaments are signs of slavery, whereas the energetic shadows of the Gothic reveal 'the life and liberty of every workman who struck the stone; a freedom of thought and rank in scale of being, such as no laws, no charters, no charities can secure, but which it must be the first aim of all Europe at this day to regain for her children'.[56] This is a powerful rhetorical shift. Venice, religiously 'disinfected', is an island trading state and naval power like Britain. Engaging with the Gothic shadow switches Venice to England; labour and the worker become visible, and the reader, enjoined to look outwards, is simultaneously compelled to look inward and examine his own conscience. Ruskin produces a progressive, modern Gothic that is capable of reconnecting the alienated industrial working 'hand' with his eye and heart to, as he puts it, 'make a man of him'.[57] Ruskin's attention to political economy intensifies after 'The Nature of Gothic' and his moral challenge to contemporary capitalism becomes stronger, but his vision of a solution is not a democracy. His statement in *Unto This Last* (1860), 'THERE IS NO WEALTH BUT LIFE', embodies his position.[58] Despite intense feeling for workers (which led him to a brief sympathy with the Paris Commune) and his efforts to engage them, as in the *Fors Clavigera: Letters to the Workmen and Labourers of Great Britain* (1871– 84), his vision, realised in the medieval-style Guild of St George that he founded in 1878, was one of a mutually dependent hierarchical society. As with his idiosyncratic definitions of Catholicism, politically, Ruskin called himself both 'a violent Tory of the old school' and 'a communist of the old school'.[59] His description of the 'old school' as that 'of Sir Walter Scott and

---

55 Cook and Wedderburn (eds), *The Works*, vol. 10, p. 242.
56 Cook and Wedderburn (eds), *The Works*, vol. 9, pp. 193–4.
57 Cook and Wedderburn (eds), *The Works*, vol. 9, p. 192.
58 Cook and Wedderburn (eds), *The Works*, vol. 17, p. 105.
59 Cook and Wedderburn (eds), *The Works*, vol. 5, p. 13, vol. 27, p. 116.

Homer' makes sense of the apparent contradiction. He sees in Scott's work a coherent community and in Homer the epic expression of the life and values of a people.

William Morris

It is, however, William Morris who perhaps has a better claim than Ruskin to being a member of the 'old school' of Homer and Scott. A reviewer of Morris's *The Story of Sigurd the Volsung and the Fall of the Niblungs* (published 1876; dated 1877) suggests that 'To call him a Gothic Homer would perhaps be a little hyperbolical', but praises 'the genuinely Gothic spirit which breathes from every verse, and stirs the hidden Gothic fibres in our own nature'.[60] Not everyone wished to have their Gothic fibres stirred; another reviewer condemned Morris's translation of the *Odyssey* because it had 'overlaid Homer with all the grotesqueness, the conceits, the irrationality of the Middle Ages'.[61]

Morris recapitulates the terms of the Gothic Revival in the course of his own career. Starting with childhood reading of Scott, he moved rapidly through High Church religious enthusiasm when at Oxford, where he and Edward Burne-Jones planned to found a monastic settlement, through the reading of Carlyle and Ruskin, producing writing influenced by medieval romances to a short apprenticeship with the architect George Street. Leaving professional architecture in 1856, Morris turned to painting through involvement with the Pre-Raphaelite Brotherhood, commissioned the building of the Red House and founded 'The Firm', a more commercially organised version of Ruskin's Guild. Importantly, in both the Red House and The Firm, design was led by a Gothic ethos of production, rather than a desired appearance of Gothic leading, or even disregarding, the methods of its making. This was to be influential on the Arts and Crafts movement of the late century.

Morris also pursued Ruskin's vision of the northern Gothic, travelling in Iceland, learning Icelandic and translating some of the sagas. His interest in the sagas, as with his continued interest in the Classical epics, resided in the capacity of art to express the completeness of the life of a people, and for that

---

60 Peter Faulkner (ed.), *William Morris: The Critical Heritage* (London: Routledge and Kegan Paul, 1973), p. 263.
61 Mowbray Morris, in an unsigned review in *Quarterly Review* 167:334 (1888): 398–426 (p. 407).

artefact then to continue to invigorate succeeding generations. Morris wrote in the Preface to his translation of the *Volsunga Saga* that it was:

> The Great Story of the North which should be to all our race what the Tale of Troy was to the Greeks, to all our race first, and afterwards, when the change of the world has made our race nothing more than a name of what has been – a story, too, – then it should be to those that come after us no less than the Tale of Troy has been to us.[62]

Reviews of Morris's own *Sigurd the Volsung* show how familiar the speculative geography of Gothic had become. Henry Hewlett, for example, appreciated that 'The great Gothic Epos has at least obtained incorporation into the literature of the only important nation of Gothic origin from which it was absent.' Hewlett goes on, however, to suggest that work only appealed as 'a more or less successful attempt at antiquarian restoration', concluding that 'The opportunity of employing a great racial, pre-historic myth as a potent engine of modern ideas is one that might have tempted a less ambitious poet than Mr. Morris. His artistic aims, are however, different from these, and he has chosen not to avail himself of the occasion.'[63]

Hewlett was only half right; Morris was not seeking antiquarian restoration of any kind. Believing, as had Ruskin, that architectural 'restoration' was both impossible and morally wrong, in 1877 he founded the Society for the Protection of Ancient Buildings in direct opposition to the actions of George Gilbert Scott, the most prolific 'Gothic' architect of the day. For Morris, history was a melancholy record of loss and medieval life could no more successfully be restored than could its architecture. He was, nevertheless, seeking to use the past as a potent engine of modern ideas, to locate the progressive manifestation of Gothic in the present. In 1883 he became a Socialist, joining the Democratic Federation, reading the work of Karl Marx, and coming into close contact with many left-wing thinkers and activists, including Friedrich Engels and George Bernard Shaw. Morris publicly reflected many times on his political evolution, as in this lecture of 1889:

> I know that I had come to these conclusions a good deal through reading John Ruskin's works, and that I focussed so to say his views on the matter of my work and my rising sense of injustice, probably more than he intended, and that the result of all that was that I was quite ready for Socialism when

---

62 William Morris, *Collected Works of William Morris*, 24 vols (London: Longmans, 1912), vol. 7, p. 286.
63 Faulkner (ed.), *Critical Heritage*, p. 255.

I came across it in a definite form, as a political party with distinct aims for a revolution in society.[64]

Socialism, with its orientation towards the future, made sense because it offered a reconceptualising of history. Morris absorbed the historical materialism of Marx and Engels that saw history as successive stages, each containing both an advancement of society and the seeds of the collapse of the stage. The past is thus not a record of irretrievable loss nor a place of escapist fantasy, but proof of change to come. Such historical unfolding also allowed Morris to bypass the difficult religious questions of Gothic; he came to regard religion as a necessary phase, the useful ethical dimension of which would be absorbed when supplanted by Socialism.[65] He had no wish to return to medievalism feudalism, as has often been claimed, but instead anticipated the coming of a utopian future. His essay in *Commonweal*, 'How We Live and How We Might Live' (1887), is one of many versions of *Contrasts*, but, as the title shows, the contrast is now not between the past and the present – rather between the present and the future.

The relationship is clear in the two lectures on the Gothic Revival that Morris gave in March 1884, after a year of his intense reading of Marx.[66] In them he identifies the stages of the Revival alongside the Marxian stages, describing too the dialectic of change within them. Gothic thus becomes something like the force of change, as he says in the opening line of the first lecture: 'By [Gothic Revival] I understand all those attempts to break down the slavery imposed on us first by the Italian Renaissance.'[67] But, in dialectical fashion, the Renaissance also contained the beginning of an 'intellectual revolt', through which 'a real living history became possible to us'. The Gothic Revival was both founded upon and fostered this 'new feeling'.[68] It is still a Ruskinian engagement with the energetic shadow of occluded history but Morris, unlike Ruskin, sees in it a fully democratic liberty and the 'life' of Gothic as a truly progressive driving force, unfolding inevitably through time. In the first Revival lecture, he gives the characteristics of Gothic art:

64 Paul Meier, 'An unpublished lecture of William Morris', *International Review of Social History* 16 (1971): 217–40 (pp. 225–6).
65 Norman Kelvin (ed.), *The Collected Letters of William Morris*, 4 vols (Princeton, NJ: Princeton University Press, 1984–96), vol. 2, p. 777.
66 E. P. Thompson, *William Morris: Romantic to Revolutionary* (London: Merlin, 1971), p. 270.
67 William Morris, 'The Gothic Revival I and II', in Eugene D. LeMire (ed.), *The Unpublished Lectures of William Morris* (Michigan: Wayne State University Press, 1969), pp. 54–94 (p. 54).
68 Morris, 'Revival I', pp. 55–6.

'It was common to the whole people; it was free, progressive, hopeful, full of human sentiment and humour', eclipsed by the 'death sickness' of the Renaissance that sacrificed collective genius for individual brilliance and the common good for capitalist accumulation.[69] In his projection of the fourth stage of the Gothic Revival, he registers 'the hope of many people that a new style of art is forming which will be at once beautiful and at the same time fitting to the life of our own times', concluding in the second lecture that if art 'is not of the people, it is an idle and worthless toy. Therefore the progress, nay, the very existence of art depends on the supplanting of the present capitalist system by something better, depends on changing the basis of society'.[70]

Morris's fictional work of the 1880s and 1890s shows clearly the shift in his thought. *A Dream of John Ball* (1888), *News from Nowhere* (1890) and the romances of the 1890s become increasingly dislocated from actual time and place, but they are neither nostalgist utopias nor strict prescriptions of ideal societies. Instead, they are dramatisations of historical process, integrations of past and present and future. In *News from Nowhere*, the time-travelling narrator speaks with a woman he has met in the future, who says to him 'You have begun again your never-ending contrast between the past and this present. Is it not so?'[71] From Pugin's definite *Contrasts* of towns in 1440 and 1840, we come to Morris's never-ending, non-specified contrasts of the past and *this* present, whenever this 'present' should be. For Morris the work of Gothic is clear. As he writes in 1890: 'we shall be our own Goths, and at whatever cost break up again the new tyrannous Empire of Capitalism'.[72]

Afterlives

The turn away from the Victorian in the twentieth century left its architecture, as Kenneth Clark put it in 1928, as 'unsightly wrecks stranded on the mud flat of Victorian taste', an offence to 'the sensitive eye'.[73] For him the Revival is 'interesting' and Pugin, Ruskin and Morris its 'best spirits',[74] but its legacy was not beauty, only conviction: 'The great heaps of clinkers which it left all over the country once burned with fiery belief, and we may still feel the warmth of a few embers.'[75] In 1936, Nikolaus Pevsner published *Pioneers of*

---

69 Morris, 'Revival I', pp. 65–6.   70 Morris, 'Revival II', p. 93.
71 William Morris, *News from Nowhere* (London: Kelmscott Press, 1893), p. 294.
72 William Morris 'The development of modern society', *Commonweal* 6:240 (1890): 260–1 (p. 261).
73 Clark, *Revival*, p. xxii.   74 Clark, *Revival*, p. 201.   75 Clark, *Revival*, p. 206.

the *Modern Movement: From William Morris to Walter Gropius,* boldly claiming Morris for Modernism and annexing the influence of Pugin and Ruskin. In order to make Morris Modern, however, he argued that we must put aside the half of him 'committed to nineteenth-century style and nineteenth-century prejudices'.[76] But by the middle of the twentieth century, the Victorian mudflat had become considerably more attractive. When Clark re-issued *The Gothic Revival* in 1950, he acknowledged the influence of John Betjeman in enabling him to see through the 'distorting fog of fashion' and to find its value.[77] In 1958, Betjeman and Pevsner (endorsed by Clark) were among the founders of the Victorian Society, dedicated to the defence of Victorian architecture. Pevsner's reasoning here was that 'It was that age that made them. It was in that age that they, and the whole of Britain, prospered more than in any age before or after. If we let the buildings of that age go we destroy the visual record of Britain's leadership in the civilised world.'[78] The conviction is the same as it was for Pugin, for Ruskin and for Morris, that the meaning of architecture is the product and expression of the life of a society, but the character of the age celebrated by Pevsner is precisely the condition of England that they challenged in their engagement with Gothic. In a context of post-war Socialism, what the mid-twentieth-century revivalists wanted to preserve was simply the *Victorian* and not the Gothic that Pugin, Ruskin or Morris had struggled to define.

76 Nikolaus Pevsner, *Pioneers of the Modern Movement: From William Morris to Walter Gropius* (London: Faber & Faber, 1936), p. 16.
77 Clark, *Revival*, p. xvii.
78 Susie Harries, *Nikolaus Pevsner: The Life* (London: Pimlico, 2013), p. 571.

2.6
Gothic Fiction, from Shilling Shockers to Penny Bloods

ANTHONY MANDAL

Though they were among the most circulated and consumed artefacts of the nineteenth-century literary marketplace, Gothic chapbooks and penny bloods have nonetheless occupied a critical blindspot in literary histories.[1] Despite their evanescence, these forms of short, cheap Gothic fiction proliferated from the 1770s to the 1880s, appearing in millions of copies to satisfy the demands of a rapidly expanding reading public. A number of factors played a role in enlarging the reading public in Britain from the start of the eighteenth century to the end of the nineteenth: population growth, particularly in urban locations like London; economic diversification and technological development; improvements in agricultural productivity; and a fall in infant mortality.[2]

The growth in, and the improving quality of, life for this reading public saw a correlative rise in literacy. Around 1715, adult literacy rates in England (counted as the ability of individuals to sign their names in marriage registers) was around 45 per cent for men and 25 per cent for women. Between 1800 and 1830, these rates increased by nearly half for men (to around 66 per cent) and doubled for women (50 per cent); by 1900 the percentage was 97 per cent for both sexes. In Scotland, literacy rates were harder to calculate, but the increase in literacy between 1700 and 1830 has been estimated by scholars at 260 per cent.[3] Philanthropic and civic attempts to improve the literacy of the

[1] For some noteworthy exceptions, see Franz J. Potter, *The History of Gothic Publishing, 1800–1835: Exhuming the Trade* (Basingstoke: Palgrave Macmillan, 2005); Diane Long Hoeveler, *Gothic Riffs: Secularizing the Uncanny in the European Imaginary, 1780–1820* (Columbus, OH: Ohio State University Press, 2010); Robert J. Kirkpatrick, *From the Penny Dreadful to the Ha'penny Dreadfuller: A Bibliographic History of the Boys' Periodical in Britain 1762–1950* (London: British Library; New Castle, DE: Oak Knoll Press, 2013).
[2] See Michael F. Suarez S. J., 'Introduction', in Michael F. Suarez S. J. and Michael L. Turner (eds), *The Cambridge History of the Book in Britain, Volume V: 1695–1830* (Cambridge: Cambridge University Press, 2009), pp. 1–35 (pp. 3–5).
[3] See Suarez, 'Introduction', pp. 8–11; Simon J. Eliot and Andrew Nash, 'Mass Markets: Literature', in David McKitterick (ed.), *The Cambridge History of the Book in Britain,*

mass public met with some success, but it was in fact literature on the street that played a bigger role in accomplishing this outcome. The spread of print through the land, especially in urban areas, both increased the demand for skilled readers and led to domestic consumption at home.[4] Accompanying this expansion in literacy was the growth in the purchasing power of this emergent audience: in the 1840s, a penny could merely secure a broadside; by the 1860s, it could unlock a 7,000-word serial instalment; and by the 1880s, an entire novelette of 20,000 words.[5]

The origins of these cheap fictions lay in the broadside ballads and chapbooks peddled by itinerant vendors – 'chapmen' – who wandered from street to street and from village to village from the early days of print. These works, printed on cheap paper and often accompanied by crude illustrations, were by 1800 absorbed into the increasingly industrialised systems of modern print culture. This literature continued during the nineteenth century through a vibrant culture of 'street Gothic', which manifested in the 'shilling shocker' bluebooks of the 1770s–1820s, the penny bloods of the 1840s–60s and the penny dreadfuls of the 1860s–80s.[6] Combining a tradition rooted in oral culture with the technologies of modern publishing, these Gothics formed part of the complex, class-cutting ecosystem of nineteenth-century print. David Vincent observes that

> Some of the hostility to the broadsides and penny dreadfuls was merely a consequence of publishers making visible what previously had been hidden in the oral tradition ... The delight in the bizarre and the violent long predated mass literacy; the achievement of the new era was the infusion of the fabulous with a particular sense of everyday reality.[7]

The shift towards industrialised technologies of printing enabled transformations in the material conditions for popular fiction, leading from small chapbooks manufactured in limited runs to mass-produced penny fictions, which

---

Volume VI: 1830–1914 (Cambridge: Cambridge University Press, 2009), pp. 418–19; David Vincent, *Literacy and Popular Culture: England 1750–1914* (Cambridge: Cambridge University Press, 1989), pp. 22–9.

4 Stephen Colclough and David Vincent, 'Reading', in David McKitterick (ed.), *The Cambridge History of the Book in Britain, Volume VI*, pp. 281–323 (p. 301).

5 See Richard D. Altick, *The English Common Reader: A Social History of the Mass Reading Public, 1800–1900* (Chicago: Chicago University Press, 1957), pp. 294–317.

6 Gary Kelly uses the term 'street Gothic' to describe the chapbook industry that spanned four hundred years, drawing on oral and manuscript traditions, before colliding with mass print culture around 1800. See Gary Kelly (ed.), *Varieties of Female Gothic, Volume 2: Street Gothic: Female Gothic Chapbooks* (London and Brookfield VT, Pickering & Chatto, 2002), p. vii.

7 Vincent, *Literacy and Popular Culture*, p. 205.

benefited from stereotyping, machine-made paper and steam-printing in the opening decades of the Victorian period. The ephemeral artefacts generated by this print culture disrupt our understandings of genre and medium, which indeed coalesced much later in the period. Categories like 'novel', 'tale' and 'novelette', as well as 'periodical' and 'chapbook', occupied a far more diffuse taxonomy than they do today. Roy Bearden-White reminds us that 'During the eighteenth century, very little difference existed between a chapbook series and a periodical, except semantics.'[8] Likewise, during the Victorian period, the blurring of boundaries between formats renders such concepts as anachronistic, as Graham Law and Robert Patten have pointed out: 'Both parts and periodicals are generally formatted so that either the purchaser or the vendor can have them bound up into volumes when the sequence is complete.'[9]

The Age of the 'Shilling Shocker': Gothic Bluebooks, 1770–1830

> He was very fond of reading, and greedily devoured all the books which were brought to school after the holidays; these were mostly blue books. Who does not know what blue books mean? but if there should be anyone ignorant enough to know what those dear darling volumes, so designated from their covers, contain, be it known, that they are or were to be bought for sixpence, and embodied stories of haunted castles, bandits, murderers, and other grim personages – a most exciting and interesting food for boys' minds.[10]

Thomas Medwin's famous recollection of the avid consumption of Gothic bluebooks by his childhood friend Percy Bysshe Shelley while he was a pupil at Syon House Academy at the start of the nineteenth century forcefully captures the appeal held by these cheap, bloody narratives. Indeed, the yet-to-be Romantic poet was not alone in his predilections for bluebooks, sharing this childhood passion, as he did, with other future luminaries such as Walter Scott, William Wordsworth, John Clare, Edmund Burke, George Crabbe, William Godwin and Samuel Taylor Coleridge, among many others.

As noted earlier, bluebooks descended from the older tradition of chapbooks, which typically ran between eight and twenty-four pages in length and were sold to the lower classes by itinerant pedlars known as 'chapmen' on

---

8   Roy Bearden-White, 'A history of guilty pleasure: chapbooks and the Lemoines', *Papers of the Bibliographical Society of America* 103 (2009): 284–318 (p. 314).
9   Graham Law and Robert L. Patten, 'The Serial Revolution', in David McKitterick (ed.), *The Cambridge History of the Book in Britain, Volume VI*, pp. 144–71 (p. 144).
10 Thomas Medwin, *The Life of Percy Bysshe Shelley* (London: Newby, 1847), pp. 29–30.

street corners, at festivals and in marketplaces. Although their dimensions varied, the majority of chapbooks were around 3½ by 5½ inches in size, and were sold in their thousands for anything from a few farthings to a shilling. While the quality of print and paper were generally poor, these stories captured the attention of their eager readers, comprising mournful ballads, folk and fairy tales, picaresque adventures, didactic lessons, terrifying hauntings and gruesome crimes, alongside redactions of popular novels such as *Robinson Crusoe* and *Gulliver's Travels*. The text was often prefixed with a frontispiece or illustrated title page, made up from a crude woodcut that might be recycled from work to work, often regardless of applicability to the tale in question. Sellers of chapbooks, broadsides and ballads would purvey their wares to passers-by, declaiming grim scenes, singing out verses and performing narratives. Captivated listeners would be led to part with their money for the printed sources, sharing them in turn with family members and co-workers.[11] While chapbooks might easily be dismissed as insubstantial literature for the lower classes, in actuality they spread more diffusely among multiple readerships. As William St Clair has observed, they were read by 'adults in the country areas, and young people in both the town and the country. It would be a mistake, therefore, to regard the ancient popular print as confined to those whose education fitted them for nothing longer or textually different. Many readers whether adults or children, lived at the boundary between the reading and the non-reading nations.'[12] During the mid-eighteenth century, pioneers such as John Newbery made innovative use of the chapbook format by redirecting it towards juvenile readers, with popular works tracing the uplifting stories of *Goody Two-Shoes*, *Puss-in-Boots* and *Dick Whittington*. Simultaneously drawing on the chapbook's fabular traditions and small format, Newbery replaced the crude woodcuts and broken type of his antecedents with elaborately engraved frontispieces and delicate typography.

By 1800, the chapbook industry as peddled by itinerant vendors had all but disappeared. Instead, bluebooks – having emerged simultaneously with the mainstream Gothic novel in the 1770s and lasting until the 1820s – could now be bought and borrowed alongside the triple-decker Gothic novels at the circulating library, as well from booksellers and at bazaars. Bluebooks were pitched to multiple audiences: in addition to the traditional chapbook readers drawn from the lower orders, a more polite readership emerged. Indeed,

---

[11] See Vincent, *Literacy and Popular Culture*, p. 202.
[12] William St Clair, *The Reading Nation in the Romantic Period* (Cambridge: Cambridge University Press, 2004), pp. 343–4.

Franz J. Potter has noted that the bluebook industry formed a large secondary market for middle-class readers of the Gothic.[13] The bluebooks were slightly larger and longer than their chapbook predecessors, typically spanning thirty-six or seventy-two pages. The first variant sold for sixpence and the second for a shilling: hence, the bluebooks' alternative descriptor as 'shilling shockers'.[14] While a three-volume Gothic novel in 1800 might cost up to two weeks' wages for a labourer, expenditure of sixpence or a shilling equated to the price of a meal or a cheap theatre seat.[15] Angela Koch suggests that, in this iteration, bluebooks represented the merging of two antecedent traditions into 'a new type of cheap popular literature: whereas the bluebook's size of thirty-six to seventy-two pages recalls the eighteenth century chapbook tradition, their inevitable blue covers, copperplate frontispieces, and above all their contents, derive from the late-eighteenth- and early-nineteenth-century Gothic romance'.[16] Each bluebook might comprise multiple short narratives or a single extended tale of up to 30,000 words, occasionally followed by a short sketch or anecdote to fill otherwise blank pages. Material was gleaned from a panoply of sources: items previously issued in magazines, redactions of full-length romances or original copy written specifically for the bluebook. Demand for Gothic material in both novel and bluebook form culminated between 1803 and 1805,[17] with bluebooks counting for over half the output of new Gothic fiction published between 1800 and 1834. Potter goes on to identify three key stages in the production of bluebooks: a serialised phase (1802–5); production of standalone bluebooks, coinciding with a sudden peak in Gothic novel production (1809–12); and a period of decline (from 1820). According to analysis by Diane Long Hoeveler, at least one thousand individual bluebooks were produced in Britain alone in this period.[18]

A handful of publishers were responsible for a large proportion of this output, many of them operating in the shadow of more successful firms such as William Lane's Minerva Press or more respectable ones like Longmans or John Murray. Bearden-White observes that 'Very few chapbook publishers

---

13 Potter, *History of Gothic Publishing*, pp. 10, 21–31.
14 William Whyte Watt, *Shilling Shockers of the Gothic School: A Study of Chapbook Gothic Romances* (Cambridge, MA: Harvard University Press, 1932), p. 11.
15 Diane Long Hoeveler, 'More gothic gold: the Sadleir-Black chapbook collection at the University of Virginia Library', *Papers on Language and Literature* 46 (2010): 164–93 (p. 177).
16 Angela Koch, 'Gothic bluebooks in the princely library of Corvey and beyond', *Cardiff Corvey: Reading the Romantic Text* 9 (December 2002) <www.romtext.org.uk/articles/cc09_no1\> (last accessed 10 June 2019).
17 Potter, *History of Gothic Publishing*, p. 47.   18 Hoeveler, 'More gothic gold', p. 171.

successfully navigated repeated crossings of ... social categories. Collectively, that part of the printing industry that dealt with popular street literature survived and eventually grew stronger. Individually, however, chapbook publishers did not fare as well.'[19] Nearly two-thirds of the bluebook market was controlled by a handful of publishers: John Bailey, Dean and Munday, Ann Lemoine and Thomas Tegg, with the remainder made up of a wider network of firms, such as Simon Fisher, Thomas Hughes and John Ker.[20] It is perhaps worth pausing over the two most prolific of these London firms, Thomas Tegg and Ann Lemoine, who each controlled around 20 per cent of the market.

In a career spanning from 1800 to 1840, Tegg famously made a fortune as a dealer in remaindered books, alongside issuing reprints of out-of-copyright works and publishing original publications. Tegg produced numerous bluebooks, mainly in partnership as 'Tegg and Castleman' (1801–4) and as a sole trader,[21] with indicative titles including *Albani; or, The Murderer of his Child* (1803); *Almagro & Claude; or, Monastic Murder* (1803); *Lewis Tyrrell; or, The Depraved Count* (1804); *The Nun; or, Memoirs of Angelique* (1805); *The Castle of the Apennines* (1810); and *The Daemon of Venice* (1810). Many of these titles, including *Almagro & Claude* and *The Daemon of Venice*, were redactions of longer Gothic fictions, in these particular cases Matthew Gregory Lewis's *The Monk* (1796) and Charlotte Dacre's *Zofloya; or, The Moor* (1806) respectively. Lemoine, by contrast, remains a ghostly presence in the annals of the book trade, yet is nonetheless conspicuous as one of a few women booksellers in the era. Following the bankruptcy of her husband Henry – a hack writer and trade bookseller – around 1798, Lemoine issued more chapbooks than any other London publisher, before leaving the marketplace around 1820. Bearden-White estimates that she published around four hundred bluebooks, for a total of around one million copies, with the high point of production occurring *c.* 1804–5, broadly coinciding with the peak production of mainstream Gothic novels in 1805–8.[22] Often in partnership with John Roe, Lemoine applied the technologies and aesthetics of the carriage book trade

---

19 Bearden-White, 'History of guilty pleasure', p. 293.
20 Potter, *History of Gothic Publishing*, p. 44.
21 James J. Barnes and Patience P. Barnes, 'Reassessing the reputation of Thomas Tegg, London publisher, 1776–1846', *Book History* 3 (2000): 45–60 (p. 46).
22 Bearden-White, 'History of guilty pleasure', pp. 290–3, 299. For figures regarding the output of the mainstream Gothic novel, see Peter Garside, 'Introduction: Consolidation and Dispersal', in Peter Garside, James Raven and Rainer Schöwerling (eds), *The English Novel, 1770–1829: A Bibliographical Survey of Prose Fiction Published in the British Isles*, 2 vols (Oxford: Oxford University Press, 2000), vol. 2, pp. 1–103 (p. 56); and Potter, *History of Gothic Publishing*, p. 15.

to produce higher-quality bluebooks, including works such as: *The Black Valley; or, The Castle of Rosenberg* (1801); *The Life, Surprising Adventures, and Most Remarkable Escapes of Rinaldo Rinaldini, Captain of a Banditti of Robbers* (1801); *Subterranean Passage; or, The Gothic Cell* (1803); *The Robbers of the Forest; or, the Unfortunate Princess* (1805); *The Tomb of Aurora; or, The Mysterious Summons* (1807); and *The Witch of Rona; or, The Magic Spell* (1810). Significantly, both Tegg and Lemoine also gathered together previously published chapbooks into annually published anthologies directed towards the wealthier patrons of circulating libraries: Tegg's *The Marvellous Magazine and Compendium of Prodigies* appeared in four volumes (1802–4), while Lemoine issued collections such as the four-volume *English Nights Entertainments* (1802) and *The Tell-Tale Magazine* (1803–6).

Many bluebooks recycled material that was by now decades old: *Lovel Castle; or, The Rightful Heir Restored* (1818) is a retelling of Clara Reeve's *The Old English Baron* (1778), while *The Midnight Assassin; or, Confession of the Monk Rinaldi* (1822) draws on Ann Radcliffe's *The Italian* (1796–7). Perhaps the single most popular source for redaction or extraction was Lewis's *The Monk*, with additional bluebook adaptations including *The Castle of Lindenberg; or The History of Raymond and Agnes* (1798), a verbatim plagiarism of *The Monk*'s Bleeding Nun story; *Father Innocent, Abbot of the Capuchins; or, The Crimes of Cloisters* (c. 1805); and Sarah Wilkinson's *Castle of Lindenberg; or, The History of Raymond and Agnes* (c. 1820). Indeed, in cases where bluebooks were abridgements of full-length works, publishers often traded on the original author's name (such as Lewis's) to promote sales. Compression of the original triple-decker narratives meant that narrative pacing was often haphazard, with William Watt contending that 'the plots of most of the shockers are far too complicated to have been conceived on any scale but that of a full-length novel. At all events, there is nothing original in the stories of the shilling shockers. All the Gothic machinery and characters appear again, preserved intact, but often exaggerated to an amazing degree.'[23] Likewise, Frederick S. Frank observes that 'It did not matter that almost every shilling shocker was a plagiarized reduction of *The Monk* or one of Mrs. Radcliffe's romances or a tawdry compression of Shakespeare's *Titus Andronicus, Hamlet, Measure for Measure*, or *Cymbeline*.'[24] However, such dismissive pronouncements on the bluebook phenomenon are challenged by Koch, whose first-hand examination of some 217 bluebooks located in the Corvey Collection in Germany

---

23 Watt, *Shilling Shockers*, p. 21.
24 Frederick S. Frank, 'Gothic gold: the Sadleir-Black Gothic collection', *Studies in Eighteenth-Century Culture* 26 (1997): 287–312 (p. 296).

reveals that only about one-third were actually redacted from full-length Gothic novels.[25] Anthony Jarrells similarly defends the bluebooks from charges of mere derivativeness: 'Shortened and plagiarized they may have been. Yet these little Gothics were not completely devoid of formal innovation or narrative complexity.'[26]

Whatever their provenance, bluebooks were typically medieval in setting, and placed little emphasis on character, preferring instead rapidly unfolding plots that involved knights, spectres, gloomy castles, mysterious lights and ominous sounds. *The Black Forest; or, The Cavern of Horrors* (1802) is a paradigmatic example, supplying a highly charged narrative that begins with Sir Henry Mountford en route to the Castle of Gotha, when he witnesses a preternatural-seeming meteor fall into the entrance of the eponymous Cavern. As he is informed by a domestic at the Castle, 'That Cavern is assuredly the habitation of the infernal spirits. Sometimes there have been heard in it hollow groans, or shrieks of anguish; sometimes, noises resembling the rushing of torrents, or the rumbling of pent-up vapours.'[27] These supernatural phenomena had initially been observed when the current Baron of Gotha took his title: naturally, it transpires that Henry is the true owner of the Castle, his father having been murdered by his uncle who then assumed the title. Recognising the now-adult Henry, the Baron sets assassins upon his nephew but they mistakenly murder the Baron's lustful son, who had disguised himself as Henry in order to abduct Henry's paramour Lady Theresa. Upon discovering this, the Baron stabs himself with his brother's sword and declares Henry the true heir, enabling the now-restored knight to marry Theresa.

Watt notes that 'The shilling shocker in its simplest form is an uneven battle between the hero and heroine with their faithful seconds on the one hand, and a host of aggressive foes – murderous monks, cruel abbesses, bluebeard barons, tyrannical parents, sorceresses, and bandits – on the other.'[28] Indeed, *Captive of the Banditti*, a story left incomplete by the essayist and physician Nathan Drake and finished by 'Another Hand' for publication in 1801, focuses more on chivalry than supernaturalism. Montmorency and his attendants encounter a bandit troop that has abducted a young woman,

---

25 Koch, 'Gothic bluebooks'.
26 Anthony Jarrells, 'Short Fictional Forms and the Rise of the Tale', in Peter Garside and Karen O'Brien (eds), *The Oxford History of the Novel in English, Volume II: English and British Fiction, 1750–1820* (Oxford: Oxford University Press, 2015), pp. 478–94 (p. 487).
27 Anon., *The Black Forest; or, The Cavern of Horrors* (London: Lemoine and Roe, 1802), p. 9.
28 Watt, *Shilling Shockers*, pp. 31–2.

Dorothee: 'One, who had the aspect and the garb of their leader, and who, waving his scimitar, seemed menacing the rest, held on his arm a massy shield, of immense circumference, and which being streaked with recent blood, presented to the eye an object truly terrific.'[29] After a short skirmish, Montmorency is captured, but evades his captors with the aid of Dorothee, who reveals that the bandit captain is her debauched and rejected fiancé, Count Edelbert. A second battle ensures, resulting in Edelbert's defeat, and in due course hero and heroine are married.

Indeed, the most common theme of these short fictions is that of deserving love thwarted by villains whose schemes combine usurpation, neglectful parenting and destructive desire. Schoolmaster, hack writer and alleged plagiarist, Isaac Crookenden wrote at least ten bluebooks.[30] In one of these, *The Mysterious Murder; or, The Usurper of Naples* (1808), Estaphana is abducted by her betrothed the Duke de Savelli, while her lover Belfoni is imprisoned by her father Lusigni. In a pivotal scene, the Duke is about to rape Estaphana, when it is revealed that she is his daughter, who as an infant had been kidnapped by Jaquilina, one of the Duke's abandoned lovers, and left at the doorstep of Lusigni (who is later revealed as Belfoni's usurping uncle):

> 'Accursed woman!' said the Duke to Jaquilina, 'I take the reward of thy treachery!' (at the same time he stabbed her in the breast) 'for it could have been nobody but you who stole my infant. And this, too, heaven requires!' (stabbing himself); now I am but half a monster!' – 'O villain!' said Jaquilina, faintly, while the purple stream gushed from her wound, 'is this your gratitude for my preventing you from deflouring [sic] your own child?'[31]

Similarly, in Crookenden's earlier tale, *The Vindictive Monk; or, The Fatal Ring* (1802), the titular cleric Sceloni is a man of 'gloomy character, and who was never seen once to smile'.[32] He serves at the whim of the 'lascivious' Holbruzi, who desires the innocent Alexa and seeks to abduct her away from her beloved, Calini. Slighted by his master, Sceloni plots a gruesome

---

29 'Another Hand' [Nathan Drake], *Captive of the Banditti*, in Peter Haining (ed.), *The Shilling Shockers: Stories of Terror from the Gothic Bluebooks* (London: Gollancz, 1978), pp. 61–71 (p. 64).
30 Frank accuses Crookenden of being a serial plagiarist, who not only copied other authors' works but also sold the same stories multiple times to different publishers. See Frank, 'Gothic gold', p. 296.
31 Isaac Crookenden, *The Mysterious Murder; or, The Usurper of Naples: An Original Romance. To Which Is Prefixed, The Nocturnal Assassin; or, Spanish Jealousy* (London: Lee, 1808), p. 21.
32 Isaac Crookenden, *The Vindictive Monk; or, The Fatal Ring*, in Peter Haining (ed.), *The Shilling Shockers: Stories of Terror from the Gothic Bluebooks* (London: Gollancz, 1978), pp. 21–31 (p. 24).

revenge, first shooting Holbruzi dead and then 'His vindictive spirit resolving upon a double revenge, marked Calini for a second victim.' About to deal the killing blow, Sceloni spots a ring on his victim's finger, which reveals him as his son, whom he had abandoned after murdering his wife.[33] Just as the name of the eponymous villain recalls that of Radcliffe's Father Schedoni from *The Italian*, so *The Vindictive Monk* fits clearly within a Radcliffean framework of corrupt parents realising the errors of their ways before their banishment to the margins of the narrative world.

Even more prolific than Crookenden was Sarah Wilkinson, who wrote nearly thirty volumes of Gothic fiction and around one hundred short works, including over fifty bluebooks.[34] Heavily immersed in the literary market, Wilkinson worked with around twenty-five publishers, including Lemoine, for whom she issued eighteen bluebooks between 1803 and 1806.[35] Throughout her career, she adapted a number of Gothic texts by other writers (such as Thomas Skinner Surr and Lewis) into short, fast-paced bluebooks. Potter argues that 'What Wilkinson does is to blend the pleasing aesthetics and the enticing suspension of terror found in Radcliffe and the rapidity of horrifying shocks distinctive of Lewis.'[36] Constance, the aptly named titular heroine of *The Mysterious Novice; or, Convent of the Grey Penitents* (1809), draws the attention of Adolphus, Count d'Erfeldt, while singing a hymn in the convent chapel. When Adolphus attends the deathbed of his grandfather, Marquis Sperreth, he learns of the terrible connection that the three share. The recently deceased abbess Ursula was Sperreth's daughter, originally Lady Vitoria, who as a young woman had eloped with the Protestant Count Kempenfeldt. The zealously Catholic Sperreth disavowed Vitoria and arranged the assassination of the Count. Moreover, the new abbess Lady Josephina, who has taken to persecuting Constance, had been engaged to Kempenfeldt when he eloped with Vitoria. Armed with this news, Adolphus and a monk return to the convent to find his beloved (cousin) imprisoned by the vengeful Josephina:

> Having procured the key, they proceeded to the dungeon, where they found the wretched Constance lying on a miserable mattress, praying for death to relieve her sufferings. Adolphus supported her to the parlour. The state of

---

33 Crookenden, *Vindictive Monk*, p. 31.
34 Diane Long Hoeveler, 'Gothic Adaptation, 1764–1830', in Glennis Byron and Dale Townshend (eds), *The Gothic World* (Abingdon and New York: Routledge, 2014), pp. 185–98 (p. 188).
35 Bearden-White, 'History of guilty pleasure', p. 357.
36 Potter, *History of guilty pleasure*, p. 116.

her garments testified the cruelty of the abbess, who, with the vile sister Clara, was degraded to the station of a lay sister, by the bishop ...[37]

In this conventual-Gothic tale in the Radcliffean tradition, Wilkinson combines a melodramatic style with some nuanced characterisation and intriguing plot twists, weaving together numerous Gothic devices that include peripatetic adventures, inset tales and disguised identities.

Gary Kelly identifies two traditions that collide in the bluebooks, both of which reflect their mixed class origins. On the one hand, he describes what he terms the 'lottery mentality' of the older chapbooks, which emphasised 'destiny, chance, fortune and levelling forces such as death, express[ing] the centuries-old experience of common people who lived, near, at, and sometimes over the edge of bare subsistence'. This perspective is represented in the use of repetitive narrative patterns, episodic or anecdotal structures, dehistoricised settings and an anonymous authorial body. On the other hand, the bluebooks from the turn of the nineteenth century also inflect an 'investment mentality', which spoke to the middle-class readership that they simultaneously targeted. We see the tension between these two mentalities when the bluebooks take on tropes, features and values found in the mainstream Gothic novels, which addressed 'those with access to and an interest and stake in self-improvement, self-advancement, modernisation and the benefits of self-discipline in an increasingly capitalist economy and society'.[38] Hoeveler builds on Kelly's reading by summarising the cultural labour undertaken by the authors and publishers of this form of Gothic: 'It was a literary technology that was predicated on the notion that many different belief systems could coexist, and that the mixing of traditional spirituality with newer rationalistic approaches to life would allow them to remake themselves as effective citizens of the new nation-state.'[39]

In his study of the rise of the short story in the early nineteenth century, Tim Killick notes that the genre was able 'to consolidate and refine a multitude of disparate precursory influences': European translations, eighteenth-century essays, oral traditions and short descriptive sketches. He points to the imbrication of various factors – the shift from orality and print, as well as the influence of native British and pan-European (particularly German) traditions – which created the

---

37 Sarah S. Wilkinson, *The Mysterious Novice; or, Convent of the Grey Penitents*, in Peter Haining (ed.), *The Shilling Shockers: Stories of Terror from the Gothic Bluebooks* (London: Gollancz, 1978), pp. 32–60 (p. 60).
38 Kelly, 'Introduction', p. x.   39 Hoeveler, *Gothic Riffs*, p. 228.

conditions that stimulated the emergence of short fiction in the British literary marketplace.[40] In an otherwise excellent study, Killick pays only passing attention to the contribution made by the Gothic bluebook to this longer achievement. Yet, as Jarrells observes, the bluebook links the multi-volume Gothic novels that filled circulating-library shelves with literary phenomena that were characteristic of the print-saturated nineteenth century, most notably the infamous 'tale of terror' pioneered by *Blackwood's Edinburgh Magazine* during the 1820s and 1930s: 'The latter tales condensed the horror and terror of the Gothic novel into original, focused, and often highly stylised short fictions. Their impact on the short story can be seen in the work of Edgar Allan Poe.'[41]

The Penny Blood and the Serial Revolution, 1840–1870

In many ways, *Blackwood's* pioneering role in publishing short stories within the periodical format was not groundbreaking: as Robert D. Mayo points out, fiction had appeared in magazines since the 1740s.[42] However, these early examples were not representative of their period, unlike the serialised fiction that characterised the 1840s to 1870s. The serial revolution emerged through the industrialisation of a number of print technologies in the early decades of the new century. Taken up as regular practice from the later 1820s, stereotyping involved the casting of metal facsimiles of pages that could make up thousands of copies and be reused if needed or melted down if not. Paper manufacture (the most expensive component of book production) shifted from a manual to a mechanised industry, thanks to the introduction of Fourdrinier machines around 1801, making paper more cheaply available in much greater quantities. Finally, steam-printing, initially used to produce Britain's first national daily newspaper *The Times* in 1814, slowly superseded the iron hand-press in producing the printed page.

Louis James suggests that, for working-class readers, the sixpenny or shilling bluebooks were displaced by cheaper penny publications, such as *The Penny Novelist* (1832–4), *The Calendar of Horrors* (1835–6) and *The*

---

40 Tim Killick, *British Short Fiction in the Early Nineteenth Century: The Rise of the Tale* (Aldershot and Burlington, VT: Ashgate, 2008), pp. 11–14.
41 Jarrells, 'Short Fictional Forms', p. 488.
42 See Robert D. Mayo, *The English Novel in the Magazines, 1740–1815* (Evanston: Northwestern University Press, 1962).

Romancist, and Novelist's Library (1839–40).[43] These works often recycled tales taken from magazines or collections aimed at upper- and middle-class readers, making them available to a new audience at a fraction of the original price. From the mid-1830s, this kind of cheaply reprinted fiction was replaced by a new form of publication: the penny blood.[44] The terms 'penny bloods' and 'penny dreadfuls' are often treated as synonymous with cheap, sensational fiction sold to the working classes between 1830 and 1910. However, Helen Smith notes that the terms refer to two discrete yet overlapping periods and genres, '"bloods" denoting material aimed at adult readers from the 1830s to about 1870 and "penny dreadfuls" the later fiction, primarily written for boys'.[45] The bloods initially presented gruesome tales, typically printed on eight pages of cheap paper. Blending Gothicism with criminal melodrama, they continued the street tradition of the bluebooks, but were also influenced by the 'Newgate novels' of crime popularised by writers such as William Harrison Ainsworth and Edward Bulwer-Lytton from the later 1820s onwards. Early bloods included *Love and Crime; or, The Mystery of the Convent* (1839), Edward Montague's *The Demon of Sicily* (c. 1840), *Angela, the Orphan; or, The Bandit Monk of Italy* (1841) and Thomas Peckett Prest's *Ela, the Outcast* (c. 1841). Simon Eliot and Andrew Nash observe that these works 'resembled modern soap operas in the sense that they had no predetermined shape or end and would run just as long as there was a demand for their weekly instalments'.[46]

As was the case with bluebooks, the penny revolution was driven by a cluster of entrepreneurial publishers who became firmly associated with cheap fiction, among them George Vickers, John Dicks, Edward Lloyd and Edwin J. Brett. As Altick notes, the penny publishers availed themselves of the paraphernalia of Victorian print culture: promoting new serials by selling two numbers for the price of one, giving away free samples and previews, and advertising through posters, handbills and the wrappers of other serials. Serials were also kept alive by being reissued at regular intervals or under new titles. 'Despised though they were by the regular firms, these parish publishers in London's lower depths were the shrewdest businessmen the trade had ever known.'[47] Indeed, their tactics were eminently successful.

---

43 Louis James, *Fiction for the Working Man, 1830–1850: A Study of the Literature Produced for the Working Classes in Early Victorian Urban England* (London: Oxford University Press, 1963), p. 72.
44 James, *Fiction for the Working Man*, p. 73.
45 Helen R. Smith, *A Feast of Blood* (London: Jarndyce Antiquarian Booksellers, 2002), p. 1.
46 Eliot and Nash, 'Mass Markets', p. 421.   47 Altick, *English Common Reader*, p. 292.

Thomas Paine achieved a weekly circulation of 14,000 with the neo-Radcliffean *Angela, the Orphan*. George Vickers and his successors collaborated with the radical author G. W. M. Reynolds on the first two series of the bestselling *Mysteries of London* (1844–8). While the firm continued publication of a third series without Reynolds's involvement, the author published a sequel with the rival firm of Dicks: the even more successful *The Mysteries of the Court of London* (4 series, 1848–56). This was followed by *Wagner, the Wehr-Wolf* between 1846 and 1847. The success of their collaboration transformed Dicks from a minor publisher to one of the largest London firms from the 1850s.[48] Perhaps the most notorious penny publisher was Edward Lloyd, who, from the later 1830s, issued around two hundred novels in weekly penny numbers, most famously *Varney, the Vampyre; or, The Feast of Blood* (1845–7) and *The String of Pearls* (1846–7). Such was Lloyd's acumen that he recognised how his literateness might actually mitigate understanding his publications' potential success, employing ingenious ways of ameliorating such risk, as recalled by one of his employees:

> Our publications circulate among a class so different in education and social position from the readers of three-volume novels that we sometimes distrust our own judgement and place the manuscript in the hands of an illiterate person – a servant, or machine boy, for instance. If they pronounce favourably upon it, we think it will do.[49]

From the start of his career in 1832, Lloyd had also extended his publishing network beyond fiction into newspapers and magazines, most notably with *The Penny Sunday Times and People's Police Gazette* and *Lloyd's Illustrated London Newspaper*. Despite humble origins, Lloyd's ability to turn print into profit meant that by the time of his death in 1890 he bequeathed his inheritors an estate valued at over half a million pounds.

Modelled on Eugène Sue's sprawling *Les Mystères de Paris* (1842–3), G. W. M. Reynolds's *The Mysteries of London* was first published in weekly penny numbers between October 1844 and September 1848. The serial was incredibly popular, selling 30–40,000 copies per week upon first publication, and being frequently reprinted throughout the century.[50] According to Anne

---

48 Victor E. Neuberg, *Popular Literature: A History and Guide* (Harmondsworth: Penguin, 1977), pp. 174–7.
49 Thomas Frost (1860), quoted in Neuberg, *Popular Literature*, p. 172.
50 See Anne Humpherys, 'An Introduction to G. W. M. Reynolds's "Encyclopaedia of Tales"', in Anne Humpherys and Louis James (eds), *G. W. M. Reynolds: Nineteenth-Century Fiction, Politics and the Press* (Aldershot and Burlington, VT: Ashgate, 2008), pp. 123–32 (p. 126).

Humpherys, in attempting to capture the complexity and inequalities of urban life, 'Reynolds's work integrates all the seemingly random and fragmented genres, lives, stories and fates into one comprehensible whole, an encyclopaedia of genres unified by its insistent theme.'[51] As well as being a prolific author and editor, Reynolds was a radical journalist who decried numerous social inequalities in his writing. In his view, evil is an institutionalised malignancy that oppresses the poor, weak and vulnerable: arbitrary and capricious power lies in the hands of an aristocratic oligarchy, whose instruments are the Church, the law and the middle classes. *The Mysteries of London* distinguishes itself from earlier Gothic's concentration of evil in a single villain; instead, Reynolds's corruption is systemic: hence, his villains are politicians, financiers, lawyers and venal public servants. Yet, as Ruth Doherty has suggested, Reynolds implicates his readers into this fallen world, by merging the macroscopic view of the labyrinthine city with the microscopic scrutiny of its denizens: 'In Volume 1 of *Mysteries*, expansions and contractions and sudden zooms from the general to the particular insistently call the reader's attention to the fact that he/she is reading a narrative, while also reminding him/her of just what narrative is capable of doing.'[52] Indeed, Reynolds imbricates the scientific with the Gothic when applying the metaphor of the microscope to his study of urban life:

> A drop of purest water, magnified by that instrument some thousands of times, appears filled with horrible reptiles and monsters of revolting forms. Such is London.
> Fair and attractive as the mighty metropolis may appear to the superficial observer, it swarms with disgusting, loathsome, and venomous objects, wearing human shapes.[53]

Such structural and discursive dynamics are inflected at the level of plot through the ubiquitous instances of disguise and doubling, which makes the urban world appear even larger and more amorphous. The novel opens with Eliza Sydney, disguised as her brother Walter, entering a deserted house in Smithfield. Reynolds deploys various inter- and intratextual cues, which play not only upon the mind of Walter/Eliza but also the reader, who would have

---

51 Humpherys, 'An Introduction', pp. 127, 132.
52 Ruth Doherty, 'Reading Reynolds: *The Mysteries of London* as "Microscopic Survey"', in Paul Raphael Rooney and Anna Gasperini (eds), *Media and Print Culture Consumption in Nineteenth-Century Britain: The Victorian Reading Experience* (Basingstoke: Palgrave Macmillan, 2016), pp. 147–63 (p. 152).
53 G. W. M. Reynolds, *The Mysteries of London*, 4 vols (London: George Vickers, 1844–8), vol. 1, p. 58.

been reading *Mysteries* alongside other fictional and non-fictional texts in the shared reading world of Victorian London:

> He was alone – in an uninhabited house, in the midst of a horrible neighbourhood; and all the fearful tales of midnight murders which he had ever heard or read, rushed to his memory; then, by a strange but natural freak of the fancy, those appalling deeds of blood and crime were suddenly associated with that incomprehensible black square upon the floor.[54]

This sense of indeterminacy – which veers between the playful and the horrifying – extends beyond sexually indeterminate figures like Eliza/Walter. *Mysteries'* other heroine, Ellen Monroe, simultaneously encodes a paradigmatic femininity while disrupting conventional mores: as an artists' model, she bucks the typical Victorian narrative of the 'fallen woman', bearing a child out of wedlock, yet securing a prosperous future. Unlike other penny fiction, in which the heroine's purity is maintained in the face of all forms of adversity, *The Mysteries of London*, according to Ellen Bayuk Rosenman, 'offers an unorthodox version of female sexuality that nevertheless emerges from the logic of prevailing representational codes', while 'London offers itself up as a pornographic text in its deployment of vision and space, as the libertine's gaze … roams freely throughout urban spaces'.[55]

Indeed, roaming freely through the cityscape is Anthony Tidkins, the novel's Gothic 'Resurrection Man', and the nemesis of its hero Richard Markham. The pair first encounter each other when Markham is remanded in Newgate prison for the alleged theft of £500:

> In the course of the afternoon Markham was accosted by one of his fellow-prisoners, who beckoned him aside in a somewhat mysterious manner. This individual was a very short, thin, cadaverous-looking man, with coal-black hair and whiskers, and dark piercing eyes half concealed beneath shaggy brows of the deepest jet. He was apparently about five-and-thirty years of age. His countenance was down-cast; and when he spoke, he seemed as if he could not support the glance of the person whom he addressed. He was dressed in a seedy suit of black, and wore an oil-skin cap with a large shade.[56]

Tidkins trades in cadavers, exhuming fresh corpses, or, when the need arises, producing them from live bodies. In this context, we might consider Sally Powell's suggestion that depictions of corpses in penny-blood fiction

---

54 Reynolds, *Mysteries*, vol. 1, p. 4.
55 Ellen Bayuk Rosenman, 'Spectacular women: *The Mysteries of London* and the female body', *Victorian Studies* 40:1 (Autumn 1996): 31–64 (pp. 32, 38).
56 Reynolds, *Mysteries*, vol. 1, p. 70.

'constitute an articulation of the threat posed by city commercialism to the sanctity and survival of the working-class individual'.[57] A cog in the monstrous machine of Victorian urban capitalism, Tidkins ensures that bodies keep circulating around the city to satisfy the needs of their consumers (in this case, anatomists and their students) – in a manner uncannily akin to the circulation of penny fictions among their readership.

In James Malcolm Rymer's *Varney, the Vampyre*, the equivalence between money and bodies manifests itself in the circulation of blood as capital. According to Deborah Lutz:

> Rymer, in *Varney*, finds so many excuses for exhumation – important documents buried with the body, body-snatchers, confirmation to see if a person is really dead, scientific interest, etc. – that this one act becomes the propelling force of the narrative. Readers of the serial get drawn into consuming (and buying) further parts because they must know: will he or she rise again?[58]

The serial's cover image of Sir Francis Varney presents him as a living cadaver, a being whose humanity – unnaturally extended post-mortem – represents the decay and rot of the body politic at the hands of its vampiric capitalist structures. Rymer introduces his villain in appropriately Gothic fashion: a storm rages around a mansion house while a beautiful young woman, Flora Bannerworth, sleeps fitfully; lightning flashes trace the movement of a sinister, gaunt figure as he steals into her bedchamber. Awakened, Varney's victim catches a sight of her persecutor before he feasts upon her:

> The figure turns half round, and the light falls upon the face. It is perfectly white – perfectly bloodless. The eyes look like polished tin; the lips are drawn back, and the principal feature next to those dreadful eyes is the teeth – the fearful looking teeth – projecting like those of some wild animal, hideously, glaringly white, and fang-like. It approaches the bed with a strange, gliding movement. It clashes together the long nails that literally appear to hang from the finger ends. No sound comes from its lips.[59]

---

57 Sally Powell, 'Black Markets and Cadaverous Pies: The Corpse, Urban Trade and Industrial Consumption in the Penny Blood', in Andrew Maunder and Grace Moore (eds), *Victorian Crime, Madness and Sensation* (Aldershot and Burlington, VT: Ashgate, 2004), pp. 45–58 (p. 45).
58 Deborah Lutz, 'Gothic Fictions in the Nineteenth Century', in John Kucich and Jenny Bourne Taylor (eds), *The Oxford History of the Novel in English, Volume 3: The Nineteenth-Century Novel 1820–1880* (Oxford: Oxford University Press, 2012), pp. 76–89 (p. 81).
59 James Malcolm Rymer, *Varney, the Vampyre; or, The Feast of Blood* (London: Edward Lloyd, 1845–7), p. 3.

Royce Mahawatte reminds us that 'Cheap literature, of course, had its literal monsters. Rymer's Lord Francis Varney was *the* Victorian vampire, not Polidori's Lord Ruthven nor Bram Stoker's *Dracula*.'[60]

In his never-ending quest to satiate his blood-cravings, Varney returns to his ancestral home to persecute his descendants, the Bannerworths. His Gothic doubleness is effectively, if obviously, relayed in the illustration that accompanies the scene: a portrait of the haughty *living* Varney gazes upon the scene of a bestial *revenant* feasting upon one of his scions. If not quite as explicitly radical as Reynolds's *The Mysteries of London*, Rymer's novel nonetheless details how middle-class consumption turns upon itself, in a scene that weaves together cannibalism, voyeurism and quasi-incestuous sexual violence. Yet, this doubling – between the living and undead Varney – is only one instance of his complex alterity. Sara Hackenberg notes that 'Varney's status as embodied history grows increasingly complex as the serial continues.'[61] A protean figure, he first appears in the novel as the Bannerworths' undead ancestor, then disguises himself as a human acquaintance of their deceased father, before occupying the role of a friend to the family. When he leaves the Bannerworths, Varney takes on the various other guises, playing a Teutonic aristocratic, a disfigured colonel in the Indian army, the sinister Mr Black and a Gothic Italian monk. As Varney's identities proliferate, we are presented, as Hackenberg argues, with two possible explanations for his vampiric state: 'the "scientific" hypothesis of revival by an experimenting anatomist, and the "supernatural" version whereby Varney's resurrection is also his punishment for having murdered his wife in a jealous rage.'[62]

If *The Mysteries of London* was the best-selling novel of its time and if *Varney* gave the Victorians their paradigmatic vampire, the longest-lived penny blood must surely be Rymer's *The String of Pearls*, later made famous under its revised title *Sweeney Todd, the Demon Barber of Fleet Street*. The tale of the eponymous homicidal barber and his accomplice Mrs Lovett, who turns Todd's victims into her famously delicious meat pies, has been adapted into a chapbook, plays, films and of course a long-running musical by Stephen Sondheim. Andrew King sees the novel as a 'warning about the

---

60 Royce Mahawatte, 'Horror in the Nineteenth Century: Dreadful Sensations, 1820–80', in Xavier Aldana Reyes (ed.), *Horror: A Literary History* (London: British Library, 2016), pp. 77–101 (pp. 96–7).
61 Sara Hackenberg, 'Vampires and resurrection men: the perils and pleasures of the embodied past in 1840s sensational fiction', *Victorian Studies* 52:1 (2009): 63–75 (p. 70).
62 Hackenberg, 'Vampires and resurrection men', p. 70.

dangers of capitalism in a city where people are reduced to commodities and alienated from the production processes of what they consume'.[63] One of the most morbidly entertaining scenes occurs towards the end of the novel, shortly after Todd has murdered Mr Wrankley the tobacconist and comforts his (unknowing) widow with some gruesome advice:

> '[M]y poor, dear, handsome Wrankley! Oh, I shall never be myself again; I have not eaten anything since he went out.'
> 'Then buy, a pie, madam,' said Todd, as he held one close to her. 'Look up, Mrs. Wrankley, lift off the top crust, madam, and you may take my word for it you will soon see *something* of Mr. Wrankley.'[64]

The second chapter introduces us to Johanna Oakley, who believes that her lover, the sailor Mark Ingestrie, is lost at sea; however, circumstances lead her to suspect far more sinister reasons for his disappearance. Johanna is assisted in her detections by Colonel Jeffery and the magistrate Sir Richard Brown; meanwhile, Todd's young apprentice Tobias, who has discovered his master's grim secret, escapes the madhouse to which he has been confined and alerts the authorities about Todd's misdeeds. Towards the end of the novel, we learn that a recently returned Ingestrie had in fact been forced into servitude by Mrs Lovett in her subterranean bakery, where he identifies the secret of her delectable main ingredient. Frustrated by the lack of progress in discovering Ingestrie's fate, Johanna enters Todd's employ disguised as a boy. Exploring the productive role of dread in the novel, Samantha Morse notes how the gender politics of the penny blood challenge the conventional Victorian coding of femininity: 'Instead of remaining passively "embittered" by uncertainty, Johanna actively ventures toward the "dreadful mystery". Most strikingly, the moment that Johanna *seeks* rather than *encounters* dread, she cross-dresses as a boy.'[65] At the novel's conclusion, Ingestrie reifies the consumptive economy that has reduced human flesh to meat by securing his escape while hidden among a tray full of pies called up by Mrs Lovett for her unsuspecting patrons:

> They came up upon a large tray, about six feet square, and the moment Mrs. Lovett ceased turning the handle, and let a catch fall that prevented the

---

63 Andrew King, '"Literature of the Kitchen": Cheap Serial Fiction of the 1840s and 1850s', in Pamela K. Gilbert (ed.), *A Companion to Sensation Fiction* (Malden, MA: Wiley-Blackwell, 2011), pp. 38–53 (p. 44).
64 James Malcolm Rymer, *The String of Pearls*, 2nd edition (Ware: Wordsworth Editions, 2010), p. 244.
65 Samantha Morse, 'Affective ethics and democratic politics in *Sweeney Todd* and the Victorian penny press', *Journal of Victorian Culture* 24:1 (January 2019): 1–17 (p. 8).

platform receding again, to the astonishment and terror of everyone, away flew all the pies, tray and all, across the counter, and a man, who was lying crouched down in an exceedingly flat state under the tray, sprang to his feet.

Mrs. Lovett shrieked, as well she might, and then she stood trembling, and looking as pale as death itself. It was the doomed cook from the cellars, who had adopted this mode of escape.

The throngs of persons in the shop looked petrified, and after Mrs. Lovett's shriek, there was an awful stillness for about a minute, and then the young man who officiated as cook spoke.

'Ladies and Gentlemen – I fear that what I am going to say will spoil your appetites; but the truth is beautiful at all times, and I have to state that Mrs. Lovett's pies are made of *human flesh!*'[66]

While the majority of penny bloods remain either anonymous or have been attributed to a predominantly male authorship, Mary Elizabeth Braddon entered the twilight of the bloods with her debut novel *Three Times Dead; or, The Secret of the Heath* (1860), which was revised and reissued in 1861 under its better-known title *The Trail of the Serpent*. Writing as Lady Caroline Lascelles, she published *The Black Band; or, The Mysteries of Midnight* with the *Halfpenny Journal* (1861–2), working on it alongside her middle-class sensation novels, *Lady Audley's Secret* (1861–2) and *Aurora Floyd* (1862–3). Centred upon the titular secret society led by the Austrian spy Colonel Oscar Bertrand, *The Black Band* makes effective use of the tropes established two decades previously in order to explore class and gender within an exploitative and extractive milieu. Bertrand describes the Black Band as part of a network so powerful that it can literally redirect people's destinies at a whim, as he tells the beautiful but corrupt Lady Edith Merton:

> 'I am the chief of a sect so powerful, Madam, that princes acknowledge, though they fear to share, its power ... I have but to stretch out one of these fingers' – extending his slender and dazzlingly white hand as he spoke – 'and the man you love will drop dead in the streets of London, on his way home from this house, and to-morrow morning the newspapers will be filled with the account of a terrible and mysterious murder.'[67]

In one of the novel's many sub-plots, the virtuous ballerina Clara Melville is persistently harassed by Frederick Beaumorris, who is unaware that he is her uncle: she is providentially saved from rape by Bertrand, who reveals to Beaumorris his connection to Clara. Robin Barrow notes that 'The narrative

---

66 Rymer, *String of Pearls*, pp. 256–7.
67 Mary Elizabeth Braddon, *The Black Band; or, The Mysteries of Midnight* (London: George Vickers, 1864), p. 47.

pleasure of Clara's predicament is located in her objectification, and her choice to be an unwilling victim merely generates a sadistic response to virtue in distress.'[68]

Penny Dreadfuls, 1860–1900: The Youth Market and the Waning of the Gothic

The popularity of the penny bloods had waned among adult readers by the 1860s, and the penny publishers shifted their attentions to the youth market. Serials like *The Wild Boys of London; or, The Children of the Night* (1864–6) and *The Poor Boys of London; or, Driven to Crime* (1866) supplied melodramatic stories to boys thirsting for adventure. *Wild Boys* 'was a lurid and violent tale focussing on a gang of street urchins who lived in London's sewers, and who made a living selling stolen property and corpses salvaged from the Thames, while fighting off murderers, kidnappers, grave-robbers and child molesters'.[69] Once working-class boys established themselves as the primary audience for penny dreadfuls from the 1860s, child characters increasingly took up the mantle of protagonists in these criminal narratives. In 1866, Edwin J. Brett began publishing *The Boys of England*, which introduced the figure of the crime-busting outlaw Jack Harkaway, who became beloved by a generation of young readers. One of the most popular penny dreadfuls was *Black Bess; or, The Knight of the Road* (1867–8), a 254-part serial that told the story of the notorious highwayman and murderer, Richard 'Dick' Turpin (1705–39). Such was the character's popular appeal that in the pages of later dreadfuls, he was recast from a criminal bandit into a modern-day Robin Hood, protecting the weak and poor.

Lucy Andrew notes that 'Penny dreadfuls that celebrated crime and criminals were denounced for their pernicious influence on impressionable young readers who were encouraged, critics argued, to follow in the footsteps of their fictionalized criminal heroes through the texts' glorification of crime.'[70] Numerous essays from the closing decades of the century consider the vexed issue of penny dreadfuls' beguiling influence on the youth of the day. In an article entitled 'The Influence of the

---

68 Robin Barrow, 'Braddon's haunting memories: rape, class and the Victorian popular press', *Women's Writing* 13:3 (2006): 348–68 (p. 359).
69 Kirkpatrick, *Penny Dreadful*, p. 74.
70 Lucy Andrew, '"Away with dark shadders!": juvenile detection versus juvenile crime in *The Boy Detective; or, The Crimes of London. A Romance of Modern Times*', *Clues* 30:1 (April 2012): 18–29 (p. 19).

Penny Dreadful' (1888), the anonymous writer discusses juvenile defendants who claim that their reading of penny dreadfuls had prompted them to commit acts of murder, arson and burglary. Even worse, the writer expostulates, are those who actually 'play the murderer or the thief. More commonly they only swagger and pretend', wasting precious police time while garnering notoriety for themselves. Instead of censorship, the author recommends corporal punishment – not just for the juvenile delinquents but for the publishers of penny dreadfuls themselves.[71] In a piece entitled 'How to Counteract the "Penny Dreadful"' (1895), Hugh Chisholm cites a coroner's inquest into a recent case of matricide, in which the jury called for legislators to ban penny dreadfuls: in the murderer's room, police found 'a pile of cheap romances, reeking with bloodshed and all modes of criminal horrors'.[72] A lengthy survey of penny fiction in the *Quarterly Review* in 1890 concluded that the best solution to the dreadful malaise was to 'begin in the school-room – not necessarily by yielding to the popular cry for technical education for boys and cookery classes for girls at the public expense – but by encouraging the growth of something resembling culture'.[73] Such negativity, however, was not universal. Undertaking an empirical analysis for *Time* in 1888, Thomas MacKay suggested that the works of Henry Rider Haggard and Anthony Trollope contained as much violence and murder as penny fictions: 'I had always thought that the Penny Dreadful was a very immoral and disgusting publication. As well as I can make out, this is far from the case; if there are any such books, I have not come across them.'[74] Indeed, in his volume of *Defences*, G. K. Chesterton pointed to the hypocrisy of such hysteria to what he perceived as a far less invidious form of writing than so-called 'serious literature':

> At the very instant that we curse the Penny Dreadful for encouraging thefts upon property, we canvass the proposition that all property is theft. At the very instant we accuse it (quite unjustly) of lubricity and indecency, we are cheerfully reading philosophies which glory in lubricity and indecency. At the very instant that we charge it with encouraging the young to destroy life, we are placidly discussing whether life is worth preserving.[75]

---

71 Anon., 'The Influence of the Penny Dreadful', *Saturday Review*, 20 October 1888, p. 458.
72 Hugh Chisholm, 'How to counteract the "penny dreadful"', *Fortnightly Review* 58:347 (1895): 765–75 (p. 765).
73 Anon., 'Article VI: penny fiction', *Quarterly Review* 171:341 (1890): 170.
74 T. MacKay, 'Penny dreadfuls', *Time* 19:44 (1888): 225.
75 G. K. Chesterton, 'A Defence of Penny Dreadfuls', in *The Defendant* (London: Dent, 1907), pp. 8–17 (p. 15).

Potter has talked powerfully about the crucial role played by trade Gothic and its symbiotic relationship with mainstream Gothic literature, noting that 'distinguishing between canon and trade, legitimate and corrupt, and popular and disreputable tends to isolate prevalent and popular manifestations of the Gothic potential, eventually marginalising the unadorned and corrupted forms of the Gothic and uniformly narrowing the scope of the Gothic fiction'.[76] The cheap book revolution of the nineteenth century stimulated a demand for affordable literature that, in turn, stimulated a transformation in publishers' practices. Subaltern literary forms they may have been, but the Gothic bluebook and penny blood met not only working-class readers' appetites for entertainment, but also their hunger for literacy and, thus, social power. Despite their often-outlandish plots, grisly happenings and stock characters, these fictions – whether short and telegraphed or rambling and tentacular – spoke meaningfully to the experiences and perspectives of the readers of a rapidly urbanising and industrialising nation. It is satisfying to see, despite heated disparagement during the nineteenth century and critical inattention during the twentieth, that recent and ongoing scholarship is, at last, acknowledging the central and transformative role played by street fiction in the history of Gothic, pushing beyond rigid definitions of canonicity and allowing us instead to understand the Gothic as always elastic, diverse and organic.

---

76 Potter, *History of Gothic Publishing*, p. 39.

2.7

The Theatrical Gothic in the Nineteenth Century

KELLY JONES

In his play-going diary for 1852, Henry Morley records his distaste for the dramatic fare offered at the Princess Theatre in London on 19 June, a revival of 'spectral melodrama' with a play called *The Vampire*:

> Unfortunately the mischief of such a piece, produced at a respectable theatre, does not end with the weariness of the spectators, who come to shudder and remain to yawn; for it is not only 'beside the purpose of playing', but directly contravenes it; and, though it may be too dull to pervert the tastes of those who witness its vapid extravagances, it has power to bring discredit on the most genial of arts.[1]

This was an early performance of Dion Boucicault's *The Vampire: A Phantasm Related in Three Dramas*, adapted from *Le Vampire* (1820), a play by Pierre Carmouche, Achile de Jouffroy and Charles Nodier which was duly abbreviated and renamed under the catchier title of *The Phantom* for its American presentation. Not everyone shared Morley's aversion, however, and Queen Victoria herself saw the production on 14 June, returning for a second performance a week later. Boucicault's playing as his own titular character, Alan Raby, clearly made an impression on the Queen, as she would sketch the likeness of this dashing, moustachioed villain on her embossed headed note paper.[2] Morley was altogether less enamoured with Raby, though, and writes of how the character 'passes all bounds of tolerance' through the representation of

> an animated corpse which goes about in Christian attire, and although never known to eat or drink or shake hands, is allowed to sit at good men's feasts; which renews its odious life every hundred years by sucking a young lady's

---

[1] Henry Morley, *The Journal of a London Playgoer From 1851–1866* (London: George Routledge & Sons, 1866), p. 55.
[2] See Royal Collection Trust <www.rct.uk/collection/980008-ad> (last accessed 24 May 2019).

blood, after fascinating her by motions which resemble mesmerism burlesqued; and which, notwithstanding its well-purchased longevity, is capable of being killed during its term in order that it may be revived by moonbeams.[3]

In 1852, the Gothic evidently continued to exercise an unsettling presence on the British stage past its designated golden period of the 1790s to 1830s.[4] Nevertheless, it was rare to see a Gothic drama so brazenly exhibited in full light in the mid-nineteenth century. For, with the proliferation of the domestic melodrama, the Gothic was increasingly perceived as old-fashioned and overly fanciful. Among the targets for Morley's annoyance at the drama's assault on 'the possible' was the audacity on behalf of the playwright to set the third part of the drama in 1860, thus placing it eight years in the future, and thereby representing a Gothic world that not only refused to stay assigned to the archaic past, but which also, more troublingly, is shown to re-emerge in a time that is yet to come!

Despite its seeming defeat at the hands of the new melodrama and, later, the emerging stage realism, the Gothic continued to stalk the stage well into the nineteenth century. Christine Gledhill remarks on how 'Gothic traces infused the domestic with the sensation, mystery, and excitement that made it melodrama', continuing that 'if the castle disappeared, the country house or cottage lay near a murky wood, and, not far off, the town featured a courthouse, a gaol, and an asylum; and if ghosts and specters vanished, premonitions, memories, and dreams kept the warning presences of the dead close at hand'.[5] Shape-shifting and refusing to die outright, the Gothic mode would inform melodrama, domestic drama, sensation drama and even the emerging realist dramas to the end of the century. Moreover, while according to received narratives of theatre history, the new modes of realism would claim a victorious precedence over the drama of the shudder, I argue in this chapter that as the fin de siècle loomed, attempts to repress the Gothic on stage were met with an increasingly Gothic representation of the theatre itself within the wider popular and literary imagination.

---

3 Morley, *Journal*, p. 54.
4 See Jeffrey N. Cox, 'English Gothic Theatre', in Jerrold E. Hogle (ed.), *The Cambridge Companion to Gothic Fiction* (Cambridge: Cambridge University Press, 2002), pp. 125–44 (p. 125).
5 Christine Gledhill, 'Domestic Melodrama', in Carolyn Williams (ed.), *The Cambridge Companion to English Melodrama* (Cambridge: Cambridge University Press, 2018), pp. 61–77 (p. 64).

The Legacy of the Eighteenth-Century Gothic Stage

Morley's complaint that the 'vapid extravagances' of *The Vampire* threatened the aesthetic integrity of the theatre seems somewhat short-sighted if we understand that theatricality is seminal to the effect of the Gothic aesthetic, a point that Diego Saglia notes in relation to the fictional Gothic in particular.[6] We might look to a text such as Matthew Lewis's *The Monk* (1796), with its heightened awareness of the dangers of seductive illusion and artificial façade, together with its realisations of bodies in spaces such as the claustrophobia of Agnes's dungeon and the proximity of Ambrosio and Matilda in his monastic cell, to understand how the Gothic impulse oscillates with and responds to the spatial, sensual and dramatic textures of theatrical performance.

Moreover, if the Gothic, as Fred Botting has argued, is characterised by excess, the theatre, like no other medium, can exploit its rich abundance of sensational effect through its material representations.[7] The dramas that emerged in the late eighteenth century and into the nineteenth were able physically to heighten the already excessive renderings of spaces, bodies and liveness to be found in the literary Gothic mode. Through emerging developments in stage technology, the Romantic, exotic locales that typified the early Gothic imagination – spaces such as the dungeon, forest, castle, graveyard, clandestine passageway and crypt – were given a graphic and thrilling spatial materiality through stage-craft and the scene-painter's art. Matthew Lewis's 1797 crowd-pleaser *The Castle Spectre* stages its ultimate scene in '*A gloomy subterraneous Dungeon, wide and lofty: The upper part of it has in several places fallen in, and left large chasms*' as Angela discovers Reginald, her tortured, emaciated father, imprisoned in the bowels of the castle of the villainous Osmond.[8] Representative time in performance, moreover, developed a quality of Gothic excess, arguably one that was more keenly felt by an audience watching the action unfold in front of them. Often, this involved the overwhelming surfeit of long-repressed secrets bursting their tenements over a condensed time frame, such as in Charles Maturin's *Bertram; or, The Castle of St. Aldobrand* (1816), in which passions that have been long subdued bring the characters to bloody catastrophe over the course of a couple of hours when the dark, Byronic anti-hero rekindles his passionate love affair with

---

6 Diego Saglia, 'Gothic Theatre, 1765–Present', in Glennis Byron and Dale Townshend (eds), *The Gothic World* (Abingdon and New York: Routledge, 2014), pp. 354–65 (p. 354).
7 Fred Botting, *Gothic*, 2nd edition (London and New York: Routledge, 2014), pp. 6–7.
8 Matthew Lewis, *The Castle Spectre: A Drama. In Five Acts* (London, Printed for J. Bell, 1798), Act 5, scene 3.

the now-married Imogine. Meanwhile, bodies of actors on the stage embraced an excessive visual rhetoric to be read by an audience through the use of heightened physical gesture, elaborate costume and representations of gory assault. As Bertram stands over the mutilated body of Imogine's husband St Aldobrand, Imogine herself is appalled by his betrayal, and with *'Her hair dishevelled, her dress stained with blood'*, she flees with her young child to the Forest of the Dark Knight. Bertram's own 'speechless horror' as he watches Imogine's descent into madness (having, as she perceives, lost her infant in the cavern of the 'forest fiend'), illustrates the devastating pathos conveyed by the bodies on the stage in the play's conclusive moments:

> Imogine: (Raising herself at the sound of his voice.) Bertram.
> *He rushes towards her, and first repeats 'Imogine' feebly, as he approaches, he utters her name again passionately, but as he draws nearer and sees her look of madness and desperation, he repeats it once more in despair, and does not dare to approach her, till he perceives her falling into Clotilda's arms, and catches her in his.*
> Imogine: 'Have I deserved this of thee?' – *She dies slowly with her eyes fixed on Bertram, who continues to gaze on her unconscious of her having expired.*[9]

Meanwhile, James Boaden's *Fontainville Forest* (1794) brazenly eschewed the explained supernaturalism of Ann Radcliffe's *The Romance of the Forest* (1791) when he staged the spectre that appears before Adeline in his adaptation of the novel. Here, rather than being an invention of the heroine's distressed imagination, the phantom assumes material form as it *'glides across the dark part of the stage'*.[10] Such an excessive use of Gothic spectacle led to a critical squeamishness regarding the staging of ghosts and other supernatural manifestations. A critic for the *Analytical Review*, for example, censured Harriet Lee's *The Mysterious Marriage* (1798) 'for perverting the simplicity of the drama by the introduction of visionary and phantastic beings', eventually cautioning the periodical's readers as follows: 'let ghosts and hobgoblins people the pages of a romance, but never let their forms be seen to glide across the stage'.[11]

---

9 This example follows the 1816 first edition that Maturin prepared in response to revisions suggested by Sir Walter Scott, George Lamb and George Byron. See Charles Robert Maturin, 'Bertram; or, The Castle of St. Aldobrand', in Jeffrey N. Cox (ed.), *Seven Gothic Dramas 1789–1825* (Athens: Ohio University Press, 1992), pp. 315–83 (Act 5, scene 3).
10 James Boaden, *Fontainville Forest: a play, in five acts* (London: Hookham and Carpenter, 1794), Act 3.
11 The article from *Analytical Review* 27 (1798): 295–6 is reprinted in E. J. Clery and Robert Miles (eds), *Gothic Documents: A Sourcebook 1700–1820* (Manchester and New York: Manchester University Press, 2000), p. 197.

Such censoriousness did little to vanquish the popularity or the theatrical currency of the Gothic during the first three decades of the new century, both on the popular and on the legitimate stage. Spectre-riddled dramas such as Matthew Lewis's *The Wood Daemon; or, The Clock Has Struck* (1807) and imported horrors such as Carl Maria von Weber's opera *Der Freishütz* (1824) – an international hit that spawned various English adaptations – abounded even as the Gothic mode crept into the most aesthetically elevated tragedies of Joanna Baillie, Percy Bysshe Shelley and Mary Russell Mitford. When, in 1802, Thomas Holcroft introduced melodrama to the London stage with *The Tale of Mystery*, an adaptation of René-Charles Guilbert de Pixérécourt's *Cœlina, ou l'enfant du mystère* (1800), this new drama too was infused with the hallmarks of the Gothic. It featured a sublime alpine landscape, a troop of dastardly bandits, a brooding aristocrat with a dark history, a persecuted heroine, a mute, impoverished hero and humorous interjections from the domestic hands who temper the darker moments of the plot with more quotidian dilemmas. The Gothic mode fuelled the new melodrama and it was not until Douglas Jerrold's world-wide hit *Black-Ey'd Susan* in 1829 that the nautical and domestic would usurp the Gothic's hold on the theatrical imagination.

Gothic Melodrama: A Problem with Taxonomy

Perhaps the reticence with which theatre history admits the long-reaching influence of the Gothic across the nineteenth century may be in part due to uncertainties regarding melodrama's formal relationship to, and distinction from, the contemporary genres of tragedy and Romantic drama.[12] It is difficult, therefore, to track the wider influence of the Gothic into the nineteenth century within this matrix of unclear (and at times, unhelpful) binaries, including the popular versus the legitimate stage, the Romantic drama and the melodramatic.[13] Furthermore, there remains some residual confusion regarding assumptions that the melodrama was the natural progeny of the late eighteenth-century Romantic drama. Such assumptions may be a consequence of the marginalisation of both the Gothic mode and the melodrama

---

12 For an example of an attempt to mark distinctions between melodrama and tragedy, see Robert B. Heilman, *Tragedy and Melodrama: Versions of Experience* (Seattle, WA and London: University of Washington Press, 1968).

13 This point is made by Jeffrey N. Cox, 'The Death of Tragedy; or, the Birth of Melodrama', in Tracy C. Davis and Peter Holland (eds), *The Performing Century: Nineteenth-Century Theatre's History* (Basingstoke: Palgrave Macmillan, 2007), pp. 161–81 (pp. 161–2); as well as by Diego Saglia, 'Gothic theatre', p. 356.

in favour of the perceived revolutionary potential of social and aesthetic realism in the nineteenth-century theatre.

Nevertheless, despite the shared neurosis that, together with their mutual Gothic proclivities, characterises both early melodrama and the more poetic Romantic tragedy, Jeffrey N. Cox problematises the interchangeabilty of the two forms while remaining careful to distance the new melodrama from both the Gothic and from Romantic tragedy. He draws upon Charles Nodier's avowed distaste for the Romantic drama's 'artificial pomp of lyricism' and his championing of the clear sense of moral responsibility that he ascribes to melodrama by comparison.[14] Elsewhere, Cox argues that there is an ethical ambiguity pertaining to the Gothic drama of the late eighteenth and early nineteenth centuries that would unsettle the moral incline of the new melodrama: 'the Gothic and the melodrama part company over the latter's commitment to "ordinary morality"', and while '[t]he Gothic always explores the extraordinary, the extreme ... melodrama displays the ordinary, the norm'.[15] Part of this ambivalence towards the conventional moral order, Cox explains, is in the drama's treatment of villainy. He notes of villain-heroes such as Mortimer in Francis North's *The Kentish Barons* (1791) and Osmond in Lewis's *The Castle Spectre* that the individual liberty that they pursue offers a radical (though ultimately tragic) zeal, claiming that 'We are invited to admire these oppressors, for they embody the possibility of an individual revolt counter to the communal liberation celebrated in hymeneal union and uncovered social identities.'[16] There is, for instance, a psychological depth to the hatred that torments De Monfort in Baillie's 1800 play of that name, an interiority that considerably complicates his villainy; similarly, there is no clear moral dimension to the punishment meted out by the murderers of the house of Cenci in Shelley's 1819 tragedy as the victim of incestuous rape is not spared the wrath of the law.

This ambiguous treatment of villainy is accompanied by (and perhaps feeds) the abstruse generic identity of the drama. Cox argues further that the Gothic drama that emerged in the 1790s, with its hybridity and its collapse of high and low cultural forms, responded to and reflected the chaos engendered by political upheaval on the Continent, furthermore observing that

---

14 Charles Nodier, 'Introduction', Charles Guilbert de Pixérécourt, *Théâtre Choisi*, 4 vols (Geneva: Slatkine Reprints, 1971), vol. 1: p. vii cited in Cox, 'The Death of Tragedy', p. 164.
15 Jeffrey N. Cox (ed.), *Seven Gothic Dramas 1789–1825* (Athens, OH: Ohio University Press, 1992), p. 42.
16 Cox, *Seven Gothic Dramas*, p. 31.

'the essentials of the Gothic setting and plot – the castle, the villain, the heroine's capture and escape – could be read as embodying the rhythms of the Revolution and its liberation of enclosed spaces from the powers of the past'.[17] By comparison, he ascribes the conservative tendencies of melodrama at the dawn of the subsequent century to a need to assuage contemporary anxieties provoked by Napoleonic wars following the Treaty of Amiens of 1802, as well as to the cultural neuroses of melodrama itself and its obsession with legitimising its status as a form of theatrical performance.

In what follows, I do not seek to redefine or to deny such distinctions, but instead to investigate how residual and dissonant Gothic impulses continue to haunt the content, the style and the medium of presentation of emergent dramatic forms, whatever the fixity of their generic identity, well into the nineteenth century and beyond. Moreover, despite sometimes conflicting agendas, both Romantic tragedy and melodrama possess a shared visual language that expands upon the excessive primacy of affect and sensation within the narrative itself. Advocating a phenomenological approach to the field, Jacky Bratton writes of the problems attendant upon reading melodrama as a literary form, claiming that to impose such definitions is to misread a drama 'which took sensuous and spectacular performance to new heights of illusion' as a transgressive breaker of the rules by which we judge 'good' writing for the theatre.[18] The Gothic spectacle of the castle crypt in George Colman the Younger's *Bluebeard; or, Female Curiosity* (1798) is representative of the thrilling (and gruesome) scale of this ocular abundance:

> SHACABAC *puts the key into the lock; the door instantly sinks with a tremendous crash, and the Blue Chamber appears streaked with vivid streams of blood. The Figures in the Picture over the door, change their position, and* ABOMELIQUE *is represented in the action of beheading the Beauty he was, before, supplicating. The Pictures, and Devices of Love, change to subjects of Horror and Death. The interior apartment (which the sinking of the door discovers,) exhibits various Tombs, in a sepulchral building; – in the midst of which ghastly and supernatural forms are seen; – some in motion, some fixed. –In the centre, is a large Skeleton, seated on a Tomb, (with a dart in his hand) and over his head, in characters of blood is written* 'THE PUNISHMENT OF CURIOSITY'.[19]

---

17 Cox, *Seven Gothic Dramas*, p. 18.
18 Jacky Bratton, 'Romantic Melodrama', in Jane Moody and Daniel Quinn (eds), *The Cambridge Companion to British Theatre, 1730–1830* (Cambridge: Cambridge University Press, 2007), pp. 115–27 (p. 117).
19 George Colman the Younger, *Blue-Beard; or, Female Curiosity! A Dramatick Romance* (London: Printed by T. Woodfall for Cadell and Davies, 1798), Act 1, scene 3.

Elsewhere, Isaac Pocock's *The Miller and His Men* (1813) culminates in an explosion as the villain's jilted lover, Ravina, sets alight the fuse that will exterminate the mill owned by the treacherous Grindoff. Richard Brinsley Peake's *Presumption; or, The Fate of Frankenstein* (1823), in addition to the spectacular avalanche that 'annihilates' Frankenstein and his Demon at the play's conclusion as they meet at 'the very extremity of the stage', treated audiences to the spectacle of the Demon's daring rescue of the heroine as she swoons on her encounter with the creature and tumbles into a rivulet, as well as the vision of the creature's revenge as the De Laceys' cottage is consumed in flames.[20] Meanwhile, in Edward Fitzball's *The Flying Dutchman; or, The Phantom Ship* (1827), another blazing torch ignites the stage spectacle as the hero Varnish sets fire to the mystic book of the demonic Captain Vanderdecken to unleash 'agitated waters ... covering the stage to the orchestra', all to the accompanying effects of peels of thunder and the ominous sound of a gong as Vanderdecken is entombed beneath the waves to join the sea-witch, Rockalda.[21] Later, Bram Stoker describes the full sacks of salt that were used to create the thick snow in the wintry landscape of Henry Irving's elaborate revival of Dion Boucicault's 1852 'Dramatic Romance' *The Corsican Brothers* at the Lyceum, London, in 1880.[22]

Such spectacle was undoubtedly served by the expansion of the theatres. The theatre at Drury Lane was rebuilt by Henry Holland in 1794, and by Benjamin Wyatt in 1812. The 1866 Select Committee list reports the theatre's capacity to be 3,800 (though 3,600 may have been closer to the mark).[23] New theatres such as the Britannia in Hoxton, capitalised on the rapid urban growth and the Committee list suggests that this particular venue could accommodate up to 3,900 patrons. However, even smaller-scale, non-patented theatres such as the Sans Pareil in the Strand, under the management of Jane Scott, would become synonymous with lavish Gothic drama such as Scott's own *The Old Oak Chest* (1816).

Meanwhile, the introduction of gas lighting in 1817 at the Lyceum, followed by limelight in 1837, and then later in 1848, the electric carbon-

---

20 Richard Brinsley Peake, *Presumption; or, The Fate of Frankenstein*, edited by Stephen C. Behrendt, Romantic Circles Edition <https://romantic-circles.org/editions/peake/index.html> (last accessed 7 June 2019), Act 3, scene 5; Act 2, scene 5.
21 Edward Fitzball, *The Flying Dutchman; or, The Phantom Ship: A Nautical Drama* (London: G. H. Davidson, n.d.), Act 3, scene 4.
22 Quoted in Michael R. Booth, 'Aspects of Staging in Irving's *The Corsican Brothers*', in Michael R. Booth (ed.), *English Plays of the Nineteenth Century II: Drama 1850–1900* (Oxford: Clarendon Press, 1969), pp. 71–5 (p. 72).
23 See Michael R. Booth, *Theatre in the Victorian Age* (Cambridge: Cambridge University Press, 1991), p. 61.

arc and the carbon-filament light in the 1880s, allowed for tighter control over the direction and intensity of the illumination and abetted experimentation with colour.[24] Examples of such lighting effects include the 'thunder and flames of red fire' that are called for in the final scene of Fitzball's *The Flying Dutchman* as Vanderdecken sinks within the altar, and the 'blue ethereal flame' (Act 2, scene 7) that accompanies the Bleeding Nun as she appears for the play's final image in later versions of W. H. Grosette's dramatic adaptation of Lewis's *The Monk* in *Raymond and Agnes, or the Bleeding Nun of Lindenberg; an Interesting Melodrama* (1811).[25] Scene-painting too, as pioneered and inspired by Philip James de Loutherbourg's experiments at Drury Lane in the 1770s, and equally significant when Lewis's *The Castle Spectre* was performed there in 1797, explored the impact of focused illumination upon gauze and silk screens.

The actor, forced to compete with the seductive glitter of the spectacle of lighting, scenery and costume, became part of the stage picture, a component in service to the all-consuming image. That the autonomy of the actor's body became threatened further underscores the Gothic dimension of the new technology even as, ironically, it was the Gothic drama that would inspire such innovations in stagecraft. The vampire trap was created for James Robinson Planché's *The Vampire; or, The Bride of the Isles* (1820) as a device that would enable the performer to disappear down a carefully constructed aperture in the stage to give the illusion of the vanishing body. Boucicault's *The Corsican Brothers* introduced the ghost glide, while Fitzball's *The Flying Dutchman* made use of the phantasmagoria to create the phantom ship. The aural dimension of the theatrical experience, too, was seminal to its overall effect, particularly in melodrama where, as Bratton explains, 'the music does not accompany but actively participates in the scene, shaping the narrative and extending what the characters do and say as well as framing the audience's responses'.[26] The sonic life of the drama subsumed the audience in the complete theatrical effect.[27]

---

24 Michael R. Booth, *Victorian Spectacular Theatre 1850–1910* (Boston, London and Henley: Routledge & Kegan Paul, 1981), pp. 24–6.
25 Fitzball, *The Flying Dutchman*, Act 3, scene 4; W. H. Grosette, *Raymond and Agnes; or, the Bleeding Nun of Lindenberg; A Melodrama in Two Acts* (London: Thomas Hailes Lacy, n.d.), Act 2, scene 7.
26 Bratton, 'Romantic melodrama', p. 120.
27 On the power of aural innovations in the Gothic drama, see Michael Gamer, 'Gothic Melodrama', in Williams (ed.), *The Cambridge Companion to English Melodrama*, pp. 31–46 (pp. 36–8).

Changing Perspectives: Dark Domesticities

Even as they seduced and dazzled their spectators, these dramas, inflected with Gothic tropes, enabled a more radical though not always overt political perspective as the theatre provided a space to explore the tensions between the dominant ruling class and the emerging agency of the honest, humble, working-class man. Labyrinthine castles, abbey ruins and dank dungeons, spaces associated with the feudal past and the Old Religion, were ubiquitous as sites of incarceration and torture, usually of the female body. With her morbid fascination for ghost stories, the titular heroine in Baillie's Gothic tragedy *Orra* (1812) is imprisoned in a castle that is said to be haunted as punishment for her refusal to marry her guardian's son. Orra in her dungeon descends into madness as her supernatural terrors are compounded by the very worldly fears of a potential rapist: dressed as a spectral huntsman, her would-be-rescuer emerges from the shadows ill-advisedly to rescue her from her plight. While Baillie's *Orra* is shocking precisely because the liberty of her body comes at the expense of her sanity, Gothic-infused melodrama, in line with its more assertive moral dimension, typically depicted the lowly hero's successful penetration of the castle (here a symbol of aristocratic despotism) and the relief of the female character from her bondage, leaving her supposedly free to marry, though, curiously, as with Romantic dramas, the act of marriage is not always directly confirmed. Michael Gamer notes that a later version of Grosette's *Raymond and Agnes* 'rejects the most traditional of comic endings, marriage' and that while 'the closing embrace of Raymond and Agnes may forecast their happy end ... the dramatic focus sits squarely with resolving suspense and overcoming danger'.[28]

If the man-made structures of the castle and dungeon are sites of menace, nature too has the potential to provide a hostile ecology. Even as the claustrophobia of the crypt is contrasted with the sublime scale of alpine landscapes, dark forests and treacherous ravines, these natural spaces too could prove disorientating and deadly. The dark forest of Maturin's *Bertram* presents a nightmarish landscape for Imogine and her child. The natural world again seeks retribution in Peake's *Presumption* as the snow-capped mountain collapses to engulf both Frankenstein and his creature in an icy tomb. The natural world in both cases is aligned with the moral universe and is punitive towards those characters that disturb its laws.

---

28 Gamer, 'Gothic Melodrama', p. 42.

The humble woodsman's cottage, by contrast, offered up an image of the domestic sphere in harmony with the natural world, an alternative space as respite from aristocratic tyranny. Often subject to assault, such as in William Dimond's *The Foundling of the Forest* (1809), Isaac Pocock's *The Miller and His Men* (1813) and Scott's *The Old Oak Chest*, here was the space of the working-class, humble hero, plain of speech, a figure who embodied, as Bratton notes, 'the Rousseuvian appeal to the language of the heart, rejecting the potential deceptiveness of words ... on the melodramatic stage, where all resources of music, spectacle and pantomime action could spell out the message that here was innocence threatened but for ever true to itself'.[29]

As later melodramas would eschew Gothic castles and landscapes for the more familiar settings of the domestic melodrama such as factories, London streets and country villages, populating the stage with shopgirls and factory workers, with plots that focused upon social problems such as gambling, alcohol abuse and urban crime, the domestic space both onstage and off continued to be vulnerable to external threats. The explosion of newsprint culture augmented this invasion of everyday space with sensational stories of crime, assault and murder. Grim real-life tales of domestic violence, such as the Red Barn Murder in 1827 and of folk-demons such as Spring-heeled Jack in the late 1830s, captured the public imagination and made their way into dramatisation in the middle of the nineteenth century as examples of home-grown barbarism, turning the city streets of London or the rural farmhouse into sites of horror. Bratton explains that as

> Melodramatists of the second generation, like William Moncrieff, Douglas Jerrold and Edward Fitzball, were advised to scour the newspapers to find their stories ... melodramas resembled and drew upon contemporary visual culture: Jerrold's *Rent Day*, for example, staged at Drury Lane in January 1832 at the height of the democratic excitement over parliamentary reform, comments from his own radical position upon the class tensions, oppressions and aspirations which filled the newspapers.[30]

In Jerrold's play, Gothic monstrosity is replaced with capitalist ogres, and yet a Gothic rhetoric persists. As Bullfrog and Burly, the bailiffs, under orders from Old Crumbs, the bookkeeper, take possession of the Heywood's family farmhouse, Toby Heywood labels them 'Blood-suckers!' Rachel Heywood speaks of wandering around her own house 'like a restless ghost', as her

---

29 Bratton, 'Romantic melodrama', p. 119.   30 Bratton, 'Romantic melodrama', p. 125.

husband, Martin Heywood, describes the terror that haunts him as rent-day approaches: 'There appeared a something hanging over me – about me; heavy and stifling it seemed, – and my blood would run hot and cold – and so I've lain and watched, and prayed the daylight in.'[31] Meanwhile, dark secrets of past aristocratic tyranny tumble out in the final moments of the play as Old Crumbs reveals his late wife's affair with Lord Grantley senior as his rationale for seeking retribution in bringing Grantley's son to financial ruin.

Another play, though not as popular as Jerrold's and enjoying only three performances at the Drury Lane, was John Walker's *The Factory Lad* that appeared in the same year. Published seven years prior to its premiere, this is a play that responds to the Luddite uprisings of the 1810s. Although the play signals a departure from Walker's earlier Gothic-infused melodramas, *The Factory Lad* draws upon a Gothic Romanticism as it distils the threats to domestic harmony that emerge as factory-owner Squire Westwood overturns his father's investment in his workforce and seeks to replace the manual labourers with machines. Factory worker George Allen is roused to action by outcast and poacher Will Rushton and leads a rebellion in which the workmen set the workplace alight. The men are eventually arrested and brought to account for their actions before the darkly named Justice Bias. Allen's fate, as the dispossessed working-class hero, looks bleak as the curtain falls. Walker's play is unusual for its ethical ambiguity and for its critique of a justice system that seems at odds with moral rectitude. Westwood, who occupies the conventional status of the villain, possesses the legal integrity and the play facilitates his articulate defence of the age of steam and the pressure of industrial competition. In the closing moments, Westwood is shot by Rushton, the dissident pariah who possesses the internal torment of Lewis's Osmond or Baillie's De Monfort, and who embodies a Gothic charge that seems to overwhelm this domestic tragedy. Casting Westwood's capitalist opportunism in the guise of aristocratic tyranny, rehearsing intones of the fear of foreign monsters and haunted by the 'pale spectre' of his wife and the 'mangled forms' of his children, he leads the cry for revenge as the factory burns:

> Ha, ha! This has been a glorious night, to see the palace of a tyrant levelled to the ground – to hear his engines of gain cracking – to hear him call for help, and see the red flame laugh in triumph! Ah, many a day have I lain upon the

---

31 Douglas Jerrold, *The Rent Day: A Domestic Drama, in Two Acts* (London: Printed for C. Chappel, 1832), Act 1, scene 5; Act 2, scene 1; Act 1, scene 5.

cold damp ground, muttering curses – many a night have I called upon the moon, when she has frenzied my brain, to revenge my wrongs ...[32]

Rushton dominates the closing tableau of the drama with his hysterical laughter as the soldiers level their muskets, and Allen, his family and his associates look on in shock.

The Gothic overtures continue as Jane Allen, discovering her husband's arrest, collapses and revives to enact Gothic distraction: 'Your father! [*Screams.*] Ah, I now remember all! They are tearing him from me, to take him to a loathsome dungeon! All now crosses me like a wild dream. The factory – the red sky – flames whirling in the air! My eye-balls seem cracked – my brain grows dizzy – I hear chains and screams of death!'[33] With echoes of Baillie's distracted Orra and the wildness of Bertram's Imogine, Jane Allen exemplifies the impact of external threats on the perceived sanctity of the domestic sphere. While in the plays of the late eighteenth century, Gothic heroines, having been removed from this space of safety, often run mad, dramas such as Walker's and Jerrold's rehearse threats of the monstrous penetrating and usurping the harmony of the domestic space also seen in more overtly Gothic works such as Planché's *The Vampire*.

Other examples that dramatise this threat to the integrity of the familial sphere demonstrate how, once penetrated by a sense of worldliness, the home can become a disorientating prison for internal torment, the site for the return of the repressed or the space to inspire madness, and from where the taboo of assertive female sexuality is enchained, demonised or vanquished or in which the monstrous maternal is punished by death or exile. T. A. Palmer's stage adaptation of Mrs Henry Wood's sensation novel *East Lynne* (1874) represents the moral chaos that haunts and overwhelms its heroine when she transgresses from her position as 'The Angel in the House', a reference that was eulogised in Coventry Patmore's 1854–62 paean to female forbearance in his narrative poem of that name. Following her elopement with the dastardly Levison, Lady Isabel is forced to feign death to reinvent herself as governess to her own children in order to gain re-entry to the domestic sphere. Lynne Wood, meanwhile, where Levison frames Richard Hare for his murder of Old Hallijohn, provides the Gothic forest in the play, a space of chaos and intrigue, to confirm the necessity of the marital harmony in the familial home at Castle Marling that serves to make Lady

---

32 John Walker, 'The Factory Lad: A Domestic Drama in Two Acts', Booth (ed.), *English Plays of the Nineteenth Century* 1, pp. 201–33, Act 1, scene 6; Act 1, scene 5; Act 2, scene 1.
33 Walker, 'The Factory Lad', Act 5, scene 3.

Isabel's fall from grace all the more appalling when she renounces its secular sacredness. On her return to the space of the home – the nursery – her relationships with others, particularly her children, become imbued with Gothic overtones of the uncanny, and riddled with disorientation and alienation. C. H. Hazlewood's *Lady Audley's Secret* (1863), a dramatic adaptation of Mary Elizabeth Braddon's sensation novel of 1862, similarly rehearses and thereby conservatively prohibits the threat to order in the home from a woman who has brought shameful secrets into the domestic space. The guilt of Henrik Ibsen's heroines is much more ambiguous, and his plays *The Doll's House* (1879) and, to a certain extent, *Hedda Gabler* (1890), focus upon their heroines' steady realisations of their own imprisonment. Despite the social and aesthetic realism that such dramas brought to the stage, the extent to which such plays were populated with hauntings, dark secrets and spectacles of incarcerated women for whom home becomes dungeon suggests that the Gothic impulse was never exorcised in its entirety.

While stage melodrama continued to offer an uncompromising moral perspective in championing conventional domestic order over the monstrous threats to that order, examples emerge of the genre that complicated sympathies for the monster. Leopold Lewis's *The Bells* in 1871, an adaptation of Erckmann-Chatrian's 1867 'dramatic study' *Le Juif Polonais*, explored the guilt and psychological impact of the return of the repressed, anticipating the advent of that most Gothic of all sciences, psychoanalysis.[34] The play opens upon preparations for the wedding celebrations of Christian, the quartermaster of the gendarmes, and Annette, the daughter of Mathias, the burgomaster. For Mathias, this marriage offers an opportunity for safety in appealing to Christian's position to conceal his undisclosed murder of a Polish Jew 16 years earlier. Noticeably, the cosy domestic interior of Mathias's home represses the sublime Gothic wilderness outside by allowing the audience only glimpses of a snowy landscape through its windows. The chaos becomes psycho-somatic torment as the chambers of the stage mirror Mathias's haunted mind. The thin layers between the real and the non-real, separated by a flimsy sheet of gauze, become increasingly confused, as Mathias is subjected to spectral memories made visual, the sound of sleigh bells and a dream of his reckoning in a chamber of court. The play culminates in a thrilling denouement as, in a double layering of the unconscious, he is

---

34 See Roger Luckhurst, 'Psychoanalysis', in William Hughes, David Punter and Andrew Smith (eds), *The Encyclopedia of the Gothic*, 2 vols (Malden, MA and Chichester: Wiley-Blackwell, 2016), vol. 2, pp. 526–31 (p. 526).

mesmerised in a dream into confessing his crime and dies of heart-failure as he enacts his suffocation on an imagined hangman's rope.

Leopold Lewis's representation of ghosts and ghostliness as symptoms of psychological trauma shares much in common with the literary ghost stories that emerged from writers such as Charles Dickens, Wilkie Collins, Sheridan Le Fanu and Henry James. That is not to suggest that these writers were censorious of the theatrical effect of their ghost stories: Dickens's *The Haunted Man* (1848) was used as a vehicle to showcase the new technology of Dr Henry Pepper's Ghost, while his much-loved *A Christmas Carol* (1843) was adapted for the stage numerous times following its publication. Dickens and Collins themselves would collaborate in 1855 with the staging of Collins's macabre play about an old lighthouse keeper who confesses to playing a part in a murder at Tavistock House, as well as in co-writing the script of *The Frozen Deep* (1855). Dickens, himself, relished the dramatic impact of the Gothic in his longer novels, as evident from his vivid rendering of the tattered Miss Havisham in *Great Expectations* (1860–1) and the melodramatic relish with which he portrays the murder of Nancy in *Oliver Twist* (1837–9).

As the excess of Gothic theatricality was increasingly repressed or denounced in dramatic performances, it surfaced in non-fictional performance entertainments. Magic shows, displays of mesmerism, and, perhaps, most notoriously, the Spiritualist *séance*, responded to, energised and perhaps exploited a continuing fascination with the unknown, sensations of (predominantly female) entrapment and a heightened theatricality designed to unnerve audiences. By contrast, palaces of science and exhibition constructed to dazzle audiences with Gothic effects under the auspices of edification combined entertainment with instruction, as such illusions were conjured up with a formal explanation of their manufacture. The Royal Polytechnic Institution and The Egyptian Hall, in the later years of the century, hosted lectures to accompany spectacular live performances and exhibitions associated with the supernatural and the occult, such as Pepper's Ghost and the magic shows of John Nevil Maskeylne. The latter's scepticism regarding the supernatural was well documented, and he played a considerable part in exposing countless Spiritualist mediums as charlatans and their *séance* performances as theatrical trickery. In 'My Reminiscences' for *The Strand Magazine* in 1910, Maskeylne writes, 'Here may I say that since I have been in London I have never known a medium, and have never seen a performance in which trickery could not enter. Indeed, I would go further still and add that every one that I have taken up I have succeeded in exposing.'[35] The iteration of such effects as humbug rehearses an anti-theatrical rhetoric, a denouncing of theatricality as associated with charlatanism and the theatre itself as a space of seductive illusion, which itself seems an irony in an age in which the emerging realist dramas sought an imitation of real life on the stage. Such associations serve to illustrate the argument that, despite the repression of the influence of the Gothic towards the latter part of the nineteenth century as rehearsed in narratives of theatre history which emphasise the triumph of social and aesthetic realism on the stage, the Gothic impulse returns as embodied in the apparatus of the theatre itself.

Our Haunted Houses

Arthur Wing Pinero's comedy *Trelawny of the 'Wells'* (1898) depicts the fortunes of stage ingénue, Rose, as she leaves the theatre for a new life as a respectable lady of the upper echelons. When she discovers the suffocating regulations that threaten her physical and psychological well-being in the household of Sir William Gower, a place where, to Rose's dismay, even sneezing is prohibited, she abandons her fiancé and returns to the Wells Theatre. However, she is appalled to discover that her time spent incarcerated in a life of aristocratic ennui has compromised her ability outwardly to project her emotion in the acting style required of the sensational, supernaturally inflected melodrama for which the theatre is renowned.

In Act Two, the Gowers' household in Cavendish Square becomes a playful reference to the archaic Gothic castle within which the heroine is immured, as Rose herself, rehearsing her theatrical vocabulary, refers to Sir William as a 'fiend, a vampire' and threatens that her prospective in-laws 'are killing me – like Agnes in The Spectre of St. Ives'.[36] Rose's 'rescue' at the hands of her old theatre chums takes place against a backdrop of flashes of lightning and crashes of thunder. And yet, the play dramatises the theatre's inability to offer a satisfactory alternative space to the Gothic household. Descriptions of the theatrical setting foreground the gaudy, faded grandeur of the theatre, '*the soiled theatrical finery*' described at the opening of the play's first act, threatening to burst out of trunks (old oak chests?);[37] the ancient actors,

---

35 John Nevil Maskelyne, 'My reminiscences', *The Strand Magazine* 39 (1910): 17–24 (p. 21).
36 Arthur Wing Pinero, 'Trelawny of the "Wells"' in *Pinero: Three Plays* (London: Methuen, 1988), pp. 159–245, Act 2.
37 Pinero, 'Trelawny', Act 1.

gargoyle-like with their archaic acting style that is monstrous in its hyperbole, turn the theatre itself into a site of Gothic ruin. When the budding playwright Tom Wrench acquires the Pantheon Theatre in a venture patronised by a repentant Sir William, he enlists Rose as his leading lady in a drama that is much more realistic in its psychological complexity.

The opening stage descriptions of Act Four show that the Pantheon, even more so than the Wells, is an image of degeneration and darkness, as the wings and borders *'and any other scenic appointments which may be shown, should suggest by their shabbiness a theatre fallen into decay'*, all lit by a *'dismal light'*. Pinero's stage directions emphasise the overlapping of the actual theatre with that of the Pantheon: *'The SCENE represents the stage of a theatre, the footlights and proscenium arch of the actual stage being the proscenium arch and the footlights of the mimic stage.'*[38] Although the Court, where the play was first staged, was a relatively new theatre space, having been rebuilt and reopened in 1888, the effect staged must have emphasised something of a dissonance between the old and new, where innovations in playwriting clash with the dustiness of the represented theatrical space.

The Gothic proclivities of theatre buildings themselves were further emphasised in the late Victorian period as tales of theatre ghosts in both London and regional theatres proliferated, continuing to the present day to attest to what Aoife Monks describes as 'the longstanding image of the theatre as a superstitious and haunted world'.[39] Accounts of ghosts at the Theatre Royal, Drury Lane, have circulated since the end of the nineteenth century. Richard Huggett, in his lively account of tales of hauntings in London's theatres, describes how, in 1900, two elderly women caught a glimpse of an old man 'dressed in nineteenth-century clothes' who 'had white hair and a square white face'.[40] Distracted momentarily by the play, these women, when they looked back, found that the figure had disappeared without passing them to the sole exit from the stalls. 'Later', Huggett relates, 'they compared their memories with a portrait in the Garrick Club – it was Charles Kean, who had died thirty years earlier'.[41] More enigmatic is the theatre's Man in Grey, a pale spectre decked in a tricorne hat, powdered wig, dress coat, riding boots and sword, rumoured to be the ghost of the murdered

---

38 Pinero, 'Trelawny', Act 4.
39 Aoife Monks, 'Collecting ghosts: actors, anecdotes and objects at the theatre', *Contemporary Theatre Review* 23:2 (2013): 146–52 (p. 146).
40 Richard Huggett, *Supernatural on Stage: Ghosts & Superstitions of the Theatre* (New York: Taplinger, 1975), p. 130
41 Huggett, *Supernatural*, p. 130.

man whose skeletal remains were discovered in the mid-nineteenth century in the right-hand wall of the Upper Circle. A spectacle of Gothic horror, the corpse was interred with a dagger stuck through the ribs and surrounded by golden guineas on the floor, interspersed with some playing cards. Despite this dark history, the appearance of the Gentleman in rehearsal is said to proffer a good omen for a production. Other ghosts reported to haunt the theatre include that of Charles Macklin (1700–97), Joseph Grimaldi (1778–1837) and that of a more recent stage celebrity, Dan Leno (1861–1904). Herbert Beerbohm Tree was reportedly plagued by a ghost here that kicked him during a Shakespearean gala matinée in the 1890s. The story led his contemporary, Henry Irving, with mischievous opprobrium, to label the spectre a critic.[42] The ghost of Sarah Siddons (1755–1831), too, was reported to have appeared in 1960. Siddons, evidently industrious in the afterlife, is also the resident phantom of Bristol Old Vic, and is said to have returned to the site of her lover's suicide. Another ghost said to haunt the neighbouring Adelphi Theatre is that of William Terriss who, in 1897, was murdered outside the stage door by jealous fellow actor Richard Prince, a crime that resonated as a real-life *fin-de-siècle* horror in the contemporary media. A less tragic figure is the ghost of John Baldwin Buckstone (1802–79), actor, playwright and manager, who is said to frequent his old dressing room in the Theatre Royal, Haymarket. One of the more grotesque tales of a theatre ghost emerged from the Lyceum Theatre where, in the 1880s, a gentleman 'whose name has been lost in time, looked down into the stalls and was shocked to see the severed head of a cavalier, sitting in the lap of a lady watching the performance'.[43] Irrespective of the veracity of such ghost stories, their dissemination serves to construct and figure the theatre as a space invested with a Gothic charge.

The Lyceum had long associations with the supernatural and the uncanny: it was here that Madame Tussaud displayed her waxwork creations in the country for the first time in 1802. Planché's *The Vampire* and Lewis's *The Bells* premiered in the theatre, and actor-manager Henry Irving commissioned a revival of Boucicault's *The Corsican Brothers* in 1880. Meanwhile, Irving himself fuelled fantasies of the supernatural both offstage and on. His mesmeric personality fascinated his business partner Bram Stoker, whose famous vampire was supposedly inspired by his dealings with the theatrical knight. Catherine Wynne suggests that the Count is entirely a product of 'Stoker's Gothic imagination, the Lyceum's cult of the supernatural and the nineteenth

---

42 Huggett, *Supernatural*, p. 129.
43 Ian John Shillito and Becky Walsh, *Haunted West End Theatres* (Stroud: The History Press, 2011), pp. 10–11.

century's immersion in melodramatic excess'.⁴⁴ Wynne details the tensions that reportedly emerged between the two men when, in 1897, Stoker, anticipating the publication of his novel, adapted *Dracula* for stage presentation and hosted a preliminary performed recitation of the script: 'Legend has it that Irving made negative comments on the dramatic reading of *Dracula*' and that 'when Irving was asked for his opinion, he allegedly replied that it was "Dreadful!"'⁴⁵

Irving's criticism is intriguing, yet it is the framing of the event as legend here that is significant as an anecdotal device that contributes to the idea of theatre as Gothic space. Anecdotes, pre-performance rituals, the use of lucky talismans and superstition (the suspicion of peacock feathers on stage, the naming of the Scottish play, the kissing of a stage noose, the sighting of the ghostly Man in Grey) all speak, as Monks suggests, of a need to navigate 'the uncertainties of the acting profession by setting up lines of inheritance from one generation of actors to the next, by establishing a professional identity for actors, and by appeasing the anxiety of the stage through the transmission of rituals of superstition'.⁴⁶ As Monks continues, such investment in the secular supernatural is fuelled by the more prosaic fears of the instability of labour value in the theatrical workplace. Here she draws upon Jacky Bratton's study of the relationship between the theatrical anecdote, theatrical objects and labour conditions that emerged in the early nineteenth century as a response to the deregulation of systems of patronage in favour of a free-market economy, particularly in London, where, as playwright James Boaden, himself a pioneer of Gothic drama, would in 1825 explain, the actor 'took his talent, as everything else is taken, to an open market, where the demand for the supply would always produce its exact value'.⁴⁷ There is a Gothic aura that surrounds the imbuing of objects and stories with magical agency to ward against such uncertainty. Indeed, such Gothic elements become particularly pronounced when Monks speaks of 'the ghostly properties' of the theatrical anecdote as a tool that 'shores up hierarchies of the profession': as a response to the precarious nature of the acting profession itself, such devices enable those who relate such stories to interact with and

---

44 Catherine Wynne, 'Dracula on Stage', in Roger Luckhurst (ed.), *The Cambridge Companion to Dracula* (Cambridge: Cambridge University Press, 2017), pp. 165–78 (p. 166).
45 Wynne, 'Dracula', p. 168. 46 Monks, 'Collecting Ghosts', p. 147.
47 James Boaden, *Memoirs of the Life of John Philip Kemble, esq., including a history of the stage, from the time of Garrick to the present period*, 2 vols (London: Longman, Hurst, 1825), vol. 1, p. 29, cited in Jacky Bratton, *New Readings in Theatre History* (Cambridge: Cambridge University Press, 2003), p. 122.

even to inherit their position within long-established acting dynasties with their own Gothic heroes and tyrants.[48]

As the *fin de siècle* approached, this Gothicization of the venue of theatrical performance as site for Gothic disturbance appeared in a series of prominent Gothic-infused fictions, including Oscar Wilde's *The Picture of Dorian Gray* (1890), George du Maurier's *Trilby* (1894) and, perhaps most famously, in Gaston Leroux's imagining of the Palais Garnier in *The Phantom of the Opera* (1910). Meanwhile, both the cinematic and the small screen have continued to perpetuate the association of the theatre as Gothic space with examples such as Tod Browning's *Dracula* (1931), where Harker, Lucy and Mina encounter Bela Lugosi's Dracula for the first time, or in Douglas Hickox's *Theater of Blood* (1973), Anne Rice's *Interview with the Vampire* (1976) which inspired Neil Jordan's 1994 film adaptation, and John Logan's HBO television series *Penny Dreadful* (2014–16).

Most poignant of all is the extent to which more recent Gothic drama underscores the Gothic inflections of the nineteenth-century British theatre by using the theatrical medium itself to intensify the experiential impact of the horror.[49] Audiences, for example, are playfully threatened with the falling chandelier in performances of Andrew Lloyd Webber's musical adaptation of *The Phantom of the Opera* (1986). In Stephen Mallatratt's *The Woman in Black* (1989), a stage adaptation of Susan Hill's 1983 ghostly novella and a play in which the very act of performance invokes the old curse of the benighted spectre, the theatre itself becomes an uncanny space as the woman herself ranges through the theatre, declining to confine her presence to the stage and compromising the extent to which audiences can feel complicit in the game of pretence. The latter opens, emphatically, in 'a small Victorian theatre' where there is no attempt made to disguise the nineteenth-century theatrical space as the ultimate haunted house.[50] Such examples highlight the ways in which the theatrical Gothic of the previous century insistently, irrepressibly, continues to haunt the imagination of play-going audiences.

---

48 Monks, 'Collecting Ghosts', pp. 149, 147.
49 For a similar argument, see Emma McEvoy, 'Contemporary Gothic Theatre', in Catherine Spooner and Emma McEvoy (eds), *The Routledge Companion to Gothic* (Abingdon and New York: Routledge, 2007), pp. 214–22 (p. 215).
50 Susan Hill and Stephen Mallatratt, *The Woman in Black* (London: Samuel French, 1989), p. 1.

2.8

'Spectrology': Gothic Showmanship in Nineteenth-Century Popular Shows and Media

JOE KEMBER

I am, I believe, a normal being of the recognised cottage garden variety, the only abnormality about me being an abnormal taste for the abnormal.[1]

Writing on behalf of the show-going public of Plymouth in the south-west of Britain during 1898, Denarius, the nom de plume of the roving correspondent for *The Western Figaro*, encapsulated an apparent paradox that had preoccupied audiences for well over a century: that 'abnormality' was a perfectly normal and desirable component of popular entertainments. Across a series of articles, Denarius had reported on all of the attractions available to Plymothians, from the grand, newly built variety theatre, to the massive exhibition space at St James's Hall, where dioramas, concerts, big-name lecturers and other performers had appeared for some decades. However, it was when he came to the numerous penny shows available on the same streets – theatricals, waxwork galleries, freak shows, cinematograph shows, and finally, Signor Durland's entertainment at the Plymouth Egyptian Hall – that his reportage took on this confessional tone, sharing an undisguised delight with readers who, most likely, felt much the same:

> To put it plainly, I have an inordinate bent for the marvellous, the mystical, the enigmatical; consequently when I saw, a few days ago, in Signor Durland's mysterious establishment in Union-street, an announcement to the effect that the proprietor of this unique temple of amusement has 'just secured at enormous expense, for a short time only', the following gigantic attractions to wit 'The Skeletograph or Rontgen Light', 'The Electric Lady', 'Professor Cyril, the world renowned exponent of the Magic Art of Palmistry', and above all, 'Minnie Warren, the only original relic of the

[1] Denarius, 'Random sketches by our special commissioner', *The Western Figaro* (4 March 1898), pp. 15–17 (p. 15).

late lamented Tom Thumb' I concluded that a man must be niggardly indeed who, for the sake of an "umble brown', would refrain from sampling the above intellectual fare.

Each turn on the programme had its own spectacular appeal: the 'Skeletograph' made reference to the recently discovered technology of X-rays, but was most likely a new variant of an old ghost illusion;[2] the 'Electric Lady' was a new version of an old fairground trick where every touch was rewarded with an electric shock; 'Professor Cyril' enthralled customers by reading their minds; and the small-statured 'Minnie Warren' made a spectacle of her bodily otherness and also told anecdotes about her career. Denarius's open pleasure in 'slumming it' was surely a part of this appeal, but at the centre of such shows, too, were spectacular, enigmatic, macabre or grotesque features, an apparently unsettling set of 'Gothic' qualities nonetheless regarded as good, clean fun.

Shows like these could be found in every major city and on most fairgrounds across Britain in the latter decades of the nineteenth century, with other variants also common across Europe, the United States and throughout the colonial world. They derived from a long line of performance and display traditions, including the cabinet of curiosities, freak show, magic theatre, fairground booth, waxwork gallery, the scientific show, the phantasmagoria and the penny theatrical, each of which had developed at different times and in quite different cultural and institutional contexts. For David Annwn Jones, whose compendious transhistorical study of 'dark visibilities' tracks key Gothic motifs and media across several centuries, the nineteenth-century market for popular shows is particularly significant. Defining 'Gothic' in the broadest of terms, Jones finds visual traces of it everywhere, from waxworks to theatre, linking such phenomena to a miscellany of other texts and artefacts.[3] This chapter will adopt a similarly inclusive definition of Gothic, but will focus on the distinct institutional formations of nineteenth-century shows, arguing that Gothic features were an entirely mainstream component of popular media and entertainments from the late eighteenth century. Responding to Chris Baldick and Robert Mighall's call for a thorough historicisation of the Gothic, it seeks to reposition the Gothic as a category that

---

2 Thanks to Evelien Jonckheere for information on this trick, which is likely to have been a type of metempsychosis illusion.
3 For an open definition, see David Annwn Jones, *Gothic Effigy: A Guide to Dark Visibilities* (Manchester: Manchester University Press, 2018), pp. 4–5. For similarly broad accounts, see also Mervyn Heard, *Phantasmagoria: The Secret Life of the Magic Lantern* (Hastings: The Projection Box, 2006), pp. 117–97; and Richard D. Altick, *The Shows of London* (Cambridge, MA: Belknap Press, 1978), pp. 217–20.

was, first and foremost, *useful* to the showmen, since it allowed them to attract and fascinate their varied audiences in many different ways, depending on local circumstances.[4] As Timothy G. Jones has argued in relation to Gothic fiction, 'Gothic ... ought to be understood, not as a set form, nor as a static accumulation of texts and tropes, but as a historicised practice which is durable yet transposable: a habitus that orchestrates the generation of various texts and variant readings over the course of time.'[5] In relation to Gothic shows, this type of commercial versatility and functional fluency in response to demand is best understood as a key strategy of competent showmanship, a professional enterprise I have defined at length elsewhere in terms of its open-ended appeal to audiences, its mastery of assorted performative registers and its happy, self-proclaimed *savoir faire*.[6] In this context, the Gothic might best be regarded not in generic or stylistic terms, nor even, as Jones's volume suggests, in terms of visuality, but as a uniquely valuable and fluid performative resource, which allowed the showmen and women to entice varied audiences into very different types of show.

The following sections will suggest some key dimensions of the usefulness of the Gothic to popular showmen, focusing in turn on the transferability of varied types of ghost show between different showland institutions, and on the intermedial shift of Gothic tropes and ideas into new generations of entertainments featuring mass projection media. These examples are hardly sufficient as an archaeology of Gothic showmanship or media, nor are they intended to provide an exhaustive survey of multifarious Gothic aspects across the whole entertainment landscape, but they each point decisively to the adaptability of Gothic in the context of popular shows and media, a property highly prized by the equally versatile showmen and with a widespread cultural influence hitherto little considered.

Ghosts on Tour

In the craze for the phantasmagoria that swept Britain during late 1801 and 1802, a series of ghostly shows were presented to audiences, a trend that would persist, in varied forms, throughout the century: 'phantoms, or

---

4 Chris Baldick and Robert Mighall, 'Gothic Criticism', in David Punter (ed.), *A New Companion to the Gothic* (Oxford: Blackwell, 2012), pp. 265–87.
5 Timothy G. Jones, 'The canniness of the gothic: genre as practice', *Gothic Studies* 11:1 (2009): 124–33 (p. 127).
6 Joe Kember, *Marketing Modernity: Victorian Popular Shows and Early Cinema* (Exeter: University of Exeter Press, 2009), pp. 95–111.

apparitions of the dead or absent', according to the advertising for Paul de Philipsthal's wildly successful 1801 show at the London Lyceum Theatre, 'such as imagination alone has hitherto been able to paint them'.[7] These shows were by no means the first to project or illuminate phantoms using magic lanterns and other apparatuses,[8] and such descriptions hint at the complexity of the relationship that had already developed between showmen and audiences during the late eighteenth century. The phantasmagoria promised to actualise spectral imaginings, lifting them out of the lore of witchcraft or the rituals of freemasonry, or even from the pages of Gothic romance. Taking the oxymoronic forms of 'real apparitions', these ghosts were not what they seemed – that is, not only were they not ghosts, but they were also not fakes, intended to deceive; rather, they were fictions: delightful, spectacular visions whose ontological status was acknowledged and agreed upon by showman, audience and venue, as well as by the publicity and press apparatuses surrounding them. Within this relationship, it was not necessary for audiences to understand the exact nature of the optical illusion, the ingenious operation of the magic lantern on the other side of the screen, but only for them to know that it was illusory, so that when the showmen offered rational explanations for sensational ghostly effects, this tended to foster conditions of mutual knowingness, if not actual knowledge, of the show's mechanics.[9]

Philipsthal's several imitators proved highly adept at reproducing not only the illusions and stage management required by his show but also this central characteristic of his showmanship, the calculated appeal to a knowing audience. Several of them copied his advertising directly, with one advising audiences in Canterbury and Dover in April 1802 that since it was 'absolutely necessary that the Theatre should be entirely darkened—no person can be admitted behind the scenes', thus protecting the secret operations of magic lanterns and screens. Yet, while the mechanics were conducted privately, audiences were openly encouraged to apply a distinctly modern expertise in relation to archaic views:

> This Specterology, which professes to expose the practice of artful impostors and pretended exorcists, and to open the eyes of those who still foster the

---

7 'Novel Exhibition. Lyceum, Strand', *Morning Post* (23 October 1801), p. 1.
8 On the long history of spectral projections, see Hermann Hecht, 'The history of projecting phantoms, ghosts, and apparitions – Part 1', *The New Magic Lantern Journal* 3:1 (1984): 2–6; and Hermann Hecht, 'The history of projecting phantoms, ghosts, and apparitions – Part 2', *The New Magic Lantern Journal* 3:2 (1984): 2–6.
9 See Heard, *Phantasmagoria*, pp. 85–116.

absurd belief in ghosts, or disembodied spirits, will, it is presumed, afford to the spectator an interesting and pleasing entertainment; and in order to render these apparitions more interesting, they will be introduced during the progress of a thunder storm, accompanied with vivid lighting, hail, &c.[10]

Plunged into darkness, and following this atmospheric crescendo of storm effects, the audience was then confronted by 'most wonderful appearances' of historical figures, including Shakespeare and Henry VIII but also Joseph Wall, the notorious Lieutenant Governor of Gorée, who had been hanged in front of massive crowds just two months earlier for cruelty towards his own soldiers. For another audience in Gloucester, the effect of these projections, in the words of one reviewer, was 'so strong' that 'several persons in the gallery were fully persuaded the figures were there also, and actually attempted to grasp them'.[11] The show delivered sensational effects, for sure, encouraging a haptic response to audio-visual materials, and sometimes drawing on contemporary controversies to spice things up, but the term, 'specterology' (or 'spectrology', as advertising for the Gloucester show had it)[12] still implied a rather more balanced, studious or contemplative attitude and an entertainment more 'interesting and pleasing' than it was supernatural, uncanny or bloodthirsty.

Since Terry Castle's influential 1988 account of the phantasmagoria, Gothic criticism has routinely addressed this type of contract between phantasmagores and their audiences, in which the enlightened disenchantment of unseen spirit worlds coincided with the emergence of modern forms of expertise, and the showman capitalised upon both by gifting to audience members their pervasively knowing attitude to the show.[13] Castle acknowledges early in her article that the shows presented 'mock exercises in scientific demystification, complete with preliminary lectures on the fallacy of ghost-belief', but argues that the effectiveness of the illusions also created a realisation of the Gothic imagination that went hand in hand with the subsequent 'spectralization or "ghostifying" of mental space' that followed it.[14] Marina Warner's *Phantasmagoria: Spirit Visions, Metaphors, and Media into the Twenty-First Century* tends to present the phantasmagoria relatively simply and conventionally as a form of sublime experience, inspiring qualities of

---

10 'Theatre, Canterbury', *Kentish Weekly Post or Canterbury Journal* (2 April 1802), p. 4. See, also, 'My Notes', *Kentish Gazette* (25 June 1802), p. 4.
11 'Gloucester, Monday, February 15th', *Gloucester Journal* (15 February 1802), p. 3.
12 'Phantasmagoria Improved', *Gloucester Journal* (15 February 1802), p. 3.
13 Terry Castle, 'Phantasmagoria: spectral technology and the metaphorics of modern reverie', *Critical Inquiry* 15:1 (1988): 26–61.
14 Castle, 'Phantasmagoria', pp. 29, 30.

terror or dread, but, even here, the broader project is both more mundane and more complex, seeking to explain the curiosity concerning spirits and the supernatural that persisted into the scientific age.[15] Most recently, Peter Otto has broadly adopted Castle's point concerning the scientific demystification of spirits, but has emphasised this point as the principal structuring feature of the shows. Concentrating especially on the major shows in London and Paris of both Philipsthal and Etienne-Gaspard Robertson, the two major pioneers of the ghost show as public entertainment, Otto has argued that the first halves of these shows deliberately positioned the audience 'at a distance from the spectacle, in a world that is public, urbane, and modern'.[16] The shows, he suggests, therefore framed the spectres in terms of a pleasurable 'conflict between incredulity and credulity', a disjunctive experience that he equates with 'astonishment', another prime characteristic of the sublime.[17]

These accounts are by no means equivalent, but they share at least one common ambition insofar as they seek to reconcile the affective impact of the shows' spectacles with the rationalist scepticism of modern audiences. Whether the net effect of this confrontation is read as a reflection of Romantic and post-Romantic philosophies of the sublime or of internal contradictions within modernity (and Gothic critics have tended to regard these as interrelated phenomena, emphasising one or the other dependent on subject matter) the problems, from a media-historical point of view, remain largely the same. On the one hand, they tend to essentialise spectatorship in service of broader cultural themes. Picking on samples of selected shows, with the phantasmagorias of Philipsthal and Robertson especially favoured, characteristics are described that allow for the designation of idealised modes of viewing, defined variously according to the cultural formation privileged. On the other hand, because these accounts are chiefly interested in modes of spectatorship rather than in varied forms of showmanship or specificities of the media and venues involved, they tend to miss the variety of shows taking place with alternative modes of operation, or outside of major cities, or in extra-theatrical venues across the nineteenth century.

Emphasising these variations instead tends to expand our understanding of what the phantasmagoria (and the Gothic, in the case of these shows) actually was. For example, Philipsthal's imitators during 1802 may have reproduced

---

15 Marina Warner, *Phantasmagoria: Spirit Visions, Metaphors, and Media into the Twenty-First Century* (Oxford: Oxford University Press, 2006), pp. 147–9.
16 Peter Otto, *Multiplying Worlds: Romanticism, Modernity, and the Emergence of Virtual Reality* (Oxford: Oxford University Press, 2011), p. 117.
17 Otto, *Multiplying Worlds*, p. 118.

his advertising almost word for word across British regions, but their shows are most interesting for the changes introduced on each occasion: in Gloucester the spectres appeared as 20-minute preludes to an unrelated play;[18] in Canterbury, they concluded a series of performances featuring Mr T. Russell of the Theatre Royal, Drury Lane, a form of theatrical variety show featuring adventure and comic pieces as well as comic songs;[19] in Edinburgh, the show took place independently in rented rooms, and to relatively intimate groups of no more than sixty, sometimes taking bookings from smaller groups.[20] The modes of showmanship adopted in each of these three cases, the expectations associated with each venue and the likely affects upon audiences, were all quite different, even though the attractions advertised were ostensibly identical. In each case, the shows were intended to exploit a recent novelty, but it makes little sense to identify qualities such as astonishment, dread, credulity or incredulity as inevitably significant in such cases; rather, these may best be regarded as potential affective resources for the showmen, who may also have drawn on qualities of dramatic action, comedy or parody, as well as aspects of face-to-face banter and repartee in pursuit of their audiences. As Mervyn Heard has argued in the most rigorous account to date of the varied forms of the phantasmagoria, such shows were 'fully-fledged multimedia' events by 1801: they promised 'all that was new, exciting, daring, and revolutionary', but also 'had much to offer the inquisitive amateur of technology and science', whereas, for other audiences, 'the attraction was the sheer novelty of attending a public entertainment conducted entirely in the dark'.[21] Even in these early years, ghostly effects proved a surprisingly versatile commodity, and this quality also explains their longevity, as showmen across the century crafted diversifying methods to 'reel 'em in'.

The phantasmagoria was far from the only spectral illusion on offer, and the venues hosting these shows were equally diverse. Variants persisted throughout the first half of the nineteenth century: notably, Henri Robin's 'Living Fantasmagoria' was staged in Paris and London from 1847, and included mirror-effects permitting a new generation of ghostly apparitions to appear before the public;[22] in the United States a series of showmen also

---

18 'Phantasmagoria Improved', *Gloucester Journal* (15 February 1802), p. 3.
19 'Theatre, Canterbury', *Kentish Weekly Post or Canterbury Journal* (2 April 1802), p. 4.
20 'Phantasmagoria', *Caledonian Mercury* (17 July 1802), p. 1.
21 Heard, *Phantasmagoria*, p. 9.
22 Hermann Hecht, 'Stage magic and illusions', *The New Magic Lantern Journal* 6:3 (1992): 10–13 (p. 10).

produced shows inspired by Philipstahl and Robertson.[23] Alongside such projections and reflections, various trap and other mechanical ghost effects retained their popularity in theatres and music halls throughout the century.[24] Other glass-reflection and mirror illusions became a staple of magic theatre from the 1860s through to the 1910s across Europe and in the United States, with Gothic imagery a regular component.[25] Among these, the technology of Pepper's Ghost became especially popular, perhaps because, like the phantasmagoria, it proved capable of transferring between very different institutional contexts and reaching multiple audiences with equal efficacy. Indeed, this type of transition occurred very rapidly in the case of Pepper's Ghost, even within the show's first and best-known institutional home, London's Royal Polytechnic Institution.

The basic technology of the Pepper's Ghost illusion had been developed by Henry Dircks and John Henry Pepper, with the first appearance of the full show at the Polytechnic taking place in December 1862 (Fig.8.1).[26] There were several variants of the apparatus, with Alfred Silvester's version in particular substantially improving on the original design. The concise description and image of Silvester's apparatus published in Atkinson's *Natural Philosophy for General Readers and Young Persons*, one of several handbooks on popular science to include a demystification of modern ghost-raising, will suffice to provide a sense of its basic mode of operation:

> On the floor of the stage, not seen by the spectators, is an actor covered by a sheet, and intended to represent the ghost. Between the actor and the public is the magic lantern, illuminated by lime light, which gives an extremely bright light. An assistant directs the light upon the actor and the white cloth, thus powerfully illuminated, sends its rays towards an inclined plate of glass, placed near the assistant. The glass, which is silvered, sends almost all the reflected light towards a second plate which is not silvered, on the same scene. This latter plate acts like those in carriages and in shop windows ... and, being traversed by the greater part of the incident rays, sends but little light towards the spectators. Yet, as during this time care is taken that the

---

23 X. Theodore Barber, 'Phantasmagorical wonders: the magic lantern ghost show in nineteenth-century America', *Film History* 3:2 (1989): 73–86.
24 Ray Johnson, 'Tricks, traps, and transformations: illusion in Victorian spectacular theatre', *Early Popular Visual Culture* 5:4 (2007): 151–65.
25 Albert A. Hopkins, *Magic: Stage Illusions and Scientific Diversions including Trick Photography* (London: Sampson, Low, Marston and Co, 1897).
26 See Jeremy Brooker, *The Temple of Minerva: Magic and the Magic Lantern at the Royal Polytechnic Institution, London 1837–1901* (London: The Magic Lantern Society, 2013), pp. 111–19. See, also Brooker, 'The polytechnic ghost: Pepper's ghost, metempsychosis and the magic lantern at the Royal Polytechnic Institution', *Early Popular Visual Culture* 5:2 (2007): 189–206.

Fig.8.1: Pepper's Ghost illusion. Image courtesy of the Bill Douglas Cinema Museum.

illumination in the room is very faint, the light is sufficient to give a cloudy image of the actor placed under the stage.[27]

The illusion could prove highly effective, presenting audiences with living, moving spirits that could interact with other performers actually on the stage, a deception best practised during dramatic pieces. Even at the Polytechnic, arguably the venue that best embodied the principles of rational recreation in Britain during the mid-nineteenth century, and where Pepper's introduction to the spectacle inevitably took on the form of a scientific lecture, the illusion itself appeared in a series of sketches. By 1863, according Jeremy Brooker's exhaustive account of shows at the Polytechnic, the scientific frame had destabilised further, with an 'air of self-parody' permeating the lectures and 'with Pepper becoming a protagonist in his own demonstrations (effectively playing a stage version of himself), and the demonstrations filled with self-referential in-jokes'.[28]

---

27 Edmund Atkinson, *Natural Philosophy for General Readers and Young Persons* (London: Longmans, Green, and Co, 1884), p. 423. See, also, Fulgence Marion, *The Wonders of Optics* (London: Sampson Low, Son, and Marston, 1868); and Theodore Eckardt, *Physics in Pictures: The Principal Natural Phenomena and Appliances described and illustrated by thirty coloured plates for ocular instruction in schools and families*, trans. by A. H. Keane (London: Edward Stanford, 1882).

28 Brooker, *Temple of Minerva*, p. 114.

Changes such as these speak eloquently to the versatility of both the showman and the Gothic tropes he presented. While Pepper would continue throughout the remainder of his career in Britain and Australia to promote himself principally as an inventor and prominent scientific lecturer, the most important property of the Ghost was that it continued to attract and consolidate the attention of paying audiences, and it was Pepper's competent showmanship that allowed him to exploit spectacular, scientific, dramatic, comedic and even parodic or self-reflexive registers in order to accomplish this. Leaving open the possibility that some audience members might yet feel aspects of shock and surprise occasioned by the appearance of the Ghost, Pepper proved able to adapt, and the Gothic imagery the apparatus had been designed to reproduce proved equally effective in each new articulation.

From the 1860s onwards, spectacular hauntings became regular occurrences in the Victorian market for popular shows. The wave of popularity for magic theatre in these years coincided with the rapid international advancement of the Spiritualist movement, with many *séances* taking place both in private and on the public stage. These two practices of theatrical ghost-raising defined themselves outwardly very differently. Magicians such as Neville Maskelyne of the Egyptian Hall proudly advertised themselves as 'anti-Spiritualists', claiming that their shows would debunk the effects produced during *séances*. Like the phantasmagores long before them, most stage magicians therefore flattered their audiences that they, too, could be 'in on the trick' (presumably unlike those convinced by Spiritualist deceptions) though the exact mechanism of the trick nevertheless remained secret.[29] For example, David Devant's illusion, 'The Artist's Dream', which featured the portrait of the artist's dead wife magically coming to life, was first performed at Maskelyne and Cooke's Egyptian Hall in 1893 but remained in repertory until 1919, an enduring illusion that always acknowledged itself a fiction, but never revealed the secrets of its deception.[30] But Simone Natale has uncovered a similarly knowing relationship at work during commercial theatrical *séances*: while mediums worked hard during performance to convince their audiences that their shows were authentic, in some cases 'spectators were encouraged to actively question the reality of spirit manifestations

---

29 Dan North, 'illusory bodies: magical performance on stage and screen', *Early Popular Visual Culture* 5:4 (2007): 175–88; Lynda Nead, *The Haunted Galley: Painting, Photography, Film c. 1900* (London: Yale University Press, 2007), pp. 82–3; Joe Kember, 'Productive intermediality and the expert audiences of magic theatre and early film', *Early Popular Visual Culture* 8:1 (2010): 31–46.
30 Nead, *Haunted Gallery*, pp. 82–8.

and the claims of spiritualism', an ambivalent quality of the shows that made the line between Spiritualist and magic showmanship increasingly hard to draw, especially when the actual stage effects produced were similar or identical.[31] The Spiritualist/magic show divide therefore exemplifies the fluid model of Gothic showmanship thus far outlined: though they made different claims for authenticity, entertainments of both types drew upon a similar palette of audience engagement, ranging from healthy scepticism or knowing humour as much as shock, sensationalism, or the reassuring charm of rational explanation. The important point in the commercial world occupied by both groups of showmen was that audiences continued coming to the shows, regardless of the understandings they were encouraged to take from them.

Following its success at the Polytechnic, the spread of Pepper's Ghost was rapid, with some performances licensed by the technology's various patent-holders and others taking place without permission, though largely without penalty.[32] Larger civic venues hosted ghost shows regularly from the late 1860s, with one theatrical author complaining to the showland trade journal, *The Era*, that there were 'more than a dozen ghost shows running through the country', none of which were paying copyright fees for using his spectral dramas, but that the showmen were a 'slippery lot', always moving on before court proceedings could begin.[33] Such comments might equally be regarded as a measure of the resilience and adaptability of the showmen, bringing the illusion and its variants to all types of shows and for very different audiences. Indeed, studies of Pepper's Ghost have tracked this technology from the 1860s not only in legitimate and magic theatres[34] but also across touring entertainments as diverse as diorama shows[35] and opera companies.[36] During 1863, the Ghost was shown throughout Britain, but also appeared in the

---

31 Simone Natale, *Supernatural Entertainments: Victorian Spiritualism and the Rise of Modern Media Culture* (University Park, PA: Pennsylvania State University Press, 2016), p. 30. See, also, Simon During, *Modern Enchantments: The Cultural Power of Secular Magic* (Cambridge, MA: Harvard University Press, 2002), pp. 149–56.
32 Brooker, *Temple of Minerva*, p. 125.
33 William Davis, 'Pilfering Author's Rights', *The Era* (17 July 1870), p. 10.
34 See, for example, During, *Modern Enchantments*, pp. 143–9; Beth A. Kattelman, 'Spectres and Spectators: The Poly-Technologies of the Pepper's Ghost Illusion', in Kara Reilly (ed.), *Theatre, Performance, and Analogue Technology* (Basingstoke: Palgrave Macmillan, 2013), pp. 198–213; and Allan Sutcliffe, 'The ghost illusion on the Birmingham stage', *The New Magic Lantern Journal* 10:1 (2005): 7–11.
35 Hudson John Powell, *Poole's Myriorama!* (Bradford on Avon: ELSP, 2002), pp. 35–45, 72–80.
36 R. Burdekin, 'Pepper's ghost at the opera', *Theatre Notebook* 69:3 (2015): 152–64.

United States and France, with a variety of ghostly illusions appearing across Europe in the following decades.[37]

While ghost effects retained their currency in legitimate theatres, as well as in the relatively upmarket context of anti-Spiritualist shows like Maskelyne and Cooke's, the most marked proliferation was in the world of town-centre shop shows (often known as 'penny gaffs') and fairgrounds between the 1870s and early 1900s, where the ghost shows were a regular feature alongside waxworks, freak shows, boxing booths and, eventually, moving pictures. Scholarship on this type of show is sparse, partly because they were seldom reported upon, but a combination of existing reviews in local newspapers, reports in trade journals, and occasional accounts of criminal cases involving the shows (which became more frequent as pressure mounted during these decades to close them down) give us some indication of the fluidity of the showmen and show-women's practices within. In these environments, spectral entertainments became mobile in two senses: first, they were itinerant, moving with the fairs or with individual showmen to different locations across Britain and well beyond; second, and partly for this reason, they were also malleable, adapting fluidly in relation to varied showmen, venues and audiences.

Though they varied considerably in size, longevity and legitimacy, penny gaffs often housed ghost shows for periods of a few months during the 1880s and 1890s, but attractions would rotate between locations and showfolk on a regular basis: ghost show equipment and personnel, among a number of other gaff favourites, were frequently advertised in the trade press.[38] Often, ghosts in venues such as these were needed to add spice to penny theatricals, tending to pull in large juvenile audiences. However, a secondary advantage was that the production of short plays and sketches as a 'ghost show' did not tend to fall foul of theatrical copyright laws, much to the chagrin of authors and legitimate theatre venues.[39] More generally, ghost illusions seem to have been regarded as relatively harmless among the sideshows. The penny show of Helen Eveleigh in

---

37 George Speaight, 'Professor Pepper's ghost', *Theatre Notebook* 43:1 (1989): 16–25 (p. 21).
38 These often passed through the hands of showman/auctioneer, Tom Norman. See, for example, 'Sale of Nail's Bioscope', *The Era* (28 March 1908), p. 25. For an excellent account of the shift of ghost illusions from theatrical settings into the hands of showmen, including details of the simplification of the apparatus, see Evelien Jonckheere and Kurt Vanhoutte, 'Metempsychosis as attraction on the fairground: the migration of a ghost', *Early Popular Visual Culture* 17:2 (2019): 261–78.
39 For an extensive account of a penny theatrical ghost show and its large audience of young boys, see 'The Juvenile Drama', *The Birmingham Mail* (23 March 1887), p. 4.

Shoreditch consisted of a very common mirror illusion in which, for three pence, 'a man was there seen to enter a coffin and a moment later was changed to a skeleton', a spectacle which only came to the attention of the courts when the crowds outside blocked the thoroughfare.[40] By contrast, more gruesome attractions, such as waxwork 'chambers of horrors', which often referenced contemporary murders, were reported upon widely. In 1889, in the immediate aftermath of the Ripper murders in Whitechapel, one showman on Whitechapel Road added to his retinue of penny theatricals, waxworks and boxing exhibits with a series of paintings depicting the murders, including one 'which showed six women lying down injured and covered in blood, and with their clothes disturbed'.[41]

At the top end of the showland ghost business were the large-scale entertainments provided by showmen such as Randall Williams and Harry Wall. The earliest references to Williams's 'Hobgoblinscope' appear in 1872, when he was fined for not removing his travelling canvas booth from Barnsley when requested.[42] From 1873 the show became a regular feature at London's Agricultural Hall, a massive exhibition space renowned for its popular entertainments, but Williams also continued to tour other British cities and fairgrounds.[43] According to reviews, the earlier shows comprised attractions such as stagings of the Dickens Christmas stories, phantoms projected onto transparencies (later advertised as an improvement on Pepper's Ghost)[44] and paraders outside performing assorted conjuring tricks.[45] By the 1890s, Williams's ghost show, alongside those of his competitors, had become the most elaborate of all theatrical fairground spectacles, comprising not only paraders on the outside designed to draw thousands of customers to the ghost illusions within, but a wide variety of musical and variety performers appearing alongside the ghosts and a spectacular frontage designed to draw the eye.

At the fairground, the ghost show's grand appearance was required in order to stand out among the competing attractions on offer. At the

---

40 'London's "Side-shows"', *Leigh Chronicle and Weekly District Advertiser* (22 March 1895), p. 7.
41 'A Penny Show', *The Era* (9 February 1889), p. 17.
42 'A "Ghost" Proprietor in Court', *Sheffield Independent* (13 December 1872), p. 3.
43 Vanessa Toulmin, *Randall Williams King of Showmen: From Ghost Show to Bioscope* (London: The Projection Box, 1998), p. 7.
44 'Amusements', *Aberdeen Press and Journal* (17 September 1880), p. 1.
45 See, for example, 'The Hobgoblinscope', *Bolton Evening News* (3 January 1873), p. 3; 'The Sheffield Fair', *Sheffield Daily Telegraph* (25 November 1874), p. 3.

Nottingham Goose Fair in 1876 – by no means the largest of the fairs, and perhaps 20 years before the fairgrounds were at their grandest – the reviewer for the *Nottinghamshire Guardian* found Williams's show competing with at least one other ghost show, a panoply of Merry-go-Rounds, a shooting gallery, performing animals, not to mention 'the ugliest vermin possible – two savage water rats having tails a foot long, with an obese American boy and a walking skeleton thrown in', a tattooed man, various other fat and thin men and women, the 'Viennese Giantess', and a waxwork show depicting various murderers and their victims.[46] In such an environment, one might legitimately ask what characteristics apparently 'Gothic' entertainments had in common, but come up with only the broadest of answers. The reviewer's assessment of the fairground audience seems appropriately open: 'Of course there are palaces innocent of the promised enchantment, and chambers destitute of the nominated horrors; but is there not everywhere joyful, curious, bewildered, disappointed or perhaps disgusted humanity about you, each of whose moods might occupy a philosopher for a twelvemonth?'[47] The macabre, the grotesque, the horrific, the supernatural and the spectacular gave the showmen a flexible purchase on the milling crowds, maintaining the definitively open strategies of Gothic showmanship, which by the early 1900s had endured for over a century in the ghost show. Whether they evoked joy, bewilderment or curiosity, these strategies also remained highly profitable: by 1883, even during the off season, Williams could expect takings of £25 a day.[48]

Gothic Mass Media in the Late Nineteenth Century

Gothic showmanship, I have argued, was characterised by a pragmatic capacity to solicit the attention of audiences by any means possible, and hence to avoid boredom or apathy. By the mid-nineteenth century, the strategies deployed by the showmen to accomplish this were highly sophisticated and varied, having much in common, in fact, with Catherine Spooner's description of contemporary, post-millennial Gothic 'as a mobile and sometimes contradictory discursive site', more playful than anxious, and in which 'the alternative becomes indistinguishable from the mainstream'.[49]

---

46 'Goose Fair', *Nottinghamshire Guardian* (6 October 1876), p. 3.
47 'Goose Fair', *Nottinghamshire Guardian* (6 October 1876), p. 3.
48 'Summary of News', *The Sheffield Telegraph* (6 January 1883), p. 2.
49 Catherine Spooner, *Post-Millennial Gothic: Comedy, Romance, and the Rise of Happy Gothic* (Oxford: Bloomsbury, 2017), pp. 6, 7.

Moreover, Spooner's argument that happy, post-millennial Gothic has been dismissed by scholars as 'debased or diluted' partly because of its association with women's cultures seems to be mirrored in work concerning the nineteenth century, too, though here the critical inattention to popular shows (as opposed to Gothic literature or legitimate drama, for example) seems best explained by the still-too-easy dismissal of working-class media and forms as shallow or naïve.[50]

Of course, there are also profound differences between late nineteenth-century Gothic showlands and the twenty-first century Gothic mediascape, not least of which is the massive scale of modern mass media enterprise: texts and objects created centrally but distributed transnationally to many millions. However, a more thorough historicisation of the popular late-Victorian Gothic also pinpoints the origins of Gothic mass media initially in the hands of many of the same showmen and women; this was a period in which the function of the Gothic to attract crowds passed gradually from exhibitors to new generations of media producers. Thus, while the centuries-old trajectory of Gothic media has long been recognised, not least by Spooner, a great deal of research is still required on the transitions between older entertainment institutions and new media, especially in the last decades of the nineteenth century, when techniques of mass reproduction developed especially rapidly.[51] While a detailed account of such transitions is beyond the scope of this chapter, I will suggest that the open strategies of Gothic showmanship, the ability to address all types of audience through employing varied modes of address, were highly influential on media producers. As a result, the remediation of Gothic benefited a wide range of institutions, with Gothic influences just as likely to appear in the magic-lantern shows of religious and welfare organisations as in the film shows of the demotic, celebratory environments of the fairground and the variety theatre.

As we have seen, the projection of light via the magic lantern had been intrinsic to Gothic shows from before the nineteenth century, a tradition which the phantasmagoria and later ghost shows redeveloped and refined. However, whereas earlier traditions had relied upon expensive, hand-painted slides, the development of cheaper mass-reproduction techniques, including photographic imagery, transformed the market for lantern slides from the 1870s, making the

50 Spooner, *Post-Millennial Gothic*, p. 8.
51 Fred Botting and Catherine Spooner, 'Introduction: Monstrous Media/Spectral Subjects', in Fred Botting and Catherine Spooner (eds), *Monstrous Media/Spectral Subjects: Imaging Gothic Fictions from the Nineteenth Century to the Present* (Manchester: Manchester University Press, 2015), pp. 1–12.

provision of lantern shows an increasingly everyday occurrence, more likely to take place in a village hall or school room than in a travelling ghost show. From the late 1880s, it also became possible to rent lantern slides even more cheaply, meaning that the capacity to put on a show was well within the reach of domestic middle-class consumers, as well as an ever-widening group of religious, welfare and educational institutions, many of which developed their own slide libraries. A brief survey of the lantern slide catalogues available internationally reveals both the scale of this marketplace, and also the remarkably wide range of subject matter projected onto the lantern screen.[52]

One widespread model for the projection of Gothic imagery derived directly from literary sources: the lantern excelled in realising supernatural elements during popular readings. Especially popular among these were lantern readings based on the stories of Charles Dickens, with frequent reproductions of *A Christmas Carol* (1843) reproduced by several slide manufacturers from the 1860s, some, like the set produced by Newton and Son from 1888, drawing directly from John Leech's ghostly illustrations from the original novella.[53] From the 1880s onwards photographic versions of such stories, known as 'life model' sequences, staged the action using live models and painted backdrops, a format which allowed for the projection of real individuals and painted phantoms on the same screen. Sometimes, as in T. T. Wing's *Roger's Ghost* slide set, photographic double exposure was applied instead, so that the phantom appeared semi-transparent on the screen – a combination reminiscent of the uncanny actor/phantom interactions of Pepper's Ghost, but now available to anyone with the small means required to hire these materials.[54]

But the Gothic crept into other, very different modes of lantern performance, too. According to Mervyn Heard and Richard Crangle, the growth of welfare causes linked to the abolition or moderation of alcohol usage provoked nothing less than a 'temperance phantasmagoria' from the lantern trade, intended to bring home the message as forcefully as possible.[55] While the

---

52 See, for example, the selection of lantern slide catalogues available at the Media History Digital Library <http://mediahistoryproject.org/> (last accessed 28 May 2019).
53 'A Christmas Carol' slide set available to view at the Lucerna Magic Lantern Web Resource <www.slides.uni-trier.de/set/index.php?language=EN&id=3005238> (last accessed 28 May 2019).
54 'Roger's Ghost', slide set available to view at the Lucerna Magic Lantern Web Resource, <www.slides.uni-trier.de/set/index.php?language=EN&id=3004229> (last accessed 28 May 2019).
55 Mervyn Heard and Richard Crangle, 'The Temperance Phantasmagoria', in Richard Crangle, Mervyn Heard and Ine van Dooren (eds), *Realms of Light: Uses and Perceptions of the Magic Lantern from the 17th to the 21st Century* (London: The Magic Lantern Society, 2005), pp. 46–55.

Fig.8.2: 'The Whiskey Demon; or, The Dream of the Reveller' (Newton and Co., 1888), slide 12 of 12. Philip and Rosemary Banham Collection, reproduced by permission.

narratives of temperance sequences frequently played out a formulaic narrative of mental and economic decline, often featuring the deaths of the drinkers or of family members either by murder or neglect, individual images sometimes depicted alcoholics beset by demons, linking supernatural imagery with internal conflicts and personal torment. In the case of Newton and Co.'s *The Whiskey Demon; or, The Dream of the Reveller*, a slide set intended to illustrate Charles Mackay's 1860 poem and drawn directly from the illustrations in this publication, the demon appears as a grinning, emaciated figure looming over his victims and pouring liquor into their mouths throughout their descent into the prison, the madhouse and, ultimately, the grave (Fig.8.2).[56] Grim as such

[56] 'The Whiskey Demon; or, the Dream of the Reveller', slide set available to view at the Lucerna Magic Lantern Web Resource <www.slides.uni-trier.de/set/index.php?language=EN&id=3005710> (last accessed 28 May 2019).

imagery was, especially in the context of temperance meetings designed to convince drinkers of their fate, it is important to remember that sets such as these tended to be performed alongside more uplifting material – if not other slides then the collective singing of hymns, or the provision of tea and treats.

If Gothic imagery, however, was a routine component of cautionary literary and temperance tales, it also remained significantly attached to the same populist traditions that had generated the ghost shows. It was still possible to purchase phantasmagoric lantern slides from certain dealers, even in the 1890s, though these tended to appear in sections of catalogues dedicated more generally to comic and moving slides.[57] These included the usual range of skeletons and demons, but as the century progressed the attractions of the ghost show were increasingly marketed for children's entertainments, especially over the Christmas period. Other comic slides did not always incorporate obviously supernatural elements, but throughout the century they frequently included outlandish and laughable caricatures of bodies and faces. Moving slides exaggerated these features: noses and bellies distended and shrank while audiences watched; mouths opened absurdly wide, then snapped shut; eyes grew wide with horror or surprise or darted surreptitiously around the room. In other slides, heads and limbs were chopped, sometimes magically reappearing or being replaced by new body parts to create unsettling or comic hybrids. Bodies and faces were thus distorted and disassembled, emphasising grotesquely mobile, bestial or morbid features, but all in the service of the lantern show's unique model of folk laughter. In perhaps the most popular of all comic slides, a sleeping man lying comfortably in bed begins to snore, accompanied on most occasions by sound effects provided live by the lanternist. As the sleeper's mouth opens, a series of rats leaps from below his bed and down his throat accompanied by loud gulping noises: a spectacle that still arouses laughter and disgust in equal measure from audiences today.

The slide became an established favourite of children's entertainments and was reproduced in different forms by many different manufacturers: a freakish spectacle akin to the lowest of all sideshow attractions – the man or woman eating live rats and other animals[58] – but successfully remediated

---

57 See, for example, *Illustrated Catalogue of Magic Lanterns* (Chicago, IL: McIntosh Battery and Optical Company Co., 1890), p. 166.
58 This practice seems to have been very rare and to have passed into a type or urban myth about the sideshows, but occasional reports confirm that it did take place. See, for example: 'Disgusting Exhibition. Eating Live Rats', *Stirling Observer* (28 July 1864), p. 6; 'Disgusting Cruelty to a Rabbit', *Westmorland Gazette* (24 September 1864), p. 3; 'A Man Who Eats Live Rats', *Dundee Courier* (3 December 1896), p. 5.

and repackaged for delivery to mainstream audiences at all types of venue, from variety theatres, to lecture halls, to the neighbourhood and the home.

In massifying the practices of Gothic showmanship in this type of way, making such projections available to international audiences by means of industrial methods of production, the lantern slide manufacturers were careful not to sacrifice the open-ended adaptability that had characterised the shows from the beginning. Manufacturers and distributors served a fragmented marketplace composed of both amateur and professional exhibitors, many of whom had very different objectives, and they created material suited for each niche, utilising the Gothic by deploying its various capacities to intrigue, shock, amuse, bewilder and disgust as and when it was useful to do so. Of course, final decisions about the presentation of this material rested with the exhibitors and, as in the case of the phantasmagoria and generations of macabre entertainments, it remains important to resist reading these materials as productive of any one *dispositif*: they were productive of many, from the children's Christmas show to the temperance meeting. As mechanical reproduction of projection media became more prominent during the 1880s and 1890s, it remained vital for media producers to retain this adaptability, and therefore to meet this range of existing needs.

Film arrived in a similarly fragmented market during 1895 and was embraced by a similarly varied group of exhibitors. Of course, the spectacle of movement in Gothic images was nothing new: moving lantern slides along with a series of other technologies, from optical toys to the kinetoscope or mutoscope 'peepshow' machines that appeared in parlours throughout the United States and Europe in the 1890s, had already developed their own ghostly or gruesome routines.[59] However, it was certainly the projection of film that most effectively developed the massification of Gothic showmanship, remediating old attractions for remarkably wide audiences. Indeed, it was often the most eminent late-century showfolk that first embraced the new medium. In Britain, Randall Williams was the first fairground showman to adopt film, making his customary appearance at the Agricultural Hall in Christmas 1896 having 'abandoned the spectral business' in favour of moving pictures, presumably in order to capitalise on the novelty that had been taking variety theatres and town halls by storm across the country.[60] By 1898, numerous fairground showfolk had followed Williams into the film business, with the grand fairground 'Bioscopes', as they became known, supplanting

---

59 Jones, *Gothic Effigy*, pp. 118–21.   60 'World's Fair', *The Era* (26 December 1896), p. 18.

the ghost shows as the grandest theatrical attractions at the fair.[61] At London's Egyptian Hall, the anti-Spiritualist magic theatre had introduced films as early as March 1896, and in the years that followed the company launched a series of touring outfits that brought magic and moving pictures to town halls throughout the regions.[62] The popular mesmerists Mr and Mrs Victor André also introduced moving pictures by November 1896 to a travelling show that for years had included hypnotism, clairvoyance and popular magic.[63] Across the board, film was inserted into all manner of entertainments, indicating that manufacturers had largely been successful in marketing their products to the variety of niches occupied by exhibitors.

It is tempting to read this sudden shift across such varied showland institutions, especially those that had provided Gothic thrills, as part of a reaction to the uncanny new medium of film. In a much-cited review of the Lumière cinematograph when it appeared on a Russian fairground, novelist Maxim Gorky wrote concerning the 'kingdom of the shadows' it revealed: 'Curses and ghosts, the evil spirits that have cast entire cities into eternal sleep, come to mind and you feel as though Merlin's vicious trick is being enacted before you.'[64] The films themselves were simple renderings of scenes from everyday life, and Gorky's response, though relatively unusual among initial reviews of film, remains an important document of the uncanny effects frequently associated with new photographic media – of media that are almost, but not quite, a representation of real life. In addition, as numerous film historians have now established, Gothic subject matter was a prime fascination for early audiences, with films by George Albert Smith in Britain, Georges Méliès in France and the Edison Studios in the United States receiving particular attention for their inclusion of trick effects depicting ghosts, demons, dismemberments and supernatural happenings of all kinds.[65]

---

61 Toulmin, *Randall Williams*, p. 31. See, also, Peter Yorke, *William Haggar: Fairground Film Maker* (Bedlinog: Accent Press, 2007); and Vanessa Toulmin, 'Telling the tale: the story of the fairground bioscope shows and the showmen who operated them', *Film History* 6:2 (1994): 219–37.
62 John Barnes (ed.), *The Beginnings of the Cinema in England 1894–1901*, 5 vols (Exeter: University of Exeter Press, 1998), vol. 2, pp. 134–9.
63 Advertisement, *Berkshire Chronicle* (21 November 1896), p. 4.
64 Maxim Gorky, 'Newspaper review of the Lumière programme at the Nizhni-Novgorod Fair, *Nizhegorodski listok*, 4 July 1896', in Colin Harding and Simon Popple (eds), *In the Kingdom of Shadows: A Companion to Early Cinema* (London: Cygnus arts, 1996), pp. 5–6 (p. 5).
65 See, for example, Elizabeth Ezra, *Georges Méliès: The Birth of the Auteur* (Manchester: Manchester University Press, 2000); Jacques Malthête and Laurent Mannoni, *Méliès, Magie et Cinéma* (Paris: Paris-Musées, 2002); and Dan R. North, *Performing Illusions: Cinema, Special Effects, and the Virtual Actor* (London: Wallflower Press, 2008), pp. 24–94.

For Matthew Solomon, filmmakers such as Méliès were playing with the 'tradition of skepticism' that had long characterised anti-Spiritualist magical traditions.[66] By contrast, Kendall R. Phillips tends to emphasise the uncanny and 'horrific' components of such films, but also finds that these filmmakers 'worked along the broad cultural fault lines ... between the love of the marvellous and the fear of excessive credulity'.[67] Both accounts are striking for their resemblance to studies of earlier Gothic shows, replicating some aspects of Terry Castle's and Peter Otto's work on the phantasmagoria, for example, in their understanding of the films as symptoms of a broader confrontation between superstition and variously defined ideas of modernity. However, once again, while all such readings are valid and based on sound evidence, it is important to contextualise this idea among the multitudinous responses to early film, which included aspects of fascination, bewilderment and curiosity, as well as laughter or parody, just as traditions of Gothic showmanship had done throughout the century.

As in the case of the magic-lantern industry, the Gothic retained its breadth of appeal within moving pictures, becoming a pervasive component of a wide range of emergent genres. The re-enactment of horrific scenes, as in the Edison Company's *Execution of Czolgosz, with Panorama of Auburn Prison* (1901) or the presentation of disturbing realities in such titles as *Electrocuting an Elephant* (Edison, 1903), were loaded with the bloodthirsty topicality of the chamber of horrors. In comic films such as the self-explanatory *How it Feels to be Run Over* (Cecil Hepworth, 1900) or George Albert Smith's *Mary Jane's Mishap* (1903) when the titular heroine accidentally blows herself up, the body becomes endlessly subject to all kinds of violence, but without obviously evincing any horrific effect (indeed, Mary Jane winks conspiratorially at the camera as she pours on the fuel!). As Phillips notes, other comic subjects, like Smith's *Photographing a Ghost* (1898), in which a spirit photographer struggles to capture an uncooperative spectre on film, tips over decisively into parody.[68] Even Méliès's films were far from unified in their exploitation of Gothic ideas. His *Le Manoir du Diable* (1896) included many of the phantasmagoric diableries for which he is now best known: magical appearances and disappearances, transformations and a panoply of supernatural figures including an imp, a skeleton and, presiding, over all, Mephistopheles, who

---

66 Matthew Solomon, *Disappearing Tricks: Silent Film, Houdini, and the New Magic of the Twentieth Century* (Urbana: University of Illinois Press, 2010), p. 6.
67 Kendall R. Phillips, *A Place of Darkness: The Rhetoric of Horror in Early American Cinema* (Austin, TX: University of Texas Press, 2018), p. 60.
68 Phillips, *A Place of Darkness*, p. 54.

enters the scene in the form of a giant bat. By contrast, *L'Homme à la Tête de Caoutchouc* (1898) depicts the irresistibly comic spectacle of Méliès himself removing and then inflating his own head with a giant bellows, the face swelling and becoming more distressed, before the inevitable explosion.

Given this array of productions, each of which drew on Gothic registers with a long nineteenth-century pedigree, it seems apparent that the adaptability of the Gothic, which had made it uniquely valuable to generations of showmen, persisted into the twentieth century with the emergence of the new mass medium of film, informing production strategies in a host of interrelated ways. For the exhibitors, of course, the films represented a useful continuation of Gothic performance styles with which audiences were most often already familiar, and they tended to sit alongside many other types of film, or other forms of performance, in the course of a typical ciné-variety programme. Significantly, however, as distribution of films rapidly expanded during the late 1890s into international markets, filmmakers also found Gothic components to be a productive resource, allowing them to connect with enormous mainstream audiences, often from quite different cultures. This insight ought to lead future research in this field in two directions. On the one hand, the remediation of Gothic shows at the end of the nineteenth century requires us to expand our interrogation of twentieth-century Gothic well beyond the domain of 'dark' or body genres such as horror. On the other, we need to reconsider the idea of Gothic eclecticism as a primarily twentieth- or twenty-first-century phenomenon, tied, for example, to postmodern ideas of pastiche and the emptying of affect: the Gothic shows of the nineteenth century were already, variously, bizarre, unsettling, confusing, curious, funny, parodic and happy, and the showmen and women that created them deserve serious consideration in relation to these much longer, mass media trajectories that they initiated and popularised.

2.9

The Gothic in Victorian Poetry

SERENA TROWBRIDGE

Victorian poetry has rarely been considered as a serious and prominent example of the Gothic literary aesthetic, a consequence, perhaps, of the critical tendency to compartmentalise literature into distinct periods and genres. While, in the American context, critics have frequently addressed, say, the early Gothic poetry of Edgar Allan Poe or Emily Dickinson's concerns with death, mourning and spectrality, few have extended such Gothic investigations into the poetry of nineteenth-century Britain. Suspending traditional concepts of both time and form, however, opens up the possibility of fresh readings of Victorian poetry, and permits an historical approach to the significance of Gothic for nineteenth-century British poets. The Gothic mode's startlingly mercurial ability to adapt and transform itself to reflect contemporary mores and concerns is nowhere more prevalent than in the mid-Victorian period. While its expression in poetry has largely been read as a purely aesthetic trope, this chapter will construct an argument for the reflection of deeper social concerns and values in Gothic poems of the period.

As Julian Wolfreys has argued, it is now almost customary to read the nineteenth century as an age that was saturated with the aesthetics of the Gothic, an impulse seemingly prompted by:

> all that black, all that crepe, all that jet and swirling fog. Not, of course, that these are gothic as such, but we do think of such figures as manifestations of nineteenth-century Englishness. These and other phenomena, such as the statuary found in cemeteries like Highgate, are discernible as being the fragments and manifestations of a haunting, and, equally, haunted, 'gothicized' sensibility.[1]

---

[1] Julian Wolfreys, *Victorian Hauntings: Spectrality, Gothic, the Uncanny and Literature* (Basingstoke: Palgrave MacMillan, 2002), p. 25.

The nineteenth century looks decidedly 'Gothic', then, but as Wolfreys points out, there are deeper implications behind these aesthetic hauntings, implications that indicate a pressing unease with social change, faith and death, with nineteenth-century culture simultaneously looking backward to the Gothic past and forward to an uncertain future. Exploring these indications of anxiety relocates Victorian Gothic as an acutely contemporary mode, one in which fragments of Gothic find their way into every aspect of literary culture. This relates to Harold Bloom's concept of Victorian belatedness, according to which the Victorian – and inevitably male – poet is haunted by anxieties concerning his poetic predecessors.[2] Isobel Armstrong has gone further, however, in arguing that the concept of belatedness must be extended beyond the struggle of the individual poet, and conceived instead as the position of the entire culture of the period.[3] It is in this context – reading Victorian poetry as post-Romantic, and consequently post-Gothic, a gesture based on the once-prevalent assumption that the Gothic's so-called 'first wave' ended in 1820 – that this essay will approach nineteenth-century poetry, exploring the development of the Gothic aesthetic in a selection of poems from the period. The situating of Victorian poetry on this boundary aligns it conveniently – perhaps too conveniently – with Gothic, a literary mode that engages with the present while considering the future, yet which is also continuously looking over its shoulder at sometimes nightmarish, sometimes idealised, versions of the past. Victorian culture, and particularly Victorian poetry, does this too: one need only think of the medievalised ballads of the Rossettis, of William Morris, of Alfred, Lord Tennyson and Robert Browning, poems set in a visually pleasing historical moment, yet picking up threads that resonate with their own culture. These are all texts that are strongly aware of their modernity, yet which look forward, too, to future social transformations.

Poetic form, itself, seems to present such an undertaking with a number of difficulties, not least of all the assumption that 'Gothic' is an exclusively fictional or prose-based aesthetic. Martin Willis has pointed out the inherent difficulties of pinning Gothic to a particular form, period or even writer. In place of the critical gesture that he has characterised as 'simply pointing at, say, Dickens's work and exclaiming that he is being Gothic here, look, and there', or 'importing Gothic meaning into a text rather than discovering the

2 Harold Bloom, *The Anxiety of Influence: A Theory of Poetry* (Oxford: Oxford University Press, 1973).
3 Isobel Armstrong, *Victorian Poetry: Poetry, Poetics and Politics* (London: Routledge, 1993), p. 3.

text's own natural resources',[4] this chapter will argue that Gothic can be inherent in poetry too, its singular features and concerns seeping through both form and content. Though much Victorian poetry has a narrative element, much of it does not, and it is thus necessary to consider how Gothic plots and aesthetic tropes might exist independently of narrative or 'story' to indicate wider anxieties while resonating with the socially responsive nature of the genre. With its fragmented approach to form and subject, poetry provides a particularly fertile soil for Gothic writing, with cracks and disturbances in the textual surface offering rich seams of darker material to be mined and untangled by the reader. Elizabeth Napier argues that Gothic, by its very nature, is 'disruptive and subversive to read', often fractured to breaking-point in manuscripts that abruptly end in texts that cannot be read, or in indecipherable letters and overheard words.[5] The task of the Gothic reader is thus often to unpick and to find sense in the form, an heuristic approach that can be effectively applied to the reading of poetry too. To read Victorian poetry as Gothic, then, is to discover points of entrance into the darker anxieties of the age, anxieties represented in miniature, with poems reflecting splinters of larger Gothic preoccupations.

Poets in the period frequently explored a particular aspect of Gothic, focusing on the setting or the character, for example, or adorning their poems with Gothic trappings. These poetics indicate a range of ways in which Gothic becomes nuanced in the Victorian age to suit the period and the poet, and I will argue that that use of Gothic aesthetics becomes a form of signalling to the reader the influences and preoccupations of the work. This chapter will focus particularly on the landscape and characters of Gothic, and consider how they can be read together to form an image of a society beset with social anxieties. In the poems under discussion below, the poets both celebrate and mourn the past, engaging with a Gothicized view of history while simultaneously writing with an awareness of the multiple traditions in which their work is situated. An unease with the present time is apparent in the works of many, if not most, Victorian poets, but in this chapter the focus is on particular poets who self-consciously write in, and identify with, a Gothic literary tradition.

---

4 Martin Willis, 'Victorian Realism and the Gothic', in Andrew Smith and William Hughes (eds), *The Victorian Gothic: An Edinburgh Companion* (Edinburgh: Edinburgh University Press, 2012), pp. 15–28 (p. 17).
5 Elizabeth R. Napier, *The Failure of Gothic: Problems of Disjunction in an Eighteenth-Century Literary Form* (Oxford: Clarendon Press, 1987), p. 44.

Poetry and the Gothic Landscape

In the Gothic romances of Ann Radcliffe, landscape and the natural world offer a form of access to the spiritual or the sublime; as they traverse the mountainous regions of Italy and France, Radcliffe's heroines frequently reflect upon their awe-inspiring surroundings, connecting these directly both to God and to a sense of earthly fear in responses that often forecast their impending trials in the plot. Poetry is central to this process, be that the extracted verses of eighteenth-century poets that serve as chapter epigraphs, or the original poetry with which Radcliffe intersperses her prose. Landscape is evoked in Gothic frequently for its effects on the reader, as well as for its ability to evoke the sublime and picturesque responses of the characters. Such an approach is what John Ruskin in the third volume of *Modern Painters* (1856) described as the 'pathetic fallacy', the tendency within much Romantic and post-Romantic poetry and art to attribute human emotions to insensate objects in the natural world. A 'philosopher', according to Ruskin, may say 'that everything in the world depends upon his seeing or thinking of it', relating all objects, particularly of the natural world, to human comprehension.[6] This tendency, in Ruskin's estimation, is fallacious, since it is the innate power of the object, and not the secondary interventions of the poet, that provoke this sensation; the examples that he offers are the power of a gentian to appear blue, or of gunpowder to explode. The ability of objects to evoke emotion has been extrapolated by poets, he suggests, some successfully and some less so: it is an adherence to truth that matters, and which permits the use of pathetic fallacy to strike the right note for the reader. Giving an example, he explains: 'The state of mind which attributes to it these characters of a living creature is one in which the reason is unhinged by grief.'[7] Consequently, poets offer landscape as a reflection of human characteristics to demonstrate passionate feeling: if it is done coldly, the effect is false.

While the use of landscape as an emotionally charged setting would no doubt have provoked Ruskin's censure, this became an important aspect of early Gothic writing. Indeed, Radcliffe herself had theorised an earlier and equivalent version of Ruskin's pathetic fallacy in her posthumously published essay 'On the Supernatural in Poetry' (1826), locating in her notion of 'accordant circumstances' – that is, the connections and correspondences between setting, landscape and powerful emotion often witnessed in

---

6 John Ruskin, *Modern Painters*, 5 vols (London: J. M. Dent, 1907), vol. 3, pp. 145–6.
7 Ruskin, *Modern Painters*, vol. 3, p. 148.

Shakespearean tragedy – a key quality of sublime literature and art. In Ruskin's estimation, the pathetic fallacy could be traced back to the Romantic and Gothic writers of the late eighteenth century, and was most successfully deployed in the work of his contemporary, Tennyson. Its origins may be traced back even further, and at least to Thomas Gray's 'Elegy Written in a Country Churchyard' (1751), a belated manifestation of the 'Graveyard' school of poetry that, like other poems of its ilk, exhibits tropes and aesthetics that we now identify with the Gothic, including churchyards, bats and an 'ivy-mantled tow'r' (l. 9).[8] In Gray's poem, these serve as an appropriate context in which to muse upon the fleetingness of life, the fickleness of human society and the inevitable approach of death. Such landscapes, then, are integral to an understanding of the Gothic, being 'a means by which political, psychological, social, and cultural ideals are laid bare, transmitted, and often critiqued'.[9] Moreover, as Yang and Healey have argued, 'associations with Gothic landscapes have become so deeply embedded in Western culture that authors, sometimes intentionally and sometimes automatically, use these landscapes in non-Gothic texts as invaluable, powerful shorthand to evoke in their readers horror, alienation, or uncertainty at the grotesquery, instability and corruption of their worlds'.[10] Landscape, however, need not refer only to natural setting: encompassing Walpole's Castle of Otranto, the lofty mountains of Radcliffe, or the cells and dungeons of Matthew Lewis, the category includes the material culture that constitutes the aesthetics of the Gothic, from bats to candlesticks and beyond. This focus on small spatial areas or individual objects is one that is particularly appropriate to poetry, offering a glimpse through the keyhole into a Gothic world that is necessarily restricted by form, but one which opens out onto an index of wider tropes through its relations to the larger, more pervasive fictional genre.

Together with the work of Poe and Dickinson, Emily Brontë's poetry offers a kind of 'Victorian meta-Gothic', in which, as Caroline Franklin has put it, 'we are plunged into intimate experience of a universe with its own Gothic microclimate, where we see-saw sickeningly from homely to

---

8 Thomas Gray, *The Complete English Poems of Thomas Gray*, edited by James Reeves (London: Heineman, 1973). All further line references are placed parenthetically in the body of the text.
9 Sharon Rose Yang and Kathleen Healey, 'Introduction: Haunted Landscapes and Fearful Spaces – Expanding Views on the Geography of the Gothic', in Sharon Rose Yang and Kathleen Healey (eds), *Gothic Landscapes: Changing Eras, Changing Cultures, Changing Anxieties* (Basingstoke: Palgrave Macmillan, 2009), pp. 1–18 (p. 1).
10 Yang and Healey, *Gothic Landscapes*, pp. 11–12.

horror'.[11] Her poem 'Remembrance' (1846), for example, offers a glimpse of mourning in the constructed persona of 'Augusta', one of her most significant characters from the 'Gondal' saga, and a figure who 'ultimately reinforced the disturbing connection between mortality and the feminine'.[12] Yet this poem lacks 'the desperate desire for the grave' that marks the character's other poems,[13] instead insisting on continuing to live and even 'learn how existence could be cherished, / Strengthened, and fed without the aid of joy' (ll. 23–4). The poet-queen of Gondal may be a prototype for the Gothic heroine of *Wuthering Heights* (1847), but she is also a reflection of suffering womanhood, whose life must continue despite her grief. Chichester points out how the early loss of mother and sisters may have provided Brontë with a model for feminine mortality, and it is true that in her novel, as in the Gondal saga and in her poetry, the heroines both mourn and themselves die. Yet the death of the mother, as Carolyn Dever suggests, opens up possibilities for the child, making them vulnerable but also offering freedom and opportunities.[14] 'Remembrance' is a poem of mourning for a husband, but the ability to recover and continue is apparent: the Gothic landscape of the grave and of loss that permeates the first few stanzas is left behind for a new, if joyless, embracing of the world. Other poems offer considerably less hope: while 'Remembrance' moves away from the tomb, 'I Am the Only Being Whose Doom' (1839) finds a sepulchre in the speaker's psyche, where it is 'worse to trust to my own mind / And find the same corruption there' (ll. 23–4). An emotional entombment, a form of 'living death', is worse, it seems, than physical death, and the poem leads one through the speaker's emotional development until the reader, too, is trapped within the persona's deadened brain. In contrast, 'The Night is Darkening Round Me' (1837) maps the speaker's psychological disintegration onto the landscape, with the winds, trees and clouds echoing her distress in a wild setting, yet without using the pathetic fallacy in any direct sense; here, Brontë sets up a distinction between the poet's psyche and the setting, each acting upon the other and creating a 'meta-Gothic' atmosphere that is inescapable in its interiority.

The poetry of Thomas Hood (1799–1845) is most often noted for its humour, and in his 'Prefatory Note' to Hood's poems, William Michael

---

11 Caroline Franklin (ed.), *The Longman Anthology of Gothic Verse* (Harlow: Pearson, 2011), p. 16.
12 Teddi Lynn Chichester, 'Evading "earth's dungeon tomb": Emily Brontë, A. G. A., and the fatally feminine', *Victorian Poetry* 29:1 (Spring 1991): 1–15 (p. 5).
13 Chichester, 'Emily Bronte', p. 10.
14 Carolyn Dever, *Death and the Mother from Dickens to Freud: Victorian Fiction and the Anxiety of Origins* (Cambridge: Cambridge University Press, 1998).

Rossetti described both his work and his personality as 'whimsical' and 'absurd' even as he notes that his life was 'dark with lengthening and deepening shadow of death'.[15] Rossetti evidently struggled to reconcile the very different tones of Hood's poems, ranging as they do from the witty to the farcical, the sentimental to the terrifying, commenting that 'into his grave and pathetic poems he can import qualities still loftier ... though even here it is not often that he utterly forswears quaintness and oddity'.[16] Hood's 'The Bridge of Sighs' (1844) offers a fragmented and ambiguous narrative of the death by drowning of a nameless woman, probably a prostitute, 'a class of women of whom the least that was said the better', according to one reviewer.[17] The poem is one of several by Hood that deals with the problem of poverty, a concern in this case exemplified by the narrator's assumption that the young woman, like many others in such straightened circumstances, committed suicide by jumping from Waterloo Bridge ('The Bridge of Sighs') in order to escape her plight. The tone of the poem is one of sympathy, and its moral admonition to withhold judgement and implicitly to regard the 'black flowing river' (l. 66) as having symbolically washed away her past sins is one that had a clear appeal for nineteenth-century readers. Yet the text calls attention to the helplessness of the woman, a figure who is constructed as a heroine in distress: fallen in more ways than one, she is aestheticised, her body, like that of Tennyson's Lady of Shalott, outlined and framed by her dripping garments, her face and hair indicating her beauty even in death. Objectified and mute, she is transformed by death into a work of art, despite the poem's invocation to mourn over her state. As Eve Kosofsky Sedgwick has observed, the life of the Gothic heroine frequently begins 'with a blank'.[18] In this case, however, blankness also marks the end of the heroine's existence, her character washed clean by the filthy water. And yet the reader cannot help but be aware that pity is provoked more for her death than for her life, despite the poet's attempts, that is, to summon up charity for her and her impoverished sisters.

Hood's poem is one of surfaces and depths: the woman is dragged from the depths of the water, and the aesthetic surface is what the reader is presented

---

15 Thomas Hood, *The Poetical Works of Thomas Hood*, edited by William Michael Rossetti (London: Ward, Lock, and Co., 1870), p. xiii. All further line references are placed parenthetically in the body of the text.
16 Hood, *Poetical Works*, xxi.
17 Anon., 'Hood's "Bridge of Sighs"', *The Aldine* 5:3 (March 1872): 50.
18 Eve Kosofsky Sedgwick, 'The character in the veil: imagery of the surface in the gothic novel', *PMLA* 96:2 (1981): 255–70 (p. 261).

with. The poem evokes the urban landscape as a metaphor for the busy and uncaring bustle in which she existed:

> Where the lamps quiver
> So far in the river,
> With many a light
> From window and casement,
> From garret to basement,
> She stood, with amazement,
> Houseless by night.   (ll. 56–62)

The lights from the houses are contrasted in the following stanza with 'the bleak wind of March' (l. 63) and the 'dark arch' (l. 65) of the bridge itself. The lighted windows stand synecdochally for the uncaring world, indicating an urban centre in London around the Thames. The industrialisation of the city, which offers work and implies progress, is here conjured as a contributing factor for poverty in an environment that is largely oblivious to her suffering. Moreover, at a time when the Thames was a grave environmental concern, spreading disease in the city, the woman is equated with the river, figured as an unclean and polluting taint within the environs of respectability. The clear indication of the poem is that 'Death has left on her / Only the beautiful' (ll. 25–6), purifying her to make her an appropriate object for a poem. Unlike the decaying corpses that appear throughout Gothic fiction, this beautiful corpse that inspired many artworks (including George Frederic Watts's *Found Drowned* [1848–50] and John Everett Millais's *The Bridge of Sighs* [1858]), is rescued from the city's inhumanity. The vision of history to which the poem gives expression is one that is occasionally glimpsed in Gothic fiction. As Maggie Kilgour has argued, the Gothic, when not detailing the horrid excesses of what Horace Walpole in *The Castle of Otranto* (1764) had termed 'the darkest ages of Christianity', is 'symptomatic of a nostalgia for the past which idealises the medieval world as one of organic wholeness, in which individuals were defined as members of the "body politic", essentially bound by a symbolic system of ideologies and correspondences to their families, societies, and the world around them'.[19] The poem's call to recognise the plight of such women can be read as just such a desire for a simpler past and an attendant critique of modern society, yet it also focuses on the idealised, mute and thus compliant woman who reappears throughout nineteenth-century poetry and visual art.

---

19 Maggie Kilgour, *The Rise of the Gothic Novel* (London: Routledge, 1995), p. 11.

A similar approach to the Gothicized urban city and its horrors can be seen in 'The City of Dreadful Night' (1874), a lengthy poem by the now-obscure nineteenth-century poet James Thomson (1834–82). Thomson is often referred to pseudonymously as B. V. or Bysshe Vanolis, the name by which he is distinguished from the eighteenth-century poet of the same name. This complex poem navigates an inhuman city, opening with an epigraph from Dante's *Inferno*, 'Per me si va nella città dolente' ['Through me you pass into the city of woe'], which indicates a sense of alienation from both the present and the self. The 'City' of the poem is one characterised by an absence of hope, and offers a 'myth of entropy' in which death is the only solution, one that is longed for by the City's inhabitants.[20] The despairing, necromantic *flâneur* who narrates the poem acts as a guide to this particular Purgatory, and it is clear that the poem owes much to Dante, among other sources, though it was Percy Bysshe Shelley who provided most inspiration to Thomson, giving rise to the 'Bysshe' in his pseudonym. The poem is divided into twenty-one parts, alternating between recollections of the narrator's visit to the City and the lost souls that he encounters, and a description of the City and its inhabitants. The form is regular but uneven, with some sections in seven-line stanzas, some six-line stanzas, and some in triplets; the changing form engenders the 'disruptive' effect of Gothic reading to which Napier refers, requiring the reader to adjust their pace repeatedly. This echoes the poem's inconsistent approach to time: 'A night seems termless hell' (I, l. 74),[21] and the City's occupants face interminable darkness in which is witnessed in a dissolution of night and day. Moreover, time is meaningless in the depths of melancholy that the City represents:

> Take a watch, erase
> The signs and figures of the circling hours,
> Detach the hands, remove the dial-face;
> The works proceed until run down; although
> Bereft of purpose, void of use, still go.   (II, ll. 32–6)

Yet in the exhortation to suicide that one character presents, and in the figure of the crawling man searching for a thread to return him to infancy and the safety of his mother's breast, it is clear that time still matters; there is no

---

20 Jerome J. McGann, 'James Thomson (B.V.): the woven hymns of night and day', *Studies in English Literature, 1500–1900* 3:4 (Autumn 1963): 493–507 (p. 498).
21 James Thomson (B. V.), *The City of Dreadful Night and Other Poems* (London: Watts, 1932). All further line references are placed parenthetically in the body of the text.

escape from it except in death, and a death, moreover, that will be slow in coming.

The city itself seems to be a hellish vision of London, the city to which Thomson himself was sent at the age of eight, and where he lived out his melancholy life in the Royal Caledonian Asylum. It is a place where light is artificial, serving only to illuminate the corners of despair:

> The street-lamps burn amid the baleful glooms,
>   Amidst the soundless solitudes immense
> Of ranged mansions dark and still as tombs. (I, ll. 43–5)

As these lines suggest, the City, though clearly delineated, remains obscure throughout. It is, as Raymond Williams states, 'a symbolic vision of the city as a condition of human life'.[22] The poem psychologically maps out the territory in the City where Faith, Love and Hope have died, indicating that it is their absence that has caused the living death of the inhabitants. In fact, for a nightmarish vision, the poem also offers some remarkably clear images of a city, a locale that ominously incorporates the River of Suicides:

> Although lamps burn along the silent streets,
>   Even when moonlight silvers empty squares
> The dark holds countless lanes and close retreats;
>   But when the night its sphereless mantle wears
> The open spaces yawn with gloom abysmal,
> The sombre mansions loom immense and dismal,
> The lanes are black as subterranean lairs. (III, ll. 1–7)

Yet this familiarity with the City that the first three lines above indicate is undermined by the final part of this stanza; the psychological distancing here is through the familiar being rendered strange, even uncanny, by the darkness, a darkness that is as much emotional and existential as it is literal. The 'countless lanes' in the dark are akin in their way to the subterranean passages and dark tunnels of Gothic fiction, architectural representations of what Valdine Clemens has described as the 'descent into the unconscious, away from the socially constructed self toward the uncivilized, the primitive'.[23]

Intimations of psychological complexity, sexual anxiety and emotional distress are aspects that are brought out later in the poem. The penultimate section offers an example of the grotesque, a sphinx before which a stone

---

22 Raymond Williams, *The Country and the City* (New York: Oxford University Press, 1973), p. 236.
23 Valdine Clemens, *The Return of the Repressed: Gothic Horror from The Castle of Otranto to Alien* (New York: New York University Press, 1999), p. 7.

angel disintegrates, first wings, then sword, then body, a powerful and complex image that may be read as representative of the earlier deaths of Faith, Hope and Love that the poem explores. In the grounds of the cathedral, the sphinx is unexpected; huge and implacable, it stands in for the immovability of the universe, its failure to empathise with humanity writ large. With its 'cold majestic face / Whose vision seemed of infinite void space' (XX, ll. 47–8), the creature of stone is both uncanny and grotesque, opening a space for the reader, alongside the speaker, to contemplate the vast emptiness of the universe.

The poem further manifests a close relationship with the Gothic mode through the description of the mansion that appears in section X: 'The hall was noble, and its aspect awed, / Hung round with heavy black from dome to floor' (ll. 15–16). The description of the deserted hall is one of Gothic splendour and melancholy that does justice to Walpole's *The Castle of Otranto* with its magnificent but doomed structure. The speaker overhears a young man who maps this building explicitly onto his own psyche, describing it as 'The chambers of the mansion of my heart' and 'The inmost oratory of my soul' (ll. 42, 46). It is here that he encounters the 'Lady of the images', a concept made more resonant by the poet's insistence that the City itself is a vision, and consequently its structures and inhabitants metaphoric and symbolic. This beautiful, dead woman, representing perhaps the death of false hope, is doubled, at the end of the poem, with the enormous statue of 'Melencolia', based on Albrecht Dürer's 1514 engraving of the same name. This final image offers a terrifying closure to the poem: as McGann has observed 'Because the vision is mythic, however, the statue is made to preside over the whole of reality as well. This is why the lines are so alarming.'[24]

Images are, perhaps, a last resort for Thomson in the poem; in Section XVI the 'pulpit speaker' is heckled by a listener who asks that he 'Speak not of comfort where no comfort is, / Speak not at all: can words make foul things fair?' (ll. 39–40). Words are useless in the face of despair, just as time is meaningless and light cannot illumine. In the following section, the narrator removes another potential source of comfort, by describing the moon and stars in all their glory and mocking men who 'think the heavens respond to what they feel' (XVII, l. 7). Not only does this undermine the notion that God has sympathy for his creation (a concept that the previous section denies even more explicitly), but it also suggests that the pathetic fallacy is of human

---

24 McGann, 'James Thomson', p. 504.

devising and, as such, inconsequential and meaningless: to take comfort from the beauty of nature is falsely to deceive oneself, since nature is unaware of our existence. The argument here is paradoxical, however, since the city itself reflects so closely the contorted psyche of the despairing visitor, and consequently reflects in Ruskin's truest sense the alignment between humanity and its landscape, expressing the reality of the soul in despair.

Thomson's vision is simultaneously of its time and eternal; despair does not change through the centuries, but the aestheticisation of misery is a trope to which poets consistently return. The poetry of Alfred, Lord Tennyson (1809–92) has become the face of medievalised Gothic in nineteenth-century poetry.[25] Written before the accession of Victoria to the throne, but popular with readers and artists throughout the nineteenth century, 'Mariana' (1830) has become emblematic of a Gothic aesthetic in which the landscape is used to reflect the interiority of character situated within it, along with 'The Lady of Shalott' (1833; 1842). These poems indicate Tennyson's nostalgic desire for a medieval past that is both comforting and threatening, and, most significantly, aesthetically appealing. To his friend James Knowles, Tennyson said that it was 'the distance that charms me in the landscape, the picture and the past, and not the immediate to-day in which I move'.[26] Townend has briefly acknowledged the role that the eighteenth-century Gothic played in Victorian constructions of the medieval, and this is particularly apparent in Tennyson's work, as well as in that of William Morris.[27]

Mariana herself is a minor character in Shakespeare's *Measure for Measure*, and in this poem the unification of landscape, or setting, and character reaches its pinnacle, though this itself is an irony since Mariana is separated from the wider open landscape by seclusion, the claustrophobic enclosure that characterises the situation of Gothic heroines from Sophia Lee and Ann Radcliffe onwards. While 'Mariana' contains no intimations of Gothic terror or horror, it contains at its heart an ambiguity that opens itself up into a nameless dread, at least for nineteenth-century women. The decay of the building ('Weeded and worn the ancient thatch / Upon the lonely moated

---

25 For further discussion of medieval Victorian poetics, see Matthew Townend, 'Victorian Medievalisms', in Matthew Bevis (ed.), *The Oxford Handbook of Victorian Poetry* (Oxford: Oxford University Press, 2013), pp. 166–83 and Florence S. Boos (ed.), *History and Community: Essays in Victorian Medievalism* (Abingdon: Routledge, 2016).
26 James Knowles cited in Bernard Richards, *English Poetry of the Victorian Period, 1830–1890* (London: Longman, 1988), p. 98.
27 Townend, 'Victorian Medievalisms', p. 168.

grange' [ll. 7–8]),[28] the stasis and grief of the heroine, and her inability to act upon her misery, are combined to delineate a character whose life is determined for her. As Tucker points out, a comparison with the work of Robert Browning indicates that, while Tennyson could create character and sustain its moods, 'he could not dramatize it beyond a relatively narrow range of internal and external action – a range of action that is most compelling, in fact, when it addresses those conditions or psychological mechanisms that thwart change'.[29] Tucker's claim is that Tennyson's characters are bound by their past lives and by their situation; like many Gothic heroines, then, Mariana is able only to reflect on the inevitability of her situation, a predicament that cannot be relieved unless it be through the actions of a hero. This fairy-tale construction owes much to Gothic in its retelling of the Arthurian myth of the Maid of Astolat. It also indicates the complex relationship between women and the natural world; Mariana is presented as detached from her surroundings rather than comfortable in them, and she is constructed as oppositional to the birds whose voices are heard in the poem. Visually, however, she melts into the background, becoming of the same colours and disintegrating state as the Gothic building that she occupies even as she remains, paradoxically, restrained by them. Moreover, her character is constructed as exterior and objectified, with any sense of her voice muted by the noise of the landscape that surrounds her. The setting and stock characters of Gothic are juxtaposed here, and the effect is that of approaching doom and hopelessness. Tennyson transforms the pathetic fallacy into a poetic device that retains echoes of Gothic origins.

The Gothic Character

This is a very different approach to Gothic character from those exemplified by other poets of the period. Robert Browning's dramatic monologues, for instance, especially 'Porphyria's Lover' (1836) and 'My Last Duchess' (1842), offer strong male characters who appear to represent Gothic villains: unchivalrous towards women, proud of their own strength and virility, and anxious to emphasise their own value in a rigid patriarchal system. These men are able to transcend their historical

---

28 Tennyson, Alfred Lord, *Selected Poems*, edited by Christopher Ricks (London: Penguin, 2007). All further line references are placed parenthetically in the body of the text.

29 Herbert F. Tucker, 'Tennyson and the measure of doom', *PMLA* 98:1 (1983): 8–20 (p. 9).

situation through their vocal abilities, and Browning's speakers' attributes 'even seemed to go some way towards extenuating villainy'.[30] As Kilgour writes, 'The gothic villain is frequently an example of the modern materialistic individual taken to an extreme, at which he becomes an egotistical and wilful threat to social unity and order.'[31] Though this comment refers to the villains in such late nineteenth-century Gothic fictions as Bram Stoker's *Dracula* (1897), this is equally true of Browning's speakers, and it is worth considering the ways in which these exaggerated characteristics manifested in Victorian poetry might be read. Certainly the implication is that these villains, through the use of irony, both reinforce and undermine patriarchal authority over women.

Richards's claim that 'there is a strongly escapist vein in Victorian poetry with historical settings' is perhaps overstating the case.[32] For example, a feminist reading of poems such as 'Porphyria's Lover' and 'My Last Duchess', or indeed 'The Bridge of Sighs' and 'Mariana', texts that exemplify the powerlessness of Victorian women in a patriarchal society, is easily paralleled with feminist readings of the role of the Gothic heroine, in which the enforced inertia of the heroine underlines women's situation and thus draws attention to it. 'Porphyria's Lover', like several of the poems under discussion in this chapter, refers to women's hair, which when let down becomes 'a Victorian code for released sexual feeling'.[33] In Browning's poem, the relaxation of loose hair prefigures death, indicating hypocritical moral codes that condemn women for expressions of sexuality; such an indictment is apparent in 'The Bridge of Sighs' and also Dante Gabriel Rossetti's 'Jenny' (1870). The woman's passivity may be contradicted by the languorous and enticing loosening of the hair, and yet it proves fatal, both morally and physically.

Contrastingly, the *femme fatale* is a figure that recurs throughout Gothic fiction, but which also appealed greatly to Victorian poets. Dante Gabriel Rossetti (1828–82), whose paintings of seductive yet dangerous women are his most famous works, draws on the pre-Raphaelite interest in the occult to create characters who also owe much to the Gothic aesthetic. Along with his sister Christina, Rossetti read Gothic novels avidly in his youth (a common factor with many of the poets of the period), and takes an historical and Gothicized approach in many of his poems, often in ballad form, as well as his paintings; this is also apparent in poems such as 'Rose Mary' and 'The

---

30 Richards, *English Poetry*, p. 107. 31 Kilgour, *Gothic Novel*, p. 12.
32 Richards, *English Poetry*, p. 103. 33 Armstrong, *Victorian Poetry*, p. 242.

Portrait'. The same is true of other contemporary Pre-Raphaelite poets, including Algernon Swinburne and William Morris.

The Gothic Supernatural

Dante Gabriel Rossetti's 'Sister Helen' (1870) is structured around questions from a 'little brother' concerning his sister's witchcraft, followed by her answers and, in parentheses, an invocation to 'Mother Mary'. The poem constructs a growing 'atmosphere of doom, sometimes using foreshadowing and dramatic irony'.[34] The character of Sister Helen is strongly delineated throughout, and contrasted with the naïveté of her sibling who does not understand why she must 'melt a waxen man' (l. 1).[35] The structure of the poem allows the reader to hear her voice directly. She speaks calmly and firmly to her brother:

>   'Oh the waxen knave was plump to-day,
>   Sister Helen;
>   How like dead folk he has dropped away!'
>   'Nay now, of the dead what can you say,
>   Little brother?'
>   (O Mother, Mary Mother,
>   What of the dead, between Hell and Heaven?)   (ll. 22–8)

With its formula of question, answer and aside, the poem's structure is deceptively simple, yet the form permits multiple voices to be heard, fragmenting perspective while keeping the focus on the witch and her actions. The setting evokes that of Gothic novels, with Helen recumbent in a high chamber while the wind whistles and the moon looks down, and three riders on horseback gallop across the hills towards them. The men have come, one by one, to ask her to spare Keith of Ewern, whose life is dwindling as the wax figure melts. Helen's answers are wry and sparse:

>   'The wind is loud, but I hear him cry,
>   Sister Helen,
>   That Keith of Ewern's like to die.'
>   'And he and thou, and thou and I,
>   Little brother.'   (ll. 85–9)

---

34 Clyde K. Hyder, 'Rossetti's "Rose Mary": a study in the occult', *Victorian Poetry* 1:3 (1963): 197–207 (p. 207).
35 Rossetti, Dante Gabriel, *Poems*, edited by William Michael Rossetti (London: Ellis & Elvey, 1891). All further line references are placed parenthetically in the body of the text.

The narrative continues in balladic tone, outlining how Helen has bewitched Keith of Ewern's soul to exist in torment while his body wastes away, since he abandoned her to marry another woman; this is a revenge narrative, then, in which the fallen woman uses her dark magic to punish her unfaithful lover. The abandoned woman is also explored by Christina Rossetti in 'Cousin Kate' and 'Maude Clare' (both published 1862), but although these characters are vengeful, their behaviour does not extend to witchcraft; the poet in these cases is more interested in exposing the hypocrisy of double standards than evoking the fearful glamour of the supernatural *femme fatale*. Poetry is less likely than the novel to offer a version of the 'explained supernatural', and as Jarlath Killeen has argued, evidence of witchcraft means that 'the rational views of the Victorian present about the superstitions of the past are suddenly turned upside down, and it is the superstitions which turn out to be accurate indications of the true make-up of reality'.[36] The folkloric, balladic tone of the poem belies any sense of reality, but the character of Helen speaks with the cynicism of a betrayed woman, in terror-inducing circumstances that would be all too familiar to Victorian readers.

The brother and father of the afflicted man have no success, and so the dying man's new wife begs Helen for mercy, an ill-judged move; the Lady of Ewern, like Cousin Kate, is doomed because she accepted a man who was morally, if not legally, bound to another. Helen delights in the woman's misery, situating herself as the wronged woman, and will not refrain. Her refusal to help the woman is perhaps more shocking than her mocking resistance of the men:

> 'And her moonlit hair gleams white in its flow.'
> 'Let it turn whiter than winter snow,
>   Little brother!'   (ll. 240–2)

A previous reference to the Lady of Ewern's hair refers to its golden colour; in this, Rossetti seems to be indicating the loose hair of a sexually promiscuous woman, as in 'The Bridge of Sighs' and 'Porphyria's Lover', but the circumstances here suggest that it is the married woman who is fallen, morally if not legally. This, then, is a poem about women who have fallen, though not from a conventional viewpoint, like his poem 'Jenny'; Helen holds the power here and exults in it, while the brother hopes that the Virgin Mary may offer help. Ultimately, however, Keith of Ewern and his spurned mistress are brought

---

36 Jarlath Killeen, *Gothic Literature 1825–1914* (Cardiff: University of Wales Press, 2009), p. 38.

down equally in their guilt; the poem's closing lines suggest that their wickedness is alike, and that both must suffer as a result:

> 'Ah! what white thing at the door has cross'd,
>   Sister Helen?
> Ah! what is this that sighs in the frost?'
> 'A soul that's lost as mine is lost,
>   Little brother!'
> *(O Mother, Mary Mother,*
> *Lost, lost, all lost, between Hell and Heaven!)*   (ll. 295–301)

The soul that enters is the final Gothic touch: it recalls the German ballads, such as Gottfried August Bürger's 'Lenore' and Johann Gottfried Herder's *Volkslieder* of which the Rossettis were so fond, of lost souls which come to claim their sweethearts; the final crossing of the threshold unites them in an unholy relationship, with Sister Helen's demoniac vengeance 'bought only at the price of her own soul'.[37] Rossetti's interest lies, it seems, in the mental strength of a woman whose desire for revenge is stronger than her life, mortal or eternal.

The poetry of Mary Elizabeth Coleridge (1861–1907) was described by Robert Bridges as 'wonderously [*sic*] beautiful ... but mystical rather and enigmatic'; her work contains an occult strain that clearly owes its dark aesthetics to the Gothic mode.[38] Her short poem 'The Witch' (1893) offers a rather different approach to the wicked woman from that of Rossetti; this witch conforms to female stereotypes: she is 'not tall or strong' (l. 2),[39] she claims that 'I am but a little maiden still, / My little white feet are sore' (ll. 12–13), and begs, 'Oh, lift me over the threshold, and let me in at the door!' (l. 7). Since she has positioned herself as a helpless heroine in need of rescuing, the (presumably male) narrator is blinded by her innocence and child-like appeal and admits her. The poem's title, of course, has warned the reader, yet the narrator remains in ignorance until it is too late; the reader must question whether the poem is an indication of the hidden strength of women beneath their apparent frailty, or a revival of folkloric tales of terror, akin to some of

---

37 Rodolphe Louis Mégroz, *Dante Gabriel Rossetti: Painter Poet of Heaven in Earth* (New York: Haskell House, 1971), p. 262.
38 Catherine Phillips, *Robert Bridges: A Biography* (Oxford: Oxford University Press, 1992), p. 175.
39 Breen, Jennifer (ed.), *Victorian Women Poets 1830–1900: An Anthology* (London: Everyman, 1994). All further line references are placed parenthetically in the body of the text.

the poems of her great-uncle, Samuel Taylor Coleridge. The poem is, of course, a warning – the concluding lines are ambiguous yet terrifying:

> She came — she came – and the quivering flame
> Sunk and died in the fire.
> It never was lit again on my hearth
> Since I hurried across the floor,
> To lift her over the threshold, and let her in at the door. (ll. 17–21)

The terror of the unknown and the unexplained leaves the reader's imagination to occupy the empty space once the poem concludes, making the inferences drawn from it all the more terrifying. This approach, which was popularised by the late nineteenth-century ghost story, is manifested effectively in poetry, with this example also showing the influence of Christina Rossetti. For both Rossetti and Coleridge, to cross a threshold (typically denoting the entrance of a bride to her marital home) is often a moment of crisis, in which the woman's fate is determined. In fact, a Gothic reading of this poem offers a somewhat different approach to it: Eugenia DeLamotte claims that 'The Gothic novelist always pauses at the threshold of the villain's dim domain, allowing the heroine and the reader to shudder with sudden intuitive horror.'[40] This suggests a reversal of roles: the woman may be a witch, but who or what is the speaker? Is it in fact the 'little maiden' who is condemned by entering the room? If Gothic novels by women insinuate that domesticity and marital bondage are fates worse than death, this opens up a potential new approach to the poem; similar ambiguity is apparent in Mary Elizabeth Coleridge's poems 'Wilderspin' (1899) and 'The Other Side of a Mirror' (1896), among others.

Smith and Hughes have emphasised modern critics' approaches to the Victorian period as 'inherently Gothic', even though, as Killeen acknowledges, Victorian men and women 'were more likely to think of themselves as living in an age of civilised progress rather than Gothic barbarism'.[41] This is, of course, indicative of changing views of both Gothic and the Victorians, but the use of Gothic as a poetic trope also indicates the genre's tendency to use distance in both time and place to create a space in which to offer social criticism of contemporary society. Robert Mighall argues that Victorian Gothic fiction 'reinforces the strangeness of the [urban] environment and

---

40 Eugenia C. DeLamotte, *Perils of the Night: A Feminist Study of Nineteenth-Century Gothic* (Oxford: Oxford University Press, 1990), p. 41.
41 Andrew Smith and William Hughes, 'Introduction: Locating the Victorian Gothic', in Smith and Hughes (eds), *Victorian Gothic*, pp. 1–14 (p. 2), citing Killeen, *Gothic Literature*, p. 4.

its inhabitants and establishes a distance between the respectable and the outcast, the observer and the observed'.[42] This is apparent in 'The Bridge of Sighs', in which the poem's narrator cries out to the (distanced, respectable) inhabitants of the urban space to show charity; it is also a significant aspect of many of the poems of Christina and Dante Gabriel Rossetti, among others. This distance is a familiar technique, and one that is used increasingly throughout the poetry of the nineteenth century.

There is a clearly delineated emphasis on the historical aspects of Gothic in many of the poems discussed above, and one that points time and again to contemporary anxieties. Richards suggests that 'the passion for the past among these Victorian poets is directly related to their sense of alienation and their desire for some kind of escape'.[43] Their sense of alienation from their present is apparent in all the poems under discussion here, along with many others not included, and indicates the position of many poets who saw themselves as social critics, outsiders to a problematic society, even if this is not aligned with how we regard them now. Armstrong has argued that Gothic can be read as 'an art of *resistance* to bondage ... a moment when the individual consciousness gave material form to art within a corporate social organisation and found a way of representing certain aspects of freedom'.[44] She refers, here, to Ruskin's conceptions of Gothic that he explored in 'The Nature of Gothic' (1853), and the work of the craftsmen of Venice, but the concept also bears examination in the light of poetry and its ability to use both Gothic and the grotesque to test the limits of freedom in the society in which it first existed. The poetry of the nineteenth century that most strongly shows the hallmark of its Gothic origins is that which not only manifests the aesthetics of the genre, but which also situates its crucial arguments and concerns in an historical past that provides a disguised replica of its own time.

Together with many others, the nineteenth-century poems discussed in this chapter indicate an anxiety about social conditions, including gender, poverty and sexuality; they also tend towards morbid expression that intimates a death-wish or anxieties about death as an unwanted journey or union with an unknown 'Other'. Armstrong claims that 'an obsession with death is the logical outcome of the oppressed condition';[45] though not all of the poets of the period can be described as oppressed in a material sense, many saw the

---

42 Robert Mighall, *A Geography of Victorian Gothic Fiction: Mapping History's Nightmares* (Oxford: Oxford University Press, 2003), p. 63.
43 Richards, *English Poetry*, p. 99.   44 Armstrong, *Victorian Poetry*, p. 237.
45 Armstrong, *Victorian Poetry*, p. 239.

condition of living within Victorian society as itself oppressive, to the artist as well as to marginalised groups. For those writers for whom death became a fascination, it is not always the primary focus of the text, but becomes a liminal concept, existing just beyond the bounds of the text: in few poems do we directly see, or experience, a death, though it is implied in nearly all of them. Edmund Burke described the terrible sublime as 'an apprehension of pain or death', though 'death is in general a much more affecting idea than pain'.[46] The Gothic as a genre or a mode 'allowed writers to engage with death-related subject matter considered too macabre, controversial, or sensitive' by making use of its exaggerated and excessive form to emphasise the taboo or the otherwise unacceptable.[47] The concentrated fragments of Gothic matter offered by poetry of the Victorian period are saturated with this anxiety around social issues, closely related to changing post-Enlightenment approaches to faith.

---

46 Edmund Burke, *A Philosophical Inquiry Into the Origin of Our Ideas of the Sublime and the Beautiful* (London, 1824), pp. 54, 34.
47 Carol Margaret Davison, 'Introduction: The Corpse in the Closet: The Gothic, Death, and Modernity', in Carol Margaret Davison (ed.), *The Gothic and Death* (Manchester: Manchester University Press, 2017), pp. 1–18 (p. 7).

2.10

The Genesis of the Victorian Ghost Story

SCOTT BREWSTER

In the Victorian period, the figure of the ghost and the category of the supernatural were subjected to rigorous scientific and philosophical scrutiny, but it was also a time in which the ghost story flourished as a specialised literary form and as a marketable cultural commodity. It prospered amid an array of discourses of the unseen, including the science of optics, the advent of 'invisible' technologies that constituted a form of modern supernatural, and the rise of spiritualism and psychical research. For women writers, the ghost story becomes a tale of increasing *visibility* and opportunity: women occupied a prominent role in the growth of the ghost story, exploiting the growing demand for shorter forms of fiction, encouraged by a burgeoning periodical culture. Victorian literary ghosts have tended to be treated as metaphors or ciphers for 'a spectrum of social anxieties of the day' that include the decline of the Christian faith, the contested political, social and legal position of women, and the increasing invisibility of financial exchange.[1] As Andrew Smith argues, however, while Victorian ghost stories are often concerned with money and property, they are not simply 'encrypted economic narratives';[2] in a similar vein, Nina Auerbach has emphasised that these narratives are not only about marginalised or disenfranchised women, for 'to be haunted in the nineteenth century was to be human'.[3] Recent critical studies have highlighted the imbrication of Victorian ghost narratives in wider debates concerning scientific knowledge and literary realism. This chapter examines how the ghost story encompasses wider questions of

[1] Eve M. Lynch, 'Spectral Politics: The Victorian Ghost Story and the Domestic Servant', in Nicola Bown, Carolyn Burdett and Pamela Thurschwell (eds), *The Victorian Supernatural* (Cambridge: Cambridge University Press, 2004), pp. 67–86 (p. 68).
[2] Andrew Smith, *The English Ghost Story 1840–1920: A Cultural History* (Manchester: Manchester University Press, 2010), p. 29.
[3] Nina Auerbach, 'Ghosts of ghosts', *Victorian Literature and Culture* 32:1 (2004): 277–84 (p. 280).

knowledge and belief in the period and traces its role in the formal and conceptual development of nineteenth-century Gothic.

Pleasing Terrors

The opening sentence of Dickens's *A Christmas Carol* (December 1843) encapsulates the perplexing status of the ghost: 'Marley was dead, to begin with.' The tale epitomises the Victorian ghost story, in that it bears on the nature, function and veracity of ghosts and ghost-seeing. While Marley's status seems incontrovertible – he is 'dead as a door-nail' – the manifestation of his restless spirit poses questions about the afterlife, the relationship between spirit and matter, and between seeing and believing that all preoccupy Victorian culture. Marley does business with a world that declares him dead, gone, his account settled. In Marley's end, we might say, is his beginning, at least in narrative terms: 'There is no doubt that Marley was dead. This must be distinctly understood, or nothing wonderful can come of the story I am going to relate.'[4] Is this 'wonderful' a disclaimer, suggesting that the spectral return of spirits of the night is imaginary or fantastic, or does it suggest that ghosts are transformative, an open rather than closed question of understanding? Normally, the ghost story relies upon the testimony of a living witness to the supernatural, but in his daily transactions Scrooge is already haunted long before Marley appears in spectral form. Scrooge is defined by his endless commerce with his late partner, commerce that includes the ongoing exchange between the living and the dead. Marley may be one of 'the limited dead', but he clings to some form of life and renewal, and is stubbornly up-to-date: he is clad with clanking chains, typical of the traditional ghost, but these chains are the trappings – both visible expression and constraints – of modern capitalism.[5] Scrooge is equally modern in his attempts to explain Marley as a disorder of the senses, demonstrating his awareness of contemporary scientific thought regarding ghosts: 'There's more of gravy than the grave about you, whatever you are!'[6] As Scrooge realises, however, to deal with the ghost is to live 'in the Past, the Present and the Future'.[7] His personal epiphany also reflects what Luke Thurston and I term the 'Janus-faced' position of the

---

4 Charles Dickens, 'A Christmas Carol', in *A Christmas Carol and Other Christmas Books*, edited by Robert Douglas-Fairhurst (Oxford: Oxford University Press, 2006), pp. 5–83 (p. 9).
5 Jennifer Bann, 'Ghostly hands and ghostly agency: the changing figure of the nineteenth-century specter', *Victorian Studies* 51:4 (Summer 2009): 663–85 (p. 663).
6 Dickens, *A Christmas Carol*, p. 21.   7 Dickens, *A Christmas Carol*, p. 77.

Victorian ghost story: 'poised on the threshold of modern culture, it was able both to draw on the ancestral treasure-trove of Gothic style and to invent new forms of "pleasing terror"'.[8]

Dickens's exploitation of the Christmas ghost story is precisely a combination of innovation and reversion to tradition. In 'A Christmas Tree' (1850), Dickens writes of 'telling Winter Stories – Ghost Stories, or more shame for us – round the Christmas fire' in an old house.[9] He recalls the supernatural tales celebrated in Thomas K. Hervey's *The Book of Christmas* (1836), which sees the fireside as a fitting place for 'impressions of the wild and shadowy and insubstantial' that give rise to tales of terror.[10] Washington Irving earlier records the Christmas festivities and storytelling traditions in rural England in *The Sketch Book of Geoffrey Crayon, Gent* (1820), a text that may have influenced Dickens's first ghostly tale set at Christmas, the 'Story of the Goblins Who Stole a Sexton', which appeared in the tenth instalment of *The Pickwick Papers* in December 1836. While Dickens's Christmas tales draw on older folkloric traditions, their commercial success also builds on a well-established print history: ghost stories had been a staple feature of Christmas annuals from the 1820s, and the print history of Christmas stretches back to the 1730s.[11] Dickens's Christmas books, and his regular commissioning of ghost tales as editor of *All The Year Round* and *Household Words*, nonetheless find a new niche, selling the idea of Christmas to bourgeois consumers.[12] *A Christmas Carol*, priced at five shillings, exceeded the purchasing power of working- and lower-middle-class readers, targeting more affluent consumers whose ideology the tale at once challenges and affirms. In his Preface, Dickens characterises the tale as a 'pleasant' haunting, suggesting it is designed to divert rather than frighten. When the spirits visit Scrooge, the reform of one individual by extension addresses broader social ills, and the ghostly is used to foster 'social stability and continuity' rather than dramatise division or conflict.[13]

---

8 Scott Brewster and Luke Thurston, 'Introduction', in Scott Brewster and Luke Thurston (eds), *The Routledge Handbook to the Ghost Story* (New York and London: Routledge, 2017), pp. 1–15 (p. 5).
9 Charles Dickens, 'A Christmas Tree', in David Pascoe (ed.), *Charles Dickens: Selected Journalism, 1850–1870* (Harmondsworth: Penguin, 1997), pp. 3–16 (p. 11).
10 Thomas K. Hervey, *The Book of Christmas*, reprint of 1836 edition (Boston, MA: Roberts Brothers, 1888), pp. 237–8.
11 See Tara Moore, *Victorian Christmas in Print* (Basingstoke: Palgrave Macmillan, 2009) and David Parker, *Christmas and Charles Dickens* (New York: AMS Press, 2005).
12 Dewi Evans, 'The Victorian Ghost Story and the Invention of Christmas', in Scott Brewster and Luke Thurston (eds), *The Routledge Handbook to the Ghost Story* (New York and London: Routledge, 2017), pp. 78–86 (p. 79).
13 Dewi Evans, 'The Victorian Ghost Story and the Invention of Christmas', p. 81.

Yet this is not the whole story. In their oscillation between estrangement and reconciliation, social commentary and festive celebration, Dickens's Christmas tales represent a defining moment for the Victorian ghost story. Does the ghost story intend to terrify or to instruct, to entertain or to confront difficult questions? Michael Newton points out that the ghost no longer had a stock purpose in the nineteenth century.[14] A minister of justice in the early modern period, exposing or avenging injustices, restoring family inheritances or enabling redemption, the ghost's role in Gothic fiction is 'primarily to frighten and horrify rather than teach moral lessons'.[15] In December 1847, Sheridan Le Fanu declared that Christmas ghost stories should not try 'to make the reader a better man, but merely a more uneasy one'; their aim is 'not to improve, but to frighten him'.[16] At the end of the century, Henry James's *The Turn of the Screw* (1898) inherits this model of the enigmatic, purposeless or incalculable ghost that offers no closure or moral improvement, while, in comedic form, Oscar Wilde's 'The Canterville Ghost' (1887) parodies the notion of purposeful haunting. Dickens's ghosts retain a homiletic function, but after *A Christmas Carol* this becomes more strained. In *The Haunted Man and the Ghost's Bargain* (19 December 1848) the solitary Redlaw is offered the choice of forgetting the pain of the past and its 'intertwisted chain of feelings and associations', but this bargain withers compassion, sympathy and fellow feeling in others.[17] The tale ends with partially restored memory and familial reconciliation, but its muted tone marks a transition in the treatment of the ghost: festive, nostalgic communality does not banish the shadows and only partially salvages the protagonist.

Even if the spectre is characterised by its impalpability and its ties to the past, Antony Mandal has shown how the history of the ghost story is 'quintessentially shaped by the materiality and modern technologies and processes of the Victorian print culture from which it emanated'.[18] Victorian Gothic tales and ghost stories were a core element in

---

14 Michael Newton 'Introduction', in Michael Newton (ed.), *The Penguin Book of Ghost Stories* (Harmondsworth: Penguin, 2010), pp. xv–xxxv (p. xx).
15 Nick Freeman, 'The Victorian Ghost Story', in Andrew Smith and William Hughes (eds), *The Victorian Gothic: An Edinburgh Companion* (Edinburgh: Edinburgh University Press, 2012), pp. 93–107 (p. 94).
16 Sheridan Le Fanu, 'Fireside horrors for Christmas', *Dublin University Magazine* 30:180 (December 1847): 631–46 (p. 640).
17 Charles Dickens, 'The Haunted Man and the Ghost's Bargain', in *A Christmas Carol and Other Christmas Books*, edited by Robert Douglas-Fairhurst (Oxford: Oxford University Press, 2006), pp. 323–408 (p. 344).
18 Anthony Mandal, 'The Ghost Story and the Victorian Literary Marketplace', in Brewster and Thurston (eds), *The Routledge Handbook to the Ghost Story*, pp. 29–39 (p. 39).

periodical publishing across the later nineteenth century, building on the success of Dickens's Christmas books. Ghost stories featured in a wide range of outlets, including *Blackwood's* (1817–1980); *The Dublin University Magazine* (1833–82); *Household Words* (1850–9); *All The Year Round* (1859–70); *Macmillan's Magazine* (1859–1907); *Cornhill Magazine* (1860–1975); *Temple Bar* (1860–1906); *St James's Magazine* (1861–82); *Argosy* (1865–1901); *Belgravia* (1867–99); *Tinsley's* (1868–84); *Collier's Weekly* (1888–1957); *Strand Magazine* (1891–1950); and *Pall Mall* (1893–1914). Many carried Christmas issues featuring ghost stories; one of the most notable, *The Haunted House*, in *All The Year Round* (1859), included tales by Dickens, Wilkie Collins and Elizabeth Gaskell. Ghost stories appearing in these magazines were also pirated and reprinted by American publishers.[19] Periodical culture engendered a high demand for short fiction, and the ghost story was sensitive to market conditions. Its more explicit treatment of violence and sex in the 1890s was a response to the relaxation of censorship following the collapse of the library system, a decrease in the space allocated to fiction by magazines, the wider use of illustration, and more graphic reporting of crime by the popular press.[20] Magazines and periodicals afforded significant opportunities for women to forge careers as professional authors, and a number became among the most prolific writers of ghost stories in the period. Writers such as Charlotte Riddell; Elizabeth Gaskell; Amelia Edwards; Rhoda Broughton; Mary Elizabeth Braddon and Mrs Henry (Ellen) Wood; Margaret Oliphant; Vernon Lee (Violet Paget); and, in north America, Harriet Beecher Stowe; Louisa May Alcott; Mary E. Wilkins Freeman; and Charlotte Perkins Gilman played a major role in shaping the ghost story both stylistically and thematically. In a climate of social and political reform, with campaigns for women's rights to education, suffrage and employment, and married women's property bills, these writers could cast light on 'social problems and inequalities through the figure of the ghost'.[21] As we shall see, many ghost stories by women examine, often in veiled fashion, the material and social conditions of their existence.

---

19 Jeffrey Andrew Weinstock, *Scare Tactics: Supernatural Fiction by American Women* (New York: Fordham University Press, 2008), p. 5.
20 Nick Freeman, 'E. Nesbit's new woman gothic', *Women's Writing* 15:3 (2008): 454–69 (p. 463).
21 Melissa Edmundson Makala, *Women's Ghost Literature in Nineteenth-Century Britain* (Cardiff: University of Wales Press, 2013), p. 19.

Seeing and Believing

Victorian ghost stories are primarily a matter of vision, whether in terms of social visibility, theories of optics, or the relationship between the explained and unexplained supernatural. Walter Scott's experiments with the supernatural encounter in the 1820s, which revolve around seeing, believing and witnessing, establish the formal and conceptual framework for the ghost story across the nineteenth century. 'Wandering Willie's Tale' features as an episode in Scott's novel *Redgauntlet* (1824); its use of Scots draws on oral storytelling tradition, but the tale is related in a letter that displays the writer's 'distinct narrative tone of voice'.[22] Scott had declared his preference for the careful blending of folklore and written literary tradition two decades previously, claiming in 1801 that ghost stories are 'ill-timed & disgusting when not managed with moderation & ingrafted upon some circumstances of popular tradition or belief'.[23] The tale of haunting that plays a role within a larger narrative, and which combines oral and written traditions, anticipates Catherine Earnshaw's spectral appearance to Lockwood in Emily Brönte's *Wuthering Heights* (1847). Lockwood, who listens avidly to Ellen Dean's storytelling, nonetheless tries to shut out Catherine's spirit with books.

In 'The Tapestried Chamber' (1828), Scott presents the ghostly tale as a discrete form of short fiction. Replete with Gothic features, from the setting in an 'ancient feudal fortress' to its grim family secret, the story involves a night in a haunted room and a visitation by a 'spectral hag', but the truth is only revealed in the retelling the following day, 'contrary to the custom of this species of tale'.[24] The room was the scene of 'incest' and 'unnatural murder', and the terrifying spirit is a 'wretched ancestress' of the current owner Woodville, the 'black and fearful catalogue' of her crimes recorded in a family history.[25] Scott's tale, however, stresses its modernity, prefiguring the ways in which Victorian culture will think about ghosts and the supernatural. The chamber combines a 'modern air of comfort with venerable antiquity', and Woodville is eager to remove 'unpleasant rumours' about the room's history among the

---

22 Walter Scott, *Redgauntlet*, edited by G. A. M. Wood with David Hewitt (Edinburgh: Edinburgh University Press, 1997), p. 87.
23 Walter Scott, quoted in Fiona Robertson, *Legitimate Histories: Scott, Gothic, and the Authorities of Fiction* (Oxford: Clarendon Press, 1994), p. 65.
24 Walter Scott, 'The Tapestried Chamber', in Michael Cox and R. A. Gilbert (eds), *The Oxford Book of English Ghost Stories* (Oxford: Oxford University Press, 2008), pp. 1–12 (p. 1).
25 Scott, 'The Tapestried Chamber', pp. 12–13.

domestic staff and surrounding neighbourhood.[26] Woodville admits that he has subjected his unfortunate visitor General Browne to an experiment to test the bedroom's legend, rather in the manner that the Society for Psychical Research conducted investigations into haunted houses in the last two decades of the nineteenth century. Browne is a suitable test subject, given his reputation for 'cool judgement under the most imminent dangers'.[27] Despite his fear, he is able to distinguish between the genuine spirit, and 'the deceptions of my fancy and over-excited nerves', thus affirming his credentials as a credible witness to the existence of spirits.[28] Browne's experience proves to Woodville the 'better judgement' of previous generations, and he restores the room to its gloomy solitude.

Scott's ghost-hunting scenario, later revisited in Edward Bulwer Lytton's 'The Haunted and the Haunters: or, The House and the Brain' (1865); H. G. Wells's 'The Red Room' (1896); and Perceval Landon's 'Thurnley Abbey' (1908), draws on an 'investigative' culture of ghost-seeing that can be traced back to German Romanticism and foreshadows the connections between detective fiction and the ghost story from the mid-Victorian period onwards.[29] Srdjan Smajić observes that both modes seek 'to make the dead speak in order to reveal a truth', but 'either implicitly or explicitly articulate the notion that vision, bluntly put, is a messy affair'.[30] As Terry Castle has shown, ghosts had been treated as 'figments, or phantasmata, produced by a disordered or overwrought brain' from the late eighteenth century, and 'The Tapestried Chamber' demonstrates Scott's keen awareness of contemporary debates about vision, knowledge and delusion.[31] Although Browne's account of his haunted-house experience seems compelling, in *Letters on Demonology and Witchcraft* (1830) Scott deems ghost-seeing a result of faulty perception: 'there certainly exists more than one disorder known to professional men, of which one important symptom is a disposition to see apparitions'.[32] David Brewster's *Letters on Natural Magic* (1832), which is addressed to Scott, similarly contends that sightings of spectres are explicable in physiological terms, constituting, as such, what he terms 'optical illusions'. The eye,

---

26 Scott, 'The Tapestried Chamber', pp. 5, 10.
27 Scott, 'The Tapestried Chamber', p. 4.   28 Scott, 'The Tapestried Chamber', p. 9.
29 Shane McCorristine, *Spectres of the Self: Thinking about Ghosts and Ghost-Seeing in England, 1750–1920* (Cambridge: Cambridge University Press, 2010), p. 9.
30 Srdjan Smajić, *Ghost-Seers, Detectives, and Spiritualists: Theories of Vision in Victorian Literature and Science* (Cambridge: Cambridge University Press, 2010), pp. 181–2, 4.
31 Terry Castle, *The Female Thermometer: Eighteenth-Century Culture and the Invention of the Uncanny* (New York and Oxford: Oxford University Press, 1995), p. 170.
32 Walter Scott, *Letters on Demonology and Witchcraft Addressed to J. G. Lockhart, Esq.* (London: John Murray, 1830), p. 16.

Brewster argues, is 'the principal seat of the supernatural'.[33] As Henry Ferris observes in 1845 in the *Dublin University Magazine* – a regular outlet for Victorian ghost stories – 'The ghost which we see (the nightmare, for instance) is not without us, but within.'[34] Similarly, Charles Ollier asserts in 1848 that 'anyone who thinks he has seen a ghost, may take the vision as a symptom that his bodily health is deranged ... To see a ghost, is, *ipso facto*, to be a subject for the physician'.[35] Smajić argues that this optical theory, whereby ghosts 'are exemplars of things that look real enough but exist only in the deceived or diseased eye of the beholder', has a crucial influence on the development of the ghost story in the nineteenth century.[36]

Le Fanu's 'Green Tea' (1872) centres on the treatment of ghosts as physical or psychological aberrations. The tale is presented as a case study; its frame narrator is a physician, the inheritor of the papers of Martin Hesselius, a self-proclaimed 'medical philosopher' who can be seen as the forerunner of psychic doctors or detectives like Algernon Blackwood's *John Silence: Physician Extraordinary* (1908) or William Hope Hodgson's *Carnacki the Ghost-Finder* (1913).[37] Hesselius recounts the torment of Reverend Jennings, a clergyman plagued by visions of a monkey of 'unfathomable malignity', the creature binding him in 'satanic captivity' until he commits suicide.[38] While an eminent medical authority, deemed by Jennings a *'mere* materialist', attributes the sight of this ghostly familiar to 'optic nerves', Hesselius notes that Jennings has highlighted passages from Emanuel Swedenborg's *Arcana Coelestia* (1749–56) that deal with interior vision and evil spirits assuming bestial form.[39] He diagnoses Jennings's suffering as an addiction to green tea, which has induced 'spectral illusions' and triggered 'hereditary suicidal mania'.[40] To be haunted, then, involves disordered vision, whether that is 'physiological, corporeal, retinal' in origin or, in Hesselius's view, the disturbed equilibrium of the 'inner eye'.[41]

Hesselius does not conduct a formal treatment and his diagnosis comes too late to cure the patient of his delusions, but, while he fails as 'a therapist or exorcist', he might be said to succeed as 'a detective of

---

33 Sir David Brewster, *Letters on Natural Magic Addressed to Sir Walter Scott, Bart*, reprint of 1832 edition (New York: Harper and Brothers, 1842), p. 21.
34 Henry Ferris, 'Of the nightmare', *Dublin University Magazine* 25 (1845): 32–44 (p. 40).
35 Charles Ollier, *Fallacy of Ghosts, Dreams, and Omens* (London: Charles Ollier, 1848), p. 10.
36 Smajić, *Ghost-Seers*, p. 4.
37 Sheridan Le Fanu, 'Green Tea', in Newton (ed.), *The Penguin Book of Ghost Stories*, pp. 105–39 (p. 108).
38 Le Fanu, 'Green Tea', pp. 126, 125.   39 Le Fanu, 'Green Tea', pp. 117, 128.
40 Le Fanu, 'Green Tea', pp. 137, 138.   41 Smajić, *Ghost-Seers*, p. 5.

the *causes* of occult phenomena and motivations for actions and behaviours'.[42] Victorian ghost stories, however, typically tend to depict medical or scientific authority as struggling to account for ghosts and ghost-seeing. Arthur Conan Doyle's 'The Captain of the *Polestar*' (1883) has scientific naturalism confronting the unnerving experience of the supernatural. Doyle was a strong advocate of Spiritualism, which regarded interior vision as precisely the way to validate the existence of ghosts, and this story stages a struggle between two kinds of seeing. Icebound in the Arctic, the ship's doctor views himself as a dispassionate observer of the superstitious crew and the captain's obsessive desire to be reunited with his dead fiancée, whose spirit he believes to be haunting his craft. The captain is 'a psychological study' and the doctor reflects that, with a 'demented captain and a ghost-seeing mate', he may be 'the only really sane man aboard the vessel'.[43] Presenting himself as a trustworthy eyewitness, he nonetheless acknowledges that his report will seem invented back home: 'My inferences are my own but I shall be answerable for the facts.'[44] Although lacking the apparently delusional 'eyes of love' to glimpse the ghost, the dead woman's portrait in the captain's cabin, exhibiting 'incredible' strength of will, throws a 'glamour' over the medical student.[45] Subsequently, he hears a 'ghastly scream' and perceives a 'dim nebulous body devoid of shape' keeping pace with the craft.[46] Later discovering the captain's corpse on the ice, the doctor sees a snow-drift which the crew-members claim has 'the shape of a woman'.[47] Ghost-seeing has become contagious; the doctor's final diary entry describes him as 'still starting at times and fancying I hear the quick nervous step of the dead man upon the deck above me'.[48] In a Postscript, the doctor's father claims his son to be 'a strong-nerved and unimaginative man, with the strictest regard for veracity', and a fellow physician implicitly lends credence to the story, corroborating the facts of the Captain's doomed love.[49] Julia Briggs views the

---

42 Smajić, *Ghost-Seers*, p. 152.
43 Arthur Conan Doyle, 'The Captain of the *Polestar*', in Michael Cox and R. A. Gilbert (eds), *The Oxford Book of Victorian Ghost Stories* (Oxford: Oxford University Press, 2003), pp. 283–302 (pp. 285, 295).
44 Conan Doyle, 'The Captain of the *Polestar*', p. 299.
45 Conan Doyle, 'The Captain of the *Polestar*', p. 293.
46 Conan Doyle, 'The Captain of the *Polestar*', pp. 296, 299.
47 Conan Doyle, 'The Captain of the *Polestar*', p. 301.
48 Conan Doyle, 'The Captain of the *Polestar*', p. 302.
49 Conan Doyle, 'The Captain of the *Polestar*', p. 302.

development of the ghost story as a reaction against Enlightenment thinking, but the relationship between the ghost and Enlightenment is not one of straightforward opposition.[50] As Doyle's tale suggests, rationalism never succeeds in exorcising phantoms, but rather than dismissing the supernatural, it keeps the ghost alive as an active question. Just as the wraith accompanies the *Polestar*, flickering in and out of view, so the ghost story is the intimate counterpart of reason, not its excluded other.

As 'Green Tea' and 'The Captain of the *Polestar*' demonstrate, the Victorian ghost story is 'a medium of epistemological interrogation'.[51] The open-ended titles of many ghost stories, including Fitz-James O'Brien's 'What Was It?' (1859); Charles Dickens's 'To Be Taken with a Grain of Salt' (1865; originally published as 'The Trial for Murder'); Ellen Wood's 'Reality or Delusion?' (1868); Rhoda Broughton's 'The Truth, the Whole Truth, and Nothing but the Truth' (1868); and Amelia B. Edwards's 'Was It an Illusion?: A Parson's Story' (1881), maintain a careful balance between credulity and scepticism, capturing this interrogative approach to the supernatural in Victorian culture. Literary ghost tales confront questions of testimony and illusion similar to those faced by spiritualists and psychic researchers, suggesting that the 'truth' of ghosts depends upon persuasion and conviction as much as it involves the scrupulous presentation of credible evidence.[52] Edith Nesbit's 'The Shadow' insouciantly privileges the power of narrative over the careful amassing of evidence: 'This is not an artistically rounded off ghost story, and nothing is explained in it, and there seems to be no reason why it should not be told.'[53] Victorian ghosts are thus a matter of seeing, believing and, crucially, the pleasure of telling.

Debates about ghosts and the supernatural consistently gravitate around the question of storytelling. Andrew Lang makes the connection explicit, reflecting that 'We seem to need a name for a new branch of the science of Man, the Comparative Study of Ghost Stories.'[54] Lang and other commentators were keen, however, to establish a proper distance between ghost stories as a cultural practice, respectable medical and scientific enquiry into the supernatural, and the pseudo-sciences of Spiritualism and psychical research. The *Pall Mall Gazette* concludes that ghost stories 'are matter for some science

---

50 Julia Briggs, 'The Ghost Story', in David Punter (ed.), *A New Companion to the Gothic* (Oxford: Wiley-Blackwell, 2012), pp. 176–85 (p. 179).
51 Smith, *The English Ghost Story*, p. 3.   52 McCorristine, *Spectres of the Self*, p. 16.
53 Edith Nesbit, *The Power of Darkness: Tales of Terror*, edited by David Stuart Davies (Ware, Herts: Wordsworth, 2006), p. 169.
54 Andrew Lang, 'The comparative study of ghost stories', *The Nineteenth Century* 17 (1885): 623–32 (p. 623).

or other', and when studied by anthropologists they 'do actually yield scientific material of a very valuable sort'. When approached by psychical researchers, contrastingly, 'the belief in ghosts ... is a continuous inheritance of our race from a very remote and savage period', and merely reflects the 'superstitious fears of the dark' acquired from our ancestors.[55] In *Blackwood's*, a central forum for the Victorian ghost story, Lang lamented that 'the most frivolous pastimes now have a habit of degenerating into scientific exercises ... Even ghost stories, the delight of Christmas Eve, have been ravaged and annexed by psychology'.[56] For all this determination to categorise ghost stories as unashamed entertainment rather than as serious examinations of the occult or the complexities of the human mind, the boundaries between literary tales, 'true' accounts and the scientific study of apparitions become increasingly blurred in the later Victorian period.

Catherine Crowe's *The Night Side of Nature: Or Ghosts and Ghost Seers* (1848) exemplifies this mingling of narrative forms, pursuing a distinctive formal and conceptual approach to ghosts. Gillian Bennett observes that the book marks a transition from legendary ghosts to personal experiences 'and the more subjective types of supranormal encounter' that were uncommon until the later nineteenth century.[57] Crowe's 'authentic' ghost stories, a collage of newspaper reports, letters, family legends, literary and scholarly sources, tales from classical antiquity, extracts from a church register, medical reports and individual testimony, inhabit the uncertain ground between unverifiable 'fact' and fiction. *The Night Side of Nature* mirrors many of the generic features of ghost stories, demonstrating the cultural exchange between 'real' and fictional tales of spectres. Its accounts of ghosts are carefully mediated, and a number, such as 'Round the Fire', have been anthologised alongside literary ghost stories.[58] Crowe's diffuse, self-conscious narratives, however, sit alongside a taxonomic desire to classify ghosts, with chapter titles that include 'Apparitions', 'Troubled Spirits' and 'Haunted Houses'. Crowe does not consider the phenomena under investigation 'supernatural': 'I am persuaded that the time will come, when they will be reduced strictly within the bounds of science.' For her, science is a domain 'in which nothing is stable', and she envisages a future moment 'when we shall no longer deny, but be able to

---

55 Leader Comment, 'Psychical research', *Pall Mall Gazette* (21 October 1882): 278.
56 Andrew Lang, 'Ghosts Up to Date', *Blackwood's Edinburgh Magazine* 155 (1894): 47–58 (p. 47).
57 Gillian Bennett, 'Introduction', in Catherine Crowe (ed.), *The Night Side of Nature; or, Ghosts and Ghost Seers* (Ware, Herts: Wordsworth, 2000), pp. 9–14 (p. 13).
58 Catherine Crowe, 'Round the Fire', in Richard Dalby (ed.), *The Virago Book of Victorian Ghost Stories* (London: Virago, 1992), pp. 34–43.

account for, phenomena apparently prodigious'.[59] She explicitly rejects John Ferriar's *An Essay Towards a Theory of Apparitions* (1813) and Samuel Hibbert-Ware's *Sketches of the Philosophy of Apparitions* (1832), which treat ghost-seeing as a result of diseased or over-active minds. Intriguingly, however, while Ferriar treats phantoms as the product of individual delusions, he also suggests that apparitions are a question of narrative. His explanation of the supernatural avoids the 'vulgar machinery' of trapdoors and sliding panels often associated with early Gothic, but he relocates spirits into a homely setting that will frame so many Victorian ghost stories, 'authentic' and literary: 'Nay, a person rightly prepared may see ghosts, while seated comfortably by his library-fire, in as much perfection, as amidst broken tombs, nodding ruins, and awe-inspiring ivy.'[60] Spectral impressions, here, may result from sleepiness (as with Scrooge), but equally a storytelling circle may be gathered round this 'library-fire' to share tales of ghosts.

Dickens's review of Crowe's book in *The Examiner* in February 1848 owes a clear debt to the 'spectral illusion' thesis: 'Doubtful and scant of proof at first, doubtful and scant of proof still, all mankind's experience of *them* is, that their alleged appearances have been, in all ages, marvellous, exceptional, and resting on imperfect grounds of proof; that in vast numbers of cases they are known to be delusions superintended by a well-understood, and by no means uncommon disease.'[61] Dickens would later circulate reports of Crowe's apparent breakdown, implicitly connecting her belief in the supernatural with psychological instability. His criticism of Crowe's study, however, overlooks his use of similar methods, such as collecting ghost stories and consulting contemporary medical and philosophical literature on the strange capacities of the mind, to investigate apparitions, spirits, mesmerism and clairvoyance. Equally, the 'anecdotal' ghost story deployed by Crowe featured widely in medical writing about mental disorder. Dickens also claimed to be 'perfectly unprejudiced and impressible on the subject' of ghosts and readily exploited the popularity of the ghost story for commercial advantage.[62] Thus Crowe's serious interest in ghosts and the supernatural,

---

59 Catherine Crowe, *The Night Side of Nature; or, Ghosts and Ghost Seers* (Ware, Herts: Wordsworth, 2000), p. 22.
60 John Ferriar, *An Essay Towards a Theory of Apparitions* (London: Cadell and Davies, 1813), pp. 15, vi, viii.
61 Charles Dickens, *The Examiner*, 26 February 1848, in Michael Slater (ed.), *Dickens' Journalism: The Amusements of the People and Other Papers: Reports, Essays and Reviews 1834–51, Vol. II* (London: J. M. Dent, 1996), pp. 80–91 (p. 83); original italics.
62 Charles Dickens, Letter to William Howitt, 6 September 1859, in *The Letters of Charles Dickens, vol. IX*, edited by Graham Story, Margaret Brown and Kathleen Tillotson (Oxford: Clarendon Press, 1965–99), pp. 116–17.

rather than representing an embarrassing aberration associated with her femininity, can be seen as sharing in a broader fascination with the supernatural.

Alongside Crowe's challenge to male authority, the tales that she recounts also shine an oblique light on class relations, since many are communicated via servants and domestic staff. The orality of such stories, as Vanessa Dickerson remarks, renders them 'a type of communal property not as valued by the literary establishment as were other written narratives'.[63] As if to illustrate this dismissive attitude to the residual folkloric aspects of the ghost story, Michael Cox and R. A. Gilbert declare that 'The working class and those in trade are generally too busy to concern themselves with ghosts', unlike the leisured middle classes of independent means.[64] Yet ghostly tales mediated, at least partially, through the voices of those below stairs prove a recurrent feature of Victorian ghost stories, especially those written by women. Domestic servants experience hauntings, circulate tales, represent a repository of local knowledge and often display more sympathetic and intuitive understanding than their social superiors. They appreciate ghosts, argues Eve Lynch, since their own role is to be 'the apparition appearing out of nowhere'.[65] In Nesbit's 'Man-Size in Marble' (1893), the housekeeper Mrs Dorman embodies the traditional lore harboured by the local community. She tells the husband, rather than his wife, about the haunting of the knights on All Hallows' Eve; the previous occupant, an independent woman, learned the story first-hand and survived. In Margaret Oliphant's 'The Open Door' (1882), Colonel Mortimer declares that 'it is impossible to fathom the minds of rustics', yet the coachman Jarvis and his wife know the ghostly secret of his house, which hinges on the story of a housekeeper's prodigal son. Jarvis declares that there are 'awfu' [sic] strange things in the world. An unlearned person doesna ken what to think', yet 'the minister and the gentry they just laugh in your face'.[66] The open door is a former servants' entrance, and the current staff have an economic reason to maintain silence about the ghostly voice heard in the grounds, ensuring that the occupants stay in residence.[67]

---

63 Vanessa D. Dickerson, *Victorian Ghosts in the Noontide: Women Writers and the Supernatural* (Columbia and London: University of Missouri Press, 1996), p. 111.
64 Michael Cox and R. A. Gilbert, 'Introduction', in Cox and Gilbert (eds), *The Oxford Book of English Ghost Stories*, pp. ix–xvii (p. xv).
65 Eve M. Lynch, 'Spectral politics', p. 67.
66 Margaret Oliphant, 'The Open Door', in *A Beleaguered City and Other Stories*, edited by Merryn Williams (Oxford: Oxford University Press, 1988), pp. 115–59 (pp. 128, 133).
67 Melissa Edmundson, 'The "uncomfortable houses" of Charlotte Riddell and Margaret Oliphant', *Gothic Studies* 12:1 (2010): 51–67 (p. 60).

Elizabeth Gaskell's 'The Old Nurse's Story' is narrated by the eponymous servant Hester to the children of her original charge; she was initially recruited in a schoolroom, chosen as a 'scholar who would do for a nurse-maid'.[68] These stories disclose the complex relationship between social class and belief in the supernatural in the Victorian period.

Crowe's work was eclipsed by the arrival of Spiritualism from the United States. *The Night Side of Nature* was published in the same year as Kate and Maggie Fox claimed that they could communicate with a spirit in their home in Hydesville, New York. Fuelled by the preoccupation with death and mourning on both sides of the Atlantic, the Spiritualist movement found enthusiastic followers particularly among middle-class women, but also among the working classes in northern England during the latter decades of the nineteenth century. From the outset, Spiritualism and the technologies of writing were closely associated. In the United States, the 'Hydesville rappings' were characterised as a 'spiritual telegraph' between this world and the spirit world, coming only four years after a telegraph link had been established between Baltimore and Washington.[69] Melissa Edmundson argues that the fervour for Spiritualism is 'integral to an understanding of why Victorian women were so attracted to the ghost story': mediums and writers were given a purpose outside traditional family roles, as well as the opportunity to earn money independently, and their work enabled a temporary escape from strict moral codes.[70] *Séances*, like ghost stories, brought spirits into intimate domestic settings, and the medium's performance, like 'real' and literary accounts of ghosts, represented a blend of belief and communal storytelling that challenged the senses and the boundaries of established knowledge. Diana Basham discerns an affinity between ghosts and the social position of Victorian women, arguing that both were subject 'to the same kind of criticism and liable to be met with the same dismissive hostility in their attempts to gain recognition'.[71]

In response to the rise of Spiritualism, a number of social clubs and learned groups, such as the Ghost Society (Cambridge 1851–c. 1860s); the Phasmatological Society (Oxford, 1879–85); and the Ghost Club (London,

---

68 Elizabeth Gaskell, 'The Old Nurse's Story', in *Gothic Tales*, edited by Laura Kranzler (Harmondsworth: Penguin, 2000), pp. 11–32 (p. 11).
69 Anthony Enns, 'The Undead Author: Spiritualism, Technology and Authorship', in Bown, Burdett and Thurschwell (eds), *The Victorian Supernatural*, pp. 55–78 (p. 60).
70 Melissa Edmundson, 'Women Writers and the Ghost Story', in Brewster and Thurston (eds), *The Routledge Handbook to the Ghost Story*, pp. 69–77 (p. 72).
71 Diana Basham, *The Trial of Woman: Feminism and the Occult Sciences in Victorian Literature and Society* (Baltimore: Johns Hopkins University Press, 1993), pp. 151–2.

1882–1936), were formed in order to investigate supernatural phenomena. The Ghost Society, or the Cambridge Association for Spiritual Inquiry, was founded by Edward White Benson, father of the ghost story writers E. F., A. C. and R. H. Benson; as Archbishop of Canterbury, Benson would caution against spiritualism in the first issue of W. T. Stead's *Borderland* in 1893.[72] Famously, Benson made a central contribution to the Victorian ghost story by relating to Henry James the story that would become *The Turn of the Screw*. The Society for Psychical Research (SPR), founded in 1882 by Henry Sidgwick (Chair of Moral Philosophy at Cambridge), and the Classicists Frederic Myers and Edmund Gurney, was the most prominent and long-lasting body devoted to psychical research, 'the exemplary marginal science of the fin de siècle'.[73] It attracted an eclectic membership from the worlds of science, politics and letters, including Alfred Russel Wallace; Eleanor Balfour Sidgwick (mathematician, Principal of Newnham College and elected President, 1908–9); William Gladstone; Arthur Balfour; William James; Arthur Conan Doyle; Robert Louis Stevenson; Alfred Tennyson; and John Ruskin. *Phantasms of the Living* (1886), which ran to two volumes and 1,400 pages, and the Committee on Haunted Houses reports in 1882 and 1884, demonstrated the SPR's aspiration to 'modernise the ghost story within the precepts of scientific naturalism', taking apparitions 'away from popular spiritualist beliefs and into the realms of scientific possibility'.[74] Yet unimpeachable proof remained elusive, and left the SPR sharing problems of credibility with Spiritualism. William James reflected on the flickering, enigmatic status of the supernatural and its ability to frustrate verification: 'although ghosts, and clairvoyances, and raps and messages from spirits, are always seeming to exist and can never be fully explained away, they also can never be susceptible of full corroboration'.[75]

Many ghost story writers express a resistance to approaching ghosts in pseudo-scientific fashion. In *Hauntings* (1890), Vernon Lee claims that 'My four little tales are of no genuine ghosts in the scientific sense; they tell of no

---

72 Janet Oppenheim, *The Other World: Spiritualism and Psychical Research in England, 1850–1914* (Cambridge: Cambridge University Press, 1985), p. 68.
73 Sally Ledger and Roger Luckhurst (eds), *The Fin-de-Siècle Reader: A Reader in Cultural History, c. 1880–1900* (Oxford: Oxford University Press, 2000), p. 269.
74 McCorristine, *Spectres of the Self*, p. 140.
75 William James, 'The Confidences of a "Psychical Researcher"' (1909), in *Essays in Psychical Research*, edited by Frederick Burkhardt and Fredson Bowers (Cambridge and London: Harvard University Press, 1986), pp. 361–75 (pp. 361–2).

haunting such as could be contributed by the Society for Psychical Research.'[76] Henry James's 1909 Preface to *The Turn of the Screw* notes the shift in ghost stories across the century: the new type is 'the mere modern "psychical" case, washed clean of all queerness as by exposure to a flowing laboratory tap, and equipped with credentials vouching for this – the new type clearly promised little, for the more it was respectably certified the less it seemed of a nature to rouse the dear old sacred terror'.[77] James's preference is to render the modern ghost incalculable or inexplicable, returning it to 'a realm in which the supernatural was both mysterious and terrifying'.[78] Yet this advocacy of older traditions of terror is qualified by his close personal relations to psychical research. Apart from his family connections, he had close friends in the SPR, was familiar with its reports and would deliver an address if his brother William was absent. Wilde's 'The Canterville Ghost' is similarly equivocal; while the tale parodies ghost-hunting, his wife Constance joined the SPR in the 1890s and subscribed to Stead's *Borderlands*, which blended respectable science and the occult.

Victorians were also 'haunted' by the uncanny ability of modern science and technology to collapse time and space.[79] The telegraph and telephone, carrying invisible or disembodied signals and voices from afar, blurred distinctions between science and magic, and between modernity and superstition. In this sense, the ghost is 'entangled with the "real world" of science and progress ... in its mirroring of the communicational technologies of the second half of the nineteenth century'.[80] The uncanny properties of the telephone and telegraph linked them to other phenomena – telepathy, hypnosis, second sight, spirit photography, spirit rapping and planchette writing – that offered ways of communicating with and representing ghosts, of bridging that chasm between the living and the dead. The impact of these strange effects, provoking both fascination and disquiet, can be discerned in Dickens's 'No. 1 Branch

---

76 Vernon Lee, *Hauntings and Other Fantastic Tales*, edited by Catherine Maxwell and Patricia Pulham (Peterborough, Ont.: Broadview, 2006), pp. 39–40.
77 Henry James, 'Preface', in *The Turn of the Screw*, edited by Peter G. Beidler (Boston and New York: Bedford/St Martin's, 2004), pp. 179–86 (pp. 179–80).
78 Bridget Bennett, '"The Dear Old Sacred Terror": Spiritualism and the Supernatural from *The Bostonians* to *The Turn of the Screw*', in Tatiana Kontou and Sarah Willburn (eds), *The Ashgate Research Companion to Nineteenth-Century Spiritualism and the Occult* (Farnham: Ashgate, 2012), pp. 311–31 (p. 314).
79 Nicola Bown, Carolyn Burdett and Pamela Thurschwell, 'Introduction', in Bown, Burdett and Thurschwell (eds), *The Victorian Supernatural*, pp. 1–19 (p. 1).
80 Steven Connor, 'The Machine in the Ghost: Spiritualism, Technology and the "Direct Voice"', in Peter Buse and Andrew Stott (eds), *Ghosts: Deconstruction, Psychoanalysis, History* (London: Macmillan, 1999), pp. 203–25 (p. 211).

Line: The Signal-Man' (1866), which opens with a voice of uncertain origin and location that immediately precedes 'a violent pulsation' produced by a passing train.[81] Witness to several fatalities and accidents, the signal-man may suffer from 'commotion shock' or succumb to spectral illusion, but the lonely signal-man's case is not reducible to straightforward psychological explanation.[82] The ghost manifests itself as a surfeit *and* absence of signals that evade full comprehension. The narrator 'diagnoses' the signal-man's ghostly premonition through existing optical theory – 'a disease of the delicate nerves that minister to the functions of the eye' – and attributes the imaginary cry to the uncanniness of new technology: 'do but listen for a moment to the wind in this unnatural valley while we speak so low, and to the wild harp it makes of the telegraph wires!'[83] Yet the narrator becomes part of this ghostly chain of communication: his opening words in the narrative repeat those haunting the signal-man, and are then uttered as a vain warning by the engine-driver before the signal-man's death. In the signal-box, the bell rings exclusively for the signal-man, but it is also a *visible* sound unheard by others. Highly experienced, and utterly conscientious in discharging his duties, the signal-man is nonetheless confounded by these inscrutable intimations of the supernatural that confuse the senses and defy reason. Faced with ambiguous or unfathomable signs, he fails to 'see' properly, but what form would 'proper' understanding assume? Its purpose misinterpreted, the ghost cannot, or does not, 'mean' anything, posing a fundamental epistemological problem.

Ghosts and the Gothic

This dialogue surrounding the explained and unexplained supernatural in Victorian culture shapes the relationship between the ghost story and the Gothic tradition. Julia Briggs has proposed that between 1830 and 1930, 'it could be argued that the most characteristic form taken by the Gothic ... is the ghost story'.[84] While ghost tales may constitute 'a special category' of Gothic, the Victorian ghost story progressively eschews the 'lurid fictionality' and 'fantastic tropes' associated with the early Gothic in favour of modern

---

81 Charles Dickens, 'No. 1 Branch Line: The Signal-Man', in Newton (ed.), *The Penguin Book of Ghost Stories*, pp. 91–104 (p. 91).
82 See Catherine Aird, 'Dickens and railway spine neurosis', *The Dickensian* 108:486 (Spring 2012): 25–8 and Louise Henson, 'Investigations and Fictions: Charles Dickens and Ghosts', in Bown, Burdett and Thurschwell (eds), *The Victorian Supernatural*, pp. 44–63 (p. 57).
83 Dickens, 'No. 1 Branch Line', p. 97. 84 Briggs, 'The Ghost Story', p. 177.

scepticism, making the documentary-style presentation of the ghost more powerful and frightening.[85] The gradual disenchantment of the supernatural has to be set against Victorian culture's fascination with the occult, but towards the end of the century the ghost story becomes increasingly preoccupied with the nature of fiction itself, and with the psychological complexity of its protagonists. M. R. James's comments exemplify these formal and tonal shifts away from the early Gothic: he favours 'reticence' over 'blatancy', observing that 'the weltering and wallowing that I too often encounter merely recalls the methods of M. G. Lewis'.[86] James's 'The Mezzotint' (1904) epitomises this understated presentation of the ghostly. The unremarkable picture in the tale shows a Queen Anne manor house rather than a Gothic pile, but it still tells of an old family terror. Over the course of a day, the picture progressively changes to show a skeletal wraith, whose movements take place out of direct sight, approaching and leaving the house with malign intent. The mezzotint's owner is determined to conceal this 'impossible' occurrence from the Phasmatological Society, but it is the enigmatic glimpses of the phantom at work, and the reticence and emotional detachment of the academics witnessing the unfolding scene of child abduction, that intensify the horror of the tale.[87]

With some exceptions, the Victorian ghost story operates on an intimate, domestic scale, far from the castles and catacombs of the early Gothic novel: ghosts now frequent more modest middle-class town houses and country estates, and haunting becomes 'a feature of less exclusive addresses'.[88] The ghost story's relocation to domestic surroundings mirrors that of sensation fiction, which similarly 'brought dislocation and menace to the very heart of the family home', although sensation novels deal in the explained supernatural, as in the spectral appearances of Anne Catherick in Wilkie Collins's *The Woman in White* (1860).[89] The contrast between Le Fanu's 'Squire Toby's Will' (1868) and 'An Account of Some Strange Disturbances in Aungier Street' (1853) illustrates the ghost story's change of location. While 'Squire Toby's

---

85 Luke Thurston, *Literary Ghosts from the Victorians to Modernism* (New York and London: Routledge, 2012), pp. 1–2.
86 M. R. James, 'Some Remarks on Ghost Stories', in *Collected Ghost Stories*, edited by Darryl Jones (Oxford: Oxford University Press, 2011), pp. 410–16 (pp. 414–15).
87 M. R. James, 'The Mezzotint', in M. R. James, *Collected Ghost Stories*, edited by Darryl Jones (Oxford: Oxford University Press, 2011), pp. 24–34 (p. 31).
88 Steven Connor, 'Afterword', in Bown, Burdett and Thurschwell (eds), *The Victorian Supernatural*, pp. 258–77 (p. 259).
89 Jennifer Uglow, 'Introduction', *The Virago Book of Victorian Ghost Stories*, edited by Richard Dalby (London: Virago, 1988), pp. ix–xvii (p. xiv).

Will' recounts a typical Gothic tale of secrets and disputed inheritance in an ancient house in northern England, in the latter story property changes hands at the whim of the market. The haunted house, owned by the Lord Mayor of Dublin during the reign of James II, has Jacobite associations, but the current tenants are only temporarily imperilled by the weight of that past, and several years later the house is burned down by a subsequent tenant. This typifies many Victorian ghost tales with modern urban settings, such as the anonymous 'The Story of Clifford House' (1878) and Charlotte Riddell's 'The Old House in Vauxhall Walk' (1882). Rented houses may harbour ghosts, but it is another family's secret which sustains spirits in that place, rather than the crimes or misfortunes of one's own parents and ancestors.

Henry James's *The Turn of the Screw* is self-aware about the seductions of Gothic romance. The governess's 'fancies' about Bly and its 'gingerbread antiquity', and her notion that the house conceals 'a mystery of Udolpho', cannot account meaningfully for the sight of Quint on the battlements.[90] The governess's subsequent experience strips away her illusions, and registers the distance between early Gothic and the realist framework of the later Victorian ghost story. Whether her vision is 'real' or not, the veiled horror of the story is rooted in the everyday, which James regarded as the mark of quality: 'A good ghost-story, to be half as terrible as a good murder-story, must be connected at a hundred points with the common objects of life.'[91] The 'small sympathy with monkish times' shown in Mary Elizabeth Braddon's 'At Chrighton Abbey' is by no means uniform;[92] Vernon Lee places the phantom in a distinctly Gothic setting and atmosphere: 'a ghost is the sound of our steps through a ruined cloister ... it is the scent of mouldering plaster and mouldering bones from beneath the broken pavement'.[93] Nonetheless, for Lee and many women writers the ghost story is a means of resituating established Gothic motifs and preoccupations in recognisably modern contexts.

Vanessa Dickerson sees Victorian women writers as 'the real ghosts in the Victorian noontide', rendered invisible by the 'neo-Gothic condition' of

---

90 Henry James, 'The Turn of the Screw', in *The Turn of the Screw and Other Stories*, edited by T. J. Lustig (Oxford: Oxford University Press, 2008), pp. 113–236 (pp. 136, 138).
91 Henry James, 'Review of *Aurora Floyd*', in Mark Wilson and Leon Edel (eds), *Literary Criticism: Essays on Literature, American Writers, English Writers* (New York: Library of America, 1984), pp. 741–6 (p. 742).
92 Mary Elizabeth Braddon, 'At Chrighton Abbey', in Cox and Gilbert (eds), *The Oxford Book of Victorian Ghost Stories*, pp. 163–89 (p. 166).
93 Vernon Lee, 'Faustus and Helena', in *Hauntings*, pp. 309–10.

economic and legal enslavement in marriage that is only partly mitigated by legislative changes to married women's property rights.[94] In their ghost stories, women writers revise the 'property plot', involving wealth and authorship, identified by Ellen Moers as central to the emergence of Female Gothic.[95] Inheritance and property rights remain acute concerns in many stories, but Diana Wallace remarks that the ghost story is an exception to the rules of Female Gothic, the form allowing women writers 'license to use the *unexplained* supernatural and to evade the marriage ending'.[96] Equally, the ghost story and supernatural tale enabled a number of women to pursue careers as professional authors. Histories of the ghost story have often overlooked the sophistication, inventiveness and breadth of women's ghost stories, and their integral role in the genre's stylistic development in the Victorian period. Nickianne Moody critiques the tendency to regard male practitioners as 'serious' and women writers as 'commercial', arguing instead that the ghost story can be seen as 'an experimental as well as formulaic narrative framework for women's writing'.[97]

Edith Nesbit kept her distance from politicised New Women writers, but a story such as 'Man-Size in Marble' shines a harsh light on marriage and its containment of women's creative ambitions.[98] For all the couple's modish trappings and apparent equality, the female voice is silenced in the tale. Laura's husband 'explains' her death at the hands of unholy knights who reputedly 'walk' on All Saints' Eve, conveniently overlooking his failure to warn his wife about the legend. While it is Laura who learns that the cottage they inhabit 'was a big house in Catholic times, and there was a many deeds done there', her reward is to become the victim of a feudal history hostile towards an independent woman who privileges writing over domestic work, a past symbolised by the effigies of the knights in the nearby church.[99] While the story rehearses the early Gothic trope of the heroine imperilled by oppressive, atavistic powers, however, Nick Freeman argues that it can also

---

94 Dickerson, *Victorian Ghosts in the Noontide*, pp. 30, 137.
95 Ellen Moers, *Literary Women: The Great Writers* (New York: Oxford University Press, 1976); see also Lauren Fitzgerald, 'Female Gothic and the institutionalization of Gothic studies', *Gothic Studies* 6:1 (2004): 8–18.
96 Diana Wallace, 'Uncanny stories: the ghost story as female gothic', *Gothic Studies* 6:1 (2004): 57–68 (p. 58).
97 Nickianne Moody, 'Visible Margins: Women Writers and the English Ghost Story', in Sarah Sceats and Gail Cunningham (eds), *Image and Power: Women in Fiction in the Twentieth Century* (London and New York: Longman, 1996), pp. 77–90 (p. 77).
98 Victoria Margree 'The feminist orientation in Edith Nesbit's Gothic short fiction', *Women's Writing* 21:4 (2014): 425–44 (p. 426).
99 Edith Nesbit, 'Man-Size in Marble', in *The Power of Darkness*, p. 11.

be read 'as a narrative of the insurmountable obstacles facing the radical woman of the period'.[100] In Amelia B. Edwards's 'The Phantom Coach' (1864), the newly married narrator becomes lost while hunting on a northern moor and seeks refuge with a reclusive scientist, leaving his wife waiting anxiously at a lonely inn. The couple are 'very much in love and, of course, very happy', but the husband has broken his promise to return before dusk.[101] Tempting though it is to view the marooned scientist, ostracised because of his belief in the traditionally 'feminine' arts of the occult, as a marginalised figure like the new bride, this is a story of male self-absorption. The scientist expounds his philosophy like an 'inspired dreamer', his beguiling eloquence holding the narrator's imagination 'captive'.[102] The husband never tells his wife about his terrifying experience aboard the phantom coach – nor his accident in the snow, partly resulting from the strong whisky he is given in the remote farmhouse – excluding her in the same fashion as Nesbit's Laura, an evident irony given that women were perceived as more 'sensitive' to the supernatural.

In Nesbit's 'The Ebony Frame' (1893), the desire of the ghostly woman to be reunited with her reincarnated lover in the present day is thwarted due to a fire ignited by the candle of a 'nightly-studious housemaid'.[103] The woman had been burned as a witch in the seventeenth century because of her interest in astronomy, but her spirit is kept alive within a picture whose frame is fashioned by the Devil. Intellectual ambition is presented as dangerous or challenging for women, and their choices are tightly circumscribed compared to those of the protagonist, who casually inherits property while listlessly courting his present-day fiancée. To risk his soul for a lost love seems an 'imbecility' in 'our "so-called nineteenth century"'.[104] Unlike the women of the tale, held within various frames, the man can have his dreams of what might have been and his dull reality (marriage, wealth) too. The ghostly encounter in these stories exposes what is 'unseen' and 'less than satisfying' in middle-class marriage for women.[105] Obliquely but powerfully, women's lack of social agency emerges in anamorphic form through these ghost stories, a

---

100 Nick Freeman, 'E. Nesbit's New Woman Gothic', p. 466.
101 Amelia B. Edwards, 'The Phantom Coach', in Cox and Gilbert (eds), *The Oxford Book of English Ghost Stories*, pp. 13–24 (pp. 13–14).
102 Edwards, 'The Phantom Coach', pp. 18, 20.
103 Nesbit, 'The Ebony Frame', in *The Power of Darkness*, p. 152.
104 Nesbit, 'The Ebony Frame', in *The Power of Darkness*, p. 149.
105 Emma Liggins, 'Gendering the spectral encounter at the *fin de siècle*: unspeakability in Vernon Lee's supernatural stories', *Gothic Studies* 15:2 (2013): 37–52 (p. 38).

negative or spirit image of the freedoms enjoyed by men. Once again, the Victorian ghost is fundamentally a matter of vision.

Conclusion

Ghosts are treated as a question of the veridical in the latter part of the nineteenth century, and Victorian culture offers remarkable hospitality to these homely interlopers. A preoccupation with death and mourning, and the shift in science towards the invisible, accounts only partially, however, for the familiarity and rude health of spirits in the period. It is the enigmatic refusal of 'full closure and disclosure' that gives ghosts their distinctive power.[106] A modern enchantment, the ghost story resituates the Gothic in modest country houses, drawing rooms and gaslit urban streets. This spatial relocation away from cataracts and ruined abbeys mirrors the formal compression of the ghost story: spectral encounters are usually fleeting, and ghosts show, rather than tell, their tales of 'old sacred terror'. Unlike Jacob Marley, these apparitions tend to be cryptic, incalculable, hovering at the edge of established regimes of knowledge. Crucially, too, the ghost story examines the subjective life – fear, loss, yearning and regret – with a concentration and intensity unmatched by the novel. In 'real' and fictional form, the Victorian ghost story grants momentary, haunting glimpses of the forgotten, hidden and excluded. For the Victorians, then, ghosts are something 'to begin with'; rather than being consigned definitively to the past, they enable a reimagining of the present and the future.

---

106 Dara Downey, '"Taking Noiseless Turns in the Passage": Phantoms and Floor Plans in Henry James's *The Turn of the Screw*', in Helen Conrad O'Briain and Julie Anne Stevens (eds), *The Ghost Story from the Middle Ages to the Twentieth Century* (Dublin: Four Courts Press, 2010), pp. 189–202 (p. 190).

2.11

Charles Dickens and the Gothic

JOHN BOWEN

Gothic, Horror and Laughs

Dickens and Gothic: one of the great unwritten books of criticism. This is perhaps not so surprising, given the simultaneous paucity and complexity of Dickens's engagement with Gothic material. The word itself appears no more than six or seven times in his work, usually in trivial adjectives to describe 'gothic' windows in Wemmick's suburban castle in *Great Expectations* (1860–1) and Sleary's circus in *Hard Times* (1854). References to the Gothic are equally rare in his letters, where they are typically a cue for laughter, as in his view of Charles Maturin's *The Fatal Revenge* (1807), a novel which he thought 'very bad' because its characters

> are so very convulsive and tumble down so many places, and are always knocking other people's bones about in such a very irrational way, that I object. The way in which earthquakes won't swallow the monsters, and volcanoes in eruption won't boil them, is extremely aggravating. Also their habit of bolting when they are going to explain anything.[1]

Dickens could find an 1852 stage adaptation by Dion Boucicault of John Polidori's *The Vampyre* (1819) 'very picturesque and romantic',[2] but otherwise vampires are mainly a comic matter: the fleas that tormented his pet dog, he recounts in *Pictures From Italy* (1846), made 'feasts of blood' until eventually 'it seemed as if the two hind legs and the tail of the dog were lifted off the ground by the muscular power of these thirsty vampires'.[3] Dickens never wrote a Gothic novel, and like many of his post-Romantic generation, often

---

1 Charles Dickens to B. W. Procter, 15 April 1854, in Graham Storey, Kathleen Tillotson and Angus Easson (eds), *The Letters of Charles Dickens, Volume VII: 1853–35* (Oxford: Clarendon, 1993), p. 314.
2 Charles Dickens to Dion Boucicault, 29 April 1862, in Graham Storey (ed.), *The Letters of Charles Dickens, Volume X: 1862–64* (Oxford: Clarendon, 1998), p. 74.
3 See F. G. Kitton, *Charles Dickens by Pen and Pencil*, 13 parts (London, 1889–90), II, p. 8, cited in Kathleen Tillotson (ed.), *The Letters of Charles Dickens, Volume IV: 1844–46* (Oxford: Clarendon, 1977), pp. 156–7.

saw it as an outdated and intermittently absurd literary form. In his writing, as in the popular theatrical culture in which he was saturated, there was, as William St Clair puts it, 'a general muddling of gothic, of horror, and of laughs'.[4] When Dickens recalls his childhood reading, for example, there are no Gothic texts mentioned. Instead, the iconic works are novels by Daniel Defoe, Henry Fielding and Tobias Smollett, together with *The Arabian Nights' Entertainment* and James Ridley's pastiche *The Tales of the Genii* (1764): not Gothic, but either comic and picaresque, or oriental and exotic.[5] This is in contrast to his younger friend and later collaborator Wilkie Collins, for example, who recounted in an early letter his delight in reciting 'the most terrible parts of the Monk and Frankenstein', giving his relatives 'a hash of diablerie, demonology, & massacre with their Souchong and bread and butter'.[6]

Yet Gothic elements are present throughout Dickens's work, particularly at affectively charged moments, such as Miss Havisham's first appearance to Pip's wondering eyes in *Great Expectations*:

> I saw that the bride within the bridal dress had withered like the dress, and like the flowers, and had no brightness left but the brightness of her sunken eyes. I saw that the dress had been put upon the rounded figure of a young woman, and that the figure upon which it now hung loose had shrunk to skin and bone. Once, I had been taken to see some ghastly waxwork at the Fair, representing I know not what impossible personage lying in state. Once, I had been taken to one of our old marsh churches to see a skeleton in the ashes of a rich dress that had been dug out of a vault under the church pavement. Now, waxwork and skeleton seemed to have dark eyes that moved and looked at me. I should have cried out, if I could.[7]

A complex psychological process of memory and apprehension (in both the older narrating Pip and the suffering child) is tracked by this passage, through two material, embodied memories of things that resemble living humans but are not. The passage draws subtly but decisively on Gothic in the 'dark eyes' of the 'waxwork and skeleton' that 'moved and looked at me'. It is the

---

4 William St Clair, *The Reading Nation in the Romantic Period* (Cambridge: Cambridge University Press, 2004), p. 370.
5 See John Bowen, 'Chapter 1: The Life of Dickens 1: Before Ellen Ternan', in Sally Ledger and Holly Furneaux (eds), *Dickens in Context* (Cambridge: Cambridge University Press, 2011), pp. 3–10 (p. 4).
6 William Baker and William W. Clarke (eds), *The Letters of Wilkie Collins*, 2 vols (Basingstoke: Macmillan, 1999), vol. 1, p. 14.
7 Charles Dickens, *Great Expectations*, edited by Margaret Cardwell (Oxford: Oxford University Press, 1994), p. 57.

Gothic mode that has been disciplined – rhythmically, emotionally and intellectually – to follow the disturbed processes of Pip's intimate remembering. It works not to make us cry out, if we could, but to feel the continuing power of these characters' and our own vulnerabilities and memories, as abandoned woman, working-class child, and reader. Gothic is here *staged*, in great part by Miss Havisham herself, as a privileged idiom of suffering and grievance by a woman who has been sexually and financially betrayed. Her tattered seclusion, her abject grandiosity, both embody and display her pain. She consciously theatricalises her grief, in a victimhood simultaneously imposed, consciously taken up and, in her dealings with Pip, weaponised. She is one of Dickens's supreme creations, and the Gothic is essential to her characterisation, self-presentation and self-understanding.

Dickens is often seen as a great humanist writer, the creator of vividly individual characters, but he is equally interested in exploring the limits of the human. His novels are full of those who exist at the margins or limits of both Victorian and our own understandings and categories of human life and being. Gothic motifs, tropes, plottings and characterisations are essential to this work of exploration, and are used in inventive and controlled ways throughout his career. Dickens's writing repeatedly returns to the depiction of power relations that are profoundly asymmetrical, simultaneously intimate and domineering: Quilp and Little Nell; Dombey and Florence; John Jasper and Rosa Bud. In his late work, they often dramatise exquisite exactions of pain, such as Pip's and Estella's 'romance', Miss Havisham's predatory love for Estella or the passionately eroticised rivalry of Bradley Headstone and Eugene Wrayburn in *Our Mutual Friend* (1864–5). He is not content to explore in conventionally Gothic ways what Judith Wilt calls 'the suffering of Power in the male and the power of Suffering in the female': characters and states of mind, like those of Miss Havisham or Pip, which cannot easily be put in either category, matter as much, or more.[8] His victims are often also his tyrants.

Like the 'great spirt of blood' that periodically bursts from Bradley Headstone's nose, these relations can break out into explosive violence.[9] Still shocking, the most extreme of these is Bill Sikes's killing of his lover Nancy in *Oliver Twist*. After Nancy dies, Sikes is haunted and pursued by her spectral eyes, which eventually drive him to his death. An intensely private haunting that dominates the latter stages of the novel climaxes in a

---

8 Judith Wilt, 'Love/slave', *Victorian Studies* 33:3 (Spring, 1994): 451–60 (p. 452).
9 Charles Dickens, *Our Mutual Friend*, edited by Michael Cotsell (Oxford: Oxford University Press, 1989), p. 637.

spectacular public hanging, an act both of popular justice and mob rule. It is not clear to what degree we should think of Nancy's eyes as a 'real' haunting and how much a psychological projection by Sikes, for their fictional power stems from their undecidability and our uncertainty. The writing drives Sikes's sordid murder of a poor prostitute onto both outer and inner stages: on the one hand, that of the outraged London mob which pursues him to his final self-lynching, and on the other the idea that he might be a soul in torment, a figure of agonising, newly-discovered inwardness:

> Every object before him, substance or shadow, still or moving, took the semblance of some fearful thing; but these fears were nothing, compared to the sense that haunted him of that morning's ghastly figure following at his heels. He could trace its shadow in the gloom, supply the smallest item of the outline, and note how stiff and solemn it seemed to stalk along. He could hear its garments rustling in the leaves, and every breath of wind came laden with that last low cry. If he stopped it did the same. If he ran, it followed – not running too, that would have been a relief, but like a corpse endowed with the mere machinery of life, and borne upon one slow melancholy wind that never rose or fell.[10]

There are objects and the substance of material reality here, but more powerful are the unseen traces, shadows and semblances, the melancholy wind and the mechanical corpse. It is a typical extension through Gothic by Dickens of the affective range of the book, both for its characters and readers.

Michael Hollington has shown how Dickens in his very first book *Sketches by Boz* (1836–8) treats Radcliffean terror with irony, while repurposing it into social critique. This Hollington christens, after the prison reformer Elizabeth Fry, 'Mrs Fry Gothic', which captures well both the ironic treatment of his Romantic precursors in Dickens's early work, and its use in the service of a radical, campaigning anger.[11] This can be lost if we think of it simply as 'Urban Gothic', the more usual term applied to Victorian fiction of this nature, although that captures well its characteristic landscape of social decay and squalor within labyrinthine streets and institutions.[12] Dickens was also drawn to the 'energetic grotesquery' of the Gothic Revival in

---

10 Charles Dickens, *Oliver Twist*, edited by Philip Horne (Harmondsworth: Penguin, 2002), p. 402.
11 Michael Hollington, 'Dickens's gothic gargoyles', *Dickens Quarterly* 16:3 (September 1999): 160–77 (p. 162).
12 Allan Pritchard, 'The urban gothic of *Bleak House*', *Nineteenth-Century Literature* 45:4 (March 1991): 432–52. See, too, Robert Mighall, *A Geography of Victorian Gothic Fiction: Mapping History's Nightmares* (Oxford: Oxford University Press, 2003), pp. 39–45 and 69–77.

architecture, as well as to the possibilities of picturesque illustration and juxtaposition that it offered.[13] This is particularly clear in his two most profusely illustrated novels, *The Old Curiosity Shop* (1840–1) and *Barnaby Rudge* (1841). Quilp, the demonic villain of *The Old Curiosity Shop*, is just such a grotesque, and *Barnaby Rudge* repeatedly disrupts historical and causal understanding of the past with the energies of the Gothic, in the shape of strange hauntings and repetitions, talking animals and the living dead.[14]

Although Gothic colours were thus always part of the palette of Dickens's fiction, they were rarely allowed to dominate it. One important reason for this was that prisons were for him not just a significant cluster of literary conventions and possibilities but a lived reality. They could be the stuff of fantasies and projections as well, of course, but they were first known and feared locations in the London of his childhood. He knew them as a 12-year old boy after his father, John Dickens, was imprisoned for debt and taken to the Marshalsea prison, together with his wife Elizabeth and their younger children. Dickens himself was sent out to work in a rat-infested warehouse on the banks of the Thames, visiting his captive family every Sunday for the six months of their incarceration, an experience that he could never directly speak about, or forget.[15]

Such violently asymmetrical power relations were ubiquitous in the exploitative, slave profiting, patriarchal, fiscal–military state that Dickens was born into, as they were in the nascent industrial economy that so transformed Victorian Britain. State violence and radical economic inequality are figured in the ubiquity and importance of children, prisoners, working people and the dispossessed in his work; Gothic is often a way to bring the reality of their lives uncannily or shockingly home to his readers. Gothic is rarely exotic or foreign in Dickens, but rather deployed to dramatise the often-archaic social fabric and institutions of early and mid-Victorian England, and the exploitation and suffering that ensued. As reporter, journalist and traveller in his adult life, Dickens saw many prisons – Newgate, the Fleet, the King's Bench, and the New Jail or House of Correction at Clerkenwell – which he named in his fiction, and knew from the inside, both literally and psychologically. There is a strong continuity, not a binary opposition, between the 'realism' of Dickens's work and its Gothicism. They

---

13 Rodney Stenning Edgecombe, 'Anti-clerical gothic: the tale of the sisters in *Nicholas Nickleby*', *Modern Language Review* 94:1 (January 1999): 1–10 (p. 4).

14 See John Bowen, *Other Dickens: Pickwick to Chuzzlewit* (Oxford: Oxford University Press, 2000), pp. 171–74.

15 John Forster, *The Life of Charles Dickens* (London: Chapman & Hall, 1908), pp. 16–18.

form a spectrum both of fictional motifs and modes, and of psychic states and possibilities, a spectrum that can also be a labyrinth, a disturbance, a hope, or a joke.

Radical, Virtual Gothic

Critics have often returned to the same familiar places in Dickens's fiction when they come to talk about his Gothic affiliations, above all to the ghosts of *A Christmas Carol* (1843) and the urban decay and interminable legal procedures of the Court of Chancery in *Bleak House* (1852–3). *Little Dorrit* (1855–7), its successor among Dickens's great mid-period multi-plot social novels, lures readers with Gothic possibilities in its depiction, not of the Marshalsea prison where much of the first volume is set, but in the mercantile bourgeois Clennam household. Mrs Clennam has not moved from her room 'in a dozen years', and her enigmatically powerful servant Jeremiah Flintwinch 'had a weird appearance of having hanged himself at one time or other, and of having gone about ever since halter and all, exactly as some timely hand had cut him down'.[16] Flintwinch's wife Affery has been forced into marriage by 'them two clever ones', and is perpetually terrified of Flintwinch's abusive violence.[17] The guilty secrets and recurrence of 'strange noise . . . and curious movement' in the house suggest both morbid decay and either ghostly or imprisoned presences hidden within.[18] Flintwinch also seems to have an uncanny twin or double, and Affery secretly watches 'Mr Flintwinch awake . . . watching Mr Flintwinch asleep'.[19] The backstory that is eventually revealed is a terrible one: that Arthur was effectively seized as a baby from his real mother by Mrs Clennam. Brought up by her, he had a miserable childhood, full of 'all the old dark horrors' of punitive evangelical Christianity.[20] Arthur's unnamed real mother suffered even more, in the care of Flintwinch's twin brother who 'speculated unsuccessfully in lunatics' but had 'got into difficulty about over-roasting a patient to bring him to reason'.[21] It is not the story that Arthur thought he would discover – of some wrong or fraud committed against the imprisoned family of Amy Dorrit, whom he comes to love – but instead a stranger and more disturbing family story, and with very different scenes of imprisonment from those of the

---

16 Charles Dickens, *Little Dorrit*, edited by Peter Harvey Sucksmith (Oxford: Oxford University Press, 1982), p. 50.
17 Dickens, *Little Dorrit*, p. 51.   18 Dickens, *Little Dorrit*, p. 190.
19 Dickens, *Little Dorrit*, p. 54.   20 Dickens, *Little Dorrit*, p. 49.
21 Dickens, *Little Dorrit*, p. 765.

Marshalsea. Almost entirely offstage from the main plot is its haunting origin and shadow in Arthur's mother's story, that of an illegitimate birth and the ensuing violence against the unnamed, unmarried mother, who was 'always writing, incessantly writing' to Arthur, her lost son, 'mostly letters of confession . . . and Prayers for forgiveness'.[22]

A Christmas Carol is, as its title page tells us, 'A Ghost Story for Christmas', but it is also an 'allegory or a parable . . . or a conversion narrative, or a dream vision, or a melodrama, or a ghost story, or of a Gothic tale, or the text for a dramatic reading or monologue', and indeed a 'Carol', whatever that might mean.[23] The suffering of Scrooge's late partner Jacob Marley, however, stems from a distinctively new poetics or politics of the ghostly: his seemingly eternal pains stem from having to witness urgent human suffering, which as a disembodied spirit he is unable to help or diminish. Scrooge looks out of the window to see the air 'filled with phantoms, wandering hither and thither in restless haste, and moaning as they went . . . The misery with them all was, clearly, that they sought to interfere, for good, in human matters, and had lost the power for ever.'[24] The Spirits of Christmas Past, Present and Yet to Come in turn stimulate memory, through Scrooge's return to childhood; invoke his compassion by showing the suffering that surrounds him; and, climactically, force him to confront the fact of his own mortality. Dickens is often thought to be a sentimental writer, but there is nothing sentimental in the two 'wretched, abject, frightful, hideous, miserable' children, Ignorance and Want, who are 'Yellow, meagre, ragged, scowling, wolfish'.[25] Scrooge at times finds what he sees unbearable, exclaiming 'No more! . . . No more. I don't wish to see it. Show me no more!', but he is not allowed to flinch away because, the narrator tells us, 'the relentless Ghost pinioned him in both his arms, and forced him to observe what happened next'.[26] The final, silent and hooded phantom, of Christmas Yet to Come, takes Scrooge to see the selling of his effects – bed-curtains, blankets, even the shirt that he was to have been buried in – by a charwoman, laundress and undertaker's man, who are like 'obscene demons, marketing the corpse'.[27] He is not really dead, of course, but an unseen presence, at a virtual or possible ending to his life. Tropes of haunting are here mobilised to create the hope and possibility of radical social

---

22 Dickens, *Little Dorrit*, p. 765.
23 J. Hillis Miller, 'The genres of *A Christmas Carol*', *Dickensian* 89:431 (Winter 1993): 193–206 (p. 199).
24 Charles Dickens, *A Christmas Carol and Other Christmas Writings*, edited by Michael Slater (Harmondsworth: Penguin, 2003), p. 52.
25 Dickens, *A Christmas Carol*, p. 92.   26 Dickens, *A Christmas Carol*, p. 67.
27 Dickens, *A Christmas Carol*, p. 102.

and personal change, in a highly innovative narrative form, both proto-filmic and proto-Brechtian.

Haunting, though, is not something that happens just to Scrooge in this text, for Dickens embeds it deeply in the whole process of reading fiction:

> The curtains of his bed were drawn aside; and Scrooge, starting up into a half-recumbent attitude, found himself face to face with the unearthly visitor who drew them: as close to it as I am now to you, and I am standing in the spirit at your elbow.[28]

Reading itself is thus like the experience of a benevolent haunting, as the preface to the story suggests:

> I have endeavoured in this Ghostly little book, to raise the Ghost of an Idea, which shall not put my readers out of humour with themselves, with each other, with the season, or with me. May it haunt their house pleasantly, and no one wish to lay it.[29]

The book is a ghost, its narrator is like a ghost, and the story itself is full of ghosts. Indeed, when Scrooge is taken by the first spirit to see his younger self, he is

> intent upon his reading. Suddenly a man, in foreign garments: wonderfully real and distinct to look at: stood outside the window, with an axe stuck in his belt, and leading an ass laden with wood by the bridle. 'Why, it's Ali Baba!' Scrooge exclaimed in ecstasy.[30]

The fictional Scrooge sees something like a ghost or spectre of his past self who, in turn, is haunted by a benevolent spectre from his reading, that of Ali Baba from 'Ali Baba and the Forty Thieves'.[31] In and through these multiple embedded hauntings, of a ghost or spirit (Scrooge) accompanied by a ghost or spirit (Christmas Past) beside a ghost or spirit (his younger self) visited by a ghost or spirit (Ali Baba) within a ghost or spirit (the text itself), Scrooge for the first time shows compassion for another, and begins to change.

Gothic, then, is a pervasive and inventively used presence in Dickens's work, rarely a mere convention. In *Great Expectations*, for example, Magwitch reappears to Pip, who is appalled to learn that the transported convict has bankrolled his gentility for many years. In recounting his shocked recoil, Pip reaches for an analogy from Mary Shelley's *Frankenstein* (1818):

---

28 Dickens, *A Christmas Carol*, p. 54.   29 Dickens, *A Christmas Carol*, p. 29.
30 Dickens, *A Christmas Carol*, p. 58.
31 See Michael Slater, 'Dickens in Wonderland', in Peter L. Caracciolo (ed.), *The Arabian Nights in English Literature* (Basingstoke: Palgrave Macmillan, 1988), pp. 130–42.

'The imaginary student pursued by the misshapen creature he had impiously made, was not more wretched than I, pursued by the creature who had made me, and recoiling from him with a stronger repulsion, the more he admired me and the fonder he was of me.'[32] The second half of this remarkable sentence undoes the first half; first, Pip thinks of himself as like Frankenstein, a character who creates, then abandons, a monster and is then hunted down by him. But the second half of the sentence glimpses a more terrifying prospect – that Pip 'is pursued by the creature who had made me'. Magwitch is still merely a creature, like the monster, but Pip now becomes the monster's creation: a monster's monster, in short.

More properly Gothic tropes and motifs, particularly those of the diabolical and uncanny, irrigate Dickens's work throughout his career. In *Oliver Twist* (1837–9), the two villains of the book, Fagin and Oliver's half-brother Monks, suddenly and mysteriously appear at the sleeping boy's window. At the very moment that he seems to be most secure from their power, resting in the cottage of his recently discovered relatives the Maylies, he seems to be teleported back into their clutches:

> Oliver knew perfectly well that he was in his own little room, that his books were lying on the table before him, and that the sweet air was stirring among the creeping plants outside, – and yet he was asleep. Suddenly the scene changed, the air became close and confined, and he thought with a glow of terror that he was in the Jew's house again. There sat the hideous old man in his accustomed corner pointing at him, and whispering to another man with his face averted, who sat beside him.
>
> 'Hush, my dear!' he thought he heard the Jew say; 'it is him, sure enough. Come away.'
>
> 'He!' the other man seemed to answer; 'could I mistake him, think you? If a crowd of devils were to put themselves into his exact shape, and he stood amongst them, there is something that would tell me how to point him out. If you buried him fifty feet deep, and took me across his grave, I fancy I should know, if there wasn't a mark above it, that he lay buried there?'[33]

Gothic force crackles through this passage in Monks's name, in Oliver's hypnagogic state, and in Monks's fantasies of Oliver's cloned devils and self-revealing corpse. Monks, perhaps the most conventionally Gothic of all Dickens's villains, seems to haunt or terrify himself in this passage, and his and Fagin's manifestation at Oliver's window remains unexplained by the

---

32 Dickens, *Great Expectations*, p. 335, and St Clair, *The Reading Nation in the Romantic Period*, pp. 367–73.
33 Dickens, *Oliver Twist*, p. 283.

text. Oliver wakes to the briefest of recognition scenes – 'an instant, a glance, a flash' – but no naturalistic explanation of their intrusion is given; no footsteps are found, nor 'the slightest mark which would indicate that any feet had pressed the ground'.[34] It is a brilliantly uncanny effect, unassimilated by, unassimilable to, the novel's plot.[35]

There is a similarly creative use of Gothic in *Bleak House* (1852–3), which comes at the end of chapter 37, well over half, almost two-thirds, of the way through the book. By this point, readers may well imagine that they have already met all the significant characters of the narrative and are pressing on to the conclusion in the company of familiar names and faces. But there is one more major character introduced to the plot, another lawyer whom Dickens calls, in his chapter plan, 'the evil genius'.[36] His name is Mr Vholes, and he works for Richard Carstone, the young hero of the book, who has now fallen deep into the toils of the Court of Chancery, which will prove fatal to him. Vholes epitomises everything that drives or draws Richard away from his love for his cousin Ada, from the novel's narrator and moral core Esther Summerson, from 'fire and laughter' and life.[37] He has 'a lifeless manner, and a slow fixed way ... of looking', with 'an inward manner of speaking' and a 'buttoned-up half-inaudible voice as if there were an unclean spirit that will neither come in nor speak out'.[38] His body is 'bloodless and gaunt', and he acts 'as if there were not a human passion or emotion in his nature'.[39] His 'dead glove' at one point 'scarcely seemed to have any hand in it', but even that seems reassuring compared to the moment when, in an extraordinary act of figurative self-vivisection, Vholes 'takes off his close black gloves as if he were skinning his hands' and 'lifts off his tight hat as if he were scalping himself'.[40]

There is, evidently, a good deal of Gothic colouring to Vholes, which is made explicit when Esther says that she felt 'as if Richard were wasting away beneath the eyes of this adviser and there were something of the Vampire in him'.[41] Vampiric perhaps, but Vholes is no seductive aristocrat like Lord Ruthven in Polidori's *The Vampyre*, or Sir Francis Varney in James Malcolm Rymer and Thomas Peckett Prest's popular 1847–8 *Varney the Vampire*. He is

---

34 Dickens, *Oliver Twist*, pp. 283, 285.
35 John Sutherland, 'Is Oliver dreaming?', in *Is Heathcliff a Murderer?: Great Puzzles in Nineteenth-Century Literature* (Oxford: Oxford University Press, 1996), pp. 34–45.
36 Charles Dickens, *Bleak House*, edited by George Ford and Sylvère Monod (New York: Norton, 1977), p. 798.
37 Dickens, *Bleak House*, p. 471.   38 Dickens, *Bleak House*, pp. 469, 470, 485.
39 Dickens, *Bleak House*, p. 720.   40 Dickens, *Bleak House*, pp. 543, 484.
41 Dickens, *Bleak House*, p. 720.

not charming, compelling or sexy, but a 'very respectable' middle-aged bourgeois man, with three daughters and a 'father ... in the Vale of Taunton', a man who 'never takes any pleasure' and 'never misses a chance in his practice'.⁴² Dickens is here concerned with the professionalised, interminable legal and social vampirism of the Court of Chancery, of which Vholes is both climax and epitome. Vampirism is as banal as it is pervasive in his life and work and that of the law, which he represents. His desk, he tells Richard 'is your rock, sir!' but when he gives it a rap 'it sounds', the narrator tells us, 'as hollow as a coffin'.⁴³

Queer, Uncanny Gothic

Dickens's uses of Gothic in his work of the 1860s releases powerful possibilities for subsequent authors. With Wilkie Collins, he is one of the creators of 'sensation fiction', which so successfully channelled Gothic into a contemporary world of adultery, illegitimacy and divorce. Dickens's later work has also proved particularly fertile for understanding 'paranoid Gothic', that privileged mode of exploring suppressed homoerotic desire within modern male heterosexual identity.⁴⁴ Although Dickens's fiction shows many happy queer relationships, particularly in his early and middle-period novels, things are markedly darker in *Our Mutual Friend* and the unfinished *The Mystery of Edwin Drood* (1870).⁴⁵ As Eve Kosofsky Sedgwick has influentially argued, these novels show how in 'male homosocial bonds are concentrated the fantasy energies of compulsion, prohibition, and explosive violence; all are fully structured by the logic of paranoia'.⁴⁶ Although there are problems with Sedgwick's evidence for the overarching claim that *Our Mutual Friend* is a novel 'about the whole issue of anal eroticism', she nevertheless brilliantly highlights a key structuring dynamic of these works, epitomised by the violent sexual rivalry between John Jasper and his nephew Edwin Drood and the 'hungry, exacting, watchful, and yet devoted affection' that accompanies it.⁴⁷

---

42 Dickens, *Bleak House*, p. 482.   43 Dickens, *Bleak House*, p. 485.
44 Eve Kosofsky Sedgwick, *Between Men: English Literature and Male Homosocial Desire* (New York: Columbia University Press, 1985), pp. 161–200.
45 See Holly Furneaux, *Queer Dickens: Erotics, Families, Masculinities* (Oxford: Oxford University Press, 2009).
46 Sedgwick, *Between Men*, p. 162.
47 Sedgwick, *Between Men*, p. 164; Charles Dickens, *The Mystery of Edwin Drood*, edited by Margaret Cardwell (Oxford: Oxford University Press, 1982), p. 6.

One of Dickens's greatest short stories from this period, 'No. 1 Branch Line: The Signal-Man' (1866), also mobilises the uncanny to powerful effect to shape a tale of two men bound together in equivocal, anxious and ultimately fatal ways. It is a ghost story, with the Gothic's characteristic interest in new technology, set in a remote railway cutting, where an isolated signal-man responds to the electric bell, telegraph, flag and lamp that structure his daily work. Some of the signals that he sees are ghostly ones, given by spectres who portend deaths on the line, but this is far from a straightforward tale of haunting. For it is difficult not to read its landscape in bodily, indeed anal, terms, set as it is in a 'steep cutting' or 'deep trench' with an 'earthy, deadly smell', a place which, the narrator tells us, 'became oozier and wetter as I came down'.[48] Looking down on it, he 'feels a vague vibration' which quickly changes into 'a violent pulsation . . . as though it had force to draw me down'.[49] He enters the cutting, in one direction of which is 'a crooked prolongation of this great dungeon'; in the other 'a gloomy red light, and the gloomier entrance to a black tunnel', from which death will emerge three times.[50] Matching the three deaths, there are three fantasised beds in the story, each located in the moist, deep cutting and its dark tunnel: that of the signal-man, who, recounting his misspent youth, concludes that he has 'made my bed and must lie on it'; that of the narrator who thinks he 'should have slept poorly if my bed had been' in the cutting; and that of the corpse of the signal-man at the end of the story, which is placed inside a 'little hut' that is 'no bigger than a bed'.[51] Death and desire here meet in a rectum that is also a grave.[52]

The narrator is a deeply enigmatic figure, whose self-characterisation on meeting the signal-man for the first time is positively Jamesian in its ambiguities: 'In me, he merely saw a man who had been shut up within narrow limits all his life, and who, being at last set free, had a newly-awakened interest in these great works.'[53] '[H]e merely saw': that was all he saw, but was that all there was to see? Do the 'narrow limits' in which the narrator has lived mean that he is now simply retired and looking for a change; or that he has escaped from incarceration of some sort; or that he is dead and now out of the tomb? Or did the signal-man, or indeed the narrator, misread the other

---

48 Charles Dickens, 'No. 1 Branch Line. The Signal-Man', in *Christmas Stories*, edited by Ruth Glancy (London: Everyman, 1996), pp. 656–69 (pp. 656, 658).
49 'The Signal-Man', p. 656.   50 'The Signal-Man', p. 658.
51 'The Signal-Man', pp. 660, 667, 668.
52 Leo Bersani, 'Is the rectum a grave?', *October* 43 (Winter 1987): 197–222.
53 'The Signal-Man', p. 658.

man's signals completely? The motives and relationship of the two anonymous men are profoundly uncertain: what kind of literal or figurative finger, for example, might it be when the narrator tells us that on his first nocturnal visit he was 'Resisting the slow touch of a frozen finger tracing out my spine'?[54] Doubling or trebling our doubts, the narrator adds that on looking at the signal-man: 'the monstrous thought came into my mind, as I perused the fixed eyes and the saturnine face, that this was a spirit, not a man. I have speculated since, whether there may have been infection in his mind.'[55] The most banal of encounters – a man shouting down to another in a railway cutting – releases 'monstrous' thoughts of spirits, mental infection and slow touchings of the spine. The signal-man seems to look at the narrator, the latter says, 'as if you had a dread of me'. He replies: 'I was doubtful ... whether I had seen you before.'[56] Such uncanniness is structural to the narration and to the men's relationship, and it is intensified, not resolved, as the story progresses.

Doubt, like anxiety, infects the reader as much as the protagonists. We too don't know how to read the signals of the story. Like the signal-man, we also can feel 'oppressed beyond endurance by an unintelligible responsibility involving life'.[57] A workaday modern world that requires 'exactness and watchfulness' in its workers produces at every turn cognitive uncertainty, existential 'anxiety' and erotic possibility, each figured through the Gothic.[58] The 'red light near the mouth of the tunnel' of 'these lower shadows' hints at the diabolic, but more important are the repetitions and variations of the ways in which a single phrase, 'Halloa! Below there!', returns to both structure and derange the lives and narration of the story.[59] These words, by which the narrator first hails the signal-man, seem innocent enough until he asks the narrator if he felt 'they were conveyed to you in any supernatural way?'[60] They are, the signal-man tells him, the identical words shouted out by the spectral figure who appeared to him before. Who or what is the ghost here?

The paranoid possibilities of the story, its vibrations and pulsations of narrative uncertainty, draw the reader down to a performative climax in its final words, when the narrator tells us that, shortly before the signal-man's death:

---

54 'The Signal-Man', p. 663. 55 'The Signal-Man', p. 659. 56 'The Signal-Man', p. 659.
57 'The Signal-Man', p. 666. 58 'The Signal-Man', p. 660.
59 'The Signal-Man', pp. 656, 661, 662, 665, 669. 60 The Signal-Man', p. 661.

the warning of the Engine-Driver included, not only the words which the unfortunate Signal-man had repeated to me as haunting him, but also the words which I myself – not he – had attached, and that only in my own mind, to the gesticulation he had imitated.[61]

It ends, and so we end, with no guidance whatsoever about the insight or affect – pleasure? guilt? – attached to those words that existed only in the narrator's mind. Are they a matter of mere chance, or of foreknowledge? And if foreknowledge, conscious or not? We cannot know at this point if he is a haunting or haunted being, malevolent, telepathic, or simply mystified. It is a remarkable supplement to the two late novels – *Our Mutual Friend* and *The Mystery of Edwin Drood* – that it bisects, innovatively reworking within two brief encounters the characteristic material of paranoid Gothic of two men uncannily bound together in a mysterious, highly anxious relationship that ends with the death of one of them, into whose thought-processes the other seems to have supernatural insight or foreknowledge. The melancholy whole of 'The Signal-Man' hangs from its hyphen, between the signals – flag, bell, shout, wave, look, touch – and the man or men, if they are men, who use, or are used by them, and who fail to understand what they might mean, until it is too late, if then.

Meta-, Diabolic Gothic

What were the sources of Gothic in Dickens's imagination? The 'Tales of Terror' in *Blackwood's Magazine* (1817–32) were important to him and influenced directly the 'interpolated tales' of *The Pickwick Papers* (1836–7).[62] Although he was sceptical about the truth of ghost stories, he loved to tell them, and they are appear regularly in the magazines that he edited, *Household Words* and *All the Year Round*.[63] Although the 1859 *All the Year Round* special Christmas number is called 'The Haunted House', for example, none of the tales told is shown to be a true haunting; each ghost, rather, is a figure for memory.[64]

---

61 'The Signal-Man', p. 669.
62 Harvey Peter Sucksmith, 'The secret of immediacy: Dickens' debt to the tale of terror in *Blackwood's*', *Nineteenth-Century Fiction* 26:2 (September 1971): 145–57.
63 Forster, *Life*, p. 656. See John Bowen, 'Uncanny Gifts, Strange Contagion: Allegory in Dickens's *The Haunted Man*', in Deirdre David and Eileen Gillooly (eds), *Contemporary Dickens* (Columbus: Ohio State University Press, 2009), pp. 75–92 (p. 85).
64 Charles Dickens, 'The Haunted House', in *Christmas Stories*, edited by Ruth Glancy (London: Everyman, 1996), pp. 307–39.

But Dickens seems to have been drawn to Gothic, or rather had it imposed upon him, at a much earlier age and in less literary a way. There are two important sources for this possibility. Although neither can be taken as straightforward autobiographical transcription, both accounts seem to draw on his early childhood memories. In the co-authored 1855 Christmas number of *Household Words*, his first contribution is a memory piece by an anonymous 'Guest' that recalls how as a small child he was told stories 'at the knee of a sallow woman with a fishy eye, an aquiline nose, and a green gown', who 'had a Ghoulish pleasure, I have long been persuaded, in terrifying me to the utmost confines of my reason'.[65] This she achieves through free adaptations of the stories of Sweeney Todd and Bluebeard, but her speciality was to tell the boy an 'authentic anecdote within her own experience, founded, I now believe, upon Raymond and Agnes, or the Bleeding Nun'.[66] The most famous episode from Mathew Lewis's foundational horror Gothic *The Monk* (1796) had a lengthy afterlife in chapbooks, short Gothic theatrical entertainments and Gothic bluebooks.[67] Dickens here completes a circuit of fictional recycling: over half a century or so, the bleeding nun moves from novel to drama to chapbook to oral narration, and back, in Dickens's hands, to the written literary text that we are reading. But we are not allowed to forget the power and ensuing terror of this scene of working-class female narration and popular literary appropriation: the effect of the stories is to make the child's 'faculties . . . so frozen with terror . . . that the power of listening stagnated within me for some quarter of an hour'.[68]

In 'The Holly-Tree Inn', terror is played for laughs, mostly, but when Dickens revisits this material in 'Nurse's Stories' (1860), later collected in *The Uncommercial Traveller* (1860), it is with very different effect. 'Nurse's Stories' is a story about story-telling, and one acutely aware of the power of narrative repetition and its capacity to take on at times a 'daemonic' or diabolic force, a compulsive, inexorable negating pressure.[69] Like Freud's 'Beyond the Pleasure Principle' (1920), 'Nurse's Stories' is a text both about the devil and repetition, and diabolical and repetitive in the way it is told. A story about

---

65 Charles Dickens, 'The Holly Tree Inn', in *Christmas Stories*, pp. 83–121 (pp. 92–3).
66 Dickens, 'The Holly Tree Inn', p. 93.
67 See, for example, the anonymous chapbook *The Bleeding Nun, of the Castle of Lindenberg; or, The History of Raymond & Agnes. By the author of the Castle Spectre* (London: Hodgson & Co., [1823]).
68 Dickens, 'The Holly Tree Inn', p. 94.
69 Sigmund Freud, 'Beyond the Pleasure Principle', in *Pelican Freud Library Volume XI: On Metapsychology*, edited by Angela Richards (Harmondsworth: Penguin, 1984), pp. 271–338 (p. 307).

how stories are told to children and the power they have to return without choice in pleasurable or unpleasurable ways, the paper consists of a set of memories of scenes of narration between a woman – the *Uncommercial's* Nurse, Mercy – and the child in her care. It narrates various stories of the 'utterly impossible places and people, but nonetheless alarmingly real – that I found I had been introduced to by my nurse before I was six years old, and used to be forced to go back to at night without at all wanting to go'.[70] Explicitly a story about narrative origins, it is an account of the earliest scenes of narration in any autobiographical piece of writing by Dickens. Its central concerns are the unconscious and repetitious compulsions at work and at play in storytelling, what Dickens calls 'the dark corners we are forced to go back to, against our wills'.[71]

'Nurse's Stories' is a kind of meta-Gothic text that stems from the period when Dickens was meditating the novel that would become *Great Expectations*, his deepest exploration of the self-deluding nature of autobiographical recollection and most subtly Gothicizing creation. Like *Great Expectations*, 'Nurse's Stories' is delicately pitched between tragedy and comedy, is concerned with the potentially traumatic nature of early childhood experience and draws on significant material from Dickens's own childhood years. In both texts, the devil and the diabolic arrive early and stay late. In *Great Expectations*, Magwitch's first words to Pip, the very first piece of quoted speech in the novel, are 'Hold your noise! . . . Keep still, you little devil.'[72] A little later, when he limps away from Pip, 'he looked . . . as if he were eluding the hands of the dead people, stretching up cautiously out of their graves, to get a twist upon his ankle and pull him in'.[73] At the end of the same extraordinary opening chapter of the book, the still unnamed Magwitch seems to the young Pip to head towards 'a gibbet, with some chains hanging to it which had once held a pirate . . . as if he were the pirate come to life, and come down, and going back to hook himself up again'.[74] This is part of the wider *Hamlet*-infected revenge-plotting of the book, in which, as Catherine Gallagher puts it, the orphaned Pip 'replaces the father's ghost with a whole demoniacal society, any member of which might suddenly rouse himself to deliver the hapless child over for judgement'.[75]

---

70 Charles Dickens, 'Nurse's Stories', in *The Uncommercial Traveller and Other Papers 1859–70*, edited by Michael Slater and John Drew (London: Dent, 2000), pp. 169–80 (p. 173).
71 Dickens, 'Nurse's Stories', p. 173.   72 Dickens, *Great Expectations*, p. 4.
73 Dickens, *Great Expectations*, p. 7.   74 Dickens, *Great Expectations*, p. 7.
75 Catherine Gallagher and Stephen Greenblatt, *Practicing New Historicism* (Chicago: Chicago University Press, 2000), p. 177.

In 'Nurse's Stories' the devil and the demonic are even more fully at work. The first story, for example, that the merciless Mercy tells the child in her care is about a certain Captain Murderer, 'the first diabolical character who intruded himself on my peaceful youth'.[76] It is a version of the Bluebeard story in which Captain Murderer marries, kills and then eats a succession of virgin brides; he is finally defeated by the twin-sister of his last bride who takes poisons so that when she is killed and eaten:

> Captain Murderer ... began to swell, and to turn blue, and to be all over spots, and to scream. And he went on swelling and turning bluer, and being more all over spots and screaming, until he reached from floor to ceiling and from wall to wall; and then, at one o'clock in the morning, he blew up with a loud explosion.[77]

Mercy's – and the *Uncommercial*'s – centrepiece, however, is the story of Chips and the devil. Chips is a carpenter at Chatham dockyard, where, although the story doesn't tell us, Dickens's own father worked. Chips's father, grandfather and great-grandfather – all also called Chips – have in turn sold their souls to the devil in exchange for 'an iron pot and a bushel of tenpenny nails and half a ton of copper and a rat that could speak'.[78] In this family you inherit labour, name and damnation. Chips at first unsurprisingly tries to resist the devil's offer, but eventually succumbs, overwhelmed by desire, for 'nails and copper are a shipwright's sweethearts'.[79] His intended marriage is broken off and, after various episodes in which he seeks desperately to escape his fate and is pursued remorselessly by rats, he is finally left dead on a beach with an 'immense overgrown' talking rat sitting on his chest, reciting his demonic jingle for the fourth time in the story:

> A Lemon has pips,
> And a Yard has ships,
> And *I*'ll have Chips![80]

It is a compulsively repetitious story about compulsive repetition, which leads only to death and yet more repetition. The stories themselves are repetitious and diabolical; their afterlife in the mind equally so. After the first story that Mercy tells him, the little Uncommercial adds:

---

76 Dickens, 'Nurse's Stories', p. 173.
77 Dickens, 'Nurse's Stories', p. 175. On Dickens and Bluebeard, see Shuli Barzilai, *Tales of Bluebeard and His Wives from late Antiquity to Postmodern Times* (London: Routledge, 2009), pp. 22–43.
78 Dickens, 'Nurse's Stories', p. 176.   79 Dickens, 'Nurse's Stories', p. 177.
80 Dickens, 'Nurse's Stories', p. 177.

> Hundreds of times did I hear this legend of Captain Murderer, in my early youth, and added hundreds of times was there a mental compulsion upon me in bed, to peep in at his window as the dark twin peeped, and to revisit his horrible house.[81]

Mercy, like the talking rat, repeats herself continually; the child who hears them feels driven to repeat what he has heard; all of these repetitions are repeated both by the narrator and the reader or hearer of the paper. Mercy takes him to, he takes himself back to, we take ourselves back to diabolical stories of cannibalism, seduction, damnation, death, mass murder, twins and a talking rat. Here, Gothic terror, Gothic laughter, narrative force and diabolic repetition are inextricably and compulsively entwined, synonyms almost.

Much of the power of Dickens's texts stems from repetition – lexical, syntactical, grammatical, familial, paternal, narrative – a repetition charged with a kind of diabolical energy that the texts seek simultaneously to accelerate, exorcise and master: Gothic on speed. 'Nurse's Stories' makes these concerns thematic and more than thematic. The child is repeatedly told stories whose distinctiveness is that they are both about demonic power and demonic in their power. They cannot be ignored, prevented or evaded: 'I sometimes used to plead I thought I was hardly strong enough and old enough to hear the story again just yet. But she never spared me one word of it.'[82] They can only repeat and be repeated. That diabolical energy – imposed, shaped and deeply identified with – irrigates much of Dickens's work. Indeed, almost nothing he ever wrote seems wholly free of the demonic or diabolical in some form or other. Quilp in *The Old Curiosity Shop*, for example, is 'like some familiar demon, invisible to all eyes', 'grinning like a devil'.[83] In *Oliver Twist*, Oliver himself is called a 'young devil' and is haunted and pursued by Fagin, who looks with 'devilish anticipation' and who is repeatedly described as demoniacal and diabolical ('worse than devil', according to Nancy, who is herself described as a 'she-devil').[84] Doubling the diabolical energies once more, Fagin says that he too is 'bound . . . to a born devil' in the shape of that 'writhing and foaming' diabolical villain, Monks.[85] Oliver is the devil, Nancy is the devil, Fagin is the devil, and Monks is the devil, the word itself appearing more than thirty times in the course of the book. In *The Mystery of Edwin Drood*, like *Oliver Twist*, one of Dickens's most diabolic texts, the

---

81 Dickens, 'Nurse's Stories', p. 175.   82 Dickens, 'Nurse's Stories', p. 175.
83 Charles Dickens, *The Old Curiosity Shop*, edited by Norman Page (Harmondsworth: Penguin, 2000), pp. 367, 32.
84 Dickens, *Oliver Twist*, pp. 78, 393, 385, 396.   85 Dickens, *Oliver Twist*, pp. 210, 270.

villain John Jasper, is compared to a devil, finds the music he plays in the Cathedral 'quite devilish' and thinks of 'carving demons ... out of my heart'.[86]

Both 'Nurse's Stories' and the Guest's story in 'The Holly-Tree Inn' are tales about oral narration, about the power of servants, and about paternal inheritance, told by women. They are stories of work – of nursing children, of being a ship's carpenter – as well as, and as much, about 'ghoulish pleasures', sexual violence and living up to dad. In both, Dickens dramatically stages the incitement of the child's fears, while simultaneously registering his later, and our current, ironic or comic distance from them. What is so remarkable about 'Nurse's Stories' is the sophistication of its recognition of the continuing power of Gothic for both narrator and reader: the child's fears are also the narrator's own. Adulthood in Dickens, as in Freud, is never free of its childhood experiences, and this truth is often compellingly realised through imaginings, borrowings and reworkings of the Gothic mode. Children, women and the poor, in particular, can sometimes find in Gothic a way to speak directly or indirectly of their deep fears, desires or hopes. But Dickens's characters, like his readers, can also be trapped or compelled in ways that they do not want by Gothic's narrative and figurative power. His kind of Gothic is never simply Gothic; instead, it both mobilises and reflects on the needs and compulsions of its tellers, readers and listeners. Its power of compulsive, at times demonic, repetition illuminates as it deranges the lives and stories through which it moves.

86 Dickens, *The Mystery of Edwin Drood*, p. 10.

2.12
Victorian Domestic Gothic Fiction

TAMAR HELLER

In 1865, Henry James hailed Wilkie Collins as the progenitor of a new type of Gothic:

> To Mr. Collins belongs the credit of having introduced into fiction those most mysterious of mysteries, the mysteries which are at our own doors. This innovation gave a new impetus to the literature of horrors. It was fatal to the authority of Mrs. Radcliffe and her everlasting castle in the Apennines. What are the Apennines to us, or we to the Apennines? Instead of the terrors of *Udolpho,* we were treated to the terrors of the cheerful country house and the busy London lodgings. And there is no doubt that these were infinitely the more terrible. Mrs. Radcliffe's mysteries were romances pure and simple; while those of Mr. Wilkie Collins were stern reality.[1]

Significantly for the purposes of this chapter, the borderline between private and public spheres in James's description of the new Gothic is ambiguous. The phrase 'at our own doors' identifies Collins's innovation as his revelation of the mysteries *inside* houses. At the same time, the word 'at' in 'at our own doors' could refer to an invader from *outside*, a metaphoric barbarian at the gate who threatens what is within – an appropriate association, given that the term 'Gothic' derives from the Goths whose incursion into Rome famously toppled that empire. By portraying the home – in domestic ideology a refuge from the outside world – as in fact the site of violence, duplicity, familial dysfunction, infidelity and repression, Victorian domestic Gothic reflects the era's anxieties and debates about the relation of domesticity to the tumultuous public sphere. Indeed, during the Victorian period the private space of the home increasingly became the locus of heated public controversy, especially on topics relating to the nature and role of women, the group

---

1 Henry James, 'Miss Braddon', in Norman Page (ed.), *Wilkie Collins: The Critical Heritage* (London: Routledge, 1974), pp. 122–4 (pp. 122–3).

defined by domestic ideology as upholders of the sanctity of the private sphere.

This chapter examines the dialogue of mid-Victorian domestic Gothic fiction with the nineteenth-century debates about gender known as the Victorian Woman Question. I define 'Victorian domestic Gothic fiction' in much the same way as James does Collins's work, as fiction with a contemporary setting (or one in the fairly recent past) that portrays the home using such classic Gothic themes as family secrets, familial violence and domestic claustrophobia. I am particularly interested in exploring representations of failed marriage: marriage was a major issue in the Woman Question, and the focus of important legislation such as the Infant Custody Act of 1839 and the Matrimonial Causes Act of 1857, the latter either cheered or excoriated, depending on commentators' ideological allegiances, for challenging the legal principle of coverture, which defined married women as having no separate legal, social or economic identity apart from their husbands'. My exploration of such topical concerns in domestic Gothic as marriage, adultery and women's economic disenfranchisement spans the late 1840s through the 1860s, and traces the transformation of Brontëan Gothic into sensation fiction, the genre to whose inaugural text, Wilkie Collins's *The Woman in White* (1860), James refers, and which I represent here by two novels with prominent depictions of failed marriages, Mary Elizabeth Braddon's *Lady Audley's Secret* (1862) and Ellen Wood's *East Lynne* (1861).

My discussion of Victorian domestic Gothic, however, draws on a different model of origins and influence than that provided by James. Perhaps reflecting his tendency to devalue women 's writing,[2] James dismisses Radcliffean Gothic, with its foreign and historically distant settings, as irrelevant to modern-day experience ('What are the Appenines to us, or we to the Appenines?'). As feminist critics have noted, though, there is a strong continuity between Radcliffean and Victorian Gothic depictions of the 'feminine carceral', as D. A. Miller calls representations of domesticity in female Gothic.[3] The degree to which Radcliffean Gothic reads as a fictional version of the feminist critique of Radcliffe's contemporary Mary Wollstonecraft – herself an erstwhile writer of politically charged Gothic fiction – makes it a clear precursor to the Gothic representations of women's disadvantaged legal, economic and sexual status in the era of the Woman Question.

2 For more on James and women writers, see Alfred Habegger, *Henry James and the 'Woman Business'* (Cambridge: Cambridge University Press, 1989).
3 D. A. Miller, '*Cage aux folles*: sensation and gender in Wilkie Collins's *The Woman in White*', *Representations* 14 (1986): 107–36 (p. 120).

At the same time, the feminist elements of Victorian domestic Gothic are complicated by the genre's ambivalent, and often negative, depiction of female sexuality. Female sexuality was the locus of considerable panic in Victorian culture. Opponents of expanding women's power and public role averred that such changes would render women unchaste and lead to social disintegration. The frequent depiction of bigamous and adulterous women in sensation fiction made the genre a common target for critics who accused it of corrupting female readers. In one such diatribe against sensationalism in 1867, Margaret Oliphant declared that the genre's 'unseemly references and exhibitions of forbidden knowledge' threatened the female chastity that was 'of such vital consequence to a nation'.[4] Yet sensation novels themselves often harshly reprove female transgression. To some extent, such moralistic portrayals reflect authors' attempts to placate a social and publishing environment hostile to representations of sexuality. Nonetheless, sensation fiction, like Victorian domestic Gothic more generally, is often animated by anxieties about the danger of female sexuality and, particularly, the socially disastrous potential of the deviant married woman to collapse boundaries between home and public sphere.

Rooftop Feminists and Restive Wives: Brontëan Domestic Gothic

Dismissing one female precursor – Ann Radcliffe – as passé, Henry James ignores others when he credits Wilkie Collins with launching an updated version of Gothic. While Collins's contribution to the development of Victorian Gothic is undeniable,[5] the Brontë sisters preceded him in the late 1840s in pioneering what Carol Margaret Davison calls the 'generic fusion' of Gothic convention with nineteenth-century 'social realism'.[6] Of the three texts I discuss in this section – Charlotte Brontë's *Jane Eyre* (1847), Emily Brontë's *Wuthering Heights* (1847) and Anne Brontë's *The Tenant of Wildfell Hall* (1848) – I focus on *Jane Eyre* as pivotal to the history of domestic Gothic. Not only is *Jane Eyre* an enduringly influential precursor to female Gothic in

---

4 Margaret Oliphant, 'Novels', *Blackwood's Edinburgh Magazine* 102 (September 1867): 257–80 (pp. 258, 275).
5 For more on Collins's important revision of female Gothic and its representation of women's oppression, see Tamar Heller, *Dead Secrets: Wilkie Collins and the Female Gothic* (New Haven: Yale University Press, 1992).
6 Carol Margaret Davison, 'The Victorian Gothic and Gender', in Andrew Smith and William Hughes (eds), *The Victorian Gothic: An Edinburgh Companion* (Edinburgh: Edinburgh University Press, 2012), pp. 124–41 (p. 127).

the nineteenth century and after, but its nascent feminism anticipates the subversive features of sensationalism. In the attack on sensation fiction to which I referred earlier, Margaret Oliphant dates the erosion of feminine modesty in that genre to 'the time when Jane Eyre made what advanced [feminist] critics call her "protest" against the conventionalities in which the world clothes itself'.[7]

One scene in *Jane Eyre* – possibly the one that Oliphant had in mind when she alluded to the heroine's 'protest' against convention – explicitly refers to contemporary debates about the status of women. Pacing the ramparts of Thornfield Hall while longing for a 'power of vision' that surpasses the 'limit' of feminine experience, Jane anticipates not only the rebellious women of sensation fiction, but the discontented protagonists of novels by George Eliot and New Woman writers:

> Women are supposed to be very calm generally; but women feel just as men feel; they need exercise for their faculties, and a field for their efforts as much as their brothers do ... and it is narrow-minded ... to condemn them ... if they seek to do more or learn more than custom has pronounced necessary for their sex.[8]

Responding to this passage in *A Room of One's Own* (1929), Virginia Woolf objects to the juxtaposition of Gothic machinery with feminist sentiment, finding it 'upsetting'[9] that Jane's musings are interrupted by the 'low, slow "ha ha"' she thinks is Grace Poole's laugh, but which we later learn is that of Bertha, Rochester's insane wife.[10] Feminist critics, however, most notably Sandra Gilbert and Susan Gubar, have not been surprised by the intersection of Jane's story with that of an incarcerated wife – an intersection, in narrative terms, of the feminist *bildungsroman* with the classic female Gothic plot of the woman confined, by husband or other male authority figure, in a home, convent, or, like the protagonist of Mary Wollstonecraft's *The Wrongs of Woman, or Maria* (1798), a madhouse. In the scene above, Brontë connects the two genres through a kind of Gothic spatiality. Roaming the manor house's rooftop, a liminal space between public and private realms, Jane yearns for experience outside domesticity directly over the site of the secret confinement of

---

7 Oliphant, 'Novels', p. 258.
8 Charlotte Brontë, *Jane Eyre*, edited by Beth Newman (Boston: Bedford/St. Martin's, 1996), pp. 116–17.
9 Virginia Woolf, *A Room of One's Own* (New York: Harcourt Brace Jovanovich, 1929), p. 72.
10 Brontë, *Jane Eyre*, p. 117.

the 'madwoman in the attic', as Gilbert and Gubar call her.[11] Indeed, it is from the ramparts where Jane expresses her discontent that Bertha leaps to her death, having first set fire to Thornfield.

Reading Bertha as the embodiment of the childhood rage that Jane has learned to suppress but which she still feels, Gilbert and Gubar famously label Rochester's first wife Jane's 'truest and darkest double'.[12] Yet we can also read Jane's relationship to Bertha as a variant of the mother–daughter plot in female Gothic. Claire Kahane in fact includes *Jane Eyre* among classic examples of this plot, which she defines as the heroine's discovery, while dealing with an alluring, possibly dangerous male, of a mysterious, 'dead–undead mother' or mother-figure.[13] Several of Ann Radcliffe's novels depict a daughter unearthing evidence of a mother, or mother-figure's, oppression as a wife. In *A Sicilian Romance* (1790), the protagonist learns that her father has long imprisoned her missing mother in the dungeons beneath his castle; in *The Mysteries of Udolpho* (1794), Emily, the heroine, witnesses the grim fate of an aunt starved to death by her husband, Emily's guardian, while he attempts to deprive his ward of her inheritance. As I have argued elsewhere, in both *A Sicilian Romance* and *The Mysteries of Udolpho* the mother-daughter plot is matrophobic, as the mother's fate, which emblematises women's disadvantaged economic, legal, and sexual status, is one the daughter fears to repeat.[14] In *Jane Eyre*'s version of the mother–daughter plot, Bertha, a woman of an earlier generation than the heroine, implicitly warns that marriage can become a prison, while also, significantly, modelling rebellion against confinement.

Bertha appears most explicitly as a monitory figure several nights before the public revelation of her existence derails Jane and Rochester's planned wedding. Invading Jane's bedchamber, Bertha tries on Jane's wedding veil before ripping it in two and trampling it underfoot.[15] A garment that covers and obscures, the wedding veil is an apt symbol for the legal doctrine of coverture, which collapsed a married woman's legal identity into her husband's. Yet this wedding veil points, even more specifically, to gender inequalities that vex Jane and Rochester's relationship during their

---

11 I refer to the title of Sandra M. Gilbert and Susan Gubar's *The Madwoman in the Attic: The Woman Writer and the Nineteenth-Century Literary Imagination* (New Haven: Yale University Press, 1979).
12 Gilbert and Gubar, *Madwoman*, p. 360.
13 Claire Kahane, 'The Gothic Mirror', in Shirley Nelson Garner, Claire Kahane and Madelon Sprengnether (eds), *The (M)Other Tongue: Essays in Feminist Psychoanalytic Interpretation* (Ithaca, NY: Cornell University Press, 1985), pp. 43–64 (pp. 334, 336).
14 Heller, *Dead Secrets*, pp. 17–20.   15 Brontë, *Jane Eyre*, p. 281.

engagement and threaten to do so after their marriage as well. A 'costly' gift from Rochester, the veil recalls the extravagant clothes and jewels that he tries to shower on Jane during a shopping trip that overwhelms her with 'degradation' by emphasising her economic inferiority and making her feel like a 'doll', or sexual object.[16] During this scene, Brontë uses the same metaphor of the 'seraglio', or harem, which Mary Wollstonecraft employs in *A Vindication of the Rights of Woman* (1792) to convey women's erotic and economic subjugation.[17] Not only does Jane think that Rochester treats her with the condescension with which a 'sultan' might 'bestow upon a slave his gold and gems had enriched', but Rochester himself exclaims that he prefers 'this one little English girl' to 'the grand Turk's whole seraglio', an 'eastern allusion' that prompts Jane to snap that she would like to 'go out as a missionary to preach liberty to them that are enslaved—your harem inmates amongst the rest' and 'stir up mutiny'.[18] Yet it is Bertha, rather than Jane, who overtly rebels against Rochester's economic and sexual domination by tearing asunder the expensive veil, allowing Jane to substitute a plainer one that she prefers. As Gilbert and Gubar claim, 'What Bertha now *does* [tear the veil] ... is what Jane wants to do.'[19]

That Jane's reservations about Rochester's domination lead to the revelation of Bertha's existence – which in turn derails Jane's marriage – further interlaces the two women's stories. Jane's sense of being prostituted during the shopping trip inspires her to announce her marriage to the uncle in Madeira whose heiress she is, thinking 'if I had but a prospect of one day bringing Mr. Rochester an accession of fortune, I could better endure to be kept by him now'.[20] This letter ensures the exposure of Rochester's attempted bigamy, as Jane's uncle alerts Bertha's brother, who journeys to England in time to halt the marriage. Only after the fire that ends Bertha's life and maims Rochester will Jane wed a chastened, diminished man who does not represent the same threat to her autonomy that he did earlier.

Still, even as Bertha acts out Jane's resentment of male domination, Brontë obscures the parallels between the two women by portraying Bertha as an immoral – and promiscuous – foil to Jane's incarnation of virtue and chastity. In this sense, *Jane Eyre* exemplifies the tension I noted earlier in Victorian

---

16 Brontë, *Jane Eyre*, pp. 278, 267.
17 Mary Wollstonecraft, 'A Vindication of the Rights of Woman', in Mary Wollstonecraft, *A Vindication of the Rights of Woman and The Wrongs of Woman, or Maria*, edited by Anne K. Mellor and Noelle Chao (New York: Pearson Longman, 2007), p. 47.
18 Brontë, *Jane Eyre*, p. 267.   19 Gilbert and Gubar, *Madwoman*, p. 359.
20 Brontë, *Jane Eyre*, p. 267.

domestic Gothic between a feminist critique of marriage on the one hand and a misogynist demonisation of female sexuality on the other. '[I]ntemperate and unchaste', as Rochester describes her in the account to Jane of his marriage, Bertha was apparently an adulteress, and only the onset of insanity prevented her husband from taking 'legal proceedings' – in other words, divorce – to 'rid' himself of association with one whom he considers 'gross, impure, depraved'.[21] Rochester is, of course, biased in his portrait of Bertha. But Brontë herself codes Bertha as excessively appetitive. 'Corpulent', with 'bloated features', Bertha is, in dualistic terms, an inferior body to the petite Jane's superior incarnation of mind and soul.[22] The racial imagery that Brontë uses to describe Bertha's 'savage', 'discoloured' face and 'dark, grizzled hair' links this voraciousness to her tropical origins. Whether one reads Bertha (as critics variously have) as a signifier for the black or native woman, or for the dissolute white colonist, her West Indian background associates her with Victorian anxieties about female sexuality and loss of racial purity.[23] In a misogynist variant on the mother–daughter plot of female Gothic, Bertha's promiscuity is represented as an inheritance from her insane – and presumably licentious – mother; Rochester, indeed, calls Bertha the 'true daughter of an infamous mother'.[24]

Yet, even while emphasising Jane's spirituality and intellect over Bertha's corporeality, Brontë does not wholly desexualise her heroine. Jane's attraction to Rochester is indubitably physical, and during their separation after the abortive wedding, she refers to 'strange' – apparently erotic – dreams of 'being in his arms'.[25] Still, Brontë frames the distinction between Jane and Bertha as the difference between an adulteress – Bertha – and a woman who refuses to commit adultery – Jane. Jane's refusal, once she finds out that Rochester is married, to become his mistress frees her from the sexual objectification that she dreaded, but also reinforces the traditional distinction between the chaste heroine and the unchaste woman who can never achieve heroine status.

---

21 Brontë, *Jane Eyre*, p. 302. This split between pure and impure woman already exists in Radcliffean Gothic (see Heller, *Dead Secrets*, pp. 21–3), but Victorian writers give the theme greater emphasis.
22 Brontë, *Jane Eyre*, p. 281.
23 For a reading of Bertha as a figure for the native woman, see Susan Meyer, *Imperialism at Home: Race and Victorian Women's Fiction* (Ithaca, NY: Cornell University Press, 1996), pp. 60–95; for a reading of Bertha as a figure for a decadent colonial aristocracy, see Sue Thomas, 'The tropical extravagance of Bertha Mason', *Victorian Literature and Culture* 27:1 (1999): 1–17.
24 Brontë, *Jane Eyre*, p. 302.   25 Brontë, *Jane Eyre*, p. 359.

Domestic Gothic by the other Brontë sisters, Emily and Anne, is also marked by a split between virtuous and transgressive women, though *Wuthering Heights* goes farther than perhaps any other nineteenth-century Gothic fiction to trouble this distinction. In that novel, Catherine Earnshaw unabashedly yearns for Heathcliff even after marrying Edgar Linton: indeed, when Heathcliff returns to Wuthering Heights a wealthy man and visits the Lintons, Cathy seems genuinely surprised that anyone would think it improper for her to voice her rapture in front of her husband.[26] Emily Brontë also dares to disregard a long-standing – and still prevalent – taboo against depicting a mother as a sexual being: Cathy is pregnant by her husband in a scene in which Heathcliff embraces her with 'frantic caresses' while Nelly Dean stands at the door anxiously watching for Linton's return.[27] At the same time, even in *Wuthering Heights* the transgressive woman is, like Bertha, killed off, as Cathy dies after giving birth. This maternal death can be read either as a containment of Cathy's desire or as a strategy for depicting adulterous love more sympathetically by rendering it ethereal instead of corporeal (once Cathy dies, the lovers can only be united in the afterlife). The woman who is allowed to have a corporeal union with a man of her choice is the second Cathy, daughter of the mother who dies in childbirth: recalling the matrophobic mother–daughter plot of female Gothic, the younger Cathy, in wedding Hareton, avoids her mother's fate of marrying a man whom she does not passionately love. Still, this happy ending is less satisfying than it might be, given that the second Cathy is a more conventional character than the first, and the contrast between mother and daughter reinstates the narrative divide between pure woman and impure counterpart.

Anne Brontë's *The Tenant of Wildfell Hall* (1848) is a strikingly innovative domestic Gothic in not relying on traditional paraphernalia as a setting for the feminine carceral. The most Gothic space in the novel, Wildfell Hall – a 'superannuated' and 'gloomy' Elizabethan mansion[28] – is the refuge to which Helen Huntingdon flees to escape her abusive marriage, not its backdrop. In an important departure from her sisters' version of domestic Gothic, too, Anne Brontë refuses to represent the domineering male protagonist as darkly

---

26 Emily Brontë, *Wuthering Heights*, edited by Ian Jack (Oxford: Oxford University Press, 1995), pp. 84–7. For more on female sexuality and the Gothic in the novel, see Tamar Heller, 'Haunted Bodies: The Female Gothic of *Wuthering Heights*', in Sue Lonoff and Terri A. Hasseler (eds), *Approaches to Teaching Emily Brontë's Wuthering Heights* (New York: MLA Press, 2006), pp. 67–74.
27 Brontë, *Wuthering Heights*, p. 142.
28 Anne Brontë, *The Tenant of Wildfell Hall*, edited by G. D. Hargreaves (Harmondsworth: Penguin, 1979), p. 45.

alluring. Byronic precursors of many a craggy, troubled romance-novel hero, Rochester and Heathcliff are undoubtedly in love with the women whom they consider soulmates, and thus depicted at least somewhat positively, even though their treatment of women leaves much to be desired. This is especially the case with Heathcliff, who, in order to gain control of the Linton fortune, becomes a Radcliffean villain, subjecting Isabella Linton to an abusive marriage and later forcing the second Cathy to wed his own dying son. In contrast, *The Tenant of Wildfell Hall* does not romanticise Helen's husband Arthur: though handsome, he not only lacks Rochester and Heathcliff's broody magnetism, but helps Anne Brontë to make the point that a key tenet of domestic ideology – that women can redeem men through moral influence – may be myth rather than reality. Although Rochester eventually turns to God after Jane refuses to commit adultery with him, Arthur Huntingdon – despite his wife's pious hopes to 'save him' from his bad ways[29] – only shows a lukewarm interest in religion on his deathbed, and cannot, during his lifetime, be weaned from alcoholism and profligacy.

In its harrowing portrayal of a ruined marriage, moreover, *The Tenant of Wildfell Hall* is the most clearly topical of the three examples of Brontëan Gothic considered here. Set in the late 1820s, around a decade before the passage of the Infant Custody Act of 1839, the story of a wife's flight from a failed marriage and attempt to retain custody of her infant son evokes the real-life history of Caroline Norton, a wife who, in accordance with the legal precedents of the time, lost custody of her children after the breakdown of her marriage, and whose strenuous campaigns to bring the inequalities of the legal situation of wives and mothers to the attention of the public contributed to the passage of both the Infant Custody Act and the Matrimonial Causes Act of 1857. As Elisabeth Rose Gruner argues, Helen's plight in *The Tenant of Wildfell Hall* not only resembles Norton's, but mirrors the contradictions of Norton's relation to domestic ideology. A 'public domestic figure', as Gruner calls her,[30] Norton aired her private woes in published appeals that, paradoxically, brought her outside the domestic sphere in the service of protecting wives and mothers within it. At the same time, Norton's public stance, and her own history, placed her in a liminal space between respectability and notoriety, particularly since she came to public notice when her husband sued her for adultery; although he lost

---

29 Brontë, *Tenant*, p. 167.
30 Elisabeth Rose Gruner, 'Plotting the mother: Caroline Norton, Helen Huntingdon, and Isabel Vane', *Tulsa Studies in Women's Literature* 16:2 (Autumn 1997): 303–25 (p. 309).

his case, Norton's association with even the potential for fallenness underscored the dangers of a wife's visibility in the public sphere. In *The Tenant of Wildfell Hall*, Helen similarly risks classification as a fallen woman when her neighbours, suspicious of her evident concealment of a past history, assume that the brother who visits her is in fact her lover. Only, as Gruner points out, when Helen, like Norton, makes a written record of her private experience public is she vindicated; loaning her diary to Gilbert Markham – who in turn shares it with a friend and, by extension, the reader – Helen clears herself of accusations of sexual misconduct and, moreover, defends a flight from her husband that might otherwise be labelled immoral.[31] Still, the indeterminate status of Helen's story – caught between private and public space – recalls the uneasy relation to domesticity that characterised Norton's career as a wronged wife.

Unsurprisingly, given the risk of linking Helen with sexual impropriety, Anne Brontë represents her as a model of chastity and piety. To the extent that female sexual transgression is depicted in *The Tenant of Wildfell Hall*, it is associated with Annabella, Lady Lowborough, who commits adultery with Helen's husband, and who, as the novel's resident fallen woman, is thoroughly demonised. It would remain for sensation fiction – after Brontëan Gothic, the genre's 'second major metamorphosis in the domain of the Victorian mainstream novel'[32] – to trouble more overtly the distinction between chaste heroine and unchaste foil.

The Adulteress in the House: Marriage and Female Sexuality in Sensation Fiction

Consider two narrative trajectories. In the first, a young woman with an infant son is abandoned by a husband who sails to Australia to mine for gold and vanishes for three years, during which she neither hears a word from him nor receives a penny of support. After struggling to eke out a living as a music teacher, she entrusts her son to her father's care and takes positions as a school teacher and governess, receiving, in the latter post, a marriage offer from a middle-aged aristocrat. Thinking it reasonable to believe her first husband dead, she accepts the proposal, but the husband returns to England soon after the marriage, discovers her whereabouts, and bruises her arm in an

---

31 Gruner, 'Plotting the mother', p. 311. 32 Davison, 'Victorian Gothic and Gender', p. 132.

angry confrontation. Eventually, following a perfunctory ten-minute interview with a doctor, the young woman is 'buried alive' in an insane asylum, where she dies within a year.[33]

In the second narrative trajectory, a scheming wife adopts a false identity as a single woman after her husband sails to Australia. While employed as a governess, she accepts a proposal of marriage from a middle-aged aristocrat without ascertaining that her first husband is dead. When he returns to England shortly after her marriage, she arranges for a dying woman to be buried under her own legal name, leaving the husband heartbroken over her apparent demise. After he discovers that she is still alive and threatens to reveal her bigamy, she sends him plummeting to the bottom of a well, later attempting to kill the young man who investigates his friend's suspicious disappearance. Although it turns out that her first husband survives his fall, the murderous and duplicitous wife is punished with confinement in an insane asylum.

Both narrative trajectories summarise a single novel – Mary Elizabeth Braddon's *Lady Audley's Secret* (1862), one of the first and most famous sensation fictions – but each tells the tale by emphasising a different set of conventions. The first summary isolates aspects of Braddon's tale that recall the female Gothic plot of the marital carceral: spousal neglect and cruelty, a wife's disadvantaged economic situation, incarceration in an insane asylum without adequate medical rationale. In this summary of *Lady Audley's Secret*, the female protagonist, a governess wooed by an older aristocrat, is a version of Jane Eyre, as well as a variant on Anne Brontë's Helen Huntingdon, who supports herself and her infant son under an assumed name following the collapse of her marriage.[34] To the extent that Lady Audley evokes Bertha in this account of the novel, she does so by evoking the female Gothic convention of the wife immured in a madhouse. In the second summary of Braddon's novel, however, Lady Audley loses any resemblance to Jane Eyre and resembles Bertha in her incarnation as a femme fatale, sharing with Rochester's first wife an insane mother and a penchant for violence and arson (Lady Audley tries to kill her first husband's friend by setting fire to the inn where he is sleeping, reminiscent of Bertha's attempt to kill Rochester by setting fire to his bed and her later torching of Thornfield Hall). Significantly,

---

33 Mary Elizabeth Braddon, *Lady Audley's Secret*, edited by Natalie Houston (Peterborough, Ont.: Broadview, 2003), p. 387.
34 Could Braddon actually be referring to *The Tenant of Wildfell Hall*? The surname Lady Audley adopts while working as a governess, Graham, is the same that Helen Huntingdon assumes when she flees her marriage.

too, Lady Audley is, also like Bertha, an adulteress, although ironically her adultery consists of committing the sexual transgression – bigamy – that Rochester failed to commit when he attempted to marry Jane during Bertha's lifetime.

The conflation of female Gothic heroine and femme fatale is one of Braddon's most important revisions of Brontëan domestic Gothic. Whereas *Jane Eyre* differentiates these figures, in Braddon's text, as one Victorian reviewer complained, 'Lady Audley is at once the heroine and the monstrosity of the novel', a combination that he found 'noxious'.[35] While to Victorians the notion of a female reader sympathising with a criminal female protagonist was one of the more unnerving aspects of sensation fiction, it has been a subject of particular interest to feminist critics reevaluating the genre. In one of the earliest such analyses, Elaine Showalter labels Lady Audley's efforts to free herself from disadvantaged economic and social positions as one of the 'fantasies of protest and escape' that sensation novels provide their female audience.[36] At the same time, there are fantasies that *Lady Audley's Secret* debunks, including the myth that Jan Cohn sees as central to narratives of bourgeois romance, that the heroine is motivated by love to the exclusion of economic self-interest.[37] Whereas Charlotte Brontë's virtuous Jane loves Rochester regardless of wealth and position, Braddon's determinedly unidealised Lady Audley, also initially a governess, acknowledges the lure of her aristocratic's suitor's status, confessing, when he proposes, 'I *cannot* be disinterested.'[38]

Nevertheless, the covert critique of women's economic dependence in *Lady Audley's Secret* is complicated by the novel's overt condemnation of its anti-heroine. Not only do we see much of the action through the masculine, and decidedly misogynist, perspective of Robert Audley, the friend who investigates the disappearance of Lady Audley's first husband, but the narrator repeatedly describes the bigamous wife with words such as 'selfish' and 'wicked', and Braddon herself makes her protagonist a homicidal sociopath.[39] In accounting for this demonisation of Lady Audley, we cannot forget the

---

35 W. Fraser Rae, 'Sensation novelists: Miss Braddon', *North British Review* (September 1865), in *North British Review* New Series, Vol. IV (September–December 1865): 180–204 (pp. 186, 187).
36 Elaine Showalter, *A Literature of Their Own: British Women Novelists from Brontë to Lessing* (Princeton: Princeton University Press, 1977), p. 159.
37 See Jan Cohn, *Romance and the Erotics of Property* (Durham, NC: Duke University Press, 1988), esp. pp. 127–41.
38 Braddon, *Lady Audley's Secret*, p. 52.
39 Braddon, *Lady Audley's Secret*, pp. 310, 378, 397.

pressures on authors, particularly female ones, to avoid positively portraying a transgressive woman. Yet *Lady Audley's Secret* also recirculates potent cultural anxieties about marriage and female sexuality that were at a high level when it was published, anxieties which Lady Audley embodies both by being an adulteress and becoming one in order to escape a failed marriage. Departing from the tendency of feminist critics to read Braddon as subversive, Lillian Nayder argues that *Lady Audley's Secret* is a 'conservative' response to the passage of the Matrimonial Causes Act of 1857 and the Indian Mutiny, both of which occurred in the same year and which fanned 'patriarchal anxieties' about the weakening of the marriage bond at home and imperial power abroad.[40] When Lady Audley propels her husband down a well, Nayder claims, Braddon invokes an iconic image of post-Mutiny English propaganda, the Well of Cawnpore, into which Indians rebels tossed the bodies of murdered Englishwomen and children.[41] Nayder interprets the 'racial and sexual inversion' of the Cawnpore Massacre in Braddon's novel – an inversion in which an English husband is attacked by his runaway wife – as implying that 'the real threat posed to the British empire in the 1860s does not come from unruly natives in the colonies but from Englishwomen agitating for their rights'.[42]

While I see *Lady Audley's Secret* as more ambivalent in its portrayal of the rebellious wife than does Nayder, the context in which she situates the novel – the 'moral panic', as Lynda Nead calls it, generated by the conjunction of the Matrimonial Causes Act and the Indian Mutiny[43] – is crucial to sensation fiction. Because of its controversial changes to marriage law, the Matrimonial Causes Act is particularly relevant to a genre notable for, as one reviewer grumbled, 'the insecurity given to the marriage relation'.[44] Like sensation fiction, too, the Act offers contradictory messages about gender, and, indeed, is readable as ideologically fissured domestic Gothic in its own right. Granting women as well as men the right to divorce, the Act tacitly admitted the inadequacy of coverture to protect the interests of wives in

---

40 Lillian Nayder, 'Rebellious Sepoys and Bigamous Wives: The Indian Mutiny and Marriage Law Reform in *Lady Audley's Secret*', in Marlene Tromp, Pamela K. Gilbert and Aeron Haynie (eds), *Beyond Sensation: Mary Elizabeth Braddon in Context* (Albany: State University of New York Press, 2000), pp. 31–42 (pp. 34, 37).
41 Nayder, 'Rebellious Sepoys and Bigamous Wives', pp. 38–9.
42 Nayder, 'Rebellious Sepoys and Bigamous Wives', p. 39.
43 See Lynda Nead, *Myths of Sexuality: Representations of Women in Victorian Britain* (Oxford: Blackwell, 1988), p. 80.
44 'Our Female Sensation Novelists', in Andrew Maunder (ed.), *Sensationalism and the Sensation Debate: Varieties of Women's Sensation Fiction 1855–1890*, 6 vols (London: Pickering & Chatto, 2004), vol. 1, pp. 105–14 (p. 109).

unhappy marriages, making it, as Mary Poovey says, 'the first major piece of British legislation to focus attention on the anomalous position of women under the law'.[45] Whereas coverture assumed a benevolent husband with his wife's best interests at heart – in which case her legal non-existence through being 'covered' by his identity would not harm her – the Matrimonial Causes Act acknowledged that such was not always the case. Not only did this acknowledgement suggest the need for further changes to remedy women's legal non-identity, but it also challenged the depiction of the home as a refuge of moral sanctity, portraying it instead, in true female Gothic style, as the site of infidelity and cruelty. While it subversively expanded women's rights, however, the Matrimonial Causes Act, like many domestic Gothic narratives, highlighted the dangers posed by female, rather than male, sexuality. Preserving the double standard, the Act allowed men to divorce women in cases of adultery, but mandated that wives could only divorce their husbands if adultery were compounded by 'aggravating circumstances' such as cruelty, incest or bigamy.[46] The Act's implicit message that, as Lynda Nead says, 'the social consequences of female adultery were more serious than those of male adultery'[47] stoked anxieties about the weakening of the patriarchal family heightened by the passage of the Act itself – anxieties which infiltrated sensation fiction as well as other forms of popular culture in the late 1850s and 1860s, including the painter Augustus Egg's triptych of a modern adulteress, *Past and Present* (1858).[48]

Like sensation fiction, too, the Matrimonial Causes Act brought increased public scrutiny to female sexual transgression. Shifting divorce cases from ecclesiastical to civil court, the Act ensured that their salacious details would be more readily available to the public, who could attend trials themselves or read titillating accounts in the newspapers. Given the burden on wives divorcing husbands to provide evidence of both adultery and aggravating circumstances, it was easier for husbands to sue wives on grounds of adultery alone, and the Divorce Court thus more commonly aired women's sexual transgressions than men's.[49] Critics of sensationalism drew a parallel between the genre's depiction of risqué issues and divorce proceedings, seeing both as potentially corrupting discourses for women. For example, one clergyman

---

45 Mary Poovey, *Uneven Developments: The Ideological Work of Gender in Mid-Victorian England* (Chicago: University of Chicago Press, 1988), p. 51.
46 See Nead, *Myths of Sexuality*, p. 52. 47 Nead, *Myths of Sexuality*, p. 56.
48 See Nead's discussion of *Past and Present* in *Myths of Sexuality*, pp. 71–86.
49 In his introduction to *East Lynne* (Peterborough, Ont.: Broadview, 2000), Andrew Maunder notes that, in 1858, the year following the Matrimonial Causes Act, petitions for divorce brought by husbands accounted for 156 of an annual total of 253 (p. 26).

who claimed that sensation novels recirculated, from 'the records of the Divorce Courts, the things which twenty years ago English women did not talk of at all', attacked the works for rendering the minds of 'our sisters and daughters . . . literally "full of adultery."'[50] Although adultery cases were civil rather than criminal, their being argued in a public courtroom – a venue that, moreover, labelled adulterous acts 'criminal conversation' – linked female sexual transgression with criminality and the class degradation it implied. (Bigamy, is, of course a form of adultery that is actually a criminal offence.) In sensation fiction, the association of female adultery with crime was exacerbated by the genre's numerous 'homicidal heroines', as one journal labelled them, of whom Lady Audley was the most famous – and who, as the same journal claimed, threatened to turn 'Mr. Mudie's lending library' into a 'Newgate Calendar'.[51]

The representation of 'homicidal' women in sensation fiction was also influenced by the increased cultural visibility, in mid-century, of real-life murderesses, whose cases, like the records of Divorce Court, broadcast narratives of female deviance. In one of the most notorious Victorian murder trials, the letters of Madeleine Smith, the daughter of a respectable Glasgow family who was accused of poisoning her lover, were read aloud in court, making it all too clear that she had engaged in sex outside of marriage.[52] Braddon alludes to this context in *Lady Audley's Secret* when Robert Audley hopes to avoid bringing murder charges in his friend's death so as to escape the 'shame' of seeing his aristocratic uncle's wife 'in a criminal dock, hemmed in on every side by a sea of eager faces'[53] – a breach of domestic privacy that exposes female transgression to the glare of degrading publicity.

In its tale of a disgruntled, homicidal wife, then, *Lady Audley's Secret* both reflected and stoked cultural anxieties about female rebellion, sexuality and violence in an era of perceived threats to patriarchal law and imperial rule. Whereas Braddon's allusions to topical events provoking these anxieties are more often implied than stated, however, Ellen Wood's *East Lynne* (1861) explicitly engages divorce practices in the wake of the Matrimonial Causes Act. The novel is structured first by action leading up to, and then resulting from, Archibald Carlyle's divorce of his wife, Lady Isabel Vane, on grounds of

---

50 William Alexander, Bishop of Derby, 'Sensationalism', in Maunder (ed.), *Sensationalism*, vol. 1, pp. 263–74 (p. 269).
51 'Homicidal Heroines', in Maunder (ed.), *Sensationalism*, pp. 145–49 (p. 145).
52 For more on the Madeleine Smith case, see Mary S. Hartman, *Victorian Murderesses: A True History of Thirteen Respectable French and English Women Accused of Unspeakable Crimes* (New York: Schocken, 1977), pp. 51–84.
53 Braddon, *Lady Audley's Secret*, p. 382.

adultery. In class terms, Archibald would be one of the husbands to benefit from the Matrimonial Causes Act, which made divorce far less expensive than the previous system, under which only the wealthiest could afford the legal costs: although Archibald has purchased East Lynne, formerly the estate of Lady Isabel's aristocratic father, he is not yet rich enough to have secured a divorce under the old law. *East Lynne*, however, is not only a tale of divorce, but a tale of two marriages: after receiving what turns out to be an erroneous report that his divorced wife has been killed in a train crash, Archibald marries Barbara Hare, with whom he achieves domestic contentment. While the novel's contrast between the unfaithful and faithful wife recalls the split between chaste and unchaste women in *Jane Eyre*, *East Lynne* nonetheless disturbs that boundary, blurring the categories of female purity and impurity that supposedly structure the novel.

As in *Lady Audley's Secret*, however, subversive messages are muffled by heavy-handed condemnation of the anti-heroine. Not only does Wood's narrator berate Lady Isabel for her fall and enjoin the reader to avoid her 'far worse than death' fate,[54] Wood also drives home the absurdity of her protagonist's choice by depicting Lady Isabel's seducer, Sir Francis Levison, as a murdering cad whose ignominy throws the nobility of her betrayed husband into sharper relief. To some extent, Lady Isabel's and Sir Francis's moral frailty is overdetermined by the novel's class allegory. Andrew Maunder usefully details the ways in which *East Lynne* draws on discourses of degeneration and hereditary vice prevalent in the 1860s to construct 'a tale of identity for the newly affluent middle classes'.[55] In this narrative, the rising bourgeoisie, represented by the industrious lawyer Archibald Carlyle and his virtuous second wife, triumph over the effete aristocracy embodied by Lady Isabel and her father, Lord Mount Severn, whose gout and bankruptcy symbolise the unrestrained appetites that he presumably bequeaths to his daughter. Viewed from this perspective, Lady Isabel plays the promiscuous Bertha, scion of debauched colonial planters, to Barbara Hare's domesticated Jane Eyre.

Yet the contrast between the chaste and unchaste woman in *East Lynne* is undercut by the depiction of Barbara's own illicit desire. Prior to becoming Archibald Carlyle's wife, Barbara is unrequitedly in love with him; while this

---

54 Ellen Wood, *East Lynne*, edited by Andrew Maunder (Peterborough, Ont.: Broadview, 2000), p. 335.
55 Andrew Maunder, '"Stepchildren of Nature": *East Lynne* and the Spectre of Female Degeneracy, 1860–1861', in Andrew Maunder and Grace Moore (eds), *Victorian Crime, Madness and Sensation* (Farnham: Ashgate, 2004), pp. 59–71 (p. 63).

plot is not unusual in Victorian fiction, the degree to which the lovelorn woman voices her desire is. Geraldine Jewsbury, a redoubtable reader for Bentley's, in fact urged the publisher to ensure the removal of a scene in which Barbara confesses her love to the married Archibald in what Jewsbury called a 'violent explosion'.[56] Yet not only did this scene remain in the novel, but Wood elsewhere emphasises the intensity of Barbara's thwarted desire, calling it an 'almost idolatrous passion' and depicting the young woman's agony as she voyeuristically spots Archibald caressing his bride.[57] Viewed in this light, Barbara and Isabel are not so much different as alike: Barbara's frustrated desire for Archibald while he is married to Isabel is paralleled when the divorced Isabel, disfigured by injuries in the train wreck purported to have killed her, returns to East Lynne to care for her children disguised as a governess, and is forced to view her former husband's attentions to Barbara. Each of Archibald Carlyle's wives, in other words, is tormented by adulterous desire when she either is not, or is no longer, wed to him.

Wood also associates Barbara with adultery by suggesting that her marriage to the divorced Archibald may not be recognised by God. Although it is legally permissable for him to remarry after the divorce, Archibald announces his refusal to do so while Isabel is alive, citing the biblical verse 'Whosoever putteth away his wife, and marriest another, commiteth adultery.'[58] That Isabel, unbeknownst to him, is in fact alive when he remarries nullifies the second union according to his own definition, casting doubt on the legitimacy of the children that he has with Barbara during Isabel's lifetime. Sidestepping the theological and social implications of Archibald's remarriage, Wood does not show him questioning its validity, or his children's legitimacy, after discovering Isabel's identity on her deathbed. Nonetheless, Archibald is sufficiently rattled by this discovery to conceptualise his predicament as a kind of bigamy: 'the first clear thought that came thumping through his brain was, that he must be a man with two wives'.[59] Whatever point Wood wishes to make about remarriage following divorce, the bizarre *ménage-à-trois* that ensues upon Isabel's return to East Lynne – in which the unwitting Archibald shares the house with both his current and his ex-wife, the latter transformed into a voyeuristic, Jane Eyre-style governess – portrays the aftermath of the Matrimonial Causes Act as sexual confusion.

---

56 Geraldine Jewsbury, 'Reader's Report on *East Lynne*', Appendix B in Ellen Wood, *East Lynne*, edited by Andrew Maunder (Peterborough, Ont.: Broadview Press, 2000), pp. 698–99 (p. 698).
57 Wood, *East Lynne*, p. 180.   58 Wood, *East Lynne*, p. 372.
59 Wood, *East Lynne*, p. 680.

Making Barbara more like Isabel than the novel's sententious narrator would ever admit, *East Lynne* suggests another resemblance between Archibald's 'two wives': their stories both reveal social and economic pressures on women in conventional domesticity. Barbara grows up in a home defined by fear of the ruling patriarch; like an oppressed mother in female Gothic, Barbara's mother is frightened into invalidism by her husband's 'great storms of passion',[60] and his micromanaging household control. Barbara herself is compelled to resort to lies and secrecy in order to arrange clandestine meetings with her brother, a fugitive from a murder charge whom Barbara's inflexible father threatens to betray to the authorities. In Isabel's case, economics are paramount: Wood makes it clear that Isabel accepts Archibald's proposal not for romantic reasons – she admits to not loving him[61] – but because the marriage would spare her the homelessness and penury into which she is thrown by her father's death. Archibald himself demonstrates how even a well-intentioned man can be insensitive to women's feelings. At one point, he is unaware that Barbara has interpreted his gift of a locket, bestowed with a kiss, as a sign of romantic interest – a mistake that causes her considerable pain when he marries Isabel. Archibald is even more disastrously clueless when it comes to Isabel herself. Absorbed in his law practice, he fails to notice her misery when his unmarried sister moves in and subjects her new sister-in-law to unending criticism, all the while usurping her place as mistress of the household. Archibald is also unaware how, when he meets for long sessions with Barbara to discuss her brother's situation, he gives his insecure wife reason to believe that he is having an affair, a suspicion that precipitates her decision to elope with Sir Francis, on hand as a guest at East Lynne because Archibald ignored Isabel's pleas not to invite him.

Especially when considered alongside this male incompetence, the sheer volume of Isabel's woes – which include witnessing the slow death of her oldest child from consumption while she is unable to reveal her true identity – cannot help but unsettle the narrative's condemnation of her fall. To Margaret Oliphant, this aspect of *East Lynne* was 'dangerous'.[62] Admitting to finding Isabel more appealing than her virtuous replacement, Oliphant announced that 'Nothing can be more wrong and fatal than to represent the flames of vice as a purifying, fiery ordeal, through which the penitent is to

---

60 Wood, *East Lynne*, p. 367.   61 Wood, *East Lynne*, p. 168.
62 Margaret Oliphant, 'Sensation Novels', in Ellen Wood, *East Lynne*, edited by Andrew Maunder (Peterborough, Ont.: Broadview Press, 2000), p. 715.

come elevated and sublimed.'[63] Noting that 'nohow, except through [Isabel's] wickedness and sufferings, could she have gained so strong a hold upon our sympathies',[64] Oliphant identifies the feature of *East Lynne* that feminist critics find particularly subversive. As Lyn Pykett argues, when the reader witnesses the 'spectacle' of Isabel's suffering, she or he forms an emotional bond with the fallen woman that 'creates a space for resistance of the text's "official" morality'.[65] The 'access', as Ann Cvetcovich puts it, that Wood grants the reader to Isabel's 'psychic pain and repressed feelings'[66] has another subversive potential: to challenge the very definition of private and public spheres in domestic ideology. As demonstrated by protagonists like Isabel and Lady Audley, whose inner anguish is known to the reader but not to characters around them, the purportedly private sphere is redefined as, in fact, a public stage upon which women play roles that mask their truly private – because suppressed – selves.[67]

The light that sensation fiction sheds on female consciousness is arguably its most notable innovation. In this version of Gothic, the female protagonist not only inhabits Gothic domesticity: she *is* a symbolic Gothic dwelling, a mental habitation haunted by memories, fears and frustrated desires. This innovation would also prove influential. Earlier, I mentioned the influence of *Jane Eyre*, and its portrait of the discontented heroine, on later feminist *bildungsromans*, including the novels of George Eliot. Sensation fiction, which often itself revises *Jane Eyre*, is an intermediary between Brontë's text and such later Victorian fictions as George Eliot's *Daniel Deronda* (1876) and Thomas Hardy's *Tess of the D'Urbervilles* (1891) that address women's situation in a changing, but still confining, social environment. Not only do these later fictions absorb sensation themes and conventions, but their portrayal of the heroines' suffering is the successor to sensation fiction's depictions of women's Gothic interiority. Ann Cvetcovich, for example, reads Gwendolen's inner torment in *Daniel Deronda*, both during her marriage to Grandcourt and in her guilt following his melodramatic death, as evidence of the 'large debt' that Eliot owes to sensationalism.[68] New Woman

---

63 Oliphant, 'Sensation Novels', p. 715.   64 Oliphant, 'Sensation Novels', p. 715.
65 Lyn Pykett, *The 'Improper' Feminine: The Women's Sensation Novel and the New Woman Writing* (London: Routledge, 1992), pp. 130, 131, 132.
66 Ann Cvetcovich, *Mixed Feelings: Feminism, Mass Culture, and Victorian Sensationalism* (New Brunswick: Rutgers University Press, 1992), pp. 101, 98.
67 Feminist critics have long noted how the emphasis on women acting social roles in sensationalism destabilises domestic ideology's concept of an innate female nature; see, for example, Pykett, *The Improper Feminine*, pp. 90–4.
68 Cvetcovich, *Mixed Feelings*, p. 129.

novels of the 1890s build as well on domestic Gothic's representation of marriage as a prison for haunted wives.[69] Legatees of Victorian domestic Gothic, novels such as Eliot's and New Woman fiction in turn anticipate portrayals of female consciousness in feminist modernism.[70]

Reflecting an ever-mutating social and publishing climate, too, late nineteenth-century domestic Gothic tends to be more sympathetic to female desire than its predecessor texts, a shift in attitude that draws more on the genre's feminist aspects than its misogyny. The most negative, and explicitly anti-feminist, portrayals of female sexuality in late nineteenth-century Gothic occur in the male-oriented adventure fiction that Patrick Brantlinger labels 'imperial Gothic', and which illustrates the late-Victorian historical trend that John Tosh calls the 'flight from domesticity'.[71] But even Bram Stoker's *Dracula* (1897) – probably the most iconic *fin-de-siècle* Gothic fiction, and a text in which male bonding is inextricable from fear of female sexuality – can be read as a version of domestic Gothic, and as ambivalent, rather than wholly negative, in its depiction of the New Woman.[72] The legacy of Victorian domestic Gothic was to inspire ever more aesthetically flexible and ideologically complex ways of representing gender role controversy and change.

69 For more on this topic, see Patricia Murphy, *The New Woman Gothic: Reconfigurations of Distress* (Columbia: University of Missouri Press, 2016).
70 I am thinking in particular of the fiction of Virginia Woolf and Jean Rhys, but see also, for the influence of *East Lynne* specifically on a writer who bridges Victorian and modernist eras, Tamar Heller, 'Victorian sensationalism and the silence of maternal sexuality in Edith Wharton's *The Mother's Recompense*', *Narrative* 5.2 (May 1997): 135–42.
71 Patrick Brantlinger, *Rule of Darkness: British Literature and Imperialism, 1830–1914* (Ithaca, NY: Cornell University Press, 1988), pp. 227–53 and John Tosh, *A Man's Place: Masculinity and the Middle-Class Home in Victorian England* (New Haven: Yale University Press, 1999), pp. 170–94.
72 Despite a heavily male cast and adventure-related plot, *Dracula* contains a number of domestic scenes (some, interestingly, in a madhouse) and a major female character (Mina Harker) who is at once Angel in the House and New Woman, and who expresses her feelings at being marginalised by male vampire hunters in journal entries that recall sensationalism's depiction of female interiority. For a reading that diverges from many feminist critiques in finding Stoker ambivalent, rather than completely negative, on the New Woman, see Sos Eltis, 'Corruption of the Blood and Degeneration of the Race: *Dracula* and Policing the Borders of Gender', in John Paul Riquelme (ed.), *Dracula* (Boston: Bedford/St. Martin's, 2002), pp. 450–65.

2.13

The Gothic in Nineteenth-Century Spain

XAVIER ALDANA REYES AND ROCÍO RØDTJER

The long-held view that the Gothic occupied little space in both literary histories of Spain and in its popular imaginative output has been steadily challenged in recent years by a number of studies that have sought to establish the Gothic as a key component of the country's larger cultural production.[1] Once deemed foreign and of little import, the Gothic is now seen as a key articulator of inherently national preoccupations. As Ann Davies has argued, it is likely that such a revisionary perception owes much to a recent boom heralded by the visual excesses of the films of Guillermo del Toro, the spectral imaginings of *El orfanato* (2007) [The Orphanage] and *Los otros* (2001) [The Others], and the transnational success of Carlos Ruiz Zafón's novel *La sombra del viento* (2001) [The Shadow of the Wind].[2] Memory studies have fuelled this interest by interpreting these new Gothic incursions reflectively, reading them as a confrontation with the ghosts of the Spanish Civil War (1936–9), a traumatic period in history that continues to plague the country in its attempts to consolidate itself as a fully-fledged modern democracy. A Gothic presence in Spain, however, can in fact be traced to the closing years of the eighteenth century and the first translations of English and French works that would help to lay the foundations for later home-grown efforts. This chapter aims to provide a survey of Gothic Spanish literature of the nineteenth century, a period often overlooked in favour of its twentieth-century counterpart. In doing so, it attempts to continue the critical task of reinserting Spain within the European literary

---

1 See Abigail Lee Six, *Gothic Terrors: Incarceration, Duplication and Bloodlust in Spanish Narrative* (Lewisburg, PA: Bucknell University Press, 2010); Miriam López Santos, *La novela gótica en España (1788–1833)* (Vigo: Academia del Hispanismo, 2010); Xavier Aldana Reyes, *Spanish Gothic: National Identity, Collaboration and Cultural Adaptation* (Basingstoke: Palgrave Macmillan, 2017).
2 Ann Davies, *Contemporary Spanish Gothic* (Edinburgh: Edinburgh University Press, 2016), p. 9.

trends from which it has traditionally been separated, while contributing to the critical conception of a global Gothic composed of circulating tropes that have been inflected with local interpretations and adaptations.³

For a long time, nineteenth-century Spanish Gothic remained in the shadows, neglected in literary surveys of the period. Critics hesitated to employ the term *'gótico'* [Gothic], preferring instead the label *'fantástico'* [fantastic] to describe works that fit Gothic templates in Anglophone countries.⁴ While the term 'fantastic' has its uses insofar as it amalgamates non-realist forms of fiction, this aversion to the use of 'Gothic' implicitly isolated Spain from the transnational Gothic stream of which it was undoubtedly part. With the Gothic traditionally seen as emanating from northern Europe, Spain was rendered 'Gothic' in the largely dystopian sense of that term, becoming a favoured backdrop of decaying feudal castles, brooding counts and cruel Inquisitors in three key novels from the first wave of Gothic fiction in Britain (1764–1820), Matthew Lewis's *The Monk* (1796), William Godwin's *St. Leon* (1799) and Charles Maturin's *Melmoth the Wanderer* (1820), as well as in numerous chapbooks and dramas.⁵ Later, Spain became a popular destination for Romantic-era travellers like Prosper Mérimée, who revelled in the exotic aura of Andalusian Moorish palaces and created the sultry gypsy Carmen in the eponymous 1845 novel.⁶ 'Few, if any of these observers, were really interested in understanding Spain', observe Adrian Shubert and José Álvarez Junco, concluding instead that, 'The Spain they sought and which – naturally enough – they found was idealization, the counter-image to the quotidian reality they rejected and left behind.'⁷ This was a Spain beyond the realms of modernity.

If any overview of contemporary Spanish Gothic has to contend with the risks of simplistic readings that may reduce a national Gothic to the ongoing exorcism of fascism and Franco's dictatorship, the peripheral place of Spain in the cartography of Western modernity presents comparable challenges.⁸

---

3 Alexandra Warwick, 'Feeling gothicky?', *Gothic Studies* 9:1 (2007): 5–15 (p. 6).
4 Aldana Reyes, *Spanish Gothic*, p. 7.
5 Diane Long Hoeveler, *The Gothic Ideology: Religious Hysteria and Anti-Catholicism in British Popular Fiction, 1780–1880* (Cardiff: University of Wales Press, 2014), pp. 157–86.
6 For the engagement of Romantic British writers with Spain, see Diego Saglia, *Poetic Castles in Spain: British Romanticism and Figurations of Iberia* (Amsterdam: Rodopi, 2000) and Diego Saglia and Ian Haywood (eds), *Spain in British Romanticism, 1800–1840* (Basingstoke: Palgrave Macmillan, 2017).
7 Adrian Shubert and José Álvarez Junco, 'Introduction', *Spanish History since 1808* (London: Arnold; New York: Oxford University Press, 2000), pp. 1–16 (p. 7). Unless otherwise indicated, all English translations are the authors' own.
8 Michael P. Iarocci, *Properties of Modernity: Romantic Spain, Modern Europe, and the Legacies of Empire* (Nashville, TN: Vanderbilt University Press, 2006), p. xi.

According to what was for many years the prevalent view, Spain was never modern enough to sustain the Gothic mode. Simply put, why would a superstitious country in which the Inquisition was not formally disbanded until 1834 feel compelled to invent dark and twisted Gothic tales? Yet this narrative has been overhauled in recent years with the rise of postcolonial studies, a critical mode that has interrogated the assumption that countries such as France and England held the monopoly on modernity, and which has redrawn the European cultural map in order to reflect 'a plural panorama of cultural history' in which Spain plays an important part.[9] The evolution and trajectory of the Gothic in Spain as we present it in this chapter, from the early adapted Gothic novels to the mad doctors of the *fin-de-siècle* short story, reflect how the country followed some of the major literary trends of the nineteenth century while remaining shaped by local concerns and draconian censorship laws. The Spanish Gothic during the period is thus interesting as an example of both national specificity and transnational exchange.

The Arrival of the Gothic Novel in Spain

It would be incorrect to claim that Spain had no indigenous literary history of the supernatural prior to the arrival of the first translated Gothic novels in the mid-to-late 1780s. It is, in fact, possible to trace texts in which magic and the supernatural play either a major or an episodic role in their narratives at least as far back as the oriental tales of *Calila e Dimna* (1251) [Calila and Dimna] and the medieval moralising prose of Gonzalo de Berceo, Don Juan Manuel or the Archpriest of Hita in the thirteenth and fourteenth centuries. It could even be argued, as Abigail Lee Six has done, that the honour plays of the seventeenth century, especially the work of Lope de Vega and Calderón de la Barca, may have inspired British Gothic novelists like Matthew Lewis in their preoccupations with sexual secrets, imprisonment, prophecy and violence.[10] Spain's own 'novela cortesana' [courtly novel], developed in the early-to-mid seventeenth century and heavily concerned with gruesome revenge, has also been suggested as the origin of the horror tale as we know it.[11] It would be equally remiss to propose that it was European Romanticism that brought

---

9 Andrew Ginger, *Painting and the Turn to Cultural Modernity in Spain: The Time of Eugenio Lucas Velázquez (1850–1870)* (Selinsgrove, PA: Susquehanna University Press, 2007), p. 317.
10 Abigail Lee Six, 'The Monk (1796): a Hispanist's reading', *Ilha do Desterro* 62 (2012): 25–54.
11 Gerardo González de Vega, 'La literatura fantástica española bajo el Antiguo Régimen', *El demonio meridiano: Cuentos fantásticos y de terror en la España del Antiguo Régimen* (Madrid: Miraguano Ediciones, 2015), pp. 13–148 (p. 51).

the Gothic to Spain. Instead, it is more accurate to say that the Gothic mode fertilised the Spanish Romantic imagination, as it did in Britain and France, so that key Romantic writers such as José de Espronceda, discussed below, found in the Gothic's macabre imagery and obsession with the past an echo of emotional and artistic concerns that aligned with the Romantic spirit: melancholia, nostalgia, exacerbated passions (including love and death), and an interest in the poetics of ruins, among others.

The gradual encroachment and importation of the hugely popular British and French Gothic novels, largely via France, to Spain was key to the development of a recognisable aesthetics as well as of a series of narrative motifs and scenarios that, if never self-professedly 'Gothic', would betray an obvious influence of foreign models. This means that, first and foremost, the Gothic was introduced to Spain through the translation of predominantly British and French sources. It was also consumed in the original language (generally English, French, German or Italian) and in French translations that would have been purchased on the black market.[12] A couple of minor borderline sentimental volumes by Stéphanie Felicité, countess of Genlis, trickled through in the 1780s, and these were followed in the 1790s by translations of novels by Elizabeth Helme, François Guillaume Ducray-Duminil, Sophia Lee and Jean-Baptiste Louvet de Couvray. Particularly successful were Regina Maria Roche's *The Children of the Abbey* (1796), which was translated in 1808 and which saw at least another ten editions before the end of the nineteenth century, and above all Ann Radcliffe's *A Sicilian Romance* (1790), *The Romance of the Forest* (1791), *The Mysteries of Udolpho* (1794) and *The Italian* (1796–7), all of which appeared in translation between 1818 and 1832. So popular was Radcliffe, in fact, that four additional apocryphal texts surfaced between 1827 and 1843. Noticeably, there were no translations of key Gothic novels such as Horace Walpole's *The Castle of Otranto* (1764), William Beckford's *Vathek* (1786) or Charles Maturin's *Melmoth the Wanderer*, and only a very late one, in 1822, of Matthew Lewis's *The Monk*. This fiction, with its rampant anti-clericalism, did not sit well with the censors, and only managed to see the light of day, along with *The Italian* (trans. 1821) and W. H. Ireland's *The Abbess* (1799; trans. 1822), during the three-year window of relative freedom granted to the publishing industry by the Liberal Triennium's relaxation of publishing regulations between 1820 and 1823.

12 Santos, *La novela gótica en España*, p. 46.

It is important to note that the availability of certain authors and the total absence of others was not merely a result of the laws of supply and demand, but rather a reflection of the limitations imposed by the Inquisition's ruthless process of cultural censorship.[13] The type of Gothic novel that was translated into Spanish and therefore most widely read was, of necessity, not overtly supernatural, a tendency explained by the fact that in the nineteenth century the country's religious institutions were still waging a war against superstition. The reification of evil supernatural forces that we encounter in the Satanic manifestations of Lewis and Maturin was both inconceivable and contemptible.[14] As a result, the 'explained supernatural' of Ann Radcliffe and her followers, a heavily didactic form of literature that paid lip service to the ruling principles of Catholicism and avoided frivolous thrills, became the predominant strand of the Gothic in Spain. Like sentimental fiction, culturally sanctioned Gothic novels had to at least pretend to instruct or strengthen the character and morals of their readers. This state of affairs has led critics like David Roas rightly to conclude that 'la visión que tuvieron los españoles del genero fue bastante sesgada' [the vision of the Gothic to which the Spanish were exposed was, at best, partial].[15]

Such was the need to sanitise the excesses of the imported Gothic novel and to render them useful in the service of moral edification that editors and translators would often edit out or tone down controversial, anti-ecclesiastic or salacious passages (the torture and erotic scenes in 1822's *La abadesa*, for example), rewriting and effectively creating new versions of the novels as they did so. In the case of Agustín Pérez Zaragoza Godínez, whose *Galería fúnebre de espectros y sombras ensangrentadas* (1831) [Funereal Gallery of Spectres and Bloody Shadows] was the most successful Spanish Gothic short story collection of the early nineteenth century, the fiction of J. P. R. Cuisin and others was effectively passed off as his own. Additionally, translators and editors would feel the need to justify their choices or else legitimise the value of the volumes to which they would attach their names, if only for the sake of their reputations. These new forewords were sometimes original works and demonstrate, in addition to the expurgations and excisions of the translations, the extent to which Gothic texts that had been produced under very different national and religious contexts could be manipulated and made

---

13 See Marcelin Défourneaux, *Inquisición y censura de libros en la España del siglo XVIII* (Madrid: Taurus, 1973).
14 Santos, *La novela gótica en España*, p. 46.
15 David Roas, *De la maravilla al horror: Los inicios de lo fantástico en la cultura española (1750–1860)* (Pontevedra: Mirabel Editorial, 2006), p. 84.

to fit the coordinates of a much more conservative Spain. For example, the translator's note to *Adelina, ó, la abadía en la selva: Novela histórica*, the 1830 translation of *The Romance of the Forest*, presents Radcliffe's novel as a true story, and promises that 'encierra esta obra la moral más pura y Cristiana, y es sumamente útil para desterrar los terrores vanos y ridículos que atormentan a ciertas personas cuya educación primera ha sido descuidada o llena de preocupaciones, hijas de la ignorancia' [this work hides the purest and most Christian of morals, and is extremely useful in helping us vanish the vain and ridiculous terrors that torment certain individuals whose education has either been neglected or else is full of preoccupations, the children of ignorance].[16] The arrival of the Gothic in Spain was late by comparison with other European countries and certainly uneven. Given how contemporary socio-political forces – largely the state and the Church – made circulation difficult, it is perhaps not an exaggeration to claim that the Gothic novel was popular and thrived *despite* all the obstacles that were put in its way.

The First Spanish Gothic Writers

Since the Gothic to which Spanish authors were exposed was predominantly of the didactic, explained supernatural variety, and since the publishing context favoured moralistic rational fiction, national Gothic production largely followed Radcliffean parameters. This has led to the critical perception that Spain never truly developed a substantial or remarkable Gothic tradition of its own, at least during the late-eighteenth and early-nineteenth centuries. The difficulty of exploring the irrational at a time when this was either discouraged or forbidden, coupled with what appears to have been scant literary output with little impact, has led some critics to conclude that 'salvo en contadas ocasiones, la novela de terror española sólo es capaz de recoger los elementos o motivos adoptados por autores extranjeros' [save for a few exceptions, the Spanish horror novel was only capable of gathering elements or motifs developed by foreign authors].[17] It is true that many of the first literary experiments, from José de Cadalso's unfinished lyrical poem *Noches lúgubres* [Lugubrious Nights] in 1771 (published 1789–90) to Gaspar Zavala y Zamora's *La Eumenia, ó la Madrileña* (1805) [Eumenia, or the

16 D. Santiago de Alvarado de la Peña, 'El traductor', in Mis Ana de Radcliff [sic], *Adelina, ó la abadía en la selva: Novela histórica* (Madrid: Imprenta de I. Sancha, 1830), pp. v–viii (pp. v–vi).
17 Enrique Rubio Cremades, 'La novela histórica del romanticismo español', *Historia de la literatura española: Siglo XIX (I)* (Madrid: Espasa-Calpe, 1996), pp. 610–42 (p. 615).

Madrilenian] and Jerónimo Martín de Bernardo's *El emprendedor, ó, Aventuras de un español en el Asia* (1805) [The Entrepreneur, or Memories of a Spaniard in Asia], were only incidentally or episodically Gothic. These new hybrids, utilising elements from the historical novel, the sentimental novel and the chivalric romance, were not predominantly Gothic insofar as they neither aimed to scare readers nor conceived of fictional horror as a valid and pleasurable experience in its own right. Instead, the Gothic was evoked at the level of atmosphere, through the architectonically macabre (cemeteries, gloomy forests or dark subterranean passages) or the oneiric (visions of death and other bad omens, but also cautionary apparitions) in episodes in which characters learnt valuable lessons. In the case of the best known of these early novels, Vicente Martínez Colomer's *El Valdemaro* (1792) [Valdemaro], the fantastic moments are quickly abandoned and sometimes left unexplained, their narrative effect privileged over their metaphorical or allegorical meanings.

The influence of British and French Gothic would become more pronounced in the years to follow, after a wave of previously untranslated novels, including works by Ann Radcliffe, Catherine Cuthbertson, Mrs Harley, Walter Scott and a number of reprinted editions, began to flood the market in the late 1820s and 1830s. Of the Spanish writers who attempted to adapt the European vogue for the Gothic to Spanish letters, Pascual Pérez y Rodríguez did so most seamlessly. A priest and photographer, he published both anonymously and under the pseudonyms J. R. and P. J. P, possibly to avoid either censorship or disrepute. He wrote three novels, *La torre gótica, ó, El espectro de Limberg* (1831) [The Gothic Tower, or The Limberg Spectre], the only Spanish novel of the time to bear the word 'Gothic' in its title; *El hombre invisible, ó, Las ruinas de Munsterhall* (1833) [The Invisible Man, or The Munsterhall Ruins]; and *La urna sangrienta, ó, El panteón de Scianella* (1834) [The Bloody Urn, or the Scianella Pantheon]. The latter is one of the most 'Gothic' Spanish texts of the nineteenth century; its pages are a true catalogue of Gothic motifs, including an apparent haunting, disembodied voices and mysterious lights, gruesome murders, a dark underground chapel and an equally dismal prison, hidden doors and subterranean passages, vanishings, mistaken identities, a fortune-telling hermit who lives in a cave and the bleeding urn of the fiction's title. The novel is also framed as the contents of an Italian manuscript (translated to the Spanish from the English) that is discovered by a travelling Englishman, a narrative device probably borrowed from Radcliffe's recently translated *The Italian*. At the same time, though, Pérez y Rodríguez does not merely replicate a well-worn Gothic formula, for he is forced to adapt the product to the Spanish context, its readers and cultural arbiters. As a result, his Gothic novels are extremely didactic – the gruesomeness and thrills masquerade as moral lessons – and must explain away their hauntings. For López Santos, 'la exaltación de la religión, pero también la búsqueda incesante de la verosimilitud literaria y del realismo más palmario' [the praise of religion, but also the incessant search for literary verisimilitude and the clearest form of realism] are other key indicators of the novel's unique Spanish qualities.[18]

More radical and transgressive writings came from those authors who were forced into exile. Luis Gutiérrez, journalist and writer, published his epistolary novel *Cornelia Bororquia, o La víctima de la Inquisición* [Cornelia Bororquia, or Victim of the Inquisition] in 1801 in France. In this narrative, a pious woman, Cornelia, becomes prey to the lascivious desires of the villainous Archbishop of Seville. Stabbing him in self-defence, she is found guilty of murder and executed by the Inquisitors, who are painted as cruel, merciless and morally corrupt while Cornelia is celebrated for her martyr-like resolution and faith. Significantly, and in a plea for empathy, Cornelia is presented as a real character, her life offered up as an example of the tragedy brought about by an institutional body that is 'injusto y tiránico, ajeno de una nación libre e ilustrada' [unjust and tyrannical, alien to a free and enlightened nation].[19] This incendiary novel would not be available in Spain for 20 years and would quickly find its way into the Inquisition's list of banned books. Joseph Blanco White's *Vargas: A Tale of Spain* (1822), initially published in London in English and an effective expansion and re-imagining of the same story, was less indignant and more mordant, bringing together elements of the Gothic with narrative tropes derived from the historical novel – Blanco White was Walter Scott's first Spanish translator – but furnishing the narrative with a happy ending. Just as in Gutiérrez's novel, Cornelia's tragedy serves to present Protestantism and England as 'free and enlightened' by comparison to Spain.[20] The grotesque treatment of the members of the Inquisition and the macabre rendering of their prisons make these anticlerical texts an alternative strand of the realist Gothic. Gutiérrez and Blanco White's versions of monastic hell are based on real blood-curdling

---

18 Miriam López Santos, 'Introducción', Pascual Pérez y Rodríguez, *La urna sangrienta o el panteón de Scianella* (Madrid: Siruela, 2010), pp. 13–25 (p. 16).
19 Luis Gutiérrez, *Cornelia Bororquia, o La víctima de la Inquisición* (Madrid: Cátedra, 2005), p. 75.
20 Joseph Blanco White, *Vargas: A Tale of Spain* (London: Baldwin, Cradock and Joy, 1822), p. 296.

events (stories similar to Cornelia's were indeed recorded by historians) and may thus be read as a challenge to simplistic readings of the Gothic of the time as necessarily escapist or attenuated.

The 1830s was also a decade that witnessed a flurry of Romantic activity; in fact, in his analysis of the Romantic movement in Spain, Ricardo Navas Ruiz describes the years between 1834 and 1850 as the period of the 'triunfo romántico' [Romantic triumph].[21] Novels such as Ramón López Soler's *Los bandos de Castilla, ó El caballero del cisne* (1830) [The Clans of Castile or The Knight of the Swan], Mariano José de Larra's *El doncel de don Enrique el doliente* (1834) [Henry the Infirm's Page] and José de Espronceda's *Sancho Saldaña, ó El castellano de Cuéllar* (1834) [Sancho Saldaña, or the Castilian of Cuéllar] were technically historical novels insofar as they fictionalised 'real' historical episodes: fifteenth-century tensions between Castile and Aragon; incidents that took place during Henry the Infirm's Court in the fifteenth century; and the rivalry between Alfonso X of Castile and his son Sancho in the thirteenth century, respectively. But into their chronicles these writers wove a number of Gothic scenarios, such as the apparent return of the dead or characters with seemingly magical powers, broadly for their affective appeal. Since the remit was verisimilitudinous, supernatural elements inevitably had to be explained away – the only exception is the 'Doña Jimena' episode in *Los bandos de Castilla*, which features what appears to be a 'real' ghostly vision. The Gothic also persisted in the atmospherics of certain scenes, with thrilling moments sometimes taking place in dark, scary sepulchres and other appropriately Gothic spaces. Another of Espronceda's writings, the narrative poem *El estudiante de Salamanca* (1840) [The Student of Salamanca] that was inspired by the Don Juan legend and Gottfried August Bürger's poem *Lenore* (1774), is perhaps the most unashamedly Gothic text in early nineteenth-century Spanish letters. Not only is the rotting spectre of Don Félix's beloved portrayed as 'real' within the fictional confines of the poem, she is also described in terms of an abject and visceral horror that had previously only been conceivable in foreign literature.

Early Gothic Short Stories and the 'Folletín' Novel

The fact that there is evidence of a steady Gothic production before and after the rise and peak of Romanticism in Spain (1814–50) suggests that either the Gothic exceeded the parameters of Romanticism or that the Gothic mode

---

21 Ricardo Navas Ruiz, *El romanticismo español* (Madrid: Cátedra, 1990), p. 94.

continued to evolve even after the former's decline. One of the places to which the Gothic would migrate was the newspaper and the literary magazine, especially as literacy rose steadily throughout the following six decades.[22] The earliest Gothic short stories that we have been able to trace are the anonymous 'Cartas del otro mundo' (1818) [Letters from the Beyond]; Blanco White's 'The Fortress of Seville' (1825), written in English and published in England; the anonymous 'Diálogo de muertos' [1828] [Dialogue among the Dead]; and Serafín Estébanez Calderón's 'Los tesoros de la Alhambra' (1832) [The Treasures of the Alhambra], all of which show influences from the British and French Gothic traditions. The translation and reception of E. T. A. Hoffmann and Edgar Allan Poe's tales, which began to appear in the 1830s and 1850s respectively, provided considerable inspiration to such nineteenth-century Spanish writers as Miguel de los Santos Álvarez; Gertrudis Gómez de Avellaneda; Antonio Ros de Olano; Rafael Serrano Alcázar; Pedro Antonio de Alarcón; and Emilia Pardo Bazán.[23] The legitimisation of Hoffmann and Poe, however partial, made it possible for Spain to develop its own tradition of the 'fantastique' tale, one that, as we show below, grew to become a major artistic strand during the *fin de siècle*.

A whole new world of imaginative possibilities was also opened up by the inclusion of serialised fiction in the press as a marketing tool, a practice that started in Britain with *The Lady's Magazine* (1770–1847) in the eighteenth century and which soon travelled to Spain. The 'folletín', a word adapted from the French 'feuilleton' to encompass various types of melodramatic serialised fiction, some of which would later be published as books, peaked in popularity during the mid-1840s. It continued to be in vogue throughout the rest of the nineteenth century. Although it is tempting to compare the 'folletín' with the British 'penny blood' or 'penny dreadful', the reality is that Spain did not develop any full-blown Gothic texts the likes of James Malcolm Rymer and / or Thomas Peckett Prest's *The String of Pearls* (1846) or Rymer's *Varney the Vampire* (1847). Rather, the novels to come out of this period were much more interested in exploring ill-fated relationships, in revising the political past, such as the recent Carlist Wars of the 1830s, and in defending liberal ideas. In some respects, these preoccupations showcase the 'realist' principles that would become ingrained within Spanish letters,

---

22 Jean-François Botrel, 'Los nuevos lectores en la España del siglo XIX', *Siglo Diecinueve* 2 (1996): 47–64 (p. 50).
23 See David Roas, *Hoffmann en España: Recepción e influencias* (Madrid: Biblioteca Nueva, 2002); Roas, *La sombra del cuervo: Edgar Allan Poe y la literatura fantástica del siglo XIX* (Madrid: Devenir, 2011).

especially after the publication of Fernán Caballero's *La gaviota* (1849) [The Seagull] and Benito Pérez Galdós's *Episodios Nacionales* (1872–1912) [National Episodes]. Nonetheless, the Gothic did manifest in a number of these new fictions, much as it did in the historical novels of Larra or Espronceda, albeit episodically – to build up fear or suspense, both basic emotions in the creation of cliff-hangers, or to represent grotesque and reprehensible characters, as in Juan Martínez Villergas's *Los misterios de Madrid* (1844–5) [The Mysteries of Madrid].

The most well-known of the 'folletínes' to utilise Gothic elements took inspiration from French writers like Alexandre Dumas and Charles Paul de Kock but were particularly influenced by the publication of Eugène Sue's phenomenally successful *Les mystères de Paris* (1842–3) [The Mysteries of Paris]. The first of the novel's 150 instalments began with a warning 'alert[ing] readers to the sinister scenes that await them. If they proceed, they will find themselves in strange places, foul urban abscesses that teem with criminals as terrifying and revolting as swamp creatures.'[24] The novel does explore the underbelly of Paris, and its criminals could be compared to the aristocratic tyrants in Radcliffe, yet the emotion sought by its narrative is suspense, not fear. Similarly, the text does not resort to the supernatural, so that the principal Gothic elements remain the general premise, the revelation of a secret identity, and the titillations afforded by the author's insight into an underworld of vice. Gothic motifs are adapted to the setting of the modern metropolis – where, after all, the main 'folletín' readers resided – to give birth to the urban Gothic that would, in Britain, be explored by writers such as George W. M. Reynolds or Charles Dickens, and which may be described as 'a Gothic *of* the city'.[25] These are the parameters within which Spanish 'folletín' novels such as José Nicasio Milà de Roca's *Los misterios de Barcelona* (1844) [The Mysteries of Barcelona], Villergas's *Los misterios de Madrid* [The Mysteries of Madrid] and Antonio Altadill's *Barcelona y sus misterios* (1860) [Barcelona and Its Mysteries], comparable in their scope and thematic interests, need to be situated.[26] In them, Gothic affect does not predominate, but simply serves narrative purposes in a number of episodes.

---

24 Eugène Sue, *The Mysteries of Paris*, trans. by Carolyn Betensky and Jonathan Loesberg (London: Penguin, 2015), p. 3.
25 Robert Mighall, *A Geography of Victorian Gothic Fiction: Mapping History's Nightmares* (Oxford: Oxford University Press, 2003), p. 30; italics in original.
26 Cristina Delano, 'Gothic tales of the liberal nation in Juan Martínez Villergas's *Los misterios de Madrid* (1844–1845)', *Bulletin of Hispanic Studies* 93:3 (2016): 269–83.

Key to Sue's novel was its social awareness. *The Mysteries of Paris*'s sensational depiction of crime, prostitution, poverty and the tragic predicament of the working classes may be read as an act of exploitation, since it sensationalised the plight of those who could not represent themselves, but the text was also concerned with bringing about political change through melodramatic exposition. This was most certainly the case with some of the Spanish 'folletín' novels, which, if anything, underscored and sometimes privileged their politics and sentimentalism over narrative action. Wenceslao Ayguals de Izco's *Pobres y ricos, ó La bruja de Madrid* (1849–50) [The Poor and the Rich, or The Witch of Madrid] is a representative example. Here, the grotesque Inés, a deformed and mutilated woman forced into poverty and fortune-telling, is revealed to be Adela, the long-dead mother of a nobleman; her ability to predict the future, a supernatural trait that is explained as a mere gift for empathy and an interest in human psychology, grants her the 'witch' appellative of the title. Adela's life of misery, a direct result of the duke's reluctance to marry her because of her lower social status, is improved thanks to the charity and affections of Eduardo and his intended, Enriqueta. Adela's many bad omens regarding the possible union between Eduardo and Enriqueta end up saving them from incest as, in the end, it is discovered that Adela mothered them both. Ayguals de Izco makes the most of his character's apparent powers in passages that either describe vivid demonic nightmares or offer horrific descriptions of her body. Yet his real objective is to paint Adela as a social martyr who encapsulates the inequalities of a contemporary Spain that must embrace liberal principles in the face of systemic inequality. Appropriately, *La bruja de Madrid* is prefaced by an introduction that condemns the actions of king Ferdinand VII (suppressor of the liberal press) and makes a plea for the need to find virtue in human qualities, and not in riches, so that 'una verdadera fraternidad reemplace el odio que ciertas pasiones de índole bastarda hacen germinar entre POBRES Y RICOS' [a true fellowship may replace the hatred between THE RICH AND THE POOR that is born from certain passions of a bastardly nature].[27]

Legends and the Folkloric Gothic

The decades between the 1850s and 1870 also saw the publication of Gustavo Adolfo Bécquer's historical legends, another key manifestation of the Gothic in mid-to-late nineteenth-century Spain. Despite their

---

27 Wenceslao Ayguals de Izco, *La bruja de Madrid* (Barcelona: Editorial Taber, 1969), p. 32.

publication in the magazine *El Contemporáneo* [The Contemporary] and other periodicals, and in stark contrast to the modern urban mores of the 'folletín', Bécquer's legends are set in a mystical medieval past that is populated by lovelorn knights, moonlit ruins and malevolent spirits. Collected posthumously in the volume *Rimas y Leyendas* (1871) [Rhymes and Legends], the introspective tone and cult of sensibility that permeates these stories, together with the incorporation of historical motifs or popular folklore, have led them to be labelled a belated expression of Romanticism. Although legends had long been part of the literary landscape, they became an object of renewed interest and attention in the first half of the nineteenth century among Romantic authors, who regarded them as vessels for the *Volkgeist* – the spirit of the nation unpolluted by foreign trends. Often these stories were presented as part of an oral tradition that had been passed down by an old nursemaid or a similar metonymic embodiment of 'the people'. Like the motif of the found manuscript so popular in early Gothic literature, this was just another narrative device to deflect attention from the author and to insert the story within a wider literary tradition. The writer José Zorrilla features as a major exponent of the genre, with seven volumes of poetry that appeared between 1837 and 1840 entitled *Poesías* [Poems] and *Cantos del trovador: Colección de leyendas y tradiciones históricas* [Songs of the Troubadour: Collection of Legends and Historical Traditions]. The period also saw the publication of decidedly Gothic manifestations of the genre, such as the aforementioned 'Los tesoros de la Alhambra', together with Eugenio de Ochoa's 'El castillo del espectro' (1835) [The Castle of the Spectre] and José Augusto Ochoa's 'Beltrán: cuento fantástico' (1835) [Beltrán: A Fantastic Tale]. Yet while there is no scarcity of earlier examples, Bécquer's *Leyendas* are, together with Espronceda's *El estudiante de Salamanca*, the most overtly Gothic texts forged by Spanish Romanticism. In 'El miserere' (1862) [The Miserere] Bécquer narrates the annual rise of Templar monks from the tombs to sing the psalm of the story's title in passages that are replete with sublime horrors and terrors: 'contrastaban con sus descarnadas mandíbulas y los blancos dientes las oscuras cavidades de los ojos de sus calaveras ..., diciendo con voz baja y sepulcral, pero con una desgarradora expresión de dolor, el primer versículo del salmo de David: "Miserere mei, Deus, secundum magnam misericordiam tuam!"' [their fleshless jaws and white teeth were at odds with the dark eye sockets of their skulls ... as they uttered in a low, sepulchral voice, but with a heartrending expression of grief, the first verse of the psalm of David: 'Have mercy upon me. Oh God, according to thy loving kindness'].[28]

'El miserere' is a good example of a Catholic Gothic fiction that deftly merges thrills and scares with sacred motives, celebrating the creed as a redemptive force rather than as a symptom of superstition. 'Maese Pérez, el organista' (1861) [Master Pérez, the Organist] and 'La cruz del diablo' (1860) [The Devil's Cross] similarly weave the sinister and supernatural with Catholic iconography into a new pattern: both are unmistakably Gothic, yet patently Spanish. Terror does not always feature as the main intent in these legends – sometimes the supernatural erupts as hubristic punishment. For example, both 'La ajorca de oro' (1861) [The Gold Bracelet] and 'El beso' (1863) [The Kiss] feature reanimated statues that chastise transgressors. In the latter, a French Napoleonic officer, infatuated with the statue of a Spanish noblewoman, attempts to kiss her, only to be struck down violently by her equally lifeless spouse, who has come to life to defend her virtue. Set during the War of Independence, Bécquer's text celebrates the resistance of the Spanish population, with stone statues joining the cause.

Written at a time when the realist novel spearheaded by Benito Pérez Galdós was firmly establishing itself as the only legitimate vehicle to discuss the social issues of the day, Bécquer's legends are seen as the nostalgic escapist residue of a bygone era. This is reflected in the critical labelling of Bécquer as a 'postromantic' author. *El rayo de luna* (1862) [The Moonbeam] epitomises such a reading. It tells the tale of Manrique, the canonical Romantic hero, who chases a ray of moonlight through the eerie ruins of an abandoned Templars' monastery in the mistaken belief that it embodies his ideal woman. Manrique's musings echo the sorrows of a Wertherian martyr rather than of someone concerned with the repercussions of the Industrial Revolution. Similarly, one cannot escape the traditionalist worldview that pervades legends of a homogeneous God-fearing nation during a fabled golden age. Over time, Bécquer's collected *Leyendas* became a byword for the genre in Spain, but Bécquer himself remained far from unengaged in politics. The myth of the author as a penniless bohemian emerged only posthumously and was created by friends who deliberately omitted an extensive journalistic output in their curation of his writings.[29]

Published around the same time as Bécquer's work we find legends with very different ideological aims, such as *La dama de Amboto* (1857) [The Lady of

---

28 Gustavo Adolfo Bécquer, *Leyendas* (Madrid: Cátedra, 2002), p. 288.
29 See Rica Brown, 'The Bécquer legend', *Bulletin of Hispanic Studies* 18:69 (1941): 4–18.

Amboto], by Gertrudis Gómez de Avellaneda. Similarly set in a medieval past, it retells the myth of Abel and Cain with María Urraca, the Lady of Amboto of the title, in the role of a fratricidal sibling, driven to murder to maintain her economic independence. Frustrated that, as the male heir, her younger brother will inherit everything, María throws him off a cliff on a dark and stormy night, only later, haunted by his presence, to hurl herself from the same precipice. '¿Qué me quiere, pues, ese fantasma?' [What then does this ghost want from me?] the Lady of Amboto laments in a speech reminiscent of Lady Macbeth, '¿[c]ómo vuelve a saltar aquella sangre odiada, para salpicar mi frente, caliente y espumosa todavía?' [How can that hated blood return to spray my forehead, still warm and foamy?].[30]

Although the legend lost its discursive currency in the closing decades of the nineteenth century in favour of the novel, it remained a staple in countless periodicals, popular with readers and a profitable pursuit for writers, including realist stalwarts such as Leopoldo Alas 'Clarín', Emilia Pardo Bazán and Vicente Blasco Ibañez.[31] Nor did it remain completely removed from the present, as writers continued to revisit past episodes to comment on current affairs. Thus in *El encubierto* (1883) [The Shrouded One], the writer Julia de Asensi retells the legend of an enigmatic figure who claimed to be the legitimate heir of the Catholic Monarchs and whose appearance prompted a clash between his supporters and the government of Carlos I in the early sixteenth century. In Asensi's retelling, the pretender has been murdered by the king's men, only allegedly to haunt the room in which he met his death, his memory renewing the strife between sympathisers and detractors and even dividing families. Penned in the aftermath of the last Carlist War (1872–6), the historical parallels between the two dynastic disputes that prompted the fracturing of the country are clear. One could also argue that this continual revisiting of the Carlist Wars makes them, alongside the twentieth-century Civil War, one of the more Gothicized civil conflicts in Spanish history.

Fin-de-siècle Spanish Gothic

As the nineteenth century drew to a close, so the growing fascination with scientific progress and its capacity for disruption made the figure of the mad

---

30 Gertrudis Gómez de Avellaneda, 'La dama de Amboto', *Leyendas del siglo XIX* (Madrid: Akal, 2013), pp. 153–62 (p. 160).
31 Juan Molina Porras, 'Introducción', *Leyendas del siglo XIX* (Madrid: Akal, 2013), pp. 9–47 (pp. 15–16).

doctor as familiar to Spanish readers as it was to their continental counterparts.[32] Pérez Galdós could thus describe the abode of Dr Anselmo as resembling a 'laboratorio de esos que hemos visto en más de una novela' [one of those laboratories that we have seen in more than one novel].[33] So begins *La sombra* [The Shadow], a novella originally serialised in *La Revista de España* in 1871 and which follows the aforementioned doctor and his sinister doppelgänger – the shadow invoked in the title. *La sombra* shows that not even the main ambassadors of realism were immune to flights of fancy, and crucially it testifies to the influence of Poe in the development of the Gothic short story in Spain. Poe soon overtook Hoffmann in popularity, becoming the most translated author in the late nineteenth century.[34] This is not to say that Hoffmann did not continue to leave an imprint on the Gothic imagination. On the contrary, Hoffmann's influence was vast, and lasted well into the closing decades of the century, as illustrated by José Selgas's *Escenas fantásticas* (1876) [Fantastic Vignettes] or Carlos Coello's *Cuentos inverosímiles* (1878) [Unlikely Tales]. The Hoffmannesque irruption of the supernatural and the oneiric into the quotidian characterises these tales and many others that appeared in the press, establishing Spain's own 'fantastique' tradition.

Yet it was Poe's penchant for maniacal personalities and his distortion of reality to grotesque extremes that increasingly informed much Spanish *fin-de-siècle* Gothic writing, signalling a move inwards towards the psychic landscapes of Robert Louis Stevenson's *Strange Case of Dr Jekyll and Mr Hyde* (1886) or Oscar Wilde's *The Picture of Dorian Gray* (1890). Spanish literature did not lack obsessive scientists like Dr Jekyll, cut from the same cloth as the earlier Dr Frankenstein. In addition to Dr Anselmo, this gallery includes the optometrist Ojeda in José Fernández Bremón's short story *Un crimen científico* (1875) [A Scientific Crime], which narrates his transplants of animal eyes onto humans and whose victims predate the hubristic hybrids of the better-known H. G. Wells's novel *The Island of Doctor Moreau* (1896). Like the French-sounding Moreau, some of Fernández Bremón's unhinged explorers are of foreign extraction. In *Gestas, ó el idioma de los monos* (1872) [Gestas, or The Language of Monkeys], the half-German linguist Don Crisóstomo becomes fixated on turning the eponymous ape into the perfect gentleman so Gestas can colonise part of Africa on behalf of Spain, although his plans are foiled

---

32 Six, *Gothic Terrors*, p. 71.
33 Benito Pérez Galdós, *La sombra* (Barcelona: Ediciones Internacionales Universitarias, 1997), p. 10.
34 Roas, *La sombra del cuervo*, p. 12.

by the unscrupulous British diplomat Mr Cuckoo. In *El último mono* (1887) [The Last Monkey], Dr Oxford is revealed to be an orangutan, a product of an accelerated evolution. The story thus taps into the atavistic anxieties triggered by Darwinism. Carlos Coello's short story *Hombres y animales* (1871) [Men and Animals] follows the descent into madness of Sir James Lowe, compatriot of Mr Cuckoo and Dr Oxford, in his conviction that animals have their own language and in his attempts to decipher it. Narrated in the form of diary entries, the structure intentionally recalls the research journal that Charles Darwin kept during his voyage on the *Beagle*, while Lowe himself is a caricature of the English naturalist. The British nationality shared by all these mad doctors is no coincidence and suggests instead a wish to discredit the sanity of a key colonial rival. Spain wanted to avoid the fate of the British empire, which it figured as being in thrall to godless materialism and mercenary opportunism, and instead 'responded vigorously by rejecting the emphasis on markets and profits and defending the putative civilising mission of the Spanish conquerors'.[35] A wish to discredit rival empires and fear of barbarism are by no means a uniquely Spanish response to the period's pressures, but rather link the country to the imperial Gothic so thoroughly documented in English literature, from Bram Stoker's *Dracula* (1897) and H. G. Wells's *The Island of Doctor Moreau* to Joseph Conrad's *Heart of Darkness* (1899). In these and other stories, Gothic imagery is used to articulate fears of 'individual regression or going native' as well as 'an invasion of civilization by the forces of barbarism or demonism'.[36]

While Fernández Bremón's and Coello's grotesque vignettes are punctuated by humour, their contemporary Justo Sanjurjo López de Gomara explored the potential horrors of science in *Locuras humanas* [Human Madness]. Originally published as a short story collection in 1887 in Buenos Aires, it contains 'Vida cerebral' [Life of the Brain], a narrative that is worth highlighting for its status as the 'first truly horrific mad science short story in Spain'.[37] 'Vida cerebral' recounts the neurological experiments of the French doctor Charcot as he maintains alive the decapitated head of a criminal only to be mauled to death when freeing it from its constraints. It might not be a coincidence that the morally lax scientist shares his surname with Jean-Martin

---

35 Christopher Schmidt-Nowara, *The Conquest of History: Spanish Colonialism and National Histories in the Nineteenth Century* (Pittsburgh, PA: University of Pittsburgh Press, 2006), p. 4.
36 Patrick Brantlinger, *Rule of Darkness: British Literature and Imperialism, 1830–1914* (Ithaca, NY: Cornell University Press, 1988), p. 230.
37 Aldana Reyes, *Spanish Gothic*, p. 123.

Charcot, another foreigner and the founder of modern neurology, remembered today for his problematic experiments with hysterical women at La Salpêtrière hospital in France in the late nineteenth century.

The hysterical or swooning heroine figured as a staple in early Gothic repertoire – a language that by the second half of the century was firmly established in the popular imagination and which was ripe for parody or deconstruction. Not only a useful platform to articulate anxieties over Spain's waning colonial power, the Gothic became an equally effective tool to denounce women's continued lack of agency. Worth highlighting in this context is Emilia Pardo Bazán, one of the few women admitted to the canon thanks to a novelistic output that, like that of her male contemporaries, diligently chronicles the shifting social landscape at the turn of the century. Yet parallel to these, she produced a vast body of short stories, many of which could be labelled female Gothic, most notably 'Vampiro' (1901) [Vampire], 'La resucitada' (1908) [The Revived Woman] and 'La emparedada' (1907) [The Walled-Up Woman]. In these fictions, vampirism, demonic possession, madness, phantoms and other Gothic elements are appropriated to show the invisibility of women in contemporary society. In 'La resucitada', for example, a woman who has been buried prematurely returns home only to retrace her steps to oblivion after enduring the indifference of her family. Pardo Bazán is not the first woman to utilise the Gothic in such a way, nor was she the only writer to do so during her time. Her privileged position as a well-studied author only serves to highlight the little critical attention that, until recently, has been paid to the Gothic elements in her work, particularly to the many short stories that amply showcase her cultivation of the mode.

As this chapter has shown, unearthing the Gothic past reconnects Spanish literary production to the main intellectual streams and preoccupations of a period often disingenuously recast as essentially realist. It also prompts us to acknowledge the extent to which the Gothic mode in nineteenth-century Spain became an evocative language moulded by local events, including the practice of cultural censorship and the ongoing Carlist conflicts that would haunt the country's literary production. Recovering forgotten Gothic writers and texts sheds new light on Spain's place within the cultural coordinates of nineteenth-century Europe, and recasts the country as both an important consumer and contributor to the Gothic tradition.

2.14
The Gothic in Nineteenth-Century Italy

FRANCESCA SAGGINI

> Perhaps he lives, even then, when to his ear
> Is silent the sweet harmony of day:
> May not the cares, the vigils of his friends
> once more awaken it? Celestial
> is this communion with the cherished dead—
> a lovely and a holy gift to men.

The Italians; or, The Penitents of the Gothic: Paralipomena of an Occulted Genre

Is there an Italian Gothic of the nineteenth century? At first glance, the question may appear redundant, particularly for Anglophone readers accustomed to associating Italy not just with the Grand Tourists and nostalgic antiquarianism of the eighteenth century, but also with the imaginative geography of the Gothic canon, the cultural and topological setting of masterpieces such as Horace Walpole's *The Castle of Otranto* (1764) and the novels of Ann Radcliffe, from *A Sicilian Romance* (1790) to *The Italian; or, The Confessional of the Black Penitents* (1796–7), to mention just two authors linked by a pervasive interdiscursive and intertextual Italophile network.[1] Given its deeper implications, my opening question should therefore be broadened and qualified: was there an indigenous or autochthonous Gothic in nineteenth-century Italy, a local reworking of English (and perhaps also Continental) forms and models – a Gothic 'under the sun', so to speak,

---

* My thanks to Dr Maria Giovanna Pontesilli, Director of the Polo Bibliotecario Umanistico-Sociale of the University of Tuscia and to Dr Clotilde Valeri, for her efficient and tireless help with interlibrary loans. Without this expertise and support I would not have been able to consult so many otherwise unobtainable texts.

1 Epigraph: Ugo Foscolo, *The Sepulchres. Addressed to Ippolito Pindemonte*, trans. attrib. to Stratford Canning, Viscount Stratford de Redcliffe (London, 1820?), p. 1.

capable of exercising its aesthetic and thematic influence at a supranational level? Addressing this question is not only worthwhile in itself, but also sheds light on certain aesthetic and cultural-historical complications raised by this period. Such complications become most apparent if we consider the question from the privileged, albeit somewhat deceptive, point of view of two giants of Italian letters, here chosen as symbolic bookends of a century so crucial to Italy's political, linguistic and cultural development: the writer Alessandro Manzoni (1785–1873) and the philosopher and critic Benedetto Croce (1866–1952).

Italo Calvino, the undisputed master of twentieth-century fantastic literature, seemingly laid a tombstone over any vestige of Italian Gothic literature when he stated in 1983 that, with the exception perhaps of Arrigo Boito and a few other authors belonging to the so-called 'Scapigliatura' movement, there had been no nineteenth-century fantastic literature to speak of: were he to mention it alongside its European or American counterparts, it would be 'merely out of obligation' – to satisfy a purely parochial aspiration.[2] As if to disprove Calvino, but only in part, the following year the literary scholar Enrico Ghidetti published the collection *Notturno italiano* (1984), the first attempt to organise the corpus of Italian fantastic literature and further stimulate its study.[3] The story that opens Ghidetti's anthology, 'Narcisa' by the Milanese Luigi Gualdo, however, dates back only to 1868, as though to confirm that there was no Italian Gothic (or fantastic) literature worthy of note before the Scapigliati.

Notwithstanding Calvino's epitaph for Italian fantastic (and by extension Gothic) literature, other scholars over the past 40 years besides Ghidetti have laboured to unearth Italy's Gothic literary production from beneath the thick layers of canonical and ideologically informed generic categorisations that for decades had hidden it from sight – a fate all too common to genre literature. The result has been, on the one hand, a rediscovery of established authors, now recognised as capable of creating a distinct autochthonous Gothic typology (as we will see with *I promessi sposi* [The Betrothed] by Alessandro Manzoni and *Pinocchio* by Carlo Lorenzini, better known by his pseudonym, Collodi), and, on the other hand, an exploration of the Gothic's intersections

---

2 Italo Calvino (ed.), *Fantastic Tales: Visionary and Everyday* (Boston: Mariner Books, 1997), p. xvii.
3 Enrico Ghidetti (ed.), *Notturno italiano. Racconti fantastici dell'Ottocento* (Rome: Editori Riuniti, 1984). In addition to the excellent Preface to *Notturno italiano* (pp. vii–xii), Ghidetti also wrote *Dal racconto fantastico al romanzo popolare* (Rome: Editori Riuniti, 1987), a study that further explored the nineteenth-century genre novel.

with overlapping or adjacent genres, including the many varieties flourishing in the Anglophone world, such as sensational, detective and fantastic literature. Well before 1909–10 when the Sicilian Luigi Natoli (who wrote as 'William Galt') published *I Beati Paoli*, a dark, gripping historical-detection *feuilleton*, in the *Giornale di Sicilia*, the Italian Gothic of the nineteenth century had already provided sufficient evidence not only of its existence but also its originality.[4] We need only think of such nineteenth-century writers as Francesco Domenico Guerrazzi, Luigi Capuana, Giovanni Verga and Matilde Serao, not to mention recognised masters such as Giacomo Leopardi[5] and now-forgotten authors such as Diodata Saluzzo Roero and Vincenzo Linares; it was in fact Linares who, long before Natoli, first used the Beati Paoli sect (and title) in an 1840 story that curiously blended realism and esotericism. As with the statue of the Veiled Christ of the Cappella di Sansevero in Naples, the impartial eye can perceive the disquieting, unmistakable Gothic veining beneath the neoclassical 'moral beauty' and highly polished realism prized by the nineteenth century, as though the semes of realism, rationalism and didacticism could afford some protection from what lay beneath.

For the convenience of researchers who might be unfamiliar with nineteenth-century Italian literature, this chapter employs a two-pronged approach: on the one hand I will discuss the Gothic of the so-called classics, which developed alongside the historical novel of the first half of the nineteenth century, and for which translations are readily available. On the other hand, I will turn to 'popular' Gothic fiction, increasingly

---

4 Published as a volume in 1921, Natoli's novel has a Manichean structure pitting a heartless antagonist, don Raimondo Albamonte, against a powerful secret sect that operates underground beneath the city of Palermo. Occultism and revenge, conspiracies and persecuted maidens, physiognomic determinism and sinister landscapes: these are the familiar staples of Natoli's controversial Gothic – openly referencing Eugène Sue and the so-called 'Illuminati novels', but also the more disturbing actual abuses of a Sicilian criminal gang – discussed by Umberto Eco in the introduction to Luigi Natoli, *I Beati Paoli. Grande romanzo storico siciliano* (Palermo: Flaccovio, 1971).

5 Leopardi owned the 1804 Italian translation of Edmund Burke's 1757 *Philosophical Enquiry into the Origin of our Ideas of the Sublime and of the Beautiful*, which he drew upon in the posthumously published *Zibaldone di pensieri*, now available in several English translations, including *Zibaldone: The Notebooks of Leopardi* – edited by Michael Caesar and Franco D'Intino, trans. by Kathleen Baldwin, Richard Dixon, David Gibbons, Ann Goldstein, Gerard Slowey, Martin Thom and Pamela Williams (Harmondsworth: Penguin, 2013). Typical of Leopardi's ambivalent oscillations between Enlightenment and unreason, light and dark is the ironic 'Dialogo di Federico Ruysch e delle sue mummie' [Dialogue between Frederick Ruysch and his Mummies] (*c*. 1824; publ. in *Operette Morali*, 1827; trans. as *Essays, Dialogues and Thoughts*, by Patrick Maxwell, London: Walter Scott Ltd., 1880), in which science (the Dutch anatomist Ruysch) engages in a dialogue on and *with* death (the mummies in the scientist's study come back to life owing to a lunar alignment).

anthologised since the 1980s. Besides the shorter texts in these anthologies, I consider full-length Gothic novels first published as serials, as well as works readable within the famous 'limit of a single sitting' stipulated by Edgar Allan Poe in *The Philosophy of Composition* (1846) as indispensable to achieving the true poetic effect: short narratives, whether wholly Gothic or Gothic-inflected, that appeared in major newspapers and magazines of the time.[6] Providing a full bibliography of the latter is not possible here, though I include essential references to enable further research. In both cases, I have paid particular attention to the first half of the century; neglected by Ghidetti, these decades have long been considered the terra incognita of the Italian Gothic and therefore deserve fuller investigation. Finally, I touch on nineteenth-century Italian translations of English and European Gothic works, a field worthy of an essay in its own right, as it was precisely through these works that many of the Italian authors mentioned here approached the Gothic – whether to reject, adapt or wholly adopt it.

Enduring Delights and Fascinations of the Mind: Alessandro Manzoni and the Romantic Gothic[7]

Continuously taught in Italian secondary schools from 1870 to 2010, *I promessi sposi* (1827) [*The Betrothed*] by the Milanese Alessandro Manzoni is universally acknowledged to be the first great Italian novel, and as such it greatly influenced later authors from both a thematic-structural standpoint and a linguistic one: it served as a model for the historical fiction that was quickly rising to prominence in Italy after 1820, in an historical-political context that spurred Italian novelists to create heroic examples of resistance to (foreign)

---

6 I have consulted the following magazines: *Antologia* (Florence); *Biblioteca Italiana* (Milan); *L'illustrazione italiana* (Milan); *Domenica del Corriere* (Milan); *Fanfulla della domenica* (Rome); and the newspapers *Capitan Fracassa* (Rome); *Fanfulla* (Florence; later Rome). For the first Italian translations of some of the Gothic authors, see, in particular, the contemporary periodicals *Gabinetto di lettura*. *Miscellanea di scrittori francesi, inglesi e tedeschi recati in Italia* and *Rivista contemporanea*, both published in Turin. The cities of publication outline a geographic-editorial web of the Italian Gothic (autochthonous and in translation) closely intertwined with the democratisation of literature and with the editorial strategies of the 'popular' nineteenth century, as detailed in the last section of this essay. Further information on periodicals is given below when discussing particular authors.
7 The title is adapted from Alessandro Manzoni, 'Letter on romanticism (1823)', intro. and trans. by Joseph Luzzi, *PMLA* 119:2 (2004): 299–316. Alessandro Manzoni, 'Lettera sul Romanticismo', in *Opere varie* (Milan: Fratelli Rechiedei Editori, 1881), pp. 583–97. This edition collects all the Manzoni theoretical writings mentioned in this essay.

oppression;[8] its language, for which Manzoni chose the current Florentine literary vernacular, was widely embraced as an instrument of Italy's nascent linguistic unity, a model of cohesion and a common strategy in the service of an otherwise fragmented kingdom.[9] As such, the novel became compulsory reading in secondary schools, and it remains to this day the keystone of the national literary canon promoted by ministerial education programmes – an institutionalised, centralised canon that, if we look closely, stands on a solid Gothic foundation the reach of which extends throughout the nineteenth century.

Manzoni published the novel in two editions: the so-called Ventisettana, written between 1824 and 1827, and translated into a heavily abridged English version by Charles Swan (Pisa, Niccolò Capurro, 1828); and the so-called Quarantana, further reworked linguistically and published in instalments from 1840 to 1842. The latter was anonymously translated, in full, as *The Betrothed Lovers: A Milanese Story of the Seventeenth Century* (London, James Burns, 1844), the title later simplified to *The Betrothed*. The novel employs well-known invariants of the Gothic genre: like *The Castle of Otranto*, it features a priest with a troubled past (Walpole's father Jerome and Manzoni's father Cristoforo) who opposes the abuses, inevitably of a sexual nature, of an overbearing feudal lord (the tyrant Manfred, a character who in Manzoni is split into two – Don Rodrigo and his henchman, the Innominato, 'the unnamed', who later repents of his evil ways); and the victimiser of a virtuous young woman (Isabella in Walpole and Lucia in Manzoni, both imprisoned by order of the scheming villain). Similarly, the Radcliffe school is represented by the convention of the angelic heroine's kidnapping (Lucia is held prisoner by the Innominato, a fate she shares with Radcliffe's Emily St Aubert and Ellena di Rosalba, together with a host of other Gothic heroines) and the dual focus, with resulting structural bifurcation, which produces an independent, picaresque subplot for the male protagonists (Vivaldi and Renzo).[10] This complex

---

8 Also worth recalling in this context is *Poesie di Ossian, antico poeta celtico* [The poems of Ossian, ancient Celtic poet] (Padua, 1763), an important translation by Melchiorre Cesarotti of the first *Poems of Ossian*. Other translations of James Macpherson followed, spreading the new canon-breaking aesthetic that rose to the fore in the nineteenth century. See Enrico Mattioda, 'Ossian in Italy: From Cesarotti to the Theater', in Howard Gaskill (ed.), *The Reception of Ossian in Europe* (London and New York: Bloomsbury, 2004), pp. 274–302.

9 Also worth noting is that, according to the records in the Catalogo del Servizio Bibliotecario Nazionale, the Italian translations of Radcliffe reached a peak from the mid-1860s through the 1870s, precisely when the scholastic edition of *I promessi sposi* was most widely used.

10 While there is no clear evidence that Manzoni read the Gothic classics, it remains a distinct possibility: Milan's public libraries held translations of Radcliffe into French, a

interdiscursive grid also allows for the inclusion of various other intertextual elements – specific similarities and reuses that, as several scholars have noted, are by no means accidental.[11]

Bandits, castles, convents, corrupt religious figures, ruthless tyrants – even an introduction (the anonymous seventeenth-century 'dilavato e graffiato autografo' [faded and scratched-out manuscript])[12] reminiscent of the Preface to the first edition of *The Castle of Otranto*: Manzoni plainly adopted and transposed onto Italian soil the genre's eighteenth-century topologies and plot typologies, by now somewhat stereotyped, but recently given new life on English soil by Walter Scott, who was widely read in Italy and well known to Manzoni. Equally undeniable, however, is that the novel defuses them in

language in which Manzoni was fluent. Walpole's novel was translated into Italian by Giovanni [Jean] Sivrac (London, 1795), probably a pseudonym employed by the author and typographer Gaetano Polidori, an occasional translator living in exile in London and the father of the well-known John William Polidori. Ann Radcliffe's major novels were also translated into Italian: the Neapolitan printer Gaetano Nobile published *Emilia e Valancourt* and *Elena e Vivaldi* in the 1820s, while in Livorno Assunto Barbani had published *Udolfo* a decade earlier. Matthew Gregory Lewis, who does not seem to have influenced Manzoni directly, was not translated into Italian until mid-century (*Il frate*, 1850, for the Ferrario Brothers in Milan, but almost 30 years elapsed before a second edition). For a detailed bibliography of translations into Italian of Gothic classics in the late eighteenth and nineteenth centuries, see Francesca Billiani, 'Appendix' to 'Delusional Identities: The Politics of the Italian Gothic and Fantastic', in Igino Ugo Tarchetti's Trilogy "Love in Art" and Luigi Gualdo's Short Stories "Hallucination", "The Song of Weber" and "Narcisa"', *Forum for Modern Language Studies* 44:4 (2008): 497–9, and Gianfranco de Turris, 'Gotico popolare italiano. Appunti per una bibliostoria', in Enzo Biffi Gentili, with Giorgio Barberi Squarotti, Valter Boggione and Barbara Zandrino (eds), *Neogotico tricolore. Letteratura e altro* (Milan and Cuneo: Cassa di Risparmio di Cuneo Foundation, 2015), pp. 130–6. On the reception of the English Gothic in Italy, see Céline Rodenas, 'La traduction des romans gothiques anglais vers l'italien à la fin du XVIIIe siècle et au début du XIXe siècle. Échanges culturels entre l'Angleterre et l'Italie. "Il Castello di Otranto" (1795) et "La foresta" (1813)', *Cercles* 34 (2015): 170–86. Finally, on Italian translations of Radcliffe, see also Rosamaria Loretelli and John Dunkley, 'Translating Ann Radcliffe's *The Italian*: André Morellet and Giovanni De Coureil', in Lidia De Michelis, Lia Guerra and Frank O'Gorman (eds), *Politics and Culture in Eighteenth-Century Anglo-Italian Encounters. Entangled Histories* (Newcastle: Cambridge Scholars, 2019), pp. 2–46. I thank my colleagues Loretelli and Dunkley for sharing their research with me.

11 Among the most convincing is Mariarosa Bricchi, '"Come una magnifica veste gittata sopra un manichino manierato e logoro". I "Promessi Sposi", il gusto gotico e Ann Radcliffe', *Autografo. La letteratura italiana e l'Europa nell'Ottocento* 31 (1995): 29–70. Bricchi references an idea expressed by Mario Praz in *The Romantic Agony* (Italian edition 1930, English trans. 1933): 'Manzoni's masterpiece is a magnificent garment over a mannered and worn-out lay figure'. Praz was the first critic to dwell on the Gothic antecedents of *I promessi sposi* from a comparatist perspective.

12 Alessandro Manzoni, *I promessi sposi, 1. Fermo e Lucia. Appendice storica sulla colonna infame; 2. I promessi sposi nelle due edizioni del 1840 e del 1825–27 raffrontate tra loro. Storia della colonna infame*, edited by Lanfranco Caretti, 2 vols (Turin: Einaudi, 1971), vol. 2, p. 5.

order to normalise and stabilise the more subversive and 'explosive' aspects of the genre, recoding them in line with a more emphatically Christian and providential literary typology.[13]

This is why the draft of *I promessi sposi* (traditionally referred to as *Fermo e Lucia* [Fermo and Lucia]) is of particular interest to scholars of the Gothic. Written between April 1821 and September 1823, just as the historical novel was gaining traction in Italy, this first version of the novel is filled with melodramatic contrasts, lurid overtones and long digressions that veer into sensationalism. These elements give *Fermo e Lucia* a blatantly *noir* flavour,[14] which Manzoni subsequently toned down or wholly suppressed in order to emphasise its more religiously inflected rational and moralising aspects. The revisions likewise involved subordinating history to imagination and it is no coincidence that at this time Manzoni was writing 'Del romanzo storico e, in genere, de' componimenti misti di storia e d'invenzione' [On the historical novel and, in general, on compositions created by mixing history and invention], an important essay published in 1845, but written at least a decade earlier. In the Quarantana, for example, the trials of the *untori* (those suspected of spreading the plague in Milan) form a separate appendix, *Storia della colonna infame* [History of the column of infamy], in which the strange and the wonderful (in the Hoffmannian sense) give way to the Christian tragic mode that became Manzoni's hallmark.[15] Likewise, special emphasis is placed on the evil Innominato's conversion – a revised section much praised for its psychological verisimilitude and an obvious choice for the 'moral considerations' imposed on nineteenth-century students – as well as on the chapters set in the lazaretto, where the victims of the plague end their miserable days. Originally the most horrifying sections of the novel, these chapters now become its true *kairòs*, awarding greater centrality to the mystery of God's judgement. But as Manzoni acknowledged, what had interested him most, at first, was the educational value of the representation of Evil, a concern that responded directly to the

---

13 Juri Lotman, *Culture and Explosion*, edited by Marina Grishakova (Berlin: De Gruyter, 2009).
14 A note on terminology is necessary here. I will employ the French *noir* (black) to refer to the Gothic *roman noir*, also known as *littérature noire*. See Terry Hale, 'Roman Noir', in Marie Mulvey-Roberts (ed.), *The Handbook of the Gothic* (Basingstoke: Palgrave Macmillan, 2009), pp. 307–9. For the contaminations between *roman noir* and *I promessi sposi*, see Maria Antonietta Frangipani, *Motivi del romanzo nero nella letteratura lombarda* (Rome: Editrice Elia, 1981).
15 Manzoni, *I promessi sposi*, vol. 2, pp. 901–1009.

moral reservations expressed against the novel (primarily of a 'Nordic', Anglo-German kind) by Piedmontese and Lombard intellectuals:

> Siamo stati più volte in dubbio se non convenisse stralciare dalla nostra storia queste turpi ed atroci avventure; ma esaminando l'impressione che ce n'era rimasta, leggendola dal manoscritto, abbiamo trovato che era un'impressione d'orrore; e ci è sembrato che la cognizione del male quando ne produce l'orrore sia non solo innocua ma utile.[16]

> [We have often been in doubt if it were not better to remove these nefarious and appalling adventures from our history; but in examining the impression they left when reading the manuscript, we found that it was an impression of horror; and it seemed to us that the knowledge of evil, when it produces a horror of it, is not only harmless but useful.]

The rhetorical question that Manzoni raises here prefigures – and justifies – the dark tenor of many horrific episodes in *Fermo e Lucia*, which were later removed. Among these is the story of Geltrude, better known as the Nun of Monza, a lengthy digression on the well-established Gothic theme of forced monastic vows (and their criminal consequences) first introduced by Denis Diderot in *La religeuse* [The nun] (1780–2), and given a sinister twist by the Gothic's anti-Catholicism (as in the story of Beatrice de las Cisternas, the Bleeding Nun of Matthew G. Lewis's *The Monk*, 1796).[17] In the first draft of Manzoni's novel, the fall of Geltrude, who is called simply 'la Signora' [the Lady] (possibly a reference to Sister Agnes/Signora Laurentini in *The Mysteries of Udolpho*), is effectively foreshadowed through two sensationalist similes: 'aveva la passione nell'animo e il serpente al fianco; e lo colse' [she had passion in her soul and a serpent by her side;

---

16 Manzoni, *Fermo e Lucia*, in *I promessi sposi*, vol. 1, p. 204.
17 See Diane Long Hoeveler, 'Anti-Catholicism and the Gothic Imaginary: The Historical and Literary Contexts', in Brett C. McInelly (ed.), *Religion in the Age of Enlightenment*, 5 vols (New York: AMS Press, 2012), vol. 3, pp. 1–31 and bibliography. The imaginative contamination with the monastic dramas of the revolutionary period (for example the French playwrights Jacques Marie Boutet, known as Monvel, and Marie-Joseph-Blaise de Chénier) is also evident in the iconography of Geltrude, '*non molto dissimile da un'attrice ardimentosa, di quelle che nei paesi separati dalla comunione cattolica facevano le parti di monaca in quelle commedie dove i riti cattolici erano soggetti di beffa e di parodia caricata*' [*not very unlike* a bold actress, like those who in countries separated from the Catholic communion played the nun in comedies where the Catholic rites were the object of mockery and heavy-handed parody] (*Fermo e Lucia*, vol. 1, p. 138; italics mine). Manzoni was also a playwright and theorist of the theatre, having already written a historical drama (*Il conte di Carmagnola* [The Count of Carmagnola], 1816–19) and a tragedy (*Adelchi*, 1820–2). The analogy in the quotation should therefore be read in light of this theatrical context, of which I believe he was fully cognisant.

and she grasped it].¹⁸ The dark episode is made even more shocking by the nun's brutal murder of an unfortunate novice who had witnessed and exposed Geltrude's dalliance with the 'serpent-seducer' Egidio, and whose body he then buries in a dark cellar under his quarters. Then there is the bloody episode of the Conte del Sagrato (the Innominato of the Quarantana), a ruthless murderer drawn with stylised Manicheanism: 'Il Conte prese di mira [quel misero] in questo spazio, lo colse, e lo stese a terra, ... e senza scomporsi, ritornò per la sua via ...' [The count took aim [at the wretch] in this place, struck him, and felled him to the ground, ... and unperturbed, returned whence he came].¹⁹ This heinous crime, committed on the *sagrato* (outside steps) of a church, allows Manzoni to reflect on the torments of remorse, as the count falls prey to a terrifying hallucination:

> E qui cominciarono a schierarsi dinanzi alla sua memoria tutti quelli ch'egli aveva cacciati o fatti cacciare dal mondo ...; tutti con i loro volti nell'atto di morire, e quelli che egli non aveva veduti, ma uccisi soltanto col comando, la sua fantasia dava loro i volti e gli atti.²⁰

> [And now his memory began to parade before him all those he had sent out of this world, or whose death he had ordered ...; their faces in the throes of death, and those he had not seen, but killed only by command, to them his imagination gave faces and gestures.]

Finally, there is the terrible sketch *à la* Goya of the death of Don Rodrigo, whom we see in the lazaretto, a mere husk of a man, deprived of reason, barefoot and almost naked. His mad flight on a runaway horse – which evokes the motif of the demonic cavalcade – is starkly contrasted with the cynical inhumanity of the eerie, hooded monks who collect the repulsive corpse of the once-arrogant baron and callously throw him 'su la cima d'un tristo mucchio, fra lo strepito e le bestemmie' [on top of a miserable heap, amidst the general tumult and execrations].²¹

A French translation of the Ventisettana led the way for the remarkable success of Manzoni's novel in Europe. Three English translations appeared within 15 years, confirming the growing reputation of the author, the same 'Genius of the Place' to whom Edward Bulwer Lytton dedicated the

---

18 Manzoni, *Fermo e Lucia*, p. 196. The contemporary English translations retained the original Italian 'la Signora' for Geltrude.
19 Manzoni, *Fermo e Lucia*, p. 226.   20 Manzoni, *Fermo e Lucia*, pp. 281–2.
21 Manzoni, *Fermo e Lucia*, pp. 605, 608.

historical novel *Rienzi, The Last of the Roman Tribunes* (1836).[22] Another admirer was Charles Dickens, probably drawn by a poetics that seamlessly blended historical scope and moral vision with exciting plot twists. Father Cristoforo's enigmatic words, 'può esser gastigo, può esser misericordia' [it may be punishment, it may be mercy],[23] uttered by the bedside of the dying villain Don Rodrigo, would not be out of place in *Oliver Twist* (1837–9), one of the works in which Dickens employs Gothic imaginary to great effect, particularly in the episode of Oliver's visit to the imprisoned Fagin. Likewise, the blood spilled by Egidio and his accomplices inevitably leaves its mark on their faces and on their actions, just as Nancy's blood indelibly stains her murderer, Sikes.

The influence of *Fermo e Lucia*'s Gothic style on the principal Italian authors of the nineteenth century was considerable, and might be traced in Giovanni Verga's *Storia di una capinera* [History of a blackcap], a magazine serial, published as a volume in 1870, that includes forced monastic vows. Immured in a convent, where she is eagerly scrutinised through the cell's double grating by the 'viventi che si affacciano alla tomba per vedere cadaveri che parlano e si muovono' [living who peer into the tomb to see corpses that speak and move],[24] Maria has been crushed – or better, buried alive – by her impossible love for the young Nino, leading to her madness and, inevitably, death (hence the epitextual reference to the blackcap, the caged bird symbolising imprisonment), against the background of a mid-sixteenth-century cholera epidemic in the city of Catania. Well before Verga, however, the Romantic Gothic (and later the Risorgimento) had already drawn upon the early Manzoni, particularly in *La battaglia di Benevento. Storia del secolo XIII* [The battle of Benevento. A story of the thirteenth century] (Livorno, 1827–8) and *Beatrice Cenci. Storia del secolo XVI* [Beatrice Cenci. A story of the sixteenth century] (Pisa, 1853) by Francesco Domenico Guerrazzi, a keen emulator of the English schools of terror and horror, whose taste for ghastly images was more sensationalistic than cathartic, as censoriously noted by Benedetto Croce, who described him, with an unforgettable metaphor, as 'oppresso dall'incubo dell'orrendo' [oppressed by the nightmare of the horrible].[25] Even

---

22 Alessandro Vescovi, 'Dickens and Alessandro Manzoni's "I Promessi Sposi"', in Alessandro Vescovi, Luisa Villa and Paul Vita (eds), *The Victorians and Italy: Literature, Travel, Politics and Art* (Monza: Polimetrica, 2009), pp. 151–167.
23 Alessandro Manzoni, *The Betrothed*, trans. by anon. (London: Bentley, 1834), p. 421.
24 Giovanni Verga, *Storia di una capinera* (Milan: Treves, 1893), p. 140.
25 'L'orrendo, che è sparso a piene mani in tutti i suoi libri ... è un orrendo senza intimo fremito sebbene (anzi appunto perché) roboante di esclamazioni e di declamazioni. E' un orrendo di testa e non di cuore, un'escogitazione di cose terribili non ispirate da

Edgar Allan Poe, the master of the American macabre, probably took inspiration from Manzoni in his brief tale 'King Pest', first published in the *Southern Literary Messenger* in 1835 and translated in Italy as 'Re peste. Una storia che contiene un'allegoria'.[26]

By the time of the mid-century, the Gothic contagion had spread throughout the Italian peninsula. Leading the way here were the 'Scapigliati' [the dishevelled ones] (from the French *chevel*, Latin *capillus*), the name a tell-tale semantisation of the messy, unruly corporeality favoured by this northern school of artists, poets and novelists whose influence on late-century fantastic literature was such that they are often assumed to encompass the entirety of nineteenth-century Italian Gothic literature.

In the Non-thetic: Between Body and Mind at Mid-century

If the first phase of nineteenth-century Italian Gothic replicated, adapting them to its own ends, the themes, forms and discourses of late eighteenth- and early nineteenth-century English models, as the nineteenth century advanced the discourses of the body and mind became increasingly central. On the one hand, this was the result of the influence exercised on Italian writers by authors such as Poe, who explored the interior and sensory dimensions of the Gothic alongside its architectural topologies;[27] on the other, this was due to the emergence of characters in Italian literature that

reale terrore dell'anima' [The horrible, which he liberally scatters through all his books ... is a horrible lacking any inner tremors despite (or rather because) of all the loud exclaiming and declaiming. It is a horrible of the head not of the heart, a concoction of terrible things not inspired by a real terror of the soul]. Both quotations are from Benedetto Croce, 'Gli ultimi romanzi di Francesco Domenico Guerrazzi', in Benedetto Croce, *La letteratura della Nuova Italia. Saggi Critici*, 6 vols (Bari: Laterza, 1914), vol. 1, pp. 27–44 (pp. 28–9). On the influence of Radcliffe, see the first pages of Francesco Domenico Guerrazzi, *Note autobiografiche e poema* (Florence: Successori Le Monnier, 1899); on Radcliffe, see also pp. 55–8. Its magniloquence, extreme chromatic contrasts, standard appurtenances (skulls, thunder, ghosts) and paradigmatic spaces (underground vaults, a castle) make *La battaglia di Benevento*, with its Luciferesque villain Manfredi, a late, stale example of Italian hyper-Romanticism, somewhere between Radcliffe's explained supernatural and Lewis's demonic intensity.

26 See in particular the possible comparison with *Fermo e Lucia*, vol. 2, chapters II–IV. On Poe and *I promessi sposi*, specifically the plague episode, also see the anonymous review (probably by Poe himself) of George William Featherstonhaugh's translation of the novel, in *Southern Literary Messenger* 1:1 (1835): 520–2.

27 See, for example, Diodata Saluzzo Roero's *Il castello di Binasco* (1819), with its early Gothic (specifically subalpine) regionalism, and Gian Battista Bazzoni, a popular Walter Scott imitator whose *Il castello di Trezzo* (Milan, 1827) went through twelve editions.

existed at the very limit of the human, central even in one of the cornerstones of Western children's literature, *Le avventure di Pinocchio: storia di un burattino* (1883). I am referring here to what, following Jean-Paul Sartre in *Being and Nothingness* (1943), we might call the 'non-thetic turn' of the Italian Gothic of the later nineteenth century. Equally pertinent in this respect is Georges Bataille's synthesis of this friction – or fault-line – between thetic and non-thetic in his discussion of sacrifice, where he describes it as a *freeing rupture*, a 'déchirure libératrice' ('a tear, or wound, laid open in the side of the real', as Rosemary Jackson glosses it), thus accounting for the carnality and corporeality that we also find in the Italian Gothic of this period.[28] It is less a regression into the 'arid real' condemned by the classicist Vincenzo Monti in his essay *Sulla mitologia* 1825 [On mythology] than a progressive desacralisation of the world that makes the representation of the body – impenetrable, aberrant, dangerous, resistant, unstable in its exposed, continually challenged materiality that paradoxically elevates it to the stature of *mysterium* – a privileged ethical-aesthetic object. In contrast to the age of Enlightenment, the later Italian nineteenth century is captivated by the disturbing allure of animated objects and seduced by the transgressing body in all its manifestations – possessed, ill, decaying, freed from the equation 'normality = beauty' – as it prepares to encounter the insidious end-century *daimon* quietly lying in wait among the arcane and nocturnal relics of an ancient past.

At the centre of these new discourses, and partly shaped by foreign influences that, alongside Poe, included Nikolai Gogol, Charles Baudelaire and Ernst Theodor Hoffmann, was the Scapigliatura movement, active roughly from 1840 to 1860 between Turin and Milan. Inspired by European late Romanticism, the Scapigliati sought to 'de-provincialise' Italian culture as part of a broader social and intellectual effort that extended, in the arts, to poetry and music. As Francesca Billiani explains, 'this literary (and political) movement strongly rejected bourgeois social and ethical values as well as the brand of historical realism advocated by Alessandro Manzoni and his followers'.[29]

The Scapigliati effectively fleshed out the Gothic, locating it in the body and giving it a blatant and disturbing materiality that was quite distinct both

---

28 Georges Bataille, 'Le Collège de Sociologie', Mardi 4 juillet 1939, in *Le Collège de Sociologie (1937–1939)*, edited by Denies Hollier (Paris: Gallimard, 1995), pp. 533; Rosemary Jackson, *Fantasy: The Literature of Subversion* (London and New York: Methuen, 1981), p. 22.

29 Billiani, 'Delusional Identities', p. 495, n.1.

from the immateriality of Gothic historical narratives and from the spectres and phantasmagorias of the turn of the century. Texts in this tradition explore and test the limits of distorted desire, negotiating the most disturbing of proclivities and obsessive psychopathologies. We thus witness a morbid fascination with amputation ('Il pugno chiuso' [The closed fist] by Arrigo Boito and 'Storia di una gamba' [The story of a leg] by Igino Ugo Tarchetti); fetishism verging upon morphophilia (the teeth and especially the hair of Fosca, *femme fatale* 'incadaverita e consunta' [corpse-like, wasted], in the miasmatic short novel by Tarchetti, emblematic of the dismemberment and reification of the *corpus*/corpse, especially female, already inherent in the movement's name);[30] the overwrought erotic aestheticism of necrophilia ('Un corpo' [A body] by Camillo Boito, 1870, which pits science against nature, the anatomist against the artist in a highly contemporary variant on the poetic theme of the corpse of a beautiful woman); and a focus on the diseases and disfigurements of the flesh, inevitable and at the same time liberating, that fascinate and subjugate male characters ('Narcisa', Luigi Gualdo's first work, whose protagonist dies of her beauty, in a foretaste of decadentism that reworks the Scapigliatura invariant 'beauty = incompleteness').

In this interpretative scenario, the aesthetic of the ugly, the abnormal and the heretical is relentlessly and oppressively celebrated, becoming the object of the horrified and subjugated gaze. What Edward Burne-Jones's painting of 1887 termed the female 'baleful head' is clearly epitomised by Tarchetti's Fosca:

> L'esiguità del suo collo formava un contrasto vivissimo colla grossezza della sua testa, di cui un ricco volume di capelli neri, folti, lunghissimi, quali non vide mai in altra donna, aumentava ancora la *sproporzione*.[31]

> [Her slender neck formed the most striking contrast with the bulk of her head, whose rich mass of hair, black, thick, longer than I had ever seen on a woman, further augmented the disproportion.]

The term 'disproportion' is, indeed, particularly fitting for this figure's Medusa-like dismantling of Burkean notions of beauty and Vitruvian

---

30 Igino Ugo Tarchetti, *Fosca: racconto di I.U. Tarchetti. Amore nell'arte: tre racconti dello stesso autore* (Milan: Edoardo Sonzogno Editore, 1874), p. 127; the translation that I cite here is from Lawrence Venuti's English translation of the text as Igino Ugo Tarchetti, *Passion*, trans. by Lawrence Venuti (San Francisco: Mercury House, 1994), p. 9.

31 Tarchetti, *Fosca*, p. 49; italics mine; the English translation comes from Venuti's translation, p. 42. See Galia Ofek, *Representations of Hair in Victorian Literature and Culture* (Farnham: Ashgate, 2009).

conceptualisations of harmony. A note on language here can help us better understand the typology of Tarchetti's Gothic style. The adjective 'horrid', from the Latin *horridus* (Italian *orribile*), has the secondary archaic meaning of *hairy, bristling*, which, according to the *OED*, remains current. The hyperonymy *horrid hair*, a semantic tautology, thus places *Fosca*'s imagery squarely within the fold of post-Romantic European Gothic. Tarchetti's aesthetic was evidently attuned to such linguistic-rhetorical nuances, as evidenced by his translations from English (among others, Mary Shelley's short story 'The Mortal Immortal' in 1865) and, more particularly, by his proto-deconstructionist story 'La lettera U. (Manoscritto di un pazzo)' [The letter U. (Manuscript of a madman)], published posthumously in 1869 in *Racconti Fantastici* [Fantastic tales], which plays on a linguistic phobia, a lipogram that prevents the narrator from using that letter of the alphabet.[32] In Tarchetti, however, such sophisticated discursive practices are always subordinated to the Scapigliatura's anti-realist project; an example is the presence of *orrid-* within one of the novel's most recurring terms: *sorridere* [to smile], in my interpretation deconstructible into *s-orrid-ere*. There are no fewer than twenty-eight occurrences of verbs and nouns related to *sorridere/sorriso* in this *fosco* [fuscous, dark] novel. The horror of Fosca ('la luce del giorno me la mostrava in tutta la sua *orridezza*')[33] is therefore semantically/aesthetically contained within beauty and joy itself, in a plastic rendering of the binary beauty/ugliness (or rather, beauty *in* ugliness) that was central to the decadent and Romantic 'agony' (to cite Mario Praz's influential study). Fosca, in other words, is a channel of *contagion* – medical, psychic, even linguistic – and Giorgio, the narrator, ends up being himself corrupted and corroded, 'inerte, muto, *inorridito*';[34] in brief, he becomes 'foschizzato' [fosca-fied], enveloped in the arms of his horrible corpse-bride, in an ultimate transference of the malady that simultaneously enables and empowers the woman and disables and disempowers the man (where the fate of the body natural also involves that of the body politic). Giorgio encounters the horrible skull that lurks under the beautiful female face.

32 On Tarchetti's estranging and anti-domesticising practice as a translator, and on the aesthetic and political significance of his thoughts on language, see Lawrence Venuti, *The Translator's Invisibility: A History of Translation* (London and New York: Routledge, 1995), pp. 148–86.
33 'The daylight displayed her in all her *horror*'. The English translation comes from Venuti's translation, p. 87; italics mine.
34 'Inert, mute, aghast', Venuti's translation, p. 123; italics mine.

Gothic Pinocchio/Pinocchio and the Gothic

To obviate any potential transmedia and transcultural suggestions, it should be clarified immediately that the tender, colourful character created by Walt Disney in 1940 shares very little besides the name with the puppet-turned-real-boy invented by Collodi half a century earlier. The novel was published in instalments in the weekly *Giornale per i bambini* [The children's review] from 1881, later collected in a book entitled *Le avventure di Pinocchio: storia di un burattino* (1883) [The Adventures of Pinocchio: The Story of a Puppet], with illustrations by Enrico Mazzanti. To give a sense of the Gothic tone of Collodi's book as compared to Disney's film, one need only note that in the last episode of the original Pinocchio is hanged and dies.[35] Indeed, Collodi's *Pinocchio* is a grotesque and disturbing reinterpretation of the Pygmalion epyllion that was so popular in nineteenth-century Europe (for example, *La Vénus d'Ille* by Prosper Mérimée, 1837, a model for 'Lorenzo Alviati' by Tarchetti, 1869, and 'Ida' by Federico Verdinois, 1880, the latter a refined multilingual translator who introduced Italians to many European fantastic authors). It is a violent, dark story, a symbolic battlefield in which the Dionysian spirit of boyish disengagement (the *wanting* to be) clashes with, and finally succumbs to, the Apollonian mode (the *having* to be) of adult sociality and of sacrifice.

The plot recounts the misadventures of a disobedient wooden puppet whose stubbornness and misplaced sense of independence continually place him in harm's way, causing him to collide, in an adventure-filled process of *Bildung* that replicates the stages of a child's psychosocial development, with paternal (the carpenter Geppetto), maternal (the Good Fairy) and social authority (learning to interact with peers and to internalise mechanisms of repression), before he finally finds his own identity within the community. The novel develops many Gothic motifs, on which it superimposes a strict – indeed harshly repressive – pedagogical intent: alimentary metaphors (anxiety and taboos about appetite and food, with extreme bodily representations of hunger such as starvation and cannibalism); scenes of entrapment and premature burial (Pinocchio is locked in a prison and later is swallowed by the terrible Dog-fish); several near-death experiences (the puppet-master Fire-eater wants to use him as firewood); the tortured and grotesque body (the piece of pine that will become Pinocchio is already animated and talking

---

35 I quote from the first English translation of the novel: Carlo Collodi [pseud. of Carlo Lorenzini], *The Story of a Puppet or The Adventures of Pinocchio*, trans. by Mary Alice Murray, illustrated by C. Mazzanti [sic] (London: Fisher Unwin, 1892).

before Master Cherry offers the wood to Geppetto, and later the puppet is stabbed, hanged and left to die by the Cat and the Fox); and episodes of animalisation and body morphing, literal and metaphorical (Pinocchio's nose notoriously growing longer and longer is certainly the best-known example, but when he follows Candlewick to the land of Cocagne, he turns into a braying donkey, whipped and 'bought by a man who proposed to make a drum of his skin',[36] and in an earlier episode he is put on a chain to serve as a guard dog). These are just some of the Gothic horrors of which the irreverent and rebellious puppet is the subject/object. Besides the explicit didactic intent of correcting a child's misbehaviour, at work here is a constant testing of Pinocchio's ontological and physical boundaries, in a process that encapsulates – as already foreshadowed two decades earlier by the Scapigliati – the late nineteenth-century crisis of binary classifications, the perturbing and unstable porosity of the threshold between human and ab-human – a wooden object in the act of becoming alive – and what Julia Kristeva calls the abject, the limit between law and desire.[37] An example occurs in chapter 34, which tests the monstrous immortality – owing to the uncontainable, irrepressible energy of the Id – of this Creature of uncertainty (I capitalise the word in homage to a possible *Pinocchio* intertext: Mary Shelley's *Frankenstein* [1818; 1831]):

> Well, then, the good Fairy, as soon as she saw that I was in danger of drowning, sent immediately an immense shoal of fish, who, believing me really to be a little dead donkey, began to eat me. And what mouthfuls they took! I should never have thought that fish were greedier than boys! ... Some ate my ears, some my muzzle, others my neck and mane, some the skin of my legs, some my coat ... and amongst them there was a little fish so polite that he even condescended to eat my tail. ... However, I must tell you that when the fish had finished eating the donkey's hide that covered me from head to foot, they naturally reached the bone ... or rather the wood, for as you see I am made of the hardest wood.[38]

Through this sequence of transformations – theoretically interminable because oneirically reproducible to infinity, and made possible by

---

36 Collodi, *Pinocchio*, p. 190.
37 Julia Kristeva, *Powers of Horror: An Essay on Abjection*, trans. by Leon S. Roudiez (New York: Columbia University Press, 1982).
38 Collodi, *Pinocchio*, pp. 205–6. Charles Klopp also notes the possible inter-discursive relation between *Frankenstein* and *Pinocchio* in 'Workshops of Creation, Filthy and Not: Collodi's "Pinocchio" and Shelley's "Frankenstein"', in Katia Pizzi (ed.), *Pinocchio, Puppets and Modernity: The Mechanical Body* (London and New York: Routledge, 2012), pp. 63–74.

Pinocchio's uncertain ontological status – the puppet stages a protean journey that takes him from vegetable to animal (wood–> donkey–> wood) and from dead to alive (prey of the fish–> fugitive). By contesting and deconstructing already inherently mobile classifications and taxonomies, Pinocchio, an animated block of wood, an un-begotten Other, an object mediating the desire of his male creator, complicates the distinction between object and subject, between I/Other: he embodies the Freudian uncanny par excellence, even if, once again, the novel's extra-textual frame of reference recodes and dislocates the Gothic's mythopoeic and supernatural thrust. Within this narrative scheme, each adventure becomes a device to drive home the novel's moral message and to reiterate the imperatives of social utility, productivity and charity that the individual must learn to recognise and internalise, thus naturalising them. As a result, even horror and monstrosity become abstractions, discourses subjected to a transformation that re-encodes them within a modern morality.[39]

Pinocchio is, unquestionably, a humanistic metaphor *avant la lettre*, a character/trope who, even on a purely semantic level – his name's association with the pine nut – already represents a seme/seed, that of the dialogue between natural / artificial, I/other than me, desire/moral lesson: the seme/seed of modernity itself.

Further Thresholds: The Twilight of Positivism

Alongside the major narrative strands of Verismo and regional literature, the final years of the *siècle stupide* in Italy, as in Great Britain, were marked by explorations of anti-rationalist and anti-scientific discourses and hermeneutical modalities such as spiritualism, mesmerism, psychic phenomena and occultism. Vampirism was also among these, a cultural preoccupation that is worth looking at more closely, since it was the focus of an artistic subgenre that had flourished in the peninsula ever since the *Dissertazione sopra i vampiri* (1739) [Dissertation on Vampires] by the Florentine Giuseppe Davanzati, Archbishop of Trani, a scientific-ethnographic treatise first circulated in manuscript and later published in two editions (1764 and 1789).

In the wake of the success of John William Polidori's *The Vampyre* (*New Monthly Magazine*, 1 April 1819), vampires became a recurring theme in

---

39 For the 'negative aesthetics' of the Gothic, see Fred Botting, *Gothic*, 2nd edition (London and New York: Routledge, 2014), p. 8. Collodi had also translated Charles Perrault's fairy tales (*I racconti delle fate*, 1876), which, typically for the genre at this time, were expressly written as morality tales.

nineteenth-century Italy, both on the stage and in print.[40] After the appearance of the anonymous *Lord Ruthven o i vampiri di Lord Byron* [Lord Ruthven or Lord Byron's vampires] (Naples, Marotta and Vaspandoch, 1826), a text largely unrelated to Polidori's story, *The Vampyre* was translated as *Il vampiro. Novella di Lord Byron* [The vampire. A novel by Lord Byron] (Udine, 1831). The trope also appeared fairly regularly on the stage, both as free transmediations of Polidori's text (masked ballet extravaganzas staged at the royal theatres of Milan and Turin, of which only a single narrativisation, dating to the 1860s, has survived in print), and as a colourful framing device for comedies (Giovanni Carlo Cosenza, *Il vampire* [The Vampire], 1825; Angelo Brofferio, *Il vampire* [The Vampire], 1827; Cesare Vitaliani, *I vampiri del giorno* [The Vampires of the Day], 1866). In fiction, the first original Italian vampire story appeared in *I racconti del diavolo. Storia della paura* [The devil's stories. A tale of fear] (Bologna, 1861) by Franco Mistrali, the author of the first Italian vampire novel, *Il vampiro. Storia vera* [The vampire; a true story] (Bologna, 1869). Of particular interest, finally, is the story by Francesco Ernesto Morando, 'Vampiro innocente' [Innocent vampire] (published in *Fanfulla della Domenica* in 1885), in which a madman interned in an asylum tells the institution's director how his young daughter had the life sucked out of her by his vampiric son, whom the despairing father then strangled in an attempt to rid the world of the monster. The luridly sensational plot, with its almost explicit incestuous subtext, was probably rendered acceptable only by the deranged narrator's unreliability, a convenient (and common) narrative ploy that casts doubt on his understanding – and therefore the truth – of the events that he recounts, thus justifying the possibility that his son was indeed an 'innocent vampire'.

If Fosca, the deadly protagonist of Tarchetti's novel, can be associated – as victim and active carrier – with forms of physical and psychic vampirism that were also common in contemporary English literature, after the turn of the century the story 'Un vampiro' by Luigi Capuana (published in a 1907 collection by the same title) represents a new, distinctly bourgeois version of the vampire *mỳthos*. The narrative is set in post-Umbertine Italy and reconfigures the figure of the vampire according to the middle-class ideologies of domesticity and marriage, a shift shared with much Gothic and fantastic fiction of nineteenth-century Italy. In Capuana's story the vampire is thus the deceased husband of the protagonist, Luisa, newly married to her

---

40 Edoardo Zuccato, 'The Fortunes of Byron in Italy (1810–1870)', in Richard Cardwell (ed.), *The Reception of Byron in Europe*, 2 vols (London: Thoemmes-Continuum, 2004), vol. 1, pp. 80–99.

first love – a union both fulfiling and long desired, and hence *guilty*. The couple has a child, whereas her first marriage to the man whom death has transformed into a *revenant* had been childless. Like the persecution of a phantasm, always present in its absence and able endlessly to reactivate a past that must not be allowed to remain past, the torment inflicted by Capuana's vampire on the couple's son is, ideologically, the punishment that patriarchal authority reserves for the woman, guilty of a desire that is perceived as illegitimate and unnatural, and that must therefore be disciplined and punished. On an epistemological level, however, the acceptance by Dr Mongeri, the story's narrator, of the extraordinary events related by his friend, the poet Lelio Giorgi, makes him the spokesman of a new *doxa,* a modern anti-dogmatic empiricism open to other dimensions parallel to that of reason, and capable of allowing that this 'preteso caso di vampirismo' [alleged case of vampirism] belongs within a vaster and more complex natural order, of which it even represents an evolutionary stage.[41]

Salvatore di Giacomo expressed this new openness in 'La fine di Barth' [The end of Barth] (1893):

> Tutto questo, miei ottimi amici, io vi giuro di averlo *visto* e *udito*. La realtà ha tali argomenti di persuasione e di sensazioni che non ci si può permettere d'offenderla co' soliti argomenti fantastici, con le supposizioni di un sogno, d'una visione del solo spirito, della sola immaginazione esaltata.
>
> Che successe dopo? Posso io narrarvelo con la medesima precisione? No, non posso … Tutto quello che succedette alla mia visione – devo io chiamarla *visione*? – è impreciso.[42]

[All this, my good friends, I swear to have *seen* and *heard*. Reality has such arguments of persuasion and such sensations that we cannot allow ourselves

---

[41] Luigi Capuana, 'Il Vampiro', in Costanza Melani (ed.), *Fantastico italiano* (Milan: BUR Rizzoli, 2009), pp. 290–308 (p. 308). In the early editions, the story had a dedication to Cesare Lombroso, whose collaboration with Capuana I discuss elsewhere in this essay. Of the vampire fictions that I refer to, Franco Mistrali's *Il vampiro. Storia vera*, edited by Antonio Daniele (Salerno: Keres Edizioni, 2011) is currently out of print; Luigi Capuana's 'Il Vampiro' is available in several collections of nineteenth-century fantastic tales, for which, as for the other texts mentioned in this essay, see the bibliography. Especially useful is the critical introduction to Luigi Capuana, *Novelle dal mondo occulto*, edited by Andrea Cedola (Bologna: Pendragon, 2007), pp. 7–75. Some of the nineteenth-century vampire tales, including those discussed here, are in Antonio Daniele (ed.), *Vampiriana. Novelle italiane di vampiri* (Salerno: Keres Edizioni, 2011). The only scholarly text on the subgenre, though with a strong twentieth-century focus, is Giuseppe Tardiola, *Il vampiro nella letteratura italiana* (Anzio: De Rubeis, 1991).

[42] Salvatore di Giacomo, 'La fine di Barth', in Melani (ed.), *Fantastico italiano*, pp. 381–4; italics in original.

to offend it with the usual fantastic arguments, with suppositions of a dream, of a vision of the spirit alone, of exalted imagination alone.

What happened next? Can I describe it with equal accuracy? No, I cannot... All that followed my vision – must I call it *vision?* – is imprecise.]

It is with this symbolic final question, as obsessive as it is disarming, that the Italian Gothic of the nineteenth century comes to a close. The question expresses a hermeneutic and narratological incapacity, the gnoseological hesitation of a dissolve, of an evanescent body, of a gaze that *cannot* see. Not surprisingly, with positivism in full decline, the next century ushered in a new attempt scientifically to systematise spiritualism itself: the Società di studi psichici was founded in Milan in 1900. Modelled on the Society for Psychical Research in London (founded in 1882), and with its own journal, *Luce e ombra. Rivista mensile illustrata di scienze spiritualiste* (1901) [Light and darkness. Illustrated monthly review of spiritualist sciences], the Società remained active for many decades and included among its members writers of the calibre of Antonio Fogazzaro (also its honorary president), Arrigo Boito, Capuana and, among men of science, even Cesare Lombroso, the psychiatrist whose new discipline of criminal anthropology sought in the materiality of the most deterministic physical taxonomy a direct route into the *psyche*.[43] The deep crisis of traditional values that marked the end of the century was thus accompanied by a radical questioning of scientific certainties, in a context of social unease made starkly apparent by the worsening living conditions of the masses. The potentially subversive experimentation of the Gothic (and more generally, the fantastic) responds to this post-unification disillusionment and conveys the sense of crisis through anti-realist or para-realist forms and themes that grapple with and challenge not just facts but facticity itself.

No clear distinction can therefore be drawn between literary naturalism and supernaturalism in these end-century decades, nor between the standard-bearers of realism-naturalism on the one hand and the exponents of late-Romantic anti-realism on the other. But such uncertainty about 'the true', and the need constantly to review the hermeneutic paradigm and hence the boundaries of the fantastic, were already evident in Manzoni, who wrote explicitly about the frailty of Enlightenment reason: 'Non voglio dissimulare ... a me stesso, perché non desidero di ingannarmi, quanto indeterminato,

---

[43] Fascinated by the famous medium Eusapia Paladino (or Palladino), Lombroso also wrote a treatise on spiritualism, much of which concerns precisely what he called 'fenomeni spiritici eusapiani' [Eusapian spiritual phenomena]: *Ricerche sui fenomeni ipnotici e spiritici* (Turin: Unione Tipografico-Editrice Torinese, 1909).

incerto, e vacillante nell'applicazione sia il senso della parola "vero" riguardo ai lavori dell'immaginazione' [I do not want to conceal ... from myself, because I do not wish to deceive myself, how indeterminate, uncertain, and dubious in its application is the meaning of the word 'true' as regards the works of imagination].[44] Authors such as Verga, Capuana and Serao, but also the Neapolitan Salvatore di Giacomo, and, early in the next century, the Sardinian Grazia Deledda and the Sicilian Luigi Pirandello, constantly interweave apparently antithetical forms and genres in their works. Such experimental contaminations give rise to plots in which the inexplicable, the mysterious and the unknown imbue the Gothic of this time with an original and distinctly regionalist and folkloristic-popular tinge, shrouding in black the sunny, Mediterranean *genius loci* so beloved by the writers and travellers of earlier centuries. In this geolocalised rereading of the Gothic that is attentive to specific cultural nuances, traditional themes and actors are recoded: history becomes legend (sometimes brutally violent, as in *Le storie del Castello di Trezza* [The stories of the Castle of Trezza] by Giovanni Verga, 1875); supernatural events turn into miracles, if the interpretation is religious or, if secular, into the effects of omnipresent and omnipotent local forces of oppression (the post-feudal crimes of arrogant landowners or secret societies, as in *I Beati Paoli*); psychic phenomena and mesmerism are reinterpreted as beguilements; the figure of the antagonist, enveloped in an aura of superstition, becomes 'Il fatale' ('The fatal being', the title of a story by Tarchetti in *Racconti Fantastici*); the spectral, finally, may be reduced to mere passion. Once again, the work of Luigi Capuana is emblematic in this respect. A dialectologist deeply versed in Sicilian traditions, including their darker and fiercer aspects, Capuana was the acknowledged progenitor of the southern naturalist literary school, but experimented equally with fantastic as with anthropological-documentary forms, adapting characters and situations from the *fin-de-siècle* art/science dialogue to the Sicilian setting. One example is the psychopathology of a criminal explored in *Il Marchese di Roccaverdina* [The Marquis of Roccaverdina] (Treves, 1901), a novel set against the background of an archaic and feudal Sicily, and which is unanimously recognised as his masterpiece. His works exhibit his decades-long interest in the anti-materialism and anti-dogmatism of 'metapsychics' (or *metapsychique,* a term coined by the French physiologist Charles-Robert Richet, a scholar of the paranormal and winner of the Nobel Prize in 1912) and transcendentalist doctrines that interrogated the boundaries between visible and invisible, life and death,

---

44 Manzoni, 'Lettera sul romanticismo', p. 594.

between the material and an immateriality that is often dark and threatening (as in the story 'Forze occulte' [Occult powers], first published in 1902).

If the major Italian authors of the end of the century thus had no qualms about making their own incursions into the Gothic and the fantastic, it is also true that the rapidly expanding circulation of magazines and newspapers, with their serialised novels and short stories ranging in genre from horror to the exotic to proto-science fiction, contributed in no small part to the popularity of Italian genre literature. However distant from the 'high' literary canon, such reading matter was nonetheless fully attuned to the tastes of a newly literate working-class and petty-bourgeois audience. Though this wholesale production of literary 'pleasure' was scorned by militant critics, it remained in high demand by the masses.[45] It was this publishing context that gave rise to best-selling authors such as Emilio De Marchi and Carolina Invernizio, whose gripping novels freely combined *noir* with detection and romance, in a winning narrative formula first mastered in Britain by Wilkie Collins. In Invernizio's fiction, in particular, a morbid insistence on death, a theme already dear to the Scapigliati, is coupled with a focus on women's victimisation that reads as a scarcely veiled critique of the repressive institution of the family: unbridled sexual impulses that inevitably result in social transgressions (not least adultery, in plotlines revolving around typical ethical-social constructions of the time such as 'honour' and 'respectability') could thus find free expression outside the ideological and formal straightjacket of bourgeois realism. In this regard the titles of Invernizio's novels are exemplary, enticing the reader into the realm of the macabre, the anguished, the forbidden: *Il bacio d'una morta* [The kiss of the dead woman] (1886) and its sequel, *La vendetta d'una pazza* [The vengeance of a mad woman] (1894), and, among the novels on taphophobia, the 'buried alive' theme that garnered Invernizio an immense following, *La sepolta viva* [The buried alive woman] (1896) and, consequently, *La rediviva* [The revenant woman] (1906). These are works – rapidly adapted for the screen in the silent film era – that cleverly exploit a diverse range of mass-market Gothic themes and forms, blending

---

45 For a detailed and fascinating introduction to Italian 'weird' magazine literature, see Fabrizio Foni, *Alla fiera dei mostri. Racconti pulp, horror e arcane fantasticherie nelle riviste italiane 1899–1932* (Latina: Tanué, 2007), from which I draw the following information. Among periodicals of interest to Gothic scholars are *Per terra e per mare*; *Il giornale dei viaggi*, with a similar editorial thrust, and, at the cusp of the new century, *La domenica del Corriere*, supplement of the very popular Milan daily *Il Corriere della Sera*, which serialised, among others, *She* (1887) by Henry Rider Haggard, starting from n. 15 of 1901, and in 1902, from n. 44, *The Hound of the Baskervilles* (1902) by Arthur Conan Doyle, translated as *La maledizione dei Baskerville*.

the 'gaslight mysteries' *à la* Eugene Sue with the surprise endings of the *roman feuilleton* and the classic features of the sensation novel.[46]

Shadows and Glimmers: Into the Twentieth Century

> L'anima italiana tende, naturalmente, al definito e all'armonico. Bene invase e corse l'Italia, dopo il 1815, una nordica cavalcata di spettri, di vergini morenti, di angeli-demoni, di disperati e cupi bestemmiatori, e si udirono scricchiolii di scheletri, e sospiri e pianti e sghignazzate di folli e deliri di febbricitanti. Ma tutto ciò ... agitò la superficie e non le profondità.[47]

> [The Italian soul leans naturally toward the definite and harmonious. It is true that after 1815, Italy was invaded by a Northern cavalcade of ghosts, dying virgins, angel-demons, desperate and gloomy blasphemers and one could hear the creaking of skeletons, the sighing, weeping and guffaws of fools and delirious cries of feverish people ... But it only rippled the surface without touching the depths.]

So wrote Benedetto Croce, the leading Italian intellectual of the first half of the twentieth century, in 1904, reflecting on the century just past. With their icy dismissal of the unbalanced, disturbed, neurotic – in short, 'nocturnal' – side of what he defined, perhaps for lack of a better word, 'Romanticism', Croce's critical writings, thoroughly politicised and ideologically inflected, helped to establish the (or, rather, *a*) literary canon that held sway in Italy until almost the end of the last century. His condemnation carried much weight, therefore, and exemplifies a late resurgence of post-Enlightenment censure that proved so influential as to become an automatic critical response among Italian intellectuals, as we saw with Italo Calvino's views on the Italian Gothic discussed at the start of this chapter. In retrospect, however, this towering figure now paradoxically has come to resemble an *éidolon* – an anachronistic phantasm far removed from the *real*.

---

46 Carolina Invernizio's rich *oeuvre* is available in several languages, including Spanish and Portuguese, but not in English. An exception is the short story 'Punishment', translated, with some critical notes, in Cosetta Gaudenzi, 'Carolina Invernizio's "Punishment"', *Forum Italicum: A Journal of Italian Studies* 38:2 (2004): 562–81.

47 Benedetto Croce, 'Arrigo Boito', in *La letteratura della Nuova Italia. Saggi Critici*, 6 vols (Bari: Laterza, 1914), vol. 1, pp. 259–76 (p. 259). Up to the ellipsis the translation is by Remo Ceserani, 'Fantastic and Literature', in Paul Puppa and Luca Somigli (eds), *Encyclopedia of Italian Literary Studies*, gen. ed. Gaetana Marrone (London and New York: Routledge, 2007), pp. 684–8 (p. 685).

Demons and brigands, darkness and light, ecstasy and terror; superstitious horrors generated by the excesses of religion; dazzling visions emerging from dark sea's depths. As this chapter has shown, the Italian Gothic of the nineteenth century is a hybrid, bipolar genre locked into a perennial intergenerational struggle with stolid *res* – the realism, or 'dull catalogue of common things' against which John Keats in *Lamia* (1820) rebelled – at the uncertain and mobile boundary between matter and idea, Romantic and Classic, or between *griechisch* and *gotisch*, to return to the eighteenth-century aesthetic categories from which we started. From Radcliffe's Italy, the land of villains, castles and bandits – a hetero-directed vision, a cultural construction – to the post-Verist Italy of mysteries, of otherworldly psychopomps, of the crisis of epistemologies and radical questioning of the discourses of the body and of humanity, we have before us a vast chiaroscuro Gothic canvas in which the strands of ethnographic enquiry intertwine with those of social denunciation, all set against the background of the difficult construction of the new nation. Its development can be traced through a sequence of cultural interrelations, confluences, contacts, rereadings, until it gradually acquired its own strong and distinct voice, one whose history for the most part still waits be written. Replete with the unresolved paradoxes and unsolvable aporias of a land born under the sign of Saturn, where unquiet pagan gods still seem to inhabit the quivering vegetation overlooking the brilliant blue of the Mediterranean idyll, Gothic Italy lurks even beneath the sunny and fragrant Ravello of E. M. Forster's 'The Story of a Panic' (1904), the (purposely northern) gem of a story with which I conclude this journey into the Italic Gothic:

> It is not possible to describe coherently what happened next: but I, for one, am not ashamed to confess that, though the fair blue sky was above me, and the green spring woods beneath me, and the kindest of friends around me, yet I became terribly frightened, more frightened than I ever wish to become again, frightened in a way I never have known either before or after.[48]

Forster here figures a sinister, transformative encounter – simultaneously disturbing and epiphanic, once again inexorably oxymoronic – that marks a

---

48 E. M. Forster, 'The Story of a Panic', in *Selected Stories*, edited by David Leavitt and with an introduction and notes, by David Leavitt and Mark Mitchell (Harmondsworth: Penguin, 2001), pp. 1–23 (p. 6).

transition: an end that is a beginning, a flight forward, headlong into the next century, the indisputably *noir* century whose fertile soil nourished such figures as Tommaso Landolfi, Mario Bava, Dario Argento, Eraldo Baldini and Tiziano Sclavi, the new purveyors, in different media and with diverse imaginative and rhetorical talents, of chills under the Italian sun.

2.15

The Gothic in Nineteenth-Century Scotland

SUZANNE GILBERT

A pivotal moment for nineteenth-century Scottish Gothic occurred in the late Summer of 1794, when Anna Laetitia Barbauld delivered her electrifying reading of Gottfried Augustus Bürger's 'Lenore', a German supernatural ballad that had been translated into English as 'Lenora' in 1790 by Barbauld's former student William Taylor and widely circulated thereafter in manuscript.[1] Addressing members of a literary society gathered at the home of Enlightenment philosopher Dugald Stewart, Barbauld recited the heart-thumping fusion of Gothic narrative and ballad form: 'Tramp, tramp, across the land they speed; / Splash, splash, across the sea: / "Hurrah! the dead can ride apace; / Dost feare to ride with mee?"' The narrative, in itself, was compelling, but it was the sound of 'Lenore' that captivated readers too, even in the relatively restrained stanzas of Taylor's English translation. Combining a curse motif, mysterious abductor, spectral horseback ride, helpless victim, breathless suspense and horrific conclusion, and propelled along by compulsive metre, incremental repetition, internal rhyme and onomatopoeia, 'Lenore' pounded its way into the heads and hearts of that audience and beyond.

Published in the *Monthly Magazine* in 1796, Taylor's translation of 'Lenore' took the British reading public by storm, inspiring many other translations and imitations throughout Britain in the same year. As Peter Boerner puts it, 'The hoofbeats of the ghostly horse that carried Lenore to her death ... could be heard reverberating from Scotland to Wales.'[2] Famously, when Charles

---

1 The precise year in which Barbauld recited Bürger's poem in Edinburgh has been the source of considerable disagreement among critics. While some cite the year as 1793, I follow here the dates of September–October 1794, as listed in the chronology included in William McCarthy and Elizabeth Kraft's definitive edition of Barbauld's works, *Anna Letitia Barbauld: Selected Poetry and Prose* (Peterborough, Ont.: Broadview, 2002), p. 35.
2 Peter Boerner, 'Bürger's "Lenore" in Germany, France and England', in Janos Riesz and Peter Boerner (eds), *Sensus Communis: Contemporary Trends in Comparative Literature* (Tübingen: G. Narr, 1986), pp. 305–11 (p. 307).

Lamb read Taylor's English translation, he wrote to Samuel Taylor Coleridge, 'Have you read the Balad [sic] called "Leonora" in the 2d No. of the "Monthly Magazine"? – If you have – !!!!!!!!!!!!!!'[3] Later, Walter Scott recalled how accounts by those present at Barbauld's recitation in Edinburgh in 1794 fired his imagination, initiating a chain of events that would lead him to 'set up for a poet' as he graduated from translation to imitation to original poetic creation.[4] Scott's fascination with 'Lenore' led to his translation of other poems by Bürger and Johann Wolfgang von Goethe too, as well as to his meeting with James Ballantyne, who would become his lifelong publisher. It also led to Scott's production of original Gothic ballads and a brief but intense association with Matthew Gregory Lewis, a professional collaboration that, in turn, led to further publications of ballads in the Gothic vein. Scott, however, would, in time, come to reject Lewis's kind of Gothic ballad-making, aiming instead for a more authentic presentation of ballad material in the traditional ballads of his own nation's literature. As I shall address in more detail below, this move was crucial to the development of Scottish Gothic writing in the nineteenth century, and was repeated among other Scots in the period, including James Hogg and John Leyden.

Scott's apparent retreat from the mode aside, 'Lenore' ushered in a vogue for the Gothic in nineteenth-century Scotland, one expressed first through imitation and then experimentation with the Gothic possibilities within Scottish literary and cultural contexts. The encounter that Bürger's ballad offered between German Gothic, sublime aesthetics and British folk traditions became a catalyst for writers who adopted its combination of the narrative power of traditional balladry with sensational Gothic language. Beyond the sensationalism of 'Lenore', writers found in Scottish narrative traditions formed by a unique historical and cultural heritage a treasure trove of material to adapt for other purposes, as Bürger himself had done with both English and his own native German sources alike. As Scott's later fascination with collecting Border ballads attests, he was preoccupied by the notion of Scotland having its own national literature, believing that German poetic taste would help in 'renewing the spirit of our own' poetry.[5] Against the eighteenth-century backdrop of James Macpherson's Ossianic sublime and

---

3 Charles Lamb, 'Letter to Coleridge, 5 July 1796', in E. W. Marrs (ed.), *Letters of Charles and Mary Anne Lamb*, Vol. I (Ithaca, NY: Cornell University Press, 1975), p. 41.
4 Walter Scott, *Minstrelsy of the Scottish Border*, revised edition, 4 vols (Edinburgh: James Ballantyne, 1830), vol. 4, p. 24.
5 Douglass H. Thomson, 'The Gothic Ballad', in David Punter (ed.), *A New Companion to the Gothic* (Oxford: Blackwell, 2012), pp. 77–90 (p. 80).

what Ian Duncan refers to as the 'subversive outburst of energies of popular "superstition"' in the poetry of Robert Burns, Scottish writers created texts infused with the peculiar sense of national history, tradition and uncanniness, producing those textually complex engagements with the supernatural that characterise much Scottish Gothic writing.[6] The 'Lenore' moment, as I show in this chapter, coalesces strands of thematic expression that reveal how and why Scottish Gothic in the period developed quite as it did. It also provides a lens through which to trace supernatural themes and motifs, from their origins in traditional narratives to their Gothic internalisation as malevolent possession and psychological doubling in texts by later nineteenth-century writers.

Scottish Gothic: The Cultural and Critical Context

This, however, is not to overlook the extent to which the very notion of 'Scottish Gothic' has become a contested critical category over the last decade or so. For certain critics, the term itself presents something of a historical, theoretical and political conundrum,[7] while, for others, the category remains useful insofar as it attests to the considerable differences between the development across the eighteenth and nineteenth centuries of Gothic literature in England, on the one hand, and in Scotland, on the other.[8] And yet, as I demonstrate below, the differences between Scottish Gothic and the Gothic literary traditions of other nations both within and beyond the British Isles are as internal as they are external. Arguably more so than in the English, oppositions, contestation and irreconcilability run throughout this literary tradition – a fact that seems hardly surprising in view of the fact that the conjunction

---

6 Ian Duncan, 'Walter Scott, James Hogg and Scottish Gothic', Punter (ed.), *A New Companion to the Gothic*, pp. 123–34 (p. 126).
7 See, for example, Dale Townshend, 'Shakespeare, Ossian and the Problem of "Scottish Gothic"', in Elisabeth Bronfen and Beate Neumeier (eds), *Gothic Renaissance: A Reassessment* (Manchester: Manchester University Press, 2014), pp. 218–43 and Nick Groom, '"The Celtic Century" and the Genesis of Scottish Gothic', in Carol Margaret Davison and Monica Germanà (eds), *Scottish Gothic: An Edinburgh Companion* (Edinburgh: Edinburgh University Press, 2017), pp. 14–27. For an account of the broader political and antiquarian tensions between Scotland and the Gothic, see Colin Kidd, *Subverting Scotland's Past: Scottish Whig Historians and the Creation of an Anglo-British Identity, 1689–1830* (Cambridge: Cambridge University Press, 2003).
8 See, for example, Ian Duncan, 'Walter Scott, James Hogg and Scottish Gothic', in David Punter (ed.), *A New Companion to the Scottish Gothic* (Oxford: Blackwell, 2012), pp. 123–34 (p. 123) and Carol Margaret Davison and Monica Germanà, 'Borderlands of Identity and the Aesthetics of Disjuncture: An Introduction to Scottish Gothic', in Carol Margaret Davison and Monica Germanà (eds), *Scottish Gothic*, pp. 1–13 (p. 4).

of opposites has long been established in the Scottish cultural imagination.

As evident from novels such as Scott's *Waverley; or, 'Tis Sixty Years Since* (1814), Scots in the early nineteenth century, a century after the 1807 Union of Parliaments resulting in Scotland's loss of political sovereignty, were negotiating issues of identity internal to the nation, particularly what it meant to be Scottish within Britain. There was no simple or single answer to this question. Highlanders and Lowlanders, for example, experienced post-Union changes in entirely different ways. Over the previous century, the Highlands had been wracked by warfare over a series of Jacobite risings (and defeats), which dislocated the population, savaged the economy and engendered a sense of cultural anxiety and loss. The more urban Lowlands generally prospered; literature, and culture more broadly, flourished in Edinburgh and Glasgow during the Enlightenment, as intellectuals turned their attention to raising Scotland's cultural (rather than political) profile. In literature, the Highlands became associated with primitivism through the terms laid out in Adam Smith's stadial conception of societal progression; Highland banditti became a common figure in romance fiction. And in an odd conflation – one aided by Walter Scott's stage-management of King George IV's visit to Edinburgh in 1822 – the Highlands became a synecdoche for all of Scotland. Oppositions and disjunctions between Protestant and Catholic, and between the monarchy's brand of Protestantism and that of the dissenting Covenanters, had scarred the country throughout the seventeenth century, and these deep differences among Scots were felt long into the nineteenth century, not least in the 'Disruption' separating the Church of Scotland from the Free Church in 1843.

Particularly fraught during this period was language, around which no sense of national identity could be forged, as English, Scots and Gaelic (the latter completely unrelated to the other two) were all spoken and, to varying degrees, written. Scots, having been a highly developed literary language prior to the Regal Union of 1603, lost much of its prestige when Scottish King James VI moved the court and, with it, literary patronage, south to London. Many eighteenth-century Scots, among them Allan Ramsay and Robert Burns, were engaged in preserving the work of their predecessors, and in mining the language of poets such as William Dunbar and Robert Henryson for their own work. From a Highland perspective, James Macpherson's Ossian poems were designed to highlight, or make new, a stylised Celtic antiquity. But writers had to decide how to present themselves to a market centred in London, and some took other approaches; James Beattie and others methodically excised the 'Scotticisms' from their written language – even as many wrote in careful English but spoke in broad Scots.

All of these oppositions, disjunctions, and fragmentations were unique to Scotland and exerted a powerful effect on nineteenth-century writers' sense of identity. Their potency is heightened in Scottish Gothic, a mode that, at its heart, contains what Stephen Arata refers to as an 'intimate estrangement'.[9] Scottish Gothic, we might say, is itself constructed of such contestation and conflict, tensions that, in the words of Carol Margaret Davison and Monica Germanà, reflect 'not only the political bias of a dominant agenda outside Scotland, but also, and in a more complicated way, an inward-looking attitude towards national identity, whereby being Scottish becomes the equivalent, on occasion, of being foreign to oneself'.[10] Emerging via a different path from that of English Gothic, Scottish Gothic, they continue, developed an 'aesthetics of disjuncture' that looks 'both inward to the nation's own fragmented status as well as outward, offering a way of reflecting on identity that moves beyond essentialist binary forms of self-representation'.[11]

In turn, these splits, fragmentation and duality have led to a particularly complex and nuanced textuality, to forms of writing shaped by narrative strategies that heighten ambiguity and unease. Gothic balladry, for instance, taps into the narrative movement of traditional ballads, in which pace is controlled by incremental repetition and stanzaic gaps (withholding or postponing information) and 'leaping and lingering' (shifting and juxtaposing scenes). Derived also from the ballad form, dead riders, demon lovers and motifs of supernatural abduction have proven to be detachable, and useful for Scottish Gothic writing across different genres and forms. The found-manuscript conceit common in Gothic literature since Horace Walpole's *The Castle of Otranto* (1764), and occurring in Scottish literature from James Macpherson's Ossian poems of the 1760s through to Robert Louis Stevenson's *The Master of Ballantrae* (1889) and beyond, is frequently employed, but often complicated by multiple, competing narratives and intrusions of contradictory, at times vernacular, voices. These and other definitive characteristics, I argue, might all in various ways be traced back

---

9 Stephen Arata, 'Stevenson and *Fin-de-Siècle* Gothic', in Penny Fielding (ed.), *The Edinburgh Companion to Robert Louis Stevenson* (Edinburgh: Edinburgh University Press, 2010), pp. 53–69 (p. 60).
10 Davison and Germanà, 'Borderlands of Identity and the Aesthetics of Disjuncture', p. 2.
11 Davison and Germanà, 'Borderlands of Identity and the Aesthetics of Disjuncture', p. 7.

to that galvanising moment in 1794 when Bürger's 'Lenore' commenced its influential Scottish tour.

'Lenora' and the British Folkloric Tradition

Originally published in Germany in 1773, Bürger's Gothic ballad recasts another supernatural-abduction narrative, based on a common folk tale of the 'dead rider' variety, in which a deceased lover returns to reclaim his lady and bears her away on horseback.[12] 'Lenore' fuses the motifs of lovers' separation and revenant's complaint with the Gothic horror of malevolent, supernatural abduction. In Bürger's version, the grieving Lenore curses Providence when her betrothed Wilhelm is not among those returning from war. Then suddenly, at midnight, Wilhelm appears and convinces her to leave with him to seal their union. He pulls Lenore onto his horse, and they begin a harrowing journey at top speed through strange country:

> Halloo! halloo! away they goe,
> Unheeding wet or drye;
> And horse and rider snort and blowe,
> And sparkling pebbles flye.

Ultimately arriving at a graveyard, Wilhelm's appearance begins to change until he is nothing but a skeleton. The earth opens, swallowing the revenant Wilhelm and the living Lenore, now united in the grave:

> And hollow howlings hung in aire,
> And shrekes from vaults arose.
> Then knew the mayde she mighte no more
> Her living eyes unclose.[13]

As innovative as 'Lenore' seemed at the time, it nonetheless drew on a rich, varied and long-established balladic tradition, one filtered and mediated by earlier eighteenth-century antiquarian projects. Most immediately, Bürger was responding to a climate in which German writers and philosophers, most notably Johann Gottfried Herder, were urging the establishment of 'a

---

12 Boerner, 'Bürger's Ballad *Lenore* in Germany, France and England', p. 305. See also Thomson, 'The Gothic Ballad', pp. 77–90. For a description of the 'Dead Rider' theme, see Stith Thompson, *Motif-Index of Folk-Literature*, 6 vols (Bloomington: University of Indiana Press, 1955–8), vol. 2, p. 420.
13 All citations from the ballad are taken from William Taylor's English translation, 'Lenora. A ballad, from Bürger', *The Monthly Magazine, and British Register* 1 (1796): 135–7.

national poetic identity' and 'claiming a kinship with British poetry', particularly Shakespeare and shared ballad traditions;[14] accordingly, he referenced for his Gothic ballad an old German *volkslied* or folk song. But Bürger also drew heavily on those British ballad collections with which, along with Macpherson's Ossianic poetry, he was deeply familiar. In particular, it was 'Sweet William's Ghost', a ballad that had appeared in both the Scottish artist and poet Allan Ramsay's *Tea-Table Miscellany* (1723–37) and in the English collector Thomas Percy's *Reliques of Ancient English Poetry* (1765), that likely inspired him to write 'Lenore'.[15] And, in turn, Scott's own *Minstrely of the Scottish Border* (1802–3) was inspired both by Bürger and by Percy's *Reliques*. Here, Scott, with the help of his countryman James Hogg, endeavoured to reclaim for the nation the Scottish ballads that Percy had anthologised. The compulsion for preserving traditional ballads and tales had created a climate in which antiquarian collectors were repeatedly announcing the imminent death of the oral tradition.[16] In Scotland, however, the oral tradition remained functional and robust, though it was also simultaneously encouraged and altered by ballad-collecting and the endeavours of literary antiquarianism in general.

'Sweet William's Ghost' is a revenant ballad, but a romantic one in which no act of abduction occurs. William has returned, as Francis J. Child explains, 'to ask back his unfulfilled troth-plight' for reasons that are consistent with folk tradition.[17] William practices no deception; he forthrightly informs Margaret that he is 'no earthly man', and that a kiss from him will bring her death. He tells her that his 'bones are buried in yon kirk-yard / Afar beyond the sea', and that only his 'spirit' speaks to her.[18] Even as William warns her away, Margaret persists in asking to go with him, even to the grave: 'Is there any room at your head, Willie? / Or any room at your feet? / Or any room at your side, Willie? / Wherein that I may creep?'. When William vanishes and Margaret dies of sorrow, it is figured as a moment of extreme sentiment, not horror. In its migration from

---

14 Thomson, 'The Gothic Ballad', p. 79.
15 Boerner, 'Bürger's Ballad *Lenore* in Germany, France and England', p. 306.
16 For more on attitudes to the oral tradition in nineteenth-century Scotland, see Penny Fielding, *Writing and Orality: Nationality, Culture, and Nineteenth-Century Scottish Fiction* (Oxford: Oxford University Press, 1996), pp. 19–58.
17 Francis J. Child, *The English and Scottish Popular Ballads*, 5 vols (New York: Dover Publications, 1965), vol. 2, p. 227.
18 All citations from this variant of 'Sweet William's Ghost' (77A), which appeared in the tenth edition of Ramsay's *Tea Table-Miscellany* (1740), are taken from Child, *The English and Scottish Popular Ballads*, vol. 2, p. 229.

Britain to Germany, however, the ballad and the tradition on which it is founded were reshaped by Bürger and then returned as a full-blown horror story, contributing powerful elements in this way to the mix that shaped Scottish Gothic. Witnessing German writers' rediscovery of their national literature compelled Scottish writers to look with new eyes at the potential of their own literary and cultural heritage. The Gothic ballad demonstrated how the distinctive narrative features of the ballad form could be used for new kinds of storytelling and suggested the form's usefulness for stories of the supernatural. Amalgamating the strands was the sense that writers could engage in combinations of literary forms, modes and motifs, a practice in keeping with the joining of opposites so embedded in Scottish culture and literature more generally. Recognising themselves and their own richly varied culture in this new form, these writers found new ways of combining the various kinds of expression that they encountered. Gothic ballad-making, in which motifs and preoccupations peculiar to the German Gothic were wedded to traditional Scottish folklore, history and ballad form, was an important ingredient in the development of Scottish literature at the time, contributing particularly to the development of prose fiction.

Traditional forms provided structural and narrative approaches, as well as emphasis on the vernacular. In the hands of Scottish writers, such techniques proved to be genre-bending; both Hogg and Scott, for example, drew on the supernatural-abduction motif of the traditional ballads of 'Thomas the Rhymer' and 'Tam Lin', as well as the grisly black humour of 'The Twa Corbies', in their own poetry, verse romances and in their short- and longer-length prose fiction. Vernacular storytelling is embedded in Scott's *Redgauntlet* (1824) in the form of 'Wandering Willie's Tale'; in Hogg's carnivalesque oral-storytelling contest (set in the castle of the wizard Michael Scott) at the heart of *The Three Perils of Man* (1822); and in the Calvinist nightmare of Stevenson's short story 'Thrawn Janet' (1881). Such formal hybridity and experimentation reveal in the Scottish Gothic imagination what Adrienne Scullion has called 'a sophisticated engagement with the fantastic that other cultures might celebrate as magic realism'.[19]

---

19 Adrienne Scullion, 'Feminine Pleasures and Masculine Indignities: Gender and Community in Scottish Drama', in Christopher Whyte (ed.), *Gendering the Nation: Studies in Modern Scottish Literature* (Edinburgh: Edinburgh University Press, 1995), pp. 169–204 (p. 201).

Walter Scott and the Gothic

Readers of Walter Scott today will have encountered the novelist's critical comments on Gothic literature, not least in his playful account of his avoidance of the Radcliffean tradition of Gothic romance in the opening chapter of his historical novel *Waverley*:

> Had I, for example, announced in my frontispiece, 'Waverley, a Tale of Other Days', must not every novel-reader have anticipated a castle scarce less than that of Udolpho, of which the eastern wing had been long uninhabited, and the keys either lost or consigned to the care of some aged butler or housekeeper, whose trembling steps, about the middle of the second volume, were doomed to guide the hero, or heroine, to the ruinous precincts?[20]

Despite such anti-Gothic sentiments, Scott's enthusiasm, he admits, 'was chiefly awakened by the wonderful and the terrible – the common taste of children' – a confession to which he revealingly adds, 'but in which I have remained a child even unto this day'.[21] Though he was not in the audience for Barbauld's recitation of 'Lenore' in Edinburgh in 1794, Scott, entranced by the reports of those present, straightaway obtained a copy of Bürger's poems in German and, in the span of two days, produced his own translation entitled 'William and Helen', which borrowed the galloping metre of the original. To this he added another translation of a Bürger ballad, 'The Chase', later revised as 'The Wild Huntsman'. These translations were Scott's first publications, and appeared in Edinburgh in 1796 as *The Chase, and William and Helen: Two Ballads, from the German of Gottfried Augustus Bürger*. Both address didactically the consequences of rash or bold challenges to authority; in both ballads, breaking a taboo activates a curse. This element is in fact exaggerated in Scott's versions. In both cases, moreover, a wild ride on horseback propels the narrative. Scott attempts to capture the relentless rhythm of a headlong race on horseback in this favourite and often-repeated refrain: 'Tramp! tramp! along the land they rode, / Splash! splash! along the sea; / The scourge is red, the spur drops blood, / The flashing pebbles flee'.[22] Scott's attraction to 'Lenore', however, was as personal as it was poetic: he named

---

20 Walter Scott, *Waverley; or, 'Tis Sixty Years Since*, edited by Claire Lamont (Oxford: Oxford University Press, 1986), p. 3.
21 J. G. Lockhart, *Memoirs of the Life of Sir Walter Scott, Bart.* 7 vols (Edinburgh: R. Cadell, 1837-8), vol. 1, p. 8.
22 The lines from this poem are cited from Walter Scott, 'William and Helen', in J. Logie Robertson (ed.), *Scott: Poetical Works* (London: Oxford University Press, 1971), pp. 630-4 (p. 633).

his favourite horse after Bürger's eponymous heroine, while, at the time of his translation of the ballad, he was in love with Williamina Belches, who was to marry a man named William, both names recalled by the revenant 'Wilhelm' in 'Lenore'. Throughout his life, in fact, Scott frequently quoted passages from the ballad, particularly those depicting the wild horseback ride to the grave, where the lovers would be buried.

Though Scott's English translations from the German were poorly distributed and received almost no attention in their day, he followed them with other Gothic ballads, this time directly inspired by Matthew Gregory Lewis, who had included in *The Monk* (1796) his own harrowing Gothic ballad, 'Alonzo the Brave and Fair Imogine'. Lewis invited Scott to contribute to his planned anthology of supernatural poetry, initially to be called *Tales of Terror* but eventually published as *Tales of Wonder* (1801), and Scott accordingly submitted two poems set in Scotland: 'Glenfinlas; or Lord Ronald's Coronach' and 'The Eve of Saint John', along with two other pieces. 'The Eve of Saint John' represents Scott's first attempt at using ballad metre – what he referred to as 'the measure of his own favourite Minstrels' – for his own poems.[23] In Scott's literary ballad, the baron of 'Smaylho'me' has left his lady behind in the castle. Ostensibly he has gone to fight the English with 'the bold Buccleuch', but although his axe and dagger are stained with blood, 'it [is] not English gore'.[24] The baron has slain a Scot, for reasons that, true to the ballad form, go unexplained. His lady, we learn, has not been content to sit at home and wait, and in a motif that recurs throughout Scott's work, the actions of a servant within the castle complicate the dramatic situation. In this case the foot-page, 'English Will', secretly observes the lady's nightly trysts and informs the baron of the affair. The baron apparently suspects his lady, as he has asked the page to recount her movements in his absence, but he does not suspect Richard of Coldinghame, whom he has just killed.

As a revenant, Coldinghame (whose 'hame' or home is now truly cold) is compelled to wander alone on the eve of Saint John, but the lady does not recognise him as the walking dead. She insists that she will 'chain the bloodhound, and the warder shall not sound, / And rushes shall be strewed on the stair' to facilitate his clandestine entrance into the castle. The priest, who might be awakened at the knight's entrance, is away saying mass 'for the soul

---

23 Scott, *Minstrelsy of the Scottish Border*, vol. 4, pp. 158–77.
24 All quotations from the poem in this chapter are taken from Walter Scott, 'The Eve of Saint John', in Logie Robertson (ed.), *Scott: Poetical Works*, pp. 664–7.

of a knight that is slayne' – ironically, most likely the very knight before her. Like the Wife of Usher's Well, who challenges Nature itself in her passion to regain her drowned sons, the lady conjures her knight 'by the black roodstone and by holy Saint John', and it is her violation of natural and sacred law that enables the revenant to enter the castle.

The truth, however, will out. The revenant Coldinghame articulates the ballad's moral in one neat stanza. In a rhythm recalling Coleridge's Ancient Mariner – 'He prayeth best who loveth best' – Coldinghame intones, 'Who spilleth life shall forfeit life; / So bid thy lord believe: / That lawless love is guilt above, / This awful sign receive.' Then, touching the 'oaken beam' with his left hand and her arm with his right, he leaves burns on both; so branded, henceforth the lady wears 'A covering on her wrist'. The narrative then leaps abruptly to Dryburgh tower, where a nun 'Ne'er looks upon the sun', and then to Melrose tower, where a monk 'speaketh word to none'. The traditional ballad would end here, but Scott is compelled to name them: 'That nun was Smaylho'me's lady gay, / That monk the bold baron.'

Characteristically filled with the historical ballad's references to family names and battles, Scott's ballad also brings his Gothic powers to bear on the narrative. Anything inexplicable, however, is glossed in the extensive introduction, notes and appendix, paratextual elements in which Scott provides historical context, explains antiquated terms and justifies his creative and editorial choices. In the introduction he sets the scene of the ballad, 'Smaylho'me' Tower; in one footnote he glosses 'plate-jack'; in another he chronicles the history of Dryburgh Abbey; as an appendix he attaches a detailed account of the battle of Ancrum Moor. 'The Eve of Saint John' bears testimony to Scott's attraction to German Gothic, but also to local historical and romantic ballad traditions, as well as to historicising romance. The battle rages outside the poem, but the dramatic action takes place in the castle bower, a space which has been violated – literally, by the revenant's visit, and metaphorically by the lady's faithlessness and the baron's act of murder.

After long delays with Lewis's anticipated publication, Scott approached the printer James Ballantyne to produce a limited run of *An Apology for Tales of Terror* (1799), which included his translations of Bürger's ballads and 'The Erl-King', and some pieces by Lewis, Robert Southey and John Aikin, Anna Laetitia Barbauld's brother. Lewis's volume would eventually appear in 1801 under the title *Tales of Wonder*. Here, Scott's affinity for tales about demon lovers and mouldering revenants achieved its widest recognition: a critic in the *Anti-Jacobin Review* deemed Scott to be 'the best of the new species of *horror-breeding Bards'*, an appellation that, as Thomson puts it, Scott himself would later 'gladly disavow'.[25]

Indeed, Scott's association with Lewis would ultimately test and alter his assessment of the Gothic vogue. With their starkly contrasting approaches to the differences between modern ballads and 'real imitations of the ancient ballad', their aesthetic tensions soon became clear. Scott disagreed vehemently with the editorial interventions that Lewis made to four traditional Scottish ballads to be included in *Tales of Wonder*. As Thomson, citing Scott's own headnotes, observes, 'In the *Minstrelsy of the Scottish Border* (1802), Scott pointedly prints more authentic Scottish versions of all four poems with the purpose of restoring their "native simplicity" in opposition to the anglicizing and intrusively Gothic "additions and alternations"' provided by Lewis.[26] Later, in 'Essay on Imitations of the Ancient Ballad' (1830), which originally appeared as prefatory material to the fourth volume of *Minstrelsy*, Scott expressed his appreciation for Lewis's support, but also his relief at having escaped 'the general depreciation of the *Tales of Wonder*'.[27]

Scott managed to blend Germanic influence with his antiquarian enthusiasm, subsequently setting out in search of the Scottish legends and tales that would provide the subjects of his next work.[28] His 'German-mad' period behind him, he 'proceeds to the *Minstrelsy* and establishes his more reputable literary persona as collector and champion of Scotland's literary heritage'.[29] However, though he moved quickly from this point into producing *Minstrelsy of the Scottish Border*, echoes of his earlier Gothic balladry continue to reverberate in the verse romances and novels for which he was to achieve literary fame, providing as they do so a significant link to his later fictional achievements. 'Lenore' and the influence of Lewis are visible in *Marmion* (1803), for example, in the transgressive nun Constance being tried and then buried alive in a monastery wall. Scott's *The Lay of the Last Minstrel* (1805) features the wizard Michael Scott's 'black book'; its removal from his tomb 'unleashes a demonic agency', though, as Ian Duncan observes,

---

25 For the original review of Lewis's *Tales of Wonder*, see *The Anti-Jacobin Review and Magazine* (January–April 1801): 322–7 (p. 327); see, too, Thomson, 'The Gothic Ballad', p. 80.
26 Thomson, 'The Gothic Ballad', p. 80.
27 Scott, *Minstrelsy of the Scottish Border*, vol. 4, p. 76.
28 See Lockhart, *Memoirs of the Life of Sir Walter Scott*, vol. 1 p. 84; Herbert J. C. Grierson, *Sir Walter Scott, Bart* (London: Constable & Co., 1938), p. 24.
29 Thomson, 'The Gothic Ballad', p. 81. For more on Scott's retreat from the Gothic, see Michael Gamer, *Romanticism and the Gothic: Genre, Reception, and Canon Formation* (Cambridge: Cambridge University Press, 2000), pp. 163–97.

ultimately this action 'contributes to the peaceful resolution' of historical conflict.[30] In *The Antiquary* (1816), the eponymous Jonathan Oldbuck pronounces that 'every mansion in this country of the slightest antiquity has its ghosts and its haunted chamber, and you must not suppose us worse off than our [English] neighbours'.[31] And in the closing moments of *The Bride of Lammermoor* (1819), perhaps Scott's most overtly Gothic novel, the volatile young Master of Ravenswood, in furious, mounted pursuit of his antagonists, is swallowed by quicksand right before Colonel Ashton's very eyes: 'At once the figure became invisible, as if it had melted into the air.'[32] More widely, in fact, and as Fiona Robertson, Ian Duncan and others have shown, Scott employed Gothic conventions and narrative techniques extensively throughout his historical fictions, perhaps most obviously in his representations of castle ruins and breaches of security that provoked such terror in him.[33] His earlier interest in the Gothic potential of the ballad, however, was formative, and was rivalled only by that of his near-contemporary and erstwhile collaborator, James Hogg.

James Hogg's Gothic Balladry and Fiction

As Roderick Watson observes, 'Scottish culture in general in the late eighteenth and nineteenth centuries tended to play the more "rational" claims of modernity and the Enlightenment against older discourses from traditional culture, oral lore and superstition.'[34] James Hogg's first major publication, *The Mountain Bard* (1807), shows him positioning himself in his constructions and deconstructions of Scottish identity as mediator in a highly charged balancing act between his roots in oral tradition and Edinburgh's literary culture. Hogg engages both tradition-bearers and literary figures while also presenting himself as a promoter of Scottish culture, a move that marks his work with a profound ambivalence that

---

30 Duncan, 'Walter Scott, James Hogg and Scottish Gothic', p. 127.
31 Walter Scott, *The Antiquary*, edited by Nicola J. Watson (Oxford: Oxford University Press, 2002), p. 89.
32 Walter Scott, *The Bride of Lammermoor*, edited by Fiona Robertson (Oxford: Oxford University Press, 1991), p. 347.
33 See Fiona Robertson, *Legitimate Histories: Scott, Gothic, and the Authorities of Fiction* (Oxford: Clarendon Press, 1994) and Fiona Robertson, 'Gothic Scott', in Davison and Germanà (eds), *Scottish Gothic*, pp. 102–14.
34 Roderick Watson, 'Gothic Stevenson', in Davison and Germanà (eds), *Scottish Gothic*, pp. 142–54 (p. 142).

livens the many voices that he adopts. From a background steeped in oral tradition, and from decidedly underprivileged circumstances, Hogg recognised himself eminently qualified, as Douglas S. Mack phrases it, to 'challenge and subvert' the grand narrative 'by trying to gain a hearing for the subaltern voice'.[35] Thus, he was well positioned to present the traditional ballads and tales of the supernatural to a nineteenth-century audience hungry for Gothic narratives. This aim he pursued with energy, acting as mediator first in his role as informant for Scott's *Minstrelsy* and then as deliberate rewriter of folk narratives in ballad imitations, poetry and fiction.[36]

'The Pedlar', a Gothic ballad imitation included in *The Mountain Bard*, illustrates Hogg's self-fashioning as a writer both of and for traditional culture. The headnote is designed to establish the narrative's veracity and authority, noting that 'This Ballad is founded on a fact', and that, to the aged people in and around Ettrick, 'every part of it is believed by them to be absolute truth'.[37] In this amalgamation of Gothic and traditional ballad, a murdered pedlar returns to terrorise the countryside, appearing with a 'muckle green pack on his shoulders', the colour green signalling his supernatural status.[38] He is seen by members of the communities and each time vanishes: 'Then quick, wi a sound, he sank i' the ground / A knock was heard, an' the fire did flee.'[39] The murderer is revealed through a traditional ballad device: when the pedlar's skeleton is discovered and the guilty miller touches the heel-bone, it suddenly streams with blood, prompting his confession. This device recalls the traditional ballad of 'The Twa Sisters', in which a harp made of the dead sister's breastbone 'sings' the story of her murder. Hogg's closing stanza intervenes directly in contemporary arguments regarding reason, superstition and legal testimony: 'Ca't not superstition, wi' reason you'll find it, / Nor laugh at a story attestit sae weel; / For lang ga'e the *facts* in the forest been mindit / O' the ghaist an' the bane o' the pedlar's heel.'[40] The narrative voice within the ballad employs vernacular Scots freely, often in stark contrast to the headnote and seven pages of detailed notes in standard, editorial-sounding English. For *The Mountain Bard* of 1807, Hogg

---

35 Douglas S. Mack, *Scottish Fiction and the British Empire* (Edinburgh: Edinburgh University Press, 2006), p. 2.
36 Suzanne Gilbert, 'James Hogg and the Authority of Tradition', in Sharon Alker and Holly Faith Nelson (eds), *James Hogg and the Literary Marketplace: Scottish Romanticism and the Working-Class Author* (Farnham: Ashgate, 2009), pp. 93–109 (p. 94).
37 James Hogg, 'The Pedlar', in *The Mountain Bard*, edited by Suzanne Gilbert (Edinburgh: Edinburgh University Press, 2007), pp. 26–36 (p. 26).
38 Hogg, 'The Pedlar', p. 27.   39 Hogg, 'The Pedlar', p. 144.
40 Hogg, 'The Pedlar', p. 31.

had expanded the editorial apparatus; earlier, for the first appearance of 'The Pedlar', in the *Scots Magazine* in November 1804, it was introduced simply as 'A Scottish Ballad in Imitation of the Ancients', the title itself echoing a subsection in Scott's *Minstrelsy*. Assigning authority to the 'tradition' rather than 'the *best informed* old people', a footnote to the 1804 version reads, 'Thirlestane, on the banks of the Ettrick. The ballad being founded on a fact, and every circumstance of it the tradition of the country.'[41] Increasingly over time, Hogg referred to the human sources, the tradition-bearers and their testimony to establish the authenticity of traditional narratives.

One of Hogg's best-known, ballad-influenced poems, 'Kilmeny' from *The Queen's Wake* (1813, 1819), references the ballad of 'Thomas the Rhymer', a fairy-abduction narrative about the thirteenth-century Scottish poet and prophet-figure Thomas Learmont (Sir Thomas of Erceldoune), set in what is now Earlston in the Scottish Borders. Hogg's poem may be seen in the context of increased interest in fairy narratives and tales of supernatural abduction in the early nineteenth century, a vogue that was notably fostered and encouraged by an important publishing event: Walter Scott's bringing to press the manuscripts of the seventeenth-century folklorist Robert Kirk, which were published as *The Secret Commonwealth of Elves, Fauns and Fairies* in 1815. Certainly, the ballad of 'Thomas the Rhymer' enthralled both Scott and Hogg. Scott devoted fifty-two pages of the third volume of *Minstrelsy* (1803) to it, presenting the ballad in three parts, all framed by copious editorial notes. While Hogg links 'Kilmeny' to 'the old ballads of Tam Lean and Thomas of Erceldon' in his notes,[42] the poem departs from the traditional ballad in that 'Bonnie Kilmeny' disappears without explanation, and then after seven years, 'Late, late in the gloamin' and wearing a 'bonnie snood of the birk sae green', she reappears just as mysteriously.[43] She cannot describe where she has been – her account suggests elements of fairyland and also of a kind of heaven – but she has been given a vision of 'what mortal never has seen', as well as of Scotland itself. She cannot reintegrate into her family and community – 'all the land were in fear and dread, / For they kendna whether she was living or dead' – and

---

41 Hogg, 'The Pedlar', p. 143.
42 James Hogg, 'Notes', in *The Queen's Wake*, edited by Douglas S. Mack (Edinburgh: Edinburgh University Press, 2004), p. 377.
43 James Hogg, 'Kilmeny', in *The Queen's Wake*, edited by Douglas S. Mack (Edinburgh: Edinburgh University Press, 2004), pp. 288–96 (p. 289). Quotations are taken from the 1819 version of *The Queen's Wake*, for which Hogg substantially revised the 1813 version of 'Kilmeny'.

she elects to return to that otherworld, the 'land of thought'.[44] She disappears again, and this time 'on earth was never mair seen', the detail echoing the ballad lines, 'till seven years were gane and past / True Thomas on earth was never seen'.[45] While Hogg's poem does not adhere to standard ballad form, its leaping-and-lingering narrative movement, together with the use of incremental repetition, infuses it with an explanation-eluding ambiguity that is similar to that created by the ballad's gaps between stanzas.

Hogg's exploration of Gothic, of course, was not confined to any particular genre or form, and the burgeoning growth of commercial periodicals provided a market for his ballads, poems, songs, tales and essays. Scott Brewster has helpfully linked Hogg's Gothic to 'the vernacular storytelling tradition of Lowland Scotland';[46] through his close association with *Blackwood's Edinburgh Magazine*, Hogg secured some, if unreliable, financial support and a growing readership. Robert Morrison observes that 'in [Hogg's] finest *Blackwood's* tales the "uncanny" and the "unaccountable" both defy all attempts at rational explanation, and provoke the extremes of paranoia and obsession'.[47] In 'Mary Burnet', a story written for and published in *Blackwood's* in February of 1828 and in *The Shepherd's Calendar* (1829) of the following year, Hogg returns to the ballad of supernatural abduction, but employs it here for the purposes of prose narrative. As in *The Mountain Bard*, Hogg positions himself in 'Mary Burnet' as mediator between his modern, enlightened reader and traditional culture, but insists that his role is 'to cherish the visions that have been, as well as the hope of visions yet in reserve'.[48] In the story, the disreputable John Allanson wishes three times that 'some witch or fairy would influence his Mary to come to him' at a spot on the edge of St Mary's Loch. Mary suddenly appears 'with wild and eccentric motions, speeding to the appointed place', as if she has no control over her movements.[49] After he has taken full advantage of her, she is

---

44 Hogg, 'Kilmeny', p. 296.
45 'Thomas Rhymer' (variant 37C) appeared in Scott's *Minstrelsy of the Scottish Border*, vol. 2 (1802). The citation is taken from Child, *The English and Scottish Popular Ballads*, vol. 1, pp. 325–6.
46 Scott Brewster, 'Gothic Hogg', in Davison and Germanà (eds), *Scottish Gothic*, pp. 115–28 (p. 116).
47 Robert Morrison, '"The Singular Wrought Out into the Strange and Mystical": *Blackwood's Edinburgh Magazine* and the Transformation of Terror', in Davison and Germanà (eds), *Scottish Gothic*, pp. 129–41 (p. 134).
48 James Hogg, 'Mary Burnet', in *The Shepherd's Calendar*, edited by Douglas S. Mack (Edinburgh: Edinburgh University Press, 2002), pp. 200–22 (p. 200).
49 Hogg, 'Mary Burnet', p. 201.

inconsolable; throwing herself into the loch, she sinks out of sight. But when Allanson goes to give her parents the terrible news, she is found in her own bed, clothes dry and neatly folded. The next day she disappears, and the 'whole country' agrees that 'it had been the real Mary Burnet who was drowned in the loch, and that the being which was found in her bed, lying weeping and complaining of suffering, and which vanished the next day, had been a fairy, an evil spirit, or a changeling of some sort'.[50]

Hogg's narrative, then, remains rife with ambiguity. At a hiring fair, 'Mary', or something uncannily like her, appears to Allanson numerous times, wearing green, and targets his sexual predilection to lure him into a trap of enchantment. Ultimately, his 'mangled corpse' is found at the bottom of a ravine.[51] Beginning with the suggestion that Mary has been replaced by a changeling before she disappears, and then returns in garb suggesting the Fairy Queen, the story draws on 'Thomas the Rhymer' and a range of traditional fairylore. Her return after seven years (a fairy convention) to torture John Allanson is couched in decidedly supernatural terms. But, unlike 'Thomas the Rhymer', many voices jostle against one another to judge whether she is still the human Mary, a changeling or the Fairy Queen – that is, whether supernatural forces have taken vengeance for the deceased Mary. A 'little shrivelled old man', a 'creature ... was not above five spans in height' with a face 'scarcely like that of a human creature', a figure whom the reader may recognise as a brownie, arrives to tell Mary's father that she is 'living, and in good health'.[52] The reader, however, is left to weigh the vengeful pursuit of Allanson's punishment through enchantment with the actions of the 'long-lost darling', the loving daughter who visits her parents and presents to them her two sons, before disappearing again forever (on a mysterious chariot, hardly a common mode of transport in Moffat).[53]

Hogg's 'The Brownie of the Black Haggs', published in *Blackwood's* in October 1828 and then again in *The Shepherd's Calendar*, explores a toxic mix of the supernatural with the religious persecution of the Covenanters in the 1680s. Following his usual method, Hogg anchors the story in the community, citing sources and pinpointing locations as if to vouch for the authenticity of the tale: it was 'told to me by an old man, named Adam Halliday, whose great grandfather, Thomas Halliday, was one of those that found the body and buried it'.[54] In the story, the strange servant Merodach (the biblical

---

50 Hogg, 'Mary Burnet', p. 209.   51 Hogg, 'Mary Burnet', p. 217.
52 Hogg, 'Mary Burnet', pp. 217, 219.   53 Hogg, 'Mary Burnet', p. 221.
54 James Hogg, 'The Brownie of the Black Haggs', in *The Shepherd's Calendar*, edited by Douglas S. Mack (Edinburgh: Edinburgh University Press, 2002), pp. 242–55 (p. 254).

name of the god of Babylon, Jeremiah 50.2) is identifiable as a brownie, a figure, according to popular tradition, with 'the form of a boy, but the features of one a hundred years old', who eats only bread and sweet milk and is referred to throughout as a 'creature'.[55] He is 'froward [sic] and perverse in all of his actions' and '[disregards] the pleasure or displeasure of any person', but performs his work 'well, and with apparent ease'.[56] This uncanny figure appears when the wicked Lady Wheelhope, a vociferous anti-Convenanter, is tormenting, even poisoning, her religious servants until such time as 'the poor persecuted Covenanters were obliged to unite in their prayers against her'.[57] His coming prompts an uncontrollable rage in the Lady Wheelhope, and the enmity between the two spirals brutally out of control, eventually leading to her murder and burial 'like a dog'. The narrator reports that the fugitive Covenanters who found her 'rolled three huge stones upon her grave, which are lying there to this day', and that 'When they found her corpse, it was mangled and wounded in a most shocking manner, the fiendish creature having manifestly tormented her to death.'[58] It is reported that the brownie was 'never more seen or heard of in this kingdom, though all that country-side was kept in terror for him many years afterwards'.[59] The narrative voice compares the story to another that turns on a similar 'passion of inveterate malice', but abruptly overthrows the sense of authenticity that has been established by concluding that, 'upon the whole, I scarcely believe the tale can be true'.[60]

Hogg's masterpiece of Scottish Gothic, *The Private Memoirs and Confessions of a Justified Sinner* (1824), employs the same strategies found in his other work, among them diverse, multiple perspectives and competing, fractured narratives. It deals in found manuscripts, the demonic, unquiet graves, doubling, obsession and possession, all deployed in the context of Scotland's uniquely tangled political and religious history. As in the stories, Hogg in the *Confessions* frequently employs subaltern, vernacular voices to call into question the narrative voice that, at first glance, might seem to dominate. It is an approach that challenges the reader's sense of authority, authenticity and reliability, allowing Hogg to subvert Enlightenment assumptions and to decentre narrative authority. Alison Milbank in this

---

55 Hogg, 'The Brownie of the Black Haggs', p. 246.
56 Hogg, 'The Brownie of the Black Haggs', p. 244.
57 Hogg, 'The Brownie of the Black Haggs', p. 242.
58 Hogg, 'The Brownie of the Black Haggs', p. 254.
59 Hogg, 'The Brownie of the Black Haggs', p. 254.
60 Hogg, 'The Brownie of the Black Haggs', p. 255.

regard has pointed to the 'human mediation' provided by the perspectives of Arabella Logan and Arabella Calvert, characters who 'become the agents of justice, seeking to establish the truth about George Colwan's murder', and whose findings undercut the assumptions of 'The Editor's Narrative'.[61] And, famously, the character of Hogg refuses to join the Editor in the latter's increasingly obsessive quest to find the suicide's grave ('I hae mair ado than I can manage the day, foreby ganging to houk up hunder-year-auld banes').[62] The description in the shepherd's letter to *Blackwood's*, itself contested, first compels the editor to seek out the grave. When reading the letter, the editor muses, 'It bears the stamp of authenticity in every line; yet, so often had I been hoaxed by the ingenious fancies displayed in that Magazine.'[63] The letter's veracity is questioned again when the editor asks Mr L—t of C—d whether Hogg's letter is 'founded at all on truth' and is answered, 'I suppose so. For my part I never doubted the thing, having been told that there has been a deal of talking about it up in the Forest for some time past', and then, 'But, God knows! Hogg has imposed as ingenious lies on the public ere now.'[64]

The 'Auchtermuchty Tale' that is embedded in *The Private Memoirs and Confessions of a Justified Sinner* foregrounds the view presented by Robert Wringhim's servant, which subverts Wringhim's story of his victimisation. Wringham describes Scrape as 'my man, Samuel Scrape, who was a very honest blunt fellow, a staunch Cameronian, but withal very little conversant in religious matters'.[65] Scrape enquires,

> 'do you ken what the auld wives o' the clachan say about you?', adding that 'there are some o' them weel kend for witches too; an' they say, – lord have a care o' us! – they say the deil's often seen gaun sidie for sidie w'ye, whiles in ae shape, an' whiles in another. An' they say that he whiles takes your ain shape, or else enters into you, and then you turn a deil yoursel'.[66]

The tale that Scrape tells responds to Wringhim's request to know 'all that passed between you and the wives of the clachan'.[67] The tale itself is of the devil in disguise preaching in the village of Auchtermuchty, who is revealed

---

61 Alison Milbank, 'Calvinist and Covenanter Gothic', in Carol Margaret Davison and Monica Germanà (eds), *Scottish Gothic*, pp. 89–101 (p. 95).
62 James Hogg, *The Private Memoirs and Confessions of a Justified Sinner*, edited by P. D. Garside (Edinburgh: Edinburgh University Press, 2001), p. 170.
63 Hogg, *The Private Memoirs and Confessions*, p. 169.
64 Hogg, *The Private Memoirs and Confessions*, p. 169.
65 Hogg, *The Private Memoirs and Confessions*, p. 133.
66 Hogg, *The Private Memoirs and Confessions*, p. 135.
67 Hogg, *The Private Memoirs and Confessions*, p. 136.

to have cloven feet by a villager with second sight. The story over, Wringhim reclaims the narrative by dismissing 'the clown's absurd story'.[68]

Of Scottish fantasy in general, and of Hogg's novel in particular, Colin Manlove has observed that 'the fantastic experience and the world from which it emanates are very close to our own – into which they can come at any time. In the midst of an everyday experience of Edinburgh, Robert / Wringhim in Hogg's *Confessions* moves in a landscape of hell'.[69] While the novel is indeed, as Nick Groom puts it, 'persistently on the verge of releasing supernatural demonology into the plot', it is also 'doggedly mundane in its scenes and settings'.[70] In the *Confessions*, the supernatural-abduction narratives, so rooted in tradition and depicting supernatural events in a very matter-of-fact fashion, take on yet another form. The notion of there being two worlds, and of being taken from one to another, shifts when the two worlds become, uncannily, almost one and the same. In this scenario, abduction becomes a kind of possession and obsession, an external abductor (or double) turning inwards. When Wringhim remarks on Gil-Martin's 'cameleon art' of changing his appearance, an ability that amounts to Gothic shape-shifting, he replies,

> My countenance changes with my studies and sensations ... It is a natural peculiarity in me, over which I have not full control. If I contemplate a man's features seriously, mine own gradually assume the very same appearance and character. And what is more, by contemplating a face minutely, I not only attain the same likeness, but, with the likeness, I attain the very same ideas as well as the same mode of arranging them, so that, you see, by looking at a person attentively, I by degrees assume his likeness, and by assuming his likeness I attain to the possession of his most secret thoughts.[71]

For Wringhim, the joining is inescapable: 'to shake him off was impossible – we were incorporated together – identified with one another, as it were, and the power was not in me to separate myself from him'.[72] In this play of uncanniness, the boundaries between self and other disintegrate, constituting, in Ian Duncan's words, 'unstable slidings between literal and figurative meaning, the intimation of powers and causes inaccessible to consciousness'.[73] Albeit not primarily through the techniques of splitting,

---

68 Hogg, *The Private Memoirs and Confessions*, p. 140.
69 Colin Manlove, *Scottish Fantasy Literature: A Critical Survey* (Edinburgh: Canongate Academic, 1994), pp. 13–14.
70 Nick Groom, '"The Celtic Century" and the Genesis of Scottish Gothic', p. 23.
71 Hogg, *The Private Memoirs and Confessions*, p. 86.
72 Hogg, *The Private Memoirs and Confessions*, p. 126.
73 Duncan, 'Walter Scott, James Hogg and Scottish Gothic', pp. 131–2.

doubling and textual proliferation, Margaret Oliphant later in the nineteenth century would produce an equally uncanny form of Scottish Gothic fiction in and through her characteristic preoccupation with the tenuous boundaries between visible and invisible worlds.

Margaret Oliphant's Seen and Unseen Worlds

A few years before beginning work on *A Beleaguered City*, Margaret Oliphant remarked on the 1817 edition of Coleridge's 'The Rime of the Ancient Mariner', loosely quoting Coleridge's translation of the Latin epigraph that he had taken from Thomas Burnet's *Archaelogiae philosophicae* (1692):

> '*There is more of the invisible than the visible in the world about us*' ... The mind grows giddy, the imagination trembles and wavers. Our senses become confused, unable to identify what we see from what we hear; and finally, triumphantly, the unseen sweeps in and holds possession, more real, more true, and more unquestionable than anything that eye can see.[74]

Over a career that spanned much of the nineteenth century, Oliphant touched on a vast array of subjects in her fiction, essays and reviews. But her greatest contribution to Scottish Gothic came through her intense preoccupation with what she here referred to as 'the seen' and 'the unseen', and in testing the thin and sometimes indiscernible boundary between them. Her fascination with this subject was deeply personal, prompted by grief over the loss of three children, and, in the last 20 years of her life, she wrote a cluster of supernatural stories that all variously explored the theme.

By employing varied, nuanced qualities of light and darkness, Oliphant in these stories explores the distinction between the seen and the unseen, and the sensory confusion that is created when that boundary seems to be crossed or distorted. In all her narratives of the supernatural, the most sensitive, open or vulnerable characters, usually women or children, have access to this liminal space. What is seen and not seen is also related to the unspeakable, and to the functioning of community and family. Influenced by the Gothic tale, Victorian ghost stories, ballads and Calvinism, these stories illustrate the ways in which supernatural abduction may be internalised, constituting a psychological takeover of the self that approaches the Gothic motif of

---

74 Quoted in Vineta Colby and Robert A. Colby, *The Equivocal Virtue: Mrs Oliphant and the Victorian Market Place* (Hamden, Connecticut: Archon Books, 1966), p. 285.

possession.[75] Jenni Calder, characterising Oliphant's fictional reality as 'woven out of characters who exemplify the traditional readiness of the Scottish imagination to accommodate the unseen and the unexplainable', pinpoints the 'currents' that contribute to this in 'the environment, a contentious history brimming with attempts to justify unjustifiable actions, and an uncompromising religion'.[76]

Oliphant's *A Beleaguered City* first appeared in an abridged version in the *New Quarterly Magazine* in January 1879, and the full-length book was published in 1880 under the lengthy title *A Beleaguered City, Being a Narrative of Certain Recent Events in the City of Semur, in the Department of the haute Bourgogne, A Story of the Seen and the Unseen*. Prompted by a visit to Semur, France, in 1871, it features as its primary narrator the town's mayor Martin Dupin, who, like Hogg's editor in *The Confessions* and Stevenson's narrator Mackellar in the later *The Master of Ballantrae* (1889), presents himself as the rational and reliable 'head of the community'. The reader, however, finds him a rather vain and self-important character: insisting that he has 'always been noted as a man of fine perceptions' and that 'the faculty of imagination has always been one of my characteristics', he adds that 'It usually is so ... in superior minds.'[77]

Dupin's inability to fathom or otherwise conceptualise the unseen, however, becomes clear when Semur is suddenly plunged into darkness, the dead rise and invisible forces expel the people from the town. In a folktale-like trajectory, the dead return seemingly in answer to the townspeople's earlier repeated though unwitting pronouncements that observed acts of crass materialism are 'enough to make the dead rise out of their graves'.[78] These revenants, though, are not the corporeal undead of the ballad tradition. Instead, they are invisible, comprised of spirit and a restless, oppressive energy, and Oliphant depicts their effect as a sensory assault. The sceptical mayor is plunged into an unfamiliar and uncomfortable state, one in which he has no control. As he feels himself being 'softy, firmly, irresistably pushed out of the gate', he loses the ability to speak: 'I was not my own master. My tongue clave to the roof of my mouth; I could not say a word.'[79] Attempting to describe the effect

---

75 See Jenni Calder, 'Introduction', in Margaret Oliphant, *A Beleaguered City and Other Tales of the Seen and the Unseen*, edited by Jenni Calder (Edinburgh: Canongate, 2000), pp. vii–xviii (pp. x–xi).
76 Calder, 'Introduction', p. xiii.
77 Margaret Oliphant, 'A Beleaguered City', in *A Beleaguered City and Other Tales of the Seen and the Unseen*, pp. 1–105 (pp. 9, 8).
78 Oliphant, 'A Beleaguered City', p. 3.   79 Oliphant, 'A Beleaguered City', p. 28.

of the dead's occupation of Semur, Dupin remarks, 'It was rather now as if the world had become a grave in which we, though living, were held fast.'[80] It is the women of the town and one man, the visionary dreamer Lecamus, who can 'see' that the dead have reclaimed the town, and ultimately it is their understanding of what the dead want that resolves the stalemate.

Throughout her stories of the seen, the unseen and the porous boundary between them, Oliphant juxtaposes light and dark in relation to acts of sensory perception. In each case a prominent character is able to access that which ordinarily eludes vision. In 'The Open Door', a ghost story published in Blackwood's in January 1882, it is the child Roland who provides the crucial link between the two realms. The narrator, Roland's father who is said to be a 'sober man ... and not superstitious', reveals that the boy is 'fragile in body ... and deeply sensitive in mind'.[81] Judged to be suffering from 'cerebral excitement', Roland insists to his father that 'it's not illness, – it's a secret', and that there is 'some one that has been badly used' in the ruins of the old mansion.[82] Traditional knowledge and experience inform the narrative, as the father learns from his coachman and his wife that the ruin is haunted, and that during November and December 'the visitation' occurs, a time when strange, plaintive cries are heard. Jarvis tells him, 'Some people, bolder or more imaginative than the others, had seen the darkness moving.'[83] Those having this heightened perception are contrasted in the story with the proponents of science, who have 'cold-blooded confidence' but no real vision.[84]

Oliphant's 'The Library Window', which was first published in January 1896, was the last of the writer's stories of the supernatural to be published in Blackwood's and pulls together thematic strands that had run throughout her earlier Gothic writing. In its presentation of the first-person narrator's possible experiences of second sight and the traditional narrative (a family curse) that underpins it, and in its nuanced depiction of a sensitive, suggestible mind increasingly obsessed with a seeming hallucination, the story pushes further the confusion of boundaries between the seen and unseen worlds. Tamar Heller cites 'The Library Window' as an example of the 'female uncanny' and

---

80 Oliphant, 'A Beleaguered City', p. 19.
81 Margaret Oliphant, 'The Open Door', in *A Beleaguered City and Other Tales of the Seen and the Unseen*, pp. 171–210 (pp. 180, 171).
82 Oliphant, 'The Open Door', pp. 194, 178.   83 Oliphant, 'The Open Door', p. 184.
84 Oliphant, 'The Open Door', p. 205.

argues that 'the frisson of this brilliantly eerie tale is produced by its intense interiority'.[85] It shares certain features with Charlotte Perkins Gilman's 'The Yellow Wallpaper' (1892), published four years earlier in *The New England Magazine*, particularly in its use of an unnamed, female first-person narrator who has been deemed by patriarchal medical opinion to need a rest cure, and who increasingly 'sees' a human figure in an inanimate surface.

In Oliphant's story, the light and her evocations of it are among its most uncanny elements. Set in St Rules – unambiguously St Andrews in Fife on the northeast coast – during the long evenings of a Scottish summer, the narrative turns on what is revealed and not revealed by the 'soft strange' twilight or gloaming: 'in the evening in June in Scotland – then is the time to see. For it is daylight, yet it is not day, and there is a quality in it which I cannot describe, it is so clear, as if every object was a reflection of itself'.[86] Variants of the phrases 'then is the time to see' and 'a light which is daylight yet is not day' recur as a kind of refrain at key moments throughout the narrative. The unnamed narrator reflects on a time in her youth when she spent hours overlooking the High Street from a perch in the recess of her aunt's drawing-room window, a period during when she became increasingly obsessed with a window in the library across the road, but a fixture that alternatively may not be a window at all. The light presides over moments of insight and moves her towards discovery, as reflected syntactically in a drawn-out series of dependent phrases leading to the revelation, even to herself, that she has noticed the 'window':

> It was getting late, though the clear soft daylight went on and on. All through the lingering evening, which seemed to consist of interminable hours, long but not weary, drawn out as if the spell of the light and the outdoor life might never end, I had now and then, quite unawares, cast a glance at the mysterious window.[87]

She soon becomes convinced that what was once only greyness is a space that recedes back into the gloom, subsequently describing, in syntactically complex and obscure prose, 'a sort of vision, very dim, of a wall, and something against it; something dark, with the blackness that a solid article, however

---

85 Tamar Heller, 'Textual seductions: women's reading and writing in Margaret Oliphant's "The Library Window"', *Victorian Literature and Culture* 25:1 (Spring 1997): 23–37 (p. 23).
86 Margaret Oliphant, 'The Library Window', in *A Beleaguered City and Other Tales of the Seen and the Unseen*, pp. 363–402 (pp. 389, 373).
87 Oliphant, 'The Library Window', p. 369.

indistinctly seen, takes into the lighter darkness that is only space – a large, black, dark thing coming out into the grey'.[88]

At midsummer, suddenly she perceives a man in the window; over a series of sightings, she observes him 'writing, writing always' at a desk.[89] Increasingly, she is able to identify details of the man's minute movements from across the street at twilight, such as 'a faint turn of his head as he went from one side to another of the page he was writing'.[90] The narrator thinks of him in terms of her father, a writer, and invokes a story about Walter Scott's compulsive work ethic as documented in Lockhart's *Memoirs of the Life of Sir Walter Scott* (1837–8). Watching him is something that she cannot help doing: 'It become like a fascination', she writes; 'I could not take my eyes from him and that little scarcely perceptible movement he made, turning his head.'[91] This moment echoes one in Hogg's *Confessions*: when Wringhim encounters Gil-Martin during an early meeting, he reflects, 'There was ... a fascination in his look and manner, that drew me back toward him in spite of myself, and I resolved to go to him, if it were merely to speak and see who he was.'[92] Such compulsive observation of one party by another had been figured in such earlier Gothic fictions as William Godwin's *Caleb Williams* (1794) and Mary Shelley's *Frankenstein* (1818); the same sense of urgency governs the passionate curiosity of Oliphant's narrator in 'The Library Window'. The opposition that is established between the narrator's certainty that the man exists and the implied judgement that she is simply imagining things is further complicated by the baker's boy, who seems to see the window from the street below, and in fact throws a rock at it. The narrator experiences sensory confusion when she hears the thud of the stone on the 'window' and sees it strike panes of glass. But the baker's boy also sees the window open and stands 'staring up ... with his mouth open and his face full of wonder' at the moment when the narrator sees the man who 'had lifted his hand and waved it' to her across the street.[93]

A stream of visitors to the house incrementally reveals information supporting a traditionally based, supernatural cause for the narrator's sightings: a family curse. The brothers of the narrator's female ancestor killed a scholar working in the library, whom they believed to have

---

88 Oliphant, 'The Library Window', p. 370.
89 Oliphant, 'The Library Window', p. 378.
90 Oliphant, 'The Library Window', p. 379.
91 Oliphant, 'The Library Window', p. 380.
92 Hogg, *The Private Memoirs and Confessions*, p. 85.
93 Oliphant, 'The Library Window', p. 396.

responded to their sister's flirtatious wave from the window across the street. The family's women are cursed henceforth by the scholar's ghost, doomed forever to see and relive that fatal moment. As Aunt Mary eventually explains, 'we all saw him in our time – that is ... the ones that are like you and me'.[94] Of the visitors, most prominent is Old Lady Carnbee who, addressing the narrator's aunt, exclaims, 'My faith! ... there is that bairn there still like a dream. Is the creature bewitched, Mary Balcarres? and is she bound to sit there by night and by day for the rest of her days? You should mind that there's things about, uncanny for women of our blood.'[95] But the supernatural is filtered through the narrator's perception too, and her kind of seeing is telescopic, the focus moving from wide to narrow, as is apparent in her approach to other strange things: through her curious powers of defamiliarisation, she actively renders them uncanny. She is afraid of Lady Carnbee, for example, and the terror emerges slowly, with subtle shifts of light and creative perception. Beginning with simple, objective description, the narrator focuses more and more closely on the old woman's hand, which, anatomised into its distinctively shaped fingers, lifeless colour, blue veins and jewellery, increasingly becomes an object of terror: 'The hand, which seemed to come almost to a point, with this strange ornament underneath, clutched at my half-terrified imagination. It too seemed to mean far more than was said. I felt as if it might clutch me with sharp claws, and the lurking, dazzling creature bite – with a sting that would go to the heart.'[96]

As elsewhere in Oliphant's fiction, the motif of the seen and the unseen is often related to 'things that should not be spoken of' and the way in which a family or community functions. The narrator, for instance, frequently abstains from speaking. Like the curse, secrets and unfulfilled desires run in the family, as Aunt Mary makes clear when the narrator presses her for more information: 'I will not speak another word', 'I canna tell you! How can I tell you, when I know just what you know and no more? It is a longing all your life after – it is a looking – for what never comes.'[97] As I argue by way of conclusion to this chapter below, however, it is in the fiction of Robert Louis Stevenson in the last two decades of the nineteenth century that this sense of the unspeakable, together with many of the other features

---

94 Oliphant, 'The Library Window', p. 399.   95 Oliphant, 'The Library Window', p. 371.
96 Oliphant, 'The Library Window', p. 367.
97 Oliphant, 'The Library Window', p. 398.

of nineteenth-century Scottish Gothic that I have explored in this chapter, would reach their crescendo.

Robert Louis Stevenson's Gothic Culminations

Born into a family of engineers epitomising the rational, scientific ethos of the Enlightenment, but also steeped from infancy in traditional Scottish tales of the supernatural and seventeenth-century religious history, Robert Louis Stevenson was particularly well situated to negotiate and find expression for the dualities that proliferate in nineteenth-century Scottish Gothic writing. His nurse, Alison Cunningham ('Cummy') was 'a Fifer steeped in Covenanting lore', whose broad Scots speech enlivened the stories he heard and enabled his later deftness with incorporating the vernacular into his fiction.[98] To her he dedicated *A Child's Garden of Verses* (1885), some poems in which recall those frightening traditional Scottish tales and which, in retrospect, seem rather too Gothic for a book of children's verse. 'Shadow March', for instance, a poem replete with references to darkness, ominous shadows and a host of terrifying 'bogies', employs the suspenseful paranoia and supernatural creatures of folk narrative, but also the incremental repetitions and cadences of a ballad such as 'Lenore': 'The shadow of the balusters, the shadow of the lamp, / The shadow of the child that goes to bed— / All the wicked shadows coming tramp, tramp, tramp, / With the black night overhead.'[99] In addition to these balladic and folkloric influences, Stevenson as a young man was fascinated by the extreme histories of the Presbyterian martyrs, such as George Sinclair's *Satan's Invisible World Discovered* (1685) and Robert Wodrow's *The History of the Suffering of the Church of Scotland from the Restoration to the Revolution* (1721–2). His style, he told J. M. Barrie, 'is from the Covenanting writers';[100] to George Saintsbury, similarly, he wrote of the 'common devotion' that he with Hogg shared to the 'quaint unwholesome authors' of Covenanting literature, 'of which I read more when young than you could dream'.[101]

---

98 William Gray, *Robert Louis Stevenson: A Literary Life* (New York: Palgrave Macmillan, 2004), p. 52.
99 Robert Louis Stevenson, *A Child's Garden of Verses*, illustrated by Charles Robinson (New York: Charles Scribner's Sons; London: John Lane, 1895), p. 77.
100 Robert Louis Stevenson, *The Letters of Robert Louis Stevenson*, edited by Bradford Booth and Ernest Mehew, 8 vols (New Haven and London: Yale University Press, 1994–5), vol. 8, p. 205; Gray, *Robert Louis Stevenson*, p. 49.
101 *Letters of Robert Louis Stevenson*, vol. 7, p. 126; Gray, *Robert Louis Stevenson*, p. 49.

Stephen Arata observes that Stevenson's approach to Scottish subjects was 'by way of Gothic', though that approach took remarkably different forms across his writing.[102] At age eighteen, Stevenson was planning a collection of stories for *A Covenanting Storybook*;[103] later it was retitled *The Black Man and Other Tales* (in Scottish tradition and Covenanting writing, the devil often appears as a black man). The stories were never published as a group, but among them was 'Thrawn Janet', which was published in *Cornhill Magazine* in October 1881. Hearkening back to Hogg's tales that, like the 'Auchtermuchty Tale' embedded in *The Confessions*, employ traditional narratives and vernacular Scots, 'Thrawn Janet' engages with what Watson describes as 'orality, hard-core Calvinism and the Scottish Gothic'.[104] The story opens with an official, editorial-sounding voice, setting the scene in the parish of Balweary and introducing the retrospective tale of the Reverend Soulis's downfall. But the narrative is soon taken over by a folk or community voice speaking in broad Scots, 'one of the older folk' who would 'warm into courage over his third tumbler, and recount the cause of the minister's strange looks and solitary life', beginning with his hiring of a housekeeper against local advice.[105] Janet M'Clour is a solitary woman who, they say, gave birth in her youth to an illegitimate child, and whose body is twisted and her nature intractable. She has refused communion for decades and, worse, is reputedly possessed by the devil. Soulis, the educated, enlightened minister, repeatedly tries to propose rational explanations for the strange happenings that his parishioners assume are attributable to demonic influence. He then encounters the black man himself, surrounded by reeling crows: 'a man, or the appearance o' a man, sittin' … upon a grave', 'of a great stature, an' black as hell, an' his e'en were singular to see'.[106] Unsettled to the core, he begins to consider, as he watches his uncanny housekeeper washing clothes, 'what folk said, that Janet was deid lang syne, an' this was a bogle in her clay-cauld flesh'; and he watches her 'tramp-trampin'' in the cla'es, croonin' to hersel'.[107] That night, one 'that has never been forgotten in Ba'weary', he sees Janet hanging on the wall, on a nail 'held only by a single thread', her heels 'twa feet clear abune the floor'.[108] After witnessing her 'yon unhaly footstep that cam' ploddin' doun the stairs inside the manse', he, shaken and possessed by the

---

102 Arata, 'Stevenson and *Fin-de-Siècle* Gothic', p. 59.
103 Watson, 'Gothic Stevenson', p. 143.   104 Watson, 'Gothic Stevenson', p. 144.
105 Robert Louis Stevenson, 'Thrawn Janet', in Douglas Dunn (ed.), *The Oxford Book of Scottish Short Stories* (Oxford: Oxford University Press, 1995), pp. 110–17 (p. 111).
106 Stevenson, 'Thrawn Janet', p. 113.   107 Stevenson, 'Thrawn Janet', p. 115.
108 Stevenson, 'Thrawn Janet', pp. 115, 116.

horror of that moment, is forever changed. And, as the narrator initially relates, he walks after dark, 'sometimes groaning aloud in the instancy of his unspoken prayers'.[109]

Given Stevenson's upbringing and childhood preoccupations, it is no surprise that his imagination was populated by a range of Scottish 'bogles' (ghosts, spectres or phantoms that cause fright); nor that his unconscious delivered the germ of *Strange Case of Dr Jekyll and Mr Hyde* (1886) in a dream; nor that he would think of the story he composed so feverishly in terms of a legendary, dwarfish creature. 'I send you herewith a Gothic gnome', he announced in a letter to W. H. Low on 2 January 1886, referring perhaps to the narrative as a whole but also to the characters he had created: 'The gnome's name is JEKYLL & HYDE.' As he continues, 'The gnome is interesting, I think, and he came out of a deep mine.'[110] In its transferral of traditional resonances into an urban, industrial setting, and in its exploration of the extremes of splits and doubling so well established in nineteenth-century Scottish Gothic literature and culture, Stevenson's narrative, like Hogg's 'The Brownie of the Black Haggs', does, indeed, owe much to the 'deep mine' of Scottish tales of the supernatural and to Covenanting literature, and is thus a fitting point of conclusion to this discussion.

As he is described by Utterson, Hyde physically recalls the supernatural brownie of tradition, at least in its more unpleasant form: he is 'pale and dwarfish', giving the 'impression of deformity without any nameable malformation'; he has 'a displeasing smile' and demonstrates 'a sort of murderous mixture of timidity and boldness' and speaks 'with a husky, whispering and somewhat broken voice' – all characteristics shared with the brownie Merodach in Hogg's 'The Brownie of the Black Haggs'.[111] And though these are 'points against him', Utterson, in all the ineffability of the uncanny encounter, cannot identify exactly why it is that Hyde fills him with 'the hitherto unknown disgust, loathing and fear'.[112] Perplexed, he speculates: 'There must be something else ... There *is* something more, if I could find a name for it.'[113] The exact words fail him, however, and, continuing to flounder for the appropriate language, he resorts immediately to such inadequate phrases as 'hardly human' and 'Something troglodytic'.[114] The biblical

---

109 Stevenson, 'Thrawn Janet', p. 110.
110 *Letters of Robert Louis Stevenson*, vol. 2, p. 163.
111 Robert Louis Stevenson, *Strange Case of Dr Jekyll and Mr Hyde and Weir of Hermiston*, edited by Emma Letley (Oxford: Oxford University Press, 1987), p. 19.
112 Stevenson, *Strange Case*, p. 19.   113 Stevenson, *Strange Case*, p. 19.
114 Stevenson, *Strange Case*, p. 19.

note in his attempts to describe Hyde – 'mere radiance of a foul soul that thus transpires through, and transfigures, its clay continent' – echoes the language of Covenanting literature, the source, Stevenson claimed, of his own style.[115] Hyde's actions also invoke the sociopathic indifference ascribed to the more malevolent type of brownie in the Scottish tradition: he tramples 'calmly' over a young girl's body and leaves her 'screaming on the ground', while, with 'ape-like fury', he tramples another victim, Danvers Carew, under foot, 'hailing down a storm of blows, under which the bones were audibly shattered and the body jumped upon the roadway'.[116] Again, the allusions to the murders committed by Hogg's equally simian brownie Merodach are striking.

Significantly for nineteenth-century Scottish Gothic, Stevenson's novel delves philosophically into the complexity of split and doubled consciousness that was long prevalent in Scottish culture, and an element of Enlightenment-driven scientific pursuit underpins the narrative. Doomed by a horrifically botched experiment, a broken Jekyll ponders at the end of his life the nature of human existence. In 'The Full Statement of the Case', he concedes that 'man is not truly one, but truly two' (and perhaps more) existing in the same body at the same time, and is mortified that 'that insurgent horror was knit to him closer than a wife, closer than an eye, lay caged in his flesh, where he heard it mutter and felt it struggle to be born'.[117] He observes that 'of the two natures that contended' within him, 'even if I could rightly be said to be either, it was only because I was radically both'.[118] While *The Private Memoirs and Confessions of a Justified Sinner* arrives at many of the same conclusions regarding human duality, it is the ambiguity associated with the supernatural that presides over the events in Hogg's text. Narratives concerning the murder of George Colwan, for example, compete with one another for supremacy – is it Wringhim or a separate being, the shape-shifting Gil-Martin-as-Wringhim, committing the crime? – though later in Wringim's narrative there is a sense of the two being fully merged with one another. Wringhim claims to be 'utterly ignorant of the crimes' of which he is accused, defensively claiming that 'I have two souls, which take possession of my bodily frame by turns, the one being all unconscious of what the other performs.'[119] As Gil-Martin insists, 'Our beings are amalgamated, as it were, and consociated in one.'[120] Just as Stevenson's Hyde is 'closer than a wife' to

---

115 Stevenson, *Strange Case*, p. 19.   116 Stevenson, *Strange Case*, pp. 9, 26.
117 Stevenson, *Strange Case*, pp. 74–5.   118 Stevenson, *Strange Case*, p. 61.
119 Hogg, *The Private Memoirs and Confessions*, p. 132.
120 Hogg, *The Private Memoirs and Confessions*, p. 130.

Jekyll, so Gil-Martin is 'wedded' to Wringhim 'so closely' that 'I feel as if I were the same person.'[121]

Though Stevenson's *Strange Case* avoids the theological issues with which Hogg was grappling, the Calvinist influence on Stevenson's novel is nonetheless paramount. As Milbank succinctly argues, 'The "elect" Dr Jekyll does indeed devote himself to charity and increased religious practice, but the "reprobate" Hyde grows in strength'; and it is 'during a moment of self-satisfaction that he is better than other men, Jekyll spontaneously transforms into Hyde'. Thus, she argues, 'from that time forward, his neat separation explodes into warring internal enmity, which ends with Jekyll denying Hyde as a part of himself'.[122] Jekyll's attempt 'to gain holiness by denying the need for repentance mirrors Wringhim's, and the same damnation is realised in self-slaughter'.[123] In Hogg's *Confessions*, Wringhim experiences a similar high moment: assured of his 'justification', his absolute freedom from sin, he thinks of himself as 'an eagle among the children of men, soaring on high, and looking down with pity and contempt on the grovelling creatures below'.[124] Immediately after this, the visitations of the mysterious Gil-Martin begin.

Engaging so closely with Scottish folklore, literary tradition and the political and religious history of the nation, Stevenson's *Strange Case of Dr Jekyll and Mr Hyde* marked the point of culmination for Scottish Gothic writing of the nineteenth century. Powerfully galvanising the preoccupations with monstrosity, uncanny doubleness and unreliable textuality that ran throughout earlier texts in the national tradition, Stevenson's narrative bequeathed to the Gothic literary aesthetic more generally a mythos that is still culturally prevalent today.

---

121 Hogg, *The Private Memoirs and Confessions*, p. 158.
122 Milbank, 'Calvinist and Covenanter Gothic', p. 98.
123 Milbank, 'Calvinist and Covenanter Gothic', p. 98.
124 Hogg, *The Private Memoirs and Confessions*, p. 80.

2.16

The Gothic in Nineteenth-Century Ireland

CHRISTINA MORIN

> Has my Aunt seen the Romance of the Forest? It has been the fashionable novel here – Every Body read & talked of it – We were much interested in some parts of it – It is something in the style of the Castle of Otranto – & the horrible parts are we thought well worked up. But it is very difficult to keep Horror breathless with his mouth wide open through three Volumes.[1]

> My Father entertained us for several Evenings past with the story of The Monk; We do not regret that we have not the Book – I never heard anything more sublimely terrific than the animated corpse & 'Raymond! Raymond! thou art mine!' I hardly dared to go to bed after I had heard it.[2]

The Anglo-Irish novelist and educationalist Maria Edgeworth is now generally remembered as an author thoroughly committed to didactic realism and, thus, divorced from the Gothic. She was, nevertheless, an enthusiastic reader of Gothic fictions, as the excerpts from her correspondence above indicate. Novels such as Ann Radcliffe's *The Romance of the Forest* (1791), William Godwin's *Caleb Williams* (1794) and Matthew Lewis's *The Monk* (1796) thrilled her with their 'horror' and produced in her the same kind of excessive emotional state condemned by critics of terror fiction.[3] They also arguably influenced her own writing, beginning with *Castle Rackrent* (1800). Jarlath Killeen, Margot Gayle Backus and Sharon Murphy have all usefully traced references to specific Gothic texts, authors and tropes in Edgeworth's *oeuvre*. Killeen, for instance, considers the Rackrent family home in *Castle Rackrent* an authentically 'Gothic' construction dating from the period of the Norman

---

1 Letter from Maria Edgeworth to Sophy Ruxton, 14 August 1792; NLI MS 10,166/7 POS 9026, Item 94.
2 Letter from Maria Edgeworth to Mrs Ruxton, n.d. [1796]; NLI MS 10,166/7 POS 9027, Item 152.
3 Letter from Maria Edgeworth to Mrs Ruxton, n.d. [1795]; NLI MS 10,166/7 POS 9027, Item 139.

359

conquest.[4] In this, its very presence in the novel evokes contemporary understandings of the term 'Gothic' as connoting a particular relationship between past and present, a concern with which is clear in Edgeworth's subtitle: 'an Hibernian tale: taken from facts and from the manners of the Irish squires, *before* the year 1782' (emphasis added). Backus also comments on the use of architecture in *Castle Rackrent*, arguing that the novel's focus on a decaying castle as symbolic of the destructive and non-generative sociopolitical order represented by the Rackrent family significantly foreshadows the decimation of the Anglo-Irish Big House in later nineteenth-century Irish literature, while also underlining Edgeworth's production of a form of writing that Backus calls 'gothic realism'.[5] Murphy, for her part, points to Glenthorn in Edgeworth's *Ennui* (1809) as a kind of Quixotic reader misled by his immersion in Gothic romances.[6] His habit of reading such works informs his views of Glenthorn Castle, where he is lodged in a 'state tower ... hung with magnificent tapestry, but ancient tapestry. It was so like a room in a haunted castle, that if I had not been too much fatigued to think of any thing, I should certainly have thought of Mrs Radcliffe'.[7]

Edgeworth's Gothic-inflected works provide a useful point of entry into nineteenth-century Irish Gothic literature as a whole. Lest we be tempted to accord *Castle Rackrent* another 'first' – not just Edgeworth's first novel, or the first regional novel, the first Irish novel and the first Irish national tale, but also the first Irish Gothic novel – it is worth situating her engagement with the Gothic mode in the context of a well-established, if now overlooked, history of Irish Gothic writing. Although she specifically names English Gothic texts and authors in her correspondence and in *Ennui*, Edgeworth was no doubt aware of – even if she does not record reading – the works of contemporaries and near contemporaries such as Regina Maria Roche, Catharine Selden, Henrietta Rouvière Mosse, Stephen Cullen and many others who represent a vital body of 'first wave' Irish Gothic fiction. Edgeworth's apparent silence on these authors may owe something to their production of what Franz Potter has compellingly termed 'trade Gothic' – fiction produced by and for a popular readership and therefore

---

4 Jarlath Killeen, *Gothic Ireland: Horror and the Irish Anglican Imagination in the Long Eighteenth Century* (Dublin: Four Courts Press, 2005), pp. 193–97.
5 Margot Gayle Backus, *The Gothic Family Romance: Heterosexuality, Child Sacrifice, and the Anglo-Irish Colonial Order* (Durham, NC: Duke University Press, 1999), p. 106.
6 Sharon Murphy, *Maria Edgeworth and Romance* (Dublin: Four Courts Press, 2004), p. 156.
7 Maria Edgeworth, *Ennui*, in Marilyn Butler and Mitzi Myers (eds), *The Novels and Selected Works of Maria Edgeworth*, 12 vols (London: Pickering & Chatto, 1999–2003), vol. 1, pp. 157–308 (p. 191); Murphy, *Maria Edgeworth and Romance*, p. 156.

condemned as a 'low' form of literature, hence the mixed delight and disdain evident in Edgeworth's letters.[8] Contributing to the glut of Gothic romances in the last decade of the eighteenth century and the first two decades of the nineteenth, Irish-authored works such as Roche's *The Children of the Abbey* (1796), Cullen's *The Castle of Inchvally* (1796), Selden's *The English Nun* (1797), F. C. Patrick's *The Jesuit* (1799) and Rouvière Mosse's *Lussington Abbey* (1804) were dismissed by critics as hackneyed, ephemeral fictions responsible for the degradation of British literature.

Today, the stereotype of 'trade Gothic' fictions as little better than plagiarisms persists, despite notable efforts by Potter, Elizabeth Neiman and Yael Shapira, among others, to counter these perceptions.[9] In an Irish context, critical attention to the national tale, the regional novel and the Irish historical novel as forms that developed at the turn of the century in direct response to the Anglo-Irish Union (1801) has pushed late eighteenth- and early nineteenth-century Irish Gothic further off our radar. This tendency has helped to perpetuate the erroneous view of Irish Gothic as a belated subgenre of English Gothic that begins and all but ends with Charles Robert Maturin's *Melmoth the Wanderer* (1820) before being spectacularly revived in the works of Sheridan Le Fanu, Oscar Wilde and Bram Stoker. In this chapter, I adopt a broadly chronological approach to Irish Gothic literature of the long nineteenth century as a corrective to the preconceptions that have hampered recognition of the scope and diversity of Irish Gothic literary production. In the first section, I sketch what has been referred to in a British context as the 'rise of the Gothic novel' from an Irish perspective, assessing how Irish authors contributed to the development of a literary form that pleased readers as much as it angered critics. I then move on to a consideration of Irish Gothic literature after this initial heyday, analysing the continued, if less often appreciated, production of Gothic via newspaper and magazine publications, before turning to that body of literature often recognised by totalising terms such as 'the Irish Gothic' and 'Anglo-Irish Gothic': late nineteenth-century works like Le Fanu's *Uncle Silas* (1864) and *Carmilla* (1872), Wilde's *The Picture of Dorian Gray* (1892)

---

8 Franz J. Potter, *The History of Gothic Publishing, 1800–1835: Exhuming the Trade* (Basingstoke: Palgrave Macmillan, 2005).

9 See Potter, *The History of Gothic Publishing*; Elizabeth A. Neiman, *Minerva's Gothics: The Politics and Poetics of Romantic Exchange, 1780–1820* (Cardiff: University of Wales Press, 2019); Yael Shapira, 'Beyond the Radcliffe Formula: Isabella Kelly and the Gothic Troubles of the Married Heroine', *Women's Writing* (26 November 2015), <www.tandfonline.com/doi/abs/10.1080/09699082.2015.1110289> (last accessed 5 April 2019).

and Stoker's *Dracula* (1897).[10] Rather than add unduly to the considerable body of literature already focused on these fictions, I problematise and expand notions of an Irish Gothic canon or tradition comprised principally of these texts via an exploration of a cross-generic and cross-sectarian selection of lesser known works that nuance our views of Irish Gothic literary production throughout the nineteenth century.

'First Wave' Irish Gothic

While the 'origins' of Irish Gothic literature have been traced back to the 1760s and 1770s with the works of Thomas Leland and Elizabeth Griffith, production of Irish Gothic experiences a notable uptick in the 1780s and 1790s, much as is the case with English Gothic. In the works of Roche, Cullen, Anne Fuller, James White, Anna Milliken, F. C. Patrick, Sarah Green and many others, we see the significant contribution Irish writers made to the rapid expansion of the literary marketplace in this period. Despite being dismissed by critics concerned with establishing and policing 'high' and 'low' categories of literature, works by these authors demonstrate the ways in which Irish writers in the final decades of the eighteenth century began to shape a form of Gothic that departs markedly from the characteristics now conventionally associated with first wave English Gothic. Rather than single-mindedly focusing on the medieval Catholic Continental settings, overtly supernatural figures and events, and other tropes we have come to expect from Gothic fiction in its heyday, early Irish Gothic adheres closely to contemporary understandings of the term Gothic as a signifier of the past and its relationship to the present. Accordingly, works such as Green's *Charles Henley; or, the Fugitive Restored* (1790), Milliken's *Corfe Castle; or, Historic Tracts* (1793), Roche's *The Children of the Abbey* (1796) and *Clermont* (1798), Patrick's *The Irish Heiress* (1797) and *The Jesuit* (1799), and Selden's *The English Nun* (1797) contemplate the similarities and differences between present-day realities and a past variously configured as an antediluvian period of barbarity and an important moment in the progress of modern society and governance. They do so using diverse means and methods encompassing a variety of settings – local and foreign, medieval and more recent – and a general recourse to romance, rather than a strict adherence to the supernatural.

---

10 I use inverted commas around 'the Irish Gothic' and 'the Gothic novel' throughout this chapter as a way of emphasising the limitations of these labels. For a detailed exploration of this issue, see Christina Morin, *The Gothic Novel in Ireland, c. 1760–1829* (Manchester: Manchester University Press, 2018), pp. 1–9.

Patrick's *The Jesuit* provides a suggestive case study. Concerned with the tumultuous reign of Elizabeth I, the novel evidences late eighteenth-century Irish Gothic's preoccupation with the past as it relates to the present. Moreover, its contemplation of social and political progress via a description of English, rather than European, sectarian strife coupled with its eschewal of supernatural horrors in favour of the violence of religious dissension emphasises the varied forms Irish Gothic takes in this period. Raised by his bigoted Catholic father to believe in the necessity of assassinating the Queen, Anthony Babington is nevertheless horrified by the hatred animating the Catholic cause. The atrocities he observes impress him with 'the consequences of rebellion and disturbance' and leave him longing for 'a well-regulated settled government'.[11] While the novel's pronounced anti-Catholicism reads as a conventional eighteenth-century Gothic trope, as Claire Connolly suggests, the narrative also complicates the Continental displacement of barbarity usually associated with early Gothic fiction by locating sectarian violence both at home and abroad.[12] Indeed, as Babington pointedly narrates from his prison-cell at the close of the novel, 'the artifices' that eventually transformed him into a criminal and 'a monster' all took place in England.[13]

Like a number of other Irish Gothic novels of the 1780s and 1790s, including Anne Fuller's *Alan Fitz-Osborne* (1787) and *The Son of Ethelwolf* (1789) as well as Milliken's *Corfe Castle*, *The Jesuit* shares much in common with Clara Reeve's *The Old English Baron* (1778) and Sophia Lee's *The Recess* (1783–5). In particular, these works explore the English past as an important point of reference during a tumultuous period of political and social upheaval in Britain. James Watt has persuasively described such fictions as 'Loyalist Gothic romances': imaginative works that adopt English medieval settings and use 'selective historical reference' to depict 'the conflict between patriotism and a variant of misguided ambition in a period of chivalric manners' in order to emphasise the didactic lesson to be learned from this clash in the present.[14] As Watt notes, these texts are frequently seen as departures from mainstream Gothic thanks to their focus on native rather than foreign locations and their decision 'to privilege the exemplary purpose of romance' instead of

---

11 Mrs F. C. Patrick, *The Jesuit; or, the History of Anthony Babington, Esq., an Historical Novel*, 3 vols (Bath, 1799), vol. 3, p. 20.
12 Claire Connolly, *A Cultural History of the Irish Novel* (Cambridge: Cambridge University Press, 2011), p. 132.
13 Patrick, *The Jesuit*, vol. 3, p. 336; Morin, *The Gothic Novel in Ireland*, pp. 130–1.
14 James Watt, *Contesting the Gothic: Fiction, Genre and Cultural Conflict, 1764–1832* (Cambridge: Cambridge University Press, 1999), p. 58.

'exploit[ing] sensational material or provid[ing] narratives of suspense'.[15] However, in Irish Gothic terms, *The Jesuit* is rather the norm than the exception, pointing to the significant portion of Irish Gothic texts in the Romantic period that both feature primary settings in the British Isles and harness the power and potential of 'fancy' as encouraged by Horace Walpole in the Preface to the second edition of *The Castle of Otranto* (1764).[16]

Even when Irish Romantic Gothic fiction appears to play by the rules of 'the Gothic novel' as now conventionally conceived, it has tended to be dismissed as derivative. Marianne Kenley's *The Cottage of the Appenines, or, the Castle of Novina* (1806), for instance, bears all the hallmarks of contemporary Female Gothic: it is set in Italy and the Apennine region in an unspecified but clearly historical time period; it features a number of harassed female characters, including the heroine, Adela, whose escape from imprisonment by the dastardly Corsino is effected by the spectral appearance of her wronged mother, later revealed to be alive; the novel's comedic conclusion sees Adela and her mother reunited, their male persecutors punished, and Adela wed at long last to the object of her affections. Although it failed to be picked up by the reviews, the novel was nevertheless judged by comparison to Radcliffe. Robert Anderson wrote in 1820 that *The Cottage of the Appenines* 'proves [Kenley] to be a warm admirer of the celebrated Mrs Radcliffe'.[17] For Anderson, Kenley's appreciation of Radcliffe was no fault, and he further opined, 'Sensibility, vivacity and a philanthropic spirit could not fail to make MARIA the admiration of many a learned and respectable circle.'[18]

Accusations of Radcliffean imitation were usually an inverse indicator of quality and were thrown repeatedly at Kenley's Irish contemporaries. Roche's *Clermont* was memorably dismissed by the *Critical Review* as 'remind[ing] us, without any great pleasure, of Mrs. Radcliffe's romances'.[19] Cullen's *The Castle of Inchvally* was similarly if implicitly linked to Radcliffean imitation in the *Critical Review*, which began its evaluation of the novel by bemoaning the fact that, 'The success of several deservedly popular novels and romances has occasioned the reading public to be pestered with innumerable tales of distressed lovers, enchanted castles, &c. &c.' Cullen's tale

15 Watt, *Contesting the Gothic*, pp. 58–9.
16 Horace Walpole, *The Castle of Otranto*, edited by W. S. Lewis (Oxford: Oxford University Press, 2008), p. 8. See Morin, *The Gothic Novel in Ireland*, chapters 2 and 3 for a more detailed discussion of local settings and romance in Irish Romantic Gothic.
17 Quoted in Jennifer Orr, *Literary Networks and Dissenting Print Culture in Romantic-Period Ireland* (Basingstoke: Palgrave Macmillan, 2015), p. 246 n. 9.
18 Quoted in Orr, *Literary Networks*, pp. 246–7 n. 9.
19 *Critical Review* n.s. 24 (November 1798): 356.

was accordingly dismissed as not even worth the price of the paper on which it was printed.[20] Likewise, Maturin's *The Fatal Revenge* (1807) was judged by Walter Scott (1771–1832) – at least at first glance – to be just another of the countless 'flat imitations of the *Castle of Udolpho*' then overwhelming the market.[21]

Similar assessments have ensured that numerous works by Irish writers, including Roche, Selden, Mosse, Milliken, Nugent Bell and Theodore Melville, have fallen to the wayside, mere confirmation of the period's surfeit of clichéd Gothic fictions. In Maturin's case, Scott detected enough original genius in *The Fatal Revenge* to urge the author to continue to distinguish himself from his models.[22] Scott's encouragement notwithstanding, Maturin's next two novels – *The Wild Irish Boy* (1808) and *The Milesian Chief* (1812) – retained strong suggestions of the author's continued indebtedness to the Gothic mode. Tellingly, the *Critical Review* introduced its assessment of *The Milesian Chief* by assuring its 'fair' readers 'that the Milesian Chief opens with as much mystery as any reasonable person would wish, viz.: – a monk and an Italian monk, who cannot fail to prove a potent agent in all manner of mischief'. Once again drawing parallels between Maturin and Radcliffe, the review explicitly compared *The Milesian Chief* to *The Italian* (1797): 'This said arch-fiend of a monk makes his debut in the first chapter and though he may not appear quite so exquisite a devil as Schedoni in the romance of The Italian, yet he performs the part allotted to him with perfect *nonchalance*.'[23]

Despite contemporary readers' continued association of Maturin's fiction with Radcliffe and the Gothic, more recent scholarship has tended to view *The Wild Irish Boy* and *The Milesian Chief* as unsuccessful pastiches of the national tales of Edgeworth and Sydney Owenson. This inclination suggests both the difficulty that Maturin had in convincing critics of his innovation and the extent to which formal labelling has hindered a full understanding of Irish Romantic literature. As I have argued elsewhere, attention to the development of regional and national forms in Ireland in the years surrounding the Anglo-Irish Union (1801) has effectively erased the continuing influence and production of Gothic literature in early nineteenth-century Ireland.[24] For this reason, it is still entirely possible to speak of writers like Maturin and Roche as

---

20 *Critical Review* 20 (May 1797): 118.
21 Sir Walter Scott, Review of *The Fatal Revenge; or, the Family of Montorio: a Romance*, *Quarterly Review* 3:6 (1810): 339–47 (p. 341).
22 Scott, Review of *The Fatal Revenge*, p. 347.
23 *Critical Review*, 4th ser. 1 (April 1812): 388–97 (pp. 388–9).
24 See Christina Morin, *Charles Robert Maturin and the Haunting of Irish Romantic Fiction* (Manchester: Manchester University Press, 2011), pp. 8–9 and chapter 3.

having careers that split generically into Gothic and national phases. Our perceptions of *Melmoth the Wanderer* (1820) as an anomaly in both Irish and Gothic literary history are also owing to this tendency to view Gothic and national modes as inherently distinct. When placed in the context of nationally minded Gothics such as *The Children of the Abbey*, *The Castle of Inchvally*, Henrietta Rouvière Mosse's *The Old Irish Baronet; or Manners of my Country* (1808) and Owenson's *O'Donnel* (1814), not to mention Maturin's own *The Wild Irish Boy* and *The Milesian Chief*, *Melmoth* appears not so much an oddity – a belated intrusion of the Gothic on a now largely national or regional literary production – as simply the most prominent example of a well-established and constantly evolving fusion of Gothic and national forms or modes in this period.

Irish Gothic in the Periodical Press

Maturin's success with *Melmoth the Wanderer* may be gauged by the fact that the novel is still in print today and, indeed, continues to exert a considerable fascination for scholars and readers alike, as might be judged by recent adaptations and re-workings, including Sarah Perry's *Melmoth* (2018) and the Big Telly Theatre Company's 2012 production, *Melmoth the Wanderer*. The novel's continued availability and accessibility belies the fate of countless other Irish Gothics of the early nineteenth century and reflects, at least in part, the vagaries of the market and the importance of publishers. Largely through Scott's influence, Maturin had published *Melmoth* with Archibald Constable, by then a well-established figure in the production of 'respectable' popular literature, including the Waverley Novels.[25] In contrast, the leading publisher of Irish Gothic fiction of the Romantic period was William Lane's notorious Minerva Press, publication with which has almost invariably condemned a work to oblivion. Figured by Romantic-era critics as the quintessential trade Gothic, Minerva fictions have continued to suffer from their reputation as lowbrow circulating library 'fluff' in modern scholarship.[26] New research has demonstrated, however, that Lane's tireless – if not entirely selfless – entrepreneurial efforts in expanding the circulating library

---

25 William St Clair, *The Reading Nation in the Romantic Period* (Cambridge: Cambridge University Press, 2004), p. 327.
26 For recent scholarship that probes many of our assumptions about the Minerva Press, see the essays in Elizabeth A. Neiman and Christina Morin (eds), *Romantic Textualities: Literature and Print Culture, 1780–1840* – Special Issue on 'The Minerva Press and the Romantic-era Literary Marketplace' (forthcoming).

system at home and abroad brought *The Children of the Abbey*, *The Old Irish Baronet* and Selden's *Serena* (1800), among many other Irish Minervas, a truly global and long-lasting popular acclaim.[27]

With the press's new direction under A. K. Newman, who took over from Lane in 1809 and, in 1829, removed 'Minerva' from its branding, a pivotal chapter in the production of Irish Gothic novels came to a close. Not coincidentally, this corresponded with Catholic Emancipation (1829) and what Connolly frames as the end of 'a formative phase of the history of the Irish novel'.[28] From the 1820s, as Jarlath Killeen and Siobhàn Kilfeather have both noted, Irish Gothic fundamentally changes, becoming more diffuse and less readily recognised than 'the Gothic novel'. From being a largely novelistic form, Killeen writes, Irish Gothic '[takes] up ghostly habitations elsewhere, indeed everywhere, in nineteenth-century culture'.[29] Kilfeather has similarly remarked that the majority of Irish Gothic literature of the early to mid-nineteenth century is notably multi-modal: 'For most of the nineteenth century, Irish Gothic cannot be defined so much in terms of a subgenre as much as in terms of an extra dimension apparent in many works of Irish fiction.'[30]

While it is customary to view Irish Gothic as entering a fallow period in the years between the publication of *Melmoth the Wanderer* and *Uncle Silas*, therefore, the Gothic remains a central point of return for Irish writers as they negotiate, among other things, national politics, class relations and the effects of migration, emigration, famine and persistent social upheaval. Thus, for instance, Carleton's *The Black Prophet: A Tale of the Irish Famine* (1847) and *The Emigrants of Ahadarra* (1848) invoke the Gothic as part of the author's notoriously heterogeneous style in order to confront present-day realities and challenge political figures to engage more directly with the crises at hand.[31] Historical, realist and Gothic modes are similarly blended in Le Fanu's early novels and in the nineteenth-century fiction of Emily Lawless, Samuel Lever and Thomas Moore.[32] Meanwhile, popular folklore collections, including Thomas Crofton Croker's *Fairy Tales and Legends of the South of Ireland*

---

27 I address this issue in *The Gothic Novel in Ireland*, chapter 4.
28 Connolly, *A Cultural History of the Irish Novel*, p. 196.
29 Jarlath Killeen, *Gothic Literature 1825–1914* (Cardiff: University of Wales Press, 2009), p. 3.
30 Siobhán Kilfeather, 'The Gothic Novel', in John Wilson Foster (ed.), *The Cambridge Companion to the Irish Novel* (Cambridge: Cambridge University Press, 2006), pp. 78–96 (p. 86).
31 Jason King, 'Emigration and the Anglo-Irish novel: William Carleton, "home sickness", and the coherence of gothic conventions', *The Canadian Journal of Irish Studies*, 26:2/27:1 (2000–1): 104–18.
32 Kilfeather, 'The Gothic Novel', pp. 86–7.

(1825) and Samuel Lover's *Legends and Stories of Ireland* (1832), as well as tales of Irish life, such as Anna Maria Hall's *Sketches of Irish Character* (1829) and *Stories of the Irish Peasantry* (1840), and Carleton's *Traits and Stories of the Irish Peasantry* (1830–3), also draw substantially upon the Gothic in their depictions of rural Irish society and traditions.

Tellingly, many of these works have their origins in magazine publications, and a number of the authors named above built their careers on packaging and re-packaging tales and serialised novels first published in the periodical press. Their ability to do so underlines the central role that nineteenth-century periodicals played in the experimentation with, and production of, the Gothic mode in Ireland.[33] In the 1830s, the legacy of Romantic-era Gothic is clear in stories such as James Clarence Mangan's 'Love, Mystery, and Murder. A Tale (Foundered on Facts)' (*Weekly Dublin Satirist*, 1834) and 'The Man in the Cloak' (*Dublin University Magazine*, 1838) as well as William Maginn's 'The New Frankenstein' (*Fraser's Magazine*, 1838). These tales revive earlier fictions – Schiller's *Der Geisterscher* (1787–8), Maturin's *Melmoth* via Balzac's *Melmoth Réconcilié* (1835), and Mary Shelley's *Frankenstein* (1818), respectively – as they re-imagine them for a new audience.[34] In doing so, they adopt, in Kilfeather's terms, 'the language of haunting, terror, dismemberment and monstrosity' to reflect, however obliquely, on questions of cultural and national identity.[35] Other significant periodical publications of the 1830s include Maginn's 'A Night of Terror' (*Bentley's Miscellany*, 1838); Carleton's 'Confessions of a Reformed Ribbonman' (*Dublin Literary Gazette*, 1830) – later revised as 'Wildgoose Lodge' and included in *Traits and Stories of the Irish Peasantry* (2nd series, 1833); the various stories by Isaac Butt published in the *Dublin University Magazine* between 1834 and 1837 and later collected as *Chapters of College Romance* (1863); and Le Fanu's 'A Chapter in the History of a Tyrone Family' (*Dublin University Magazine*, 1839).

In the 1840s, 1850s and 1860s, Le Fanu was arguably the most well-known producer of periodical press Gothic fiction. As a contributor to the *Dublin*

---

33 Kilfeather, 'The Gothic Novel', p. 87. Magazines were an important venue for Romantic-era Gothic fictions as well, as discussed in Robert D. Mayo, 'Gothic romance in the magazines', *PMLA* 65:5 (1950): 762–89.

34 On the intertextuality of 'Love, Mystery, and Murder', see Andrew Cusack, 'Cultural Transfer in the *Dublin University Magazine*: James Clarence Mangan and the German Gothic', in Andrew Cusask and Barry Murnane (eds), *Popular Revenants: The German Gothic and Its International Reception, 1800–2000* (Rochester, NY: Camden House, 2012), pp. 87–104 (p. 93). Jack Fennell notes the divergence between 'The New Frankenstein' and Shelley's original in *A Brilliant Void: A Selection of Classic Irish Science Fiction* (Dublin: Tramp Press, 2018), p. 2.

35 Kilfeather, 'The Gothic Novel', p. 87.

University Magazine from 1838 to 1869, Le Fanu published a significant body of Gothic tales, as is evident from even a brief listing: 'A Passage in the Secret History of an Irish Countess' (1838), later expanded into *Uncle Silas* (1864); 'The Fatal Bride' (1848); 'The Mysterious Lodger' (1850); 'Ghost Stories of Chapelizod' (1851); 'An Authentic Narrative of a Haunted House' (1862); and 'Wicked Captain Walshawe, of Wauling' (1864). Under Le Fanu's editor-ownership between 1861 and 1869, moreover, the *Dublin University Magazine* became an important venue for the publication of Gothic and sensation fiction – both Le Fanu's own and that of several budding sensation fiction writers, including Rhoda Broughton – even as it debated the relative worth of such fiction in terms that echo Romantic-era discussions of high versus low literature.[36] Le Fanu himself was keen to present his works as the literary offspring of Scott's historical novels, a position he asserts very clearly in 'A Preliminary Word' appended to *Uncle Silas*. Objecting to the label of 'sensation fiction', Le Fanu encourages his readers to understand his fiction in the more respectable terms of Scott's realist and historical modes; 'sensation' is, he argues, a 'degrading term' that does injustice to a 'legitimate school of tragic English romance, which has been ennobled, and in great measure founded, by the genius of Sir Walter Scott'.[37]

Gender, Genre and Creed

Le Fanu's defensiveness about genre did not prevent the text's reception as a thoroughly Gothic one, as is suggested most clearly by Elizabeth Bowen's later assessment of it: '*Uncle Silas* is a romance of terror', Bowen asserted in her introduction to the 1947 Cresset Press edition of the novel, before comparing Maud Ruthyn to the heroines of earlier 'gothic romances' and drawing parallels between Le Fanu's novel and Emily Brontë's *Wuthering Heights* (1847).[38] Bowen's comments on *Uncle Silas*, as well as her subsequent claim that *Uncle Silas* is 'an Irish story transposed to an English setting', have profoundly shaped modern conceptualisations of Irish Gothic as linked – emotionally and psychologically – to Ireland and Irish politics even when not

---

36 Elizabeth Tilley, 'J. S. Le Fanu, Gothic, and the Irish Periodical', in Christina Morin and Niall Gillespie (eds), *Irish Gothics: Genres, Forms, Modes, and Traditions, c. 1760–1890* (Basingstoke: Palgrave Macmillan, 2014), pp. 130–46.
37 Joseph Sheridan Le Fanu, *Uncle Silas*, edited by Victor Sage (London: Penguin Books, 2000), p. 4.
38 Elizabeth Bowen, 'Introduction to the Cresset Press edition of *Uncle Silas*, by Sheridan Le Fanu, 1947', in Eibhear Walshe (ed.), *Elizabeth Bowen's Selected Irish Writings* (Cork: Cork University Press, 2011), pp. 143–57 (p. 143).

ostensibly about Ireland at all.[39] Irish Gothic, or 'the Irish Gothic', is accordingly read as exploring and expressing, however obliquely, Anglo-Irish – and by extension, English – anxieties in the face of a recalcitrant native Catholic population. Thus, for instance, Stoker's *Dracula* (1897), though set in Transylvania and England, and having no obvious connection to Ireland beyond its author's Irishness, has been interpreted as a narrative of 'reverse colonisation' concerned with questions of British imperialism and conquest with direct import to Ireland. As Stephen D. Arata has influentially claimed, 'Dracula's journey from Transylvania to England could be read as a reversal of Britain's imperial exploitations of "weaker" races, including the Irish', thereby awakening in Stoker's English and Anglo-Irish readers 'seldom dormant fears of an Irish uprising'.[40] Such readings have encouraged an understanding of Irish Gothic as a peculiarly Protestant and Anglo-Irish mode of writing, as is suggested by the typical list of 'major' Irish Gothicists: Maturin, Le Fanu, Stoker, Wilde and Bowen. Recent scholarship has begun to trouble this limited lineage by exploring the Gothic works of a number of Irish Catholic writers, including Mangan, the Catholic-born and later Protestant convert Carleton, the Banim brothers – John and Michael – and Gerald Griffin.

In addition to Mangan's 'The Man in the Cloak', noted above, key examples of early nineteenth-century Catholic Gothic include Griffin's 'The Brown Man' (1827) and *The Collegians* (1829); John Banim's *The Fetches* (1825), *The Nowlans* (1826) and *The Boyne Water* (1826); and Carleton's 'The Lianhan Shee' (1830). These works mobilise the Gothic mode to explore fears about present-day Catholic realities and to register resentment over Ireland's colonial situation. Carleton's 'The Lianhan Shee', for instance, provides a telling example of the manner in which Catholic Gothic frequently dwells upon a supernaturalism linked to Catholicism and folkloric traditions in order to express concerns about social and psychological regression to an atavistic identity from which the new Catholic middle class sought to distance itself.[41] The story plots an explained supernatural narrative centred on the folkloric figure of the Lianhan Shee: 'some sthrange bein' from the good people, or fairies, that sticks to some persons' thanks to a quasi-Satanic 'bargain' made between

---

39 Bowen, 'Introduction', p. 144.
40 Stephen D. Arata, 'The occidental tourist: "Dracula" and the anxiety of reverse colonization', *Victorian Studies* 33:4 (Summer 1990): 621–45 (pp. 634, 633).
41 Jim Shanahan, 'Suffering Rebellion: Irish Gothic Fiction, 1799–1830', in Morin and Gillespie (eds), *Irish Gothics*, pp. 74–93 (pp. 88–9).

them.⁴² When the former nun, Margaret, returns to her rural home town, she appears to carry a Lianhan Shee on her back: 'look! look!' she tells Mary O'Sullivan as 'she point[s] with a shudder that almost convulsed her whole frame, to a lump that rose on her shoulders: this, be it what it might, was covered with a red cloak, closely pinned and tied with great caution about her body'.⁴³ Ultimately, the lump is revealed to be the habit she had worn as a nun, before she and the parish priest, Father Philip O'Dallaghy, had an affair and he attempted to kill her. Concluding with O'Dallaghy's descent into madness and ensuing suicide, the story 'emphasize[s] the need to outgrow superstition and Catholicism', as Richard Haslam notes.⁴⁴

Griffin's 'The Brown Man', on the other hand, deploys Irish folklore and superstition as a kind of resistance writing focused on a symbolic depiction of 'the oppression of Ireland ... by an exploitative, alien aristocratic class'.⁴⁵ First published in *Holland-Tide; or, Munster Popular Tales* (1827), the story is a brief but thoroughly terrifying tale of an innocent young peasant woman, Nora Guare, lured into marriage with the titular 'Brown Man'. He is, on first appearance, a wealthy gentleman who promises to relieve Nora's extreme want: 'You'll not refuse [my proposal]', he tells Nora's mother, as he 'flung a purse of gold into the widow's lap'.⁴⁶ By the end of the tale, however, not only has he betrayed his promise to 'make [Nora] a lady, with servants at her call, and all manner of fine doings about her', but he is also revealed as a malicious cannibalistic figure who feeds off corpses in the nearby cemetery of Muckross Abbey.⁴⁷ The story concludes with Nora's subjection to her husband's unnatural appetites: 'He just looked at her one moment, and then darted his long fingers into her bosom, from which the red blood spouted in so many streams. She was very soon out of all pain, and a

---

42 William Carleton, 'The Lianhan Shee: An Irish Superstition', *Traits and Stories of the Irish Peasantry*, 2nd series, 2nd edition, 3 vols (Dublin: William Wakeman, 1834), vol. 2, pp. 3–44 (p. 32). The story first appeared in 1830 in the *Christian Examiner and Church of Ireland Gazette*.
43 Carleton, 'The Lianhan Shee', p. 9.
44 Richard Haslam, 'Maturin's Catholic Heirs: Expanding the Limits of Irish Gothic', in Morin and Gillespie (eds), *Irish Gothics*, pp. 113–29 (p. 118).
45 Sinéad Sturgeon, '"Seven devils": Gerald Griffin's "The Brown Man" and the making of Irish gothic', *The Irish Journal of Gothic and Horror Studies* 11 (2012):18–30 (p. 21), <https://irishgothichorror.files.wordpress.com/2016/04/ijghsissue11.pdf> (last accessed 13 May 2019).
46 Gerald Griffin, 'The Brown Man', in *Holland-Tide; or, Irish Popular Tales*, 2nd edition (London: Saunders and Otley, 1827), pp. 295–307 (p. 299).
47 Griffin, 'The Brown Man', p. 299.

merry supper the horse, the dog, and the Brown Man had that night, on all accounts.'[48]

Griffin's Gothicization of the Irish landscape and his depiction of it as heaving with dead bodies used to feed a race of cannibals echoes other Romantic-era constructions of Ireland as a fundamentally Gothic space inhabited by vampiric forces and riven by bloody political and sectarian strife. Owenson famously declared in 1807 that 'it was ever, as it is now, the singular destiny of Ireland to nourish within her own bosom her bitterest enemies, who, with a species of political vampirism, destroyed that source from whence their own nutriment flowed'.[49] Influenced by similar ideas and imagery, Irish Jacobin writers harnessed the Gothic as, in Niall Gillespie's terms, the most appropriate 'language in which to describe the military and paramilitary outrages that the state was spreading throughout the nation' in the years surrounding the 1798 Rebellion.[50] In poetry such as William Drennan's 'Wake of William Orr' (1797), William Hamilton Drummond's *Hibernia* (1797), Henrietta Battier's *The Lemon, A Poem* (1798) and, later, the short stories collected in *The Terrific Register, or, Record of Crimes, Judgements, Providences and Calamities* (1825), the Gothic is deployed to radical ends as the bloody effects of political tyranny on the Irish landscape are evocatively described.[51] Maturin's *The Milesian Chief* offers a similar reflection from a divergent perspective, depicting, in one memorable scene, a peasant woman presenting the dead body of her son to the novel's hero and rebellion-leader, Connal O'Morven: 'there he lies: you have laid him there. There is the feast I promised you: you may devour him yourself, for that is all you have left me to give you.'[52]

Ireland's Gothic topography is also a focal point in landscape poetry of the Romantic-era and beyond. This is particularly the case, as Julia M. Wright has demonstrated, in verse set in or about Glendalough, as in Drennan's 'Glendalloch' (1806), Moore's 'By that Lake whose Gloomy Shore' (1811), Edmund Armstrong's 'Glandalough: A Story of Wicklow' (1877) and Dora Sigerson Shorter's 'The Deer-Stone: A Legend of Glendalough' (1919). In

---

48 Griffin, 'The Brown Man', p. 307.
49 Quoted in Claire Connolly, 'Writing the Union', in Daíre Keogh and Kevin Whelan (eds), *Acts of Union: The Causes, Contexts, and Consequences of the Act of Union* (Dublin: Four Courts Press, 2001), pp. 171–86 (p. 185).
50 Niall Gillespie, 'Irish Jacobin Gothic, c. 1796–1825', in Morin and Gillespie (eds), *Irish Gothics*, pp. 58–73 (p. 62).
51 See Gillespie, 'Irish Jacobin Gothic'.
52 Charles Robert Maturin, *The Milesian Chief*, introduced by Robert Lee Wolff, 4 vols (New York: Garland, 1979) vol. 4, p. 120.

these poems, Wright convincingly argues, 'death is the keynote ... and the gothic is the defining mode', as Glendalough is constructed and reconstructed as a sublime natural landscape through which usefully 'to ponder Irish history' and to explore 'the paralysis of the national subject by an unproductive terror'.[53] Elsewhere, poetry witnessing to and remembering the Irish Famine (1845–51) frequently calls upon the Gothic mode to describe the death, destruction and inhumanity of the Famine as well as its aftereffects. Mangan's 'The Funerals' (1849), for instance, evocatively and near prophetically registers the Famine death toll:[54]

> Here were the FUNERALS of my thoughts as well!
> The Dead and I at last were One!
> ...
> On, on, still on and on they swept,
>   Silently, save
> When the long FUNERAL chant rose up to Heaven,
> Or some wild mourner shrieked and wept –
> Earth had become one groanful grave –
> The isles and lords were left bereaven.[55]

Gothic imagery of death, corpses, skeletons and graves is difficult to avoid in these first-hand accounts of the Famine, and poets from Thomas D'Arcy McGee to Lady Jane Wilde and Richard D'Alton Williams use such provocative illustrations directly to confront those they held responsible. Lady Wilde's 'The Famine Year (The Stricken Land)' (1847), for example, boldly condemns Anglo-Irish landowners who have only an eye on their own profit:

> Weary men, what reap ye? – Golden corn for the stranger.
> What sow ye? – Human corses that wait for the avenger.
> Fainting forms, hunger-stricken, what see you in the offing?
> Stately ships to bear our food away, amid the stranger's scoffing.[56]

In the closing decades of the century, several poets return to the Irish folklore and mythology that had inspired numerous antiquarian collections of the Romantic period as the bedrock of the early Irish Revivalist project. Ireland is

---

53 Julia M. Wright, *Representing the National Landscape in Irish Romanticism* (Syracuse, NY: Syracuse University Press, 2014), pp. 48, 52.
54 Ellen Shannon-Mangan, *James Clarence Mangan: A Biography* (Dublin: Irish Academic Press, 1996), p. 206.
55 James Clarence Mangan, 'The Funerals', in Christopher Morash (ed.), *The Hungry Voice: The Poetry of the Irish Famine* (Dublin: Irish Academic Press, 1989), pp. 133–4 (p. 133).
56 Lady Jane Wilde, 'The Famine Year (The Stricken Land)', in Morash (ed.), *The Hungry Voice*, pp. 221–2 (p. 221).

constructed as a fundamentally supernatural space in poetry collections such as Katherine Tynan's *Shamrocks* (1887) and *Ballads and Lyrics* (1891), Sigerson Shorter's *The Fairy Changeling and Other Poems* (1898) and W. B. Yeats's *The Wanderings of Oisin and Other Poems* (1898). Elsewhere in Revivalist poetry, history is used as a kind of Gothic prompt to consider present-day Irish politics and to contemplate the connections between past and present, as in, for instance, Alice Milligan's 'At Midnight Hour', published posthumously in 1954, and Lawless's 'After Aughrim' (1902) and 'Dirge of the Munster Forest. 1581' (1902).

These examples of poetry in the Gothic mode are worth dwelling upon, albeit briefly, as they spotlight an area of Gothic literary production that is often overlooked in our emphasis on 'the Gothic novel', in much the same way as conventional readings of Irish Gothic exclude Catholic writers. The traditional marginalisation of both of these bodies of work from the literary historiography of Irish Gothic draws attention to other omissions as well, particularly in the latter half of the nineteenth century. If, in the Romantic period, Irish Gothic is almost exclusively – and pejoratively – linked to women writers, by the *fin de siècle* there appears to have been a masculinist takeover, inaugurated much earlier in the century by Maturin's *Melmoth*.[57] The 'major' Irish Gothicists of this period are thus both Protestant and male, and female contribution to late nineteenth-century Gothic literary production in Ireland is accordingly assumed to be negligible until Bowen publishes her first 'Big House Gothic' novel in 1929, *The Last September*.[58] However, there are a number of Irish women writers who anticipate Bowen's Gothic novels and her later ghost stories, including, perhaps most notably, Rosa Mulholland and Charlotte Riddell. Riddell's prolific career, driven by extreme personal and financial circumstances, includes a significant number of Gothic short stories and novels that are of particular interest for their use of supernatural modes to investigate issues of patriarchal society and women's rights. *The Uninhabited House* (1875), for instance, presents a play on the typical concerns of the Irish Big House novel, depicting the heroine's inheritance of a house haunted by the ghost of her brother-in-law. Ousting this ghost is

---

57 Jacqueline Pearson, 'Masculinizing the novel: women writers and intertextuality in Charles Robert Maturin's *The Wild Irish Boy*', *Studies in Romanticism* 36:4 (1997): 635–50. On male dominance of the Gothic more generally at the close of the century, see Cindy Hendershot, *The Animal Within: Masculinity and the Gothic* (Ann Arbor, MI: University of Michigan Press, 1998).

58 Vera Kreilkamp, 'The Novel of the Big House', in John Wilson Foster (ed.), *The Cambridge Companion to the Irish Novel* (Cambridge: Cambridge University Press, 2006), pp. 60–77 (pp. 67–9).

necessary to Miss Blake's social and financial independence, thus illustrating, as Killeen asserts, 'Riddell's use of the ghost to represent, not female liminality, but male power and its danger to women.'[59]

Conclusion

Despite recent efforts to revive scholarly and popular interest in Riddell, including the anthologisation of ghost stories like 'The Banshee's Warning' (1898) and 'The Open Door' (1882) as well as Tramp Press's publication in 2017 of a new edition of *A Struggle for Fame* (1883), she remains relatively neglected and her contribution to the development of nineteenth-century Irish Gothic largely overlooked. This owes, in part, to continued scholarly attachment to labels such 'the Gothic novel' and 'the Irish Gothic', which, as I have suggested here, do frank injustice to the range and breadth of Irish Gothic literary production in the long nineteenth century. Regrettably, there has not been space to consider every aspect of Irish Gothic in this period. Drama and Irish-language Gothic are a particular omission, considered in brief and inter alia elsewhere.[60] Both certainly invite greater attention, particularly as scholarship continues to probe, nuance and stretch traditional parameters of English, Irish and European Gothic literary production. Acknowledging the diverse means and methods by which Irish writers in the nineteenth century utilised the Gothic mode in formally, generically and thematically varied ways allows us to begin to appreciate the Gothic's centrality to nineteenth-century Irish literary production. It furthermore encourages a reintegration of authors and texts traditionally marginalised for their apparent deviation from the norm – of 'the Gothic novel', of 'the Irish Gothic' and of the putatively prevailing literary forms of nineteenth-century Irish literature.

---

59 Killeen, *Gothic Literature 1825–1914*, p. 138.
60 See, for instance, Claire Connolly, 'Theater and nation in Irish romanticism: the tragic drama of Charles Robert Maturin and Richard Lalor Shiel', *Éire-Ireland* 41:3&4 (2006): 185–214 and Kilfeather, 'The Gothic Novel', pp. 91–3.

2.17

The Gothic in Nineteenth-Century America

CHARLES L. CROW

The collision between Enlightenment and revolutionary Romantic values that produced the Gothic also produced the United States. Indeed, recent scholarship has asserted that that 'the definitions of America and those of Gothic are so closely related as to be inseparable', and that the 'American Dream was from its inception a haunted, Gothic endeavour'.[1] American Gothic disrupts the dominant American narrative of technological and social progress, and reveals what is hidden or omitted by this narrative. It engages the large and inescapable facts of the emerging American nation: the twinned original sins of African enslavement and native American removal, the shifting frontier between settlement and wilderness, the rise of cities and of modern capitalism, poverty, disease and the changing roles of women. The repressed truth that American Gothic exposes is that Americans are not the people they believe themselves to be, either as individuals or as a society.

Thus it could be argued, as I do, that the Gothic was even more essential to the American imagination in the nineteenth century than it was to that of Britain. The first great American novels were Gothic, and the centrality of the Gothic is obvious in the works of the Dark Romantics, Poe, Hawthorne and Melville. The importance of Gothicism continued, perhaps surprisingly, in the decades after the Civil War (1861–5), a period often described as the 'Age of Realism'. The Gothic, from the beginning, drove technical innovation in American literature, and is responsible for some of its greatest works.

---

[1] Joel Faflak and Jason Haslam, 'Introduction', in Joel Faflak and Jason Haslam (eds), *American Gothic Culture: An Edinburgh Companion* (Edinburgh: Edinburgh University Press, 2016), pp. 1–22 (pp. 2–3). My approach also has been influenced by the work of Teresa A. Goddu, Eric Savoy and Leslie A. Fiedler.

Charles Brockden Brown

Discussion of nineteenth-century American Gothic must begin with Charles Brocken Brown. He was not the first American Gothicist, nor the best-selling author of his day. Scholars such as Cathy N. Davidson and Benjamin F. Fisher have pointed out that Gothic themes appeared in popular theatre and popular fiction before Brown.[2] Nonetheless, Brown was the innovative 'godfather' of American Gothic, as Carol Margaret Davison calls him,[3] who brought its issues into sharp focus. Written in a burst of creative energy on the cusp of the new century, his four Gothic novels – *Wieland* (1798), *Arthur Mervyn* (1799), *Ormond* (1799) and *Edgar Huntly* (1799) – solved the problem of adapting a European form to the American social and physical landscape. Brown articulated most of the subsequent major themes of American Gothic. His characters confront outward horrors – menacing villains and frightening events in the night, as always in Gothic literature – but the horror often lies within. As Jeffrey Andrew Weinstock demonstrates, 'Brown—over thirty years before Poe—powerfully developed a model of the haunted mind ...'[4] Moreover – and this is Brown's key technical innovation – his narrators, and his protagonists, cannot be trusted. Clara Wieland may be the first unreliable narrator in American literature.[5] Arthur Mervyn presents himself as a bumbling naïf who always tries to do the right thing, but he may be the alpha confidence man in a novel filled with rascals. Brown develops his sleepwalking action hero Edgar Huntley as a double to the homicidal maniac Clithero, and some readers have suspected that Edgar himself, not a faceless Indian raider, committed the murder that sets the plot in motion. We are deep into *Wieland* before realising that Wieland, not the stalker and potential rapist Carwin, is the true villain of the novel. Brown infuses his novels with a doubt, shared by characters and readers alike, that a rational, unified consciousness, upon which Enlightenment values are based, even exists.

---

2 See Benjamin F. Fisher, 'Early American Gothic Drama', in Charles L. Crow (ed.), *A Companion to American Gothic* (Malden, MA: Wiley Blackwell, 2014), pp. 96–109 and Cathy N. Davidson, *Revolution and the Word: The Rise of the Novel in America* (New York: Oxford University Press, 1987), pp. 212–53.
3 Carol Margaret Davison, 'Charles Brockden Brown: Godfather of American Gothic', in Charles L. Crow (ed.), *A Companion to American Gothic*, pp. 110–23.
4 Jeffrey Andrew Weinstock, *Charles Brockden Brown* (Cardiff: University of Wales Press, 2011), p. 93.
5 Weinstock, *Charles Brockden Brown*, p. 3.

Crossing the Line

Frederick Jackson Turner famously asserted that the Western movement of the frontier was the crucial factor in shaping the character of Americans and their political institutions. The frontier – as a place and as a trope – is also essential to American Gothic. As a shifting line between settlement and wilderness, the frontier is an obvious metaphor for other boundaries: between self and other, human and inhuman, conscious and unconscious, living and dead, male and female, black and white.[6]

The earliest English settlers saw the frontier thus, as both a physical and a metaphysical boundary. Recalling his first view of the New England coast from the deck of the *Mayflower*, William Bradford saw a forest filled with devils and wild beasts and wild men, a place where his little band would have its faith tested. The fear of losing faith in the wilderness, and of even becoming the Other – which Nathaniel Hawthorne would later allegorise in 'Young Goodman Brown' (1835) – was the Puritans' greatest nightmare, and underlies the seventeenth-century proto-Gothic captivity narrative of Mary Rowlandson, as well as the Salem witch trials of the early 1690s.

The Gothic view of wilderness as a place of wonder and terror and dissolution runs though Brown to the Dark Romantics, and beyond. American quest stories are often redemptive journeys into nature, in which the hero is tested, enlightened and transfigured; but in the Gothic inversion of this narrative, heroes risk transformation into the savage Other, or discover that they have been savages all along. Brown's Edgar Huntly sleepwalks into the forest, awakens in the darkness of a womb-like cavern, kills a mountain lion and eats it raw, and emerges into a nearly endless night of warfare, in which he dispatches Indian after Indian in encounters of escalating brutality. Self-consciously aware of the 'transition' that he has 'undergone',[7] Brown can scarcely recognise himself in the ruthless warrior that he has become; neither can his friends, who open fire on him in the darkness, mistaking him for an Indian raider.

Wilderness narratives usually end with Indians defeated and melting into the forest, as if they had never existed, creating the blank space upon which the history of the westward-moving American civilisation will be written. Thus is created what Renée L. Bergland calls the 'National Uncanny', in

---

6 See David Mogen, Scott P. Sanders and Joanne B. Karpinski (eds), *Frontier Gothic: Terror and Wonder at the Frontier in America* (Rutherford, NJ: Farleigh Dickinson University Press, 1993).

7 Charles Brockden Brown, *Three Gothic Novels: Wieland, Arthur Mervyn, Edgar Huntly*, edited by Sydney J. Krause (New York: Library of America, 1998), p. 809.

which the Indian is made to disappear, but always threatens to reappear, in reality or in nightmare. This pattern – familiar to contemporary readers from such works as Stephen King's *Pet Sematary* (1985) – can be seen, for example, in William Cullen Bryant's story 'The Indian Spring' (1830), in which the narrator is chased through a forest by an Indian warrior, losing the trappings of civilisation (fowling piece, hat and shoes) and is unable to determine whether the encounter was real or a dream. The nightmare history of invasion and genocide experienced by the Indians would be told at a later time, often in Gothic terms.

From Brown to the Dark Romantics: Mysteries of Philadelphia – and of the Hudson Valley

In the early years of the nineteenth century, Gothic continued to drive innovation in American letters. While Brown was a strong feminist, his successors divided by gender, with women developing the female Gothic, and men – with interesting exceptions – engaging the themes of frontier Gothic.[8] Many of these women writers sank into obscurity and have only recently been rediscovered. The only known novel by Philadelphian Rebecca Rush, *Kelroy* (1812), is a sentimental-Gothic hybrid that shows a socially ambitious mother destroying the lives of her daughter and her daughter's lover. Harriet Prescott Spofford had a long and protean career, beginning as a romantic writer and later remaking herself as a regional realist. Her early story 'The Amber Gods' (1863) is lush and erotic, with a supernatural twist at the end. 'Circumstance' (1860) returns to the colonial past and blends the supernatural with Indian warfare and an encounter with a panther that recalls the cave sequence in *Edgar Huntly*.

Spofford's 'The Moonstone Mass' (1868), like Lydia Maria Child's novel *Hobomok* (1824), demonstrates that feminist writers could challenge the male-dominated realm of frontier and wilderness Gothic.[9] The novels of Robert Montgomery Bird (*Nick of the Woods* [1837]), William Gilmore Simms and the immensely popular James Fenimore Cooper do not challenge gender

---

8 See Weinstock, *Charles Brockden Brown*, pp. 119–46, for a full account of Brown's feminism.

9 For a reading of *Hobomok* against Cooper's *The Wept of Wish-Ton-Wish*, see Renée L. Bergland, *The National Uncanny: Indian Ghosts and American Subjects* (Hanover, NH: University Press of New England, 2000), especially pp. 69–108. For 'The Moonstone Mass', see Jeffrey Andrew Weinstock, 'The queer time of lively matter: the polar erotics of Harriet Prescott Spofford's "The Moonstone Mass"', *Women's Studies* 46:8 (2018): 752–66.

stereotypes, and usually seem to support the dominant narrative of American conquest. Yet there is considerable ambiguity here, since, as in Brown, the adventures in the wilderness often lead to disturbing transformations of character. Cooper's Leatherstocking novels both support and regret the retreat of the frontier.

As the forests receded, the importance of cities grew, and the urban Gothic, which began with Brown's *Arthur Mervyn* and *Ormond*, produced the most popular American novel before Harriet Beecher Stowe's *Uncle Tom's Cabin* (1852). George Lippard's *The Quaker City; Or, the Monks of Monk Hall* (1845) is a sprawling maze of a novel, the structure of which echoes the building of its title. Monk Hall is a den of crime presided over by a monster named Devil-Bug. The novel's several plotlines involve rape or seduction, and Lippard's novel is probably the most erotic work to have been legally published in the United States in the nineteenth century. Yet Lippard's purpose is moral, and exposes the corruption of the modern city.[10]

Meanwhile, in New York, Washington Irving worked out his own adaptations of European Gothic to the American landscape. Some of his sketches, in fact, including 'The Adventure of the German Student' (1824) and 'The Spectre Bridegroom' (1820), retain a European setting. His much-loved tales 'Rip Van Winkle' (1819) and 'The Legend of Sleepy Hollow' (1820) are comic Gothics, in which characters experience terror that is not shared by the readers. Irving had a great influence on the American Gothic tradition through his development of the frame-story device, which was adapted by writers from Sarah Orne Jewett to William Dean Howells and greatly complicated by Henry James. The masculine, privileged, clubby atmosphere of Irving's narrative frames would be deconstructed by Edith Wharton in 'The Eyes' (1910).

The Power of Blackness

In the decades before the American Civil War, the ideological debate between Enlightenment Rationalism and Romanticism that produced the first period of the Gothic was restaged in a quarrel between two factions of American Romantic thought. The Transcendentalists, for whom Ralph Waldo Emerson was the central figure (and *Nature* [1836] the central text),

---

10 See Chad Luck, 'George Lippard and the Rise of the Urban Gothic', in Crow (ed.), *A Companion to American Gothic*, pp. 124–36 and Leonard Cassuto, 'Urban American Gothic', in Jeffrey Andrew Weinstock (ed.), *The Cambridge Companion to American Gothic* (Cambridge: Cambridge University Press, 2017), pp. 156–70.

refuted the doctrine of Original Sin professed by their Puritan ancestors, and believed that the innocence of Eden was recoverable. Nature was still unfallen, and the physical facts of nature could lead to spiritual truths beyond, ultimately to a platonic union with the Oversoul. There was no sin and no darkness, only human errors that distance us from the realm of truth and beauty. The Dark Romantics, Edgar Allan Poe, Nathaniel Hawthorne and Herman Melville, shared the Transcendentalists' symbolic view of the world, and to some degree their Platonism. They differed radically from Emerson, though, in their scepticism about human and social perfectibility. Eden, for them, could not be restored; as it was for many Gothic writers, evil was all too real a threat. The poet Emily Dickinson shares many of these values, and, while recognising her unique sensibility, she can be viewed as a distant member of this category.

Melville's 1850 review of Hawthorne's *Mosses from an Old Manse* (1846), 'Hawthorne and His Mosses', is an unintentional manifesto of the Dark Romantics. In spite of the 'Indian-Summer sunlight on the higher side of Hawthorne's soul', Melville wrote, 'the other side—like the dark half of the physical sphere—is shrouded in a blackness, ten times black'. This 'power of blackness' that Melville identified in Hawthorne fascinated him. Thus Melville located the key idea in the Dark Romantics – fascination with evil, the dark side – that defined them as Gothic writers. He also used the key trope of doubleness that marks their difference from the Transcendentalists. Here, it is not circles, the frequent image of Emerson and Thoreau, that abound but notions of duality: the light and dark hemispheres of the earth, two sides of a tortoise (in Melville's 'The Encantadas' [1854]), the eyes of whale looking two ways at once, the House of Usher breaking in two and collapsing into the tarn, the doppelgängers of Poe's 'William Wilson' (1839).

In his poem 'Israfel' (1831), itself something of a manifesto in verse, Poe acknowledges a realm of perfect Platonic forms, where an angel poet might sing. But, he insists, we live in 'a world of sweets and sours' in which perfection is impossible.[11] The 'romantic agony' created by the striving for the unobtainable is a common theme in Poe's verse, as it is for many Romantic poets. But since the world of ideals is impossible, most of his poetry and fiction is concerned with our sublunary world, where things and people fragment and decay.

---

11 Edgar Allan Poe, 'Israfel', in *Poe: Poetry and Tales*, edited by Patrick F. Quinn (New York: Library of America, 1984), pp. 62–4 (p. 64).

Poe did not invent the unreliable narrator, as is often claimed, but he extended Charles Brockden Brown's experiments to great effect. Many of his narrators insist upon their sanity, while revealing, by their actions, that they are stark lunatics. 'Why *will* you say that I am mad?', asks the narrator of 'The Tell-Tale Heart' (1843).[12] The answer, of course, is because he clearly is. His tale, like that of the narrator of 'The Black Cat' (1843), will lead to the uncanny revelation of his victim's concealed corpse, and the exposure of his pretence to be a rational man. Poe's most elaborate treatment of this theme is in 'The Fall of the House of Usher' (1839), with the house of the title allegorised as a human head and mind. The narrator is a double for Roderick Usher, and the uncanny escape of Madeleine Usher from the crypt leads to the collapse of the house, allegorising his (and the narrator's) descent into madness. As Alfred Bendexen notes, this most impressive, and influential, of Poe's tales is another representation of the fragmenting of a hero's identity, the common theme of American Gothic.[13] It is the secular equivalent of the Puritan's fear of losing faith in the woods.

All four of Hawthorne's romances (i.e. Gothic novels) show the inescapable weight of the past and the deep flaws in human character. The most Emersonian moment of *The Scarlet Letter* (1850), when Hester and Dimmesdale meet in the forest, is filled with sunlight and colour. The scene's promise of freedom and fulfilment in the woods proves an illusion; however, as the light dies, Hester resumes her scarlet stigma, and she, Dimmesdale and Pearl return through the dark forest to the even darker village.

Hawthorne's 'Young Goodman Brown', a perfect summation of Dark Romanticism, follows a frequent pattern of American Gothic: the failed or inverted rite of passage. Beginning, as many of Hawthorne's narratives do, with a threshold crossing, Brown leaves his home in Salem Village, Massachusetts, and enters the forest. His adventure recreates Puritan history in miniature: an errand to the wildness, filled with wild beasts, wild men and devils, where he will have his faith tested. He loses faith because he cannot accept the truths that Puritan history suppresses, and with which the Devil taunts him. Though he tears himself away from the Satanic initiation rite (whether this is a dream or not is irrelevant), Brown returns from the forest a confused and bitter man, who has failed to create in himself the new man promised by the new world. 'In the

---

12 Poe, 'The Tell-Tale Heart', in *Poetry and Tales*, pp. 555–9 (p. 555).
13 Alfred Bendixen, 'Romanticism and the American Gothic', in Weinstock (ed.), *The Cambridge Companion to American Gothic*, pp. 31–43 (p. 36).

woods we return to reason and faith', Emerson wrote.[14] Brown's story is quite the opposite.

Emily Dickinson is increasingly seen as a Gothic writer, and, while it is difficult to confine her to any category, she shares many of the core beliefs of the Dark Romantics.[15] She, like them, sees nature as essentially alien. In her poem 1400 ('What Mystery Pervades a Well!' [1877]), for example, she stresses the veiled quality of nature and its unbridgeable strangeness. Yet for Dickinson, as for all writers of American Gothic, the mind is the place of greatest terror, and she uses, like Poe, the metaphor of the mind as a haunted house, as in her often-quoted poem 'One need not be a Chamber—to be Haunted—' (1862). A notable eccentric herself, she knew and feared the power of a patriarchal society to enforce its standards of normalcy:

> Assent—and you are sane—
> Demur—and you're straightway dangerous—
> And handled with a Chain—[16]

The madhouse, or at least the threat of it, is a theme of female Gothic, and to be seen, for example, in Louisa May Alcott's 'A Whisper in the Dark' (1877), and, later, in Charlotte Perkins Gilman's 'The Yellow Wallpaper' (1892).

The Silence of Babo: Black Gothic and Southern Gothic

Melville's 'Benito Cereno' (1855) is a Gothic sea tale, with the Spanish slave ship the San Dominick the equivalent of a Gothic castle, containing secrets, veiled images, terrified captives and a skeleton. But it is essential to note that the San Dominick was already a Gothic site before Babo's rebellion. Slavery, as Teresa Goddu and others have observed, is inherently a Gothic institution.[17] And slavery, and its aftermath, is one of the great dismal subjects of American history and literature. Following his capture, Babo is mute. To whom would he tell his story? Certainly it was not told by the mass of court records, which convey the facts of the rebellion but none of its essential

---

14 Ralph Waldo Emerson, 'Nature', in Joel Porte (ed.), *Emerson: Essays and Lectures* (New York: Library of America, 1983), pp. 9–49 (p. 10).
15 See Daneen Wardrop, *Emily Dickinson's Gothic: Goblin with a Gauge* (Iowa City: University of Iowa Press, 1996).
16 Emily Dickinson, *The Poems of Emily Dickinson: Reading Edition*, edited by R. W. Franklin (Cambridge, MA: The Belknap Press of Harvard University Press, 1998), poem 435.
17 See Teresa A. Goddu, 'The African American Slave Narrative and the Gothic', in Crow (ed.), *A Companion to American Gothic*, pp. 71–83.

truths. Amasa Delano, the optimistic, typically American sea captain whose sailors suppress the slave rebellion, cannot understand the horrors on the San Dominick, thus cannot understand why Benito Cereno, though rescued, remains sunk in a profound depression. Cereno, however, traumatised as he gazes at Babo's severed head, has lived through a Gothic narrative that has disrupted the structure of his world.

The question we ask of Babo – to whom would he tell his story? – is the problem of Black American literature of the nineteenth century. Who will hear of the horrors of slavery? The literature of race in America, both before and after the Civil War, is contested ground, with African American voices, and those of sympathetic white writers and editors, struggling to find an audience and competing with a southern narrative that idealised plantation life, and, in the post-bellum period, surrounded it with a nostalgic haze. The Plantation School, or School of Southern Nostalgia, presented a sentimental view of the old order and, at least implicitly, endorsed the repression of southern blacks that began with the end of the Reconstruction era in the late 1870s.

Gothic literature, of course, is inherently anti-nostalgic. In the last decades of the century we find both sympathetic white authors and emerging black writers who expose, once again, the brutality of slavery and of the segregated, lynch-law period after Reconstruction. They also turn to the mixed-race population that was nearly invisible in the binary, white-and-or-black vision of the Old South. To this end they often employed Gothic tropes such as masks, masquerades and doubles, and revisited the trope of the haunted house to expose the secrets that lay in its crypts.

The ghosts of slaves haunted southern houses. Many in the south knew the history of 'The "Haunted House" in Royal Street', as retold by George Washington Cable in his *Strange True Stories of Louisiana* (1889). While the citizens of New Orleans drove the infamous Madame Lalaurie from the city, the horrors of her town house, filled with dead and dying slaves, were only an extreme departure from what had become a brutal norm.

The supernatural was not needed to horrify visitors to the plantation house. In Thomas Nelson Page's 'No Haid Pawn' (1887), a terrified boy is forced to spend the night in an abandoned mansion that is believed to be haunted. While we understand that the boy sees not a ghost dragging a headless body, but an escaped slave dragging a slaughtered stolen hog, the story depicts horrors enough: the deaths of slaves who constructed the mansion and tried to clear and work fields in the disease-ridden swamp;

and the brutal last owner who cut off a slave's head, and was himself decapitated when hanged for his crimes.[18]

The sexual exploitation of enslaved women was a repressed fact of southern life, and the 'colour line' was one of the nation's uncanny frontiers. Racial laws defining a person of mixed race as black produced many absurd situations, and an unintentional critique of the idea of whiteness. As one extreme example, we might consider the real-life fate of Salome Mueller, a German immigrant orphan who was sold into slavery, and who was raised believing herself to be black, until rescued, after a widely reported legal struggle, by fellow immigrants who recognised her. American Gothic is filled with individuals whose ambiguous racial identity asks the question, who and what am I? Often characters cross the colour line unwittingly from white to black, as in Grace King's 'The Little Convent Girl' (1893), or in Kate Chopin's brilliant and often-anthologised 'Désirée's Baby' (1893).

George Washington Cable's complex novel *The Grandissimes* (1880) begins with a masked ball, a scene suitable for a narrative about concealed identity. Much of the novel is told from the point of view of a German immigrant, who struggles to learn the complexities of Creole society in pre-war New Orleans. We learn, with him, that there are two characters named Charles Grandisson, one black, one white. While their half-brother relationship is acknowledged, others are only hinted at, dimly seen through the veil of Creole silence. Similarly, in Mark Twain's most Gothic novel, *Pudd'nhead Wilson* (1894), two babies, one considered black, one white, are switched in the cradle, and grow up in an unwitting masquerade. This changeling device sets in motion events that are filled with other cross-racial and gender disguises, until all is revealed by the title character in a melodramatic courtroom scene. Such stories are necessarily uncanny since they contain and disclose family secrets that should not be revealed. Charles Chesnutt's 'conjure woman' tales of 1899 reveal many such hidden secrets. Thus we learn, only by guarded references, of a master's impregnation of his slave Phyllis (in 'The Marked Tree' [1924–5]) and, years later, of his sale of the resulting slave son to pay for the wedding of his white heir.

Such stories of 'suppressed genealogy', as I have called them,[19] were everywhere known and seldom spoken of in the South. A very different

---

18 See Carol Margaret Davison, 'Southern Gothic: Haunted Houses', in Susan Castillo Street and Charles L. Crow (eds), *The Palgrave Handbook of the Southern Gothic* (Basingstoke: Palgrave Macmillan, 2016), pp. 55–67.
19 See Charles L. Crow, 'Under the Upas Tree: Charles Chesnutt's Gothic', in Joseph R. McElrath, Jr (ed.), *Critical Essays on Charles Chesnutt* (New York: G. K. Hall, 1999), pp. 261–70.

form of brutality was lynch law, by its nature public and intended to intimidate. This horror, graphically depicted by Paul Laurence Dunbar in 'The Lynching of Jube Benson' (1904), would be visited again in the twentieth century by writers as diverse as Richard Wright, Jean Toomer and William Faulkner. These two forms of Southern Gothic, the story of concealed genealogy and that of lynching, were combined in Chesnutt's 'The Sheriff's Children' (1889), which shows a heroic southern sheriff defending a black prisoner from a mob. The comfortable stereotypes used to present the sheriff – like those that Melville used to describe his Captain Delano – are shattered when the mulatto prisoner is revealed to be the sheriff's own son Tom, sold by the sheriff before the war to the rice swamps of Alabama, with his mother, who died under the lash. After a series of plot reversals in which Tom is wounded, Tom tears off his bandages and allows himself to bleed to death at night in his cell. His mute defiance, like Babo's, leaves the sheriff, and the reader, without an easy escape from guilt and history.

Gothic in the Age of Realism

The tumultuous period of change that the United States entered after the Civil War produced divergent literary responses, among them local colour (of which the plantation school was a part), realism and naturalism. These literary styles or traditions were at war with antebellum Romanticism and its legacies, and at times with each other. All of them would seem to be inconsistent with the Gothic. The nostalgia that fuels most local colour (or 'regional realism') – the longing for a simpler past – is the opposite of Gothic dread or terror. Howellsian realism, with its stress on the observable norms of experience, and its successor Naturalism, which insisted on scientific determinism, likewise seem to exclude the mystery and ambiguity on which the Gothic mode thrives.[20]

Yet these contradictions are more apparent than real. The Gothic, indeed, exposes the common themes and the shared fears of Americans in the decades after the Civil War, as it did before, and helps to clarify the literary history of the period. As before the War, many of the finest works of American literature of the remaining decades of the century are Gothic, as we have seen already with Chesnutt and Chopin. Virtually every writer of the Age of Realism, from Sarah Orne Jewett to Henry James, wrote ghost stories,

---

20 For a full discussion of realism, naturalism and the Gothic, see Monika Elbert and Wendy Ryden (eds), *Haunting Realities: Naturalistic Gothic and American Realism* (Tualoosa: University of Alabama Press, 2017).

and some, such as M. E. Wilkins Freeman, published volumes of them. We should remember, moreover, that the 'real', that plane of experience that realism supposedly reflects, is a constructed and changing concept. Certainly ghosts were real for many Americans at the time, as demonstrated by the resurgence of Spiritualism after the War. The Society for Psychical Research seemed to offer scientific justification for such a belief.

While local colour (regional realism) became intensely popular after the War, and Bret Harte for a time was the best-paid author in the country, its roots go back to the 1850s. Among the early writers of this tradition is Alice Cary, whose two volumes of tales about the fictional Clovernook, Ohio (1852, 1853) illustrate its contradictory tensions. While Cary and her readers may be drawn to the memory of the simple and snug life of the village (the word 'nook' in its name would suggest as much), she, like the later Mark Twain, has a counterbalancing realistic impulse to describe the details of this life, which were at times squalid and vicious. Thus her story 'Uncle Christopher's' (1853) reveals a family that is blighted by the narrowness and stinginess of its patriarch. The snugness of Clovernook can undergo the *unheimlich* inversion, in which what is concealed can be exposed – an unsettling or uncanny turn that is always a possibility in nostalgic local colour. In Cary's 'The Wildermings' (1852), we sense something uncanny about the new neighbours, something involving a past sexual transgression, but which is never quite explained, and remains part of the mystery of repressive village life.

In the short stories of New England regional realists, there is often a celebration of the snug comfort and plain values of the village, but also the acknowledgment that, in Jewett's words, 'there was little real comfort in a community where the sterner, stingier, forbidding side of New England life was well exemplified'.[21] Often, as in Alice Cary's frontier Ohio, the burden of this sternness and stinginess falls upon women.

Mary E. Wilkins Freeman wrote ghost stories collected in *The Wind in the Rose-Bush* (1903), including, among her tales of village life, some Gothic works that were supernatural, some grimly realistic. 'Luella Miller' is a vampire story, in which the beautiful doll-like woman of the title sucks the life out of a series of victims. In 'Old Woman Magoun', a heroic woman tries to defend her granddaughter from sexual enslavement, ultimately allowing her to die from eating deadly nightshade rather than falling into the power of a degenerate village rake.

---

21 Sarah Orne Jewett, 'In Dark New England Days', in Peter Straub (ed.), *American Fantastic Tales: Terror and the Uncanny, From Poe to the Pulps*, 2 vols (New York: Library of America), vol. 1, 112–30 (p. 121).

There is a strong feminist element in the writing of Jewett and Freeman, as there certainly was in that of Charlotte Perkins Gilman. Gilman is not usually regarded as a regional realist, but it is instructive to consider her in this context. In 1891 and 1892 the *New England Magazine* devoted several issues to the two-hundredth anniversary of the Salem witchcraft trials, and published both historical essays and fiction devoted to those dark old times. Among other stories, including one by the still neglected Alice Brown, was Gilman's 'The Giant Wisteria' (1891), a ghostly Gothic tale that is essentially a rewriting, in miniature, of *The Scarlet Letter* – except that the Hester character apparently drowns her child in a well to prevent being separated from it by her stern Puritan father.

'The Giant Wisteria' is a haunted-house story, and recently Agnieszka Soltysik Monnet has argued that Gilman's most famous story, 'The Yellow Wall-Paper' might be situated in that tradition too.[22] The haunted house, in fact, evolves in innovative ways in late nineteenth-century American fiction. It is, of course, a central trope in Southern Gothic, with Poe's 'The Fall of the House of Usher' becoming the ruined plantation house of the declining, or decadent, southern aristocracy, a trope continuing into the twentieth century in Faulkner's Yoknapatawptha County. In another strain, anticipated by Fitz-James O'Brien's 'The Lost Room' (1858), a domestic space, a room or a house disappears or mutates. Emma Dowson's 'An Itinerant House' (1897), Madeline Yale Wynne's 'The Little Room' (1895), Elia W. Peattie's 'The House That Was Not' (1898) are all, like 'The Yellow Wall-Paper', feminist fables about the oppression of women at the century's end.[23]

Gothic at the Heart of Realism

W. D. Howells used his position as editor of *The Atlantic*, and then of *Harper's Monthly*, to promote the theory and practice of realism, both through the publication of younger writers, as well as through his own editorial columns. He is remembered now largely for his realistic novels,

---

[22] Agnieszka Soltysik Monnet, *The Poetics and Politics of the American Gothic: Gender and Slavery in Nineteenth-Century American Literature* (Farnham and Burlington: Ashgate, 2010), p. 106.

[23] See Jeffrey Andrew Weinstock, *Scare Tactics: Supernatural Fiction by American Women* (New York: Fordham University Press, 2008), pp. 56–81 and Dara Downey, *American Women's Ghost Stories in the Gilded Age* (Basingstoke: Palgrave Macmillan, 2014), pp. 121–78.

especially *The Rise of Silas Lapham* (1885) and *A Hazard of New Fortunes* (1890). Nonetheless there is a Gothic side to Howells – though he would not have called it so – that runs back to Hawthorne, and owes something also to his experience of popular Spiritualism. He co-edited a collection of Gothic tales, *Shapes that Haunt the Dusk* (1907), and included several supernatural or Gothic psychological tales in two collections of his own stories, *Questionable Shapes* (1903) and *Between the Dark and the Daylight* (1907). His early novel *The Undiscovered Country* (1880) is, in part, a homage to Hawthorne's *The Blithedale Romance* (1852). His novella *The Shadow of a Dream* (1899), in which the recurring dream of one character destroys the lives of three, is a story of veiled and suppressed homosexual longing.[24]

Henry James wrote his own homage to *Blithedale* in *The Bostonians* (1886). James's early novel *The American* (1877) begins in apparent realism and darkens into the Gothic (though James used the Hawthornian term 'romance' to describe it), in which a murder is discovered through a long-concealed letter. *The Aspern Papers* (1888) uses Gothic devices such as a cache of secret documents and concealed paternity. His late and important tale *The Jolly Corner* (1908) employs the motif of the double, familiar in American literature from Poe's 'William Wilson', in which two versions of the main character, representing alternative life choices, haunt each other through an empty New York townhouse.

James's *The Turn of the Screw* (1898) uses almost every trope of English and American Gothic, and takes them to excruciating levels of complication, resulting in a novella that has generated as much scholarly attention as any work of fiction in the English language. There is, from the beginning, the question of the narrative voice, which joins the unreliable narrator, explored by Charles Brockden Brown and Poe, to the frame-story device developed by Washington Irving. The nameless governess is familiar from such English Gothic fictions as Charlotte Brontë's *Jane Eyre* (1847), as is the lonely country estate, which here becomes a haunted house, haunted by *something*, either the mad governess herself, or the ghosts of Peter Quint and Miss Jessel. Certainly Bly and its angelic, all-too-perfect children conceal some uncanny secret, and a nasty hint of paedophilia lurks behind the more obvious secret of Quint's and Jessel's transgressions.

---

24 See George Spangler, 'The shadow of a dream: Howells' homosexual tragedy', *American Quarterly*, 23 (1971): 110–19.

Gothic Naturalism

The generation of writers that we call Naturalists was at war with its literary fathers. Born within a few years of 1870, they were believers in social Darwinism, usually learned from Herbert Spencer, and often accepted in a kind of conversion experience. They detested the timidity of Howellsian realism, as they saw it. They lived in an amoral universe of natural, social, and economic forces, and they needed to shock their readers into an awareness of this truth. To them, ugliness could be more valid than beauty, pain more valuable than pleasure. The Naturalists' vision of a world in which great forces batter the individual could be expressed in Gothic tropes, and Naturalists and earlier Gothic writers shared common images of prisons, traps and cages. Their work had been anticipated by the proto-Naturalist Rebecca Harding Davis, whose *Life in the Iron Mills: Or, The Korl Woman* (1861) presented an industrial wasteland where the artist-hero, Wolf, is driven by economic forces to commit a theft and to kill himself in a prison cell. He leaves behind his statue of a woman hacked from korl (apparently a regional term for slag, the by-product of iron production). The statue, with its unrefined technique, crude material and raw emotion, is a fitting emblem for the later Naturalists' aesthetic.

Among Naturalists, most, including E. A. Robinson, Stephen Crane, Frank Norris, and Jack London, experimented with the Gothic. Robinson and Crane crafted variations on regional realism. Crane's imagined Whilomville, like Alice Cary's Clovernook, suggests in its name the comfortable hometown, remembered with nostalgia, that may produce *unheimlich* discoveries. In his novella *The Monster* (1899), Crane presented a Frankensteinian story set in the small, fictional town of Whilomville, New York. The monster is a black man without a face, burned away in a fire, who becomes an image of the feared Other to the community. He is driven out, and the doctor who saved his life is ostracised. The story is a fable about loss of identity, race and mob psychology.

Robinson's poems about Tilbury Town depict characters defeated by change and time. There are ghosts in some of his poems, like 'Luke Havergal' (1897). Others are Gothic without being supernatural. 'The Mill' (1920) shows the crushing effect of industrialisation on the craft tradition of milling. Robinson contrasts the sad double suicide of the miller and his wife with a gorgeous description of the starry night sky reflected in the mill pond, in which she drowned. Nature may be lovely, but, as always in Naturalism, it is indifferent.

Frank Norris was drawn to the Gothic from his earliest work. His juvenile story 'Lauth' (1893) shows the influence of Poe and, like Crane's *The Monster*, Mary Shelley. Set in the Middle Ages, 'Lauth' depicts an attempt by a young scientist and his friends to revive one of their classmates, who has been killed in an insurrection, by giving him blood transfusions and stimulants. While he seems at first to respond, ultimately he subsides to a quivering puddle of protoplasm. 'Lauth' unites a particular Naturalistic fear, an atavistic descent back down the evolutionary scale, with a Gothic fascination with disease and bodily corruption. What, after all, is more threatening to identity than disease or decay? And what could be more uncanny? Charles Brockden Brown used descriptions of Philadelphia's yellow fever epidemics in the 1790s to great and disgusting effect in *Arthur Mervyn* and *Ormond*, while Poe described the collapse of a body into a sickening mass of corruption in 'The Facts in the Case of M. Valdemar' (1845).

Yellow fever and, especially, tuberculosis, were omnipresent in the nineteenth century, and both illnesses remained without a cure. Nearly every biography of a nineteenth-century person will reveal some relative or friend who died of tuberculosis, a lingering, wasting disease that could turn a healthy young person into a pale shadow, like a ghost or wraith. Faye Ringel has traced a New England tradition of vampire stories back to the continuing tuberculosis epidemic, a tradition that would be drawn upon in the early twentieth century by Edith Wharton in 'Bewitched' (1925), which also pays homage to Hawthorne.[25]

A number of other infectious diseases could not be named in nineteenth-century fiction. Not even Émile Zola, Frank Norris's idol, could bring himself to have his eponymous prostitute-heroine die of syphilis in *Nana* (1880), though the plot clearly indicates it; instead, she dies of smallpox. It was daring, therefore, for Norris to write of an artist who contracts syphilis, and who is turned into a kind of werewolf when the disease attacks his nervous system. Norris knew, of course, that *Vandover and the Brute* (1914) could not be published at the time, and it was issued, with some bowdlerising, a dozen years after his death. Elaine Showalter notes that vampires often function in the nineteenth century as metaphors for syphilis.[26] In the twentieth century, vampires and werewolves return with the AIDS epidemic.

---

25 Faye Ringel, *New England's Gothic Literature: History and Folklore of the Supernatural from the Seventeenth Through the Twentieth Centuries* (Lewiston, Queenston and Lampter: Edwin Mellen Press, 1995), pp. 137–56.
26 Elaine Showalter, 'Syphilis, Sexuality, and the Fiction of the Fin de Siècle', in Ruth Bernard Yeazell (ed.), *Sex, Politics, and Science in the Nineteenth-Century Novel* (Baltimore: Johns Hopkins University Press, 1986), pp. 88–115.

Most of the Gothic fiction of Jack London, the youngest of the major Naturalists, was published in the twentieth century, and is thus beyond the purview of this essay, but we should note that *The Sea Wolf* (1904) is a continuation of the sea Gothic tradition developed by Poe in *The Narrative of Arthur Gordon Pym of Nantucket* (1838) and Melville in *Moby-Dick* (1851).

Weird Tales

The genre of the weird tale derives, like much American Gothic, from Poe. Usually using heightened, poetic language, and often featuring a mysterious narrator, the weird tale builds towards a chilling, usually supernatural, revelation.[27] The weird tale thrived in the last decades of the nineteenth century, sometimes in the work of writers who also wrote in the Naturalist tradition. Ambrose Bierce wrote tales based on his Civil War experience, including the non-supernatural Gothic 'Chicamagua' (1889) and 'An Occurrence at Owl Creek Bridge' (1890), as well as the ambiguously supernatural 'The Death of Halpin Frayser'. He was a master of the haunted-house story. But it was Bierce's 'An Inhabitant of Carcosa' (1886) that was particularly important in the development of the weird tale.

The narrator of 'An Inhabitant of Carcosa' discovers his own tombstone. He is a ghost, wandering among ruins. Robert W. Chambers took the idea of the lost Carcosa for his interlocking series of four stories, *The King in Yellow* (1895). In all of these weird tales there is reference to a forbidden play, also called *The King in Yellow*, which is the ultimate Gothic text. To read it is to be driven mad, and to open a portal to Carcosa, through which horrors may enter our own world, including the terrible Yellow King himself. These stories had great influence on twentieth-century writers of weird tales, including H. P. Lovecraft.

Another practitioner of the art of the weird was Greek-born Lafcadio Hearn, who, though a wanderer who ultimately became a citizen of Japan, always considered himself an American author. His story 'The Ghostly Kiss' (1880), like Bierce's 'An Inhabitant of Carcosa', is told by a narrator who discovers that he is a ghost. In Japan, Hearn translated and collected Japanese ghost stories in *Kwaidan*, which means 'weird tales'. Hearn in turn influenced the Japanese writer whose pen name was Edogawa Rampo (1894–1965), a phonetic rendering of the name 'Edgar Allan Poe' when pronounced with a

---

27 See S. T. Joshi, *The Weird Tale: Arthur Machen, Lord Dunsany, Algernon Blackwood, M. R. James, H. P. Lovecraft* (Austin: University of Texas Press, 1990).

thick Japanese accent. Some of Rampo's tales have been translated into English, serving as one illustration, among many, of the ways that nineteenth-century American Gothic has interacted with world literature.

Conclusion

American culture, like that of the Old South, wraps itself in nostalgia and denial. We often think, like W. D. Howells, that the 'smiling aspects of life' are more typically American, and that, as Hawthorne said, America lacks 'deep and gloomy' wrongs. Both writers knew better, of course, but these statements of American optimism, and faith and amnesia demonstrate the need then, as of now, for Gothic. American writers of Gothic literature, from the late eighteenth century to the early twentieth century and beyond, have met that need with works of great originality and enduring power.

2.18

Nineteenth-Century British and American Gothic and the History of Slavery

MAISHA WESTER

Related by historians and travellers in accounts overflowing with Gothic terms and descriptions, the Haitian Revolution (1791–1804) was the unspeakable monster that lurked beneath nineteenth-century terrors. Its ramifications as just one of an increasing number of slave rebellions permanently changed the Gothic mode in both Britain and America. While the Gothic's turn to bloodshed is partially explained through the anxiety generated by the turmoil in revolutionary and post-revolutionary France, the revolts of enslaved populations in the colonies introduced a particularly racialised discourse to the genre that worked in tandem with the excessive white-on-white French violence. Haiti's rise – built upon a refutation of racial constructions, anger at multiple betrayals by their former rulers/owners, and an utter rejection of the previous socioeconomic and racial structures – generated troubling discourses about the difference between free and enslaved, civilised and savage, justice and lawlessness, revolution and submission, in both sociopolitical and Gothic discourses that invariably read these questions through the lens of race. More importantly, Gothic texts from the nineteenth century onwards reveal that such questions have yet to be answered; in troubling the line between white/owner and black/beast (of burden), the Haitian Revolution generated the nightmare that plagued a nascent modernity and the era beyond. Thus the Gothic became, and indeed remains, haunted by an ever-present racialised discourse, one that reveals the horror of modernity's constructions and their inheritances, and which anxiously investigates (the lie of) racial difference.

Nineteenth-century British and American Gothic texts invariably embedded the Caribbean's racial turbulence in their narratives. On the one hand, texts such as Charlotte Dacre's *Zofloya; or, The Moor* (1806), Edgar Allan Poe's *Narrative of Arthur Gordon Pym of Nantucket* (1838) and Herman

Melville's 'Benito Cereno' (1855) depict black rebellion in unequivocal tones of horror, their black (enslaved) characters assuming the place of the utterly monstrous. On the other hand, novels like Mary Shelley's *Frankenstein* (1818; 1831) and Emily Bronte's *Wuthering Heights* (1847) worry over the blurred line separating blacks from whites and thus anxiously debate the justice of violent black revolution. Indeed, such texts seem plagued by the notion that, while slavery itself may be responsible for the violence of the enslaved, slavery may in fact debase white subjects as well. By the end of the nineteenth century, fictions such as Florence Marryat's *The Blood of the Vampire* (1897) depict slavery as a horrifying spectre haunting the edges of civil white society, threatening destruction in the contaminating, usurping figures of miscegenated characters who migrate from the colonies to the seat of empire.

Each narrative centres around an anti-hero or villain who is either literally or symbolically a person of colour. Dacre's Zofloya is an actual black slave (or Moor) from Africa; Poe's novel is populated by people of colour, including a particularly murderous black cook who drives the crew to mutiny, a half-savage mixed-race figure who becomes Pym's protector, and an island of murderous, ferocious blacks whose location and description are notably suggestive of Haiti. Melville likewise invokes the spectre of Haiti by naming the ship the *San Dominick* and by populating the story primarily with insurrectionary black slaves. And while there has been much critical discussion about Heathcliff's race, his dark visage and appearance on the streets of Liverpool in 1801 – a time when Liverpool's industry was thriving as a consequence of its role in the slave trade – strongly support arguments in favour of reading him as a black person. Lastly, although Marryat's character Harriet Brandt looks white upon first appearance, the narrative reveals that she is, in fact, a quadroon. Shelley's Creature in *Frankenstein* is the only figure here that is symbolically a person of colour even as he is literally painted with colours, having black lips, yellow skin and bloodshot red eyes.

The texts' concerns with slavery are readily apparent. In cases such as *Zofloya*, 'Benito Cereno' and *The Blood of the Vampire*, slavery and slave rebellion are explicitly referenced if not represented. Meanwhile *Pym* reproduces the scene of slave insurrection in the black cook's mutiny and islanders' assaults. Similarly, *Frankenstein* and *Wuthering Heights* attribute traits typical to enslaved people to their villains: both are unnamed, Heathcliff being named after a son that died. Thus, in Heathcliff's case, the Earnshaws essentially re-label him with their own familial name, and while the choice of moniker may be read as a sign of Heathcliff's immediate threat as a usurper, it also signals the extent to which he has been claimed and objectified as property. Likewise, the Creature in Shelley's novel learns to speak in ways similar to how slaves often learned to write – that is, through eavesdropping and subterfuge. More importantly, he becomes aware of his difference in a way that predicts Frantz Fanon's concept of the racial subject becoming 'black'. In *Black Skin, White Masks* (1952; trans. 1967) Fanon explains that blackness does not exist ipso facto, but rather that the black subject must encounter the self amid the white world to learn the s/he is black.[1] The Creature makes a similar discovery, having 'admired the perfect forms' of the white family before observing his own reflection.[2] Equally important, he learns the 'fatal effects of [his] miserable deformity'[3] only through actual engagement with the cottagers as the first among many to reject him based upon his physical difference. Thus, slavery and enslaved subjects haunt Gothic writing through much of the nineteenth century.

Gothic in the Age of Revolutions and Rebellions

Born out of, and informed by, the Enlightenment, British and American Gothic literature reflected the era's conflicted thoughts about racial difference. The Enlightenment's basic notion was 'that of the "sameness" of humanity'.[4] Yet this sameness seemed to reach its limits when racial difference entered the equation. Thus French writers like Hippolyte Taine critiqued such notions, and 'the word "civilization" came to be geographically and historically inflected ... to turn "white skin" into "both a marker and a product" of civilization, with civilization being defined "through difference, against a hierarchy that invokes the state of other, historical or non-European, societies"'.[5] The Gothic mode, arising as it does in the midst of the slave trade and rising racialist notions, reflects such ideologies. The need to rationalise the continued existence of slavery in the face of increasingly widespread slave rebellions, which pointed to the dangers of maintaining the institution, resulted in contradictory ideas about blacks in particular. Political authors such as Bryan Edwards, a staunch supporter of the slave trade, emphasised the brutality of blacks, enslaved and otherwise. In *An Historical*

---

1 Frantz Fanon, *Black Skin, White Masks*, trans. by Charles Lam Markmann (New York: Grove Press, 1967), p. 109.
2 Mary Shelley, *Frankenstein*, edited by D. L. Macdonald and Kathleen Scherf (Peterborough, Ont.: Broadview Press, 2005), p. 139.
3 Shelley, *Frankenstein*, p. 139.
4 Tabish Khair, 'Summing Up', in *The Gothic, Postcolonialism and Otherness: Ghosts from Elsewhere* (New York: Palgrave Macmillan, 2009), pp. 157–74 (p. 157).
5 Khair, 'Summing Up', p. 157.

Survey of the French Colony in the Island of St. Domingo (1797), his study of the rebellion in Saint Domingue, for instance, Edwards describes the black rebels as 'savage people, habituated to the barbarities of Africa, [who] avail themselves of the silence and obscurity of the night, and fall on the peaceful and unsuspicious planters, like so many famished tigers thirsting for human blood'.[6] Nor is Saint Domingue the sole, or even the first, point of horror for the era. The Caribbean was plagued by poison plots, such as Makandal's 1759 conspiracy against white colonialists in Saint Domingue. In 1760, Tacky's Rebellion, an uprising of Akan slaves, gave rise to stories of black atrocities committed against white planters in Jamaica. And the year 1831 witnessed the Baptist War, known today as Sam Sharpe's Rebellion or the Christmas Rebellion, in which an enslaved African Jamaican man led an insurrection against slavery.

Consequently, by the nineteenth century, dominant opinion viewed blacks as 'egregiously cruel and vindictive', and marked by 'unnatural cruelty'.[7] By many accounts, black subjects were barely human. In *The History of Jamaica; or, General Survey of the Ancient and Modern State of that Island* (1774), Edward Long characterised blacks as fetid-smelling brutes covered in 'wool, like bestial fleece';[8] incapable of civility, much less of scientific or philosophical thought, blacks were supposedly void of any moral system. Furthermore, blacks drank excessively and were supposedly idle. Long concludes that they are 'the vilest of the human kind, to which they have little more pretension of resemblance than what arises from their exterior form'.[9] Yet the profitable nature of the slave trade required a way to calm fears of violence, and so produced conflicting depictions of black bodies. Enslaved people were deemed 'universally deceitful and ruled by transitory appetites and terrors',[10] yet also docile, dependent, faithful and selfless; in fact, they were eulogised and deemed legendary for these later traits,[11] even as they were demonised and rendered monstrous for the former. Thus, notable American Gothic writer Edgar Allan Poe explained that the negro differs in

---

6 Bryan Edwards, *An Historical Survey of the French Colony In the Island of St. Domingo* (London, 1797), p. 63.
7 Sara D. Schotland, 'The slave's revenge: the terror in Charlotte Dacre's *Zofloya*', *The Western Journal of Black Studies* 33:2 (2009): 123–31 (p. 128).
8 Quoted in Maja-Lisa von Sneidern, '*Wuthering Heights* and the Liverpool slave trade', *ELH* 62:1 (1996): 171–96 (p. 190).
9 Quoted in Von Sneidern, '*Wuthering Heights* and the Liverpool slave trade', p. 191.
10 Von Sneidern, '*Wuthering Heights* and the Liverpool slave trade', p. 179.
11 Von Sneidern, '*Wuthering Heights* and the Liverpool slave trade', p. 179.

passions and wants and feelings and tempers in all respects from the white man. These differences create a relationship of loyal devotion on the part of the slave to which the white man's heart is a stranger, and of the master's reciprocal feeling of parental attachment to his humble dependent ... [T]hese sentiments in the breast of the negro and his master, are stronger than they would be under like circumstances between individuals of the white race.[12]

Such competing ideas were partially resolved through the mystification of black rebellion. White planters and colonists attempted to account for slave rebellion by explaining such violence as the outgrowth of 'magical' practices such as Voudou and Obeah. Thus Makandal was rumoured to be a potent voudoun and accounts of Tacky's Rebellion emphasised Obeah men's role as rebel leaders. The 1789 *Report of the Lords* explained that such leaders 'induce[d] many to enter into that rebellion on the assurance that they were invulnerable, and to render them so, the Obeah man gave them a powder with which to rub themselves'.[13]

Abolition, moreover, saw a rise in support in the years following the Haitian Revolution as white European and American populations became increasingly wary of the effect of prolonged exposure to 'colonial societies, nonwhite races, non-Christian belief systems, and the moral evils of slavery'; 'The fear of miscegenation', Lizabeth Paravisini-Gebert concludes, 'with the attendant horror of interracial sexuality, enters public discourse at about the time Walpole began the Gothic novel.'[14] Indeed, in *Candid reflections upon the judgement lately awarded by the Court of King's Bench in Westminster-Hall on what is commonly called the Negroe Cause* (1772), Edward Long categorises 'the horrors of sexual miscegenation as an infectious disease'.[15] Therefore, terror of the violence arising from slave rebellion was accompanied by concerns that whiteness would be contaminated through cultural (and sexual) miscegenation. Charlotte Smith's novella 'The Story of Henrietta' (1800) evokes both the horror of rebellion and cultural contamination via its setting in Jamaica's Blue Mountains. As Paravisini-Gebert explains, both the heroine's (and Smith's) 'fears of Jamaica's African-derived magicoreligious practice of

---

12 Quoted in Von Sneidern, '*Wuthering Heights* and the Liverpool slave trade', p. 190.
13 Lizabeth Paravisini-Gebert, 'Colonial and Postcolonial Gothic: The Caribbean', in Jerrold E. Hogle (ed.), *The Cambridge Companion to Gothic Fiction* (Cambridge: Cambridge University Press, 2002), pp. 229–58 (pp. 234–5). Awareness of the roles of such magicoreligious systems led colonialists to outlaw the practice of Voudou and Obeah in places like Saint Domingue and Jamaica.
14 Paravisini-Gebert, 'Colonial and Postcolonial Gothic', p. 230.
15 Paravisini-Gebert, 'Colonial and Postcolonial Gothic', p. 230.

Obeah and the possibility of sexual attack by black males' further aggravate her terror of slave rebellion.[16] Anti-slavery proponents thus presented arguments defining the enslaved as a human deserving of freedom – the more commonly emphasised argument in modern discussions of Abolitionism – alongside arguments demonising the enslaved as a debased and destructive being born out of the corrupting system of slavery.

Gothic texts similarly pondered over the cause of slave rebellion, essentially reducing the issue to an irresolvable question of nature versus nurture. The very question destabilised the concept of race and racial superiority, since 'such speculation places the savage origin of black Africans and the primitive origin of Anglo-Saxons in a very dangerous and threatening proximity. Race itself becomes a superstition, and brutality, ignorance and treachery characteristics of degeneration in the potential of any culture'.[17] *Wuthering Heights* provides a significant example of the impact of the nature /nurture debate as its terror arises not from monstrous beings threatening damnation nor from damsels pursued across vast landscapes by unrelenting would-be rapists; instead, its horrified plot arises from its assault on the racial 'knowledge' of the era, for Catherine and Hindley prove as degenerate as Heathcliff. The last third of Melville's 'Benito Cereno' struggles with this assault, consisting of court documents that recount the uprising's beginning as well as interviews with its victims and leaders. What troubles most in these seemingly banal documents is Babo's silence because, in refusing to speak, he impedes the attempts of legalistic (and, implicitly, pseudoscientific) discourses to re-contain him as a known entity. Babo and his band of rebels were barbarous and brilliant, savage and orderly. Thus Melville's rebellious slave terrifies, even in his death, by refusing to participate in racial discourses that firmly affixed civility according to racial nature.

The Gothic mode, struggling to contain the proliferation of meanings stemming from racialised discourses, became populated by barbarous and liberty-seeking dark anti-heroes.[18] *Frankenstein* invites readers to understand that the Creature's violence stems not just from his monstrous birth but from being abandoned by his creator/father for the first two years of his life. Indeed, accosting Victor as wicked for his wanton assaults upon him, the Creature explains, 'I was benevolent and good; misery made me a fiend.'[19]

---

16 Paravisini-Gebert, 'Colonial and Postcolonial Gothic', p. 229.
17 Von Sneidern, '*Wuthering Heights* and the Liverpool Slave Trade', p. 177.
18 Laura Doyle, 'At world's edge: post/coloniality, Charles Maturin, and the gothic wanderer', *Nineteenth-Century Literature* 65:4 (March 2011): 513–47 (p. 525).
19 Shelley, *Frankenstein*, p. 126.

While *Wuthering Heights* opaquely defines the inevitability of Heathcliff's moral decline, Hindley's mistreatment of him certainly accelerates his fall. Abuse encourages Heathcliff to forget the kindness and curiosity fostered by his early education with Mr Earnshaw. Under Hindley's despotic insistence on 'continual hard work, begun soon and ended late', Heathcliff develops an 'impression of inward and outward repulsiveness' and exaggerates 'his naturally reserved disposition ... into an almost idiotic excess of unsociable moroseness'.[20] The change leads Nelly to conclude that Heathcliff's pleasure soon lies 'in exciting the aversion rather than the esteem of his few acquaintances'.[21] Importantly, Cathy rejects the essentialising biologism in nineteenth-century racial constructs, blaming Heathcliff's environment for his degradation.[22]

Frankenstein implicitly addresses the question of racial difference and social condition in both the figure of the Creature and in the character of Justine, a white female servant. Indeed, Justine occupies a significant position in the text, as a member of an inferior class whose childhood and 'employment' are reminiscent of slavery. Adopted from impoverished parents as a young girl, Justine is treated much like a pet, though she never accesses the same status as Elizabeth, Frankenstein's fostered cousin.[23] As an adult, and not unlike a slave, she is technically employed by the family whom she has been serving since childhood. In introducing Justine, Victor remarks that 'there is less distinction between the several classes of [Geneva's] inhabitants; and the lower orders, being neither so poor nor so despised, their manners are more refined and moral. A servant in Geneva does not mean the same thing as a servant in France and England'.[24] This comment significantly contextualises servitude/slavery and thus also contextualises the nature of the servant/slave relation. A social inferior, Justine is nonetheless equal to her employers, proving as refined in her manners as a consequence of national and social environment. Yet, even here, Shelley is unable to escape the racial discourses of her era; the question of servitude and violence can only be advanced when it is read through a white female body, not through a black body. The text seems aware of this contradiction and, more importantly, of how the

---

20 Emily Brontë, *Wuthering Heights*, edited by Currer Bell (New York: Barnes and Noble Books, 1993), p. 57.
21 Brontë, *Wuthering Heights*, p. 57.
22 Von Sneidern, '*Wuthering Heights* and the Liverpool slave trade', p. 177.
23 Notably, the question of Justine's social standing is further emphasised when juxtaposed with Elizabeth in the 1831 version of the text; in that later edition, Elizabeth is also adopted from impoverished parents.
24 Shelley, *Frankenstein*, p. 92.

racialised discourses of a nation impede complete access to the discussion. While the social position and nature of a servant differs depending on the country and its treatment of social inferiors, the Creature, as a person of colour, is hated and despised across borders and so 'every country must be equally horrible'.[25]

The insurrectionary slave as monster appears in texts like *Zofloya*, *Frankenstein*, 'Benito Cereno', and *The Narrative of Arthur Gordon Pym*, while counterarguments positing the slave as (hu)man appear in novels such as *Wuthering Heights* and *Frankenstein*;[26] yet both sides stand in terrible awe of the enslaved. The horror of these depictions lies in the possibility that the slave, even when depicted as inhuman and thus inferior, may nonetheless be more than man, as is the case in many ways in *Frankenstein* and *Zofloya*. Though both the Creature and the Moor are monsters – one proving a Golem of sorts,[27] the other being the Devil – they are also more powerful than average men. As the Creature reminds Victor, his sheer physicality

---

25 Shelley, *Frankenstein*, p. 163.
26 Shelley particularly adopts much of the humanising, Abolitionist rhetoric about slavery, for the Creature explicitly defines his oppression and marginalisation as contingent upon his appearance in his conversation with the blind patriarch of the De Lacey family from whom he seeks assistance. Victor's response to his creation further affirms the Abolitionist rhetoric; the moment in which the novel's violence becomes inevitable occurs as a consequence of Victor's visual prejudice: 'His words had a strange effect upon me. I compassionated him and sometimes felt a wish to console him, *but when I looked upon him*, when I saw the filthy mass that moved and talked, my heart sickened and *my feelings were altered to those of horror and hatred*', Shelley, *Frankenstein*, p. 171; emphasis added.
27 A number of scholars have identified Frankenstein's Creature as a kind of Golem. For instance, Stephen Bertman argues that Mary Shelley likely discovered the Golem through its appearance in nineteenth-century German literature as well as through Percy Shelley's poetry on the 'Wandering Jew'. Likewise, Ruth Anolik notes that stories such as the 'Golem of Prague' may have influenced Mary Shelley. Explaining that Golem criticism persistently associates Golem folktales with Shelley's novel, Anolik posits that the Golem legends and Shelley's novel centre around similar Gothic tropes, such as 'preoccupation with possession of the body and of the narrative, anxieties of female authority, [and] the presence of supernatural powers resulting in transgressive and destructive creations'. Perhaps most strikingly, Anolik observes that, as in *Frankenstein*, 'in some versions of the golem story, the golem destroys his creator'. Thus scholars such as Jane Davidson term Frankenstein's Creature 'a "golem" of considerable notoriety'. For more, see Stephen Bertman, 'The role of the golem in the making of *Frankenstein*', *Keats-Shelley Review* 29:1 (2015): 42–50; Ruth Bienstock Anolik, 'Reviving the golem: cultural negotiations in Ozick's *The Puttermesser Papers* and Piercy's *He, She and It*', *Studies in American Jewish Literature* 19 (2000): 37–48 (p. 40); and, Jane P. Davidson, 'Golem–Frankenstein–golem of your own', *The Journal of the Fantastic in the Arts* 7:2/3 (1995): 228–43 (p. 228). Also see Ruth Bienstock Anolik, 'Appropriating the golem, possessing the dybbuk: female retellings of Jewish tales', *Modern Language Studies* 312 (2001): 39–55 (p. 43); and, Byron L. Sherwin, 'Golems in the biotech century', *Zygon: Journal of Religion and Science* 42:1 (2007): 133–43.

demands respect: 'thou hast made me more powerful than thyself; my height is superior to thine, my joints more supple'.[28] Such comments recall the physical realities of the black body, made physically powerful through excessive labour, and of slavery itself, which sees the masters always outnumbered and thus outmanned by their slaves.

In these novels, enslavement and racial superiority become a privilege that is granted at the behest of the seeming servant. This dynamic disrupts easy assumptions about the seat of power, for while Zofloya does Victoria's bidding, he is nonetheless rhetorically right to declare 'am I not thy equal?—Ay, thy superior!—proud girl, to suppose that the Moor, Zofloya, is a slave in mind'.[29] Although Frankenstein's Creature offers an attitude of submission, claiming that 'I am thy creature, and I will be even mild and docile to my natural lord and king if thou wilt also perform thy part, the which thou owest me',[30] his offer is contingent upon Victor's compliance. Terror arises not just from the question of the fiction of race (and racial superiority) but from the reality that the slave may become the master of his supposed 'natural lord'.

Slave insurrection presented the very real possibility of the master losing power to his slaves. This was the lesson of the revolution in Saint Domingue, where Europeans were toppled from their positions of power, brutally exiled from their former lands and doomed to watch from afar while the location underwent a profound regime change as Saint Domingue transformed into Haiti. Thus rebel leader Babo in 'Benito Cereno' daily threatens Cereno that failure to obey Babo's command will result in 'follow[ing] your leader' to his death.[31] The threat functions as a signifier of regime-change and Cereno's racial superiority is doubly challenged, for the utterance constructs Cereno, as ship captain, as nonetheless the servant of a now-dead leader. Furthermore, as a result of the insurrection, black Babo now assumes the role of leader and superior to the white aristocrat Cereno. Similarly, Zofloya's status as a royal slave disrupts normative power dynamics from his first appearance, while 'Henriquez treats him as "a friend" and "an equal", rather than "an inferior"', with disastrous consequences.[32] While Zofloya's status as a slave of royal origins mediates his access to equality and power, his

---

28 Shelley, *Frankenstein*.
29 Charlotte Dacre, *Zofloya, or The Moor*, edited by Adriana Craciun (Peterborough, Ont.: Broadview Press, 1997), p. 234.
30 Shelley, *Frankenstein*, p. 126.
31 Herman Melville, 'Benito Cereno', in *Billy Budd and Other Tales* (New York: New American Library, 1961), pp. 141–223 (p. 212).
32 Schotland, 'The slave's revenge', p. 124.

origins provide little comfort to nineteenth-century white readers and slave owners. Indeed, the nature of the slave trade was such that an owner could never be certain if royalty was among their stock.

In *Wuthering Heights* Nelly muses about the regal possibilities of Heathcliff's parentage, and Heathcliff responds by claiming the power to resist his abuser. In an early encounter with Hindley, Heathcliff stands against him, threatening to betray his abuse to Mr Earnshaw and concluding that 'I'll tell how you boasted that you would turn me out of doors as soon as he died, and see whether he will not turn you out directly.'[33] Although Heathcliff does not explicitly invoke the question of his heritage, he nonetheless claims control over Hindley in his ability to exile him through his access to Mr Earnshaw. As an adult, Heathcliff completes his usurpation of Hindley's power, becoming master of the property and reducing Hindley to a dependent pauper. More importantly, he plans to enslave the Earnshaw and Linton families in a reversal of established power dynamics, declaring 'I want the triumph of seeing my descendant fairly lord of their estates; my child hiring their children to till their fathers' lands for wages.'[34] Perhaps more distressing, however, are the ways in which Heathcliff reveals himself to be a superior master. Where Hindley proves a slovenly leader of the household, the home falling into disrepair under his rule, the villagers affirm that Heathcliff is a methodical, though cruel, master; under his ownership 'the house ... regained its ancient aspect of comfort under female management, and the scenes of riot common in Hindley's time were not now enacted within its walls'.[35] Such insurrectionary moments are horrifying in the texts most clearly because of the violence that they bring and the usurpation of power that they reveal. But implicit in the issue of usurpation lies another, more distressing problem: the erasure of racial difference and consequent dissolution of white identity. As the texts reveal, black insurrection dismantles the very concepts upon which racial superiority and whiteness themselves depend.

Who Is Free, Who Is 'Me'?: The Nightmare of Sameness

Throughout nineteenth-century Gothic and sociopolitical texts alike, the black subject, as Other, existed in relation to white subjects as part of

---

33 Brontë, *Wuthering Heights*, p. 33.   34 Brontë, *Wuthering Heights*, p. 179.
35 Brontë, *Wuthering Heights*, p. 170.

what Abdul JanMohamed terms 'the manichean allegory', a framework 'consist[ing] of interchangeable oppositions between white/black, good/evil, superiority/inferiority, civilization/savagery, intelligence/emotion, rationality/sensuality, self/Other, subject/object'.[36] In deploying this allegory, colonial authors accessed 'the benefits proffered by the ideological machinery that generates the stereotypes', namely 'metonymic displacement and metaphoric condensation', ultimately producing destructive commodifying stereotypes that helped them 'maintain a sense of moral differences … [and] transform social and historical dissimilarities into universal, metaphysical differences, forcing the Other to remain forever the "negative reflection, the shadow of the British self-image"'.[37] Thus the black Other was consistently portrayed as 'the dustbin or antithesis of the European Self. Pejorative terms—cannibalism, human sacrifice, superstition, irrationality etc.—accreted to it, while positive terms—civilisation, rationality, truth, religion etc.—remained the explicit or implicit preserve of the European'.[38]

Such allegories are rampant throughout the nineteenth-century Gothic. Encountering Linton when they are children, Heathcliff's height, powerful shoulders and dirty visage only highlight Edgar Linton's sweet, doll-like image – though Heathcliff is a year younger than Linton – so that Catherine inevitably marked their contrast, which 'resembled what you see in exchanging a bleak, hilly, coal country for a beautiful fertile valley'.[39] Harriet Brandt in *The Blood of the Vampire* doubly serves as a negative reflection, her excessive (sexualised) affection and consuming energies serving as a marker for proper English womanhood.[40] Like Heathcliff, her appearance helps to define the white female face, only this time in destructively sexual terms. Ralph Cullen, unabashedly attracted to Harriet despite his engagement to Elinor, exclaims 'Ah! a drop of Creole blood in her then, I daresay! You never see such eyes in an English face.'[41] Such descriptions appear in sharp contrast to earlier descriptions of Elinor, who has

> an exceptionally cold face, and it matched her disposition. She had attractive features;—a delicate nose, carved as if in ivory—brown eyes, a fair rose-tinted complexion, and a small mouth with thin, firmly closed lips. Her hair was bronze-coloured, and it was always dressed to perfection. She had a

---

36 Lori Pollock, '(An)Other politics of reading *Jane Eyre*', *The Journal of Narrative Technique* 26:3 (1996): 249–73 (p. 250).
37 Pollock, '(An)Other Politics of Reading *Jane Eyre*', p. 250.
38 Khair, 'Summing Up', pp. 171–2.   39 Brontë, *Wuthering Heights*, pp. 47, 59.
40 Notably, the excessively cold and distant British woman Elinor Leyton serves as the opposite extreme on the spectrum.
41 Florence Marryat, *The Blood of the Vampire* (Leipzig: Bernhard Tauchnitz, 1897), p. 83.

good figure too, with small hands and feet—and she was robed in excellent taste. She was pre-eminently a woman for a man to be proud of as the mistress of his house, and the head of his table.[42]

Although the novel is critical of Elinor's excessive concern with, and exercise of, propriety, her excesses nonetheless fit within the concept of Englishness. In contrast, the novel not only hypersexualises Harriet's excesses but, more importantly, marks them as both dangerously consuming and as standing in stark contrast to proper social exchanges. Pontificating upon Harriet's nature allows Doctor Philips better to define the typical exchanges of energy that occur among members of civil society:

> There are some born into this world who nourish those with whom they are associated; they give out their magnetic power, and their families, their husbands or wives, children and friends, feel the better for it. There are those, on the other hand, who draw from their neighbours, sometimes making large demands upon their vitality—sapping their physical strength, and feeding upon them, as it were, until they are perfectly exhausted and unable to resist disease.[43]

Figures such as Harriet and Heathcliff, then, serve not just as markers of (negative) visual and cultural difference, but as signifiers of difference around the very essence of social relationships.

The very concept of the 'Other' insisted upon the 'ineradicability of difference', and thus a relationship between 'the Self and the Other [that] cannot be reduced to sameness'.[44] Consequently, Zofloya's observation that Victoria's 'co-operation with me can alone render me powerful'[45] terrifies because of its implications of the shared traits between him and Victoria. After all, there must be a similarity between the black slave and the white mistress in order for them to engage in communion. This, precisely, is the terror beneath slave insurrection, for it reveals the lie of the binary logic that constructs blackness as irreparably different from (and inferior to) whiteness. In the face of insurrection, the desires, ideals and violent struggles of the racial Other mirror the desires, ideals and violence of the Self.

Zofloya's comments also reveal the ways in which Otherness remains intact even in the midst of supposedly humanitarian causes, for such causes maintained 'the great white illusion of imperial necessity and generosity, and the refutation of lack that underscored the unidirectional and utterly false

---

42 Marryat, *The Blood of the Vampire*, p. 39. 43 Marryat, *The Blood of the Vampire*, p. 273.
44 Khair, 'Summing Up', p. 158. 45 Dacre, *Zofloya*, p. 168.

logic of imperialism: we are doing *them* a service'.[46] Such reflection is significant in the face of nineteenth-century Abolition, which saw slavery as a great evil, but not necessarily because of the injustice that it dealt to a population that was deemed to be similar to free white subjects. Britain and the United States shared the idea that abolition should be gradually accomplished through the goodwill of a generous white population. In such mindsets, the black subject functioned as a kind of ghost – an intangible influence that haunts through its difference – rather than a double to whiteness for, as Tabish Khair explains 'what is more terrifying, being confronted with the Other—in this case a "ghost"—or the realisation that the Other is related to your Self as a double.[47] Indeed, for Khair, the Gothic genre's preoccupation with shadows and doubles alludes to this exact anxiety – is the double a spectre or is it the Self? Thus horror arises when slaves gain their freedom through their own means, for it signals a violent disruption of the racial boundaries as black will and behaviour prove similar to that of whites. For instance, Zofloya's threat comes not from his savageness but his civility. Endowed with 'superior qualities', Zofloya proves an 'elegant person' who 'could dance with inimitable grace' and whose musical skills enchant listeners.[48] In manners, he is thus on a par with his white masters and his previous and current master 'considered him rather as a friend than an inferior'.[49] Such equality of status proves disastrous in the novel as it grants Zolfoya access to, and influence in, elite white society, culminating in the death of his innocent owner.

Centred on white subjects, Gothic texts invariably encounter this anxiety from the position of the white body that performs in ways that are aligned with blackness. Thus a supreme moment of revulsion in Poe's *Pym* circles around a scene of cannibalism. Though necessary for their survival, the fact of white cannibalism requires punishment, especially as it occurs in the presence of a mixed-race character. Consequently, the white sailor who first verbalises the idea is the one who draws the short straw and is eaten, and another suffers a grotesque death in which his body changes colour and literally falls apart. Such moments of white cannibalism may be read as expressions of the anxiety haunting enlightened but slave-holding republics: their viability and profit were only made possible 'by grim or "Gothic" practices of plantation and sexual slavery, genocide, forced emigration, and all kinds of

---

46 Melissa Free, '"Dirty linen": legacies of empire in Wilkie Collins's *The Moonstone*', *Texas Studies in Literature and Language* 48:4 (2006): 340–71 (p. 340).
47 Khair, 'Summing Up', p. 159.   48 Dacre, *Zofloya*, p. 148.   49 Dacre, *Zofloya*, p. 150.

brutal punishment'.[50] As often as accounts of the Haitian Revolution decried the extreme violence committed by the black rebels, there remained excessive and horrific violence on both sides. As such, the figures on the stern-piece of Melville's 'Benito Cereno' – a masked figure 'holding his foot on the prostrate neck of a writhing figure, likewise masked'[51] – poses a significant question to white supremacy: given the terrifying violence of slavery and slave insurrection, who has his foot on whose neck? Which figure in the exchange is the brute, if either (or both) can be termed 'civilised'?

The question proves particularly recurrent throughout *Frankenstein*, in which Victor repeatedly proves as monstrous as his creation, if not more so. Where the Creature kills dispassionately, Victor suffers animal-like fury:

> I gnashed my teeth, my eyes became inflamed, and I ardently wished to extinguish that life which I had so thoughtlessly bestowed. When I reflected on his crimes and malice, my hatred and revenge burst all bounds of moderation ... I wished to see him again, that I might wreak the utmost extent of anger on his head.[52]

Victor attempts to rationalise such violence as a response to the Creature's crimes, yet the Creature also rationalises his own violence, rhetorically enquiring 'Shall I not then hate them who abhor me?'[53] The Creature's violence is merely a response to the violence that all of society offers him as a consequence of his physical difference, and Victor perpetuates that assault. Indeed, it is Victor's vehemence that extends the Creature's attacks on him. The Creature only resumes his murderous assaults, ripping Victor's life to shreds, after Victor literally rips the Creature's would-be wife and sole companion apart.

Furthermore, whereas the Creature provides an explanation for his violence, disdain for and violence towards the Other seems inherent within whiteness, as evidenced in the Creature's encounter with Victor's young brother William. Espying William, the Creature assumes 'that this little creature was unprejudiced, and had lived too short a time to have imbibed a horror of deformity. If, therefore, I could seize him, and educate him as my companion and friend, I should not be so desolate in this peopled earth.'[54] Yet even the child is already corrupted by prejudice: '"Let me go," he cried; "monster! Ugly wretch!" ... The child still struggled and loaded me with

50 Doyle, 'At World's Edge', p. 516. 51 Melville, 'Benito Cereno', p. 144.
52 Shelley, *Frankenstein*, p. 119. 53 Shelley, *Frankenstein*, p. 127.
54 Shelley, *Frankenstein*, pp. 166–7.

epithets which carried despair to my heart.'[55] William's violently prejudiced and hateful reaction upon first encountering the Creature further reflects upon Victor's immediate rejection of the being that he created. As murderous as the Creature may be, so too are his supposed superiors. What's more, the viciousness proves inherent in his superiors, unlike the Creature who mourns the loss of himself in his pursuit of revenge:

> Once I falsely hoped to meet with beings who, pardoning my outward form, would love me for the excellent qualities which I was capable of unfolding. I was nourished with high thoughts of honour and devotion. But now crime has degraded me beneath the meanest animal ... When I run over the frightful catalogue of my sins, I cannot believe that I am the same creature whose thoughts were once filled with sublime and transcendent visions of the beauty and the majesty of goodness.[56]

Victor, in contrast, asks Captain Walton to finish his mission and destroy the Creature. Indeed, only the crew's determination to return to England, a direction away from the Creature's path, quiets Victor's dying pleas.

The consequence of such encounters is the dissolution of whiteness and white identity. Having been ultimately outwitted by the Creature, Victor dies. Similarly, the Grange cannot resume its traditions of white patriarchy so long as Heathcliff lives; rather, its white inhabitants remain in a state of sunken degeneracy under his presence. Only after his death can the surviving heirs of the Lintons and the Earnshaws marry, 'restor[ing] an illusion of happiness and proper English complacence'.[57] Pym's tale – after narrating his cannibalism, his adventures and companionship with Augustus, and his confrontation with the intelligent, insurrectionary black Tsalal natives – ends suddenly in his death, which occurs as he describes rushing into a white abyss from whence a gigantic white figure arises. Having repeatedly narrated encounters that reveal the lie of racial difference, the narrative crumbles at the point of encountering whiteness. Incapable of proceeding past the monstrous truth, the text instead awkwardly concludes with an editorial note explaining Pym's sudden death in the midst of relaying this portion of the tale. Melville is even starker in his detailing of such encounters. Having suffered enslavement at the hands of Babo and his black rebels, Cereno never recovers. Instead, he convalesces in a home, haunted by the events until his premature death. When Delano declares 'you are saved: what has cast such a shadow upon you', Cereno only utters in horror, 'the

---

55 Shelley, *Frankenstein*, p. 167.   56 Shelley, *Frankenstein*, p. 174.
57 Paravisini-Gebert, 'Colonial and Postcolonial Gothic', p. 249.

Negro'.[58] The lesson, here, is that such encounters with insurrectionary blackness, even when unsuccessful, can only mean the death of white identity.

Spectres of Slavery: The Creole Case

By the end of the nineteenth century, the African slave trade and slavery among the colonial powers had been abolished. Deemed part of a brutal past, 'the fiendish, monstrous, inhuman practice was … suppressed, and those with sunny dispositions imagined that it was dead and buried'.[59] Yet the Gothic, participating in 'the volume of discourses related to slavery and the Anglo-Saxon myth of racial superiority', testified to the 'unquiet slumber' of slavery and its racial ideologies.[60] The representation of the Creole in texts of the era particularly illustrates this haunting. As (white) people who originated in the colonies, Creoles came to signify all that was degenerate and horrific about slavery and slave ownership.

Even before slavery's end, Creoles occupied a peculiar racialised space in colonial nations. Originally a term used to classify the descendants of Europeans who settled in the colonies, Creoles were defined as 'sunk in sloth … satisfied with the revenues of their personal estates'.[61] They were culturally miscegenated as a result of environments in which they were greatly outnumbered by enslaved blacks. Thus the habit of social critics such as Bryan Edwards to explain Creole degeneracy as a result of 'the influence of climate', may be read as a signifier of black influence, given that 'The climate, in Edwards's view, encourages early intellectual precociousness, but "the want of proper objects for exercising the faculties" and "the contagion and enervating effects of youthful excesses" (a "propensity" for "licentiousness" "undoubtedly" encouraged by the climate) mitigates against "mental improvement"'.[62] Such ideologies manifest themselves in Gothic texts in which Creoles reveal extravagant tastes, volatile temperaments, bestial sexual appetites and atrocious fits of passion. Creolised women such as Harriet Brandt in *The Blood of the Vampire* prove sexually licentious and vengeful, while the men are weak but brutal, and both genders are

---

58 Melville, 'Benito Cereno', p. 222.
59 Von Sneidern, '*Wuthering Heights* and the Liverpool slave trade', p. 187.
60 Von Sneidern, '*Wuthering Heights* and the Liverpool slave trade', p. 187.
61 Quoted in Thomas Tracy, '"Reader, I buried him": apocalypse and empire in *Jane Eyre*', *Critical Survey* 16:2 (2004): 59–77 (p. 2).
62 Tracy, 'Reader, I buried him', p. 3.

inhuman in their despotic exercise of power. Like enslaved blacks, Creole savagery proves so deeply ingrained that, as Harriet's story reveals, they are forever beyond the reach of civilisation. They may be reintroduced to proper society, but their brutal appetites can never be tamed.

As the white Other, Creoles functioned as abject bodies onto which 'proper' white Westerners could project all the evils of slaveholding culture. Novels such as Charlotte Brontë's *Jane Eyre* (1847) 'link[ed] the degenerate moral and intellectual character of the white Creole with the cruelties of the slave-labour system in Jamaica, and with historical ... slave rebellions figured through metaphor and allusion'.[63] Marryat's *The Blood of the Vampire* particularly illustrates this troping in its depiction of Harriet's parents. Explaining Harriet's vampiric origins, Doctor Phillips recalls

> when this girl was a child of six years old, running half naked about her father's plantation, uncared for by either parent, and associating solely with the negro servants. Brandt was a brute—the perpetrator of such atrocities in vivisection and other scientific experiments, that he was finally slaughtered on his own plantation by his servants, and everyone said it served him right. The mother was the most awful woman I have ever seen ... She was the daughter of a certain Judge Carey of Barbados by one of his slave girls, and Brandt took her as his mistress before she was fourteen. At thirty, when I saw her she was a revolting spectacle. Gluttonous and obese—her large eyes rolling and her sensual lips protruding as if she were always licking them in anticipation of her prey. She was said to be 'Obeah' too by the natives and they ascribed all the deaths and diseases that took place on the plantation, to her malign influence. Consequently, when they got her in their clutches, I have heard that they did not spare her, but killed her in the most torturing fashion they could devise ... [The father] had been known to decoy diseased and old natives into his laboratory, after which they were never seen again, and it was the digging up of human bones on the plantation, which finally roused the negroes to such a pitch of indignation that they rose en masse, and after murdering both Brandt and his abominable mistress, they set fire to the house and burned it to the ground.[64]

The passage is worth quoting at length for its representation of the Othering that Creoles incur. The opening sentence marks the Creole as being beyond hope, for their childhood is spent in savagery, surrounded and cared for by blacks. While the mother's degeneracy and grotesqueness also participates in discourses surrounding the mixed-race body, the father's absolute corruption is unaccounted for within the text; rather, his subhuman, criminal behaviour

---

63 Tracy, 'Reader, I buried him', p. 1.   64 Marryat, *The Blood of the Vampire*, p. 129–30.

reflects popular notions about Creoles in general. Likewise, the passage echoes notions of the Creole body as culturally, and later racially, miscegenated, given that the mother practices Obeah. But the passage's indictment of slavery as a corrupter of whiteness is equally important. As much as the mother's origins can be understood within the problematic sexual culture of slave-owning society, the text's observation that she was not even fourteen when Brandt took her for a mistress implicitly critiques such sexual practices as part of a heinous culture.

Significant, too, is the explanation that the passage offers for slave insurrection. The Creoles are cannibalistic figures who, when juxtaposed with the violence of the rebelling slaves, prove far more ghastly. Although the passage marks the violence of the insurrection as horrific, the slaves' violence is outweighed by the terrible deeds of the Creole slave owners. The text consequently reproduces the kinds of discourses that circulated around slave rebellion in an attempt to re-contain it within racial ideologies. In such cases, slave insurrectionists are reduced to the position of a brutalised dog that finally snaps the hand of its master. In describing the events of the Haitian Revolution, British scholars tended to indict the French Creole's brutal mistreatment of their slaves as the reason that blacks rebelled, even as the Creole's laxness was blamed for the insurrection's success. Marryat almost perfectly reproduces these notions for, although the natively British Brandts are slave owners in Jamaica, the text associates Harriet and her family with French Creoles. Harriet, skilled in French, speaks English with an accent, explaining that 'We always spoke French in the Convent, and it is in general use in the Island. But I thought—I hoped—that I spoke English like an English woman! I am an Englishwoman, you know.'[65] As a Creole, Harriet may be a British subject but she is not English, and her accent suggests that she is more akin to a French Creole than a Briton.

So influential is the discourse around Creoles that they haunt other texts that include no actual Creole characters. For instance, Hindley, Catherine and even Isabella in *Wuthering Heights* degenerate into a kind of creolised profligacy in Heathcliff's presence. Both Hindley and Catherine prove abusive to Heathcliff, their assaults upon him growing more intense the longer he is in their home. Likewise, Isabella deteriorates in the plantation-like isolation of the Heights[66] until she shows signs of the kinds of sexual

---

65 Marryat, *The Blood of the Vampire*, p. 23.
66 Von Sneidern observes that 'The Grange, like Mother England, is an estate isolated from a planter economy by both breeding and seeming cultural independence. At one point Isabella writes that the distance between the Heights and the Grange is

misbehaviour that is typically attributed to Creole (and black) women. Living, like the Creoles, 'in such close, unremitting and, finally, sexual proximity to the racial other' Isabella is 'Stripped of the prerogatives of her race, class and gender ... and the racialist and misogynistic commentary about the lasciviousness of black women so rampant in Edward Long's *History of Jamaica* are cathected onto her'.[67] Exiled to the Heights, Isabella degenerates from True Womanhood into 'a thorough little slattern'.[68] Isabella's arc, in particular, reveals the degeneration that Britons suffer when exposed to the contaminating 'climate' of the slaveholding Caribbean for too long.

By the end of the nineteenth century, the Creole's cultural miscegenation becomes actual racial miscegenation. While this may be taken as a comment upon the problem of proximity, it is also a critique of the sexual (mis)behaviour attributed to Creole populations from the eighteenth century onwards. Indeed, as the relationship between young Heathcliff and Catherine reveals, the regional isolation, power dynamics and interracial nature of the slaveholding Caribbean produced a dynamic in which 'The bond between mistress and bondsman transcends the laws of nature, and transgresses the bonds of matrimony'.[69] Accordingly, the Caribbean 'climate' resulted in disastrous sexual liaisons and a population increasingly identified as mixed-race. Moreover, Gothic depictions of mixed-race Creoles repeated dominant ideas about miscegenation; the taint of blackness meant that characters were not just morally degenerate, but physically and psychologically degraded too. Thus Heathcliff's son Linton, miscegenated though not literally Creole, is weak and effeminate yet vicious in his cravings to see others suffer.

As a mixed-race Creole, Marryat's Harriet is one the 'Gothic Unnaturals' that populate these later nineteenth-century texts, figures who, according to H. L. Malchow, 'stand in that contradictory space between "loyal subject and vengeful rebel," the tainted product of the undisciplined sexual passions of their white fathers and the "savage inheritance of their non-white mothers"'.[70] As a quadroon, she is nearly white, yet the shadow of blackness reveals itself in the excessiveness of her features, as Doctor Phillips notes: 'she shews it distinctly in

tantamount to "the Atlantic"', Von Sneidern, '*Wuthering Heights* and the Liverpool slave trade', p. 174.
67 Von Sneidern, '*Wuthering Heights* and the Liverpool slave trade', p. 182.
68 Brontë, *Wuthering Heights*, p. 126.
69 Von Sneidern, '*Wuthering Heights* and the Liverpool slave trade', p. 179.
70 Paravisini-Gebert, 'Colonial and Postcolonial Gothic', pp. 231–2.

her long-shaped eyes with their blue whites and her wide mouth and blood-red lips! Also in her supple figure and apparently boneless hands and feet ... I can tell you by the way she eats her food, and the way in which she uses her eyes, that she has inherited her half-caste mother's greedy and sensual disposition.'[71] Importantly, these features are a physical marker of her excessive appetites and thus Phillips warns that 'in ten years' time she will in all probability have no figure at all! She will run to fat'.[72] The text also replicates the pseudoscience informing these discourses as Doctor Phillips is typically the one to explain Harriet's nature, validating his claims on the premise that 'We medical men know the consequences of heredity.'[73]

Harriet's vampirism illustrates dominant notions of the threats that miscegenated people pose to society. Like Dracula, she feeds on English society, but her threat is even more insidious for Harriet never bears fangs. She clings to women in ways that are deemed peculiar, and behaves intimately with new acquaintances. Within hours of meeting Margaret Pullen, Harriet behaves as if they are dear friends, wrapping her arms around Margaret's waist and laying her head on her shoulder.[74] Such physical affection makes Margaret uncomfortable, and constructs Harriet as a queering sexual threat. While Harriet seduces men, threatening to steal Ralph from Elinor before turning her hunger upon Baronness Gobelli's son, she tends to feed on women. Margaret catches Harriet looking at her 'full of yearning and affection—almost of longing to approach her nearer, to hear her speak, to touch her hand'.[75] The look suggests queer desire; thus Margaret recalls 'hear[ing] of cases, in which young unsophisticated girls had taken unaccountable affections for members of their own sex'.[76] Phillips's contention that Harriet 'must be an epitome of lust'[77] further marks her as a queer threat, for his comment fails to specify a gender towards which such lust is oriented.

Ultimately, Harriet feeds on Europe itself, given that her looks greatly improve during her time in Brussels and England. After several weeks, her complexion develops a healthy blush, her eyes glow, her hair seems to have caught some of the sun's fire and her figure grows fuller, suggesting that she has been fattening herself on the energies surrounding her, growing more powerful the longer that she is in Europe. Harriet, it is clear, feeds on European culture itself, adopting its manners so that 'her manner was altogether more intelligent'.[78] As much as the Caribbean 'climate' produced

---

71 Marryat, *The Blood of the Vampire*, p. 130. 72 Marryat, *The Blood of the Vampire*, p. 130.
73 Marryat, *The Blood of the Vampire*, p. 118. 74 Marryat, *The Blood of the Vampire*, p. 28.
75 Marryat, *The Blood of the Vampire*, p. 38. 76 Marryat, *The Blood of the Vampire*, p. 38.
77 Marryat, *The Blood of the Vampire*, p. 120. 78 Marryat, *The Blood of the Vampire*, p. 215.

degeneracy in the white subject in earlier discourses, the European climate falls prey to the mixed-race subject whose animal appetites seem unquenchable. As much as Harriet has grown fat on white energy, her 'dark eyes were still looking for their prey, and the restless lips were incessantly twitching and moving one over the other'.[79] More distressingly, Harriet also feeds on white futures; she is particularly fond of children, and coos incessantly over Margaret's infant daughter to such an extent that Olga correctly quips, 'I think she would like to eat them.'[80] In consuming infants, Harriet consumes the future English population around her, for she prefers white children, deeming black children smelly and untouchable.[81] The unintended consequence, of course, is that black children and the futures they represent, are safe from assault. Harriet's presence thus offers racial imbalance in the seat of empire itself.

Unlike Bram Stoker's Dracula, the imperceptible nature and unintentionality of Harriet's vampirism makes her impossible to defend against. Indeed, as Doctor Phillips notes, the only solution is absolute exile, for even true love cannot quell Harriet's appetite. Yet the solution also reveals the real anxiety latent in Harriet and others like her. As much as these figures seem to condense typical anxieties surrounding racial mixing, they also conceal a concern about the haunting of history. Creatures such as Harriet Brandt represent anxieties about the genetic, sexual and social repercussions of slavery as they would appear in later generations – the literal products of slavery's evil – as much as earlier figures like Babo and Frankenstein's Creature revealed a concern about the immediate repercussions of slavery. Similarly, *Wuthering Heights*, like *Jane Eyre*, sets its plot during the era of the slave trade, though both were written a decade after Britain abolished slavery throughout its empire. Thus Lori Pollock questions whether such texts 'reveal a sense of historical embarrassment surrounding slavery'.[82] We may, in fact, find a solution to this question in *Frankenstein*, particularly in Victor's frequent complaints concerning the position of 'miserable slavery' that he occupies in relation to his creation, whose colouring and marginalised status mark him as the figure more physically similar to the enslaved population.

Victor's complaints reveal the true horror that much Gothic literature of the nineteenth century grapples with, beyond even the issue of racial difference: the question of responsibility for the chaos and violence arising from

---

79 Marryat, *The Blood of the Vampire*, p. 215.   80 Marryat, *The Blood of the Vampire*, p. 97.
81 Marryat, *The Blood of the Vampire*, p. 23.
82 Pollock, '(An)Other Politics of Reading *Jane Eyre*', p. 256.

slavery and its inevitable insurrections. We may read Victor's anxiety about helping to birth a new race of devils through this lens, given that he predicts the end of 'man' as a consequence. Remembering that 'man' was still a racially qualified term at the time of Shelley's writing, we see that Victor's angst also articulates concern about the end of whiteness. Even Victor's claim of responsibility for the Creature's hateful colouring assumes significant meaning, given that it was through white social discourses that blackness, and its accompanying physical attributes, became hateful.[83] Yet he, and we, cannot forget Victor's role as creator of the Creature in his own pursuit of modernity, a pursuit that the novel marks as supreme ruler (and destroyer) of whiteness: 'I [Victor] was the slave, not the master, of an impulse which I detested yet could not disobey.'[84] Thus, like the wielders of the lash, the captains of the ships and the owners of the plantations who were victims to slave insurrections, Victor may be a victim of his Creature, but he is ultimately 'not in deed, but in effect ... the true murderer'.[85] This, then, is the ultimate horror of nineteenth-century Gothic fiction. Slave insurrections may be bloody, violating and seemingly incomprehensible, but their monstrous birth originates in white (mis)deeds. Whiteness is thus the source of its own dissolution, victim and villain to itself.

83 Shelley, *Frankenstein*, p. 85.   84 Shelley, *Frankenstein*, p. 142.
85 Shelley, *Frankenstein*, p. 120.

2.19

Genealogies of Monstrosity: Darwin, the Biology of Crime and Nineteenth-Century British Gothic Literature

CORINNA WAGNER

On 1 June 1865, the geologist, botanist and manufacturer of encaustic tiles, George Maw, wrote excitedly to Charles Darwin about 'a very remarkable case of animal monstrosity' that had been 'preserved in spirits'.[1] A young pig with a trunk-like snout and 'ears & mouth shaped exactly like an elephant's' had been born in a Shropshire town. Maw elaborated:

> The Sow was put to the Boar & one or two days afterwards ... Some Elephants belonging to Edmund's menagerie were quartered at the Star Hotel one of these had a peculiar antipathy to pigs & ... endeavoured to reach the sow with its trunk ... the pig appeared quite terror striken [sic] & to this is attributed the singular malformations in its young—

Darwin's response was lukewarm, for he doubted the rarity of the 'proboscis-like prolongation of the snout' and disavowed 'the effects of the imagination of the mother on the offspring'. Yet, the 250 and more times that the word *monstrous*, *monstrosity*, or *monster* appear in his correspondence would seem to indicate a deep interest in this subject.

In this chapter, I focus on how Darwin's ideas about structural and functional anomalies in plants, animals and humans inspired Gothic writers of the late nineteenth century to imagine new types of biological monsters.[2] These are a different breed of monster from those that Jeffrey

---

[1] Darwin Correspondence Project, 'Letter no. 4847' < www.darwinproject.ac.uk/DCP-LETT-4847> (last accessed 13 August 2019).

[2] As we know, Darwin's cultural influence has been immense; so too is the body of scholarship on his influence. Scholars invariably note that evolutionary theories pre-existed Darwin's work, and that terms like 'Darwinian' and 'Darwinism' indicate how his biological theories (and misinterpretations thereof) were used to justify a range of social, political and economic ideologies. Some of the key studies upon which this chapter builds are: Gillian Beer, *Darwin's Plots: Evolutionary Narrative in Darwin, George Eliot and Nineteenth-Century Fiction* (Cambridge: Cambridge University Press, 2009);

Jerome Cohen described in his influential 'Monster Culture: Seven Theses'.³ While Cohen's monsters are, above all, cultural constructs that embody social anxieties, represent a breakdown of order, and manifest fears of (and desires for) cultural, social, racial and sexual 'Others', the monsters in this chapter are distinctly biological embodiments. They claim closer kinship with those that Kelly Hurley describes as manifestations of 'an anxiety generated by scientific discourses, biological and sociomedical'.⁴ Even more specifically, I concentrate on monsters with a certain parentage: the union of Darwinian materialism and criminal anthropology. They are, for example, experimental surgeons schooled in Darwinian evolutionary biology who create hideous offspring; sadistic criminals who torture living things for pleasure; and murderous plants with animal anatomies who consume their masters. All are monstrous manifestations of the materialist views at the heart of evolutionary biology, and of the determinist implications for the new sciences it informed, particularly criminal anthropology.

I will also demonstrate the ways in which these monsters, as products of evolutionary biology, materialism and Darwinist criminal anthropology, challenged some of the most cherished ideas that Victorians held about their *cultural* history and heritage. In particular, the ideals and values of the age of chivalry, the medieval past, had to be reconsidered in the light of what was now known about human descent and evolution, the aetiology of animal and human 'monstrosity', and the criminal compulsions that dwelt in the 'protoplasm' – the biological material – that was shared by humans, animals and plants. Gothic writers constructed biological monstrosities that deconstructed the same historical past that Victorian Gothic Revivalists like John Ruskin were celebrating for bequeathing the higher-order values that supposedly defined the human as exceptional.

George Levine, *Darwin and the Novelists: Patterns of Science in Victorian Fiction* (Cambridge, MA: Harvard University Press, 1989); George Levine, *Darwin the Writer* (Oxford: Oxford University Press, 2011); Peter Morton, *The Vital Science: Biology and the Literary Imagination 1860–1900* (London: Allen & Unwin, 1984); Robert M. Young, *Darwin's Metaphor: Nature's Place in Victorian Culture* (Cambridge: Cambridge University Press, 1985); David Amigoni, *Colonies, Cults and Evolution: Literature, Science and Culture in Nineteenth-Century Writing* (Cambridge: Cambridge University Press, 2007); and Jonathan Smith, *Charles Darwin and Victorian Visual Culture* (Cambridge: Cambridge University Press, 2009).

3 Jeffrey Jerome Cohen, 'Monster Culture (Seven Theses)', *Monster Theory: Reading Culture* (Minneapolis: University of Minnesota Press, 1996), pp. 3–25.

4 Kelly Hurley, *The Gothic Body: Sexuality, Materialism, and Degeneration at the Fin de Siècle* (Cambridge: Cambridge University Press, 1996), p. 5.

Anatomical Affinities

It would be hard to picture a more quintessentially Gothic scene than this: on a dark wintry night in nineteenth-century Paris, a man slumbering at his fire is awakened by a monstrously grotesque, limping demon. Yet botanist Pierre Boitard's prehistoric novel, *Paris Before Man* (1861), takes an unexpected turn. The goat-legged Devil on Two Sticks escorts his drowsy captive on a journey into deep time, to prehistoric Paris. They encounter, among other things, a 'real' vampire: *vampirus spectrum* is a rabbit-size bat that feeds by sucking the blood of sleeping humans and animals. The 'most horrible' creatures, however, are the 'fetid' orangutan-like humans, with their bristly-haired faces, protruding lips and muzzles 'full of garbage, blood, and small pieces of dry flesh'.[5]

Although Boitard died the year in which Darwin published his *On the Origin of Species* (1859), and despite the fact that the novel was published posthumously, *Paris Before Man* has been called 'the first Darwinian narrative'.[6] The engraver's image of Boitard's fossil man (Fig.19.1) is a product of early evolutionary or 'transformist' theories associated with Jean-Baptiste Lamarck, Alfred Russell Wallace and Étienne Geoffroy Saint Hilaire, which anticipates Darwin's work. Fossil man is a fictionalised materialisation of Geoffroy's principle of 'unity of composition' or 'the unity of plan', which showed the structural similarities between human and animal, and among species. Thus, for instance, the leg bones of lizards and humans may have adapted to different environmental stimuli, but they were homologous in form.[7] As Darwin acknowledged, Geoffroy's morphology – his study of the internal structures and external forms of living things – laid an important anatomical groundwork for his own realisation that human hands, porpoise paddles and bat wings were 'constructed on the same pattern'.[8]

In the illustration (Fig.19.1), fossil man's prehistoric weapon, which is described as resembling 'the tomahawk of the Canadian savages', also reflects the rise of biological, racial and criminological anthropology.[9] Anatomical

---

5 Pierre Boitard, *Paris Avant Les Hommes*, trans. by Stephen Trussel (Paris: Passard, 1861) <www.trussel.com/prehist/boitarde.htm> (last accessed 21 February 2019).
6 Marc Angenot, 'Science fiction in France before Verne', trans. by J. M. Gouanvic and D. Suvin, *Science Fiction Studies* 5:1 (March 1978): 58–66.
7 See Toby A. Appel, *The Cuvier-Geoffroy Debate: French Biology in the Decades Before Darwin* (Oxford: Oxford University Press, 1987) and Adrian Desmond, *The Politics of Evolution Morphology, Medicine, and Reform in Radical London* (Chicago: Chicago University Press, 1989).
8 Charles Darwin, *On the Origin of Species by Means of Natural Selection*, 2nd edition (London: John Murray, 1860), p. 434.
9 Boitard <www.trussel.com/prehist/boitarde.htm>.

Fig.19.1: Moreau, *L'homme fossile*, from Pierre Boitard, *Paris Before Man* (1861). Author's photograph.

proximity between prehistoric and modern beings, and between human and animal, suggested that biological change could be regressive or atavistic rather than progressive: if hairy faces, webbed feet and vestigial tails could reappear, so too could unseen traits like bloodlust or purposeless violence. The raised weapon is not only a gesture of humanity's violent origins but also a recognition that the 'characteristics of [fossil man's] race are still found', for 'individuals, even in France, are almost as hairy as monkeys', and 'some Ethiopian Negroes still offer you the same face'.[10] Prehistoric man wears an animal skin in the image, but it is jauntily knotted about his neck in the style of a modern-day Parisian flâneur.

Three Genealogies: Evolutionary, Criminal, Medieval

The sole illustration in Darwin's *On the Origin of Species* (1859), a theoretical 'Tree of Life', makes visible the relatedness of all species, and demonstrates 'descent with modification' – or 'transmutation' (Fig.19.2). It shows the long, long reach of heredity through a history of survival marked by extinction, adaptation and variation. Darwin's comment to geologist Charles Lyell in 1860 indicates why this genealogy opened up imaginative avenues for Gothic writers: '*Our* ancestor was an animal which breathed water, had a swim-bladder, a great swimming tail, an imperfect skull & undoubtedly was an hermaphrodite!' This was, 'a pleasant genealogy for mankind', he pronounced wryly.[11] Gothic writers, as we will see, mapped some distinctly *un*pleasant genealogies for modern humans.

Another well-known genealogy that claims origins, however loosely, in Darwin's work is the sociologist Richard Dugdale's 1877 chart of six generations of the 'Jukes' family of pauper criminals (Fig.19.3). This rather elaborate eugenic family tree is, in the words of one of Dugdale's contemporaries, 'a natural history of crime', and 'a complete physiological and moral record of … degeneracy'; more recently, Paul Lombardo has called it a 'genetic morality tale'.[12] Dugdale's study is one of many criminal anthropological studies that sought biological and sociological reasons for what seemed to be a distressing rise in a criminal class that imperilled civilisation. In 1870, the Scottish surgeon

---

10 Boitard <www.trussel.com/prehist/boitarde.htm>.
11 Darwin Correspondence Project, 'Letter no. 2647' <www.darwinproject.ac.uk/DCP-LETT-2647> (last accessed 30 January 2019).
12 Elisha Harris, 'Introduction', in Richard Dugdale (ed.), '*The Jukes*': *A Study in Crime, Pauperism, Disease, and Heredity*, 3rd edition (New York: G. P. Putnam's sons, 1877), pp. v–vi (p. vi); Paul Lombardo, 'Return of the Jukes: eugenic mythologies and internet evangelism', *Journal of Legal Medicine* 33:2 (2012): 207–33 (p. 213).

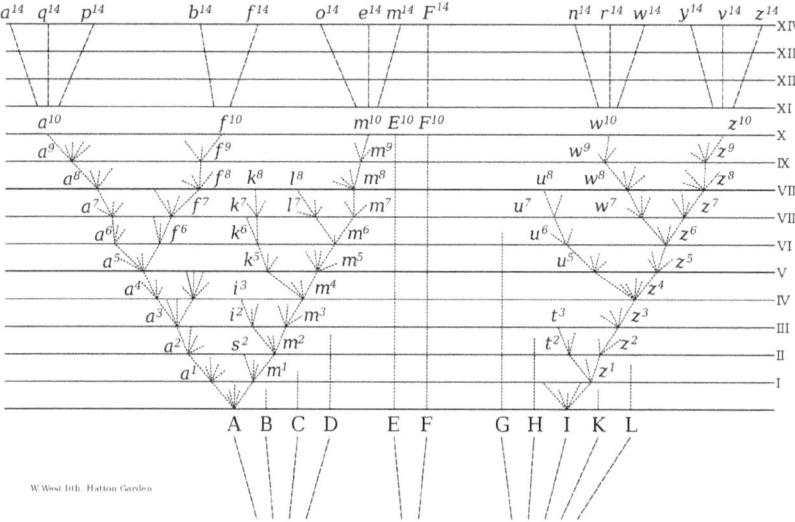

Fig.19.2: Charles Darwin, 'Tree of Life', from *On the Origin of Species* (1859). Author's photograph.

and early criminologist J. Bruce Thomson compared this class to the Old Testament wandering tribe of Ismaelites: this criminal caste, 'whose hand is against civilised men', was likewise 'opposed to all others'.[13] Dugdale's chart is a visual record of what Thomson identifies as a criminalistic decline 'from generation to generation by geometrical retrogression'.[14] A Darwinian tenor, however misguided, is unmistakable here and also in a large number of similar genealogies of hereditary decline produced in the last half of the nineteenth century.

There is yet another genealogy to bring in here, one which, like that of Darwin and Dugdale, addresses and reconfigures the past. John Ruskin, an acute critic of Darwinism and also one of the most influential proponents of Gothic Revival, expressed a growing antipathy towards anatomy, evolutionary theory and scientific materialism in his 1870s lectures and publications. As evidence of this, critics and historians have often referred to Ruskin's line condemning 'the filthy heraldries which record the relation of humanity to the ascidian [sea squirt] and

---

13 J. Bruce Thomson, 'The psychology of criminals', *The Journal of Mental Science* 16 (19 February 1870): pp. 321–50 (p. 328).
14 Thomson, 'Psychology', p. 97.

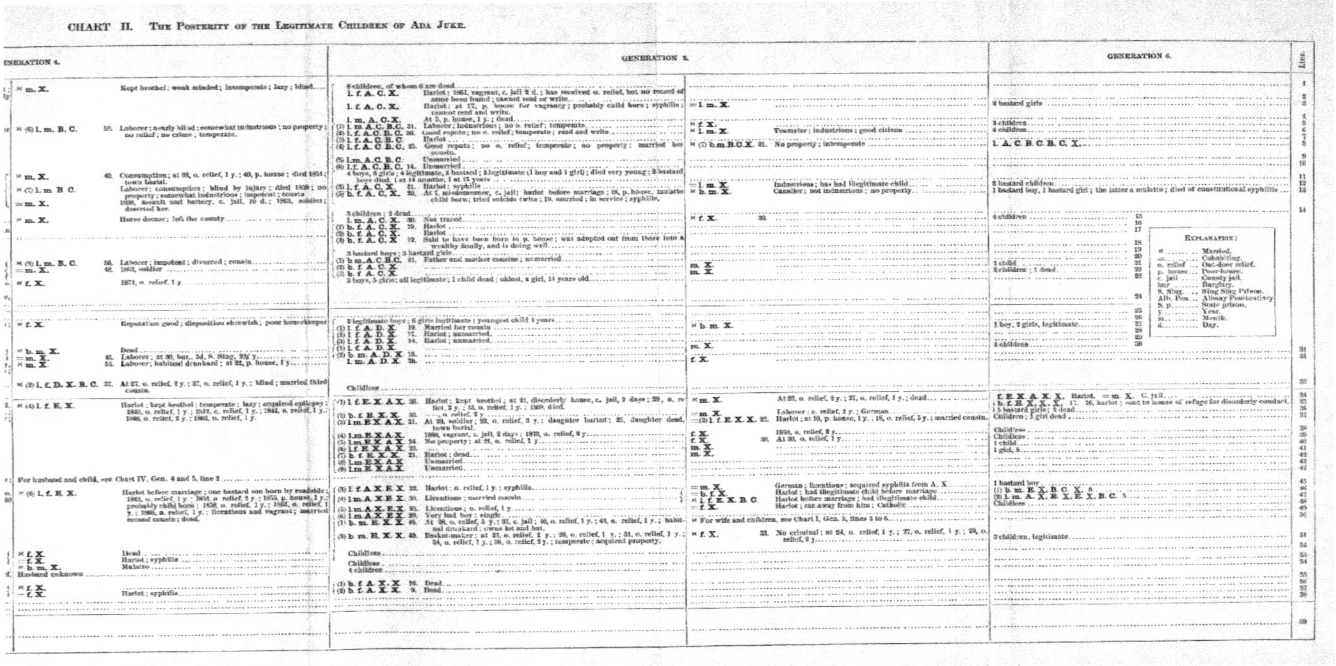
CHART II. THE POSTERITY OF THE LEGITIMATE CHILDREN OF ADA JUKE.

Generation 4.	Generation 5.	Generation 6.	Line.

EXPLANATION:

×	Married.
=	Cohabiting.
o. relief	Out-door relief.
p. house	Poor-house.
c. jail	County jail.
bur.	Burglary.
S. Sing.	Sing Sing Prison.
Alb. Pen.	Albany Penitentiary.
S. p.	State prison.
y.	Year.
m.	Month.
d.	Day.

Fig.19.3: Richard Louis Dugdale, showing the fifth to the six generations of the Juke Family, *The Jukes* (1877; 1910). Author's photograph.

the crocodile'.[15] I wish, however, to return this famous line to the slightly longer passage in *Love's Meinie* (1873) from which it is taken. Beginning with a lament 'that the whole scientific world was agog concerning the origin of species', Ruskin continues:

> While your men of science are thus ... disputing about the origin, in past ages, of what they cannot define in the present ones; and deciphering the filthy heraldries which record the relation of humanity to the ascidian and the crocodile, you have ceased utterly to distinguish between the two species of man ... of whom the one, [is] capable of loyalty and of love ... and the other, capable only of avarice, hatred, and shame.[16]

Ruskin draws an opposition here between a medieval cultural past and an evolutionary biological past: between the chivalrous, devotional and morally principled Middle Ages, with its proud armorial tradition of recording noble genealogies, and the scientific, materialist modern age that had reduced humans by including them in a family tree that included sea squirts.

The word 'meinie' in the essay's title – an Old English expression for the 'many' who serve, as courtiers or bridesmaids – invokes Geoffrey Chaucer's fourteenth-century translation of *The Romaunt of the Rose*, in which it appears. As such, this reference signals, as one biographer put it, that Ruskin's 'care was for the plumage, not for the anatomy'.[17] Ruskin pushes this opposition further: the values of an honourable people originate in a cultured, courtly history, while a materialist modernity composed of shameful degenerates originates, as evolutionary biologists have it, in the sea squirt and the crocodile.

Hereditary Tails in Gothic Tales

These three genealogies – evolutionary, criminological and medieval – feature in the work of Grant Allen, the evolutionist known for what fellow author H. G. Wells called his 'aggressive Darwinism'.[18] In Allen's 1892 story

---

15 This includes, for example, Gillian Beer, *Darwin's Plots*, p. 7; Rebecca Stott, 'Darwin's Barnacles: Mid-Century Natural History and the Marine Grotesque', in Roger Luckhurst and Josephine McDonagh (eds), *Transactions and Encounters: Science and Culture in the Nineteenth Century* (Manchester: Manchester University Press, 2002), pp. 151–81 (p. 174); John Hedley Brooke, 'Visions of the Past: Religious Belief and the Historical Sciences', in John Hedley Brooke (ed.), *Science and Religion: Some Historical Perspectives* (Cambridge: Cambridge University Press, 2014), pp. 307–73 (p. 307).
16 John Ruskin, *Love's Meinie: Three Lectures on Greek and English Birds* (New York: John Wiley, 1873), pp. 51–3.
17 Edward Tyas Cook, *The Life of John Ruskin*, 2 vols (New York: Haskell House, 1968), vol. 1, p. 239.
18 H. G. Wells, *Experiment in Autobiography* (New York: Macmillan, 1934), p. 461.

Fig.19.4: Illustration from 'Pallinghurst Barrow', *Illustrated London News* (1892). Author's photograph.

'Pallinghurst Barrow', a journalist named Rudolph Reeve is one of several cosmopolitan guests at a country manor house near the site of the ancient burial mound of the title. A man of science with a poetic soul, Reeve has romantic visions of an ancient history 'living and moving' beneath the barrow. On the night of St Michael's Eve, he attempts to gain access to the barrow by walking around it 'widershins', or against the path of the sun, according to legend. It works. Turning evolutionary time back 'ten thousand years', Reeve descends underground to stand 'face to face with a remote antiquity'.[19] Romantic visions are quickly dispelled when his forebears, with their prognathous faces and bloodthirsty expressions, attempt to murder him (Fig.19.4).

19 Grant Allen, 'Pallinghurst Barrow', *Illustrated London News*, 28 November 1892, p. 17.

Readers might reasonably identify a message of progress in Allen's tale, for Reeve is saved by reason, tools and technology. A ghostly Renaissance man dressed in sixteenth-century clothing instructs him to 'show them iron!'; Reeve subsequently brandishes his pocketknife; the savages quake in fear and he makes his escape.[20] But the narrative also suggests that primal violence has been entwined with all aspects of human history, including medieval courtly culture. Reeve discovers that long barrows, in which the ancient Picts made human sacrifice, are 'the real originals of all the fairy hills and subterranean palaces' of medieval romance.[21] Thus, in the case of the English fairy tale of Childe Roland, moderns imagine that the Dark Tower, from which the knight Roland chivalrously saves his sister Burd Ellen, is a medieval castle; in truth, the tower 'was nothing more or less than a long barrow'.[22]

Grant Allen's short story, like Robert Louis Stevenson's *Strange Case of Dr Jekyll and Mr Hyde* (1886) and Oscar Wilde's *The Picture of Dorian Gray* (1890), raises the possibility of retrogression down the evolutionary chain, and suggests that primordial atavistic traits cannot be overcome by culture or bred out of the body. In *Degeneration: A Chapter in Darwinism* (1880), the zoologist E. Ray Lankester provided evidence of biological degeneration, based upon his research of ascidians.[23] An example of retrogressive metamorphosis, these sea squirts initially had a tail with which they actively propelled through water, but they later attached themselves for life to a rock where they passively took in whatever food floated by. As Allen interprets it, the ascidian had 'grown degraded and fallen from his high estate' to become 'a blind, handless, footless and degenerate thing'.[24] And as H. G. Wells interprets it, 10 years later, ascidians provided a model for human regression: individuals begin life full of activity and imagination, but then enter a profession, marry, and settle down to quiet domesticity and passivity. In other words, writes Wells, 'the Bohemian tail is discarded'.[25] Yet, just as the ascidian carries within it the skeletal and sensory remnants of its past active life, so 'the human fœtus wears an undeniable tail' and 'novelette heroes' have birth marks.[26] These are biological remnants that suggest that, given the right conditions, an active but more aggressive past could still

---

20 Allen, 'Pallinghurst', p. 18. 21 Allen, 'Pallinghurst', p. 15.
22 Allen, 'Pallinghurst', p. 15.
23 Edwin Lankester, *Degeneration: A Chapter in Darwinism* (London: MacMillan, 1880).
24 Grant Allen, *The Evolutionist at Large* (London: Chatto and Windus, 1881), pp. 100–1.
25 H. G. Wells, 'Zoological regression', *The Gentleman's Magazine* 271 (September 1891): 246–53 (p. 249).
26 Wells, 'Zoological', pp. 249, 248.

manifest itself. Or, would modern humans continue to evolve on a similarly degenerate path as the sea squirt?

There are things about Allen's Rudolph Reeve which suggest that, in the last decades of the nineteenth century, conditions were right for a downward slide. He is prone to 'nervous breakdown'; he suffers from 'nervous inanition' and headaches of 'the worst neuralgic kind', afflictions common to writer types (and particularly those with a 'poet's soul').[27] On the evening before his adventure in the barrow, another house guest, Dr Porter, prescribes him 'Soma—the fine old trusted remedy of our Aryan ancestor', the narcotic 'Cannabis Indica'.[28] Taking more than the recommended dosage, it is a drugged Reeve, still dressed in his dinner suit and with Joseph Jacobs's *English Fairy Tales* on his mind, who enters the barrow. In these respects, Reeve is a model of the morbid moderns that Max Nordau describes in his monumental *Entartung* (1892; translated into English as *Degeneration* in 1895). Showing the mental and physical stigmata of degeneration in their bodies, nervous dispositions, use of opiates, fondness for the occult, and in their ahistorical 'predilection for the Middle Ages', these moderns often subscribed to a mystical medievalism 'peopled with queens and knights, noble damozels with coronets on their golden hair, and pages with plumed caps' – not to mention fairy barrows.[29] While Victorian medievalists like Ruskin would see chivalrous cultural history as a marker of human exceptionalism, the form that it had taken in decadent culture was for Nordau a sign that humanity was slipping back down the evolutionary scale.

'A Nasty Curious Subject': Biological Monstrosities and Criminal Doctors

In an 1845 letter to the botanist Joseph Hooker, Darwin used the term 'curious' a good deal:

> One of the subject[s] I am curious to discuss hereafter with you—is the position, as a method of induction, in which morphology stands; it seems to me a very curious point.— ... I have just finished three huge volumes by St Hilaire on animal monsters, and a nasty curious subject it is.—[30]

---

27 Allen, 'Pallinghurst', pp. 13, 16, 12.   28 Allen, 'Pallinghurst', p. 16.
29 Max Nordau, *Degeneration*, translated 2nd edition (London: William Heinemann, 1898), p. 70.
30 Darwin Correspondence Project, 'Letter no. 847' < www.darwinproject.ac.uk/DCP-LETT-847> (last accessed 9 August 2018).

Darwin refers here to Isidore Geoffroy Saint-Hilaire's *General and Particular History of Structural Monstrosities in Man and Animals* (1832–7), a compilation of case studies of morphological deviation, which laid the groundwork for the study of teratology and greatly informed Darwin's ideas on this subject.[31]

In *Origin*, Darwin differentiated variation, which was adaptive, from monstrosity, which was random and 'either injurious or not useful to the species'.[32] These classifications depended on time, place and circumstance. For example, in the 1874 edition of *The Descent of Man* (1871), he elaborates on a type of monstrosity that is 'arrested at an early phase of embryonic development'; in this state of 'reversion', the subject's form resembles 'the lower types of mankind' and 'the lower animals'.[33] In chapters on 'Reversion or Atavism' in *The Variation of Animals and Plants under Domestication* (1868), Darwin observes how cross-breeding 'often leads to the reappearance of long-lost characters', to the extent that it was 'impossible to distinguish between the reappearance of ancient characters and new characters'.[34] A child could, for example, take after a 'remote ancestor of foreign blood', so that it would seem that the parents had failed 'to transmit their own likeness'.[35] Then again, there were cases in which 'mutilations', accidents and 'injurious conditions', including 'the use and disuse of parts, and of mental habits' in one generation, were then transmitted to the offspring.[36] Such cases of acquired or transformational heredity could be relatively insignificant, or 'of the highest importance, as when affecting the brain or … the eye': these 'grave' alterations 'deserve to be called a monstrosity'.[37]

Although brief, this synopsis of Darwin's teratology indicates why and how it sparked the imagination of late nineteenth-century Gothic writers. His vocabulary of mutilations, transmutations, reversions, atavisms and malformations; his emphasis on the unpredictability, but also durability of traits; his exploration of how human intervention altered domesticated species; the tension between gradual and abrupt change; the suggestion of the plasticity of living form (and especially, what H. G. Wells referred to as 'degeneration

---

31 Isidore Geoffroy Saint-Hilaire, *Histoire générale et particulière des anomalies de l'organisation chez l'homme et les animaux* (Paris: B. Baillière, 1832–7).
32 Darwin, *Origin*, p. 44.
33 Charles Darwin, *The Descent of Man*, 2nd edition (New York: D. Appleton, 1875), pp. 35–6.
34 Charles Darwin, *The Variation of Animals and Plants under Domestication*, 2nd edition, 2 vols (London: John Murray, 1875), vol. 2, pp. 18, 39.
35 Darwin, *Variation*, vol. 2, p. 58.   36 Darwin, *Variation*, vol. 2, p. 57.
37 Darwin, *Variation*, vol. 2, p. 57.

as a plastic process') all underpin writing by Stevenson, Stoker, Wells, Machen and many others.[38] Significantly, though, this line of influence did not often produce in literature those 'spectacularly misshapen figures of the true terrata', as Erin O'Connor designates them.[39] Gothic monsters embodied reversions, mutations and accidents, yet they were rarely of a type that would include, say, Wells's Beast Folk. More often, they were aesthetes, doctors, rural Welsh children, housemaids, law students and budding scholars who hid their monstrosity within.

Surgically Modified Monstrous Genealogies

In Gothic literature, doctors who were armed with new knowledge about sensory experience, comparative anatomy and heredity, bred biological monsters, yet these experimenters also harboured a monstrous criminality within their own 'genes' (to use a word that would come into usage on the heels of Darwin's *Variation*). In Arthur Machen's 'The Great God Pan' (1894), Dr Raymond performs experimental neurosurgery on a beautiful 17-year-old housemaid in order to give her access to a metaphysical realm, an otherwise unattainable spirit-world. As a result, Mary is reduced, post-surgery, to 'a hopeless idiot' who can only lay in her bed 'wide-awake, rolling her head from side to side, and grinning vacantly'.[40] She gives birth, unconsciously, to a monstrous offspring as a consequence of a union with the god Pan. From the beginning, Helen Vaughan, Mary's child, is a dangerous degenerate driven by unquenchable compulsions; as a sadistic adult, she takes great pleasure in destroying young men, leaving them feeble-minded, insane and suicidal. This monstrous genealogy, the result of mutilations to the parent being transmitted to the offspring, ends with Helen's remarkable death, described by the attending doctor as a series of physical transformations from woman to man to beast, until flesh and bones melt into a jelly-like substance. This doctor echoes T. H. Huxley in his observation that,

---

38 Wells, 'Zoological,' p. 246; on the issue of gradual versus abrupt change, see Palmira Fontes da Costa, 'The Meaning of Monstrosities in Charles Darwin's Understanding of the Origin of Species', in Ana Leonor Pereira, João Pita and Pedro Ricardo Fonseca (eds), *Darwin, Evolution, Evolutionists* (Coimbra: Imprensa da Universidade de Coimbra, 2011), pp. 74–83.
39 Erin O' Connor, *Raw Material: Producing Pathology in Victorian Culture* (Durham, NC: Duke University Press, 2000), p. 184.
40 Arthur Machen, 'The Great God Pan', in Aaron Worth (ed.), *The Great God Pan and Other Horror Stories* (Oxford: Oxford University Press, 2018), pp. 9–54 (p. 15).

although 'the outward form' of Helen's body changed dramatically, 'the principle of life, which makes organism, always remained'.[41]

Machen's story 'The Inmost Light' (1894) belongs to a Gothic sub-genre that includes Nathaniel Hawthorne's 'The Birth-Mark' (1843) and Edward Berdoe's *St Bernard's: The Romance of a Medical Student* (1887), and which features doctors who perform experiments on beautiful and (to varying degrees) acquiescent women. In order to separate his wife's soul from her body, Machen's Dr Black forewarns her that something shameful and horrific 'would enter in' her body 'where her life had been'.[42] As prearranged, he eventually kills her, thereby releasing her from a miserable existence as a monstrous not-quite human 'satyr'. The surgeons who perform the ensuing post-mortem 'scarcely believe that the brain' of Mrs Black 'was that of a human being at all'.[43] Part of the brain was animalistic, but in other respects it 'indicated a nervous organization of a wholly different character from that either of man or the lower animals'.[44] She is, then, an unprecedented biological monstrosity that has been reduced to mere matter: a body without sensorium, what Erasmus Darwin had called the 'living principle, or spirit of animation, which resides throughout the body'.[45]

Some scholars have read Machen's stories as distinctly materialist narratives. According to Kelly Hurley, for instance, the manner of Helen's death and her transformations reflect the materialist conviction that humans shared their basic composition with all other organisms.[46] Similarly, Clive Bloom reads Helen's end as 'a Darwinian nightmare of degeneration, dissolution and sexual ambiguity, a polymorphously perverse descent into the primal sludge of creation'.[47] In contrast, other critics have emphasised the religious, metaphysical or occultic elements in such scenes. Jake Poller, for one, has argued that 'the animosity' Machen 'displayed towards scientific materialism makes it highly unlikely that he would have knowingly incorporated the concept in his work'; further, Poller argues that, since Machen had allegedly 'never

---

41 Machen, 'Great God Pan', p. 50. In his 1868 essay 'On the Physical Basis of Life', T. H. Huxley famously identified protoplasm as the 'single physical basis of life underlying all the diversities of vital existence'. See Alan P. Barr (ed.), *The Major Prose of Thomas Henry Huxley* (Athens, GA: University of Georgia Press, 1997), p. 176.
42 Arthur Machen, 'The Inmost Light', in Corinna Wagner (ed.), *Gothic Evolutions: Poetry, Tales, Context, Theory* (Peterborough, Ont.: Broadview, 2014), pp. 388–406 (p. 405).
43 Machen, 'Inmost', p. 392.   44 Machen, 'Inmost', p. 392.
45 Erasmus Darwin, *Zoonomia; or, the Laws of Organic Life* (London: Joseph Johnson, 1794–6), vol. I, p. 10.
46 Hurley, *Gothic Body*, p. 31.
47 Clive Bloom, *Victoria's Madmen: Revolution and Alienation* (Basingstoke: Palgrave Macmillan, 2013), p. 100.

heard of' theories of degeneration, those scenes of dissolution in which bodies return to 'protoplasm, are revealed to derive from alchemy'.[48] Without entering too much into this debate, I find it highly unlikely that Machen was unfamiliar with ideas about degeneration, a topic that was hotly debated across a wide variety of contemporary media, from newspapers to novels, social commentary to popular science. Moreover, animosity towards materialism does not amount to a lack of engagement with it, as Ruskin's writing, for example, makes clear.

In fact, while Dr Raymond's goal is to gain access, via the portal of the brain, to a world beyond phenomenal existence, his methods engage directly with materialist science. His surgical method – surpassing the ability of 'ninety-nine brain specialists out of a hundred' – results in a 'slight lesion in the grey matter ... a trifling rearrangement of certain cells, a microscopical alteration' in 'the physiology of the brain'.[49] The effect is physical and mental degeneracy, and as we have seen, the outcomes illustrate evolutionary principles, and clearly reflect Darwinian ideas about the aetiology of monsters. Furthermore, while the protoplasmic basis of life may itself be a source of anxiety, another must surely be that a deeply anti-social, unfeeling, merciless compulsion of the kind demonstrated by Drs Raymond and Black inheres within that protoplasm. Ruined bodies call attention to the educated perpetrators of their ruination, indicating that violent compulsions are embodied universally.

Oscar Wilde recorded his thoughts on the universality of protoplasmic inheritance in his Oxford notebooks from the 1870s: 'comparative anatomy' as much as 'the anatomy of the mind', he wrote, reveals that 'man is but the last of a long series' that begins with 'the formless speck of living protoplasm which lies on the shallow boundary between animal and vegetable life'.[50] In Wilde's *The Picture of Dorian Gray* (1890), formless protoplasmic specks take the form of destructive 'germs' inhering within the minds and bodies of modern aesthetes. Neither youthful beauty nor aesthetic sensibility can prevent the eponymous Dorian from an entropic decline that is recorded in his monstrous portrait and which results in the death of another beautiful young woman. The death by suicide of Dorian's abandoned fiancée Sibyl Vane means that she, like Machen's Mrs Black, will undergo an autopsy: in

48 Jake Poller, 'The transmutations of Arthur Machen: alchemy in "The Great God Pan" and *The Three Impostors*', *Literature and Theology* 29 (2013): 18–32 (pp. 18, 30).
49 Machen, 'Great God Pan', p. 10.
50 Philip E. Smith II and Michael S. Helfand (eds), *Oscar Wilde's Oxford Notebooks: A Portrait of the Mind in the Making* (Oxford: Oxford University Press, 1989), pp. 163–4.

death as in life, 'there are horrors in store for that little white body of hers!'[51] Even with the benefit of civilisation – education, privilege, autonomy – the Paleolithic savagery and anti-social, amoral instincts that inhere within Machen's doctors, and the 'strange poisonous *germ*' within Dorian, cannot be contained.[52] Sadistic compulsions were fixed within biological matter, waiting to be given destructive expression, whether in the form of Dorian's hedonistic, sensation-seeking experimentation, or in the medical experiments of Drs Jekyll, Moreau, Raymond and Black and their murderous, mindless and/or soulless progeny.

These characters illustrate a significant tension in *Descent of Man*. Early in the volume, Darwin identifies a genealogy of sociability: 'Primeval man, or the ape-like progenitors of man', he writes, 'must have acquired the same instinctive feelings which impel other animals to live in a [social] body'.[53] Yet Darwin famously closes *Descent of Man* with a rather wry commentary about two strands of lineage, one sociable and one irrationally violent:

> I would as soon be descended from that heroic little monkey, who braved his dreaded enemy in order to save the life of his keeper, or from that old baboon, who descending from the mountains, carried away in triumph his young comrade from a crowd of astonished dogs – as from a savage who delights to torture his enemies, offers up bloody sacrifices, practices infanticide without remorse, treats his wives like slaves, knows no decency, and is haunted by the grossest superstitions.[54]

Sociability descends with the apes, while violence descends with the human savage. Likewise, Gothic writing often challenges the idea of a natural human sociability and suggests that the structures of civilisation, which have been so painstakingly constructed over centuries, fail to curb savage impulses.

Whereas Darwin saw 'morality develop from the social instincts', Huxley conceived of the instincts more pessimistically: they were 'primeval lusts' that were 'anti-social, an amoral vestige to be repressed'.[55] Wells takes up the Huxleyan view in *The Island of Doctor Moreau* (1896); in fact, Wells's explanation of his theme could apply just as well to any number of *fin-de-siècle* Gothic stories: 'what we call morality becomes the padding of suggested emotional habits necessary to keep the round Paleolithic savage in the square hole of the

---

51 Oscar Wilde, *The Picture of Dorian Gray*, edited by Robert Mighall (Harmondsworth: Penguin, 2003), p. 105.
52 Wilde, *Dorian*, p. 137. 53 Darwin, *Descent*, p. 129. 54 Darwin, *Descent*, p. 619.
55 Adrian Desmond, *Huxley: From Devil's Disciple to Evolution's High Priest* (London: Penguin, 1998), p. 584.

civilized state'.⁵⁶ When that padding gives way, civilisation's defenders – the 'Crew of Light' in Stoker's *Dracula* or Sherlock Holmes in Sir Arthur Conan Doyle's short stories – step forward to reinforce it. Yet even when these defenders succeed in containing the villain in the square hole of civilisation, there is a sense that the tide cannot be stemmed: another and then another mercilessly vivisecting doctor, vampire or sadistic criminal will appear. In 'The Adventure of the Creeping Man' (1923), the eminently adept Sherlock Holmes acknowledges the precariousness of social order and the difficulty of keeping Paleolithic savagery at bay when he reveals the real crime of the distinguished physiologist Professor Presbury. It is not that the professor's experimentation with a monkey-based serum reveals how 'the highest type of man may revert to animal', but rather that he demonstrates how, given the right conditions, 'the material, the sensual, the worldly' individual could turn society into a 'cesspool'.⁵⁷

Sadistic Criminals and the New Normality

Cesare Lombroso thought that 'born criminals', individuals for whom crime was biological destiny, constituted the greatest threat to civilised society. But if society had a hard time containing these violent, incorrigible criminals, what of the primeval, sadistic lusts that lay hidden within what H. G. Wells called the 'undying protoplasm' of everyone and everything – capacious categories that include *normal* people?⁵⁸

Scholars who have explicated Lombroso's theories of crime have shown that he, like other early criminologists, were more or less influenced by Darwinian materialism and evolutionary ideas, at least by the 1860s.⁵⁹ The anecdote about how Lombroso lighted upon his theory of the biologically inferior and developmentally arrested 'born criminal' may be familiar to some, but it is worth sketching here briefly, for it reveals two particularly

---

56 H. G. Wells, 'Human Evolution, an Artificial Process. in *H. G. Wells: Early Writings in Science and Science Fiction*, edited by Robert Philmus and David Y. Hughes (Berkeley, CA: University of California Press, 1975), pp. 211–19 (p. 217).

57 Arthur Conan Doyle, 'The Adventure of the Creeping Man', in *The Casebook of Sherlock Holmes*, edited by W. W. Robson (Oxford: Oxford University Press, 2009), pp. 50–71 (p. 70).

58 H. G. Wells, 'Death', in *Early Writings*, pp. 137–9 (p. 139).

59 Daniel Pick, *Faces of Degeneration: A European Disorder, c. 1848–c. 1918* (Cambridge: Cambridge University Press, 1993), p. 112; see also David G. Horn, *The Criminal Body: Lombroso and the Anatomy of Deviance* (New York: Routledge, 2003) and Nicole H. Rafter, 'Introduction', in *The Origins of Criminology: A Reader* (New York: Routledge, 2009), pp. xiii–xxvi.

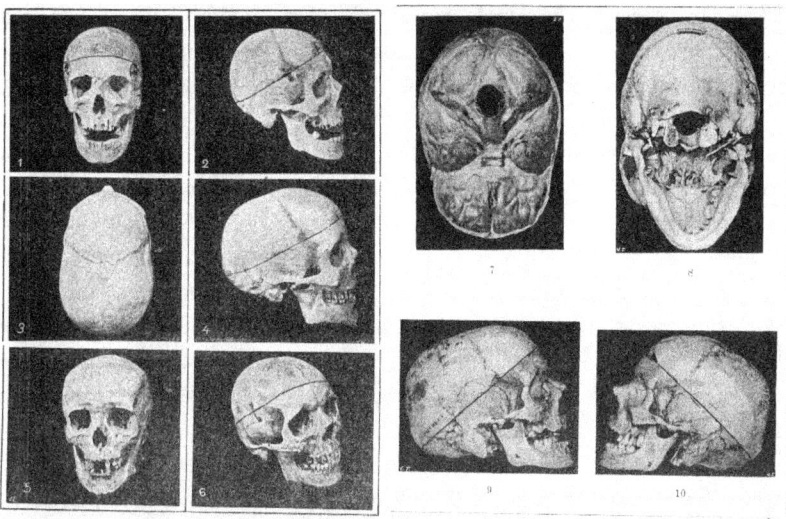

Fig.19.5: 'The skull of Villella', Gina Lombroso-Ferrero, *Criminal Man* (c. 1864–71). Author's photograph.

important things about Gothic representations of monstrosity. When the young Lombroso performed a post-mortem on the body of 'an Italian Jack the Ripper', Giuseppe Villella, he found anomalies in the cranium, including an indentation redolent of the lower types of apes and other animals (see Fig.19.5).[60] Lombroso recalled how 'at the sight of that skull', he understood 'the nature of the criminal, who reproduces in civilised times characteristics, not only of primitive savages, but of still lower types as far back as the carnivora'.[61] Thus, criminality was, first, hereditary, the result of arrested development and an expression of atavistic biological characteristics; and, second, it was indicated by a range of 'stigmata' or physical markers. These bodily, and especially facial characteristics, which recalled that of apes, birds, rodents and savages, included prognathism (protruding jaws), asymmetrical features and prominent teeth, browbones and ears. Stevenson's Edward Hyde, who has the 'face of a man without bowels of mercy', is clearly modelled upon such principles, as is Bram Stoker's Dracula, with his massive eyebrows, cruel mouth, and pointy teeth and ears.[62] For Lombroso, even

---

60 Gina Lombroso-Ferrero, *Criminal Man* (New York: G. P. Putnam's Sons, 1911), p. 6.
61 Lombroso-Ferrero, *Criminal*, p. 7.
62 Robert Louis Stevenson, *Strange Case of Dr Jekyll and Mr Hyde and Weir of Hermiston*, edited by Emma Letley (Oxford: Oxford University Press, 1987), p. 17.

habitual or occasional criminals, moral imbeciles and 'criminal epileptics' had an external and internal morphology that supposedly demarcated them from the normal population.[63]

In Darwin's materialism, his theory of descent and in his ideas about atavism and degeneration, criminologists as well as psychiatrists found biological justifications for the criminal compulsion. In *The Expression of the Emotions in Man and Animals* (1872), Darwin made important links between the internal life and its external manifestation; so too did criminologists identify the visible physical signs or anatomical anomalies that corresponded to mental anomalies. Lombroso was particularly drawn to the English school of criminal psychiatry, which had developed a theory of moral insanity. In 1885 Daniel Hack Tuke determined that those who committed the most horrifically sadistic crimes, including infanticide and parricide, had a 'congenital defect of the moral sense'.[64] In his *Psychopathia Sexualis* (1892) Richard von Krafft-Ebing determined between sane persons whose search for ever-greater sensation made them 'forget that they are human beings', leading them to commit sexually deviant acts of brutality, and those individuals whose heinous crimes were due to physiological debility and certain pathologies.[65] As such, the morally insane could not be held legally responsible for their offences.

Mason Harris observes that 'because of the monstrous nature of their crimes', Lombroso's born criminals took on 'a disproportionate importance' in the cultural imagination.[66] The same could be said for the morally insane: the unboundedness of their desires and the uninhibited, sadistic nature of their acts loomed large in the public mind. Moreover, this anxiety was compounded by the belief that the morally insane and the true-born criminal lacked higher-order emotions like shame and sympathy, felt neither remorse nor regret for their acts, and were impervious to pain. Robert Mighall has challenged what he terms the 'anxiety model' of reading Gothic literature as reflective of cultural fears, and insists that we should instead see late

---

63 See chapters on 'Criminal craniums' and 'Anthropometry and physiognomy of criminals', in Cesare Lombroso, *Criminal Man*, trans. and edited by Mary Gibson and Nicole Hahn Rafter (Durham, NC: Duke University Press, 2006).
64 D. Hack Tuke, 'Case of moral insanity or congenital moral defect, with commentary' *Journal of Mental Science* 31 (October 1885): 360–6 (p. 364).
65 Richard von Krafft-Ebing, *Psychopathia Sexualis*, trans. by Charles Gilbert Chaddock (Philadelphia, PA: F. A. Davis, 1892), p. 404.
66 Mason Harris, 'Introduction', in H. G. Wells, *The Island of Dr Moreau*, edited by Mason Harris (Peterborough, Ont.: Broadview, 2009), pp. 13–58 (p. 36–7).

nineteenth-century Gothic monsters as 'objects, de-*monst*-rating ... the truth of the sciences which produced and represented them'.[67] But, often Gothic monsters were both: they expressed cultural anxieties about deviance in modern society at the same time that they reflected key principles of evolutionary science as well as the preoccupations of the emergent fields of anthropology, criminology, psychiatry, and sexology. This is the case, for example, in Arthur Machen's complicated episodic work, *The Three Impostors; or, The Transmutations* (1895). The anxiety-inducing monstrosity of the titular three villains is compounded by the fact that they could so easily blend into the population of the city and adopt a number of false identities with such remarkable ease. In this, they express a problem faced by new disciplines that take the human as subject: that of non-coherence between internal self and external appearance.

The Three Impostors consists of four, separate, 'novels', two of which are respectively narrated by the two male impostors, Davies and Richmond, and two of which are told by the more sadistic member of the triumvirate, Helen. Together, these 'novels' comprise the belly of the text: a tangled mess of truth and fabrication that is meant to mislead Machen's writer-detective-collector-dilettante, Dyson and his friend Phillipps. This narrative structure simulates the torture performed on the body of a young, bespectacled scholar, Joseph Walters. Indeed, *The Three Impostors* is bookended by the same scene of torture: it ends where it begins, at a Gothic house on the outskirts of London, within which lies Walters's mutilated body, his entrails eviscerated by still-burning coals. As the three impostors exit the abandoned old house, they trade gruesome jokes about the sadistic torture that they have just performed, while Helen carries an 'oozing' and 'dripping' package containing one of Walters' hands, bound for the museum of their cult leader, Dr Lipsius.[68] Devoted to sadistic pleasures, Lipsius's 'acutest enjoyment' is to devise creative tortures for those who have been lured into their clubhouse.[69] Walters had been seduced to join this secret criminal society, but upon witnessing the macabre mummification of a man whom he recognises, he attempts to extract himself from the club – which is, of course, impossible.

---

67 Robert Mighall, *A Geography of Victorian Gothic Fiction: Mapping History's Nightmares* (Oxford: Oxford University Press, 2003), pp. 166–209 (p. 208).
68 Arthur Machen, 'The Three Impostors', in Worth (ed.), *The Great God Pan and Other Horror Stories*, pp. 79–196 (p. 81). This edition unfortunately drops the meaningful subtitle.
69 Machen, 'Three Impostors', p. 185.

At the end of *The Three Impostors* (chronologically, the point at which it begins), Dyson and Phillipps arrive at the abandoned house mere moments after the departure of the torturers, where they find the naked Walters:

> lying on the floor, his arms and legs stretched wide apart, and bound to pegs that had been hammered into the boards. The body was torn and mutilated in the most hideous fashion, scarred with the marks of red-hot irons, a shameful ruin of the human shape. But upon the middle of the body a fire of coals was smouldering; the flesh had been burned through. The man was dead, but the smoke of his torment mounted still, a black vapor.[70]

This is not the first body that is sadistically reduced to 'a shameful ruin of the human shape' in the story. In another of the inset narratives, the 'Novel of the White Powder', a handsome law student, Francis Leicester, is transmuted into a 'dark and putrid mass, seething with corruption and hideous rottenness neither liquid nor solid, but melting and changing … and bubbling with unctuous oily bubbles like boiling pitch'.[71] In the 'Novel of the Black Seal', a 'slimy, wavering tentacle' bursts from the convulsing, distended body of a developmentally arrested boy named Jervase Craddock, a descendant of the ancient 'Little People' of the Welsh Grey Hills. That slimy tentacle is evidence of how, though 'fallen out of the grand march of evolution', this ancient race had 'retained "miraculous" powers', including the ability to reduce a man 'to the slime from which he came'.[72]

Kelly Hurley is right to see the demise of Jervase Craddock and Francis Leicester as reflective of imperfect human evolution and as 'motif[s] of human devolution'.[73] But the three impostors, with their carefully devised identities and nefarious aims, are also models of retrogression, though of a covert (and more dangerous) kind. They adopt respectable names and identities: Mr Burton, the dealer in antiques and curiosities; Mr Wilkins, the private secretary; and in the case of Helen, both Miss Lally, the governess and Miss Leicester, the devoted sister. Convinced at one point that the bespectacled Walters is the criminal, Dyson opens his doors to the real criminal, Davies, in disguise as the antique dealer Mr Burton. A revealing point of comparison can be made between Machen's impostors and Joseph Conrad's Comrade Ossipon in *The Secret Agent* (1907). When he 'invokes Lombroso', the scientifically minded Ossipon escapes the clutches of the murderous Mrs Verloc. He reads in her features 'the sister of a degenerate, a degenerate herself—of a murdering type … He gazed at her cheeks, at her

70 Machen, 'Three Impostors', p. 196. 71 Machen, 'Three Impostors', p. 172.
72 Machen, 'Three Impostors', p. 141. 73 Hurley, *Gothic Body*, p. 63.

nose, at her eyes, at her ears ... Bad! ... Fatal!'[74] However, this is *not* the case in Machen's story, for criminality is buried within and beneath a decent, banal exterior. The three impostors fit the description of Lombroso's born criminals insofar as they are motivated by an 'irresistible craving for evil for its own sake, the desire not only to extinguish life in the victim, but to mutilate the corpse, tear its flesh, and drink its blood'.[75] Yet, unlike Mrs Verloc, they lack any revealing physical stigmata.

Charles Bernheimer has described the Lombrosian 'project of cataloguing ever more degenerates' as endlessly proliferating more of the same so that it 'risks overwhelming a shrinking center of normalcy by an expanding margin of deviance'.[76] In some ways this may be true, but Machen's unreadable identity-shifting criminals reveal that criminality also hides within the bodies of seemingly normal citizens. They reveal, too, that normalcy and deviance are oftentimes inseparable. Savage appetites refuse to be moored by moral anchors.

Remorseless Automatism: Crimes against Animals and Murderous Plants

When, in *The Secret Agent*, Mrs Verloc delivers a 'murdering mad' knife into the chest of her husband, she does so with 'all the inheritance of her immemorial and obscure descent, the simple ferocity of the age of caverns, and the unbalanced nervous fury of the age of bar-rooms'.[77] A Darwinian line of heredity, which stretches from fossil man to a modern shop in London's Soho, culminates in that fatal stab. Bare survival is unleashed as murderous impulse in a pessimistic, morbidly anxious, decadent age. While all living things compete and struggle for survival, only humans have a capacity for irrational, remorseless violence.

The lunatic Renfield remorselessly consumes crawling, buzzing, flying things in Bram Stoker's *Dracula* (1897). In his asylum cell, he cultivates a sadistic food chain: flies are fed to spiders, spiders to sparrows, and, denied a much-desired cat, he steps in to eat the sparrows raw, whole and feathered. The asylum director Dr John Seward classifies his 'curious' and 'abnormally

---

74 Joseph Conrad, *The Secret Agent*, edited by John Lyon (Oxford: Oxford University Press, 2008), p. 217.
75 Lombroso-Fererro, *Criminal*, p. xv.
76 Charles Bernheimer, *Decadent Subjects: The Idea of Decadence in Art, Literature, Philosophy, and the Culture of the Fin de Siècle in Europe* (Baltimore, MA: Johns Hopkins University Press, 2002), p. 142.
77 Conrad, *Secret*, p. 193.

cruel' patient as an 'undeveloped homicidal maniac', while Renfield rationalises his zoophagus desire:

> By consuming a multitude of live things, no matter how low in the scale of creation, one might indefinitely prolong life ... The doctor here will bear me out that on one occasion I tried to kill him for the purpose of strengthening my vital powers by the assimilation with my own body of his life through the medium of his blood.[78]

Obviously, this is a description of vampirism, but Dracula's control of Renfield is also analogous to the workings of heredity. Renfield's impulses are regulated by the automatous pull of an inborn violence that overrides the efforts of modern science, with its diagnostic taxonomies and physiological psychology. Describing Renfield's impulses as 'animalistic' is not quite right though, for his cycle of consuming is neither reasonable nor necessitous, as it is for animals. His delight in slow death – in catching and triumphantly holding aloft 'a horrid blow-fly, bloated with some carrion food' before devouring it – as well as his swing from utter calm to uncontrollable rage mark him as more savage than animal.[79] For Darwin, rage was particularly associated with irrationality, savagery, delusive jealousy, and the primitive functions. In *Expression,* he concurs with Henry Maudsley's observations that snarling, howling maniacs and developmentally arrested patients have 'the brute nature within'.[80]

Lombroso saw marked similarities between human criminality and 'the zoological world': animals committed theft, participated in organised crime, became alcoholics (bees) and coffee bean addicts (goats).[81] And from his reading of Darwin's work on botany, Lombroso drew similar comparisons between humans and plants. In fact, the chapters of Darwin's *Insectivorous Plants* (1875), on the glands, bladders, 'movements of the tentacles', digestive power, irritations, sensual responses and spontaneous movements of carniverous plants, seem to describe animal anatomy and physiology. The illustrations, such as the one by Darwin's son George, present alien life forms (Fig.19.6). This is a seething, heaving and even nightmarish realm that Tina Gianquitto describes as 'a dark world of plant digestion, replete with smotherings, crushings, drownings,

---

78 Bram Stoker, *Dracula*, edited by Roger Luckhurst (Oxford: Oxford University Press, 2011), pp. 66, 68, 218.
79 Stoker, *Dracula*, p. 67.
80 Charles Darwin, *The Expression of the Emotions in Man and Animals* (London: John Murray, 1872), p. 246.
81 Lombroso, *Criminal*, p. 172.

FIG. 1.*
(*Drosera rotundifolia.*)
Leaf viewed from above; enlarged four times.

Fig.19.6: George Darwin, for Charles Darwin, 'Drosera rotundifolia', *Insectivorous Plants* (1875). Author's photograph.

entanglings, and absorbings' – which recalls Tennyson's 'Nature, red in tooth and claw'.[82] As such, Lombroso credited carnivorous plants, which committed 'true murders of insects', as heralding the 'dawn of criminality', reasoning that they indulged in 'pre-meditation, ambush, killing for greed, and, to a certain extent, decision-making' (as in, refusal to kill insects deemed too small).[83]

---

82 Tina Gianquitto, 'Criminal Botany: Progress, Degeneration, and Darwin's *Insectivorous Plants*', in Tina Gianquitto and Lydia Fisher (eds), *America's Darwin: Darwinian Theory and U.S. Literary Culture* (Athens, GA: University of Georgia Press, 2014), pp. 235–62 (p. 236).
83 Lombroso, *Criminal*, p. 168.

Yet, in the final analysis, the acts of plants could not be considered crimes because they were 'derived completely from histology or the microstructure of organic tissue—and not from alleged will'.[84] The same applied to animals: that they killed for sexual access to females was explained by 'the Darwinian theory of sexual selection'; that they had occasion to commit infanticide and parricide was a result of 'the necessary effects of heredity—an organic structure imposed by competition for survival, by sexual selection', and by 'social necessity'.[85] Crucially, from these observations of plant and animal life, Lombroso drew pessimistic conclusions about human self-determination. Animal crimes underlined 'the absurdity of a concept of justice based on free will', he decided, and they indicated 'why we find criminal tendencies . . . even within the most civilized races'.[86] Animal crimes showed that even society's most cherished beliefs 'about bonds of blood and innate maternal and filial affection' were just 'sentimental cant'.[87] The qualities that had supposedly defined humanity as exceptional – loyalty, love, and duty – were revealed as platitudes that obscured material reality.

In the wake of these speculations, large numbers of stories featured crimes committed by plants, though often humans were ultimately responsible. For example, Lucy H. Hooper's 1889 story 'Carnivorine' features Julius Lambert, a scientist schooled 'in the Darwinian theories' and specifically Darwin's work on the Drosera plant pictured above.[88] From these studies, Lambert develops his own 'theory that the hydra, the dragon, and other monstrous forms of animal life really did exist, and that, in the evolution of ages, and by reason of geological changes . . . these creatures . . . degenerated into trees and plants'.[89] In a deserted house on the malarial plains outside Rome, Lambert attempts to make 'the link between the vegetable and the animal kingdom' by 'resuscitat[ing] the animal in the plant'.[90] He produces a huge and hungry drosera, Carnivorine, who develops limb-like appendages, paws, tentacles, powers of locomotion and something like blood pumping through 'her'. Unable to help himself, the obsessed scientist insists that 'for science, there is no such thing as a monster'; as we might expect, these are famous last words.[91] Carnivorine tears Lambert's head from his body.

---

84 Lombroso, *Criminal*, pp. 171, 168. 85 Lombroso, *Criminal*, pp. 171, 168.
86 Lombroso, *Criminal*, p. 171. 87 Lombroso, *Criminal*, p. 170.
88 Lucy H. Hooper, 'Carnivorine', in Chad Arment (ed.), *Botanica Delira: More Stories of Strange, Undiscovered, and Murderous Vegetation* (Landisville, PA: Coachwhip, 2010), pp. 73–81 (p. 73).
89 Hooper, 'Carnivorine', pp. 80–1. 90 Hooper, 'Carnivorine', pp. 79, 81.
91 Hooper, 'Carnivorine', p. 81.

For Dawn Keetley, Hooper's story illustrates Lombroso's view that 'the vestigial remains' of plant and animal 'formed an indwelling core of automatism' within the human 'that was in part characterized by an innate propensity for violence'.[92] This automatous violence motivates Lambert to attempt to resurrect the ancient dragons and hydra that had supposedly degenerated into a vegetative state. As Lambert rekindles the monster's vestigial active germ, lurking inside the drosera, he simultaneously degenerates into something of that remorseless savage that Darwin described at the end of *Descent*. For in spite of being a cultivated, educated scientist, Lambert willingly sacrifices love, family, and the safety of society in a quest to resurrect the monsters of medieval imagination.

Three Medieval Returns and *The Three Impostors*

Something medieval lurks in almost all of the texts addressed here. In this last section, let me raise three seemingly loosely related comments, each articulated within a decade, and each making a particular kind of reference to the medieval past.

First, in 1884, Cesare Lombroso claimed that criminals reproduced 'the instincts of not only prehistoric but also medieval man', which explained the resurgence of duelling: it was a result of the cultural 'reappearance of medieval passions'.[93] Second, in an 1885 article, psychiatrist Daniel Hack Tuke described patient W. B., whose long history of crimes included torturing his siblings, cutting horses, maiming birds and molesting girls, as 'a reversion to an old savage type' who was 'born by accident in the wrong century'.[94] If W. B., pictured in Fig.19.7, had been born 'in a barbaric age', he would have 'been in harmony' with his 'environment' (Fig.19.7).[95] Third, in an 1894 letter to his publisher, Arthur Machen defended his occult themes and bemoaned the demand for scientific rationality in literature: 'in the Middle Ages ... the supernatural *per se* was entirely credible ... If Mr Stevenson had written his great masterpiece about 1590–1650, Dr Jekyll would have made a compact with the devil. In 1886 Dr Jekyll sends to the Bond Street chemists for some rare

---

92 Dawn Keetley, 'Six Theses on Plant Horror', in Dawn Keetley and Angela Tenga (eds), *Plant Horror: Approaches to the Monstrous Vegetal in Fiction and Film* (Basingstoke: Palgrave Macmillan, 2016), pp. 1–30; See also T. S. Miller, 'Lives of the monster plants: the revenge of the vegetable in the age of animal studies', *The Journal of the Fantastic in the Arts* 23:3 (2012): 460–79.
93 Lombroso, *Criminal*, p. 222. 94 Tuke, 'Case of moral insanity', p. 365.
95 Tuke, 'Case of moral insanity', p. 365.

CASE OF MORAL INSANITY.

Fig.19.7: Daniel Hack Tuke, 'W. B.' 'Case of Moral Insanity' (1885). Author's photograph.

drugs.'[96] These three comments reveal the Victorian cultural investment in the Middle (or 'Dark') Ages, and demonstrate how that past was used to make sense of a world that had been irrevocably changed by Darwinist materialism and evolutionary biology.

The primeval, medieval, and modern; the biological and the cultural; and savagery and civilisation coincide in remarkable ways in 'The Novel of the Black Seal' of *The Three Impostors*. For example, almost in the same instance that Machen's Professor Gregg witnesses a slimy tentacle burst from Jervase Craddock's body, he notices 'the quaint and Gothic design, the angles between the arches, and the silvery gray' of an ancient stone bridge.[97] The slimy tentacle is a biological inheritance, as the bridge – 'a mystical allegory' of an immaterial, spiritual 'passage

---

96 Arthur Machen, *Selected Letters: The Private Writings of the Master of the Macabre*, edited by Roger Dobson, Godfrey Brangham and R. A. Gilbert (Wellingborough: Aquarian Press, 1988), p. 73.
97 Machen, 'Three Impostors', p. 129.

from one world to another' – is a cultural inheritance.[98] On another occasion, while the professor thinks, simultaneously, about ancient cultures, the powers lodged in the protoplasm of snails, and the Darwinian 'theory of reversion,' he focuses on a newspaper article about the disappearance and possible murder of a country girl from the Welsh Grey Hills:

> It was ... to all appearance the usual sordid tragedy of the village—a young girl unaccountably missing, and evil rumour blatant and busy with her reputation ... A flight to London or Liverpool, or an undiscovered body lying with a weight about its neck in the foul depths of a woodland pool, or perhaps murder.[99]

As the professor scans the newspaper report, his mind on murder, 'a flash of thought' passes through him 'with the violence of an electric shock': that the ancient 'horrible race of the hills still survived'. This extraordinary circumstance would be tantamount, he thinks, to a professor of natural science suddenly encountering in a quiet English woodland 'the slimy and loathsome terror of the ichthyosaurus, the original of the stories of the awful worms killed by valorous knights, or ... the pterodactyl, the dragon of tradition'.[100]

The juxtaposition, in the professor's mind, of all these otherwise diverse elements reveals, as Darwin's theories had, the interconnectedness of life, through time and space. In the Middle Ages, prehistoric monsters were consigned to the edges of manuscripts and frozen in stone carvings where they were vanquished by valorous knights; the ichthyosaurus and pterodactyl were made safe in myth. But Darwin had torn away the drapery of medieval myth to reveal the monstrous proximity of species. Modern humans were biologically connected, as Professor Gregg realises, to the pterodactyl as much as to the 'evil' and 'unchanged and unchangeable' ancient people 'of Gothic legend'.[101] That Gothic architecture and medieval beasts intrude in the vision and thoughts of a Victorian scientist, as he mulls over modern-day mysteries, reminds readers that savagery, criminality and violence could neither be consigned to the margins of society nor expunged by civilisation.

This significant theme takes many forms in Machen's canon and in *fin-de-siècle* Gothic literature more generally. In Machen's 'The White People' (*c*. late 1890s), an eccentric bibliophile named Ambrose suggests that 'the

---

98 Machen, 'Three Impostors', p. 129. 99 Machen, 'Three Impostors', p. 136.
100 Machen, 'Three Impostors', p. 137.
101 Machen, 'Three Impostors', p. 137; incidentally, Dyson is described as 'unchanged and unchangeable' in 'The Inmost Light'.

materialism of the age' had suppressed the extremes of 'sanctity' and 'evil', yet his own desires and the stories that he reveals indicate precisely the opposite.[102] Ambrose bemoans the fact that scientific rationality and materialism had rendered moderns incapable of feeling the heightened passions and extreme sensations that their medieval and primeval ancestors had experienced. Contemporary historians could only plod over dusty antiquarian books while palaeontologists studied fossilised bones ('no palaeontologist could show you a *live* pterodactyl').[103] The drunk labourer who 'kicks his irritating and injudicious wife to death' in some metropolitan slum could not hold a candle to historical figures and their acts of *real* monstrosity, such as those performed by the medieval knight Gilles de Rais, who fought alongside Joan of Arc, but was a sadistic serial child killer.[104] That Ambrose takes such delight in recounting, from his armchair, this history as well as the secret seductive horrors of the ancient, mysterious White People, indicates the unchanged and unchangeable quality of human violence.

The Dark Ages of Gilles de Rais was not, though, the glorious Middle Ages of Gothic Revivalists like John Ruskin. For revivalists, as for many Victorians, feudal society had developed higher-order virtues and values in its struggle against primeval lust and bloodthirsty savagery. Gothic architectural features, including flying buttresses, pointed arches, jutting towers and spires, steeply sloping roofs, decorative tracery, chimeras and gargoyles, embodied heightened passions and sensations, but these were godly. Such competing genealogies are discernible in Gothic literature that portrays the ascents and the descents, the evolutions and devolutions, of human experience. In the late nineteenth century, Gothic writers were challenged by genealogical questions, including that one posed by Darwin in the conclusion to *Descent*: could moderns claim the sympathetic baboon or the violent human savage as their forebearer? Either way, in spite of such values as sympathy, benevolence and even a 'god-like intellect', humans bore 'the indelible stamp' of their 'lowly origin' within and on the surface of their 'bodily frame'.[105] In Gothic writing, this lowly origin took modern form as sadistic criminal monsters whose degenerate minds and bodies threatened civilised society, and as atavistic flesh-eating plants whose natural 'criminality' was coaxed out by experimental scientists. These monsters were as much a reimagining of biological as cultural history.

---

102 Arthur Machen, 'The White People', in Worth (ed.), *The Great God Pan*, pp. 261–93 (p. 266).
103 Machen, 'The White People', p. 267. 104 Machen, 'The White People', pp. 265–6.
105 Darwin, *Descent*, p. 619.

2.20

Gothic and the Coming of the Railways

WILLIAM HUGHES

Railways, historically, represent change. They are a dynamic force, rendering obsolete other modes of transport and communication – the stagecoach and the canal barge, most notably – and imposing a new cultural regime founded upon a pervasive predictability manifested in regulated speed and adherence to centrally printed timetables. In the British context, the cultural changes wrought by the development of an industrialised transport network – which began in earnest in the mid-1820s and reached a speculative peak in the so-called 'Railway Mania' of the 1840s – were both profound and enduring.

The impact of railway expansion is perceptible as much in its imposition upon cultural geography as on the physical landscape. Railways impose connection not merely by way of an enclosing network of steel rails and timber cross-ties – these components in themselves being mass-produced rather than artisan consumables – but also by way of the economic interdependence through which the provinces are brought more firmly into the orbit and interests of the metropolis, and by the implicit imposition of a centralised control upon hitherto distant or neglected spaces at the borders or margins of national geography and cultural consciousness. Local independence and regional distinctions are implicitly challenged through communicative connection to the metropolitan centre or to a subaltern regional equivalent. Hence, historic place-names are formally adjusted to suit metropolitan linguistic convenience, consequently enduring the further indignity of mispronunciation and distortion.[1] Newspapers, carried by rail from the metropolis, likewise prioritise national issues as matters for immediate concern over and above specifically regional ones.[2] Finally, consulting engineers

---

1 See, for example, Thomas Morgan, *Hand-Book of the Origin of Place Names in Wales and Monmouthshire* (Merthyr Tydfil: Printed for the Author, 1887), pp. 3, 105, 122, 135.
2 According to one anonymous commentator, writing in 1883, 'As a rule, the provincial dailies will not stand comparison with the metropolitan': in England at this time roughly a third of newspapers were published from the capital city. See Anon., 'Newspapers', in

redirect established roads and waterways to facilitate the new (and significantly named) 'permanent way' of the railway, and peripatetic architects supplant traditional and localised building styles and materials in the erection of institutional edifices whose origins lie elsewhere in time and space.[3] Even in the British colonies, railway infrastructure was frequently modelled upon an Anglocentric domestic paradigm and underwritten with British capital, its presence enforcing a unifying colonist culture upon an often unwilling indigenous population.[4]

The easy cliché that railways were an unequivocal emblem of 'progress' in Victorian culture thus appears highly questionable.[5] If anything, the influence of the railways was a reflex of the power vested in distant and arbitrary institutions and individuals, these enjoying limited accountability for their actions and exercising at best a nominal duty of care with regard to customers, employees and the physical environment. Even time itself was subject to the demands placed upon its persistence by the railway companies: by the 1840s the Great Western Railway was sufficiently confident to establish a synchronised 'Railway Time' across its linear network, with regional railway clocks calibrated to Greenwich Mean Time in preference to the local solar zenith, and though the imposition of standard time across the country met with some local resistance, full compliance was achieved by 1880.[6] Such things bent the nation to a new industrial servitude. Railways, though peculiarly linked to a mobile modernity, thus simultaneously embody something of the feudal within their capacity to impose a tyranny of conformity, a culture of compliance, upon the places they connect. Their very modernity is, perversely, a reversion to Gothic modes of arbitrary power. The engines of

---

John M. Ross (ed.), *The Illustrated Globe Encyclopædia of Universal Information*, 12 vols (London: Thomas C. Jack, 1883), vol. 8, pp. 411–15 (pp. 412–13).

3 Paul Atterbury, 'Steam and Speed: Industry, Transport and Communications', in John M. Mackenzie (ed.), *The Victorian Vision: Inventing New Britain* (London: V&A Publications, 2001), pp. 147–71 (p. 159).

4 Atterbury, 'Steam and Speed', in Mackenzie (ed.), *The Victorian Vision*, pp. 159–61. Among many colonial examples, Mumbai's significantly named Victoria terminus (1878–82) was designed for the Great Indian Peninsula Railway by the English architect Frederick William Stevens in a style that imbricated European Gothic with a British interpretation of Indian elements. See Fred S. Kleiner, *Gardner's Art Through the Ages: Non-Western Perspectives*, 13th edition (Boston MA: Wadsworth, 2010), pp. 40–1.

5 The comparative punctuality of railways is, of course, a component of Jonathan Harker's ongoing critique of European difference during his journey from Exeter to Transylvania. See Bram Stoker, *Dracula*, edited by William Hughes and Diane Mason (Bath: Artswork Books, 2007), pp. 41, 43.

6 Wolfgang Schivelbusch, *The Railway Journey: The Industrialization of Time and Space in the Nineteenth Century* (Berkeley: University of California Press, 1986), pp. 42–4.

locomotion, in other words, may equally enforce the will of an effective engine of oppression.

It is this capacity to embody past and present simultaneously, to *facilitate* the intrusion of the past *into* the present, that makes railways peculiarly and perversely Gothic. Surprisingly, little has been written to date upon the Gothic nature of the British rail network itself, though the recurrent motif of *travel* by rail into an uncanny regionality *beyond* has on occasion been explored by way of the genre.[7] There remains, however, a rich and largely unacknowledged context of Gothic signification outside of this latter motif, a body of meaning which in many respects betrays its Gothic credentials far more openly than might be expected. Indeed, an essentially Gothic discourse arguably configures many aspects of how the physicality of the rail network is comprehended, and how its momentary construction and enduring infrastructure impose consequences for both the natural and the built environment – and for those who dwell in those places. The traveller, engaged in the process of travelling – rather than at the point of arrival – is likewise an individual placed in an uncanny relationship with both terrain and mode of travel, and his or her vulnerability in transit remain issues hardly touched upon in Gothic criticism. Finally, the psychological implications of industrialisation, the anxious burden of stress and obsessive observance imposed upon those who are tasked with maintaining the punctuality and good order of the railway network, demand consideration with the oppressive working environment of the Victorian period serving a function analogous to the imprisoning castles and inquisitorial chambers of the earlier Gothic genre.

Mechanical Horror: The Destructive Power of Locomotion

The railway, being both mechanical and institutional, is inhuman and inhumane. Thomas Carlyle, in *Sartor Resartus* (1836), had the fictional Herr Teufelsdröckh configure the raw power of the locomotive as a metaphor for a world perceived as both secular and meaningless in its arbitrary relationship to humanity:

---

7 See, for example, William Hughes, 'The Uncanny Space of Regionality: Gothic Beyond the Metropolis', in William Hughes and Ruth Heholt (eds), *Gothic Britain: Dark Places in the Provinces and Margins of the British Isles* (Cardiff: University of Wales Press, 2018), pp. 1–24 (pp. 11–14); Paul Young, 'Rambles beyond railways: gothicised place and globalised space in Victorian Cornwall', *Gothic Studies* 13:1 (May 2011): 55–74.

> To me the Universe was all void of Life, of Purpose, of Volition, even of Hostility: it was one huge, dead, immeasurable Steam-engine, rolling on, in its dead indifference, to grind me limb from limb.[8]

Arbitrary and totalitarian in its extensive compass of human life and aspirations, the railway is a power, as Dickens's narrator in *Dombey and Son* (1848) suggests, 'defiant of all paths and roads, piercing through the heart of every obstacle, and dragging living creatures of all classes, ages, and degrees behind it': as such it is 'a type of the triumphant monster, Death'.[9]

Death, indeed, has long occupied a place in the popular perception of the rail network. The first recorded fatality associated with rail travel occurred on 15 September 1830, the day of the ceremonial opening of the Liverpool and Manchester Railway, when the statesman William Huskisson 'missed his footing' when entering a carriage, fell backwards and was run over by Stephenson's Rocket, his body being, in the words of a contemporary newspaper report, 'left bleeding and mangled before his friends!'[10] *Dombey and Son*, published some 18 years after this fatality, includes a strikingly similar railway accident, where the treacherous Mr Carker, having also staggered backwards, 'was beaten down, caught up, and whirled away upon a jagged mill, that spun him round and round, and struck him limb from limb ... and cast his mutilated fragments in the air'.[11] Dickens's emphasis upon the frailty of the human body in the face of mobile and intractable steel is not unique: George Eliot, in *Felix Holt, The Radical* (1866), has an early nineteenth-century commentator likewise foresee a more general dismemberment following the death of Huskisson, with 'the ruined country strewn with shattered limbs' as a consequence of railway misadventure.[12] The language associated with railway accidents has a characteristically violent tone: witness, for example, the title of one article on railway safety published in Dickens's *Household Words* in 1851 which bore the uncompromising title 'Need railway travellers be smashed?'[13]

---

8 Thomas Carlyle, *Sartor Resartus: The Life and Opinions of Herr Teufelsdröckh* (London: Oxford University Press, 1943), p. 142.
9 Charles Dickens, *Dealings with the Firm of Dombey and Son, Wholesale, Retail and for Exportation*, edited by Peter Fairclough (Harmondsworth: Penguin, 1981), p. 354.
10 Anon., 'Death of Mr Huskisson', *Morning Post*, 18 September 1830, p. 3, col. 4.
11 Dickens, *Dombey and Son*, p. 875. Such accidents were far from rare. See Anon., 'Three Railway Accidents in Lancashire', *Daily News*, 15 October 1855, p. 3, col. 4.
12 George Eliot, *Felix Holt, The Radical*, edited by Peter Coveney (Harmondsworth: Penguin, 1975), p. 80.
13 Anon., [Henry Morley], 'Need railway travellers be smashed?', *Household Words* 4:88 (29 November 1851): 217–21.

Gothic and the Coming of the Railways

The capacity of the railway to impact upon collective as well as individual existence is, again, a theme sporadically taken up in Gothic-inflected nineteenth-century popular fiction. The changes brought by the construction of the permanent way and through associated civil engineering have a profound environmental and cultural impact, and even though these changes need not be literally fatal, they are invariably destructive in their effects upon landscape and social identity. Dickens is, again, a trenchant commentator upon this fearful reshaping – and redefinition – of the familiar and the established. In *Dombey and Son*, the construction of the London to Birmingham Railway by way of Camden Town in the mid-1830s is conveyed first through the language of geological upheaval and latterly in more biblical images of apocalypse. The narrator records how:

> The first shock of a great earthquake had, just at that period, rent the whole neighbourhood to its centre. Traces of its course were visible on every side. Houses were knocked down; streets broken through and stopped; deep pits and trenches dug in the ground; enormous heaps of earth and clay thrown up; buildings that were undermined and shaking, propped by great beams of wood.[14]

Though the narrator states that the 'Hot springs and fiery eruptions' that punctuate this newly made wasteland are 'the usual attendants upon earthquakes', the subsequent emphasis placed upon 'the glare and roar of flames' and 'mounds of ashes' is more redolent of a theological hell than of seismic upheaval.[15] The narrator, though, subtly turns the focus of his dis-ease from mere physical destruction to a bleaker vision of existential pointlessness. The account continues:

> Here, a chaos of carts, overthrown and jumbled together, lay topsy-turvy at the bottom of a steep unnatural hill; there, confused treasures of iron soaked and rusted in something that had accidentally become a pond. Everywhere were bridges that led nowhere; thoroughfares that were wholly impassable; Babel towers of chimneys, wanting half their height; temporary wooden houses and enclosures, in the most unlikely situations; carcases of ragged tenements, and fragments of unfinished walls and arches, and piles of scaffolding and wildernesses of bricks, and giant forms of cranes, and tripods straddling above nothing.[16]

The overwhelming chaos of the contemporary, emphasised as it is by Dickens's pointed use of semi-colons, ensheathes the more disturbing

---

14 Dickens, *Dombey and Son*, p. 120.   15 Dickens, *Dombey and Son*, p. 121.
16 Dickens, *Dombey and Son*, pp. 120–1.

implications of what is actually happening to a residential and commercial environment that had been progressively developed as such from as early as 1791. Essentially, the narrator asserts that, at the temporal point of observation, nothing is complete nor seems to be in hope of imminent completion; that demolition and construction have become elided into one chaotic mass; that there is no end to the journey – nor any substantive terminus to a railway that does not seem to have satisfactorily *begun*. What was once purposeful and meaningful is now purposeless and meaningless at the very point when it ostensibly accedes to impending futurity. What was once Camden Town is now a non-place, its former boundaries and certainties blurred and obscured by 'a hundred thousand shapes and substances of incompleteness'. As the narrator succinctly – and ironically – phrases it, 'the yet unfinished and unopened Railroad was in progress; and, from the very core of all this dire disorder, trailed smoothly away, upon its mighty course of civilisation and improvement'. Thus, the coming of the railway in all its enduring incompleteness had 'wholly changed the law and custom of the neighbourhood', even to the extent that a newly constructed local hostelry displays the implicitly anachronistic title of 'The Railway Arms', and 'the old-established Ham and Beef Shop had become the Railway Eating House'.[17] All is changed, profoundly and seemingly permanently, and what is being averred in Dickens's purple prose is that the progress of the railway, be it indefinitely deferred or ultimately irresistible, implies the destruction and dismemberment of the landmarks – literal and figurative – of any culture located in its path, just as much as it must lead to the literal death and likely dismemberment of the unfortunate individual who is thrown across its tracks.

Entrapment and Enclosure: Passengers in Peril

Similar imperilment, needless to say, may befall those members of the public who entrust their lives to the mobile security of the railway carriage, as Dickens himself was to appreciate practically in 1865, some 17 years after the publication of Dombey and Son.[18] Drawing, perhaps, upon the scandalous – and highly profitable – revelations advanced by the popular press, writers of fiction were quick to appreciate the possibilities of the railway carriage as a place of both adventure and peril. For

---

17 Dickens, *Dombey and Son*, p. 121.
18 Dickens was involved in a serious accident at Staplehurst, Kent, on the South Eastern Railway on Saturday, 9 June 1865. See John Forster, *The Life of Charles Dickens* (London: Chapman and Hall, 1892), pp. 573–4, 626.

the popular press, the carriage was a semi-public place in which the career criminal might successfully masquerade as a respectable citizen.[19] Hence, as a traveller in any class of carriage, one might be 'amused or fleeced by the acute, eager, ever-journeying swindlers who, with persuasive voice and marvellous finger dexterity, live upon the three-card trick or other thieving game'.[20] More seriously, though, the possibility of physical assault within the railway carriage became a standard of scandalous journalism and popular fiction alike.

In part, this tendency was a consequence of the physical structure of railway carriages. The modern railway carriage, in Britain at least, is what is termed an 'open' carriage – that is, one in which all the public seats are located within a relatively undivided linear space traversed by a central gangway or aisle. All those travelling, therefore, are essentially visible to their fellow passengers as well as to entrained railway officials, and thus remain theoretically safe within the gaze of altruistic community. The Victorian railway coach was, however, more often than not a version of the compartment carriage, this being a conveyance made up of several discrete spaces. Until the arrival of the longer bogie coach, these spaces were seldom accessible by way of an adjacent on-train corridor – though in Third Class the divisions between compartments might not reach to the actual ceiling of the carriage. For First- and Second-Class passengers, however, the very barriers between each compartment that ensured privacy effectively enforced imprisonment for, with external doors frequently being locked upon departure or else not being fitted with interior handles capable of releasing their locks, any passenger placed in the company of an undesirable fellow traveller had only their own resources to depend upon in the event of violence or other assault. The communication cord, a mechanical device by which a passenger might alert the driver to a problem within their carriage while

19 In Britain, railway carriages were customarily divided between First, Second and Third Class following the original fare structure of the Liverpool and Manchester Railway. Second-Class travel declined as a practice across the nineteenth century and is conventionally presumed to have finally ended in the late 1930s. British railway companies, though, retained a two-tier labelling of First and Third Class carriages and compartments until 1956: the current terminology of Standard (rather than Second) Class conveyance was initiated in 1988.
20 John Pendleton, *Our Railways: Their Origin, Development, Incident and Romance* (London: Cassell and Company, 1894), p. 5. This was a theme explored, albeit in an American context, by F. Scott Fitzgerald in his 1927 supernatural story 'A Short Trip Home', in Mike Ashley (ed.), *The Platform Edge: Uncanny Tales of the Railways* (London: British Library, 2019), pp. 257–83.

the train was in motion, became legally mandatory in the United Kingdom as late as 1868.[21]

Within the curtilage of the railway compartment, at least until the mandatory provision of the communication cord, the ambience of travel might be considered as being somewhat analogous to that of a much earlier period of history – and, indeed, to that history as reflected in the earliest phase of Gothic fiction. If the imposing façade of the British railway terminus – which frequently resembled a Gothic cathedral, palace or castle[22] – was calculated to inspire confidence both in the enduring financial stability of the operating company and the physical comforts afforded to travellers by its timetabled services, the ferro-vitreous train shed itself was characteristically more reminiscent of the airy modernity of Joseph Paxton's Crystal Palace of 1851. The passenger carriages marshalled beneath the glazed canopy of that station, though, resembled internally – and in the earliest days, externally, also – the horse-drawn coaches of the past.[23] It is in such places, and no doubt as a consequence of the supposedly libidinous effect of the badly sprung coaches in motion, that sexual adventures – consensual or otherwise – may take place. Such things have a historical resonance in Gothic. The sensible heroine of eighteenth-century Female Gothic, confined within a horse-drawn conveyance by masculine agency, is tantalised and taunted by the presence of a window that provides a view of, but no exit to, that outside world in which she might be properly protected by the indignation of moral community.[24] That heroine, however, tends to survive, her physical and moral integrity characteristically intact. In the more prosaic nineteenth century the female traveller, though possibly less likely to be actually abducted by rail, was perhaps more substantially imperilled by the amorous intentions of fellow travellers. Female passengers, indeed, were frequently impelled to remove themselves from the compartment in such cases, on occasions having to cling

---

21 Under the Regulation of Railways Act 1868, Section 22, passengers were provided with a device that communicated with the driver on trains scheduled to travel more than twenty miles in distance. In 1889 the legislation was revisited and the devices modified so that they would apply the brakes upon an alarm being raised.

22 Consider here, for example, the Gothic and Tudor façades of Temple Meads Station (1839–41), Bristol; Citadel Station (1847–8), Carlisle; and St Pancras Station (1867–76), London.

23 Anon., *Rocket 150: 150th Anniversary of the Liverpool and Manchester Railway 1830–1980: Official Handbook* (London: British Rail, 1980), pp. 6, 12, 36.

24 See, for example, Ann Radcliffe, *The Mysteries of Udolpho*, edited by Bonamy Dobrée (Oxford: Oxford University Press, 1981), pp. 224–7. With regard to the imperilled but invariably competent heroine of Female Gothic, see Ellen Moers, *Literary Women: The Great Writers* (London: W. H. Allen, 1977), pp. 126, 137–38; Carol Margaret Davison, *Gothic Literature 1764–1824* (Cardiff: University of Wales Press, 2009), pp. 84–90.

to uncertain footholds on the outside of their own or an adjacent carriage at risk to life and limb.

Such was the case, for example, when Colonel Valentine Baker attempted to molest Miss Rebecca Kate Dickinson, 'an exceedingly ladylike girl', in a First-Class railway compartment on 18 June 1875. Baker, a stranger to Miss Dickinson, first engaged her in verbal pleasantries, but then attempted to embrace and kiss her. Rebuffing his suit, she tried unsuccessfully to summon help by way of the communication cord, whereupon – in her own words – 'He forced me back into the corner [of the compartment] and pressed me to the back of the carriage.' If this were not sufficiently outrageous in itself, Baker then – as Dickinson recalled – 'kissed me on the lips', before 'he sank down close in front of me, and I felt his hand underneath by [sic] dress, on my stocking, above my boot'.[25] With remarkable courage, Miss Dickinson was able to escape from the compartment, completing her journey upon the external running board of the carriage before calling assistance to apprehend her assailant. The trial against Baker was premised upon whether he had attempted to ravish – that is, rape – Miss Dickinson; whether it was a case of indecent assault; or else one of common assault.[26] Baker was convicted of indecent assault, gaoled for a year without hard labour, and fined £500 plus costs. He quitted the country upon his release.[27]

Such accounts of predatory fellow travellers are far from rare, and attracted national as well as regional attention.[28] It is thus hardly surprising that their rhetoric informs if not generic Gothic fiction then at least an adjacent trope in later nineteenth-century writing, the pornographic memoir. The memoir *My Secret Life* (c. 1890) by the pseudonymous 'Walter' is a controversial work, as much for its uncertain bibliographical history and disputed authorship as for the somewhat graphic nature of

---

25 The lady's name is spelled as Dickenson in some accounts. Anon., 'The Charge Against Colonel Valentine Baker', *Southampton Herald*, 26 June 1875, p. 7, col. 3.

26 Anon., 'The Charge Against Colonel Valentine Baker', *Southampton Herald*, 31 July 1875, p. 7, col. 4. The act of kissing was in itself a potent indictment against Baker, for, as another newspaper noted, 'If any man kissed a woman against her will and to gratify any passion of his own that was an indecent assault.' See Anon., 'The Case of Colonel Valentine Baker', *Leeds Mercury*, 30 July 1875, p. 3, col. 6.

27 Anon., 'Trial and Conviction of Colonel Valentine Baker', *Bury and Norwich Post*, 3 August 1875, p. 8, col. 5. Upon his release, Baker enlisted in the Turkish Army, where he served with distinction. One of his obituary notices would seem to infer his social rehabilitation, his disgrace being referred to momentarily as a 'deplorable incident' quite incidental to his subsequent military career. See Anon, 'Death of General Valentine Baker', *Morning Post*, 18 November 1887, p. 2, col. 6.

28 See, for example, Anon., 'The Tamworth Railway Outrage', *Sheffield Independent*, 30 March 1892, p. 7, col. 3; Anon., 'The Assault on the Brighton Railway', *The Standard*, 13 May 1892, p. 3, col. 4.

the sexual acts it portrays and the carnal language in which these are phrased.²⁹ Though much of this ostensible memoir is scripted as preceding the general development of the railways in Britain, the narrator – the pseudonymous Walter himself – deploys rail travel as a backdrop to his improbably prolific amours in both France and England. Among these, one episode stands out as being essentially a palimpsest of the reportage surrounding the Baker case as well as other contemporary outrages. The narrator – who has expressed few, if any, qualms with regard to his own participation in sexual violence – is travelling from Aldershot to Waterloo – a route strikingly reminiscent of that taken by both Colonel Baker (who joined the London train at Liphook, but was based at Aldershot) and Dickinson (who was travelling from Midhurst to Dover via London). Like Baker, Walter joins the lady in a First-Class carriage, though the significant wink he gives the guard seems to indicate a masculine complicity in his fellow traveller's undoing. Like Baker, Walter engages the lady – whom he understands to be a kept woman – in conversation, talking, like the Colonel, of the London stage.³⁰ His suit rapidly progresses, her coquettishness facilitating an initial foray beneath her petticoats when, having squeezed or, rather, 'pinched [her] ankle', he 'rapidly ran [his] hand up to her knee, felt the garter, and just the flesh beyond'. Consensual as this encounter initially sounds – the lady, after all, willingly proffered her foot and ankle for Walter to fondle – the situation rapidly deteriorates into a more predatory violence. On his companion's again 'Coquettishly' placing her foot upon the opposing seat, Walter engages her with renewed vigour, and despite her protests – including her intention to call the guard, presumably via the communication cord, and stated intention to 'get out at the next station', Walter, in his own words, 'threw myself on my knees, lifted her petticoats, and got my face upon her thighs. Tho she resisted, my lust now unbridled made me strong. – Violently I got her thighs apart, my head between them.'³¹ Walter does not succeed (on this occasion) in literally penetrating her body, but instead exposes himself in such a way that his actions partake of both frottage and masturbation,

---

29 See Steven Marcus, *The Other Victorians: A Study of Sexuality and Pornography in Mid-Nineteenth-Century England* (London: Book Club Associates, 1970), pp. 77–82.
30 Anon., 'Alleged Outrage on a Lady', *Sheffield Independent*, 26 June 1875, Supplement, p. 9, col. 3; Anon., 'The Charge Against Colonel Valentine Baker', *The Times*, 25 June 1875, p. 11, col. 3.
31 Walter [pseud.], *My Secret Life*, vol. 7, ch. 2, excerpted in Shelly Klein (ed.), *Victorian Erotic Tales* (London: Michael O'Mara, 1995), pp. 7–20 (pp. 9, 10).

for 'I pulled out my prick and rubbed it hard against her calf.' After this, he has his fellow traveller masturbate him before he finally persuades her to engage in coitus as the train rocks unsteadily on its progress to Waterloo.[32]

Walter's frankness amplifies the somewhat more muted reportage of the court proceedings. Notably, one witness called to the trial of Colonel Baker was explicit that the defendant's 'dress was disarranged', and cross-examination of the prosecutrix in court revealed that though one of Baker's hands was deployed 'on my stockings above my boot', 'I did not see what he was doing with the other hand; but I have an impression what he was doing.'[33] Miss Dickinson's verbal coyness fails to dissipate the sense of outrage that ought to be felt by the gentlemanly, rather than caddish, reader. If *My Secret Life* is not generically a Gothic work, it – in common with the newspaper accounts of the trial of Colonel Baker – draws perceptibly upon the same suggestions of coercion, debasement and fear that manifest themselves in Gothic works from the eighteenth century through to the early twentieth.[34] In all of these works, and in contemporary newspaper reportage, the implication is that a woman is nowhere more vulnerable than when she is in transit – and where her travelling companions may be men who, for all their outward garb of status and respectability, remain a threat to her honour during the confinement of travel.[35]

---

32 Walter, *My Secret Life*, pp. 11–12.
33 Anon., 'The Charge Against Colonel Valentine Baker', *The Times*, 25 June 1875, p. 11, col. 4; Anon., 'Trial and Conviction of Colonel Valentine Baker', *Bury and Norwich Post*, 3 August 1875, p. 8, col. 5.
34 A temporally later counterpart to the eighteenth-century experiences of Ann Radcliffe's heroines might be Bram Stoker's Marjory Anita Drake, abducted by sea in a novel first published in 1902, she being ominously described as 'a bonnie bit lassie in the power o' wicked men'. See Bram Stoker, *The Mystery of the Sea*, intro. by Jessica de Mellow (Stroud: Sutton Publishing, 1997), p. 247.
35 As a coda to the Baker case and similar outrages, it might be noted that many Victorian railway companies subsequently introduced women-only compartments for the protection of female passengers. It should also be noted that blackmail might be as strong a motivation as lust, with one male commentator advising his fellows to always travel in the company of two or three others, for 'A particular sort of women [sic] invariably select either a smoking compartment, or a compartment where an unprotected man may be alone; and the male traveller must remember that no twelve men, honest and true, will believe the word of a man against the word of a fairly good-looking woman.' See Pendleton, *Our Railways*, p. 26. Characteristically, in Gothic fiction across the long nineteenth century, male travellers are more likely to face robbery than sexual assault on the railway, a consequence no doubt of the relative sexual conservatism of the period, Mary Louisa Molesworth's ambiguous 1894 tale 'The Man with the Cough' being a representative example. See Mary Louisa Molesworth, 'The Man with the Cough', in Ashley (ed.), *The Platform Edge*, pp. 87–105.

Quis custodiet ipsos custodes: Railway Servants and the Supernatural[36]

Those who travel, it is assumed, are to be protected by what have historically been termed 'railway servants' – that is, the station staff, entrained guards, signal-men and others who maintain the permanent way. Inevitably, of course, the care exercised by railway servants may be negligent – witness Charles Dickens's own involvement in a fatal accident caused by deficient signalling.[37] The railway servant is, by definition, a watchful servant – and is seldom a comedic servant in the Gothic sense. Too much of the freedom of mobility enjoyed by the traveller is contingent upon his – for in the nineteenth century most railway employees were male – submission to the discipline of responsible and unglamorous servitude.

Among the myriad employees of the railway, none engages so much mystique as the signal-man, a solitary personage whose participation in a chain of communication that literally runs parallel to the conveying rails facilitates the safe and punctual passage of traffic. Those who man the signal-box characteristically lack the garrulousness of the platform porter, the officiousness of the station master and the easy deportment of the navvy. Signal-men are solitary beings, seemingly absorbed in the railway rather than its passengers. As one Victorian commentator notes:

> The signalman is generally thoughtful. Whether his many-windowed cabin stands sentinel near the railway bridge that crosses a wide thoroughfare in a great city, and all about him is the roar of traffic and the hum of the multitude, or is perched on the breast of some crag, far away from big town and drowsy hamlet, in the midst of solitude only broken now and then by the voices of nature, or the shriek of the express engine as she tears through the dale, he gives no heed to his surroundings. His work occupies his thoughts. He moves carefully along his iron frame, which bristles with levers, pulling one this way, or pushing one that way, opening the track here, closing it there, and raising the signal to 'danger'.[38]

Indeed, 'The signalman is the last person one would suspect of frolic. To him, "life is no joke."'[39] It is 'no joke', of course, because life, much more than

---

36 Literally, 'Who shall guard the guardians themselves?': Juvenal, *The Satires*, 'Satire VI', 345, in Charles William Stocker (ed.), *The Satires of Persius and Juvenal*, 3rd edition (London: Longman, Brown & Co., 1845), pp. 204–72 (p. 240).
37 Anon., 'Dreadful Railway Accident at Staplehurst', *Caledonian Mercury*, 12 June 1865, p. 4, col. 1.
38 Pendleton, *Our Railways*, pp. 310–11.   39 Pendleton, *Our Railways*, p. 312.

punctuality, depends upon his absorption and watchfulness.[40] The signal-man polices an effective junction at which life and death may meet.

It is the this constant, isolated and anxious watchfulness that arguably motivates what is possibly the most celebrated example of railway-based Gothic, if not of British railway fiction more broadly: Charles Dickens's 'No. 1 Branch Line: The Signal-Man' (1866). Dickens's ostensibly supernatural narrative, in which the appearance of a beckoning spectre in the sight of the eponymous railway servant presages three successive fatal episodes, must necessarily be read in the light of actual events. The first of the three fictional incidents – understatedly referred to as 'The memorable accident on this Line' – is particularly reminiscent of the collision between two trains within Clayton Tunnel on the Brighton Line in 1861, the national reportage of which made much of the presence of a flag-wielding signal-man at the tunnel's mouth and the potential conflict between mechanical signalling apparatus and human judgement on the part of railway servants.[41] Dickens, though, may well have been aware of other incidents, such as the 1864 accident in Blackheath Tunnel or the 1866 collision and fire in Welwyn Tunnel, in which imperfect communications between signal-men, stations and train crews contributed to fatalities among passengers or railway employees.[42]

The physical location in which Dickens places his signal-man is, to be sure, redolent of Gothic desolation, and calculated to focus the mind upon gloomy and introspective concerns. The narrator notes how the signal-man, 'a dark sallow man', seems very much an extension or expression of the man-made environment he occupies, a railway cutting with an associated tunnel portal:

> His post was in as solitary and dismal a place as I ever saw. On either side, a dripping-wet wall of jagged stone, excluding all view but a strip of sky; the perspective one way, only a crooked prolongation of this great dungeon; the shorter perspective in the other direction, terminating in a gloomy red light, and the gloomier entrance to a black tunnel, in whose massive architecture

---

40 Railway accidents in which signal-men are questioned regarding, or censured because of, deficient signalling practice are strikingly common in Victorian newspaper reportage. See, for example, Anon., 'The Dreadful Collision on the Hampstead Junction Line', *Jackson's Oxford Journal*, 14 September 1861, p. 3, cols. 5–6; Anon., 'The Paisley Collision', *Dundee Courier*, 15 September 1880, p. 3, col. 4; Anon., 'The Binegar Railway Collision', *Southampton Herald*, 2 June 1886, p. 3, col. 7.

41 The collision occurred on 25 August 1861, the inquest being convened shortly afterwards. See Anon., 'The Railway Accident at Clayton Tunnel', *Liverpool Mercury*, 3 September 1861, p. 5, col. 2; Anon., 'The Catastrophe on the London and Brighton Railway', *Jackson's Oxford Journal*, 14 September 1861, p. 3, col. 5.

42 Anon., 'The Blackheath Tunnel Accident', *Bell's Life in London and Sporting Chronicle*, 14 January 1865, p. 5, col. 6; Anon., 'The Late Railway Accident', *Essex Standard*, 20 June 1866, p. 4, col. 3.

there was a barbarous, depressing, and forbidding air. So little sunlight ever found its way to this spot, that it had an earthy deadly smell; and so much cold wind rushed through it, that it struck chill to me, as if I had left the natural world.[43]

Such a restricted compass of vision might well serve to focus consciousness, though it is *not* the sky – freedom, the outside world – upon which this employee-prisoner fixes his obsessive gaze. Indeed, he seldom rises above his narrow enclosure and, even then, is anxiously mindful of 'being at all times liable to be called by his electric bell'.[44] It is the tunnel's mouth and the signal which anticipates, and reacts to, the sporadic passing of trains that apparently fixates him. The passage of trains, it is suggested, regulates his hours, and this timetabled man of 'exactness and watchfulness' has ostensibly contoured 'the routine of his life' around sporadic calls to action: 'To change that signal, to trim those lights, and to turn this iron handle now and then.'[45] The narrator deems him, on first acquaintance. 'a contented man', though it is the signal-man himself who corrects his misapprehension.[46]

The signal-man's 'exact and vigilant demeanour' – frequently drawn to the reader's attention by the narrator – is the telling symptom of a pathological attentiveness.[47] Such a fixed pattern of observance is hardly a sign of health but rather one of compulsive obsession, a vigilance which subsumes the present and all its certain demands into an abstracted futurity. Fundamentally, the narrator misreads the demeanour of the signal-man. He is not 'one of the safest of men to be employed in that capacity', for his morbid gaze is in fact *not* appendant upon the signal, the approaching train or the tunnel: its focus, if not the spectre itself, is the prospect of the spectre's manifestation and the assumed calamity that its presence portends.[48] If both mentally healthy and true to his professional calling, the signal-man should anticipate that which is coming with expedient immediacy: the next train, which he must allow to clear both signal and tunnel in safety in order to prevent a subterranean accident such as those at Clayton, Blackheath or Welwyn. Instead, though, he anticipates an uncertain *something* – something which may come not immediately and as predicted by the ring of a communicative electric bell, but which will appear suddenly, at some indeterminate

---

43 Charles Dickens, 'Mugby Junction. No. 1 Branch Line. The Signal-Man', in *Selected Short Fiction*, edited by Deborah A. Thomas (Harmondsworth: Penguin, 1977), pp. 78–90 (p. 79).
44 Dickens, 'The Signal-Man', p. 81.   45 Dickens, 'The Signal-Man', pp. 80–1.
46 Dickens, 'The Signal-Man', p. 82.   47 Dickens, 'The Signal-Man', p. 81.
48 Dickens, 'The Signal-Man', pp. 81–2.

point in the future and in a form neither consistent or expected, for all three fatalities associated with the spectre's appearance are different, and they follow the portent with no exactness of periodicity.[49] It is thus that the supposedly ordered and regulated mind of the signal-man is disturbed by *knowing* that the presence of this apparently supernatural messenger betokens – in the same way that the electric bell which informs the signal cabin that an approaching train has entered its specific responsibility – a coming danger whose nature and imminence are yet *not* known.

The psychological horror that afflicts the signal-man is thus premised upon existential powerlessness and pervasive uncertainty, a condition of being that contrasts markedly with the supposed puissance and requisite decisiveness associated with his vigilant guardianship of life and property. With a single action – the raising of a flag, the displaying of a lamp, the pulling of a signal lever – he may command a speeding train to a sudden and decisive halt. That imperative, however, may only be deployed in the comprehension of an actual – rather than a supposed – danger. A spectre's warning is less substantial than one derived from another signal-man. As he notes:

> 'If I telegraph danger, on either side of me, or on both, I can give no reason for it', he went on, wiping the palms of his hands, 'I should get into trouble and do no good. They would think I was mad. This is the way it would work: Message: "Danger! Take care!" Answer: "What danger? Where?" Message: "Don't know. But for God's sake take care!" They would displace me. What else could they do?'[50]

The narrator's attempts to dismiss the signal-man's visions as a disorder of the optical nerves or to subject him to conventional medical diagnosis are, again, a misreading of the whole affliction.[51] He is subject to, in his own words, 'a cruel haunting of *me*'.[52] It is not the ghost that is the problem but the ghost-seer, not the ghost's communication but the recipient's inability to pass it further down the line. The signal-man's death, beneath the very wheels of a train under his guardianship, is seemingly inevitable. If it is him rather than the line that is haunted, then his removal will literally clear the way and allow the chain of communication to persist unbroken and with certainty. Whatever the case, it is implicit that the signal-man is, in his own mind, redundant, for if he receives, he does not understand, and what he receives he fails to transmit. As the narrator observes, 'It was the mental torture of a conscientious man, oppressed beyond endurance by an unintelligible

---

49 Dickens, 'The Signal-Man', pp. 84, 85, 86.   50 Dickens, 'The Signal-Man', p. 87.
51 Dickens, 'The Signal-Man', pp. 84, 88.   52 Dickens, 'The Signal-Man', pp. 84, 88.

responsibility involving life.'⁵³ It is too easy to comprehend the signal-man's death as being a consequence of an almost mesmeric fascination with the gestures and words of the driver of the locomotive that runs him down, these being identical to those of the portentous spectre. It would be, perhaps, more just to contemplate it as a suicide, a final closure of the communication actively sought by one hitherto caught up in its uncertainty.

Though Dickens's narrative is perhaps the best-known Victorian tale of the supernatural in railway context, it is by no means the sole exemplar. Indeed, it is not unique in its specific focus upon dutiful servitude, for in the short anonymous 1878 tale 'A Desperate Run', published in the Christmas periodical *The Mistletoe Bough*, 'Evan Wynne, the pointsman' maintains his guardianship even after death, his ghost warning the tale's narrator safely to divert a train from one track to another, while the railway servant's body lies lifeless across a – no doubt self-improving – book in his trackside cabin.⁵⁴ The ambivalently possessed communicative technology of Dickens's signal box is likewise echoed in the ghost story 'Railhead' by Perceval Landon, a 1908 tale of pioneer American railroading, recounted in a British colonial context.⁵⁵ The railway servant, indeed, exhibits at times a selfless loyalty equal to that of those faithful domestic retainers to be found elsewhere in the genre.

Conclusion: Ghosts in – and on – the Machine

There ought to be no room, in a mechanical age, for a ghost *in* the machine – though supernatural fictions from the mid-nineteenth century through to the later twentieth are undoubtedly freighted with narratives of cursed engines, disappearing rolling stock and phantom expresses. Tales involving spectres *on* the machine are, if anything, even more frequently encountered in Victorian and Edwardian supernatural fiction. The footplate of the locomotive and the enclosed space of the carriage are but two arenas in which ghostly dramas characteristically – and *repeatedly* – play themselves out in the railway ghost story.

It is perhaps this repetition of manifestation that best facilitates the fictional interaction between the ambivalent presence of the supernatural and the

---

53 Dickens, 'The Signal-Man', p. 87.
54 A pointsman sets or changes points (turnouts, in American English), having a less extensive oversight than a signal-man. See Anon., 'A Desperate Run', in Ashley (ed.), *The Platform Edge*, pp. 47–50.
55 See Ashley (ed.), *The Platform Edge*, pp. 109–18 (p. 114). In this case, the ghostly telegraph communicates to warn the station master of an impending crime rather than portending an accident on the line.

uncompromising materiality of the railway itself. In Gothic fictions of the railway, ghosts seemingly aspire to a new regularity of being, an institutionalisation that makes them as purposeful as the modern infrastructure they now haunt. Far from being the dusty spectres of a distant past, they may be seen increasingly as a phenomenon whose presence is, if not actually timetabled, then at least signalled in its significance for those who approach and perceive it.[56] Ghosts are, on the whole, highly purposeful entities, their appearances inclined to inform, to remind or to provoke those who witness them. There are very few ghosts, arguably, who haunt to no purpose. Thus, though the haunted house may retain its place as a central venue for uncanny recollections of past deeds, the railway provides, particularly from the later nineteenth century, a corresponding venue in which such things may be variously exposed or revenged. Thus, in Victor Whitechurch's 'The Strange Story of Engine Number 651' (1902), a footplate murder is regularly re-enacted on the locomotive on which it took place, communicating the crime to other railway staff and, in an act of ostensible revenge for the atrocity, involving the murderer in a fatal railway accident.[57] Similarly, the events leading up to a fatal crash, this being the fault of a signal-man drunk at his post, are re-enacted each night in 'A Strange Night' (1897) by Lucy Gertrude Moberley: again, as it were, the ghost – which is explicitly a compound of the organic *and* inorganic components of an express train – is engaged in an act of communication as much as of memorialisation.[58] The ghostly, in other words, has gained meaningfulness not through mere repetition but by the coupling of that repetition with the regularities associated with the world of purposeful technology. The ghost is a servant, if not of the supernatural broadly, then of the incident with which its mortal body was associated; its manifestations are signals that record the passage of incidents, and warn of the consequences of not addressing such things. The railway – and the adoption of the railway environment as a suitable venue for the uncanny and the supernatural – has effectively industrialised the occult, bringing the ghostly into the purlieu of the modern world.

---

56 The importance of railway timetables in Gothic fiction should not be overlooked. In *Dracula* – which is perhaps the first novel in which a supernatural protagonist systematically employs the timetabled services of a commercial transporter – their global oversight of the transport network greatly assists the strategic pursuit of the vampire. See Stoker, *Dracula*, pp. 140, 376, 381, 387.

57 Victor L. Whitechurch, 'The Strange Story of Engine Number 651', in Ashley (ed.), *The Platform Edge*, pp. 13–23 (pp. 18, 20, 22, 23).

58 L. G. Moberly, 'A Strange Night', in Ashley (ed.), *The Platform Edge*, pp. 61–7 (pp. 63–4, 66–7).

It is only in the second half of the twentieth century, when the glory days of British railways had finally passed and when the ability of the network to connect efficiently the breadth and length of the country had been superseded by a yet newer technology, that railway Gothic would lose its contemporaneity, and look back with open nostalgia to an age in which the terminus, the station yard and the locomotive could satisfactorily take their cultural place alongside the country house and the coaching inn. This point represents the final integration of the railways into the genre, not in the age of Empire but in that of post-war decline, and in the reign of Elizabeth II rather than of Victoria. If Dickens alone has hitherto been recognised as a writer of railway Gothic, then his successor – and a more prolific author of ghost stories with industrial settings – should arguably be L. T. C. Rolt, a writer whose railway fiction has, it might be noted, also been singularly ignored in criticism.[59] Rolt's post-war Britain, reshaped by socialist politics and fearful in a nuclear age, in many respects recalls the uncertain cultural landscapes of the industrialising nation presented by Carlyle and Eliot. The ghosts that populate Rolt's railways, canals and foundries are the inheritors of so much that was initially exposed in Victorian and Edwardian fiction. The place of the railways in Gothic, from the nineteenth century to the contemporary, therefore, remains very much open for further exploration.

[59] Lionel Thomas Caswall Rolt (1910–74) was a railway and industrial historian with a particular concern for the dehumanising effects of British post-war nationalisation and deindustrialisation. His Gothic reputation rests upon one volume of railway, canal and industrial ghost stories, *Sleep No More*, first published in 1948.

2.21

Gothic Imperialism at the *Fin de siècle*

ANDREW SMITH

The late nineteenth century was characterised by various forms of political crisis at both home and abroad. In Britain the period was dominated by popular anxieties centred on theories of degeneration that troublingly seemed to suggest that the great colonising nation of the nineteenth century might be either growing its own degenerates or subject to an invasion of degenerate forces that threatened it with colonisation. Bram Stoker's *Dracula* (1897) reflects the presence of both these impulses, with the vampire hunters allied against the forces of degeneration represented by the Count, but also tacitly enamoured of the illicit freedoms offered by vampirism. To defeat the degenerate Count they have to become more like him, be more heroic and war-like, and this is the central conundrum of the novel: to defeat degeneracy the vampire hunters must ape its aggressive, and regressive, tendencies and so overcome their home-grown middle-class frailties. What it means to be a man (a middle-class professional, or an aristocratic warlord) is central to this paradox and this chapter charts the various ways in which images of Empire were imbricated with a discourse of masculinity. Empire, however, is not a unified concept during this period. Britain's imperial interest in India rests upon a particular set of political and territorial concerns that are, for example, different in kind to Britain's territorial interests in Egypt (which centred on ownership of the Suez Canal). British imperial history is, in reality, the case of multiple *histories* of domination generated by different economic principles and by the practical challenges of annexing often vast terrains.

How the Gothic relates to the complexities of British imperial history has been the subject of longstanding critical enquiry. The term 'imperial Gothic' was coined by Patrick Brantlinger in *Rule of Darkness: British Literature and Imperialism: 1830–1914* (1988). Here, Brantlinger identified the form's core characteristics as including a fear of Britain becoming invaded, an anxiety about cultural absorption, and a general sense of disappointment with the lack of heroism that marked the modern, bureaucratic pen-pushing world (like that of the recently promoted Solicitor, Jonathan Harker, in *Dracula*). Brantlinger identifies the time frame of the imperial Gothic as covering the period from Henry Rider Haggard's *King Solomon's Mines* (1885) to John Buchan's *Greenmantle* (1916). How these points of imperial contact can be linked to gender narratives has been explored by Ann McClintock in *Imperial Leather: Race, Gender, and Sexuality in the Colonial Contest* (1995), a study which examined conjunctions of sexuality, race and money in the establishment of colonial rule. McClintock's approach provides a helpful way to think about how a Gothic engagement with these concerns generated often highly ambivalent models of imperial rule.

At one level, the colonial might seem to be synonymous with the imperial, but as Alexandra Warwick has noted, the 'imperial Gothic is a British, perhaps even English, form, while it is possible to see colonial concerns in, for example, American writing and postcolonial concerns in many other literatures'.[1] The British, and possibly English, provenance of the imperial Gothic will be explored towards the end of this chapter in a discussion of how Stoker's Irish background only superficially complicates a model of a unified British imperialism, because ultimately the wider colonial interests of England and Ireland are aligned during the period. For this reason it is America rather than England that appears as a threat to Stoker. The focus of this chapter is on the contexts of Egypt and India and concludes with a discussion of Stoker's Ireland.

That Brantlinger would locate the beginning of the imperial Gothic in a novel by Haggard might seem reasonable enough given Haggard's seemingly impeccable imperialist credentials. Haggard had worked in the colonial service in South Africa in the 1870s, and held an administrative position in the annexation of Boer-held territories during that period. Even after he left the colonial service he was still active in supporting British imperial interests and was involved with the Council of Public Morals and the National League for the Promotion of Physical and Moral Race Regeneration.[2] Haggard's novels, however, often challenge imperialism, and the writer has posed a problem for critics who, like Tim Murray, have come to the conclusion that 'There is more to [Haggard] than his simply being a hack imperialist ..., but it is difficult

---

[1] Alexandra Warwick, 'Imperial Gothic', in William Hughes, David Punter and Andrew Smith (eds), *The Encyclopedia of the Gothic* (Oxford: Blackwell, 2016), pp. 338–42 (p. 338).
[2] On his links to these bodies, see Peter Beresford Ellis, *H. Rider Haggard: A Voice from the Infinite* (London: Routledge & Kegan Paul, 1978), pp. 6–7.

to find amongst all the imperialist puff.'³ As we shall see, Haggard's classic imperial Gothic novel *She* (1887) cannot be read as simple imperialist polemic because it frequently subverts many of the racist assumptions that supported British imperial activity.⁴

She's narrator, Ludwig Horace Holly, is a Cambridge don who resembles a baboon. These conflicting identities emphasise that he possesses both mental and physical strength and enables the novel to reclaim images of the simian for positive rather than racist ends. In part this is because Haggard was keen to challenge links that might be made between races and animals (as unevolved figures who constitute the white man's burden) but also because he explores tensions between the physical and the spiritual that run throughout the novel. The relationship between body and spirit inspires Holly's attempt to discover what wisdom Ayesha may have garnered during her 2,000-year wait for the return of her lover, Kallikrates. Beneath the ostensible imperial politics and the idea of heroic adventures that can only be found outside of the college room, there is a seriousness in *She* which is partly about imperial authority (Ayesha as an imperial Queen) and partly about the pursuit of spirituality (Holly as a seeker of non-Western-based knowledge), which articulates a more thoughtful, and ambivalent, version of the imperial Gothic. Holly pursues this line of enquiry with Ayesha only to be disappointed by the robust Darwinian position that she adopts when asserting that 'day by day we destroy that we may live, since in this world none save the strongest can endure. Those who are weak must perish; the earth is to the strong, and the fruits thereof.'⁵ Ayesha articulates a language of physical superiority that underpinned models of racial, and thus imperial, supremacy. Images of manliness, as reflected in Holly and Leo, are also closely related to imperialism. The link between imperial decline and masculine fragility is expressed as an analogy for degeneration in Edwin Lankester's *Degeneration: A Chapter in Darwinism* (1880), where he claims that:

> Any new set of conditions occurring to an animal which render its food and safety easily attained, seem to lead as a rule to Degeneration; just as an active

---

3 Tim Murray, 'Archaeology and the threat of the past: Sir Henry Rider Haggard and the acquisition of time', *World Archaeology* 25:2 (1993): 175–86 (p. 180).
4 See also Andrew Smith, 'Beyond Colonialism: Death and the Body in H. Rider Haggard', in Andrew Smith and William Hughes (eds), *Empire and the Gothic: The Politics of Genre* (Basingstoke: Palgrave Macmillan, 2003), pp. 103–117.
5 Henry Rider Haggard, *She* (Ware: Wordsworth Editions, 1995), p. 153.

healthy man sometimes degenerates when he becomes suddenly possessed of a fortune; or as Rome degenerated when possessed of the riches of the ancient world.[6]

Physical decline and imperial decline become aligned, and *She* critically examines this Darwinian position. Ayesha's symbolic correlation of humans with animals, according to which Holly is a baboon, Leo a lion, Billali (an elder of the Amahagger tribe) a goat and Job (Holly's servant) a pig, also underlines their respective social standings for Ayesha. At the end of the narrative, when Ayesha seemingly dies after attempting to re-enter the flame of life that has enabled her to live for 2,000 years, she appears to Job to be 'turning into a monkey!', as she physically shrivels and regresses.[7] And yet, for Holly, this does not represent the type of biological decline suggested by Lankester; rather, it implies a spiritual judgement on the nihilistic Darwinian position maintained by Ayesha herself, since, for him 'it requires no great stretch of the imagination to see the finger of Providence in the matter'.[8] The novel keeps in place this tension between the body and the spirit that, as discussed below, is shaped by subtle ideas of imperialism that reveal that Holly's pursuit of spiritual understanding is rooted within an imperial context.

Shawn Malley has argued that 'The universe Ayesha inhabits and explores as a eugenicist, astronomer, chemist, physicist, geologist, and archaeologist is a decidedly Darwinian one.'[9] Ayesha's manufacturing of tribes and subsequent destruction of them demonstrates this scientific and imperial aspect of her authority, one that casts her as a *fin-de-siécle* femme fatale. However, this is not the sole empire over which she exerts control. She has also, through her entry into the flame of life, exercised mastery over life and death on a spiritual as well as a physical plane. At the end of the novel, Holly considers whether Leo really is the reincarnation of Kallikrates or his biological descendant; if the former, then the implication is that the story might not have come to the end with Ayesha's apparent death so that, for Holly, 'A story that began more than two thousand years ago may stretch a long way into the dim and distant future.'[10] That Haggard had not finished with Ayesha is clear from the three sequels to *She* – *Ayesha: The Return of She* (1905), *She and Allan* (1921) and *Wisdom's Daughter* (1923). In *Ayesha: The Return of She*, Ayesha's empire has shifted from the

---

6 Edwin Lankester, *Degeneration: A Chapter in Darwinism* (London: Macmillan, 1880), p. 33.
7 Haggard, *She*, p. 222.   8 Haggard, *She*, p. 223.
9 Shawn Malley, '"Time hath no power against identity": historical continuity and archaeological adventure in H. Rider Haggard's She', *English Literature in Transition 1880–1920* 40:3 (1997): 275–97 (p. 290).
10 Haggard, *She*, p. 239.

physical Darwinian world into a more metaphysical one in which she retains her queenly status. Holly and Leo, some 20 years after the events recorded in *She*, rediscover Ayseha in the palatial 'hall of shades' where:

> She seemed a Queen of Death receiving homage from the dead. More she was receiving homage from dead or living – I know not which – for, as I thought it, a shadowy Shape arose before the throne and bent the knee to her, then another, and another, and another.[11]

In *She*, there is a blurring of the East with the West and the living and the dead and these can be contextualised within a growing Western interest in the tomb excavations in Egypt from the 1870s. David Gange has noted that the excavations were not motivated by principles of scientific enquiry but by an attempt to prove that Christianity had influenced the ancient Egyptians. In this narrative, the Old Testament was initially construed as historical fact with Rameses II cast as the pharaoh referred to in the Book of Exodus.[12] Holly's search for spirituality should be seen within this occidental context, which attempts to suggest that the Orient is related to the West through its inheritance of a hidden Western spirituality. Haggard was a keen amateur Egyptologist who made many visits to the Valley of the Kings. Holly is also an archaeologist of a kind who mines Ayesha's past for its hidden spiritual qualities. The imperial Gothic read in these terms is thus founded on an attempt to reclaim and reassert spiritual authority, not just racial or economic superiority.

She represents the position maintained by biblical scholars in the 1870s and 1880s. However, by the 1890s the picture had changed. The excavations indicated that the ancient Egyptians pre-dated the records of Christianity and so compromised the attempt to refute geological theories that had suggested that the Earth existed before the biblical Genesis. Gange notes that in the 1890s, 'late Victorian Egyptologists, painfully aware of the challenges facing contemporary religion, held up [some] aspect of ancient Egyptian culture as an ideal for Victorian Britain to aspire to, emphasizing faith, steadfastness, and tolerance'.[13] Christianity now looked like a latter-day belief – regarded as historically influenced by the cult of Mithras and the veneration of Isis.[14] British imperialism, as supported by biblical dogma, now

---

11 Henry Rider Haggard, *Ayesha: The Return of She*, intro. by David Pringle (Polegate: Pulp Fictions, 1998), p. 211.
12 David Gange, 'Religion and science in late nineteenth-century British Egyptology', *The Historical Journal* 49:4 (December 2006): 1083–103 (p. 1088).
13 Gange, 'Religion and Science', p. 1092.   14 Gange, 'Religion and Science', p. 1098.

seemed to rest on shaky ground. The solution was to argue that Christian ideas could be discerned within pre-Christian civilisations and that, therefore, one should look for points of similarity rather than difference. How to square that relationship is central to *Ayesha: The Return of She*. In Haggard's sequel Holly and Leo begin their quest for Ayesha in Tibet and during their travels reside at a number of Buddhist monasteries. J. Jeffrey Franklin has noted the prevalence of an interest in Buddhism in Britain from the 1880s and argues that the two pressing questions of the time were 'did Buddhism influence the origins of Christianity, and is India the geographical and genetic point of origin for the European Aryan race?'[15] Franklin has also noted that Haggard's novel explores tensions surrounding possible Buddhist, and indeed Egyptian, influences on Christianity by playing them out as conflicts between love (as a form of active desire) and ideas of duty (which are about denying your desires in pursuit of both nirvana, and about support for moral and social codes).[16] Imperialist issues are formally present in more conventional terms in the novel through the territorial conflicts that are fought between Ayesha and Atene, and the heroic adventures of Holly and Leo. However, imperial occidental considerations also underpin the more abstract theological considerations that focus on ownership of the soul. These tensions emerge between the spiritually open-minded Holly and the more narrow-minded Christian, Leo. Leo, as part of his marriage ceremony with Ayesha, is asked to carry a crook-shaped sceptre that evokes symbolic connections with Osiris. Leo states, 'I don't want to impersonate any Egyptian god, or to be mixed up in their heathen idolatries.'[17] Holly approves of Leo's retention of a Western faith-based morality but urges a pragmatic approach: 'Better go through with it ... probably only something symbolical.'[18] However, Leo confronts Ayesha as follows: 'Thy religion I do not understand, but I understand my own, and not even for thy sake will I take part in what I hold to be idolatry'; Ayesha, in turn, challenges this by asserting that:

> all great Faiths are the same, changed a little to suit the needs of the passing times and peoples. What taught that of Egypt, which, in a fashion, we still follow here? That hidden in a multitude of manifestations, one Power great and good, rules all the universes: that the holy shall inherit a life eternal and the vile, eternal death.[19]

---

15 J. Jeffrey Franklin, 'The Counter-invasion of Britain by Buddhism in Marie Corelli's *A Romance of Two Worlds* and H. Rider Haggard's *Ayesha: The Return of She*', *Victorian Literature and Culture* 31:1 (2003): 19–42 (pp. 23–4).
16 Franklin, 'The Counter-invasion of Britain', p. 32.   17 Haggard, *Ayesha*, p. 204.
18 Haggard, *Ayesha*, p. 204.   19 Haggard, *Ayesha*, p. 213.

This version of Ayesha is what Holly had hoped to find in *She*. The dictates of the imperial Gothic that focus on territorial acquisition have been refocused to explore the acquisition of belief. The outward adventure is replaced by an inner journey, but one in which the grounds of faith have been challenged and in which the desires of the body are transcended. Indeed, in this novel Holly no longer physically desires Ayesha, as he does in *She*, but is instead focused on her spiritual essence. However, it would be wrong to suggest that Haggard's challenge to the conventional plot devices of the imperial Gothic constitute a sustainable political radicalism, although there is an argument that Holly can only find true spirituality beyond the confines of modern Britain. The novel implies that the way forward is the way back to a primitive culture, but one which is free from the deadening world of middle-class respectability that is so frequently represented in Gothic fiction of the period. At the end of the novel Leo and Ayesha are dead and Holly is dying in a Buddhist monastery; the monk who listens to Holly's tale, and for whom the dead are not really dead but merely awaiting reincarnation, tells him, 'doubtless you are all winning merit, but, if I may venture to say so, you are winning it very slowly', indicating that there is still some way to go on the spiritual journey.[20]

Egypt and Mummy Fiction

By looking at the specific context of Egypt and the Victorian fascination with the tomb evacuations we can observe how a quite specific context shaped a strand of the imperial Gothic. *She* is set in the African interior, which reflects the colonial rush to Africa that was popular at the time. The Egyptian context is more specific and does not just relate to the archaeological excavations; there is also the matter of ownership of the Suez Canal, which was built between 1859 and 1869 and which was of considerable economic significance, as it enabled ships to move between Europe and South Asia without having to undertake an extensive detour around the African coast. In 1875 Benjamin Disraeli purchased a number of shares in the Canal Company, which ensured that Britain retained a strong economic interest in the canal. In 1882 Britain invaded Egypt after an uprising had threatened to put into a power a regime that would have been hostile to British interests. Thereafter Britain retained a military presence in the area until the Suez crisis of 1956. The military occupation

20 Haggard, *Ayesha*, p. 301.

represents the presence of a more direct form of imperial intervention than the theological deliberations of the 1870s and 1880s, which were centred on tomb excavations. However, the two impulses become aligned in the mummy fictions of the period that repeatedly address the questionable legitimacy of the British military presence, a concern that is frequently represented through often revengeful mummies seeking to reassert their historic authority. The heyday of the mummy story can be closely related to the period of the tomb excavations, ownership of the Suez Canal and the British military presence from 1882. Ailise Bulfin has noted that between 1860 and 1914 there were approximately 100 mummy stories published in the British periodical press, and that around two-thirds of these could be classified as curse narratives and the rest as romances.[21] Although Bulfin identifies some slippage between the curse and romance narratives, the gendered aspects of the romance tales, which tended to centre on alluring female mummies, also have specific imperial political connotations. Edward Said in *Orientalism* (1978) explored how the employment of female figures to represent subordinate nations constituted an imperial strategy of emphasising the masculinity of the West and the femininity of the East. The portrayal of Ayesha indicates that such figures might form, in *She*, a semi-erotic spectacle, but they are also capable of exercising considerable defiance to a putatively masculine, Western imperialist gaze.

An interesting example of the early mummy tale is Grant Allen's 'My New Year's Eve Among the Mummies' (1879), which, despite its jocular tone, is self-conscious about the ways in which Egypt was perceived in the period leading up to the occupation, and suggests that the freedoms represented by ancient Egyptian culture are a welcome relief to the constraints of Western middle-class respectability. The nameless narrator is unhappily engaged to an heiress, Editha Fitz-Simpkins, and after a row about his attendance at a dance, the narrator enters a pyramid and finds a feast taking place among its ancient occupants, who explain that they are revived once a millennia to enjoy this meal. On being told that this is their sixth feast, he initially asserts the theological complaint that 'But the world has not existed so long' before acknowledging that despite this

---

21 Ailise Bulfin, 'The fiction of gothic Egypt and imperial paranoia: the curse of the Suez Canal', *English Literature in Transition, 1880–1920* 54:4 (2011): 411–43 (pp. 418–19). For an authoritative overview of mummy fiction in the period see Roger Luckhurst, *The Mummy's Curse: The True History of a Dark Fantasy* (Oxford: Oxford University Press, 2012).

shock to his 'orthodoxy ... I had been accustomed to geological calculations, and was somewhat inclined to accept the antiquity of man'.[22] The male mummies refer to the narrator as a 'Barbarian intruder' at their feast and when the princess Hatasou complains of his treatment to her father, Thothmes, Thothmes retorts that 'Savages have no feelings.'[23] The narrator also complains of his disparaging treatment, asserting that he is from 'a modern land whose civilisation far surpasses the rude culture of early Egypt; and I am accustomed to respectful treatment from all other nationalities, as becomes a citizen of the First Naval Power in the World'.[24] However, 'Thothmes utterly refused to believe my reiterated assertion that our existing civilisation was far superior to the Egyptian'.[25] The narrator is drawn to Hatasou, who is described as 'a lovely figure, tall, queenly, with smooth dark arms and neck polished bronze: her big black eyes full of tenderness and her long hair bound up into a bright Egyptian headdress', with whom he discusses 'Egyptian love-making'.[26] The only way that he can join her is by becoming a mummy himself, but this experiment either fails, or the whole incident is the product of a feverish dream, and he regains consciousness in the world that he had hoped to leave behind, although to his relief Editha breaks off their engagement. The tale is a satire on British claims to authority and focuses on the regal qualities of ancient Egypt. The narrator effectively attempts to 'go native', and, in the end, is unable to enter the past or belong to the present. Ownership of Hatasou, so the story implies, would represent a belonging to Egypt. What is horrifying in the tale is not those at the feast but the Western world that attempted to assert authority over Egypt, which is ultimately represented, through the fun-loving narrator, as morally vacuous. After the occupation of 1882 and the establishment of a veiled British Protectorate, such tales acquire a more sinister edge.

In Eva M. Henry's 'The Curse of Vasartas' (1889), the eponymous female mummy is discovered in a tomb by Mr Blake, an amateur Egyptologist, who donates the body to the British Museum. Vasartas's body has been perfectly

---

22 Grant Allen, 'My New Year's Eve Among the Mummies', in *Lost in a Pyramid & Other Classic Mummy Stories*, edited and intro. by Andrew Smith (London: British Library, 2016), pp. 59–78 (p. 72). The tale was originally published in *Belgravia* magazine in February 1879.
23 Allen, 'My New Year's Eve Among the Mummies', pp. 68, 69.
24 Allen, 'My New Year's Eve Among the Mummies', p. 69.
25 Allen, 'My New Year's Eve Among the Mummies', p. 71.
26 Allen, 'My New Year's Eve Among the Mummies', p. 73.

preserved and the narrator, a friend of Blake, notes that 'She was apparently in the prime of life.'[27] A document buried with her indicates that whoever moves her from her tomb will be cursed and die, including their descendants. Mr Blake only gets this note translated after the mummy has been donated to the British Museum, and sends the narrator to retrieve the body. He is also asked to monitor the health of Mr Blake's daughter, Llora, and after they meet at her boarding school they fall in love. Llora becomes ill and Mr Blake is killed in a hunting accident. The matter is explained to the narrator in a letter left by Blake and the narrator ensures that Vasartas's body is returned to its tomb and the curse is lifted from Llora. In this instance, tomb-raiding is punished by a dead Queen who threatens Blake's family with destruction. The message is clear: if you tamper in the affairs of a foreign nation you will face their desire for revenge. Llora rather than Vasartas is the figure of romantic interest, but it is only Vasartas's return to the tomb that enables the romance plot to conclude. Life and happiness can only be assured by not meddling in Egyptian affairs, and such tales, as Bulfin notes, reflect anxieties about the legitimacy of the British presence in Egypt.[28]

There are important mummy novels published during this period too, including H. D. Everett's (writing as Theo Douglas) *Iras: A Mystery* (1896), which focuses on a failed romance between an Egyptologist and a mummy; Richard Marsh's *The Beetle* (1897), with its highly ambivalent representation of an Egyptian who seems to be an amalgam of male and female and human and non-human forms; and Guy Boothby's *Pharos the Egyptian* (1899), which explores the revenge of Egypt on the West sent in the form of a plague. The ambivalence with which Egypt was regarded is exemplified by the two endings of Stoker's mummy novel *The Jewel of Seven Stars* (1903, revised 1912). In the 1903 ending, the resurrection of the mummy, Tera, results in the death of all but the narrator, Malcolm Ross, who records that he finds those involved in the experiment (including Margaret, his fiancée) dead and 'gazing upward with fixed eyes on unspeakable terror'.[29] In the 1912 version, it appears as though Tera may have been destroyed in the process of resurrection, but the last words are left to Margaret, now married to Ross, who suggests that Tera may be alive in some form because 'Love and patience are

---

27 Eva M. Henry 'The Curse of Vasartas', in *Lost in a Pyramid & Other Classic Mummy Stories*, edited and intro. by Andrew Smith (London: British Library, 2016), pp. 107–25 (p. 119). The tale was originally published in *Belgravia* magazine in October 1889.
28 Bulfin, 'The Fiction of Gothic Egypt and Imperial Paranoia', p. 438.
29 Bram Stoker, *The Jewel of Seven Stars*, intro. by David Glover (Oxford: Oxford University Press, 1996), p. 211.

all that make for happiness in this world; or in the world of the past or of the future; of the living or the dead.'[30] Bradley Deane has written of the 1912 ending that:

> This happier version ... departs from the logic of the occupation: the space of adventure has now been closed, and the profound allure of Egyptian power has been reduced to a curious detour on the way to a cheerful British wedding.[31]

For Deane, this change can be attributed to a declining public interest in the drama of the British Protectorate at a time when other tensions appeared across Europe and which culminated in World War One.

The mummy narratives outlined here have focused on images of the female mummy as the site of imperial ambivalence – as an object of desire, but also one who invites care, and, if ill-treated, will seek revenge. Male mummies appear as less equivocal versions of imperial danger and are not often accorded this ambivalence. Arthur Conan Doyle produced two well-known mummy short stories, 'The Ring of Thoth' (1890) and 'Lot No. 249' (1892). The latter focuses on a male Egyptian mummy who is used by an Oxford student, Edward Bellingham, to inflict revenge on those who have upset or thwarted him. In the end Bellingham is made to destroy this mummy in a notably graphic way:

> In frantic haste he caught up the knife and hacked at the figure of the mummy ... The creature crackled and snapped under every stab of the keen blade. A thick yellow dust rose up from it. Spices and dried essences rained down upon the floor. Suddenly, with a rendering crack, its backbone snapped asunder, and it fell, a brown heap of sprawling limbs, upon the floor.[32]

The level of violence inflicted on the male mummy is beyond that found in fiction centred on female mummies, and even the femme fatale in Haggard, Henry and Stoker is accorded some sympathetic understanding. A notable example of violence towards a male mummy can be found in 'The Story of Baelbrow' (1898), by Kate and Hesketh Prichard (a mother and son writing under the names of E and H. Heron). The tale was published in a series

---

30 Stoker, *The Jewel of the Seven Stars*, p. 214.
31 Bradley Deane, 'Mummy fiction and the occupation of Egypt: imperial striptease', *English Literature in Transition 1880–1920* 51:4 (2008): 381–410 (p. 406).
32 Arthur Conan Doyle, 'Lot No. 249', in *Lost in a Pyramid & Other Classic Mummy Stories*, edited and intro. by Andrew Smith (London: British Library, 2016), pp. 127–70 (p. 168). The tale was originally published in *Harper's New Monthly Magazine* in October 1892.

featuring Flaxman Low (an investigator into the supernatural), and centres on Baelbrow, the ancestral mansion of the Swaffam family, which is reputedly haunted and which has been rented to a German professor and his family. The ghost appears to carry out a murderous attack on one of the servants, and Low and the owner of the house, Harold Swaffam, are contacted by the professor to investigate the crime. Swaffam is a young no-nonsense man who does not believe in the supernatural speculations of Low, but after Swaffam is attacked he begins to give Low's theories some credence. It transpires that Swaffam's father had established a small museum in the house composed of artefacts that he had collected from around the world. He had recently sent a mummy back to England, and the case in which it had been transported had been opened by Swaffam. The mummy had seemingly been restored to life, but Low notes that its assaults culminate in biting the victims' necks. Low concludes that because the house has been built on an ancient burial ground this has resulted in a distillation of all that was bad among the dead, now spectrally channelled in a vampiric form via the mummy. The mummy, resting between attacks, is discovered in its box and Swaffam dispatches it with some gusto. It is noted that:

> For a moment Swaffam stood over the thing: then with a curse he raised the revolver and shot into the grinning face again and again with deliberate vindictiveness. Finally he rammed the thing down into the box, and, clubbing the weapon, smashed the head into fragments with a vicious energy that coloured the whole horrible scene with a suggestion of murder done.[33]

The violence both here and in Doyle's tale seems excessive, especially as the mummy in both tales is a foil for others and is mindlessly subject to their influence. Both mummies are also artefacts taken from Egypt, a detail that, as in Stoker's *Jewel*, indicates another concern about the invasion of Britain, which Brantlinger identifies as a marker of the imperial Gothic. In these instances, Britain becomes invaded by tomb-robbed mummies. Grave-robbing thus generates horrors at home and the violent assault on these mummies implicates those who attack them 'with a suggestion of murder done'. The specific instance of Egypt generates a particular form of ambivalence about British imperialism.

---

33 Kate and Hesketh Prichard, 'The Story of Baelbrow', in *Lost in a Pyramid & Other Classic Mummy Stories*, edited and intro. by Andrew Smith (London: British Library, 2016), pp. 195–212 (p. 212). The tale was originally published under the names of E. and H. Heron in *Pearson's Monthly Magazine* in April 1898.

Kipling's India

The example of India provides another model of ambivalence, although one more directly centred on British abuses abroad and feelings of neglect at home. Rudyard Kipling's poem 'The Vampire' (1897) is a caustic riposte to Queen Victoria, who, since 1877, had been Empress of India. The poem, written in Victoria's diamond jubilee year, focuses on a woman who has effectively bled dry the men who have fought for her and for whom she has no care. This short poem's concluding stanza runs as follows:

> And it isn't the shame and it isn't the blame
> That stings like a white hot brand.
> It's coming to know that she never knew why
> (Seeing at last she could never know why)
> And never could understand.[34]

The poem is a critique of monarchical negligence and, as in all the imperial narratives explored here, relies on issues of gender authority to make its case. As in Haggard, Queens cannot be fully trusted, in part, as Kipling's poem suggests, because such power is estranged from the lived experience of those administratively and militarily involved in policing India at this time. The imperial context of India was longstanding and historically associated with trade. The East India Company had played a crucial role in focusing British rule in India from 1601 and parliament became increasingly involved in the Company's activities after granting it state financial support in the 1770s, which resulted in a growing British military presence. After the Indian rebellion against British rule in 1857 (referred to as the Indian Mutiny), Britain assumed full military and administrative control in the foundation of the British Raj from 1858 (which would last until 1947). Arthur Conan Doyle in *The Sign of the Four* (1890) explores a theft that takes place in India during the 1857 uprising, only for the booty to be stolen from the original thieves and used to fund the opulent Orientalism of Pondicherry Lodge on the outskirts of London. Doyle's novella argues that British imperialism is founded upon theft and that the misdeeds of the past play a continuing role in the present. Kipling's version of the imperial Gothic is often equally condemnatory of British rule in India.

In Kipling's 'The Strange Ride of Morrowbie Jukes' (1885), Jukes, a colonial administrator, finds himself after an accident trapped in a deep crater of sand.

---

34 Rudyard Kipling, 'The Vampire', in *The Collected Poems of Rudyard Kipling*, edited by R. T. Jones (Ware: Wordsworth, 1999), p. 232, ll. 29–33.

Jukes notices a series of tunnels from which a number of poorly-clad Indians emerge. Far from trying to help him, they ignore his authority and laugh at him: 'They cackled, yelled, whistled, and howled as I walked into their midst; some of them literally throwing themselves down on the ground in convulsions of an unholy mirth.'[35] In this strange place Jukes encounters Gunga Dass, a Brahmin who had worked for the British government and who, like Jukes, has been stripped of his signs of authority, explaining that the place is inhabited by people who have been identified as dead, but who exist in a trance-like state. Jukes proposes escaping, but is met by Dass's radical laughter as Dass 'gave vent to a low chuckle of derision – the laughter, be it understood, of a superior or at least of an equal'.[36] Jukes is in limbo, and his liminality means that others find it difficult to see him, and, if they do, they mock his pretence to imperial authority. Jukes regards himself as 'a representative figure of the dominant race, helpless as a child and completely at the mercy of his neighbours'.[37] Dass taunts Jukes that he is socially dead, and it is only with some difficulty that Jukes manages to escape this limbo world when he is rescued by his servant, Dunnoo. Although we are meant to be sympathetic to Jukes's plight it is also clear that his claims on authority are ludicrous, which is why they are subjected to sustained mockery.

In the tale, before his rescue, Jukes seems to belong nowhere in this frightening limbo world which emblematically represents India. Bart Moore-Gilbert has noted the presence of a double form of alienation for many of those who served in the British colonial service, arguing that such figures did not belong to the indigenous Indian culture and did not identify with the British metropolitan view of India. Moore-Gilbert also states that during this period the 'gothic was . . . a well-established genre in Anglo-Indian fiction'.[38] The Gothic in the Indian context explores these feelings of alienation that represent a level of self-conscious ambiguity in Kipling.

Kipling used the Gothic in order to explore these moments of ambivalence in the frequently discussed 'The Mark of the Beast' (1890), when the British Fleete, drunk on New Year's Eve, stubs out a cigar in the eye of a statue of the Monkey God Hanuman and is cursed with leprosy – a curse that can only be removed when the Indian responsible for it is tortured by Fleete's associates,

---

35 Rudyard Kipling, 'The Strange Ride of Morrowbie Jukes', in *The Phantom 'Rickshaw and Other Ghost Stories* (Fairfield, CT: 1st World Library, 2007), pp. 45–72 (p. 50). See also Andrew Smith, 'Kipling's gothic and postcolonial laughter', *Gothic Studies* 11:1 (May 2009): 58–69, special issue on 'Theorising the Gothic', edited by Jerrold E. Hogle and Andrew Smith.
36 Kipling, 'Jukes', p. 53.   37 Kipling, 'Jukes', p. 57.
38 Bart Moore-Gilbert, *Kipling and 'Orientalism'* (New York: St Martin's Press, 1986), p. 188.

who are appalled by their actions. 'My Own True Ghost Story' (1888) explores how the present is ghosted by Britain's imperial past. The narrator resides at a dâk-bungalow that, 25 years before, had been inhabited by a colonial administrator whom he suspects of haunting the property. These fears are seemingly confirmed when he retires to bed and hears what appears to be a spectral game of billiards taking place in the room next door. Ultimately, a more prosaic explanation is offered when 'the wind ran out and the billiards stopped', which suggests that the noise was caused by the wind playing against the window bolts (possibly combined with the noise of a gnawing rat).[39] A type of limbo is suggested here, albeit a metaphysical limbo rather than the social one confronted by Jukes in the earlier tale. However, the idea that one cannot be quite sure about the nature of reality is the consequence of the effects that a projected Indian past plays on the present, even if it is through the apparently harmless game of billiards. The tale has a comic aspect to it and it seems as though Kipling blends comedy with the Gothic to account for the British experience of India at this time.

Comedy, in a slightly different form, can also be discerned in Kipling's 'The Phantom 'Rickshaw' (1888), a tale which begins by asserting the apparently overtly explicable nature of India:

> One of the few advantages that India has over England is a great Knowability. After five years' service a man is directly or indirectly acquainted with the two or three hundred Civilians in his Province, all the Messes of ten or twelve Regiments and Batteries, and some fifteen hundred other people of the non-official caste. In ten years his knowledge should be doubled, and at the end of twenty he knows, or knows something about, every Englishman in the Empire, and may travel anywhere and everywhere without paying hotel-bills.[40]

The tale focuses on how limited this idea of 'knowability' is, particularly since it is defined by purely British social relations. The narrative centres on the narrator's affair with a Mrs Wessington, whom he abandons, and when she dies she haunts him by following him around in her spectral 'rickshaw. The narrator dies in despair, but the ghostly presence is not just a personal condemnation: it also suggests that the misdeeds that take place in India can never quite be forgotten or forgiven. There is a strand of comedy in Kipling's ghost stories, but the comedy is bleak and the laughter is of a type

---

39 Rudyard Kipling, 'My Own True Ghost Story', in *The Phantom 'Rickshaw and Other Ghost Stories* (Fairfield, CT: 1st World Library, 2007), pp. 35–44 (p. 44).
40 Rudyard Kipling, 'The Phantom 'Rickshaw', in *The Phantom 'Rickshaw and Other Ghost Stories* (Fairfield, CT: 1st World Library, 2007), pp. 7–34 (p. 7).

that mocks the social pretensions of the Anglo-Indian. In a 'Free Hand', published in the *Pioneer* in November 1888, Kipling imagines a conversation between Lord Dufferin, the outgoing viceroy, and his replacement Lord Landsdowne. Dufferin tells Landsdowne, 'You stand on the threshold of new experiences – most of which will distress you and a few amuse. You are [at] the centre of a gigantic *practical joke*. Strive to enter the spirit of it and jest temperately.'[41] If there is comedy here, it is notably dark.

Stoker's America

So far this chapter has focused on the well-established imperial contexts of Egypt and India. Our understanding of the imperial Gothic can be widened, however, by exploring how Ireland was related to British imperialism. Bram Stoker's writings provide a revealing example of this. Stoker's attitude towards British imperialism can be accounted for via the increasingly anti-American sentiment of his writings. Stoker's Anglo-Irish Protestant Ascendancy background underlines his establishment credentials, and his tacit support for British imperialism should be seen within that context. Stephen Howe has explored the role that the Irish played in helping to administer the British Empire in the nineteenth century. During this period there was a view that Irish interests could be met by being included within the economic ambitions of the Empire. Howe notes that this led to a broad informal Irish alliance in which Arthur Griffiths, the founder of Sinn Fein, 'for some time floated the idea of Ireland not freeing itself from the British Empire, but rather becoming an equal partner in it: a partner that is, in dominating the non-European peoples'.[42] The threat posed to this sense of the British Empire does not come through internal national tensions, but rather from America.[43]

Stoker's early writings on America praise the nation for its points of similarity to Britain. In his speech, published as a pamphlet entitled *A Glimpse of America* (1886), Stoker asserts that 'Our history is their

---

41 Rudyard Kipling, 'Free Hand' in the *Pioneer*, November 1888, cited in Lewis D. Wurgaft, *The Imperial Imagination: Magic and Myth in Kipling's India* (Middletown, CT: Wesleyan University Press, 1983), p. 129; italics in original.
42 Stephen Howe, *Ireland and Empire: Colonial Legacies in Irish History and Culture* (Oxford: Oxford University Press, 2000), p. 45
43 See Andrew Smith, 'Demonising the Americans: Bram Stoker's postcolonial gothic', *Gothic Studies* 5:2 (November 2004): 20–31, special issue on 'Postcolonial Gothic', edited by William Hughes and Andrew Smith.

history – our fame is their pride – their progress is our glory.'⁴⁴ However, in 'The Squaw' (1893), Elias P. Hutcheson, an American in Europe, is cast as a brutal villain who has killed a squaw on the American frontier and who has become bored with the genteel world of Europe. His accidental killing of a kitten and the mother cat's revenge on him result in his symbolic execution in an Iron Virgin (a type of Iron Maiden with interior spikes). Hutcheson is a precursor to the American frontiersman, Quincey Morris, in *Dracula*. Franco Moretti has claimed that Quincey is a representative figure of American imperialism. He argues that Quincey loses sight of the Count during a crucial pursuit and misses him with his gun, when he is supposed to be a marksman, because Morris shares the Count's ambition to subjugate Britain. According to Moretti:

> So long as things go well for Dracula, Morris acts like an accomplice. As soon as there is a reversal of fortunes, he turns into his staunchest enemy. Morris enters into competition with Dracula; he would like to replace him in the conquest of the Old World. He does not succeed in the novel but he will succeed, in 'real' history, a few years afterwards.⁴⁵

Stephen D. Arata has noted the fear of reverse colonialism in *Dracula* in which, in keeping with the imperial Gothic, the home front finds itself under attack from a figure from Eastern Europe.⁴⁶ However, Moretti's argument nuances and helps to explain the growing anti-American impulse in Stoker's work, which is articulated in Renfield's comment to Quincey that relations between Britain and American may improve once 'the Pole and the Tropics may hold allegiance to the Stars and Stripes [and] when the Monroe doctrine takes its place as a political fable'.⁴⁷ Renfield's apparent celebration of growing American power (from the Pole to the Tropics) and the anticipated repeal of the Monroe doctrine (which limited European influence in American affairs) would seem to be ironised given that it comes out of the mouth of Seward's pet lunatic.

Stoker, while touring America with the Lyceum Theatre company, gave a lecture on Abraham Lincoln and his praise of Lincoln should be read as support for a vision of a united America (although he stopped delivering the

---

44 Bram Stoker, *A Glimpse of America* (London: Sampson Low, Marston and Co., 1886), pp. 47–8.
45 Franco Moretti, *Signs Taken for Wonders: Essays in the Sociology of Literary Forms*, trans. by Susan Fischer, David Forgacs and David Miller (London: Verso, 1988), p. 95.
46 Stephen D. Arata, 'The occidental tourist: *Dracula* and the anxiety of reverse colonialism', *Victorian Studies* 33:4 (Summer 1990): 621–45.
47 Bram Stoker, *Dracula*, edited by Maud Ellmann (Oxford: Oxford University Press, 1996), p. 244.

lecture in America after 1887), but his look back at an old America was because the new one had become disturbing to him. Stoker's *The Mystery of the Sea* (1902) is narrated by Archibald Hunter, who falls in love with an American heiress, Marjory Drake, whom he subsequently marries. Marjory has bought a battleship for the American navy to assist them in their attempt to free Cuba from Spanish rule in what was the Spanish-Cuban-American war of 1898.[48] This was in pursuit of President McKinley's ambition to expand America's economic and political interests in establishing what looked like an Empire to many, including Stoker. The fighting in Cuba subsequently led to America battling for ownership of the Philippines in 1899–1902. Marjory (a descendant of Sir Francis Drake) informs Archibald about her recent family history: 'I come from a race of men who have held their lives in their hands from the cradle to the grave ... Their blood is in my veins, and speaks loudly to me when any sense of fear comes near me.'[49] The rhetorical similarity with Count Dracula's speech on his past is striking: 'We Szekelys have a right to be proud, for in our veins flows the blood of many brave races ... What devil or what witch was ever so great as Attila, whose blood is in these veins?'[50] Whereas the Count, and Quincey, are killed in *Dracula*, Marjory is accorded a different fate as she is forced to elude some kidnappers, which provides Archibald with the opportunity to behave bravely and so assert his manliness in ways that are reminiscent of Jonathan Harker. Finally, Marjory becomes domesticated by marriage to Archibald and loses her political power. The novel is both a supernatural romance (there are references to spirits in it) and a political fable about Britain's triumph over America – issues returned to by Stoker in *The Lady of the Shroud* (1909).

The Lady of the Shroud celebrates the reinstatement of Britain as a world power. The novel's principal narrator, Rupert St Leger, is a seven-foot-tall Union-supporting Scot of Viking descent, who helps to train an army to defend The Land of the Blue Mountains against the Turks in what was a reflection of the Bosnian crisis of 1908–9.[51] Rupert marries Teuta, a Princess of the Blue Mountains, and on marriage she renounces her authority so that Rupert can rule as King, a move that glosses the power shift between Marjory

---

48 See also Andrew Smith, 'Bram Stoker's *The Mystery of the Sea*: Ireland and the Spanish-Cuban-American War', *Irish Studies Review* 6:2 (1998): 131–8.
49 Bram Stoker, *The Mystery of the Sea*, intro. by Jessica de Mellow (Stroud: Sutton, 1997), p. 104.
50 Stoker, *Dracula*, pp. 28–9.
51 See Victor Sage, 'Exchanging Fantasies: Sex and the Serbian Crisis in *The Lady of the Shroud*', in William Hughes and Andrew Smith (eds), *Bram Stoker: History, Psychoanalysis and the Gothic* (Basingstoke: Macmillan, 1998), pp. 116–33.

and Rupert in *The Mystery of the Sea*. Once the fighting is over, the consolidation of power is celebrated through a grand ceremonial meeting that takes place between Rupert, Teuta and the King and Queen of England. This meeting is recounted by an American journalist writing for the fictitious newspaper *Free America*, who records witnessing:

> the King and Queen of the greatest nation of the earth being received by the newest King and Queen – a King and Queen who won empire for themselves, so that the former subject of another King received him as a brother-monarch on a history-making occasion.[52]

This section of the report has tellingly received an editorial correction, which changes the reference to the 'greatest nation' to the 'Greatest *Kingdom*'.[53] The real source of continuing imperial conflict thus appears in this unsubtle textual amendment. Stoker's support for Home Rule for Ireland should also be seen within this context because it too supported ultimate subservience to the British parliament. What affects Britain affects Ireland and the image of monarchical unity at the end of *The Lady of the Shroud* and the editorial disapproval that it provokes should be seen as an attempt to shore up British power at a time when it was threatened by foreign new world imperialism.

This chapter has explored a diverse range of contexts: Egypt, India and anti-Americanism in order to demonstrate how specific pressures played a role in shaping the Gothic imperialism of the time. What unites Haggard and Kipling is the ambivalence about British imperialism and the abuse of power that colours it. Stoker is less concerned with how Britain expresses its imperial power than with what threatens it, and his writing is more anxious than ambivalent about that. The global power shifts of the late nineteenth century, in which nations such as America acquired a growing international authority, effectively saw the end of the British imperial Gothic, a fictional impulse that, as Brantlinger notes, had its final manifestation in the national flag-waving of John Buchan during World War One.

---

52 Bram Stoker, *The Lady of the Shroud*, intro. by Ruth Robbins (Stroud: Sutton, 1994), p. 255.
53 Stoker, *The Lady of the Shroud*, p. 255; italics in original.

Select Bibliography

All quoted sources are referenced in full in the footnotes to the chapters in this volume. Rather than repeat that information here, this select bibliography lists only longer works, and for the most part excludes duplicate editions of the same text, as well as shorter historical reviews and articles.

Adelman, Richard, 'Ruskin & Gothic literature', *The Wordsworth Circle* 48:3 (Summer 2017): 152–63.

Adolfo Bécquer, Gustavo, *Leyendas* (Madrid: Cátedra, 2002).

Aird, Catherine, 'Dickens and railway spine neurosis', *The Dickensian* 108:486 (Spring 2012): 25–8.

Aldana Reyes, Xavier, *Spanish Gothic: National Identity, Collaboration and Cultural Adaptation* (Basingstoke: Palgrave Macmillan, 2017).

Alexander, Michael, *Medievalism: The Middle Ages in Modern England* (New Haven and London: Yale University Press, 2007).

Alexander, William, Bishop of Derby, 'Sensationalism', in Andrew Maunder (ed.), *Sensationalism and the Sensation Debate: Varieties of Women's Sensation Fiction 1855–1890*, 6 vols (London: Pickering & Chatto, 2004), vol. 1, pp. 263–74.

Allen, Grant, *The Evolutionist at Large* (London: Chatto and Windus, 1881).

Allen, Grant, 'My New Year's Eve Among the Mummies', in *Lost in a Pyramid & Other Classic Mummy Stories*, edited and intro. by Andrew Smith (London: British Library, 2016), pp. 59–78.

Altick, Richard D., *The English Common Reader: A Social History of the Mass Reading Public, 1800–1900* (Chicago: Chicago University Press, 1957).

Altick, Richard D., *The Shows of London* (Cambridge, MA and London: Harvard University Press, 1978).

Amigoni, David, *Colonies, Cults and Evolution: Literature, Science and Culture in Nineteenth-Century Writing* (Cambridge: Cambridge University Press, 2007).

Andrew, Lucy, '"Away with dark shadders!": juvenile detection versus juvenile crime in *The Boy Detective; or, The Crimes of London. A Romance of Modern Times*', *Clues* 30:1 (April 2012): 18–29.

Andrews, Stuart, *Robert Southey: History, Politics, Religion* (New York: Palgrave Macmillan, 2011).

Angenot, Marc, 'Science fiction in France before Verne', trans. by J. M. Gouanvic and D. Suvin, *Science Fiction Studies* 5:1 (March 1978): 58–66.

Select Bibliography

Anon., *The Black Forest; or, The Cavern of Horrors* (London: Lemoine and Roe, 1802).
Anon., *The Bleeding Nun, of the Castle of Lindenberg; or, The History of Raymond & Agnes. By the author of the Castle Spectre* (London: Hodgson & Co., [1823]).
Anon., *Lord Ruthven o i vampiri di Lord Byron* (Napoli: R. Marotta and Vaspandoch, 1826).
Anon., *Il vampiro. Novella di Lord Byron tradotta dall'inglese* (Udine: Fratelli Mattiuzzi, 1831).
Anon., *Rocket 150: 150th Anniversary of the Liverpool and Manchester Railway 1830–1980: Official Handbook* (London: British Rail, 1980).
Anon., 'A Desperate Run', in Mike Ashley (ed.), *The Platform Edge: Uncanny Tales of the Railways* (London: British Library, 2019), pp. 47–50.
Apel, Johann August and Friedrich Laun, *Gespensterbuch*, 5 vols (Leipzig: Göschen, 1810–15).
Appel, Toby A., *The Cuvier-Geoffroy Debate: French Biology in the Decades Before Darwin* (Oxford: Oxford University Press, 1987).
Arata, Stephen, 'Stevenson and *Fin-de-Siècle* Gothic', in Penny Fielding (ed.), *The Edinburgh Companion to Robert Louis Stevenson* (Edinburgh: Edinburgh University Press, 2010), pp. 53–69.
Arata, Stephen D., 'The occidental tourist: *Dracula* and the anxiety of reverse colonialism', *Victorian Studies* 33:4 (Summer 1990): 621–45.
Armstrong, Isobel, *Victorian Poetry: Poetry, Poetics and Politics* (London: Routledge, 1993).
Atkinson, Edmund, *Natural Philosophy for General Readers and Young Persons* (London: Longmans, Green, and Co., 1884).
Atterbury, Paul, 'Steam and Speed: Industry, Transport and Communications', in John M. Mackenzie (ed.), *The Victorian Vision: Inventing New Britain* (London: V&A Publications, 2001), pp. 147–71.
Auerbach, Nina, *Our Vampires, Ourselves* (Chicago: University of Chicago Press, 1995).
Auerbach, Nina, 'Ghosts of ghosts', *Victorian Literature and Culture* 32:1 (2004): 277–84.
Ayguals de Izco, Wenceslao, *La bruja de Madrid* (Barcelona: Editorial Taber, 1969).
Backus, Margot Gayle, *The Gothic Family Romance: Heterosexuality, Child Sacrifice, and the Anglo-Irish Colonial Order* (Durham, NC: Duke University Press, 1999).
Baker, William and William W. Clarke (eds), *The Letters of Wilkie Collins*, 2 vols (Basingstoke: Macmillan, 1999).
Baldick, Chris and Robert Mighall, 'Gothic Criticism', in David Punter (ed.), *A New Companion to the Gothic* (Oxford: Blackwell, 2012), pp. 265–87.
Bann, Jennifer, 'Ghostly hands and ghostly agency: the changing figure of the nineteenth-century specter', *Victorian Studies* 51:4 (Summer 2009): 663–85.
Bann, Stephen, *Romanticism and the Rise of History* (New York: Twayne Publishers, 1995).
Barber, X. Theodore, 'Phantasmagorical wonders: the magic lantern ghost show in nineteenth-century America', *Film History* 3:2 (1989): 73–86.
Barnes, James J. and Patience P. Barnes, 'Reassessing the reputation of Thomas Tegg, London publisher, 1776–1846', *Book History* 3 (2000): 45–60.
Barnes, John (ed.), *The Beginnings of the Cinema in England 1894–1901*, 5 vols (Exeter: University of Exeter Press, 1998).
Barr, Alan P. (ed.), *The Major Prose of Thomas Henry Huxley* (Athens, GA: University of Georgia Press, 1997).
Barrow, Robin, 'Braddon's haunting memories: rape, class and the Victorian popular press', *Women's Writing* 13:3 (2006): 348–68.
Barzilai, Shuli, *Tales of Bluebeard and His Wives from Late Antiquity to Postmodern Times* (London: Routledge, 2009).

Basham, Diana, *The Trial of Woman: Feminism and the Occult Sciences in Victorian Literature and Society* (Baltimore: Johns Hopkins University Press, 1993).

Bataille, Georges, 'Le Collège de Sociologie', Mardi 4 juillet 1939, in *Le Collège de Sociologie (1937–1939)*, edited by Denies Hollier (Paris: Gallimard, 1995).

Bate, Jonathan, *Romantic Ecology: Wordsworth and the Environmental Tradition* (London: Routledge, 1991).

Bearden-White, Roy, 'A history of guilty pleasure: chapbooks and the Lemoines', *Papers of the Bibliographical Society of America* 103 (2009): 284–318.

Beatty, Bernard and Vincent Newey (eds), *Byron and the Limits of Fiction* (Liverpool: Liverpool University Press, 1988).

Beer, Gillian, *Darwin's Plots: Evolutionary Narrative in Darwin, George Eliot and Nineteenth-Century Fiction* (Cambridge: Cambridge University Press, 2009).

Belcher, Margaret (ed.), *The Letters of A. W. N. Pugin, 1830–1842*, 5 vols (Oxford: Oxford University Press, 2001).

Bendixen, Alfred, 'Romanticism and the American Gothic', in Jeffrey Andrew Weinstock (ed.), *The Cambridge Companion to American Gothic* (Cambridge: Cambridge University Press, 2017), pp. 31–43.

Bennett, Bridget, '"The Dear Old Sacred Terror": Spiritualism and the Supernatural from *The Bostonians* to *The Turn of the Screw*', in Tatiana Kontou and Sarah Willburn (eds), *The Ashgate Research Companion to Nineteenth-Century Spiritualism and the Occult* (Farnham: Ashgate, 2012), pp. 311–31.

Bennett, Gillian, 'Introduction', in Catherine Crowe, *The Night Side of Nature; or, Ghosts and Ghost Seers* (Ware, Herts: Wordsworth, 2000).

Bergland, Renée L., *The National Uncanny: Indian Ghosts and American Subjects* (Hanover, NH: University Press of New England, 2000).

Bernheimer, Charles, *Decadent Subjects: The Idea of Decadence in Art, Literature, Philosophy, and the Culture of the Fin de Siècle in Europe* (Baltimore, MA: Johns Hopkins University Press, 2002).

Bersani, Leo, 'Is the rectum a grave?', *October* 43 (Winter 1987): 197–222.

Bertman, Stephen, 'The role of the golem in the making of *Frankenstein*', *Keats-Shelley Review* 29:1 (2015): 42–50.

Bienstock Anolik, Ruth, 'Reviving the golem: cultural negotiations in Ozick's *The Puttermesser Papers* and Piercy's *He, She and It*', *Studies in American Jewish Literature* 19 (2000): 37–48.

Bienstock Anolik, Ruth, 'Appropriating the golem, possessing the dybbuk: female retellings of Jewish tales', *Modern Language Studies* 31:2 (2001): 39–55.

Billiani, Francesca. 'Delusional identities: the politics of the Italian gothic and fantastic', in Igino Ugo Tarchetti's trilogy 'Amore nell'arte' and Luigi Gualdo's short stories 'Allucinazione', 'La canzone di Weber' and 'Narcisa', *Forum for Modern Language Studies* 44:4 (2008): 497–9.

Birch, Dinah (ed.), *John Ruskin: Selected Writings* (Oxford: Oxford University Press, 2004).

Bizup, Joseph, *Manufacturing Culture: Vindications of Early Victorian Industry* (Charlottesville and London: University of Virginia Press, 2003).

Blanco White, Joseph, *Vargas: A Tale of Spain* (London: Baldwin, Cradock and Joy, 1822).

Bleasdale, John, '"To Laughter": Shelley's sonnet and solitude', *Romanticism on the Net* 22 (2001) <http://id.erudit.org/iderudit/005972ar> (last accessed 19 September 2019).

Bloom, Clive, *Victoria's Madmen: Revolution and Alienation* (Basingstoke: Palgrave Macmillan, 2013).
Bloom, Harold, *The Anxiety of Influence: A Theory of Poetry* (Oxford: Oxford University Press, 1973).
Bloom, Harold, *A Map of Misreading* (Oxford: Oxford University Press, 1975).
Boerner, Peter, 'Bürger's "Lenore" in Germany, France and England', in Janos Riesz and Peter Boerner (eds), *Sensus Communis: Contemporary Trends in Comparative Literature* (Tübingen: G. Narr, 1986), pp. 305–11.
Boitard, Pierre, *Paris Avant Les Hommes*, trans. by Stephen Trussel (Paris: Passard, 1861) <www.trussel.com/prehist/boitarde.htm> (last accessed 21 February 2019).
Boos, Florence S. (ed.), *History and Community: Essays in Victorian Medievalism* (Abingdon: Routledge, 2016).
Booth, Michael R., 'Aspects of Staging in Irving's *The Corsican Brothers*', in Michael R. Booth (ed.), *English Plays of the Nineteenth Century II: Drama 1850–1900* (Oxford: Clarendon Press, 1969), pp. 71–5.
Booth, Michael R., *Victorian Spectacular Theatre 1850–1910* (Boston, London and Henley: Routledge & Kegan Paul, 1981).
Booth, Michael R., *Theatre in the Victorian Age* (Cambridge: Cambridge University Press, 1991).
Botrel, Jean-François, 'Los nuevos lectores en la España del siglo XIX', *Siglo Diecinueve* 2 (1996): 47–64.
Botting, Fred, *Gothic*, 2nd edition (London and New York: Routledge, 2014).
Botting, Fred and Catherine Spooner, 'Introduction: Monstrous Media/Spectral Subjects', in Fred Botting and Catherine Spooner (eds), *Monstrous Media/Spectral Subjects: Imaging Gothic Fictions from the Nineteenth Century to the Present* (Manchester: Manchester University Press, 2015), pp. 1–12.
Bowen, John, *Other Dickens: Pickwick to Chuzzlewit* (Oxford: Oxford University Press, 2000).
Bowen, John, 'Uncanny Gifts, Strange Contagion: Allegory in Dickens's *The Haunted Man*', in Deirdre David and Eileen Gillooly (eds), *Contemporary Dickens* (Columbus: Ohio State University Press, 2009), pp. 75–92.
Bowen, John, 'Introduction to the Cresset Press edition of Uncle Silas, by Sheridan Le Fanu, 1947', in Eibhear Walshe (ed.), *Elizabeth Bowen's Selected Irish Writings* (Cork: Cork University Press, 2011), pp. 143–57.
Bowen, John, 'Chapter 1: The Life of Dickens 1: Before Ellen Ternan', in Sally Ledger and Holly Furneaux (eds), *Dickens in Context* (Cambridge: Cambridge University Press, 2011), pp. 3–10.
Bown, Nicola, Carolyn Burdett and Pamela Thurschwell, 'Introduction', in Nicola Bown, Carolyn Burdett and Pamela Thurschwell (eds), *The Victorian Supernatural* (Cambridge: Cambridge University Press, 2004), pp. 1–19.
Braddon, Mary Elizabeth, *The Black Band; or, The Mysteries of Midnight* (London: George Vickers, 1864).
Braddon, Mary Elizabeth, *Lady Audley's Secret*, edited by Natalie Houston (Peterborough, Ont.: Broadview, 2003).
Braddon, Mary Elizabeth, 'At Chrighton Abbey', in Michael Cox and R. A. Gilbert (eds), *The Oxford Book of English Ghost Stories* (Oxford: Oxford University Press, 2008), pp. 163–89.

Brantlinger, Patrick, *Rule of Darkness: British Literature and Imperialism, 1830–1914* (Ithaca, NY: Cornell University Press, 1988).

Bratton, Jacky, *New Readings in Theatre History* (Cambridge: Cambridge University Press, 2003).

Bratton, Jacky, 'Romantic Melodrama', in Jane Moody and Daniel Quinn (eds), *The Cambridge Companion to British Theatre, 1730–1830* (Cambridge: Cambridge University Press, 2007), pp. 115–27.

Breen, Jennifer (ed.), *Victorian Women Poets 1830–1900: An Anthology* (London: Everyman, 1994).

Brewster, David, *Letters on Natural Magic Addressed to Sir Walter Scott, Bart*, reprint of 1832 edition (New York: Harper and Brothers, 1842).

Brewster, Scott, 'Gothic Hogg', in Carol Margaret Davison and Monica Germanà (eds), *Scottish Gothic: An Edinburgh Companion* (Edinburgh: Edinburgh University Press, 2017), pp. 115–28.

Brewster, Scott and Luke Thurston, 'Introduction', in Scott Brewster and Luke Thurston (eds), *The Routledge Handbook to the Ghost Story* (New York and London: Routledge, 2017), pp. 1–15.

Bricchi, Mariarosa, '"Come una magnifica veste gittata sopra un manichino manierato e logoro". I 'Promessi Sposi', il gusto gotico e Ann Radcliffe', *Autografo. La letteratura italiana e l'Europa nell'Ottocento* 31 (1995): 29–70.

Briggs, Julia, 'The Ghost Story', in David Punter (ed.), *A New Companion to the Gothic* (Oxford: Wiley-Blackwell, 2012), pp. 176–85.

Brontë, Anne, *The Tenant of Wildfell Hall*, edited by G. D. Hargreaves (Harmondsworth: Penguin, 1979).

Brontë, Charlotte, *Jane Eyre*, edited by Beth Newman (Boston: Bedford/St. Martin's, 1996).

Brontë, Charlotte, *Shirley*, edited by Herbert Rosengarter, intro. by Margaret Smith (Oxford: Oxford University Press, 1981).

Brontë, Emily, *Wuthering Heights*, edited by Ian Jack (Oxford: Oxford University Press, 1995).

Brooke, John Hedley, 'Visions of the Past: Religious Belief and the Historical Sciences', in John Hedley Brooke, *Science and Religion: Some Historical Perspectives* (Cambridge: Cambridge University Press, 2014), pp. 307–73.

Brooker, Jeremy, 'The polytechnic ghost: Pepper's Ghost, metempsychosis and the magic lantern at the Royal Polytechnic Institution', *Early Popular Visual Culture* 5:2 (2007): 189–206.

Brooker, Jeremy, *The Temple of Minerva: Magic and the Magic Lantern at the Royal Polytechnic Institution, London 1837–1901* (London: The Magic Lantern Society, 2013).

Brooks, Chris, *The Gothic Revival* (London: Phaidon, 1999).

Brown, Charles Brockden, *Three Gothic Novels: Wieland, Arthur Mervyn, Edgar Huntly*, edited by Sydney J. Krause (New York: Library of America, 1998).

Brown, Rica, 'The Bécquer legend', *Bulletin of Hispanic Studies* 18:69 (1941): 4–18.

Browning, Robert, *The Poems of Robert Browning* (Oxford: Oxford University Press, 1928).

Bulfin, Ailise, 'The fiction of gothic Egypt and imperial paranoia: the curse of the Suez Canal', *English Literature in Transition, 1880–1920* 54:4 (2011): 411–43.

Burdekin, R., 'Pepper's Ghost at the opera', *Theatre Notebook* 69:3 (2015): 152–64.

Burke, Edmund, *Philosophical Enquiry into the Origin of Our Ideas of the Sublime and Beautiful*, edited by Adam Phillips (Oxford: Oxford University Press, 1998).

Select Bibliography

Burke, Peter, 'A Short History of Distance', in Mark Salber Phillips, Barbara Caine and Julia Adeney Thomas (eds), *Rethinking Historical Distance* (Basingstoke and New York: Palgrave Macmillan, 2013), pp. 21–33.

Butler, Marilyn, 'The first *Frankenstein* and radical science', *Times Literary Supplement* 9 (April 1993), pp. 12–14.

Byron, Lord George Gordon, *The Prisoner of Chillon and Other Poems* (London: Printed for John Murray, 1816).

Byron, Lord George Gordon, '"A Fragment", June 17, 1816', in Mary Shelley, *Frankenstein; or, The Modern Prometheus: The 1818 Text*, edited by James Rieger, Phoenix edition (Chicago: University of Chicago Press, 1982), pp. 260–5.

Byron, Lord George Gordon, *Lord Byron: The Major Works*, edited by Jerome McGann (Oxford: Oxford University Press, 2000).

Calder, Jenni, 'Introduction', in Margaret Oliphant, *A Beleaguered City and Other Tales of the Seen and the Unseen*, edited by Jenni Calder (Edinburgh: Canongate, 2000), pp. vii–xviii.

Calvino, Italo (ed.), *Fantastic Tales: Visionary and Everyday* (Boston: Mariner Books, 1997).

Camilletti, Fabio, 'Beyond the uncanny: *Fantasmagoriana*, intertextuality, and the pleasure principle', *Compar(a)ison* 1–2 (2009): 61–81.

Camilletti, Fabio, 'From Villa Diodati to Villa Gabrielli: a manuscript appendix to *Fantasmagoriana*', *Gothic Studies* 20:1–2 (November 2018), pp. 214–26.

Capuana, Luigi, *Novelle dal mondo occulto*, edited by Andrea Cedola (Bologna: Pendragon, 2007).

Capuana, Luigi, 'Il vampiro', in Costanza Melani (ed.), *Fantastico italiano* (Milano: BUR Rizzoli, 2009), pp. 290–308.

Carleton, William, 'The Lianhan Shee: An Irish Superstition', *Traits and Stories of the Irish Peasantry*, 2nd series, 2nd edition, 3 vols (Dublin: William Wakeman, 1834), vol. 2, pp. 3–44.

[Carlyle, Thomas], 'Signs of the times', *Edinburgh Review*, 49 (1829): 439–59.

Carlyle, Thomas, *Sartor Resartus: The Life and Opinions of Herr Teufelsdröckh* (London: Oxford University Press, 1943).

Carlyle, Thomas, *Reminiscences*, edited by K. J. Fielding and Ian Campbell (Oxford: Oxford University Press, 1997).

Carlyle, Thomas, *Past and Present*, edited by Chris R. Vanden Bossche (Berkeley, Los Angeles and London: University of California Press, 2005).

Cassuto, Leonard, 'Urban American Gothic', in Jeffrey Andrew Weinstock (ed.), *The Cambridge Companion to American Gothic* (Cambridge: Cambridge University Press, 2017), pp. 156–70.

Castle, Terry, 'Phantasmagoria: spectral technology and the metaphorics of modern reverie', *Critical Inquiry* 15:1 (1988): 26–61.

Castle, Terry, *The Female Thermometer: Eighteenth-Century Culture and the Invention of the Uncanny* (New York and Oxford: Oxford University Press, 1995).

Ceserani, Remo, 'Fantastic and Literature', in Paolo Puppa and Luca Somigli (eds), *Encyclopedia of Italian Literary Studies*, gen ed. Gaetana Marrone (London and New York, Routledge, 2007), pp. 684–8.

Chernaik, Judith and Timothy Burnett, 'The Byron and Shelley notebooks in the Scrope Davies find', *The Review of English Studies* 29:113 (1978): 36–49.

Chesterton, G. K., 'A Defence of Penny Dreadfuls', in *The Defendant* (London: Dent, 1907), pp. 8–17.

Chichester, Teddi Lynn, 'Evading "earth's dungeon tomb": Emily Brontë, A. G. A., and the fatally feminine', *Victorian Poetry* 29:1 (Spring 1991): 1–15.

Child, Francis J., *The English and Scottish Popular Ballads*, 5 vols (New York: Dover Publications, 1965).

Chisholm, Hugh, 'How to counteract the "penny dreadful"', *Fortnightly Review* 58: 347 (1895): 765–75.

Clark, Kenneth, *The Gothic Revival: An Essay on the History of Taste*, revised and enlarged edition (London: Constable, 1950).

Clemens, Valdine, *The Return of the Repressed: Gothic Horror from The Castle of Otranto to Alien* (New York: New York University Press, 1999).

Clery, E. J., 'The Genesis of "Gothic" Fiction', in Jerrold E. Hogle (ed.), *The Cambridge Companion to Gothic Fiction* (Cambridge: Cambridge University Press, 2002), pp. 21–40.

Clery, E. J. and Robert Miles (eds), *Gothic Documents: A Sourcebook 1700–1820* (Manchester and New York: Manchester University Press, 2000).

Cochran, Peter, *Byron and Bob: Lord Byron's Relationship with Robert Southey* (Newcastle upon Tyne: Cambridge Scholars, 2010).

Cohen, Jeffrey Jerome, 'Monster Culture (Seven Theses)', in *Monster Theory: Reading Culture* (Minneapolis: University of Minnesota Press, 1996), pp. 3–25.

Cohn, Jan, *Romance and the Erotics of Property* (Durham, NC: Duke University Press, 1988).

Colby, Vineta and Robert A. Colby, *The Equivocal Virtue: Mrs Oliphant and the Victorian Market Place* (Hamden, Connecticut: Archon Books, 1966).

Colclough, Stephen and David Vincent, 'Reading', in David McKitterick (ed.), *The Cambridge History of the Book in Britain, Volume VI: 1830–1914* (Cambridge: Cambridge University Press, 2009), pp. 281–323.

Coleridge, Samuel Taylor, *The Statesman's Manual* (London: Gale and Jenner, 1816).

Coleridge, Samuel Taylor, *On the Constitution of the Church and State*, edited by John Colmer (London and Princeton, NJ: Routledge & Kegan Paul, Princeton University Press, 1976).

Coleridge, Samuel Taylor, *Lectures 1808–1819: On Literature*, edited by R. Foakes, 2 vols (London and Princeton, NJ: Routledge & Kegan Paul, Princeton University Press, 1987).

Coleridge, Samuel Taylor, *Christabel 1816*, intro. by Jonathan Wordsworth (Oxford: Woodstock Books, 1991).

Coleridge, Samuel Taylor, *The Collected Works of Samuel Taylor Coleridge: Poetical Works; Poems (Variorum Text), Part I, Vol. XVI*, edited by J. C. C. Mays (Princeton, NJ: Princeton University Press, 2001).

Coleridge, Samuel Taylor and William Wordsworth, *Lyrical Ballads, 1798 and 1800*, edited by Michael Gamer and Dahlia Porter (Peterborough, Ont.: Broadview, 2008).

The Collected Letters of Robert Southey, 6 parts, edited by Lynda Pratt, Ian Packer, Tim Fulford and Carol Bolton, 2009–16 <www.rc.umd.edu/editions/southeys_letters/> (last accessed 22 January 2019).

Collodi, Carlo [pseud. of Carlo Lorenzini], *The Story of a Puppet or The Adventures of Pinocchio*, trans. by Mary Alice Murray, illust. C. Mazzanti [sic] (London: Fisher Unwin, 1892).

Colman, George the Younger, *Blue-Beard; or, Female Curiosity! A Dramatick Romance* (London: Printed by T. Woodfall for Cadell and Davies, 1798).

Colvin, Howard M. and John Newman (eds), *Of Building: Roger North's Writings on Architecture* (Oxford: Clarendon, 1981).
Conan Doyle, Arthur, 'The Adventure of the Creeping Man', in *The Casebook of Sherlock Holmes*, edited by W. W. Robson (Oxford: Oxford University Press, 2009), pp. 50–71.
Connell, Philip, *Romanticism, Economics and the Question of 'Culture'* (Oxford: Oxford University Press, 2001).
Conner, Patrick R. M., 'Pugin and Ruskin', *Journal of the Warburg and Courtauld Institutes* 41 (1978): 344–50.
Connolly, Claire, 'Writing the Union', in Daíre Keogh and Kevin Whelan (eds), *Acts of Union: The Causes, Contexts, and Consequences of the Act of Union* (Dublin: Four Courts Press, 2001), pp. 171–86.
Connolly, Claire, 'Theater and nation in Irish romanticism: the tragic drama of Charles Robert Maturin and Richard Lalor Shiel', *Éire-Ireland* 41:3&4 (2006): 185–214.
Connolly, Claire, *A Cultural History of the Irish Novel* (Cambridge: Cambridge University Press, 2011).
Connor, Steven, 'The Machine in the Ghost: Spiritualism, Technology and the "Direct Voice"', in Peter Buse and Andrew Stott (eds), *Ghosts: Deconstruction, Psychoanalysis, History* (London: Macmillan, 1999), pp. 203–25.
Connor, Steven, 'Afterword', in Nicola Bown, Carolyn Burdett and Pamela Thurschwell (eds), *The Victorian Supernatural* (Cambridge: Cambridge University Press, 2004), pp. 258–77.
Conrad, Joseph, *The Secret Agent*, edited by John Lyon (Oxford: Oxford University Press, 2008).
Cook, Edward Tyas, *The Life of John Ruskin*, 2 vols (New York: Haskell House, 1968).
Cook, E. T. and Alexander Wedderburn (eds), *The Works of John Ruskin*, 39 vols (London: George Allen, 1903–12).
Courthope, William John, *The Liberal Movement in English Literature* (London: John Murray, 1885).
Cox, Jeffrey N. (ed.), *Seven Gothic Dramas 1789–1825* (Athens, OH: Ohio University Press, 1992).
Cox, Jeffrey N., 'English Gothic Theatre', in Jerrold E. Hogle (ed.), *The Cambridge Companion to Gothic Fiction* (Cambridge: Cambridge University Press, 2002), pp. 125–44.
Cox, Jeffrey N., 'The Death of Tragedy; or, the Birth of Melodrama', in Tracy C. Davis and Peter Holland (eds), *The Performing Century: Nineteenth-Century Theatre's History* (Basingstoke: Palgrave Macmillan, 2007), pp. 161–81.
Cox, Michael, and R. A. Gilbert, 'Introduction', in Michael Cox and R. A. Gilbert (eds), *The Oxford Book of English Ghost Stories* (Oxford: Oxford University Press, 2008), pp. ix–xvii.
Croce, Benedetto, 'Arrigo Boito', in *La letteratura della Nuova Italia. Saggi Critici*, 6 vols (Bari: Laterza, 1914), vol. 1, pp. 259–76.
Croce, Benedetto, '*Gli ultimi romanzi di Francesco Domenico Guerrazzi*', in Benedetoo Croce, *La letteratura della Nuova Italia. Saggi Critici*, 6 vols (Bari: Laterza, 1914), vol. 1, pp. 27–44.
Crookenden, Isaac, *The Mysterious Murder; or, The Usurper of Naples: An Original Romance. To Which Is Prefixed, The Nocturnal Assassin; or, Spanish Jealousy* (London: Lee, 1808).
Crow, Charles L., 'Under the Upas Tree: Charles Chesnutt's Gothic', in Joseph R. McElrath, Jr (ed.), *Critical Essays on Charles Chesnutt* (New York: G. K. Hall, 1999), pp. 261–70.

Crowe, Catherine, *The Night Side of Nature; or, Ghosts and Ghost Seers* (Ware, Herts: Wordsworth, 2000).
Curry, Kenneth (ed.), *New Letters of Robert Southey*, 2 vols (New York and London: Columbia University Press, 1965).
Curry, Kenneth, *Southey*, 2nd edition (London and New York: Routledge, 2016).
Cusack, Andrew, 'Cultural Transfer in the *Dublin University Magazine*: James Clarence Mangan and the German Gothic', in Andrew Cusask and Barry Murnane (eds), *Popular Revenants: The German Gothic and Its International Reception, 1800–2000* (Rochester, NY: Camden House, 2012), pp. 87–104.
Cvetcovich, Ann, *Mixed Feelings: Feminism, Mass Culture, and Victorian Sensationalism* (New Brunswick: Rutgers University Press, 1992).
Dacre, Charlotte, *Zofloya, or The Moor*, edited by Adriana Craciun (Peterborough, Ont.: Broadview Press, 1997).
Daniele, Antonio (ed.), *Vampiriana: Novelle italiane di vampiri* (Salerno: Keres Edizioni, 2011).
D'Arcy Wood, Gillen, *Tambora: The Eruption that Changed the World* (Princeton, NJ and Oxford: Princeton University Press, 2014).
Darwin, Charles, *On the Origin of Species by Means of Natural Selection*, 2nd edition (London: John Murray, 1860).
Darwin, Charles, *The Expression of the Emotions in Man and Animals* (London: John Murray, 1872).
Darwin, Charles, *The Descent of Man*, 2nd edition (New York: D. Appleton, 1875).
Darwin, Charles, *The Variation of Animals and Plants under Domestication*, 2nd edition, 2 vols (London: John Murray, 1875).
Darwin, Charles, *The Origin of Species by Means of Natural Selection*, edited by John W. Burrow (Baltimore: Penguin, 1968).
Darwin Correspondence Project <www.darwinproject.ac.uk/> (last accessed 13 August 2019).
Darwin, Erasmus, *Zoonomia; or, the Laws of Organic Life* (London: Joseph Johnson, 1794–6).
Davidson, Cathy N., *Revolution and the Word: The Rise of the Novel in America* (New York: Oxford University Press, 1987).
Davidson, Jane P., 'Golem–Frankenstein–golem of your own', *The Journal of the Fantastic in the Arts* 7:2/3 (1995): 228–43.
Davies, Ann, *Contemporary Spanish Gothic* (Edinburgh: Edinburgh University Press, 2016).
Davison, Carol Margaret, *Gothic Literature 1764–1824* (Cardiff: University of Wales Press, 2009).
Davison, Carol Margaret, 'The Victorian Gothic and Gender', in Andrew Smith and William Hughes (eds), *The Victorian Gothic: An Edinburgh Companion* (Edinburgh: Edinburgh University Press, 2012), pp. 124–41.
Davison, Carol Margaret, 'Charles Brockden Brown: Godfather of American Gothic', in Charles L. Crow (ed.), *A Companion to American Gothic* (Malden, MA: Wiley Blackwell, 2014), pp. 110–23.
Davison, Carol Margaret, 'Southern Gothic: Haunted Houses', in Susan Castillo Street and Charles L. Crow (eds), *The Palgrave Handbook of the Southern Gothic* (Basingstoke: Palgrave Macmillan, 2016), pp. 55–67.
Davison, Carol Margaret, 'Introduction: The Corpse in the Closet: The Gothic, Death, and Modernity', in Carol Margaret Davison (ed.), *The Gothic and Death* (Manchester: Manchester University Press, 2017), pp. 1–18.

Davison, Carol Margaret and Monica Germanà, 'Borderlands of Identity and the Aesthetics of Disjuncture: An Introduction to Scottish Gothic', in Carol Margaret Davison and Monica Germanà (eds), *Scottish Gothic: An Edinburgh Companion* (Edinburgh: Edinburgh University Press, 2017), pp. 1–13.

Deane, Bradley, 'Mummy fiction and the occupation of Egypt: imperial striptease', *English Literature in Transition 1880–1920* 51:4 (2008): 381–410.

Défourneaux, Marcelin, *Inquisición y censura de libros en la España del siglo XVIII* (Madrid: Taurus, 1973).

DeLamotte, Eugenia C., *Perils of the Night: A Feminist Study of Nineteenth-Century Gothic* (Oxford: Oxford University Press, 1990).

Delano, Cristina, 'Gothic tales of the liberal nation in Juan Martínez Villergas's *Los misterios de Madrid* (1844–1845)', *Bulletin of Hispanic Studies* 93:3 (2016): 269–83.

Deleuze, Gilles and Félix A. Guattari, *A Thousand Plateaus*, trans. by Brian Massumi (London and New York: Continuum, 2004).

Desmond, Adrian, *The Politics of Evolution Morphology, Medicine, and Reform in Radical London* (Chicago: Chicago University Press, 1989).

Desmond, Adrian, *Huxley: From Devil's Disciple to Evolution's High Priest* (London: Penguin, 1998).

de Turris, Gianfranco, 'Gotico popolare italiano. Appunti per una bibliostoria', in Enzo Biffi Gentili, with Giorgio Barberi Squarotti, Valter Boggione and Barbara Zandrino (eds), *Neogotico tricolore. Letteratura e altro* (Milano and Cuneo: Cassa di Risparmio di Cuneo Foundation, 2015), pp. 129–42.

Dever, Carolyn, *Death and the Mother from Dickens to Freud: Victorian Fiction and the Anxiety of Origins* (Cambridge: Cambridge University Press, 1998).

Dickens, Charles, *Bleak House*, edited by George Ford and Sylvère Monod (New York: Norton, 1977).

Dickens, Charles, 'Mugby Junction. No. 1 Branch Line. The Signal-Man', in *Selected Short Fiction*, edited by Deborah A. Thomas (Harmondsworth: Penguin, 1977), pp. 78–90.

Dickens, Charles, *Dealings with the Firm of Dombey and Son, Wholesale, Retail and for Exportation*, edited by Peter Fairclough (Harmondsworth: Penguin, 1981).

Dickens, Charles, *Little Dorrit*, edited by Peter Harvey Sucksmith (Oxford: Oxford University Press, 1982).

Dickens, Charles, *The Mystery of Edwin Drood*, edited by Margaret Cardwell (Oxford: Oxford University Press, 1982).

Dickens, Charles, *Our Mutual Friend*, edited by Michael Cotsell (Oxford: Oxford University Press, 1989).

Dickens, Charles, *Great Expectations*, edited by Margaret Cardwell (Oxford: Oxford University Press, 1994).

Dickens, Charles, *Christmas Stories*, edited by Ruth Glancy (London: Everyman, 1996).

Dickens, Charles, 'A Christmas Tree', in David Pascoe (ed.), *Charles Dickens: Selected Journalism, 1850–1870* (Harmondsworth: Penguin, 1997), pp. 3–16.

Dickens, Charles, 'Nurse's Stories', in *The Uncommercial Traveller and Other Papers 1859–70*, edited by Michael Slater and John Drew (London: Dent, 2000), pp. 169–80.

Dickens, Charles, *The Old Curiosity Shop*, edited by Norman Page (Harmondsworth: Penguin, 2000).

Dickens, Charles, *Oliver Twist*, edited by Philip Horne (Harmondsworth: Penguin, 2002).

Dickens, Charles, *A Christmas Carol and Other Christmas Books*, edited by Robert Douglas-Fairhurst (Oxford: Oxford University Press, 2006).

Dickerson, Vanessa D., *Victorian Ghosts in the Noontide: Women Writers and the Supernatural* (Columbia and London: University of Missouri Press, 1996).

Dickinson, Emily, *The Poems of Emily Dickinson: Reading Edition*, edited by R. W. Franklin (Cambridge, MA: The Belknap Press of Harvard University Press, 1998).

di Giacomo, Salvatore. 'La fine di Barth', in Costanza Melani (ed.), *Fantastico italiano* (Milano: BUR Rizzoli, 2009), pp. 381–4.

Doherty, Ruth, 'Reading Reynolds: *The Mysteries of London* as "Microscopic Survey"', in Paul Raphael Rooney and Anna Gasperini (eds), *Media and Print Culture Consumption in Nineteenth-Century Britain: The Victorian Reading Experience* (Basingstoke: Palgrave Macmillan, 2016), pp. 147–63.

Downey, Dara, '"Taking Noiseless Turns in the Passage": Phantoms and Floor Plans in Henry James's *The Turn of the Screw*', in Helen Conrad O'Briain and Julie Anne Stevens (eds), *The Ghost Story from the Middle Ages to the Twentieth Century* (Dublin: Four Courts Press, 2010), pp. 189–202.

Downey, Dara, *American Women's Ghost Stories in the Gilded Age* (Basingstoke: Palgrave Macmillan, 2014).

Doyle, Arthur Conan, 'The Captain of the *Polestar*', in Michael Cox and R. A. Gilbert (eds), *The Oxford Book of Victorian Ghost Stories* (Oxford: Oxford University Press, 2003), pp. 283–302.

Doyle, Arthur Conan, 'Lot No. 249', in *Lost in a Pyramid & Other Classic Mummy Stories*, edited and intro. by Andrew Smith (London: British Library, 2016), pp. 127–70.

Doyle, Laura, 'At world's edge: post/coloniality, Charles Maturin, and the gothic wanderer', *Nineteenth-Century Literature* 65:4 (March 2011): 513–47.

Drake, Nathan, *Literary Hours; or, Sketches Critical and Narrative* (London, 1798).

Duggett, Tom, *Gothic Romanticism: Architecture, Politics, and Literary Form* (Basingstoke and New York: Palgrave Macmillan, 2010).

Duggett, Tom, 'Gothic and Architecture: Morris, Ruskin, Carlyle and the Gothic Legacies of the Lake Poets', in David Punter (ed.), *The Edinburgh Companion to Gothic and the Arts* (Edinburgh: Edinburgh University Press, 2019), pp. 15–35.

Duncan, Ian, 'Walter Scott, James Hogg and Scottish Gothic', in David Punter (ed.), *A New Companion to the Scottish Gothic* (Oxford: Blackwell, 2012), pp. 123–34.

During, Simon, *Modern Enchantments: The Cultural Power of Secular Magic* (Cambridge, MA and London: Harvard University Press, 2002).

Eastlake, Charles Locke, *A History of the Gothic Revival* (London: Longmans, Green and Co., 1872).

Eckardt, Theodore, *Physics in Pictures: The Principal Natural Phenomena and Appliances described and illustrated by thirty coloured plates for ocular instruction in schools and families*, trans A. H. Keane (London: Edward Stanford, 1882).

Edgecombe, Rodney Stenning, 'Anti-clerical gothic: the tale of the sisters in *Nicholas Nickleby*', *Modern Language Review* 94:1 (January 1999): 1–10.

Edgeworth, Maria, *Ennui*, in Marilyn Butler and Mitzi Myers (eds), *The Novels and Selected Works of Maria Edgeworth*, 12 vols (London: Pickering & Chatto, 1999–2003), vol. 1, pp. 157–308.

Edmundson, Melissa, 'The "uncomfortable houses" of Charlotte Riddell and Margaret Oliphant', *Gothic Studies* 12:1 (2010): 51–67.
Edmundson, Melissa, 'Women Writers and the Ghost Story', in Scott Brewster and Luke Thurston (eds), *The Routledge Handbook to the Ghost Story* (New York and London: Routledge, 2017), pp. 69–77.
Edwards, Amelia B., 'The Phantom Coach', in Michael Cox and R. A. Gilbert (eds), *The Oxford Book of English Ghost Stories* (Oxford: Oxford University Press, 2008), pp. 13–24.
Edwards, Bryan, *An Historical Survey of the French Colony In the Island of St. Domingo* (London, 1797).
Eimer, Manfred, 'Einflüsse deutscher Räuber- und Schauerromantik auf Shelley, Mrs. Shelley und Byron', *Englische Studien* 48 (1914–15): 231–45.
Elbert, Monika and Wendy Ryden (eds), *Haunting Realities: Naturalistic Gothic and American Realism* (Tualoosa: University of Alabama Press, 2017).
Eliot, George, *Felix Holt, The Radical*, edited by Peter Coveney (Harmondsworth: Penguin, 1975).
Eliot, Simon J. and Andrew Nash, 'Mass Markets: Literature', in David McKitterick (ed.), *The Cambridge History of the Book in Britain, Volume VI: 1830–1914* (Cambridge: Cambridge University Press, 2009), pp. 418–19.
Ellis, David, *Byron in Geneva: The Summer of 1816* (Oxford: Oxford University Press, 2011).
Ellis, F. S., *A Lexical Concordance to the Poetical Works of Percy Bysshe Shelley* (London: Bernard Quadrich, 1892; rpt. Johnson Reprint Company 1967).
Ellis, Peter Beresford, *H. Rider Haggard: A Voice from the Infinite* (London: Routledge & Kegan Paul, 1978).
Eltis, Sos, 'Corruption of the Blood and Degeneration of the Race: *Dracula* and Policing the Borders of Gender', in John Paul Riquelme (ed.), *Dracula* (Boston: Bedford/St. Martin's, 2002), pp. 450–65.
Emerson, Ralph Waldo, 'Nature', in Joel Porte (ed.), *Emerson: Essays and Lectures* (New York: Library of America, 1983), pp. 9–49.
Enns, Anthony, 'The Undead Author: Spiritualism, Technology and Authorship', in Nicola Bown, Carolyn Burdett and Pamela Thurschwell (eds), *The Victorian Supernatural* (Cambridge: Cambridge University Press, 2004), pp. 55–78.
Evans, Dewi, 'The Victorian Ghost Story and the Invention of Christmas', in Scott Brewster and Luke Thurston (eds), *The Routledge Handbook to the Ghost Story* (New York and London: Routledge, 2017), pp. 78–86.
Eyriès, Jean-Baptiste Benoît, *Fantasmagoriana, ou Recueil d'Histoires d'Apparitions de Spectres, Revenans, Fantômes, etc.; Traduit de l'allemand, par un Amateur*, 2 vols (Paris: Schoell, 1812).
Ezra, Elizabeth, *Georges Méliès: The Birth of the Auteur* (Manchester: Manchester University Press, 2000).
Faflak, Joel and Jason Haslam, 'Introduction', in Joel Faflak and Jason Haslam (eds), *American Gothic Culture: An Edinburgh Companion* (Edinburgh: Edinburgh University Press, 2016), pp. 1–22.
Fanon, Frantz, *Black Skin, White Masks*, trans. by Charles Lam Markmann (New York: Grove Press, 1967).
Faulkner, Peter (ed.), *William Morris: The Critical Heritage* (London: Routledge and Kegan Paul, 1973).

Faulkner, Peter, 'Ruskin and Morris', *Journal of the William Morris Society* 14:1 (2000): 6–17.

Feldman, Paula R. and Diana Scott-Kilvert (eds), *The Journals of Mary Shelley, 1814–1844*, 2 vols (Oxford: Clarendon Press, 1987).

Fennell, Jack, *A Brilliant Void: A Selection of Classic Irish Science Fiction* (Dublin: Tramp Press, 2018).

Ferguson, Frances, 'Shelley's "Mont Blanc": What the Mountain Said', in Michael O'Neill (ed.), *Shelley* (London: Longman, 1993), pp. 43–55.

Ferriar, John, *An Essay Towards a Theory of Apparitions* (London: Cadell and Davies, 1813).

Fielding, Penny, *Writing and Orality: Nationality, Culture, and Nineteenth-Century Scottish Fiction* (Oxford: Oxford University Press, 1996).

Fisher, Benjamin F., 'Early American Gothic Drama', in Charles L. Crow (ed.), *A Companion to American Gothic* (Malden, MA: Wiley Blackwell, 2014), pp. 96–109.

Fisher, Benjamin Franklin IV (ed.), *The Gothic's Gothic: Study Aids to the Tradition of the Tale of Terror* (New York: Routledge, 2018).

Fitzball, Edward, *The Flying Dutchman; or, The Phantom Ship: A Nautical Drama* (London: G. H. Davidson, n.d.).

Fitzgerald, F. Scott, 'A Short Trip Home', in Mike Ashley (ed.), *The Platform Edge: Uncanny Tales of the Railways* (London: British Library, 2019), pp. 257–83.

Fitzgerald, Lauren, 'Female Gothic and the institutionalization of Gothic studies', *Gothic Studies* 6:1 (2004): 8–18.

Foni, Fabrizio, *Alla fiera dei mostri. Racconti pulp, horror e arcane fantasticherie nelle riviste italiane 1899–1932* (Latina: Tanué, 2007).

Fontes da Costa, Palmira, 'The Meaning of Monstrosities in Charles Darwin's Understanding of the Origin of Species', in Ana Leonor Pereira, João Pita and Pedro Ricardo Fonseca (eds), *Darwin, Evolution, Evolutionists* (Coimbra: Imprensa da Universidade de Coimbra, 2011), pp. 74–83.

Forster, E. M. 'The Story of a Panic', in *Selected Stories*, edited, and with an introduction and notes, by David Leavitt and Mark Mitchell (Harmondsworth: Penguin, 2001), pp. 1–23.

Forster, John, *The Life of Charles Dickens* (London: Chapman and Hall, 1892).

Fosbrooke, Thomas Dudley, *British Monachism: or, Manners and Customs of the Monks and Nuns of England*, 2nd edition, 2 vols (London: John Nichols, 1817).

Foscolo, Ugo, *The Sepulchres. Addressed to Ippolito Pindemonte*, trans. attrib. to Stratford Canning, Viscount Stratford de Redcliffe (London, 1820?).

Foucault, Michel, *The Order of Things: An Archaeology of the Human Sciences* (London and New York: Routledge, 2002).

Frangipani, Maria Antonietta, *Motivi del romanzo nero nella letteratura lombarda* (Roma: Editrice Elia, 1981).

Frank, Frederick S., 'Gothic gold: the Sadleir-Black Gothic collection', *Studies in Eighteenth-Century Culture* 26 (1997): 287–312

Franklin, Caroline (ed.), *The Longman Anthology of Gothic Verse* (Harlow: Pearson, 2011).

Franklin, J. Jeffrey, 'The counter-invasion of Britain by Buddhism in Marie Corelli's *A Romance of Two Worlds* and H. Rider Haggard's *Ayesha: The Return of She*', *Victorian Literature and Culture* 31:1 (2003): 19–42.

Free, Melissa, '"Dirty linen": legacies of empire in Wilkie Collins's *The Moonstone*', *Texas Studies in Literature and Language* 48:4 (2006): 340–71.

Freeman, Nick, 'E. Nesbit's new woman gothic', *Women's Writing* 15:3 (2008): 454–69.
Freeman, Nick, 'The Victorian Ghost Story', in Andrew Smith and William Hughes (eds), *The Victorian Gothic: An Edinburgh Companion* (Edinburgh: Edinburgh University Press, 2012), pp. 93–107.
Freud, Sigmund, 'The "Uncanny"', in *Collected Papers of Sigmund Freud*, edited and trans. by Joan Riviere, 5 vols (London: Hogarth Press, 1949), vol. 4, pp. 368–407.
Freud, Sigmund, 'Beyond the Pleasure Principle', in *Pelican Freud Library Volume XI: On Metapsychology*, edited by Angela Richards (Harmondsworth: Penguin, 1984), pp. 271–338.
Frith, Richard, '"The Worship of Courage": William Morris's *Sigurd the Volsung* and Victorian Medievalism', in L. M. Holloway and J. A. Palmgren (eds), *Beyond Arthurian Romances* (New York: Palgrave Macmillan, 2005), pp. 117–32.
Fulford, Tim, 'Virtual Topography: Poets, Painters, Publishers and the Reproduction of the Landscape in the Early Nineteenth Century', *Romanticism and Victorianism on the Net*, 57–58 (February–May 2010) <http://id.erudit.org/iderudit/1006512ar> (last accessed 22 January 2019).
Furneaux, Holly, *Queer Dickens: Erotics, Families, Masculinities* (Oxford: Oxford University Press, 2009).
Gale, Steven H. (ed.), *Encyclopedia of British Humorists: Geoffrey Chaucer to John Cleese*, 3 vols (New York and London: Garland, 1996).
Gallagher, Catherine and Stephen Greenblatt, *Practicing New Historicism* (Chicago: Chicago University Press, 2000).
Gamer, Michael, *Romanticism and the Gothic: Genre, Reception, and Canon Formation* (Cambridge: Cambridge University Press, 2000).
Gamer, Michael, 'Gothic Melodrama', in Carolyn Williams (ed.), *The Cambridge Companion to English Melodrama* (Cambridge: Cambridge University Press, 2018), pp. 31–46.
Gange, David, 'Religion and science in late nineteenth-century British Egyptology', *The Historical Journal* 49:4 (December 2006): 1083–103.
Garside, Peter, 'Introduction: Consolidation and Dispersal', in Peter Garside, James Raven and Rainer Schöwerling (eds), *The English Novel, 1770–1829: A Bibliographical Survey of Prose Fiction Published in the British Isles*, 2 vols (Oxford: Oxford University Press, 2000), vol. 2, pp. 1–103.
Gaskell, Elizabeth, 'The Old Nurse's Story', in *Gothic Tales*, edited by Laura Kranzler (Harmondsworth: Penguin, 2000), pp. 11–32.
Gaudenzi, Cosetta, 'Carolina Invernizio's "Punishment"', *Forum Italicum: A Journal of Italian Studies* 38:2 (2004): 562–81.
Geffarth, Renko, 'The Masonic Necromancer: Shifting Identities in the Lives of Johann Georg Schrepfer', in Olav Hammer and Kocku von Stuckrad (eds), *Polemical Encounters: Esoteric Discourse and Its Others* (Leiden and Boston: Brill, 2007), pp. 181–97.
Gerard, Emily, 'Transylvanian superstitions', *The Nineteenth Century* 20 (July 1885): 128–44.
Ghidetti, Enrico (ed.), *Notturno italiano. Racconti fantastici dell'Ottocento* (Roma: Editori Riuniti, 1984).
Ghidetti, Enrico, *Dal racconto fantastico al romanzo popolare* (Roma: Editori Riuniti, 1987).
Ghislanzoni, Antonio, *Racconti* (Milano: Sonzogno, 1884).
Gianquitto, Tina, 'Criminal Botany: Progress, Degeneration, and Darwin's *Insectivorous Plants*', in Tina Gianquitto and Lydia Fisher (eds), *America's Darwin: Darwinian Theory and U.S. Literary Culture* (Athens, GA: University of Georgia Press, 2014), pp. 235–62.

Gilbert, Sandra M. and Susan Gubar, *The Madwoman in the Attic: The Woman Writer and the Nineteenth-Century Literary Imagination* (New Haven: Yale University Press, 1979).

Gilbert, Suzanne, 'James Hogg and the Authority of Tradition', in Sharon Alker and Holly Faith Nelson (eds), *James Hogg and the Literary Marketplace: Scottish Romanticism and the Working-Class Author* (Farnham: Ashgate, 2009), pp. 93–109.

Gillespie, Niall, 'Irish Jacobin Gothic, c. 1796–1825', in Christina Morin and Niall Gillespie (eds), *Irish Gothics: Genres, Forms, Modes, and Traditions, c. 1760–1890* (Basingstoke: Palgrave Macmillan, 2014), pp. 58–73

Ginger, Andrew, *Painting and the Turn to Cultural Modernity in Spain: The Time of Eugenio Lucas Velázquez (1850–1870)* (Selinsgrove, PA: Susquehanna University Press, 2007).

Gledhill, Christine, 'Domestic Melodrama', in Carolyn Williams (ed.), *The Cambridge Companion to English Melodrama* (Cambridge: Cambridge University Press, 2018), pp. 61–77.

Goddu, Teresa A., 'The African American Slave Narrative and the Gothic', in Charles L. Crow, *A Companion to American Gothic* (Walden, MA: Wiley Blackwell, 2014), pp. 71–83.

Gómez de Avellaneda, Gertrudis, 'La dama de Amboto', *Leyendas del siglo XIX* (Madrid: Akal, 2013), pp. 153–62.

González de Vega, Gerardo, 'La literatura fantástica española bajo el Antiguo Régimen', *El demonio meridiano: Cuentos fantásticos y de terror en la España del Antiguo Régimen* (Madrid: Miraguano Ediciones, 2015), pp. 13–148.

Gorky, Maxim, 'Newspaper review of the Lumière programme at the Nizhni-Novgorod Fair, *Nizhegorodski listok*, 4 July 1896', in Colin Harding and Simon Popple (eds), *In the Kingdom of Shadows: A Companion to Early Cinema* (London: Cygnus arts, 1996), pp. 5–6.

Goslee, Nancy Moore, *Shelley's Visual Imagination* (Cambridge: Cambridge University Press, 2011).

Gosse, Edmund, *A History of Eighteenth Century Literature (1660–1780)* (London and New York: Macmillan and Co., 1889).

Gray, Thomas, *The Complete English Poems of Thomas Gray*, edited by James Reeves (London: Heineman, 1973).

Gray, William, *Robert Louis Stevenson: A Literary Life* (New York: Palgrave Macmillan, 2004).

Greenblatt, Stephen, *Renaissance Self-Fashioning: From More to Shakespeare*, revised edition (Chicago: University of Chicago Press, 2005).

Greenblatt, Stephen, *Hamlet in Purgatory: Expanded Edition* (Princeton, NJ and Oxford: Princeton University Press, 2013).

Grierson, Herbert J. C., *Sir Walter Scott, Bart* (London: Constable & Co., 1938).

Griffin, Gerald, 'The Brown Man', in *Holland-Tide; or, Irish Popular Tales*, 2nd edition (London: Saunders and Otley, 1827), pp. 295–307.

Groom, Nick, '"The Celtic Century" and the Genesis of Scottish Gothic', in Carol Margaret Davison and Monica Germanà (eds), *Scottish Gothic: An Edinburgh Companion* (Edinburgh: Edinburgh University Press, 2017), pp. 14–27.

Groom, Nick, 'Catachthonic romanticism: buried history, deep ruins', *Romanticism* 24:2 (2018): 118–33.

Gruner, Elisabeth Rose, 'Plotting the mother: Caroline Norton, Helen Huntingdon, and Isabel Vane', *Tulsa Studies in Women's Literature* 16:2 (Autumn 1997): 303–25.

Guerrazzi, Francesco Domenico, *Note autobiografiche e poema* (Firenze: Successori Le Monnier, 1899).
Gutiérrez, Luis, *Cornelia Bororquia, o víctima de la Inquisición* (Madrid: Cátedra, 2005).
Habegger, Alfred, *Henry James and the 'Woman Business'* (Cambridge: Cambridge University Press, 1989).
Hackenberg, Sara, 'Vampires and resurrection men: the perils and pleasures of the embodied past in 1840s sensational fiction', *Victorian Studies* 52:1 (2009): 63–75.
Haining, Peter (ed.), *The Shilling Shockers: Stories of Terror from the Gothic Bluebooks* (London: Gollancz, 1978).
Hale, Terry (ed.), *Tales of the Dead: The Ghost Stories of the Villa Diodati* (Chislehurst: The Gothic Society, 1992).
Hale, Terry, 'Roman Noir', in Marie Mulvey-Roberts (ed.), *The Handbook of the Gothic* (Basingstoke: Palgrave Macmillan, 2009), pp. 307–9.
Hall, Michael, 'Introduction', in Michael Hall (ed.), *Gothic Architecture and Its Meanings, 1550–1830* (Reading: Spire Books, 2002), pp. 7–24.
Harries, Susie, *Nikolaus Pevsner: The Life* (London: Pimlico, 2013).
Harris, Elisha, 'Introduction', in Richard Dugdale, *'The Jukes': A Study in Crime, Pauperism, Disease, and Heredity*, 3rd edition (New York: G. P. Putnam's sons, 1877), pp. v–vi.
Harris, Mason, 'Introduction', in H. G. Wells, *The Island of Dr Moreau*, edited by Mason Harris (Peterborough, Ont.: Broadview, 2009), pp. 13–58.
Harson, Robert R., 'Byron's "Tintern Abbey"', *Keats-Shelley Journal* 20 (1971): 113–21.
Hartman, Mary S., *Victorian Murderesses: A True History of Thirteen Respectable French and English Women Accused of Unspeakable Crimes* (New York: Schocken, 1977).
Hazlitt, William, *Lectures on the English Poets. Delivered at the Surrey Institution* (London: Printed for Taylor and Hessey, 1818).
Heard, Mervyn, *Phantasmagoria: The Secret Life of the Magic Lantern* (Hastings: The Projection Box, 2006).
Heard, Mervyn and Richard Crangle, 'The Temperance Phantasmagoria', in Richard Crangle, Mervyn Heard and Ine van Dooren (eds), *Realms of Light: Uses and Perceptions of the Magic Lantern from the 17th to the 21st Century* (London: The Magic Lantern Society, 2005), pp. 46–55.
Hecht, Hermann, 'The history of projecting phantoms, ghosts, and apparitions – Part 1', *The New Magic Lantern Journal* 3:1 (1984): 2–6.
Hecht, Hermann, 'The history of projecting phantoms, ghosts, and apparitions – Part 2', *The New Magic Lantern Journal* 3:2 (1984): 2–6.
Hecht, Hermann, 'Stage magic and illusions', *The New Magic Lantern Journal* 6:3 (1992): 10–13.
Heilman, Robert B., *Tragedy and Melodrama: Versions of Experience* (Seattle, WA and London: University of Washington Press, 1968).
Heller, Tamar, *Dead secrets: Wilkie Collins and the Female Gothic* (New Haven: Yale University Press, 1992).
Heller, Tamar, 'Textual seductions: women's reading and writing in Margaret Oliphant's "The Library Window"', *Victorian Literature and Culture* 25:1 (Spring 1997): 23–37.
Heller, Tamar, 'Victorian sensationalism and the silence of maternal sexuality in Edith Wharton's *The Mother's Recompense*', *Narrative* 5.2 (May 1997): 135–42.

Heller, Tamar, 'Haunted Bodies: The Female Gothic of *Wuthering Heights*', in Sue Lonoff and Terri A. Hasseler (eds), *Approaches to Teaching Emily Brontë's Wuthering Heights* (New York: MLA Press, 2006), pp. 67–74.

Hendershot, Cindy, *The Animal Within: Masculinity and the Gothic* (Ann Arbor, MI: University of Michigan Press, 1998).

Henry, Eva M., 'The Curse of Vasartas', in *Lost in a Pyramid & Other Classic Mummy Stories*, edited and intro. by Andrew Smith (London: British Library, 2016), pp. 107–25.

Henson, Louise, 'Investigations and Fictions: Charles Dickens and Ghosts', in Nicola Bown, Carolyn Burdett and Pamela Thurschwell (eds), *The Victorian Supernatural* (Cambridge: Cambridge University Press, 2004), pp. 44–63.

Herr, Curt, 'Introduction', in James Malcolm Rymer, *Varney the Vampire*, edited by Curt Herr (Crestline, CA: Zittaw Press, 2008), pp. 8–27.

Hervey, Thomas K., *The Book of Christmas*, reprint of 1836 edition (Boston, MA: Roberts Brothers, 1888).

Hill, Rosemary, *God's Architect: Pugin and the Building of Romantic Britain* (London: Allen Lane, 2007).

Hill, Susan and Stephen Mallatratt, *The Woman in Black* (London: Samuel French, 1989).

Hillis Miller, J., 'The genres of *A Christmas Carol*', *Dickensian* 89: 431 (Winter 1993): 193–206.

Hoeveler, Diane Long, *Gothic Riffs: Secularizing the Uncanny in the European Imaginary, 1780–1820* (Columbus, OH: Ohio State University Press, 2010).

Hoeveler, Diane Long, 'More gothic gold: the Sadleir-Black chapbook collection at the University of Virginia Library.', *Papers on Language and Literature* 46 (2010): 164–93.

Hoeveler, Diane Long, 'Anti-Catholicism and the Gothic Imaginary: The Historical and Literary Contexts', in Brett C. McInelly (ed.), *Religion in the Age of Enlightenment*, 5 vols (New York: AMS Press, 2012), vol. 3, pp. 1–31.

Hoeveler, Diane Long, 'Gothic Adaptation, 1764–1830', in Glennis Byron and Dale Townshend (eds), *The Gothic World* (Abingdon and New York: Routledge, 2014), pp. 185–98.

Hoeveler, Diane Long, *The Gothic Ideology: Religious Hysterias and Anti-Catholicism in British Popular Fiction, 1780–1880* (Cardiff: University of Wales Press, 2014).

Hogg, James, *The Private Memoirs and Confessions of a Justified Sinner*, edited by P. D. Garside (Edinburgh: Edinburgh University Press, 2001).

Hogg, James, 'The Brownie of the Black Haggs', in *The Shepherd's Calendar*, edited by Douglas S. Mack (Edinburgh: Edinburgh University Press, 2002), pp. 242–55.

Hogg, James, 'Mary Burnet', in *The Shepherd's Calendar*, edited by Douglas S. Mack (Edinburgh: Edinburgh University Press, 2002), pp. 200–22.

Hogg, James, 'Kilmeny', in *The Queen's Wake*, edited by Douglas S. Mack (Edinburgh: Edinburgh University Press, 2004), pp. 288–96.

Hogg, James, 'The Pedlar', in *The Mountain Bard*, edited by Suzanne Gilbert (Edinburgh: Edinburgh University Press, 2007), pp. 26–36.

Hogle, Jerrold E., '"Christabel" as gothic: the abjection of instability', *Gothic Studies* 7:1 (2005): 18–28.

Hogle, Jerrold E., 'The gothic image at the Villa Diodati', *The Wordsworth Circle* 47 (2017): 16–26.

Hollington, Michael, 'Dickens's gothic gargoyles', *Dickens Quarterly* 16:3 (September 1999): 160–77.

Select Bibliography

Holmes, Richard (ed.), *Coleridge: Selected Poems* (London: HarperCollins, 1996).

'Homicidal Heroines', in Andrew Maunder (ed.), *Sensationalism and the Sensation Debate: Varieties of Women's Sensation Fiction 1855–1890*, 6 vols (London: Pickering & Chatto, 2004), vol. 1, pp. 145–9.

Hood, Thomas, *The Poetical Works of Thomas Hood*, edited by William Michael Rossetti (London: Ward, Lock, and Co., 1870).

Hooper, Lucy H., 'Carnivorine', in Chad Arment (ed.), *Botanica Delira: More Stories of Strange, Undiscovered, and Murderous Vegetation* (Landisville, PA: Coachwhip, 2010), pp. 73–81.

Hopkins, Albert A., *Magic: Stage Illusions and Scientific Diversions including Trick Photography* (London: Sampson, Low, Marston and Co, 1897).

Horn, David G., *The Criminal Body: Lombroso and the Anatomy of Deviance* (New York: Routledge, 2003).

Howe, Stephen, *Ireland and Empire: Colonial Legacies in Irish History and Culture* (Oxford: Oxford University Press, 2000).

Huggett, Richard, *Supernatural on Stage: Ghosts & Superstitions of the Theatre* (New York: Taplinger, 1975).

Hughes, William, 'The Uncanny Space of Regionality: Gothic Beyond the Metropolis', in William Hughes, and Ruth Heholt (eds), *Gothic Britain: Dark Places in the Provinces and Margins of the British Isles* (Cardiff: University of Wales Press, 2018), pp. 1–24.

Humpherys, Anne, 'An Introduction to G. W. M. Reynolds's "Encyclopaedia of Tales"', in Anne Humpherys and Louis James (eds), *G. W. M. Reynolds: Nineteenth-Century Fiction, Politics and the Press* (Aldershot and Burlington, VT: Ashgate, 2008), pp. 123–32.

Hurley, Kelly, *The Gothic Body: Sexuality, Materialism, and Degeneration at the Fin de Siècle* (Cambridge: Cambridge University Press, 1996).

Hyder, Clyde K., 'Rossetti's "Rose Mary": a study in the occult', *Victorian Poetry* 1:3 (1963): 197–207.

Iarocci, Michael P., *Properties of Modernity: Romantic Spain, Modern Europe, and the Legacies of Empire* (Nashville, TN: Vanderbilt University Press, 2006).

Illustrated Catalogue of Magic Lanterns (Chicago, IL: McIntosh Battery and Optical Company Co., 1890).

Jackson, Rosemary, *Fantasy: The Literature of Subversion* (London and New York, Methuen, 1981).

James, Henry, 'Miss Braddon', in Norman Page (ed.), *Wilkie Collins: The Critical Heritage* (London: Routledge, 1974), pp. 122–4.

James, Henry, 'Preface', in *The Turn of the Screw*, edited by Peter G. Beidler (Boston and New York: Bedford/St Martin's, 2004), pp. 179–86.

James, Henry, 'Review of *Aurora Floyd*', in Mark Wilson and Leon Edel (eds), *Literary Criticism: Essays on Literature, American Writers, English Writers* (New York: Library of America, 1984), pp. 741–6.

James, Henry, 'The Turn of the Screw', in *The Turn of the Screw and Other Stories*, edited by T. J. Lustig (Oxford: Oxford University Press, 2008), pp. 113–236.

James, Louis, *Fiction for the Working Man, 1830–1850: A Study of the Literature Produced for the Working Classes in Early Victorian Urban England* (London: Oxford University Press, 1963).

James, M. R., 'The Mezzotint', in M. R. James, *Collected Ghost Stories*, edited by Darryl Jones (Oxford: Oxford University Press, 2011), pp. 24–34.

James, M. R., 'Some Remarks on Ghost Stories', in M. R. James, *Collected Ghost Stories*, edited by Darryl Jones (Oxford: Oxford University Press, 2011), pp. 410–16.

James, William, 'The Confidences of a "Psychical Researcher"' (1909), in *Essays in Psychical Research*, edited by Frederick Burkhardt and Fredson Bowers (Cambridge and London: Harvard University Press, 1986), pp. 361–75.

Jann, Rosemary, 'Democratic myths in Victorian medievalism', *Browning Institute Studies* 8 (1980): 129–49.

Jarrells, Anthony, 'Short Fictional Forms and the Rise of the Tale', in Peter Garside and Karen O'Brien (eds), *The Oxford History of the Novel in English, Volume II: English and British Fiction, 1750–1820* (Oxford: Oxford University Press, 2015), pp. 478–94.

Jerrold, Douglas, *The Rent Day: A Domestic Drama, in Two Acts* (London: Printed for C. Chappel, 1832).

Jewett, Sarah Orne, 'In Dark New England Days', in Peter Straub (ed.), *American Fantastic Tales: Terror and the Uncanny, From Poe to the Pulps*, 2 vols (New York: Library of America), vol. 1, pp. 112–30.

Jewsbury, Geraldine, 'Reader's Report on *East Lynne*', Appendix B in Ellen Wood, *East Lynne*, edited by Andrew Maunder (Peterborough, Ont.: Broadview Press, 2000), pp. 698–9.

Johnson, Ray, 'Tricks, traps, and transformations: illusion in Victorian spectacular theatre', *Early Popular Visual Culture* 5:4 (2007): 151–65.

Jones, David Annwn, *Gothic Effigy: A Guide to Dark Visibilities* (Manchester: Manchester University Press, 2018).

Jones, David J., *Gothic Machine: Textualities, Pre-cinematic Media and Film in Popular Visual Culture, 1670–1910* (Cardiff: University of Wales Press, 2011).

Jones, Timothy G., 'The canniness of the Gothic: genre as practice', *Gothic Studies* 11:1 (2009): 124–33.

Jonckheere, Evelien and Kurt Vanhoutte, 'Metempsychosis as attraction on the fairground: the migration of a ghost', *Early Popular Visual Culture* 17:2 (2019): 261–78.

Joshi, S. T., *The Weird Tale: Arthur Machen, Lord Dunsany, Algernon Blackwood, M. R. James, H. P. Lovecraft* (Austin: University of Texas Press, 1990).

Kahane, Claire, 'The Gothic Mirror', in Shirley Nelson Garner, Claire Kahane and Madelon Sprengnether (eds), *The (M)Other Tongue: Essays in Feminist Psychoanalytic Interpretation* (Ithaca, NY: Cornell University Press, 1985), pp. 43–64.

Kaplan, Morton and Robert Kloss, *The Unspoken Motive: A Guide to Psychoanalytic Literary Criticism* (New York: Free Press, 1973).

Kattelman, Beth A., 'Spectres and Spectators: The Poly-Technologies of the Pepper's Ghost Illusion', in Kara Reilly (ed.), *Theatre, Performance, and Analogue Technology* (Basingstoke: Palgrave Macmillan, 2013), pp. 198–213.

Keetley, Dawn, 'Six Theses on Plant Horror', in Dawn Keetley and Angela Tenga (eds), *Plant Horror: Approaches to the Monstrous Vegetal in Fiction and Film* (Basingstoke: Palgrave Macmillan, 2016), pp. 1–30.

Kelly, Gary (ed.), *Varieties of Female Gothic, Volume II: Street Gothic: Female Gothic Chapbooks* (London and Brookfield VT, Pickering & Chatto, 2002).

Kelvin, Norman (ed.), *The Collected Letters of William Morris*, 4 vols (Princeton, NJ: Princeton University Press, 1984–96).

Kember, Joe, *Marketing Modernity: Victorian Popular Shows and Early Cinema* (Exeter: University of Exeter Press, 2009).

Kember, Joe, 'Productive intermediality and the expert audiences of magic theatre and early film', *Early Popular Visual Culture* 8:1 (2010): 31–46.

Khair, Tabish, 'Summing Up', in *The Gothic, Postcolonialism and Otherness: Ghosts from Elsewhere* (New York: Palgrave Macmillan, 2009), pp. 157–74.

Kidd, Colin, *Subverting Scotland's Past: Scottish Whig Historians and the Creation of an Anglo-British Identity, 1689–1830* (Cambridge: Cambridge University Press, 2003).

Kilfeather, Siobhán, 'The Gothic Novel', in John Wilson Foster (ed.), *The Cambridge Companion to the Irish Novel* (Cambridge: Cambridge University Press, 2006), pp. 78–96.

Kilgour, Maggie, *The Rise of the Gothic Novel* (London: Routledge, 1995).

Killeen, Jarlath, *Gothic Ireland: Horror and the Irish Anglican Imagination in the Long Eighteenth Century* (Dublin: Four Courts Press, 2005).

Killeen, Jarlath, *Gothic Literature 1825–1914* (Cardiff: University of Wales Press, 2009).

Killeen, Jarlath, *The Emergence of Irish Gothic Fiction: History, Origins, Theory* (Edinburgh: Edinburgh University Press, 2014).

Killick, Tim, *British Short Fiction in the Early Nineteenth Century: The Rise of the Tale* (Aldershot and Burlington, VT: Ashgate, 2008).

King, Andrew, '"Literature of the Kitchen": Cheap Serial Fiction of the 1840s and 1850s', in Pamela K. Gilbert (ed.), *A Companion to Sensation Fiction* (Malden, MA: Wiley-Blackwell, 2011), pp. 38–53.

King, Jason, 'Emigration and the Anglo-Irish novel: William Carleton, "home sickness", and the coherence of gothic conventions', *The Canadian Journal of Irish Studies*, 26:2/27:1 (2000–1): 104–18.

Kipling, Rudyard, *The Collected Poems of Rudyard Kipling*, edited by R. T. Jones (Ware: Wordsworth, 1999).

Kipling, Rudyard, *The Phantom 'Rickshaw and Other Ghost Stories* (Fairfield, CT: 1st World Library, 2007).

Kirkpatrick, Jobert J., *From the Penny Dreadful to the Ha'penny Dreadfuller: A Bibliographic History of the Boys' Periodical in Britain 1762–1950* (London: British Library; New Castle, DE: Oak Knoll Press, 2013).

Kite, Stephen, 'Shaping the Darks; Ruskin's "Energetic Shadow"', in Timothy Brittain-Catlin, Jan de Meyer and Martin Bressani (eds), *Gothic Revival Worldwide: A. W. N. Pugin's Global Influence* (Leuven: Leuven University Press, 2016), pp. 228–39.

Kitson, Peter J., 'The Victorian Gothic', in William Baker and Kenneth Womack (eds), *A Companion to the Victorian Novel* (Westport, CT: Greenwood Press, 2002), pp. 163–76.

Kleiner, Fred S., *Gardner's Art Through the Ages: Non-Western Perspectives*, 13th edition (Boston, MA: Wadsworth, 2010).

Kliger, Samuel, 'The "Goths" in England: an introduction to the Gothic vogue in eighteenth-century aesthetic discussion', *Modern Philology* 43:2 (1945): 107–17.

Klopp, Charles, 'Workshops of Creation, Filthy and Not: Collodi's "Pinocchio" and Shelley's "Frankenstein"', in Katia Pizzi (ed.), *Pinocchio, Puppets and Modernity: The Mechanical Body* (London and New York: Routledge, 2012), pp. 63–74.

Koch, Angela, 'Gothic bluebooks in the princely library of Corvey and beyond', *Cardiff Corvey: Reading the Romantic Text* 9 (December 2002) <www.romtext.org.uk/articles/cc09_n01\> (last accessed 10 June 2019).

Koselleck, Reinhart, *Futures Past: On the Semantics of Historical Time*, trans. and edited by Keith Tribe (New York and Chichester: Columbia University Press, 2004).

Kreilkamp, Vera, 'The Novel of the Big House', in John Wilson Foster (ed.), *The Cambridge Companion to the Irish Novel* (Cambridge: Cambridge University Press, 2006), pp. 60–77.

Kristeva, Julia, *Powers of Horror: An Essay on Abjection*, trans. by Leon S. Roudiez (New York: Columbia University Press, 1982).

Lang, Andrew, 'The comparative study of ghost stories', *The Nineteenth Century* 17 (1885): 623–32.

Lang, Andrew, 'Mrs. Radcliffe's novels', *The Cornhill Magazine* 9:49 (July 1900): 23–34.

Langdon, Perceval, 'Railhead', in Mike Ashley (ed.), *The Platform Edge: Uncanny Tales of the Railways* (London: British Library, 2019), pp. 109–18.

Lankester, Edwin, *Degeneration: A Chapter in Darwinism* (London: Macmillan, 1880).

Law, Graham and Robert L. Patten, 'The Serial Revolution', in David McKitterick (ed.), *The Cambridge History of the Book in Britain, Volume VI: 1830–1914* (Cambridge: Cambridge University Press, 2009), pp. 144–71.

Ledger, Sally and Roger Luckhurst (eds), *The Fin-de-Siècle Reader: A Reader in Cultural History, c. 1880–1900* (Oxford: Oxford University Press, 2000).

Lee, Vernon, *Hauntings and Other Fantastic Tales*, edited by Catherine Maxwell and Patricia Pulham (Peterborough, Ont.: Broadview, 2006).

Le Fanu, Joseph Sheridan, 'Fireside horrors for Christmas', *Dublin University Magazine* 30: 180 (December 1847): 631–46.

Le Fanu, Joseph Sheridan, *Uncle Silas*, edited by Victor Sage (London: Penguin Books, 2000).

Le Fanu, Sheridan, 'Green Tea', in Michael Newton (ed.), *The Penguin Book of Ghost Stories* (Harmondsworth: Penguin, 2010), pp. 105–39.

Le Fanu, Joseph Sheridan, *Carmilla: A Critical Edition*, edited by Kathleen Costello-Sullivan (Syracuse, NY: Syracuse University Press, 2013).

'Lenora. A Ballad, from Bürger', *The Monthly Magazine, and British Register* vol. 1 (1796): 135–7.

Leon, Derrick, *Ruskin, the Great Victorian* (London: Routledge and Kegan Paul, 1949).

Leopardi, Giacomo, *Essays, Dialogues and Thoughts*, trans. by Patrick Maxwell (London: Walter Scott, Ltd. 1880).

Leopardi, Giacomo, *Zibaldone: The Notebooks of Leopardi*, edited by Michael Caesar and Franco D'intino, trans. by Kathleen Baldwin, Richard Dixon, David Gibbons, Ann Goldstein, Gerard Slowey, Martin Thom and Pamela Williams (Harmondsworth: Penguin, 2013).

Levine, George, *Darwin and the Novelists: Patterns of Science in Victorian Fiction* (Cambridge, MA: Harvard University Press, 1989).

Levine, George, *Darwin the Writer* (Oxford: Oxford University Press, 2011).

Lévy, Maurice, '"Gothic" and the Critical Idiom', in Allan Lloyd Smith and Victor Sage (eds), *Gothick Origins and Innovations* (Amsterdam and Atlanta, GA: Rodopi, 1994), pp. 1–15.

Lewis, Matthew Gregory, *The Castle Spectre: A Drama. In Five Acts* (London, Printed for J. Bell, 1798).
Liggins, Emma, 'Gendering the spectral encounter at the *fin de siècle*: unspeakability in Vernon Lee's supernatural stories', *Gothic Studies* 15:2 (2013): 37–52.
Lockhart, J. G., *Memoirs of the Life of Sir Walter Scott, Bart.* 7 vols (Edinburgh: R. Cadell, 1837–8).
Logie Robertson, J. (ed.), *Scott: Poetical Works* (London: Oxford University Press, 1971).
Lombardo, Paul, 'Return of the Jukes: eugenic mythologies and internet evangelism', *Journal of Legal Medicine* 33:2 (2012): 207–33.
Lombroso, Cesare, *Ricerche sui fenomeni ipnotici e spiritici* (Torino: Unione Tipografico-Editrice Torinese, 1909).
Lombroso, Cesare, *Criminal Man*, trans. and edited by Mary Gibson and Nicole Hahn Rafter (Durham, NC: Duke University Press, 2006).
Lombroso-Ferrero, Gina, *Criminal Man* (New York: G. P. Putnam's Sons, 1911).
Longueil, Alfred E., 'The word "gothic" in eighteenth century criticism', *Modern Language Notes* 38:8 (December 1923): 453–60.
López Santos, Miriam, 'Introducción', Pascual Pérez y Rodríguez, *La urna sangrienta o el panteón de Scianella* (Madrid: Siruela, 2010), pp. 13–25.
López Santos, Miriam, *La novela gótica en España (1788–1833)* (Vigo: Academia del Hispanismo, 2010).
Rosamaria, Loretelli and John Dunkley, 'Translating Ann Radcliffe's *The Italian*: André Morellet and Giovanni De Coureil', in Lidia De Michelis, Lia Guerra and Frank O'Gorman (eds), *Politics and Culture in Eighteenth-Century Anglo-Italian Encounters. Entangled Histories* (Newcastle: Cambridge Scholars, 2019), pp. 2–46.
Lotman, Juri, *Culture and Explosion*, edited by Marina Grishakova (Berlin: De Gruyter, 2009).
Lucerna Magic Lantern Web Resource <www.slides.uni-trier.de/set/index.php?languag e=EN&id=3005238> (last accessed 28 May 2019).
Luck, Chad, 'George Lippard and the Rise of the Urban Gothic', in Charles L. Crow (ed.), *A Companion to American Gothic* (Malden, MA: Wiley Blackwell, 2014), pp. 124–36
Luckhurst, Roger, *The Mummy's Curse: The True History of a Dark Fantasy* (Oxford: Oxford University Press, 2012).
Luckhurst, Roger, 'Psychoanalysis', in William Hughes, David Punter and Andrew Smith (eds), *The Encyclopedia of the Gothic*, 2 vols (Malden, MA and Chichester: Wiley-Blackwell, 2016), vol. 2, pp. 526–31.
Lutz, Deborah, 'Gothic Fictions in the Nineteenth Century', in John Kucich and Jenny Bourne Taylor (eds), *The Oxford History of the Novel in English, Volume III: The Nineteenth-Century Novel 1820–1880* (Oxford: Oxford University Press, 2012), pp. 76–89.
Lynch, Eve M., 'Spectral Politics: The Victorian Ghost Story and the Domestic Servant', in Nicola Bown, Carolyn Burdett and Pamela Thurschwell (eds), *The Victorian Supernatural* (Cambridge: Cambridge University Press, 2004), pp. 67–86.
MacCarthy, Fiona, *William Morris: A Life for Our Time*, 2nd edition (London: Faber and Faber, 2010).
Macdonald, D. L., *Poor Polidori: A Critical Biography of the Author of The Vampyre* (Toronto: University of Toronto Press, 1991).

Machen, Arthur, *Selected Letters: The Private Writings of the Master of the Macabre*, edited by Roger Dobson, Godfrey Brangham and R. A. Gilbert (Wellingborough: Aquarian Press, 1988).

Machen, Arthur, 'The Inmost Light', in Corinna Wagner (ed.), *Gothic Evolutions: Poetry, Tales, Context, Theory* (Peterborough, Ont.: Broadview, 2014), pp. 388–406.

Mack, Douglas S., *Scottish Fiction and the British Empire* (Edinburgh: Edinburgh University Press, 2006).

Madden, Lionel (ed.), *Robert Southey: The Critical Heritage* (London: Routledge, 1972).

Mahawatte, Royce, 'Horror in the Nineteenth Century: Dreadful Sensations, 1820–80', in Xavier Aldana Reyes (ed.), *Horror: A Literary History* (London: British Library, 2016), pp. 77–101.

Makala, Melissa Edmundson, *Women's Ghost Literature in Nineteenth-Century Britain* (Cardiff: University of Wales Press, 2013).

Malchow, Howard L., *Gothic Images of Race in Nineteenth-Century Britain* (Stanford: Stanford University Press, 1996).

Malley, Shawn, '"Time hath no power against identity": historical continuity and archaeological adventure in H. Rider Haggard's *She*', *English Literature in Transition 1880–1920* 40:3 (1997): 275–97

Malthête, Jacques and Laurent Mannoni, *Méliès, Magie et Cinéma* (Paris: Paris-Musées, 2002).

Mandal, Anthony, 'The Ghost Story and the Victorian Literary Marketplace', in Scott Brewster and Luke Thurston (eds), *The Routledge Handbook to the Ghost Story* (New York and London: Routledge, 2017), pp. 29–39.

Mangan, James Clarence, 'The Funerals', in Christopher Morash (ed.), *The Hungry Voice: The Poetry of the Irish Famine* (Dublin: Irish Academic Press, 1989), pp. 133–4.

Manlove, Colin, *Scottish Fantasy Literature: A Critical Survey* (Edinburgh: Canongate Academic, 1994).

Mannoni, Laurent, 'The Phantasmagoria', in Laurent Mannoni, *The Great Art of Light and Shadow: Archaeology of the Cinema*, edited and trans. by Richard Crangle (Exeter: University of Exeter Press, 2000), pp. 136–75.

Manzoni, Alessandro, *The Betrothed*, trans. anon. (London: Bentley, 1834).

Manzoni, Alessandro, *Opere varie* (Milano: Fratelli Rechiedei Editori, 1881).

Manzoni, Alessandro, *I promessi sposi*, 1. *Fermo e Lucia. Appendice storica sulla colonna infame*; 2. *I promessi sposi nelle due edizioni del 1840 e del 1825–27 raffrontate tra loro. Storia della colonna infame*, edited by Lanfranco Caretti, 2 vols (Torino: Einaudi, 1971).

Manzoni, Alessandro, 'Letter on romanticism (1823)', intro. and trans. by Joseph Luzzi, *PMLA* 119:2 (2004): 299–316.

Marcus, Steven, *The Other Victorians: A Study of Sexuality and Pornography in Mid-Nineteenth-Century England* (London: Book Club Associates, 1970).

Margree, Victoria, 'The feminist orientation in Edith Nesbit's gothic short fiction', *Women's Writing* 21:4 (2014): 425–44.

Marion, Fulgence, *The Wonders of Optics* (London: Sampson Low, Son, and Marston, 1868).

Marrs, E. W. (ed.), *Letters of Charles and Mary Anne Lamb*, Vol. I (Ithaca, NY: Cornell University Press, 1975).

Marryat, Florence, *The Blood of the Vampire*, intro. by Brenda Hammack (Kansas City: Valancourt Books, 2009).

Marx, Karl, *Capital: A Critique of Political Economy, Volume I*, trans. by Ben Fowkes (Harmondsworth: Penguin, 1990).
Matthews, David, 'From mediaeval to medievalism: a new semantic history', *The Review of English Studies* 62:257 (November 2011): 695–715.
Matthews, David, *Medievalism: A Critical History* (Cambridge: D.S. Brewer, 2015).
Mattioda, Enrico, 'Ossian in Italy: From Cesarotti to the Theatre', in Howard Gaskill (ed.), *The Reception of Ossian in Europe* (London and New York: Bloomsbury, 2004), pp. 274–302.
Maturin, Charles Robert, *The Milesian Chief*, introduced by Robert Lee Wolff, 4 vols (New York: Garland, 1979).
Maturin, Charles Robert, *Melmoth the Wanderer*, edited by Douglas Grant (Oxford: Oxford University Press, 1989).
Maturin, Charles Robert, 'Bertram; or, The Castle of St Aldobrand', in Jeffrey N. Cox (ed.), *Seven Gothic Dramas, 1789–1825* (Athens, OH: Ohio University Press, 1992), pp. 316–83.
Maunder, Andrew, '"Stepchildren of Nature": *East Lynne* and the Spectre of Female Degeneracy, 1860–1861', in Andrew Maunder and Grace Moore (eds), *Victorian Crime, Madness and Sensation* (Farnham: Ashgate, 2004), pp. 59–71.
Mayo, Robert D., 'Gothic romance in the magazines', *PMLA* 65:5 (1950): 762–89.
Mayo, Robert D., *The English Novel in the Magazines, 1740–1815* (Evanston: Northwestern University Press, 1962).
Mays, Kelly J., 'How the Victorians un-invented themselves: architecture, the battle of the styles, and the history of the term "Victorian"', *Journal of Victorian Culture* 19:1 (2014): 1–23.
McCarthy, William and Elizabeth Kraft (eds), *Anna Letitia Barbauld: Selected Poetry and Prose* (Peterborough, Ont.: Broadview, 2002).
McCorristine, Shane, *Spectres of the Self: Thinking about Ghosts and Ghost-Seeing in England, 1750–1920* (Cambridge: Cambridge University Press, 2010).
McGann, Jerome J., 'James Thomson (B. V.): the woven hymns of night and day', *Studies in English Literature, 1500–1900* 3:4 (Autumn 1963): 493–507.
McGann, Jerome J., 'Poetry', in Iain McCalman (ed.), *An Oxford Companion to the Romantic Age* (Oxford: Oxford University Press, 1999), pp. 270–9.
Media History Digital Library <http://mediahistoryproject.org/> (last accessed 28 May 2019).
Medwin, Thomas, *Conversations of Lord Byron* (London: Colburn, 1824).
Medwin, Thomas, *The Life of Percy Bysshe Shelley* (London: Newby, 1847).
Mégroz, Rodolphe Louis, *Dante Gabriel Rossetti: Painter Poet of Heaven in Earth* (New York: Haskell House, 1971).
Meier, Paul, 'An unpublished lecture of William Morris', *International Review of Social History* 16 (1971): 217–40.
Melani, Costanza (ed.), *Fantastico italiano* (Milano: BUR Rizzoli, 2009).
Mellor, Anne K., *Mary Shelley: Her Life, Her Fiction, Her Monsters* (London and New York: Routledge, 1988).
Melville, Herman, 'Benito Cereno', in *Billy Budd and Other Tales* (New York: New American Library, 1961), pp. 141–223.
Meyer, Susan, *Imperialism at Home: Race and Victorian Women's Fiction* (Ithaca, NY: Cornell University Press, 1996).

Mighall, Robert, *A Geography of Victorian Gothic Fiction: Mapping History's Nightmares* (Oxford: Oxford University Press, 2003).

Milbank, Alison, 'Calvinist and Covenanter Gothic', in Carol Margaret Davison and Monica Germanà (eds), *Scottish Gothic: An Edinburgh Companion* (Edinburgh: Edinburgh University Press, 2017), pp. 89–101.

Miller, G. A., '*Cage aux folles*: sensation and gender in Wilkie Collins's *The Woman in White*', *Representations* 14 (1986): 107–36.

Miller, T. S., 'Lives of the monster plants: the revenge of the vegetable in the age of animal studies', *The Journal of the Fantastic in the Arts* 23:3 (2012): 460–79.

Mistrali, Franco, *I racconti del diavolo. Storia di paura* (Milano: F. Pagnoni, 1861).

Mistrali, Franco, *Il vampiro. Storia vera* (Bologna, Società tipografica dei compositori, 1869).

Mistrali, Franco, *Il vampiro. Storia vera*, edited by Antonio Daniele (Salerno: Keres Edizioni, 2011).

Moberly, L. G., 'A Strange Night', in Mike Ashley (ed.), *The Platform Edge: Uncanny Tales of the Railways* (London: British Library, 2019), pp. 61–7.

Moers, Ellen, *Literary Women: The Great Writers* (New York: Oxford University Press, 1976).

Mogen, David, Scott P. Sanders and Joanne B. Karpinski (eds), *Frontier Gothic: Terror and Wonder at the Frontier in America* (Rutherford, NJ: Farleigh Dickinson University Press, 1993).

Molina Porras, Juan, 'Introducción', *Leyendas del siglo XIX* (Madrid: Akal, 2013), pp. 9–47.

Monks, Aoife, 'Collecting ghosts: actors, anecdotes and objects at the theatre', *Contemporary Theatre Review* 23:2 (2013): 146–52.

Monnet, Agnieszka Soltysik *The Poetics and Politics of the American Gothic: Gender and Slavery in Nineteenth-Century American Literature* (Farnham and Burlington: Ashgate, 2010).

Moody, Nickianne, 'Visible Margins: Women Writers and the English Ghost Story', in Sarah Sceats and Gail Cunningham (eds), *Image and Power: Women in Fiction in the Twentieth Century* (London and New York: Longman, 1996), pp. 77–90.

Moore, Tara, *Victorian Christmas in Print* (Basingstoke: Palgrave Macmillan, 2009).

Moore-Gilbert, Bart, *Kipling and 'Orientalism'* (New York: St Martin's Press, 1986).

Moretti, Franco, *Signs Taken for Wonders: Essays on the Sociology of Literary Forms*, trans. by Susan Fischer, David Forgacs and David Miller (New York: Verso, 1988).

Morgan, Thomas, *Hand-Book of the Origin of Place Names in Wales and Monmouthshire* (Merthyr Tydfil: Printed for the Author, 1887).

Morin, Christina, *Charles Robert Maturin and the Haunting of Irish Romantic Fiction* (Manchester: Manchester University Press, 2011).

Morin, Christina, *The Gothic Novel in Ireland, c. 1760–1829* (Manchester: Manchester University Press, 2018).

Morley, Henry, *The Journal of a London Playgoer From 1851–1866* (London: George Routledge & Sons, 1866).

Morris, William, 'A night in a cathedral', *The Oxford and Cambridge Magazine*, vol. 5 (May 1856): 312–14.

Morris, William, 'The development of modern society', *Commonweal* 6:240 (1890): 260–1.

Morris, William, Preface to Kelmscott edition, *The Nature of Gothic* (London: George Allen, 1892).

Morris, William, *News from Nowhere* (London: Kelmscott Press, 1893).

Morris, William, *Collected Works of William Morris*, 24 vols (London: Longmans, 1912).
Morris, William, *The Ideal Book: Essays and Lectures on the Arts of the Book*, edited by William S. Peterson (Berkeley and Los Angeles: University of California Press, 1982).
Morris, William, *The Collected Letters of William Morris*, edited by Norman Kelvin, 4 vols (Princeton, NJ: Princeton University Press, 1984–96).
Morris, William, 'The Gothic Revival I and II', in Eugene D. LeMire (ed.), *The Unpublished Lectures of William Morris* (Michigan: Wayne State University Press, 1969), pp. 54–94.
Morris, William, 'The Lesser Arts', in *News from Nowhere and Other Writings*, edited by Clive Wilmer (London: Penguin, 1993), pp. 231–54.
Morris, William, *News from Nowhere and Other Writings*, edited by Clive Wilmer (London: Penguin, 1993).
Morris, William, 'The SPAB Manifesto' (1877), available from: <www.spabis.org.uk/wh at-is-spab-/the-manifesto/> (last accessed 23 January 2019).
Morrison, Robert, '"The Singular Wrought Out into the Strange and Mystical": *Blackwood's Edinburgh Magazine* and the Transformation of Terror', in Carol Margaret Davison and Monica Germanà (eds), *Scottish Gothic: An Edinburgh Companion* (Edinburgh: Edinburgh University Press, 2017), pp. 129–41.
Morse, Samantha, 'Affective ethics and democratic politics in *Sweeney Todd* and the Victorian penny press', *Journal of Victorian Culture* 24:1 (January 2019): 1–17.
Morton, Peter, *The Vital Science: Biology and the Literary Imagination 1860–1900* (London: Allen & Unwin, 1984).
Murphy, Patricia, *The New Woman Gothic: Reconfigurations of Distress* (Columbia: University of Missouri Press, 2016).
Murphy, Sharon, *Maria Edgeworth and Romance* (Dublin: Four Courts Press, 2004).
Murray, Tim, 'Archaeology and the threat of the past: Sir Henry Rider Haggard and the acquisition of time', *World Archaeology* 25:2 (1993): 175–86.
Musäus, Johann August, *Volksmährchen der Deutschen*, 5 vols (Gotha: Ettinger, 1782–6).
Napier, Elizabeth R., *The Failure of Gothic: Problems of Disjunction in an Eighteenth-Century Literary Form* (Oxford: Clarendon Press, 1987).
Natale, Simone, *Supernatural Entertainments: Victorian Spiritualism and the Rise of Modern Media Culture* (University Park, PA: Pennsylvania State University Press, 2016).
Natoli, Luigi, *I Beati Paoli. Grande romanzo storico* (Palermo: Flaccovio, 1971).
Navas Ruiz, Ricardo, *El romanticismo español* (Madrid: Cátedra, 1990)
Nayder, Lillian, 'Rebellious Sepoys and Bigamous Wives: The Indian Mutiny and Marriage Law Reform in *Lady Audley's Secret*', in Marlene Tromp, Pamela K. Gilbert and Aeron Haynie (eds), *Beyond Sensation: Mary Elizabeth Braddon in Context* (Albany: State University of New York Press, 2000), pp. 31–42.
Nead, Lynda, *Myths of Sexuality: Representations of Women in Victorian Britain* (Oxford: Blackwell, 1988).
Nead, Lynda, *The Haunted Galley: Painting, Photography, Film c. 1900* (London: Yale University Press, 2007).
Neiman, Elizabeth A., *Minerva's Gothics: The Politics and Poetics of Romantic Exchange, 1780–1820* (Cardiff: University of Wales Press, 2019).
Neiman, Elizabeth A. and Christina Morin (eds), *Romantic Textualities: Literature and Print Culture, 1780–1840* – Special Issue on 'The Minerva Press and the Romantic-era Literary Marketplace' (forthcoming).

Nesbit, Edith, *The Power of Darkness: Tales of Terror*, edited by David Stuart Davies (Ware, Herts: Wordsworth, 2006).

Neuberg, Victor E., *Popular Literature: A History and Guide* (Harmondsworth: Penguin, 1977).

Newton, Michael, 'Introduction', in Michael Newton (ed.), *The Penguin Book of Ghost Stories* (Harmondsworth: Penguin, 2010), pp. xv–xxxv.

Nicholson, William, 'Narrative and Explanation of the Appearance of Phantoms and other Figures in the Exhibition of Phantasmagoria. With Remarks on the Philosophical use of common Occurrences', *A Journal of Natural Philosophy, Chemistry, and The Arts* (London: G. and J. Robinsons, 1802), vol. 1, pp. 147–50.

Nietzsche, Friedrich, 'On the Uses and Disadvantages of History for Life', in *Untimely Meditations*, edited by Daniel Breazeale, trans. by R. J. Hollingdale (Cambridge: Cambridge University Press, 1997), pp. 57–124.

Nordau, Max, *Degeneration*, translated 2nd edition (London: William Heinemann, 1898).

Norman, Edward R., *The English Catholic Church in the Nineteenth Century* (Oxford: Clarendon, 1984).

North, Dan, 'Illusory bodies: magical performance on stage and screen', *Early Popular Visual Culture* 5:4 (2007): 175–88.

North, Dan R., *Performing Illusions: Cinema, Special Effects, and the Virtual Actor* (London: Wallflower Press, 2008).

O' Connor, Erin, *Raw Material: Producing Pathology in Victorian Culture* (Durham, NC: Duke University Press, 2000),

Ofek, Galia, *Representations of Hair in Victoria Literature and Culture* (Farnham: Ashgate, 2009).

Oliphant, Margaret, 'Novels', *Blackwood's Edinburgh Magazine* 102 (September 1867): 257–80.

Oliphant, Margaret, 'The Open Door', in *A Beleaguered City and Other Stories*, edited by Merryn Williams (Oxford: Oxford University Press, 1988), pp. 115–59.

Oliphant, Margaret, *A Beleaguered City and Other Tales of the Seen and the Unseen*, edited by Jenni Calder (Edinburgh: Canongate, 2000).

Oliphant, Margaret, 'Sensation Novels', in Ellen Wood, *East Lynne*, edited by Andrew Maunder (Peterborough, Ont.: Broadview Press, 2000), p. 715.

Ollier, Charles, *Fallacy of Ghosts, Dreams, and Omens* (London: Charles Ollier, 1848).

Oppenheim, Janet, *The Other World: Spiritualism and Psychical Research in England, 1850–1914* (Cambridge: Cambridge University Press, 1985).

Orr, Jennifer, *Literary Networks and Dissenting Print Culture in Romantic-Period Ireland* (Basingstoke: Palgrave Macmillan, 2015).

Ortenberg, Veronica, *In Search of the Holy Grail: The Quest for the Middle Ages* (London and New York: Continuum, 2006).

Otto, Peter, *Multiplying Worlds: Romanticism, Modernity, and the Emergence of Virtual Reality* (Oxford: Oxford University Press, 2011).

'Our Female Sensation Novelists', in Andrew Maunder (ed.), *Sensationalism and the Sensation Debate: Varieties of Women's Sensation Fiction 1855–1890*, 6 vols (London: Pickering & Chatto, 2004), vol. 1, pp. 105–14.

Paravisini-Gebert, Lizabeth, 'Colonial and Postcolonial Gothic: The Caribbean', in Jerrold E. Hogle (ed.), *The Cambridge Companion to Gothic Fiction* (Cambridge: Cambridge University Press, 2002), pp. 229–58.

Parins, Marylyn (ed.), *Sir Thomas Malory: The Critical Heritage* (London and New York: Routledge, 2002).

Parker, David, *Christmas and Charles Dickens* (New York: AMS Press, 2005).

Patrick, Mrs F. C., *The Jesuit; or, the History of Anthony Babington, Esq., an Historical Novel*, 3 vols (Bath, 1799).

Peake, Richard Brinsley, *Presumption; or, The Fate of Frankenstein*, edited by Stephen C. Behrendt, Romantic Circles Edition <https://romantic-circles.org/editions/peake/index.html> (last accessed 7 June 2019).

Pearson, Jacqueline, 'Masculinizing the novel: women writers and intertextuality in Charles Robert Maturin's *The Wild Irish Boy*', *Studies in Romanticism* 36:4 (1997): 635–50.

Pendleton, John, *Our Railways: Their Origin, Development, Incident and Romance* (London: Cassell and Company, 1894).

Pérez Galdós, Benito, *La sombra* (Barcelona: Ediciones Internacionales Universitarias, 1997).

Pevsner, Nikolaus, *Pioneers of the Modern Movement: From William Morris to Walter Gropius* (London: Faber & Faber, 1936).

Pevsner, Nikolaus, *An Outline of European Architecture*, revised edition (Layton, Utah: Gibbs Smith, 2009).

Phillips, Catherine, *Robert Bridges: A Biography* (Oxford: Oxford University Press, 1992).

Phillips, Kendall R., *A Place of Darkness: The Rhetoric of Horror in Early American Cinema* (Austin, TX: University of Texas Press, 2018).

Phillips, Mark Salber, *On Historical Distance* (New Haven and London: Yale University Press, 2013).

Pick, Daniel, *Faces of Degeneration: A European Disorder, c. 1848–c. 1918* (Cambridge: Cambridge University Press, 1993).

Pinero, Arthur Wing, 'Trelawny of the "Wells"', in *Pinero: Three Plays* (London: Methuen, 1988), pp. 159–245.

Poe, Edgar Allan, *Poe: Poetry and Tales*, edited by Patrick F. Quinn (New York: Library of America, 1984).

Polidori, John, *Ernestus Berchtold; or, The Modern Oedipus. A Tale* (London: Printed for Longman, Hurst, Rees, Orme, and Brown, 1819).

[Polidori, John], *The Vampyre; A Tale* (London: Sherwood, Neeley, and Jones, 1819).

Polidori, John, *The Diary of Dr John William Polidori 1816, Relating to Byron, Shelley, Etc.*, edited by William Michael Rossetti (London: Elkin Matthews, 1911).

Poller, Jake, 'The transmutations of Arthur Machen: alchemy in "The Great God Pan" and *The Three Impostors*', *Literature and Theology* 29 (2013): 18–32.

Pollock, Lori, '(An)Other politics of reading *Jane Eyre*', *The Journal of Narrative Technique* 26:3 (1996): 249–73.

Poovey, Mary, *Uneven Developments: The Ideological Work of Gender in Mid-Victorian England* (Chicago: University of Chicago Press, 1988).

Pope, Alexander, *Alexander Pope: The Major Works*, edited by Pat Rogers (Oxford: Oxford University Press, 2006).

Porter, Bernard, *The Battle of the Styles: Society, Culture and the Design of the New Foreign Office, 1855–1861* (London: Continuum, 2011).

Potter, Franz J., *The History of Gothic Publishing, 1800–1835: Exhuming the Trade* (Basingstoke: Palgrave Macmillan, 2005).
Powell, Hudson John, *Poole's Myriorama!* (Bradford on Avon: ELSP, 2002).
Powell, Sally, 'Black Markets and Cadaverous Pies: The Corpse, Urban Trade and Industrial Consumption in the Penny Blood', in Andrew Maunder and Grace Moore (eds), *Victorian Crime, Madness and Sensation* (Aldershot and Burlington, VT: Ashgate, 2004), pp. 45–58.
Prichard, Kate and Hesketh Prichard, 'The Story of Baelbrow', in *Lost in a Pyramid & Other Classic Mummy Stories*, edited and intro. by Andrew Smith (London: British Library, 2016), pp. 195–12.
Pritchard, Allan, 'The urban gothic of *Bleak House*', *Nineteenth-Century Literature* 45:4 (March 1991): 432–52.
Pugin, Auguste Charles and Edward J. Willson, *Specimens of Gothic Architecture Selected From Various Ancient Edifices in England*, 2 vols (London: J. Taylor, 1821–3).
Pugin, A. W. N., *Contrasts*, 2nd revised edition (London: Charles Dolman, 1841).
Pykett, Lyn, *The 'Improper' Feminine: The Women's Sensation Novel and the New Woman Writing* (London: Routledge, 1992).
Radcliffe, Ann, 'On the supernatural in poetry', *New Monthly Magazine* 16:1 (1826): 145–52.
Radcliffe, Ann, *The Mysteries of Udolpho*, edited by Bonamy Dobrée (Oxford: Oxford University Press, 1981).
Rafter, Nicole H., 'Introduction', in *The Origins of Criminology: A Reader* (New York: Routledge, 2009), pp. xiii–xxvi.
Reynolds, G. W. N., *The Mysteries of London*, 4 vols (London: George Vickers, 1844–8).
Richards, Bernard, *English Poetry of the Victorian Period, 1830–1890* (London: Longman, 1988).
Rieger, James, 'Dr Polidori and the genesis of *Frankenstein*', *Studies in English Literature, 1500–1900* 3:4 (1963): 461–72.
Rider Haggard, Henry, *Ayesha: The Return of She*, intro. by David Pringle (Polegate: Pulp Fictions, 1998).
Ringel, Faye, *New England's Gothic Literature: History and Folklore of the Supernatural from the Seventeenth Through the Twentieth Centuries* (Lewiston, Queenston and Lampter: Edwin Mellen Press, 1995).
Roas, David, *Hoffmann en España: Recepción e influencias* (Madrid: Biblioteca Nueva, 2002).
Roas, David, *De la maravilla al horror: Los inicios de lo fantástico en la cultura española (1750–1860)* (Pontevedra: Mirabel Editorial, 2006).
Roas, David, *La sombra del cuervo: Edgar Allan Poe y la literatura fantástica del siglo XIX* (Madrid: Devenir, 2011).
Robertston, Fiona, *Legitimate Histories: Scott, Gothic, and the Authorities of Fiction* (Oxford: Clarendon Press, 1994).
Robertson, Fiona, 'Gothic Scott', in Carol Margaret Davison and Monica Germanà (eds), *Scottish Gothic: An Edinburgh Companion* (Edinburgh: Edinburgh University Press, 2017), pp. 102–14.
Robinson, Charles E., *Shelley and Byron: The Snake and Eagle Wreathed in Fight* (Baltimore, MD: The Johns Hopkins University Press, 1976).
Rodenas, Céline, 'La traduction des romans gothiques anglais vers l'italien a la fin du XVIIIe siècle at au début du XIXe siècle. Échanges culturels entre l'Angleterre et l'Italie. 'Il Castello di Otranto' (1795) et 'La foresta' (1813)', *Cercles* 34 (2015): 170–86.

Rosenman, Ellen Bayuk, 'Spectacular women: *The Mysteries of London* and the female body', *Victorian Studies* 40:1 (Autumn 1996): 31–64.
Rossetti, Dante Gabriel, *Poems*, edited by William Michael Rossetti (London: Ellis & Elvey, 1891).
Rossetti, William Michael (ed.), *The Diary of Dr. John William Polidori, 1816, Relating to Byron, Shelley, Etc.* (Cambridge: Cambridge University Press, 2014), p. 125.
Rubio Cremades, Enrique, 'La novela histórica del romanticismo español', *Historia de la Literatura Española: Siglo XIX (I)* (Madrid: Espasa-Calpe, 1996), pp. 610–42.
Ruskin, John, 'Traffic', in *The Crown of Wild Olive: Three Lectures on Work, Traffic, and War* (London: Smith, Elder, and Co., 1866), pp. 79–138.
Ruskin, John, *Love's Meinie: Three Lectures on Greek and English Birds* (New York: John Wiley, 1873).
Ruskin, John, *Modern Painters*, 5 vols (London: J. M. Dent, 1907).
Ruskin, John, 'The Lamp of Memory', from *The Seven Lamps of Architecture*, in Dinah Birch (ed.), *John Ruskin: Selected Writings* (Oxford: Oxford University Press, 2004), pp. 24–7.
Ruskin, John, 'The Nature of Gothic', in Dinah Birch (ed.), *John Ruskin: Selected Writings* (Oxford: Oxford University Press, 2004), pp. 32–63.
Ruskin, John [Kata Phusin], 'The Poetry of Architecture: No. 1, Introduction', *The Architectural Magazine and Journal* 4 (November 1837): 505–8.
Ruston, Sharon, *Creating Romanticism: Case Studies in the Literature, Science and Medicine of the 1790s* (Basingstoke: Palgrave Macmillan, 2013).
Rutherford, Andrew (ed.), *Byron: The Critical Heritage* (London and New York: Routledge & Kegan Paul; New York: Barnes & Noble, 1970).
Rymer, James Malcolm, *Varney, the Vampyre; or, The Feast of Blood* (London: Edward Lloyd, 1845–7).
Rymer, James Malcolm, *Varney the Vampire; or, The Feast of Blood* (New York: Arno Press, 1970).
Rymer, James Malcolm, *The String of Pearls*, 2nd edition (Ware: Wordsworth Editions, 2010).
Sabor, Peter (ed.), *Horace Walpole: The Critical Heritage* (London: Routledge & Kegan Paul, 1987).
Sage, Victor, 'Exchanging Fantasies: Sex and the Serbian Crisis in *The Lady of the Shroud*', in William Hughes and Andrew Smith (eds), *Bram Stoker: History, Psychoanalysis and the Gothic* (Basingstoke: Macmillan, 1998), pp. 116–33.
Sage, Victor (ed.), *The Gothick Novel: A Casebook* (Basingstoke: Macmillan, 1990).
Saglia, Diego, *Poetic Castles in Spain: British Romanticism and Figurations of Iberia* (Amsterdam: Rodopi, 2000).
Saglia, Diego, 'Gothic theatre, 1765–Present', in Glennis Byron and Dale Townshend (eds), *The Gothic World* (Abingdon and New York: Routledge, 2014), pp. 354–65.
Saglia, Diego and Ian Haywood (eds), *Spain in British Romanticism, 1800–1840* (Basingstoke: Palgrave Macmillan, 2017).
Saint-Hilaire, Isidore Geoffroy, *Histoire générale et particulière des anomalies de l'organisation chez l'homme et les animaux* (Paris: B. Baillière, 1832–7).
Santiago de Alvarado de la Peña, D., 'El traductor', in Mis Ana de Radcliff [sic], *Adelina, ó la abadía en la selva: Novela histórica* (Madrid: Imprenta de I. Sancha, 1830), pp. v–viii.
Schivelbusch, Wolfgang, *The Railway Journey: The Industrialization of Time and Space in the Nineteenth Century* (Berkeley: University of California Press, 1986).

Schock, Peter A., *Romantic Satanism: Myth and the Historical Moment in Blake, Shelley, and Byron* (Basingstoke: Palgrave Macmillan, 2003).

Schmidt-Nowara, Christopher, *The Conquest of History: Spanish Colonialism and National Histories in the Nineteenth Century* (Pittsburgh, PA: University of Pittsburgh Press, 2006).

Schotland, Sara D., 'The slave's revenge: the terror in Charlotte Dacre's Zofloya', *The Western Journal of Black Studies* 33:2 (2009): 123–31.

Schulze, Friedrich August, *Memoiren von Friedrich Laun*, 3 vols (Bunzlau: Appun's Buchhandlung, 1837).

Scott, Walter, Review of *The Fatal Revenge; or, the Family of Montorio: a Romance*, *Quarterly Review* 3:6 (1810): 339–47.

Scott, Walter, *Lives of the Novelists*, 2 vols (Philadelphia and New York, 1825).

Scott, Walter, *Letters on Demonology and Witchcraft Addressed to J. G. Lockhart, Esq.* (London: John Murray, 1830).

Scott, Walter, *Minstrelsy of the Scottish Border*, revised edition, 4 vols (Edinburgh: James Ballantyne, 1830).

Scott, George Gilbert, *Personal and Professional Recollections* (London: Sampson Low, 1879).

Scott, Walter, *Waverley; or, 'Tis Sixty Years Since*, edited by Claire Lamont (Oxford: Oxford University Press, 1986).

Scott, Walter, *The Bride of Lammermoor*, edited by Fiona Robertson (Oxford: Oxford University Press, 1991).

Scott, Walter, *Ivanhoe*, edited by Ian Duncan (Oxford: Oxford University Press, 1996).

Scott, Walter, *Redgauntlet*, edited by G. A. M. Wood with David Hewitt (Edinburgh: Edinburgh University Press, 1997).

Scott, Walter, *The Antiquary*, edited by Nicola J. Watson (Oxford: Oxford University Press, 2002).

Scott, Walter, 'The Tapestried Chamber', in Michael Cox and R. A. Gilbert (eds), *The Oxford Book of English Ghost Stories* (Oxford: Oxford University Press, 2008), pp. 1–12.

Scullion, Adrienne, 'Feminine Pleasures and Masculine Indignities: Gender and Community in Scottish Drama', in Christopher Whyte (ed.), *Gendering the Nation: Studies in Modern Scottish Literature* (Edinburgh: Edinburgh University Press, 1995), pp. 169–204.

Sedgwick, Eve Kosofsky, 'The character in the veil: imagery of the surface in the gothic novel', *PMLA* 96:2 (1981): 255–70.

Sedgwick, Eve Kosofsky, *Between Men: English Literature and Male Homosocial Desire* (New York: Columbia University Press, 1985).

Senf, Carol, *The Vampire in Nineteenth-Century English Literature* (Madison: University of Wisconsin Press, 1988).

Seymour, Miranda, *Mary Shelley* (London: Faber and Faber, 2011).

Shanahan, Jim, 'Suffering Rebellion: Irish Gothic Fiction, 1799–1830', in Christina Morin and Niall Gillespie (eds), *Irish Gothics: Genres, Forms, Modes, and Traditions, c. 1760–1890* (Basingstoke: Palgrave Macmillan, 2014), pp. 74–93.

Shannon-Mangan, Ellen, *James Clarence Mangan: A Biography* (Dublin: Irish Academic Press, 1996).

Shapira, Yael, 'Beyond the Radcliffe Formula: Isabella Kelly and the Gothic Troubles of the Married Heroine', *Women's Writing* (26 November 2015) <www.tandfonline.com/doi/abs/10.1080/09699082.2015.1110289> (last accessed 5 April 2019).

Shaw, Thomas B., *A History of English Literature* (London: John Murray, 1864).
Shelley, Mary Wollstonecraft, *Frankenstein; or, The Modern Prometheus: The 1818 Text*, edited by James Rieger, Phoenix edition (Chicago: University of Chicago Press, 1982).
Shelley, Percy Bysshe, 'A Defence of Poetry', in Richard Herne Shepherd (ed.), *The Prose Works of Percy Bysshe Shelley, Vol. II* (London: Chatto & Windus, 1906), pp. 1–38.
Shelley, Percy Bysshe, *The Letters of Percy Bysshe Shelley*, edited by Frederick L. Jones, 2 vols (Oxford: Clarendon Press, 1964).
Shelley, Percy Bysshe, *The Complete Poetry of Percy Bysshe Shelley*, edited by Donald Reiman, Neil Fraistat and Nora Crook, 3 vols to date (Baltimore, MD: Johns Hopkins University Press, 2004).
Shelston Alan (ed.), *Thomas Carlyle: Selected Writings* (London: Penguin, 1971).
Shenton, Caroline, *The Day Parliament Burned Down* (Oxford: Oxford University Press, 2012).
Sherwin, Byron L., 'Golems in the biotech century', *Zygon: Journal of Religion and Science* 41:1 (2007): 133–43.
Shiels, William, 'Thomas More', in Gareth Atkins (ed.), *Making and Remaking Saints in Nineteenth-Century Britain* (Manchester University Press, 2016), pp. 112–26.
Shillito, Ian John and Becky Walsh, *Haunted West End Theatres* (Stroud: The History Press, 2011).
Showalter, Elaine, *A Literature of Their Own: British Women Novelists from Brontë to Lessing* (Princeton: Princeton University Press, 1977).
Showalter, Elaine, 'Syphilis, Sexuality, and the Fiction of the Fin de Siècle', in Ruth Bernard Yeazell (ed.), *Sex, Politics, and Science in the Nineteenth-Century Novel* (Baltimore: Johns Hopkins University Press, 1986), pp. 88–115.
Shubert, Adrian and José Álvarez Junco, José, 'Introduction', *Spanish History since 1808* (London: Arnold; New York: Oxford University Press, 2000), pp. 1–16.
Silver, Sean, 'The Politics of Gothic Historiography, 1660–1800', in Glennis Byron and Dale Townshend (eds), *The Gothic World* (Abingdon and New York: Routledge, 2014), pp. 3–14.
Simmons, Clare, *Popular Medievalism in Romantic-Era Britain* (New York and Basingstoke: Palgrave Macmillan, 2011).
Six, Abigail Lee, *Gothic Terrors: Incarceration, Duplication and Bloodlust in Spanish Narrative* (Lewisburg, PA: Bucknell University Press, 2010).
Six, Abigail Lee, 'The Monk (1796): a Hispanist's reading', *Ilha do Desterro* 62 (2012): 25–54.
Skarda, Patricia L., 'Vampirism and plagiarism: Byron's influence and Polidori's practice', *Studies in Romanticism* 28:2 (Summer 1989): 249–69.
Slater, Michael, 'Dickens in Wonderland', in Peter L. Caracciolo (ed.), *The Arabian Nights in English Literature* (Basingstoke: Palgrave Macmillan, 1988), pp. 130–42.
Smajić, Srjdan, *Ghost-Seers, Detectives, and Spiritualists: Theories of Vision in Victorian Literature and Science* (Cambridge: Cambridge University Press, 2010).
Smith, Andrew, 'Bram Stoker's *The Mystery of the Sea*: Ireland and the Spanish-Cuban-American war', *Irish Studies Review* 6:2 (1998): 131–8.
Smith, Andrew, 'Beyond Colonialism: Death and the Body in H. Rider Haggard', in Andrew Smith and William Hughes (eds), *Empire and the Gothic: The Politics of Genre* (Basingstoke: Palgrave Macmillan, 2003), pp. 103–17.

Smith, Andrew, 'Demonising the Americans: Bram Stoker's postcolonial gothic', *Gothic Studies* 5:2 (November 2004): 20–31.

Smith, Andrew, 'Kipling's gothic and postcolonial laughter', *Gothic Studies* 11:1 (May2009): 58–69.

Smith, Andrew, *The English Ghost Story 1840–1920: A Cultural History* (Manchester: Manchester University Press, 2010).

Smith, Andrew and William Hughes, 'Introduction: Locating the Victorian Gothic', in Andrew Smith and William Hughes, *Victorian Gothic: An Edinburgh Companion* (Edinburgh: Edinburgh University Press, 2012), pp. 1–14.

Smith, Andrew and William Hughes (eds), *The Victorian Gothic: An Edinburgh Companion* (Edinburgh: Edinburgh University Press, 2012).

Smith, Helen R., *A Feast of Blood* (London: Jarndyce Antiquarian Booksellers, 2002).

Smith, Jonathan, *Charles Darwin and Victorian Visual Culture* (Cambridge: Cambridge University Press, 2009).

Smith, Philip II and Michael S. Helfand (eds), *Oscar Wilde's Oxford Notebooks: A Portrait of the Mind in the Making* (Oxford: Oxford University Press, 1989).

Smith, R. J., *The Gothic Bequest: Medieval Institutions in British Thought, 1688–1863* (Cambridge: Cambridge University Press, 1987).

Solomon, Matthew, *Disappearing Tricks: Silent Film, Houdini, and the New Magic of the Twentieth Century* (Urbana: University of Illinois Press, 2010).

Southey, Robert (ed.), *The byrth, lyf, and actes of Kyng Arthur: of his noble knyghtes of the Rounde Table, theyr merveyllous enquestes and aduentures, thachyeuyng of the Sanc Greal; and in the end le Morte D'Arthur, with the dolourous deth and departyng out of thys worlde of them al; With an Introduction and Notes by Robert Southey, Esq. . . . Printed from Caxton's Edition, 1485*, 2 vols (London: Longman, 1817).

Southey, Robert, *The Book of the Church*, 2 vols (London: John Murray, 1824).

Southey, Robert, *The Poetical Works of Robert Southey, Collected by Himself*, 10 vols (London: Longman, Orme, Brown, Green & Longmans, 1838).

Southey, Charles Cuthbert (ed.), *Life and Correspondence of Robert Southey*, 6 vols (London: Longman, 1849–50).

Southey, Robert, *Sir Thomas More; or, Colloquies on the Progress and Prospects of Society*, edited by Tom Duggett, 2 vols (London and New York: Routledge, 2018).

Spangler, George, 'The shadow of a dream: Howells' homosexual tragedy', *American Quarterly*, 23 (1971): 110–19.

Speaight, George, 'Professor Pepper's ghost', *Theatre Notebook* 43:1 (1989): 16–25.

Speck, W. A., *Robert Southey: Entire Man of Letters* (New Haven and London: Yale University Press, 2006).

Spenser, Edmund, *Edmund Spenser's Poetry: A Norton Critical Edition*, edited by Hugh Maclean and Anne Lake Prescott (New York: Norton, 1968).

Spooner, Catherine, *Post-Millennial Gothic: Comedy, Romance and the Rise of Happy Gothic* (Oxford: Bloomsbury, 2017).

Spuybroek, Lars, *The Sympathy of Things: Ruskin and the Ecology of Design* (London and New York: Bloomsbury, 2011).

Staines, David, *Tennyson's Camelot: The Idylls of the King and Its Medieval Sources* (Waterloo, Ont.: Wilfrid Laurier University Press, 1982).

St Clair, William, *The Godwins and the Shelleys* (London: Faber and Faber, 1989).

St Clair, William, *The Reading Nation in the Romantic Period* (Cambridge: Cambridge University Press, 2004).

Stevenson, Robert Louis, *A Child's Garden of Verses*, illustrated by Charles Robinson (New York: Charles Scribner's Sons; London: John Lane, 1895).

Stevenson, Robert Louis, *Strange Case of Dr Jekyll and Mr Hyde and Weir of Hermiston*, edited by Emma Letley (Oxford: Oxford University Press, 1987).

Stevenson, Robert Louis, *The Letters of Robert Louis Stevenson*, edited by Bradford Booth and Ernest Mehew, 8 vols (New Haven and London: Yale University Press, 1994–5).

Stevenson, Robert Louis, 'Thrawn Janet', in Douglas Dunn (ed.), *The Oxford Book of Scottish Short Stories* (Oxford: Oxford University Press, 1995), pp. 110–17.

Stocker, Charles William (ed.), *The Satires of Persius and Juvenal*, 3rd edition (London: Longman, Brown & Co., 1845).

Stoker, Bram, *A Glimpse of America* (London: Sampson Low, Marston and Co., 1886).

Stoker, Bram, *The Lady of the Shroud*, intro. by Ruth Robbins (Stroud: Sutton, 1994).

Stoker, Bram, *The Jewel of Seven Stars*, intro. by David Glover (Oxford: Oxford University Press, 1996).

Stoker, Bram, *The Mystery of the Sea*, intro. by Jessica de Mellow (Stroud: Sutton, 1997).

Stoker, Bram, *Dracula*, edited by Roger Luckhurst (Oxford: Oxford University Press, 2011).

Storey, Graham (ed.), *The Letters of Charles Dickens, Volume X: 1862–64* (Oxford: Clarendon, 1998).

Storey, Graham, Kathleen Tillotson and Angus Easson (eds), *The Letters of Charles Dickens, Volume VII: 1853–55* (Oxford: Clarendon, 1993).

Stott, Rebecca, 'Darwin's Barnacles: Mid-Century Natural History and the Marine Grotesque', in Roger Luckhurst and Josephine McDonagh (eds), *Transactions and Encounters: Science and Culture in the Nineteenth Century* (Manchester: Manchester University Press, 2002), pp. 151–81.

Stuart, Roxana, *Stage Blood: Vampires of the Nineteenth-Century Stage* (Bowling Green, OH: Bowling Green State University Popular Press, 1994).

Sturgeon, Sinéad, '"Seven devils": Gerald Griffin's "The Brown Man" and the making of Irish gothic', *The Irish Journal of Gothic and Horror Studies* 11 (2012):18–30 <https://irish gothichorror.files.wordpress.com/2016/04/ijghsissue11.pdf> (last accessed 13 May 2019).

Suarez S. J., Michael F., 'Introduction', in Michael F. Suarez S. J. and Michael L. Turner (eds), *The Cambridge History of the Book in Britain, Volume V: 1695–1830* (Cambridge: Cambridge University Press, 2009), pp. 1–35.

Sucksmith, Harvey Peter, 'The secret of immediacy: Dickens' debt to the tale of terror in *Blackwood's*', *Nineteenth-Century Fiction* 26:2 (September 1971): 145–57.

Sue, Eugène, *The Mysteries of Paris*, trans. by Carolyn Betensky and Jonathan Loesberg (London: Penguin, 2015).

Summers, Montague, *The Gothic Quest: A History of the Gothic Novel*, 2nd edition (London: Fortune Press, 1968).

Sutcliffe, Allan, 'The ghost illusion on the Birmingham stage', *The New Magic Lantern Journal* 10:1 (2005): 7–11.

Sutherland, John, 'Is Oliver dreaming?', in *Is Heathcliff a Murderer?: Great Puzzles in Nineteenth-Century Literature* (Oxford: Oxford University Press, 1996), pp. 34–45.

Tarchetti, Igino Ugo, *Fosca: racconto di I.U. Tarchetti. Amore nell'arte: tre racconti dello stesso autore* (Milano: Edoardo Sonzogno Editore, 1874).
Tarchetti, Igino Ugo, *Passion*, trans. by Lawrence Venuti (San Francisco: Mercury House, 1994).
Tardiola, Giuseppe, *Il vampiro nella letteratura italiana* (Anzio: De Rubeis, 1991).
Tennyson, Alfred Lord, *Selected Poems*, edited by Christopher Ricks (London: Penguin, 2007).
[Thackeray, William Makepeace], 'Roundabout papers, No. VIII: De Juventute', *The Cornhill Magazine* 2:10 (October 1860): 501–12.
Thomas, Sue, 'The tropical extravagance of Bertha Mason', *Victorian Literature and Culture* 27:1 (1999): 1–17.
Thompson, E. P., *William Morris: Romantic to Revolutionary* (London: Merlin, 1971).
Thompson, Stith, *Motif-Index of Folk-Literature*, 6 vols (Bloomington: University of Indiana Press, 1955–8).
Thomson, James (B. V.), *The City of Dreadful Night and Other Poems* (London: Watts, 1932).
Thurston, Luke, *Literary Ghosts from the Victorians to Modernism* (New York and London: Routledge, 2012).
Tilley, Elizabeth, 'J. S. Le Fanu, Gothic, and the Irish Periodical', in Christina Morin and Niall Gillespie (eds), *Irish Gothics: Genres, Forms, Modes, and Traditions, c. 1760–1890* (Basingstoke: Palgrave Macmillan, 2014), pp. 130–46.
Tillotson, Kathleen (ed.), *The Letters of Charles Dickens, Volume IV: 1844–46* (Oxford: Clarendon, 1977).
Tosh, John, *A Man's Place: Masculinity and the Middle-Class Home in Victorian England* (New Haven: Yale University Press, 1999).
Toulmin, Vanessa, 'Telling the tale: the story of the fairground bioscope shows and the showmen who operated them', *Film History* 6:2 (1994): 219–37.
Toulmin, Vanessa, *Randall Williams King of Showmen: From Ghost Show to Bioscope* (London: The Projection Box, 1998).
Townend, Matthew, 'Victorian Medievalisms', in Matthew Bevis (ed.), *The Oxford Handbook of Victorian Poetry* (Oxford: Oxford University Press, 2013), pp. 166–83.
Townshend, Dale, 'Shakespeare, Ossian and the Problem of "Scottish Gothic"', in Elisabeth Bronfen and Beate Neumeier (eds), *Gothic Renaissance: A Reassessment* (Manchester: Manchester University Press, 2014), pp. 218–43.
Townshend, Dale and Angela Wright, 'Gothic and Romantic: An Historical Overview', in Angela Wright and Dale Townshend (eds), *Romantic Gothic: An Edinburgh Companion* (Edinburgh: Edinburgh University Press, 2016), pp. 1–34.
Tracy, Thomas, '"Reader, I buried him": apocalypse and empire in *Jane Eyre*', *Critical Survey* 16:2 (2004): 59–77.
Trautwein, Wolfgang, *Erlesene Angst. Schauerliteratur im 18. und 19. Jahrhundert* (Munich and Vienna: Carl Hanser Verlag, 1980).
Tucker, Herbert F., 'Tennyson and the measure of doom', *PMLA* 98:1 (1983): 8–20.
Hack, Tuke, D., 'Case of Moral Insanity or Congenital Moral Defect, with Commentary' *Journal of Mental Science* 31 (October 1885): 360–6.
Twitchell, James, '"Desire with loathing strangely mixed": the dream-work of *Christabel*', *Psychoanalytic Review* 61:1 (1974): 33–44.

Uglow, Jennifer, 'Introduction', *The Virago Book of Victorian Ghost Stories*, edited by Richard Dalby (London: Virago, 1988), pp. ix–xvii.

Utterson, Sarah Elizabeth Brown, *Tales of the Dead* (London: White, Cochrane, and Co., 1813).

Il Vampiro. Ballo fantastico in cinque atti di Giuseppe Rota. Con musica del Maestro Paolo Giorza (Milan: Real Stabilimento Tipografico di P. Ripamenti, Carpano, 1861?).

Il vampiro. Gran ballo romantico fantastico in otto quadri del coreografo Giuseppe Rota. Con musica appositamente scritta dal Maestro Cavalier Giorza (Torino: Tipografia Teatrale di Savojardo, 1863?).

Van Woudenberg, Maximiliaan, 'The variants and transformations of *Fantasmagoriana*: tracing a travelling text to the Byron-Shelley circle', *Romanticism* 20:3 (2014): 306–20.

Van Woudenberg, Maximiliaan, 'The Gothic Galaxy of the Byron-Shelley Circle: The Metamorphosis of Friedrich Schulze and *Fantasmagoriana*', in Maurizio Ascari, Serena Baiesi and David Levente Palatinus (eds), *Gothic Metamorphoses Across the Centuries: Contexts, Legacies, Media* (Bern: Peter Lang, 2020), pp. 53–68.

Venuti, Lawrence, *The Translator's Invisibility: A History of Translation* (London and New York, Routledge, 1995).

Verga, Giovanni, *Storia di una capinera* (Milano: Treves, 1893).

Vescovi, Alessandro, 'Dickens and Alessandro Manzoni's "I Promessi Sposi"', in Alessandro Vescovi, Luisa Villa and Paul Vita (eds), *The Victorians and Italy: Literature, Travel, Politics and Art* (Monza: Polimetrica, 2009), pp. 151–67.

Vincent, David, *Literacy and Popular Culture: England 1750–1914* (Cambridge: Cambridge University Press, 1989).

Von Krafft-Ebing, Richard, *Psychopathia Sexualis*, trans. by Charles Gilbert Chaddock (Philadelphia, PA: F. A. Davis, 1892).

Von Sneidern, Maja-Lisa, '*Wuthering Heights* and the Liverpool slave trade', *ELH* 62:1 (1996): 171–96.

Walker, John, 'The Factory Lad: A Domestic Drama in Two Acts', in Michael Booth (ed.), *English Plays of the Nineteenth Century 1: 1800–1850* (Oxford: Oxford University Press, 1969), pp. 201–33.

Walker, Malcolm Ian (ed.), *Edgar Allan Poe: The Critical Heritage* (London and New York: Routledge & Kegan Paul, 1986).

Wallace, Diana, 'Uncanny stories: the ghost story as female gothic', *Gothic Studies* 6:1 (2004): 57–68.

Walpole, Horace, *Anecdotes of Painting in England*, 4 vols (Strawberry Hill: Printed by Thomas Farmer, 1762–71 [i.e. 1780]).

Walpole, Horace, *The Castle of Otranto: A Gothic Story*, edited by W. S. Lewis with intro. and notes by E. J. Clery (Oxford: Oxford University Press, 1996).

Walter [pseud.], *My Secret Life*, vol. 7, ch. 2, excerpted in Shelly Klein (ed.), *Victorian Erotic Tales* (London: Michael O'Mara, 1995), pp. 7–20.

Ward, Matthew, 'Laughter as sympathy in Percy Shelley's poetics', *Cambridge Quarterly* 44:2 (2015): 146–65.

Wardrop, Daneen, *Emily Dickinson's Gothic: Goblin with a Gauge* (Iowa City: University of Iowa Press, 1996).

Warner, Marina, *Phantasmagoria: Spirit Visions, Metaphors, and Media into the Twenty-First Century* (Oxford: Oxford University Press, 2006).

Warter, John Wood (ed.), *Selections from the Letters of Robert Southey*, 4 vols (London: Longman, 1856).
Warwick, Alexandra, 'Feeling gothicky?', *Gothic Studies* 9:1 (2007): 5–15.
Warwick, Alexandra, 'Imperial Gothic', in William Hughes, David Punter and Andrew Smith (eds), *The Encyclopedia of the Gothic* (Oxford: Blackwell, 2016), pp. 338–42.
Watson, Roderick, 'Gothic Stevenson', in Carol Margaret Davison and Monica Germanà (eds), *Scottish Gothic: An Edinburgh Companion* (Edinburgh: Edinburgh University Press, 2017), pp. 142–54.
Watt, James, *Contesting the Gothic: Fiction, Genre and Cultural Conflict, 1764–1832* (Cambridge: Cambridge University Press, 1999).
Watt, William Whyte, *Shilling Shockers of the Gothic School: A Study of Chapbook Gothic Romances* (Cambridge, MA: Harvard University Press, 1932).
Weinstock, Jeffrey Andrew, *Scare Tactics: Supernatural Fiction by American Women* (New York: Fordham University Press, 2008).
Weinstock, Jeffrey Andrew, *Charles Brockden Brown* (Cardiff: University of Wales Press, 2011).
Weinstock, Jeffrey Andrew, 'The queer time of lively matter: the polar erotics of Harriet Prescott Spofford's "The Moonstone Mass"', *Women's Studies* 46:8 (2018): 752–66.
Wells, H. G., 'Zoological regression', *The Gentleman's Magazine* 271 (September 1891): 246–53.
Wells, H. G., *Experiment in Autobiography* (New York: Macmillan, 1934).
Wells, H. G., 'Death', in *H. G. Wells: Early Writings in Science and Science Fiction*, edited by Robert Philmus and David Y. Hughes (Berkeley, CA: University of California Press, 1975), pp. 137–9.
Wells, H. G., 'Human Evolution, an Artificial Process', in *H. G. Wells: Early Writings in Science and Science Fiction*, edited by Robert Philmus and David Y. Hughes (Berkeley, CA: University of California Press, 1975), pp. 211–19.
West, Sally, *Coleridge and Shelley: Textual Engagement* (Aldershot: Ashgate, 2007).
Whitechurch, Victor L., 'The Strange Story of Engine Number 651', in Mike Ashley (ed.), *The Platform Edge: Uncanny Tales of the Railways* (London: British Library, 2019), pp. 13–23.
Wilde, Lady Jane, 'The Famine Year (The Stricken Land)', in Christopher Morash (ed.), *The Hungry Voice: The Poetry of the Irish Famine* (Dublin: Irish Academic Press, 1989), pp. 221–2.
Wilde, Oscar, *The Picture of Dorian Gray*, edited by Robert Mighall (Harmondsworth: Penguin, 2003).
Williams, Raymond, *The Country and the City* (New York: Oxford University Press, 1973).
Williams, Raymond, *Culture and Society, 1780–1950*, 2nd edition (New York: Columbia University Press, 1983).
Willis, Martin, 'Victorian Realism and the Gothic', in Andrew Smith and William Hughes (eds), *The Victorian Gothic: An Edinburgh Companion* (Edinburgh: Edinburgh University Press, 2012), pp. 15–28.
Wilt, Judith, 'Love/slave', *Victorian Studies* 33:3 (Spring, 1994): 451–60.
Wohlgemut, Esther, 'Southey, Macaulay and the Idea of a Picturesque History', *Romanticism on the Net*, 32–33 (2003/4) <http://id.erudit.org/iderudit/009261ar; §19–20> (last accessed 22 January 2019).

Wolfreys, Julian, 'Preface: "I could a tale unfold" or, the Promise of Gothic', in Ruth Robbins and Julian Wolfreys (eds), *Victorian Gothic: Literary and Cultural Manifestations in the Nineteenth Century* (Basingstoke: Palgrave Macmillan, 2000), pp. xi–xx.

Wolfreys, Julian, *Victorian Hauntings: Spectrality, Gothic, the Uncanny and Literature* (Basingstoke: Palgrave MacMillan, 2002).

Wolfreys, Julian, 'Victorian Gothic', in Anna Powell and Andrew Smith (eds), *Teaching the Gothic* (Basingstoke: Palgrave Macmillan, 2006), pp. 62–77.

Wollstonecraft, Mary, *A Vindication of the Rights of Woman and The Wrongs of Woman, or Maria*, edited by Anne K. Mellor and Noelle Chao (New York: Pearson Longman, 2007).

Wood, Ellen, *East Lynne*, edited by Andrew Maunder (Peterborough, Ont.: Broadview, 2000).

Woolf, Virginia, *A Room of One's Own* (New York: Harcourt Brace Jovanovich, 1929).

Wordsworth, William, *Sonnet Series and Itinerary Poems, 1819–1850*, edited by Geoffrey Jackson (Ithaca, NY: Cornell University Press, 2004).

William Wordsworth, *William Wordsworth: The Major Works, including The Prelude*, edited by Stephen Gill (Oxford: Oxford University Press, 2011).

Worth, Aaron (ed.), *The Great God Pan and Other Horror Stories* (Oxford: Oxford University Press, 2018).

Wright, Angela, *Mary Shelley* (Cardiff: University of Wales Press, 2018).

Wright, Julia M., *Representing the National Landscape in Irish Romanticism* (Syracuse, NY: Syracuse University Press, 2014).

Wurgaft, Lewis D., *The Imperial Imagination: Magic and Myth in Kipling's India* (Middletown, CT: Wesleyan University Press, 1983).

Wustmann, Gustav, 'Schrepfer [a.k.a. Schröpfer], Johann Georg', in *Allgemeine Deutsche Biographie* 32 (891). <www.deutsche-biographie.de/pnd120914042.html> (last accessed 14 May 2019).

Wynne, Catherine, 'Dracula on Stage', in Roger Luckhurst (ed.), *The Cambridge Companion to Dracula* (Cambridge: Cambridge University Press, 2017), pp. 165–78.

Yang, Sharon Rose and Kathleen Healey, 'Introduction: Haunted Landscapes and Fearful Spaces – Expanding Views on the Geography of the Gothic', in Sharon Rose Yang and Kathleen Healey (eds), *Gothic Landscapes: Changing Eras, Changing Cultures, Changing Anxieties* (Basingstoke: Palgrave Macmillan, 2009), pp. 1–18.

Yorke, Peter, *William Haggar: Fairground Film Maker* (Bedlinog: Accent Press, 2007).

Young, Paul, 'Rambles beyond railways: gothicised place and globalised space in Victorian Cornwall', *Gothic Studies* 13:1 (May 2011): 55–74.

Young, Robert M., *Darwin's Metaphor: Nature's Place in Victorian Culture* (Cambridge: Cambridge University Press, 1985).

Zuccato, Edoardo, 'The Fortunes of Byron in Italy (1810–1870)', in Richard Cardwell (ed.), *The Reception of Byron in Europe*, 2 vols (London: Thoemmes-Continuum, 2004), vol. 1, pp. 80–99.

Index

Abolition of Slavery Act, England (1833), 119
Adam, Robert, 120–1
Addison, Joseph, 2
Adelman, Richard, 105
aesthetic of the ugly, 315–16
Aikin, John, 338–9
Ainsworth, William Harrison, 151
Akenside, Mark, 8–9
Alarcón, Pedro Antonio de, 294
Alastor; or, The Spirit of Solitude; and Other Poems (Shelley, P. B.), 29
Alcott, Louisa May, 228
Alexander, Michael, 103
Allen, Grant, 423–6, 470–1
Altadill, Antonio, 295
Altick, Richard D., 55
Álvarez Junco, José, 286
American Gothic. *See* United States
Ancient Architecture Restored, and Improved (Langley, B.), 121
Anderson, Robert, 364
Andrew, Lucy, 159
anti-rationalism, in Italian Gothic, 319
anti-Semitism, in *Dracula*, 82
Apel, Johann, 42–4, 47, 55, 62–3
An Apology for Tales of Terror (Scott, W.), 338–9
An Apology for the Revival of Christian Architecture in England (Pugin, A. W. N.), 126–7
Arata, Stephen, 355, 370, 479
Archaelogiae philosophicae (Burnet, T.), 348
The Architectural Antiquities of Great Britain (Britton, J.), 121
architecture, Gothic, 111, 112
  'Battle of Styles', 128–9
  Classical architecture compared to, 119–22
  Coleridge, S. T., on, 88
  'cultural Gothicism' and, 89
  definition of, 120–1
  ecclesiological movement in, 86
  'fifty-year effect' in revival of, 88–9
  Gothic Revival movement
    'fifty-year effect' in, 88–9
    Morris on, 134, 136–7
    Socialism as 'fourth stage' of, 119–20
  historical sense in, 87–9
  Medieval Court at Great Exhibition, 128
  medievalism in, 115
  Victorian, 103–4
  Morris, W., on, 107–14
    on Gothic Revival, 134, 136–7
    in *News from Nowhere*, 107, 108, 109, 110–13
    on Socialism as 'fourth stage' of, 119–20
  revivalist, 18
  romantic antiquarianism and, 88
  Romanticism and, 87
  Ruskin on, 105–7, 119
  Shelley, Percy Bysshe, on, 107–8
  SPAB and, 85–7, 135
  Strawberry Hill, 121
  systemisation of, 121
  as ultimate expression of art, 106
  Victorian, 120
    late, 105–14
Argento, Dario, 326–7
Ariosto, Ludovico, 2
Armstrong, Harold, 205
Arthur Mervyn (Brown, C. B.), 377
Asensi, Julia de, 299
An Attempt to Discriminate the Styles of English Architecture, from the Conquest to the Reformation (Rickman, T.), 121
Auerbach, Nina, 224
Austen, Jane, 3–4, 15, 89

Backus, Margot Gayle, 359–60
Baillie, Joanna, 166, 171
Baldick, Chris, 183–4

Index

Baldini, Eraldo, 326–7
balladry, in Scottish Gothic, 332, 335
   collection and preservation of, 329–30, 334
   Lenore and, 333–4
   The Monk as inspiration for, 337
   'Sweet William's Ghost', 334–5
Ballantyne, James, 329, 338–9
Bann, Stephen, 87, 92
Barbani, Livorno Assunto, 307–8
Barbauld, Anna Laetitia, 328, 338–9
Barca, Calderón de la, 287
Barnaby Rudge (Dickens, C.), 250
Barrie, J. M., 354
Barry, Charles, 18, 124
Bataille, Georges, 314
'Battle of Styles', 128–9
Baudelaire, Charles, 314
Bava, Mario, 326–7
Bearden-White, Roy, 141
Beattie, James, 331
Beatty, Bernard, 36
Beckford, William, 127
Bécquer, Gustavo Adolfo, 296–8
Being and Nothingness (Sartre, J-P.), 314
A Beleaguered City (Oliphant, M.), 349–50
Benito Cereno (Melville, H.), 383–4, 402–3, 407, 408–9
Benson, Edward White, 238
Bentley, Richard, 41
Berceo, Gonzalo de, 287
Bernardo, Jerónimo Martín de, 290–1
Bernheimer, Charles, 437
Bertram; or, The Castle of St. Aldobrand (Maturin, C. R.), 164–5
Betjeman, John, 138
The Betrothed. See I promessi sposi
Bierce, Ambrose, 392
Big House novel, 374
Billiani, Francesca, 314
Biographia Literaria (Coleridge, S. T.), 7, 89
biology
   anatomical affinities, 418–20
   biological monstrosities, 426–8
   carnivorous plants species, 437–41
   criminal doctors and, 426–8
   criminality as, 432–7
      Lombroso on, 432–4
   evolutionary theories, 418
   genealogies, 420–3
      criminal, 420–1, 422
      evolutionary, 420
      medieval, 421–3
      surgically modified monstrous, 428–32

heredity, 423–6
On the Origin of Species, 83, 418, 420
Birch, Dinah, 106
Black American Gothic, 383–6. *See also* slavery
   identity themes in, 385
   sexual exploitation of enslaved women, 385
Blackwood, Algernon, 231
Blake, William, 11
Blanco White, Joseph, 292–3
Bleak House (Dickens, C.), 79, 255–6
Bleasdale, John, 32
The Blood of the Vampire (Marryat, F.), 81, 83
Bloom, Clive, 429
Bloom, Harold, 95, 205
Bluebeard; or, Female Curiosity (Colman, G. the Younger), 168
Boaden, James, 165, 180–1
Boerner, Peter, 328–9
Boitard, Pierre, 418
Boito, Arrigo, 304, 315, 322
The Book of Christmas (Hervey, T. K.), 226
The Book of the Church (Southey, R.), 115
Botting, Fred, 164
Boucicault, Dion, 162–3, 169
Braddon, Mary Elizabeth, 158–9, 175, 228, 242, 275–9
Brantlinger, Patrick, 284, 463–4
Bratton, Jacky, 168, 180–1
Bremón, Fernández, 300–1
Brett, Edwin J., 151, 159
Brewster, David, 230–1
The Bride of Corinth (Goethe, J. W. von), 66
The Bride of Lammermoor (Scott, W.), 9
The Bridge of Sighs (Hood, T.), 210–11, 217
Bridges, Robert, 220
Briggs, Julia, 232–3, 240
Brinsley, Richard, 169
Britton, John, 121
Brontë, Anne, 267–8, 272–4
Brontë, Charlotte, 12–13, 15, 80–1
Brontë, Emily
   Remembrance, 208–9
   Victorian meta-Gothic poetry of, 208–9
   Wuthering Heights, 76–7, 105
      ghosts in, 229
      slavery themes in, 403, 411–12
Brooker, Jeremy, 190
Broughton, Rhoda, 228, 233
Brown, Charles Brockden, 377
The Brown Man (Griffin, G.), 371–2
Browning, Robert, 205, 216–17
Browning, Tod, 181
Buckstone, John Baldwin, 179

Bulwer-Lytton, Edward, 151
Bürger, Gottfried August. *See Lenore*
Burke, Edmund, 116, 141, 223
Burne-Jones, Edward, 93–4, 315
Burnett, Thomas, 348
Burns, Robert, 11, 329–30, 331
Byron, George Gordon (Lord Byron), 7, 8–9, 11, 19
  Childe Harold's Pilgrimage, 20, 32–3, 35, 39
    isolation of self in, 36–7
    nature in, 35–6
  Don Juan, 75
  editing of work by, 39–40
  Epistle to Augusta, 37–8
  Fantasmagoriana as influence on, 56
  Manfred, 20, 32, 33–5, 56, 89
  Shelley, Percy Bysshe, and, 29, 34
  The Vampyre and, 27–8
  Wordsworth and, competition with, 35–7

Cable, George Washington, 384, 385
Cadalso, José de, 290–1
Calder, Jenni, 348–9
Calila e Dimna, 287
Calvino, Italo, 304–5, 325
Camões, Luís de, 4
Campbell, Thomas, 8–9
The Captain of the Polestar (Doyle, A. C.), 232–3
Capuana, Luigi, 305, 320–1, 323–4
Carlist War, in Spain, 299
Carlyle, Thomas, 90, 95, 97–8, 447–8
  Past and Present, 92–3, 99, 127
  on political revolution in England, 119
  Signs, 99
  Southey, R., influenced by, 99–100
Carmilla (Le Fanu, J. S.), 79–80
Carmouche, Pierre, 75, 162–3
Cary, Alice, 387
Castle, Terry, 49, 186, 202, 230
The Castle of Inchvally (Cullen, S.), 364–5
The Castle of Otranto (Walpole, H.), 2–3, 4–5, 120
  excesses of, 211
  as literary influence, on future Gothic works, 3–4
  preface, 22
  reviews of, 2
  romantic elements in, 67–9
  as translation, 3
  vampires in, 65
Castle Rackrent (Edgeworth, M.), 359–60
The Castle Spectre (Lewis, M. G.), 164, 167
Catholic Emancipation, 367

Catholicism, for Pugin, A. W. N.
  conversion to, 125–6
  public reputation negatively affected by, 127–8
censorship, in Spain, of Gothic novels, 289–90
Cesarotti, Melchiorre, 307
La Chambre Grise (Apel, J.), 62–3
La Chambre Noire (Apel, J.), 62–3
The Chase, and William and Helen (Scott, W.), 336–7
Chatterton, Thomas, 87
Chaucer, Geoffrey, 2
Chaucer, Kelmscott, 94
Chernaik, Judith, 31–2
Chesterton, G. K., 160
Child, Francis J., 334–5
Childe Harold's Pilgrimage (Byron), 20, 32–3, 35, 39
  isolation of self in, 36–7
  nature in, 35–6
A Child's Garden of Verses (Stevenson, R. L.), 354
Chisolm, Hugh, 160
Christabel (Coleridge, S. T.), 9, 21, 25–6
  Frankenstein influenced by, 69–70
  vampires in, 66
  Vampyre influenced by, 69–70
Christianity, Pugin, A. W. N., and, 127
A Christmas Carol (Dickens, C.), 225–8, 252–4
The City of Dreadful Night (Thomson, J.), 212–15
Clairmont, Jane [Clair], 20, 21, 39
Clare, John, 141
'Clarín', Leopoldo Alas, 299
Clark, Kenneth, 131, 137, 138
Classical architecture, 119–22, 124
Cobbett, William, 92, 100
Coello, Carlos, 300, 301
Cohen, Jeffrey Jerome, 416
Coke, Edward, 116
Colburn, Henry, 27, 41
Coleridge, Mary Elizabeth, 220–1
  The Other Side of a Mirror, 221
  Wilderspin, 221
  The Witch, 220–1
Coleridge, Samuel Taylor, 7, 8–9, 11, 20, 87–8, 141, 220–1
  Biographia Literaria, 7, 89
  Christabel, 9, 21, 25–6
    Frankenstein influenced by, 69–70
    vampires in, 66
    Vampyre influenced by, 69–70
  on Gothic architecture, 88

Index

Hymn Before Sun-rise, in the Vale of Chamouni, 30–1
   on living symbol, 123
   The Rime of the Ancyent Marinere, 9–10, 26
   vampires in works of, 66
   at Villa Diodati, 21
Collins, Wilkie, 11–12, 176, 228, 241–2, 256, 324
   Victorian Domestic Gothic Fiction and, 265
Collins, William, 4–5, 8–9
Collodi. *See* Lorenzini, Carlo
Colloquies on Society (Southey, R.), 91–3, 95–6, 99–100
Colman, George (the Younger), 168
colonialism. *See* imperial Gothic; reverse colonialism
Colwall, Charles Voysey, 110
Comus (Milton, J.), 19
Confessions of an English Opium-Eater (De Quincey, T.), 17
Connell, Philip, 94
Connolly, Claire, 363
Conrad, Joseph, 301
consciousness. *See* female consciousness
Contrasts (Pugin, A. W. N.), 92, 124–6
Cooper, Anthony Ashley (3rd Earl of Shaftesbury), 2
Cooper, William, 4–5
cosmopolitanism, in *Frankenstein*, 8
The Cottage of the Appenines (Kenley, M.), 364
Courthope, William John, 11
courtly novel, 287–8
Cowper, William, 8–9
Cox, Jeffrey, 167
Cox, Michael, 236
Crabbe, George, 141
Crangle, Richard, 197
Creole populations, 409–15
   racial miscegenation and, 412–13
   as white Other, 410–11
criminality
   against animals, 437–41
   as biology, 432–7
Croce, Benedetto, 304, 325
Cromwell, Oliver, 92–3
Crookenden, Isaac, 147–8
Crowe, Catherine, 234–7
Cuisin, J. P. R., 289
Cullen, Stephen, 360, 361, 364–5
'cultural Gothicism', in Gothic architecture, 89
'The Curse of Vasartas' (Henry, E. M.), 470–1
Cuthbertson, Catherine, 291
Cvetcovitch, Ann, 283–4

Dacre, Charlotte, 144
La dama de Amboto (Gómez de Avellaneda), 298–9
Daniel Deronda (Eliot, G.), 283–4
Dark Romantics, 380–3. *See also specific authors*
Darkness (Byron), 19
Darwin, Charles, 416
   Descent of Man, 431
   The Expression of the Emotions in Man and Animals, 434
   global cultural influence of, 416–17
   on morphological deviation, 426–8
   On the Origin of Species, 83, 418, 420
Davanzati, Giuseppe, 319
Davidson, Cathy, 377
Davies, Ann, 285
Davison, Carol Margaret, 331, 377
De Quincey, Thomas, 17
The Defence of Guenevere (Morris, W.), 102, 103, 104
Defences (Chesterton, G. K.), 160
Deledda, Grazia, 323
Denarius, 182–3
Dennis, John, 2
Descent of Man (Darwin, C.), 431
desire. *See* erotic desire
Devant, David, 191–2
Dever, Carolyn, 209
diabolic Gothic, in Dickens's works, 259–64
The Diary of Dr John William Polidori, 1816, Relating to Byron, Shelley, Etc. (Polidori, J.), 21
Dibdin, Thomas, 102
Dickens, Charles, 16, 233
   Barnaby Rudge, 250
   Bleak House, 79, 255–6
   A Christmas Carol, 225–8, 252–4
   critical review of Crowe's works, 235–7
   early social context for, as psychological influence, 250–1
   Gothic elements in works of, 246–64. *See also specific works*
      comedic approach to, 246–51
      diabolic Gothic, 259–64
      in letters, 246
      literary influences from, for later authors, 256–9
      meta-Gothic, 259–64
      queer relationships in, 256–9
      of the supernatural, 254–5
   Great Expectations, 246, 247–8
   Hard Times, 246
   The Holly-Tree Inn, 264

523

Dickens, Charles (cont.)
  literary influences on, 247
  Little Dorrit, 251–2
  magic lantern shows and, 197
  The Mystery of Edwin Drood, 256, 259
  No. 1 Branch Line, 257–9, 457–60
  Nurse's Stories, 260–2, 264
  Old Curiosity Shop, 250
  Oliver Twist, 248–9, 254–5
  Our Mutual Friend, 248, 256, 259
  The Pickwick Papers, 226, 259
  'sensation fiction', as creator of, 247
  Sketches by Boz, 249–50
  sources of imagination for, 259
  on spectral illusion thesis, 235–7
  theatrical Gothic in works of, 176
  vampires in works of, as comic element, 246–7
Dickerson, Vanessa, 236, 242–3
Dickinson, Emily, 204, 383
Dicks, John, 151
Diderot, Denis, 310
Dimond, William, 172
Dircks, Henry, 189
Disraeli, Benjamin, 127, 469
A Doll's House (Ibsen, H.), 175
domestic melodramas, 171–7
  ghosts and ghostliness in, 176
  guilt as theme in, 175–6
  local settings in, 172–4
  natural world in, 171
  popularity of, compared to, 163
Don Giovanni, 75
Don Juan (Byron), 75
Dowden, Edward, 11
Doyle, Arthur Conan, 17, 232–3
Dracula (Stoker, B.), 65, 81–4, 120, 301
  anti-Semitism themes in, 82
  contemporary adaptations of, 14–15
  erotic desire as element in, 82
  evolutionary theory and, 83
  imperial Gothic in, 463
    America symbolism in, 479
  railways in, 461
  reverse colonialism in, 370, 479
  Transylvanian Superstitions, 81
  as Victorian Domestic Gothic Fiction, 284
Drake, Nathan, 4–5, 146–7
A Dream of John Ball (Morris, W.), 137
Dryden, John, 2
du Maurier, George, 181
Dugdale, Richard Louis, 420–1, 422
Dumas, Alexandre, 295

Dunbar, Paul Laurence, 385–6
Dunbar, William, 331
Duncan, Ian, 340

East Lynne (Wood, E.), 174–5, 279–81, 282–3
Eastlake, Charles Locke, 18, 127–8
The Ebony Frame (Nesbit, E.), 244–5
ecclesiological movement, 86
Edgar Huntly (Brown, C. B.), 377
Edgeworth, Maria
  Castle Rackrent, 359–60
  Ennui, 360–1
  Irish Gothic and, 359–61
  literary influences on, 359
Edmundson, Melissa, 237
Edwards, Amelia, 228, 233, 244
Edwards, Bryan, 396–7
Egypt, 469–74
Eliot, George, 268, 283–4
Eliot, Simon, 151
Emerson, Ralph Waldo, 380–1
Engels, Friedrich, 135–6
England. *See also* imperial Gothic; Palace of Westminster
  Abolition of Slavery Act in, 119
  Great Reform Act in, 119
  Infant Custody Act, 266, 273
  Matrimonial Causes Act, 266, 273, 277, 278
  Oxford Movement in, 127
  phantasmagoria in, 53
    expansion of, as concept and term, 54–5
  Poor Law Amendment Act in, 119, 126
  Roman Catholic Relief Act in, 119, 125
  Tractarianism in, 127
  Young England movement, 123, 127
Ennui (Edgeworth, M.), 360–1
Epistle to Augusta (Byron), 37–8
  nature in, 37–8
erotic desire, in *Dracula*, 82
The Esdaile Notebook (Shelley, P. B.), 29
An Essay on Man (Pope, A.), 36
evolutionary theory, 83
The Excursion (Wordsworth, W.), 29
The Expression of the Emotions in Man and Animals (Darwin, C.), 434
Eyriès, Jean-Baptiste Benoît, 23, 41–8, 63–4. *See also Fantasmagoriana, ou Recueil d'Histoires d'Apparitions de Spectres, Revenants, Fantômes, etc.*

The Factory Lad (Walker, J.), 173–4
The Faerie Queene (Spenser, E.), 67

Fantasmagoriana, ou Recueil d'Histoires d'Apparitions de Spectres, Revenants, Fantômes, etc. (Eyriès, J.-B. B.), 23, 41–8, 63–4
  Byron influenced by, 56
  Frankenstein and, 56–63
  German provenance of, 42–8
  Gespensterbuch, 42–4, 47
  modern editions and translations, 42
  Polidori influenced by, 56
  'shudder literature' and, 47–8
The Fatal Revenge (Maturin, C. R.), 246
Faulkner, William, 385–6
female consciousness, in sensation fiction, 283–4
female sexuality
  sexual transgression among females, as literary theme, 274
  in Victorian Domestic Gothic Fiction, 274–84
    femme fatale in, 276
  in male-oriented adventure fiction, 284
  in *The Tenant of Wildfell Hall*, 274
feminism
  in realism movement, 388
  in Victorian Domestic Gothic Fiction, 267–74
femme fatale
  female sexuality of, 276
  in Victorian Domestic Gothic Fiction, 276
  in Victorian poetry, 217–18
Fermo e Lucia. See *I promessi sposi*
Ferrar, Nicholas, 93
Ferriar, John, 235
Ferris, Henry, 231
fiction, Gothic. See also 'shilling shocker' bluebooks; Victorian Domestic Gothic Fiction; *specific countries*
  ancient provenance of, 2
  as 'German school of horror', 3–4
  invention of, 1–7
  literacy rates and, growth of, 139–40
  literary history and, 1–7. See also *specific authors; specific works*
  as modern literary genre, 5–6
  as modern romances, 3–4
  origins of, 140
  penny bloods, 140, 150–9. See also *specific works*
    popular authors, 151, 155–9
    publishers of, 152–3
    serial revolution for, 150
    'shilling shocker' bluebooks replaced by, 150–1
    traditional plot dynamics in, 153–5
  penny dreadfuls, 140, 159–61
    publishers for, 159
    violent themes in, 159–61
    youth market for, 159
  proliferation of, between 1770 and 1889, 139–40
  'street Gothic', 140
  as terrorist system of novel writing, 3–4
  urban environment in, 221–2
'fifty-year effect', in revival of Gothic architecture, 88–9
film, Gothic elements in, 200–3
'First Wave' Irish Gothic, 362–6
Fisher, Benjamin, 377
Fitzball, Edward, 169, 172
Fogazzaro, Antonio, 322
folkloric Gothic
  in Ireland, 367–8
  in Italy, 323–4
  in Spain, 296–9
'Folletín' novel, 293–6
  literary development of, 294–5
Fontainville Forest (Boaden, J.), 165
Fonthill Abbey, 127
Fors Clavigera (Ruskin, J.), 133
Forster, E. M., 326
Foucault, Michel, 87
found-manuscript conceit, 332–3
Fox, Kate, 237
Fox, Maggie, 237
Fraistat, Neil, 29
France, Spanish Gothic writers influenced by, 288, 291–2
Frankenstein; or, The Modern Prometheus (Shelley, M. W.)
  British Romanticism and, 8
  Christabel as influence on, 69–70
  contemporary responses to, 14–15
  cosmopolitan elements in, 8
  Fantasmagoriana and, 56–63
  Galvanism and, 52
  as Golem, 401
  in Gothic tradition, 27–8
  Paradise Lost in, 26–7
  preface for, 22–8, 48
  Shelley, Percy Bysshe, and, 22–8
  as slavery narratives, 399–402, 407–8, 414–15
  during Summer of 1816, 20
    climate conditions of, 24–6
  'uncanny' in, 70
  Villa Diodati and, 21

Franklin, Caroline, 208–9
Freeman, Mary E. Wilkins, 228
The French Revolution and English Literature (Dowden, E.), 11
Freud, Sigmund, 16, 70
Frith, Richard, 94
Fulford, Tim, 94
Fuller, Anne, 362

Galvanism
  Frankenstein; or, The Modern Prometheus and, 52
  Robertson and, 51–2
  Shelley, Mary Wollstonecraft, and, 56–7
Gamer, Michael, 171
Garett, Daniel, 120–1
Garnett, Richard, 27, 104
Gaskell, Elizabeth, 228, 237
Gedhill, Christine, 163
gender. *See also* women
  in Irish Gothic, 369–75
  female writers, 374
A Geography of Victorian Gothic Fiction (Mighall, R.), 17
Gerard, Emily, 81
'German school of horror', Gothic fiction as, 3–4
Germanà, Monica, 331
Germanic tribes, Gothic and, 1–2
Gespensterbuch (Apel, J. and Schulze, F.), 42–4, 47, 55
Ghidetti, Enrico, 304
ghost shows, 193–5
ghost stories. *See also Fantasmagoriana, ou Recueil d'Histoires d'Apparitions de Spectres, Revenants, Fantômes, etc.*; phantasmagoria; Victorian ghost stories
  in *Gespensterbuch*, 42–4, 47
  at Villa Diodati, 42. *See also Frankenstein*; specific works
  as challenge from Byron, 20–1, 66–9
ghosts and ghostliness
  in domestic melodramas, 176
  railways and, 460–2
  in Victorian ghost stories, 240–5
    in everyday domestic settings, 241–2
  in *Wuthering Heights*, 229
Giacomo, Salvatore di, 321–2, 323
The Giaour (Byron), 72
Gilbert, R. A., 236
Gilman, Charlotte Perkins, 228, 351
Giorgi, Lelio, 321

Glenarvon (Lamb, C.), 72
Godínez, Agustín Pérez Zaragoza, 289
Godwin, Mary. *See* Shelley, Mary Wollstonecraft
Godwin, William, 141
Goethe, Johann Wolfgang von, 20–1, 66, 87–8, 329
Gogol, Nikolai, 314
Gómez de Avellaneda, Gertrudis, 294, 298–9
Gooch, Robert, 97
Goslee, Nancy Moore, 30
Gosse, Edmund, 6–7
Gothic, as concept. *See also* specific topics
  in British culture, 14–18
    Victorianism and, 15–16
  in European culture, 14–18
  Germanic tribes and, 1–2
  historical meanings of, loss of, 4
  in King James Bible, 1–2
  meanings of
    changes to, 4–5
    historical, loss of, 4
    political, loss of, 4
  political meanings of, loss of, 4
  Teutonic tribes and, 1–2
  in US culture, 14–18
Gothic architecture. *See* architecture
Gothic balladry. *See* balladry
Gothic fiction. *See* fiction
Gothic heroine, 276
  in Spanish Gothic literary works, 302
Gothic imperialism. *See* imperial Gothic
Gothic literature. *See* literature
The Gothic Quest (Summers, M.), 13–14
The Gothic Revival (Clark, K.), 131, 138
Gothic Revival movement, in architecture
  'fifty-year effect' in, 88–9
  Morris on, 134, 136–7
  Socialism as 'fourth stage' of, 119–20
Gothic Romanticism. *See also* Summer of 1816
  in *The Factory Lad*, 173–4
The Grandissimes (Cable), 385
Gray, Thomas, 4–5, 8–9, 208
Great Britain, Gothic in, during nineteenth century, 14–18. *See also* imperial Gothic; slavery narratives
  Industrial Revolution in, 119
  Spanish Gothic writers influenced by, 288, 291–2, 300
  Victorianism and, 15–16
Great Expectations (Dickens, C.), 246, 247–8
The Great God Pan (Machen, A.), 428–9
Great Reform Act, England (1832), 119

Green, Sarah, 362
Green Tea (Le Fanu, J. S.), 231
Griffin, Gerald, 371–2
Griffith, Elizabeth, 362
Grimaldi, Joseph, 179
Groom, Nick, 87
Grosette, W. H., 170
Gruner, Elisabeth Rose, 273
Guerrazzi, Francesco Domenico, 305
Guest, William, 108
guilt as theme, in domestic melodramas, 175–6
Gurney, Edmund, 238
Gutiérrez, Luis, 292–3

Hackenberg, Sara, 156
Haggard, Henry Rider, 17, 160, 465–6, 467–9
Haitian Revolution, 394
  abolition movement after, 398–9
Hale, Terry, 42, 57–8
Hamlet (Shakespeare, W.), 23–4
Hard Times (Dickens, C.), 246
Hardy, Thomas, 283–4
Harris, Mason, 434
haunted house genre, 177–81
  theatre as haunted space, 178–81
Hawthorne, Nathaniel, 15, 381, 382–3
Hazlewood, C. H., 175
Hazlitt, William, 7–8
Heard, Mervyn, 188, 197
Hearn Lafcadio, 392–3
Heart of Darkness (Conrad, J.), 301
Heath, William, 54–5
Hedda Gabler (Ibsen, H.), 175
Henry, Eva M., 470–1
Henryson, Robert, 331
Herder, Johann Gottfried, 220
Hervey, Thomas K., 226
Hesselius, Martin, 231–2
Hewlett, Henry, 135
Hibbert-Ware, Samuel, 235
Hickox, Douglas, 181
Hill, Susan, 181
Hillard, George Stillman, 6, 17
Hindle, Maurice, 41
historical novel, Irish, 361
An Historical Survey of the French Colony in the Island of St Domingo (Edwards, B.), 396–7
history. See semantic history
History of a Six Weeks' Tour (Shelley, P. B. and Shelley, M. W.), 30

A History of Eighteenth Century Literature (Gosse, E.), 6–7
A History of English Literature (Shaw, T. B.), 8–11
A History of the Gothic Revival (Eastlake, C. L.), 18, 127–8
Hobhouse, John, 27
Hodgson, William Hope, 231
Hoeveler, Diane Long, 143
Hoffmann, E. T. A., 294
Hoffmann, Ernst Theodor, 314
Hogg, James, 17, 329, 335
  Kilmeny, 342–3
  The Mountain Bard, 340–2
  narrative ambiguity for, 344
  The Private Memoirs and Confessions of a Justified Sinner, 17, 345–8, 357–8
  supernatural themes for, 344–5
  work in commercial periodicals, 343–4
Holcroft, Thomas, 166
Holland, Henry, 169
Hollington, Michael, 249–50
The Holly-Tree Inn (Dickens, C.), 264
Holmes, Richard, 21
homicidal women, in sensation fiction, 279–80
Hood, Thomas, 209–11, 217
hope, in To Laughter, 33
Houses of Parliament, 119
  rebuilding of. See Palace of Westminster
Huggett, Richard, 178
Humphreys, Anne, 152–3
Hunt, Leigh, 103
Hurd, Richard, 6, 120
Hurley, Kelly, 429, 436–7
Hymn Before Sun-rise, in the Vale of Chamouni (Coleridge, S. T.), 30–1
Hymn to Intellectual Beauty (Shelley, P. B.), 30

I Beati Paoli (Natoli, L.), 305
I promessi sposi (The Betrothed), 306–9
  early drafts of, 309–11
  literary legacy of, influence on future works, 312–13
  publication of dual editions, 307–8
  translations of, 307, 311–12
Ibañez, Vicente Blasco, 299
Ibsen, Henrik, 175
illusions, in spectrology, 191–2
imagination
  in American Gothic narratives, 376

imagination (cont.)
  in Gothic literature, as association-driven formula, 8
  in Romantic literature, 8
imperial Gothic, at *fin de siècle* (end of the century)
  in *Dracula*, 463
  America symbolism in, 479
  Egypt and, popularity of, 469–74
  identification and definition of, 463–5
  India and, national ambivalence towards, 475–8
  in Kipling's works, 475–8
  mummy fiction and, 469–74
  in *She*, 465–6, 467–9
  in Stoker's works, 478–81
  time frame for, 464–5
  in US and, comparisons to England, 478–81
    in *Dracula*, 479
India, 475–8
Industrial Revolution, British politics influenced by, 119
Infant Custody Act, England (1839), 266, 273
Invernizio, Carolina, 324
Ireland, Gothic in, during nineteenth century
  Catholic Emancipation and, 367
  Edgeworth and, 359–61
  'First Wave', 362–6
  gender in, 369–75
    female writers, 374
  genre in, 369–75
    Big House novel, 374
  Irish historical novel in, 361
  landscape topography, as visual metaphor, 372–3
    in poetry, 372–3
  national tale in, 361
  in periodical press, 366–9
    Le Fanu and, 368–9
  poetry, 373–5
    landscape topography in, 372–3
  popular folklore collections, 367–8
  regional novel in, 361
  Romantic-era Gothic, 368
  supernatural in, 373–4
  'trade Gothic' fictions, 361–2
Irving, Henry, 169, 179–80
The Island of Dr Moreau (Wells, H. G.), 300, 301
The Italian (Radcliffe, A.), 12, 13, 24, 303
Italian fantastic style, 304–5
Italy, Gothic in, during nineteenth century. *See also* Manzoni, Alessandro
  anti-rationalism in, 319
  anti-scientific discourses in, 319
  at *fin de siècle*, 319–25
  folkloric Gothic, 323–4
  mesmerism in, 319
  metaphysics in, 323–4
  methodological approach to, 305–6
  monastic dramas, 310
  non-thetic turn of, 313–16
  occultism in, 319
  Paralipomena of an occulted genre, 303–6
  Penitents of, 303–6
  Pinocchio, 304–5, 317–19
    as humanistic metaphor, 319
    supernatural elements of, 319
  positivism and, 319–25
  Romantic Gothic, 306–13
  Scapigliatura movement, 304, 314–16
    aesthetic of the ugly, 315–16
    European Romanticism as influence on, 314
    foreign influences on, 314
    materiality of, 314–15
  scientific enquiry in, 322
  Scott, W., and, 308–9
  spiritualism in, 319, 322
  vampirism in, popularity of, 319–22
    The Vampyre as influence on, 319–20
Izco, Wenceslao Ayguals de, 296

James, Henry, 176, 238–9, 389
  The Turn of the Screw, 227, 238, 242
James, William, 238
Jane Eyre (Brontë, C.), 15, 80–1
  Victorian Domestic Gothic Fiction and, 267–8, 270–1, 283–4
  mother–daughter plot in, 269–70
Jann, Rosemary, 122
Jenny (Rossetti, D. G.), 217
Jerrold, Douglas, 166, 172–3
Jerusalem Delivered (Tasso, T.), 4
The Jesuit (Patrick, F. C.), 363–4
Jones, David, 54, 183
Jones, Timothy G., 184
Jordan, Neil, 181
Jouffroy, Achille de, 75, 162–3

Kahane, Claire, 269
Das Kapital (Marx, K.), 78
Keats, John, 11, 326
Keetley, Dawn, 441
Kelly, Gary, 140, 149
Kelly, Isabella, 3
Kelroy (Rush, R.), 379

Kenley, Marianne, 364
Kent, William, 120–1
Kidnapped (Stevenson, R. L.), 15
Kilgour, Maggie, 211
Killeen, Jarlath, 15, 359–60
Killick, Tim, 149–50
Kilmeny (Hogg, J.), 342–3
King James Bible, 1–2
Kipling, Rudyard, 17
  on imperial Gothic, in India, 475–8
  The Phantom Rickshaw, 477–8
  The Strange Ride of Morrowbie Jukes, 475–6
  The Vampire, 475
Kirk, Robert, 342
Kitson, Peter J., 16
Knowles, James, 215
Koch, Angela, 143
Kock, Charles Paul de, 295
Koselleck, Reinhart, 98
Kristeva, Julia, 70

Lady Audley's Secret (Braddon, M. E.), 175, 275–80
The Lady of Shalott (Tennyson, A.), 215
The Lady of the Shroud (Stoker, B.), 480–1
Lake Poets, 105–6, 115–16. *See also* Coleridge, Samuel Taylor; Southey, Robert; Wordsworth, William
Lamb, Caroline (Lady), 72
Lamb, Charles, 328–9
Landolfi, Tommaso, 326–7
Landon, Percival, 230
Landor, Walter Savage, 97
landscape themes, in Victorian poetry, 207–8
Lang, Andrew, 14, 233–4
Langhorne, John, 2
Langley, Batty, 121
Lankester, E. Ray, 425–6
Lascelles, Lady Caroline. *See* Braddon, Mary Elizabeth
The Last Man (Shelley, M. W.), 39–40
laughter, 31–3
Law, Graham, 141
The Lay of the Last Minstrel (Scott, W.), 9
Le Fanu, Joseph Sheridan, 79–80, 176, 227
  Green Tea, 231
  Irish Gothic and, press production of, 368–9
  Uncle Silas, 367, 369–70
Lee, Abigail, 287
Lee, Harriet, 165
Lee, Vernon, 228
Leland, Thomas, 362
Lemoine, Ann, 144–5

Lemoine, Henry, 54
Leno, Dan, 179
Lenore (Bürger, G. A.), 4–5, 57, 66, 220, 293
  Scott, W., response to, 329–30
  Scottish Gothic influenced by, 328–30, 333–5
  in ballad tradition, 333–4
  response to reading of, 329–30
Leopardi, Giacomo, 305
Leroux, Gaston, 181
Letters on Chivalry and Romance (Hurd, R.), 120
Lewis, Leopold, 175, 176
Lewis, Matthew Gregory, 5, 10, 20, 166
  The Castle Spectre, 164, 167
  The Monk, 7, 20–1, 57, 105, 144, 260, 286
  ballads inspired by, 337
  themes of, 164
  translation of works into Italian, 307–8
  at Villa Diodati, 20–1
Leyden, John, 329
The Liberal Movement in English Literature (Courthope, W. J.), 11
The Library Window (Oliphant, M.), 350–4
Linares, Vincenzo, 305
Literary Hours; or, Sketches Critical and Narrative (Drake, N.), 4–5
literature, Gothic. *See also* fiction; romance genre
  imagination in, as association-driven formula, 8
  in nineteenth century literary historiography, 7–14
  vampires in. *See also specific authors*
    from 1800–16, 66–9
    from 1816–19, 69–75
    from 1820–70, 75–9
    from 1871–97, 79–84
Little Dorrit (Dickens, C.), 251–2
Lloyd, Edward, 151, 152–3
Logan, John, 181
Lombroso, Cesare, 432–4, 441–4
London, Jack, 392
Long, Edward, 397
López de Gomara, Justo Sanjurjo, 301–2
Lord Byron. *See* Byron, George Gordon
Lorenzini, Carlo (Collodi)
  Pinocchio, 304–5, 317–19
  as humanistic metaphor, 319
  supernatural elements of, 319
Loutherbourg, Philip James de, 170
The Lusiads (Camões, L. de), 4
Lutz, Deborah, 155
Lynch, Eve, 236

The Lynching of Jube Benson (Dunbar, P. L.), 385–6
Lyrical Ballads (Wordsworth, W. and Coleridge, S. T.), 7–8, 25
Lytton, Edward Bulwer, 230, 311–12

Macauley, Thomas Babington, 91, 99–100
MacCarthy, Fiona, 94, 99
Machen, Arthur, 428–9, 435–6, 441–4
Mackay, Charles, 198–9
MacKay, Thomas, 160
Macklin, Charles, 179
Macpherson, James, 307, 329–30, 331–
magic-lantern shows, 49–53
  in mass media, 196–200
    in children's entertainment, 199–200
    of Dickens's works, 197
    showmanship in, 200–1
  necromancy in, 50
  origins of, 49–50
  stagers of, 49–52, 53. *See also* Robert, Etienne-Gaspard (Robertson)
magic shows, 176–7
Mahawatte, Royce, 156
Mallatratt, Stephen, 181
Malory, Thomas, 89, 100, 101
Mandal, Anthony, 227
Manfred (Byron), 32, 33–5, 56, 89
  Shelley, Percy Bysshe, influence on, 34
Manuel, Don Juan, 287
Manzoni, Alessandro, 304–5, 306–13, 314
  I promessi sposi (The Betrothed), 306–9
    early drafts of, 309–11
    literary legacy of, influence on future works, 312–13
    publication of dual editions, 307–8
    translations of, 307, 311–12
  literary influences on, 307–8
    Dickens, 312
    Poe influenced by, 312–13
The Marble Faun (Hawthorne, N.), 15
Marchi, Emilio De, 324
Mariana (Tennyson, A.), 215–16
marriage
  under Matrimonial Causes Act, 266, 273, 277, 278
  in Victorian Domestic Gothic Fiction, 274–84
  rebellious wife portrayal, 277–8
Marryat, Florence, 81, 83
Marshal, William, 2–3
Martínez Colomer, Vicente, 291
Martínez Villergas, Juan, 295

Marx, Karl, 78, 135–6
mass media, Gothic in, 195–203
  through film, 200–3
  magic lantern shows, 196–200
    in children's entertainment, 199–200
    of Dickens's works, 197
    massification of showmanship through, 200–1
  mesmerism and, 201
The Master of Ballantrae (Stevenson, R. L.), 332–3
Mathias, T. J., 5
Matrimonial Causes Act, England (1857), 266, 273, 277, 278
Matthews, David, 89, 115–16
Maturin, Charles Robert, 10, 302
  Bertram; or, The Castle of St Aldobrand, 164–5
  The Fatal Revenge, 246
  Melmoth the Wanderer, 10, 17, 286, 366–7
  The Milesian Chief, 365–6
  The Wild Irish Boy, 365–6
Maunder, Andrew, 280
Maw, George, 416
Mayo, Robert D., 150
Mazzanti, Enrico, 317
McGann, Jerome, 91
Medieval Court at Great Exhibition, 128
medievalism
  in Gothic architecture, 115
  Victorian medievalism, 103–4
  Ruskin on, 116
  Southey, R., on, 115–16
Medievalism (Alexander), 103
Medwin, Thomas, 141
Méliès, Georges, 201–2
Melmoth the Wanderer (Maturin, C. R.), 10, 17, 286, 366–7
melodramas, 166–70. *See also* domestic melodramas
  actors in, growing role of, 170
  Romantic tragedies and, 167
  stage spectacle as element of, 169
  treatment of villains in, 167–8
Melville, Herman, 381
  Benito Cereno, 383–4, 402–3, 407, 408–9
memory studies, on Spanish Gothic revival, 285–6
mesmerism, 176–7
  in Italy, 319
meta-Gothic
  in Dickens's works, 259–64
  Victorian poetry, 208–9
metaphysics, in Italian Gothic, 323–4

Index

Mighall, Robert, 17, 183–4, 221–2, 434–5
The Milesian Chief (Maturin, C. R.), 365–6
Miller, D. A., 266
Milliken, Anna, 362
Milner, John, 116, 121
Milton, John, 2, 19, 26–7
mirror effects, 193–4
  in phantasmagoria shows, 188–9
miscegenation fears, in slavery narratives, 398–9
  Creoles as embodiment of, 412–13
  vampirism and, 413–14
El misere (Bécquer), 297–8
Mitford, Mary Russell, 166
Modern Painters (Ruskin), 131
Moers, Ellen, 242–3
monastic dramas, 310
Moncrieff, William, 172
The Monk (Lewis, M. G.), 7, 20–1, 57, 105, 144, 260, 286
  ballads inspired by, 337
  themes of, 164
Monks, Aoife, 178
Mont Blanc (Shelley, P. B.), 30
  Romantic idea of nature in, 30–1
Monti, Vincenzo, 314
Moore, Thomas, 8–9
More, Sir Thomas, 91, 92, 99–100
Morland, Catherine, 3–4
Morley, Henry, 162
Morris, William, 18, 85–7, 90–114, 134–7. *See also* architecture
  The Defence of Guenevere, 102, 103, 104
  A Dream of John Ball, 137
  on 'fifty-year effect', in revival of Gothic architecture, 88–9
  on Gothic architecture, 107–14
    Gothic Revival, 134, 136–7
    in *News from Nowhere*, 107, 108, 109, 110–13, 137
    Northern Gothic style, 134–5
    Socialism as 'fourth stage' of, 119–20
  on late-Victorian Gothic style, 105–14
  A Night in a Cathedral, 86–7
  as Socialist, 135–6
    Socialism as 'fourth stage' of architecture, 119–20
  Southey, R., compared to, 93–105
  The Story of Sigurd the Volsung and the Fall of the Niblungs, 134
  Victorian poetry of, 205
Le Morte d'Arthur (Malory, T.), 89, 100
Mosse, Henrietta Rouvière, 360, 361

Mosses from and Old Manse (Hawthorne, N.), 381
mother–daughter plot, in Victorian Domestic Gothic Fiction, 269–70
The Mountain Bard (Hogg, J.), 340–2
Mozart, Amadeus, 75
Mulholland, Rosa, 374
mummy fiction, 469–74. *See also specific works*
Murphy, Sharon, 359–60
My Last Duchess (Browning, R.), 216–17
My New Year's Eve Among the Mummies (Allen, G.), 470–1
Myers, Frederic, 238
The Mysteries of London (Reynolds, G. M. W.), 152–3
The Mysteries of Paris (Sue, E.), 295, 296
The Mysteries of Udolpho (Radcliffe, A.), 13, 24, 269
The Mysterious Marriage (Lee, H.), 165
The Mystery of Edwin Drood (Dickens, C.), 256, 259
The Mystery of the Sea (Stoker, B.), 480

Nash, Andrew, 151
Natale, Simone, 191–2
national tale, in Irish Gothic, 361
'National Uncanny', 378–9
Natoli, Luigi, 305
naturalism, 390–2
  disease as recurring element in, 391
  regional influences on, 390
  social Darwinism, 390
nature
  in *Childe Harold's Pilgrimage*, 35–6
  in domestic melodramas, 171
  in *Epistle to Augusta*, 37–8
The Nature of the Gothic (Ruskin, J.), 92–3
Nead, Lynda, 277
necromancy, in magic-lantern shows, 50
Neiman, Elizabeth A., 361
Nesbit, Edith, 233, 243–5
Newberry, John, 142
Newey, Vincent, 36
News from Nowhere (Morris, W.), 107, 108, 109, 110–13, 137
Newton, Michael, 227
Nicholson, William, 53
A Night in a Cathedral (Morris, W.), 86–7
The Night Side of Nature (Crowe, C.), 234–5
No. 1 Branch Line (Dickens, C.), 257–9, 457–60
No Haid Pawn (Page, T. N.), 384–5
Nodier, Charles, 75, 162–3, 167
North, Francis, 167

531

North, Roger, 120–1
Northanger Abbey (Austen, J.), 3–4, 15, 89
Nurse's Stories (Dickens, C.), 260–2, 264

Oberon (Wieland, C. M.), 5
O'Brien, Fitz-James, 233
Observations on the Fairy Queen of Spenser (Warton, T.), 121
occultism in, 319
Olano, Antonio Ros de, 294
Old Curiosity Shop (Dickens, C.), 250
The Old English Baron (Reeve, C.), 4–5, 10
Oliphant, Margaret, 228, 236–7, 267, 282–3
  A Beleaguered City, 349–50
  The Library Window, 350–4
  Scottish Gothic and, 348–54
  seen and unseen in works of, 348–9, 350
Oliver Twist (Dickens, C.), 248–9, 254–5
Ollier, Charles, 231
On the Origin of Species (Darwin, C.), 83, 418, 420
operas. *See* plays and operas
Original Poetry by Victor and Cazire (Shelley, P. B.), 29
Ormond (Brown, C. B.), 377
Orra (Baillie, J.), 171
Ossenfelder, Heinrich August, 65–6
The Other Side of a Mirror (Coleridge M. E.), 221
Otto, Peter, 187, 202
Our Mutual Friend (Dickens, C.), 248, 256, 259
Owen, Robert, 93, 97, 100
Oxford Movement, 127

Page, Thomas Nelson, 384–5
Paine, James, 120–1
Paine, Thomas, 152
Palace of Westminster (House of Parliament). *See also* Pugin, A. W. N.; Ruskin, John
  design competition for, 119–22, 124
  fire at, 118
Paladino, Eusapia, 322
Pallinghurst Barrow (Allen, G.), 423–6
Palmer, T. A., 174–5
Paradise Lost (Milton, J.), 26–7
Paralipomena of an occulted genre, 303–6
Pardo Bazán, Emilia, 294, 299, 302
Paris Before Man (Boitard), 418
Past and Present (Carlyle, T.), 92–3, 99, 127
pathetic fallacy, 207–8
Patrick, F. C., 361, 362, 363–4
Patten, Robert, 141
Peacock, Thomas Love, 30

Penitents of Italian Gothic, 303–6
penny bloods (1840–70), 140, 150–9. *See also specific works*
  popular authors, 151, 155–9
  publishers of, 152–3
  serial revolution for, 150
  'shilling shocker' bluebooks replaced by, 150–1
  traditional plot dynamics in, 153–5
penny dreadfuls (1860–1900), 140, 159–61
  publishers for, 159
  violent themes in, 159–61
  youth market for, 159
Pepper, John Henry, 189–90
Pepper's Ghost illusion, 189–90, 192–3
Percy, Thomas, 6, 120, 334
Pérez Galdós, Benito, 298, 300
Pérez y Rodríguez, Pascual, 291
Petrarch, 2
Pevsner, Nikolaus, 137–8
phantasmagoria, 48–56
  in England, 53
  expansion of, as concept and term, 54–5
  magic-lantern shows, 49–53
  necromancy in, 50
  origins of, 49–50
  stagers of, 49–52, 53. *See also* Robert, Etienne-Gaspard (Robertson)
  as performance, 48–9
  spectrology and
  definition and scope of, 187–8
  mirror effects in, 188–9
  popularity of, 184–95
  Villa Diodati and, 54
The Phantom Rickshaw (Kipling, R.), 477–8
Philidor, Paul, 50
Philipsthal, Paul de, 53, 184–6, 187
Phillips, Kendall R., 202
The Philosophy of Composition (Poe, E. A.), 306
The Pickwick Papers (Dickens, C.), 226, 259
The Picture of Dorian Gray (Wilde, O.), 300, 430–1
Pinero, Arthur Wing, 177–8
Pinocchio (Lorenzini, C.), 304–5, 317–19
  as humanistic metaphor, 319
  supernatural elements of, 319
Pioneers of the Modern Movement (Pevsner, N.), 137–8
Pirandello, Luigi, 323
Pixérécourt, René-Charles Guilbert de, 166
Planché, James Robinson, 170
plays and operas, vampires in, 75–7

'pleasing terror', in Victorian ghost stories, 225–8
Pocock, Isaac, 169, 172
Poe, Edgar Allan, 15, 204, 294, 306, 381–2
    on differences between blacks and whites, 397–8
Poems of Ossian, 307
poetry, Gothic. *See also* Victorian poetry; specific genres; specific works
    death and mourning themes in, 204
    during 1816, 28–40
        of Byron. *See* Byron, George Gordon
        of Coleridge, S. T., 28–9
        of Shelley, Percy Bysshe, 29–30. *See also* specific works
    Irish, 373–5
        landscape topography in, 372–3
    Lake Poets, 105–6, 115–16. *See also* Coleridge, Samuel Taylor; Southey, Robert; Wordsworth, William
Polidori, John William, 21
    Fantasmagoriana as influence on, 56
    suicide of, 39
    translation of works into Italian, 307–8
    The Vampyre, 20, 27–8, 56
        Byron and, 27–8
        evolving tradition of vampires and, 27
        Italian Gothic influenced by, 319–20
        romantic elements of, 72–3
        at Villa Diodati, 27–8
Political Essay on the Existing State of Things (Shelley, P. B.), 29
Poller, Jake, 429–30
Poor Law Amendment Act, England (1834), 119, 126
Pope, Alexander, 36
Porphyria's Lover (Browning, R.), 216–17
Les Portraits de Famille, 58
positivism, 319–25
Posthumous Fragments of Margaret Nicholson (Shelley, P. B.), 29
Potter, Franz J., 142–3
Powers of Horror (Kristeva, J.), 70
The Prelude (Wordsworth, W.), 29
Prest, Thomas Peckett, 77–8, 151, 155–8, 255–6, 294
primitivism, Scottish Highlands and, 331
Prince, Richard, 179
The Principles of Pointed or Christian Architecture (Pugin, A. W. N.), 126–7
The Private Memoirs and Confessions of a Justified Sinner (Hogg, J.), 17, 345–8, 357–8

Pudd'nhead Wilson (Twain, M.), 385
Pugin, A. C. (Pugin the Elder), 18, 121
Pugin, A. W. N. (Pugin the Younger), 18, 86, 118–19. *See also* architecture
    An Apology for the Revival of Christian Architecture in England, 126–7
    Catholicism and
        conversion to, 125–6
        public reputation negatively affected by, 127–8
    claims on Christianity, 127
    Contrasts, 92, 124–6
    Medieval Court at Great Exhibition, 128
    The Principles of Pointed or Christian Architecture, 126–7
    Ruskin and, 130–1
The Pursuits of Literature (Mathias, T. J.), 5
Pykett, Lyn, 283

Queen Mab (Shelley, P. B.), 29
queer relationships, in Dickens's works, 256–9

Radcliffe, Ann, 5, 10, 20, 105
    access to works of, 14
    The Italian, 12, 13, 24, 303
    literary influence of, 13–14
    The Mysteries of Udolpho, 13, 24, 269
    The Romance of the Forest, 165
    Shelley, Mary, literary works influenced by, 24
    Shelley, Percy Bysshe, literary works influenced by, 24
    A Sicilian Romance, 269, 303
    Spanish Gothic writers influenced by, 291–2
    supernatural in works of, 11, 289
    translation of works into Italian, 307–8
railways, development of
    cultural changes as result of, 445–7
    destructive power of, 447–50
    fatalities as result of, 448
    in *Dracula*, 461
    entrapment and, 448
    ghosts and ghostliness of, 460–2
    No. 1 Branch Line, 257–9, 457–60
    passengers in peril, 450–5
        of sexual assault, 453–5
    psychological implications of, 447
    servants on, 456–60
    social stratification on, 451
    supernatural events on, 456–60
Ramsay, Allan, 331, 334
Ratcliffe, Eliza, 3
El rayo de luna (Galdós, B. P.), 298

realism movement, 386–9
　in collections and periodicals, 388–9
　feminist elements in, 388
　regionalism of, 387
　after US Civil War, 386–7
re-animation themes. *See also Frankenstein*
　in theatrical Gothic, 162–3
rebellious wife, in Victorian Domestic Gothic Fiction, 277–8
Redgauntlet (Scott, W.), 229–30, 335
Reeve, Clara, 3, 4–5, 10
regional novel, in Irish Gothic, 361
Reiman, Donald H., 29
Reliques of Ancient English Poetry (Percy, T.), 120, 334
Remembrance (Brontë, E.), 208–9
Reminiscences (Carlyle, T.), 95
repression, sexual, vampires as locus of, 71–3
reverse colonialism, in *Dracula*, 370, 479
Reynolds, G. W. M., 152–3
Rice, Anne, 181
Richet, Charles-Robert, 323–4
Rickman, John, 93
Rickman, Thomas, 121
Riddell, Charlotte, 228, 242, 374
Rienzi, The Last of the Roman Tribunes (Lytton, E. B.), 311–12
The Rime of the Ancyent Marinere (Coleridge, S. T.), 9–10, 26
Roas, David, 289
Robert, Etienne-Gaspard (Robertson), 50–2, 187
　Galvanism and, 51–2
　scientific technique for, 51
Robertson, Fiona, 340
Robin, Henri, 188–9
Robinson, Charles E., 29
Robinson, Henry Crabb, 53
Roca, José Nicasio Milà de, 295
Roche, Regina Maria, 360, 361
Roderick, the Last of the Goths (Southey, R.), 90–1
Roe, John, 144–5
Roero, Diodata Saluzzo, 305
Rolt, L. T. C, 462
Roman Catholic Relief Act, England (1829), 119, 125
romance genre
　The Castle of Otranto and, 67–9
　Gothic fiction as part of, 3–4
　vampires in, 72–3
　　as locus of repression, 71–3
　The Vampyre and, 72–3

The Romance of the Forest (Radcliffe, A.), 165
Romantic antiquarianism, Gothic architecture and, 88
Romantic Gothic, 103–4
　in Italy, 306–13
Romantic literature. *See also* poetry; Summer of 1816
　as anti-Classical movement, 9–10
　Dowden on, 11
　Frankenstein as central text for, 8
　imagination in, 8
　masculine elements of, 11
　in nineteenth-century literary historiography, 7–14
　writers of, 7–8. *See also specific works*; *specific writers*
Romantic movement, in Spain, 293
Romantic tragedies, 167
Romanticism. *See also* Gothic Romanticism; *specific authors*; *specific works*
　Dowden on, 11
　Gothic architecture and, 87
　in Irish Gothic, 368
　in nineteenth-century literary historiography, 7–14
　Scapigliatura movement influenced by, 314
　Spanish Gothic and, 293–4
Ronsard, Pierre de, 2
A Room of One's Own (Woolf, V.), 268
Rosenman, Ellen Bayuk, 154
Rossetti, Christina, 221
Rossetti, Dante Gabriel, 217–18
Rossetti, William Michael, 27, 209–10
Rowlandson, Thomas, 54–5
Ruiz, Ricardo Navas, 293
Rush, Rebecca, 379
Ruskin, John, 18, 87–8, 92–3, 129–34. *See also* architecture
　Fors Clavigera, 133
　on Gothic architecture, 105–7, 119
　on medievalism, 116
　Modern Painters, 131
　on pathetic fallacy, in Victorian poetry, 207–8
　Pugin, A. W. N., and, 130–1
　The Seven Lamps of Architecture, 127, 132
　The Stones of Venice, 106, 113, 123, 129–30, 132
Rymer, James Malcolm, 77–8, 155–8, 255–6, 294

Saintsbury, George, 354
Santos Álvarez, Miguel de los, 294
Sartre, Jean-Paul, 314

Index

Scapigliatura movement, 304, 314–16
  aesthetic of the ugly, 315–16
  European Romanticism as influence on, 314
  foreign influences on, 314
  materiality of, 314–15
The Scarlet Letter (Hawthorne, N.), 382
Schock, Peter, 34
Schröpfer, Johann Georg, 49–50
Schulze, Friedrich, 42–4, 47, 55
Sclavi, Tiziano, 326–7
Scotland, Gothic in, during nineteenth century
  British folkloric tradition and, 333–5
  critical context for, 330–3
  cultural context for, 330–3
  found-manuscript conceit, 332–3
  Gothic balladry, 332, 335
    collection and preservation of, 329–30, 334
    Lenore and, 333–4
    The Monk as inspiration for, 337
    'Sweet William's Ghost', 334–5
  Highlands, primitivism and, 331
  Hogg and, 340–8. See also specific works
  Lenore, 328–30, 333–5
    in ballad tradition, 333–4
    response to reading of, 329–30
    literary language in, preservation of, 331–2
    loss of political sovereignty, 331–3
  Oliphant and, 348–54
  Scott, W., and, 336–40. See also specific works
    collection of Scottish border ballads, 329–30
  Stevenson and, 354–8
Scott, George Gilbert, 128–9, 135
Scott, Jane, 169
Scott, Walter, 5–6, 7, 8–9, 15, 100, 291
  An Apology for Tales of Terror, 338–9
  The Chase, and William and Helen, 336–7
  Italian Gothic and, 308–9
  Redgauntlet, 229–30, 335
  response to *Lenore* reading, 329–30
  Scottish Gothic and, 336–40. See also specific works
    collection of Scottish border ballads, 329–30
  on supernatural, 229–30
  Tales of Wonder, 337–9
  Waverley; or, 'Tis Sixty years Since, 331, 336
Scottish Highlands, primitivism and, 331
Scullion, Adrienne, 335
Sedgwick, Eve Kosofsky, 210, 256
  seen and unseen, in Oliphant works, 348–9, 350
Selden, Catharine, 360
self, isolation of, in *Childe Harold's Pilgrimage*, 36–7
Selgas, José, 300
semantic history, 115–16
Senf, Carol, 79
sensation fiction, 274–84
  female consciousness in, 283–4
  homicidal women in, 279–80
  Matrimonial Causes Act and, 278–9
'sensation fiction', 247
Serao, Matilde, 305
Serrano Alcázar, Rafael, 294
The Seven Lamps of Architecture (Ruskin, J.), 127, 132
sexual repression. See repression
sexual transgression, among females, as literary theme, 274
sexuality. See female sexuality
Shakespeare, William, 2, 120
  Shelley, Mary Wollstonecraft, influenced by, 23–4
Shapira, Yael, 361
Shaw, George Bernard, 135–6
Shaw, Thomas B., 8–11
She (Haggard, H. R.), 465–6
Shelley, Mary Wollstonecraft, 10, 20, 21. See also *Frankenstein*
  as editor, 39–40
  Galvanism and, 56–7
  German Gothic narratives as influence on, 61–2
  The Last Man, 39–40
  Radcliffe as literary influence on, 24
  Shakespeare as literary influence on, 23–4
  at Villa Diodati, 21
  'Waking Nightmare' for, 56–7, 58, 59, 61–2, 63–4
  'walking terror' trope for, 62
Shelley, Percy Bysshe, 7, 8–9, 11, 20, 141, 166
  Alastor; or, The Spirit of Solitude; and Other Poems, 29
  Byron and, 29
  death of, 39
  editing of work by, 39–40
  The Esdaile Notebook, 29
  on Gothic architecture, 107–8
  History of a Six Weeks' Tour, 30
  Hymn to Intellectual Beauty, 30
  To Laughter, 30
  Mont Blanc, 30

Shelley, Percy Bysshe (cont.)
  Romantic idea of nature in, 30–1
  Original Poetry by Victor and Cazire, 29
  Political Essay on the Existing State of Things, 29
  Posthumous Fragments of Margaret Nicholson, 29
  Queen Mab, 29
  Radcliffe as literary influence on, 24
  St Irvyne; or, The Rosicrucian, 29
  Upon the wandering winds, 30
  Zastrozzi, 29
Shiels, Bill, 92
'shilling shocker' bluebooks (1770–1830), 140, 141–50
  audiences for, 142–3
  components of, 143
  Crookenden and, 147–8
  historical development of, 141–3
  penny bloods as replacement for, 150–1
  publishers of, 143–5
  recycled material in, 145–6
  traditional settings for, 146
  traditional themes for, 147–8, 149
  Wilkinson and, 148–9
Shirley (Brontë, C.), 12–13
Shubert, Adrian, 286
'shudder literature', 47–8
A Sicilian Romance (Radcliffe, A.), 269, 303
Siddons, Sarah, 179
Signs (Carlyle, T.), 99
Silvester, Alfred, 189
Sinclair, George, 354
Sir Bertrand (Aikin, J.), 4–5
Sister Helen (Rossetti, D. G.), 218–20
Six Months in Italy (Hillard, G. S.), 6
Skarda, Patricia L., 28
Skeletograph, 183
Sketches by Boz (Dickens, C.), 249–50
slave rebellions, 396–403
slavery narratives, in Gothic traditions
  Benito Cereno, 402–3, 407, 408–9
  black Other in, relative to white subjects, 403–9
  black subjects in, negative perceptions about, 397–8
  brutality of, 384–5
  Caribbean racial turbulence and, 394–5
  Creole populations, 409–15
    racial miscegenation and, 412–13
    as white Other, 410–11
  Haitian Revolution and, 394
    abolition movement after, 398–9
  Manichean allegory in, 403–9
  as metaphorical element, 395–6
    in *Frankenstein*, 399–402, 407–8, 414–15
  miscegenation fears and, 398–9
    Creoles as embodiment of, 412–13
    vampirism and, 413–14
  persons of colour as central characters in, 395
  slave rebellions, 396–403
    mystification of, 398
  Wuthering Heights, 403, 411–12
Smajić, Srdjan, 230
Smith, Andrew, 224–5
Smith, George Albert, 201–2
Smith, Helen, 151
Smith, R. J., 92
Soane, John, 118–19
social Darwinism, 390
Socialism
  as 'fourth stage' of Gothic Revival, 119–20
  Morris and, 135–6
    on Socialism as 'fourth stage' of architecture, 119–20
Society for the Protection of Ancient Buildings (SPAB), 85–7, 135
Solomon, Matthew, 201–2
La sombra (Pérez Galdós, B.), 300
Southern Gothic, in US, 383–6
  suppressed genealogy stories, 385–6
Southey, Henry Herbert, 97–8
Southey, Robert, 7, 8–9, 11, 20, 90–105, 114, 338–9
  The Book of the Church, 115
  Carlyle as influence on, 99–100
  Colloquies on Society, 91–3, 95–6, 99–100
  as exponent of Gothic literary experimentation, 90–1
  on 'the medieval', 115–16
  Morris compared to, 93–105
  on Owen, 93
  Roderick, the Last of the Goths, 90–1
  Thalaba the Destroyer, 66
SPAB. *See* Society for the Protection of Ancient Buildings
Spain, Gothic in, during nineteenth century
  Carlist War and, 299
  courtly novel in, 287–8
  dystopian presentations of, 286
  early short stories, 293–6
  early writers of, 290–3. *See also specific authors*
  exiled nationals as, 292–3
  Radcliffe as influence on, 291–2

at *fin de siècle*, 299–302
folkloric Gothic, 296–9
'Folletín' novel, 293–6
  literary development of, 294–5
Gothic heroine in, 302
Gothic novel in, arrival of, 287–90. *See also specific works*
  early works, 288
  from France, 288, 291–2
  from Great Britain, 288, 291–2, 300
  Spanish censorship of, 289–90
  supernatural themes in, censorship of, 289
historical legends in, 296–9
in *Melmoth the Wanderer*, 286
modern revival of, in popular culture, 285
  through memory studies, 285–6
in *The Monk*, 286
revival of interest in, 286
Romantic movement, 293
Romanticism in, 293–4
Spanish Civil War and, 285
in *St Leon*, 286
Spanish Civil War, 285
spectrology
  ghost shows, 193–5
  illusions, 191–2
  mirror effects, 193–4
  in phantasmagoria shows, 188–9
  Pepper's Ghost illusion, 189–90, 192–3
phantasmagoria shows
  definition and scope of, 187–8
  mirror effects in, 188–9
  popularity of, 184–95
  Skeletograph, 183
  theatrical spectacle of, 183–4, 187
spectral illusion thesis, 235–7
Spenser, Edmund, 2, 67, 120
spiritualism, in Italian Gothic, 319, 322
Spiritualism movement, in US, Victorian ghost story genre influenced by, 237–8
  notable English followers, 238
  social groups and societies, establishment of, 237–8
Spiritualist séance, 176–7
Spooner, Catherine, 195–6
Spuybroek, Lars, 106
St Clair, William, 142, 246–7
St Irvyne; or, The Rosicrucian (Shelley, P. B.), 29
St Leon (Godwin, W.), 286
stage realism, in theatrical Gothic, 163
Stead, W. T., 238
Stevenson, Robert Louis

A Child's Garden of Verses, 354
Kidnapped, 15
The Master of Ballantrae, 332–3
Scottish Gothic and, 354–8
Strange Case of Dr Jekyll and Mr Hyde, 300, 356–7, 358
Thrawn Janet, 355–6
Stewart, Dugald, 328
Stoker, Bram, 169. *See also* Dracula
The Lady of the Shroud, 480–1
The Mystery of the Sea, 480
The Stones of Venice (Ruskin, J.), 106, 113, 123, 129–30, 132
The Story of a Panic (Forster, E. M.), 326
The Story of Rimini (Hunt, L.), 103
The Story of Sigurd the Volsung and the Fall of the Niblungs (Morris, W.), 134
storytelling, in Victorian ghost stories, 233–4
  mingling of narrative forms, 234–5
Stowe, Harriet Beecher, 228
Strange Case of Dr Jekyll and Mr Hyde (Stevenson, R. L.), 300, 356–7, 358
The Strange Ride of Morrowbie Jukes (Kipling, R.), 475–6
Strawberry Hill, 121, 127
Street, G. E., 86
'street Gothic', as form of fiction, 140
The String of Pearls (Rymer, J. M. and Prest, T. P.), 156–8, 294
Stuart, Roxana, 75
Sue, Eugène, 295, 296
Sullivan, Lawrence, 54–5
Summer of 1816, Romantic literature output during. *See also* poetry; Villa Diodati
  Childe Harold's Pilgrimage, 20
  Christabel and, 9, 25–6
  climate events of, 19–20, 22–3
  Frankenstein and, 24–6
  Frankenstein, 20
  climate conditions and, 24–6
  Manfred, 20
  mythological status of, 19
  Satanic School established during, 20
  The Vampyre, 20
Summers, Montague, 13–14
supernatural. *See also* ghosts and ghostliness; Spiritualism
  in Dickens's works, 254–5
  in Irish Gothic, 373–4
  in Italian Gothic, 319
  James, W., on, 238
  in Radcliffe's works, 11, 289
  on railways, 456–60

supernatural (cont.)
  Scott, W., on, 229–30
  in Spanish Gothic novel, 289
  in Victorian ghost stories
    debates about, 233–4
    spectral illusion thesis on, 235–7
  in Victorian poetry, 218–23
  in weird tales, 392
supernatural themes, in theatrical Gothic, 165, 166
suppressed genealogy stories, 385–6
Sweeney Todd, the Demon Barber of Fleet Street. See *The String of Pearls*
'Sweet William's Ghost' (Child, F. J.), 334–5

Tales of the Dead (Utterson, S.), 43–4, 47, 57–8
Tales of Wonder (Lewis, M. G.), 337–9
Tasso, Torquato, 2, 4
technology, in Victorian ghost stories, 239–40
Tegg, Thomas, 144–5
Temple, William, 2
The Tenant of Wildfell Hall (Brontë, A.), 267–8, 272–4
  female sexual transgression as theme in, 274
Tennyson, Alfred (Lord), 215–16
Terriss, William, 179
terror
  in Victorian ghost stories, 225–8
  'pleasing terror', 225–8
  'walking terror' trope, 62
terrorist system of novel writing, Gothic fiction as, 3–4
Tess of the D'Urbevilles (Hardy, T.), 283–4
Teutonic tribes, Gothic and, 1–2
Thackeray, William Makepeace, 13
Thalaba the Destroyer (Southey, R.), 66
theatres, as haunted spaces, 178–81
theatrical Gothic. See also plays and operas
  in Dickens's works, 176
  domestic melodramas, 171–7
    ghosts and ghostliness in, 176
    guilt as theme in, 175–6
    local settings in, 172–4
    natural world in, 171
    popularity of, compared to, 163
  electricity as new element of, 169–70
  haunted house genre in, 177–81
    theatre as haunted space, 178–81
  legacy of, 164–6
  magic shows, 176–7
  melodramas, 166–70
    actors in, growing role of, 170
    Romantic tragedies and, 167
    stage spectacle as element of, 169
    treatment of villains in, 167–8
  mesmerism in, 176–7
  popularity of, 166
  re-animation themes in, 162–3
  Spiritualist séance, 176–7
  stage realism in, 163
  supernatural themes in, 165, 166
Thompson, E. P., 90
Thomson, James, 212–15
Thrawn Janet (Stevenson, R. L.), 355–6
The Three Impostors (Machen, A.), 441–4
The Three Perils of Man (Hogg, J.), 335
Thurston, Luke, 225–6
Tintern Abbey (Wordsworth, W.), 37
To Laughter (Shelley, P. B.), 30, 31–3
Toomer, Jean, 385–6
Toro, Guillermo del, 285
Tosh, John, 284
Tractarianism, 127
'trade Gothic' fictions, 361–2
Transcendentalists, 380–1
transumption, 95
Transylvanian Superstitions, 81
Trautwein, Wolfgang, 47–8
Tree, Herbert Beerbohm, 179
Trelawney of the 'Wells' (Pinero, A. W.), 177–8
Trollope, Anthony, 160
Tuck, Mary, 3
Tuke, Daniel Hack, 434, 441–2
The Turn of the Screw (James, H.), 227, 238, 242
Twain, Mark, 385

Uncle Silas (Le Fanu, J. S.), 367, 369–70
United States (US), Gothic in, during nineteenth century, 14–18
  Black American Gothic, 383–6. See also slavery narratives
    identity themes in, 385
    sexual exploitation of enslaved women, 385
  Brown and, 377
  after Civil War, 386–7
  Dark Romantics, 380–3
  frontier settlement as influence on, 378–9
    'National Uncanny', 378–9
    through wilderness narratives, 378–9
  in Hudson River Valley, 379–80
  imagination as foundational element in, 376
  imperial Gothic and, comparisons to England, 478–81

in *Dracula*, 479
landscape topography as element of, 379–80
naturalism in, 390–2
  disease as recurring element in, 391
  regional influences on, 390
  social Darwinism, 390
realism movement and, 386–9
  after Civil War, 386–7
  in collections and periodicals, 388–9
  feminist elements in, 388
  regionalism of, 387
Southern Gothic, 383–6
  suppressed genealogy stories, 385–6
Spiritualism movement and, Victorian ghost story influenced by, 237–8
Transcendentalists, 380–1
urban Gothic, development of, 380
weird tales, as genre, 392–3
  supernatural in, 392
women in, 379–80
  sexual exploitation of enslaved women, 385
urban environment
  in American Gothic, 380
  in Gothic fiction, 221–2
  in Victorian poetry, as thematic element, 212–15
US. *See* United States
Utopia (More, T.), 92, 97, 99–100
Utterson, Sarah, 43–4, 47, 57–8

Le Vampire (Carmouche, P., Jouffroy, A., and Nodier, C.), 162–3
The Vampire (Boucicault, D.), 162–3
The Vampire (Kipling, R.), 475
The Vampire (Ossenfelder, H. A.), 65–6
vampires
  in *Christabel*, 66, 69–70
  in Coleridge, S. T., works of, 66
  as contradictory figure, 71
  definition of, 65
  in Dickens's works, 246–7
  Dracula, 65, 81–4
    contemporary adaptations of, 14–15
    early references to, 65–6
  in Gothic literature. *See also specific authors; specific works*
    from 1800–16, 66–9
    from 1816–19, 69–75
    from 1820–70, 75–9
    from 1871–97, 79–84
  as metaphor, 78

in modern-romance genre, 72–3
  as locus of repression, 71–3
  as mutation, 74–5
  in popular culture, expansion into, 75–9
    in stage plays and operas, 75–7
  as sympathetic figure, 75–6
vampirism
  in Italian Gothic, popularity of, 319–22
  The Vampyre as influence on, 319–20
  racial miscegenation and, 413–14
The Vampyre (Polidori, J.), 20, 27–8, 56
  Byron and, 27–8
  evolving tradition of vampires and, 27
  Italian Gothic influenced by, 319–20
  romantic elements of, 72–3
  at Villa Diodati, 27–8
Vanolis, Bysshe. *See* Thomson, James
Vargas (Blanco White, J.), 292–3
Varney the Vampire (Prest, T. P. and Rymer, J. M.), 77–8, 155–8, 255–6
Vega, Lope de, 287
Verga, Giovanni, 305
Vickers, George, 151, 152
Victorian architecture, 120
  decline of, 137
  late, 105–14
Victorian Domestic Gothic Fiction
  Collins, Wilkie, and, 265
  definition of, 266
  Dracula, 284
  economic dependence of women in, 276–7
  female sexuality in, 274–84
  femme fatale in, 276
  in male-oriented adventure fiction, 284
  in *The Tenant of Wildfell Hall*, 274
  feminist themes in, 267–74
  Gothic heroine in, 276
  in *Jane Eyre*, 267–8, 270–1, 283–4
  mother–daughter plot in, 269–70
  Lady Audley's Secret, 275–80
  marriage in, 274–84
  rebellious wife trope, 277–8
  Matrimonial Causes Act and, 277, 278–9
  origins of, 266
  as sensation fiction, 274–84
  female consciousness in, 283–4
  homicidal women in, 279–80
  Matrimonial Causes Act and, 278–9
  in *The Tenant of Wildfell Hall*, 267–8, 272–4
    female sexual transgression as theme in, 274
  Women Question in, 266
  in *Wuthering Heights*, 267–8, 272

Victorian ghost stories. *See also authors; specific works*
- belief in spirits as theme, 233
- *A Christmas Carol* as, 225–8
- Christmas setting in, 225–8
- ghosts in, 240–5
  - in everyday domestic settings, 241–2
- outlets for, 228
- philosophical scrutiny of, 224–5
- pleasing terror in, 225–8
- scientific scrutiny of, 224–5
  - through investigations, 230–1
  - resistance to, 238–9
- storytelling in, 233–4
  - mingling of narrative forms, 234–5
- supernatural in
  - debates about, 233–4
  - spectral illusion thesis on, 235–7
- technology, spectral qualities of, 239–40
- terror elements of, 225–8
- US Spiritualism movement as influence on, 237–8
  - notable followers, 238
  - social groups and societies, establishment of, 237–8
- vision as theme in, 229–40
- women as subject of, 224–5
- women authors of, 224
- working class characters in, 236–7

Victorian medievalism, 103–4

Victorian poetry. *See also specific works*
- of Brontë, E., 208–9
- Gothic character in, 216–18
  - femme fatale, 217–18
- historical aspects of, 222
- of Hood, 209–11, 217
- landscape in, 207–8
- meta-gothic, of Brontë, E., 208–9
- of Morris, 205
- pathetic fallacy in, 207–8
- as post-Gothic, 205
- as post-Romantic, 205
- supernatural in, 218–23
- of Tennyson, 215–16
- theoretical approach to, 204–6
- traditional settings for, 206
- urban city themes in, 212–15

Victorianism, 15–16

Villa Diodati, during Summer of 1816, 20–1
- Coleridge, S. T., at, 21
- ghost stories at, 42
- as literary challenge, by Byron, 20–1, 66–9

Lewis, Matthew Gregory, at, 20–1
- notoriety of works presented at, 20–1, 66–9
- phantasmagorias and, 54
- Polidori at, 21
- Shelley, Mary, at, 21
- *The Vampyre* and, 27–8

Vincent, David, 140

A Vindication of the Rights of Woman (Wollstonecraft, M.), 270

vision, as theme, in Victorian ghost stories, 229–40

von Krafft-Ebbing, Richard, 434

von Stein, Laurenz, 98

von Weber, Carl Maria, 166

'Waking Nightmare', for Shelley, Mary, 56–7, 58, 59, 61–2, 63–4

Walker, John, 173–4

'walking terror' trope, 62

Wall, Harry, 194

Wall, Joseph, 186

Wallace, Diana, 242–3

Walpole, Horace, 10. *See also The Castle of Otranto*
- Strawberry Hill, 121, 127

Walton, Margaret, 24–5

Walton, Robert, 24–5

Ward, Matthew, 33

Warner, Marina, 186–7

Warner, Richard, 3

Warton, Thomas, 121

Watson, Roderick, 340

Waverley; or, 'Tis Sixty years Since (Scott, W.), 331, 336

Webber, Andrew Lloyd, 181

weird tales, as genre, 392–3
- supernatural in, 392

Wells, H. G., 230, 300, 301, 425–6

The Whiskey Demon; or, The Dream of the Reveller, 198–9

White, James, 362

The White Doe of Rylstone (Wordsworth, W.), 9

Wieland, Christoph Martin, 5

Wieland (Brown, C. B.), 377

The Wild Irish Boy (Maturin, C. R.), 365–6

Wilde, Oscar, 17, 181, 227, 300, 430–1

wilderness narratives, in American Gothic, 378–9

Wilderspin (Coleridge M. E.), 221

Wilkinson, Sarah, 148–9

Williams, Edward, 39

Williams, Randall, 194, 200
Williams, Raymond, 92, 94, 96–7, 213
Willis, Martin, 205–6
Willson, James, 118–19
Wing, T. T., 197
The Witch (Coleridge, M. E.), 220–1
Wodrow, Robert, 354
Wolfreys, Julian, 16, 204
The Woman in White (Collins, W.), 241–2
women. *See also* female sexuality; feminism
  in American Gothic movement, 379–80
    sexual exploitation of enslaved women, 385
  femme fatale character
    female sexuality of, 276
    in Victorian Domestic Gothic Fiction, 276
    in Victorian poetry, 217–18
  Gothic heroine character, 276
  in sensation fiction, 274–84
    female consciousness in, 283–4
    homicidal women in, 279–80
    Matrimonial Causes Act and, 278–9
    sexual transgression among, as literary theme, 274
  in Victorian Domestic Gothic Fiction. *See also* Victorian Domestic Gothic Fiction
    mother–daughter plot in, 269–70
    rebellious wife character, 277–8
    women's economic independence, 276–7
  Victorian ghost stories and
    as authors of, 224
    as subject of, 224–5
Women Question, in Victorian Domestic Gothic Fiction, 266
Wood, Ellen (Mrs. Henry), 228, 233
  East Lynne, 174–5, 279–81, 282–3
Wood, Gillen D'Arcy, 19
Woodward, George Moutard, 54–5
Woolf, Virginia, 268
Wordsworth, William, 7, 8–9, 20, 141
  Byron and, competition with, 35–7
  The Excursion, 29
  The Prelude, 29
  Tintern Abbey, 37
  The White Doe of Rylstone, 9
Wren, Christopher, 124
Wright, Richard, 385–6
Wuthering Heights (Brontë, E.), 76–7, 105
  ghosts in, 229
  slavery themes in, 403, 411–12
Wyatt, Benjamin, 169
Wyatt, James, 118–19
Wynne, Catherine, 179–80

The Yellow Wallpaper (Gilman, C. P.), 351
Young England movement, 123, 127
Young Goodman Brown (Hawthorne, N.), 382–3

Zafón, Carlos Ruiz, 285
Zastrozzi (Shelley, P. B.), 29
Zavala y Zamora, Gaspar, 290–1
Zofloya; or, The Moor (Dacre, C.), 144
Zorrilla, José, 297

For EU product safety concerns, contact us at Calle de José Abascal, 56–1°,
28003 Madrid, Spain or eugpsr@cambridge.org.